VISUAL
DICTIONARY

VISUAL
DICTIONARY

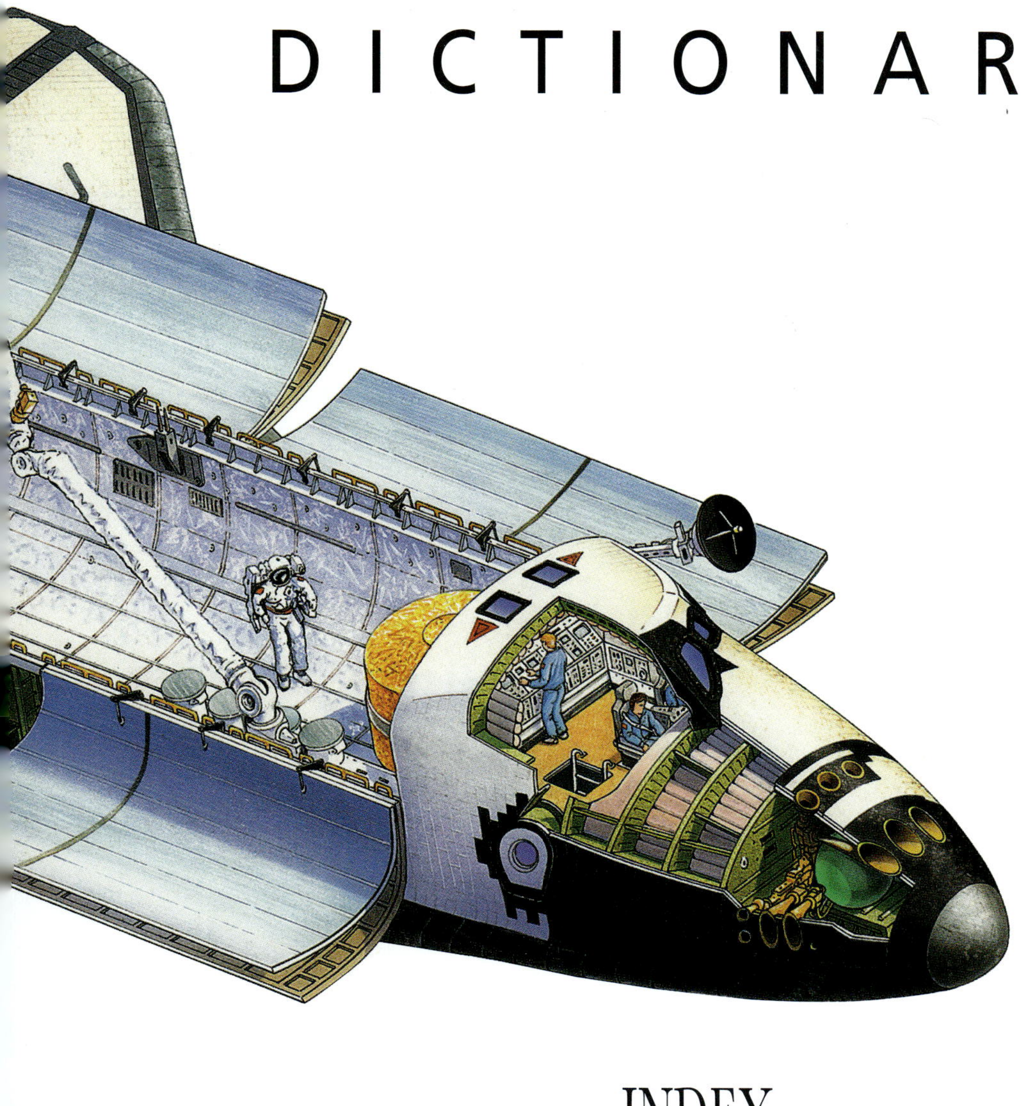

INDEX

This edition published for Index Books Ltd 2005

Produced by Fog City Press
814 Montgomery Street
San Francisco, CA 94133 USA

A catalog record for this book is available from the Library of Congress, Washington. D.C.

ISBN 1 740893 41 7

Color reproduction by Colourscan Co Pte Ltd
Printed by Tien Wah Press (PTE) Limited
Printed in Singapore

A Weldon Owen Production

WELDON OWEN PUBLISHING
Publisher: Sheena Coupe
Creative Director: Sue Burk
Project Editors: Sarah Anderson, Paul McNally
Project Designers: Suzanne Tawansi, Heather Menzies

Fog City Press
Chief Executive Officer: John Owen
President: Terry Newell
Publisher: Lynn Humphries
Managing Editors: Janine Flew, Angela Handley
Design Manager: Helen Perks
Editorial Coordinator: Jennifer Losco
Production Manager: Caroline Webber
Production Coordinator: James Blackman
Sales Manager: Emily Jahn
Vice President International Sales: Stuart Laurence

Contents

SPACE 10

The Solar System 14
Moons 40
Stars and Galaxies 50
Constellations 62
Exploring Space 80

PLANET EARTH 92

The Shifting Earth 96
Rocks and Minerals 104
Volcanoes and Earthquakes 108

ATMOSPHERE AND OCEANS 118

Weather 122
Seasons and Climate 136
Earth's Oceans 142

PREHISTORIC LIFE **148**

The Ages of Prehistory 152
Types of Dinosaurs 158
After the Dinosaurs 172

PLANTS **176**

Plant Characteristics 180
Ferns and Trees 184
Flowers and Food Plants 190
Plant Habitats 198

ANIMALS **202**

Birds 206
Mammals 240
Reptiles 280
Amphibians 298
Fishes 306
Insects and Spiders 326

THE HUMAN BODY 344

The Vital Systems 348
Bones, Muscles and Skin 362
Senses and Nerves 372

ANCIENT CIVILIZATIONS 382

Ancient Egypt 386
Ancient China 394
Ancient Greece 402
Ancient Rome 410
Native Americans 418

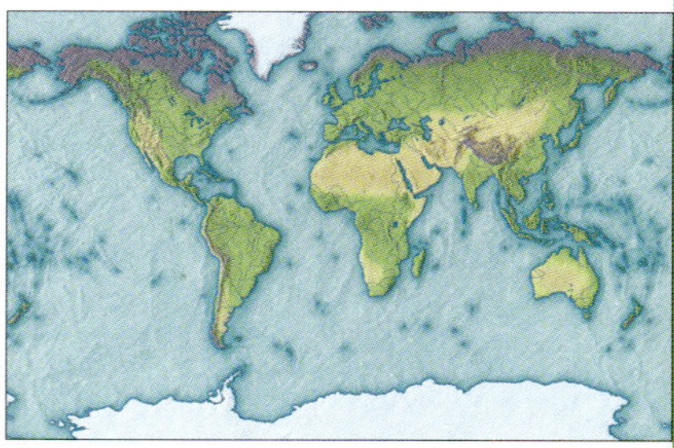

COUNTRIES OF THE WORLD 424

Europe 428
North America 446
South America 460
Asia 464
Africa 478
Australia and Oceania 482

ARCHITECTURE 486

Places of Worship 490

Public Buildings 500

Castles, Palaces and Houses 510

TECHNOLOGY AND INVENTIONS 518

Transport 522

Everyday Technology 538

Communications and Industry 546

FACT FILE 554

World 556

Universe 584

INDEX 596

Acknowledgments 608

THE SOLAR SYSTEM

Solar System 14
Mercury 16
Venus 18
Earth 20
Mars 22
Jupiter 24
Saturn 26
Uranus 28
Neptune 30
Pluto 32
Size Comparison of Planets 34
Asteroids and Meteoroids 36
Comets 38

MOONS

Earth's Moon 40
Solar and Lunar Eclipses 44
Moons 46

STARS AND GALAXIES

The Sun 50
Life Cycle of a Star 52
Stars and Supernovas 54
Clusters 56
The Milky Way 58

CONSTELLATIONS

Using a Star Map 62
Winter Stars of the Northern Skies 64
Spring Stars of the Northern Skies 66
Summer Stars of the Northern Skies 68
Autumn Stars of the Northern Skies 70
Winter Stars of the Southern Skies 72
Spring Stars of the Southern Skies 74
Summer Stars of the Southern Skies 76
Autumn Stars of the Southern Skies 78

EXPLORING SPACE

Our Place in Space 80
Astronomy from Earth 82
Astronomy from Space 84
Robot Probes 86
Spacecraft 88
Space Travel 90

Solar System

BIRTH OF THE SOLAR SYSTEM

Dust and gas collapse to form a dense core surrounded by a broad disk called the solar nebula.

The nebula's densest part attracts dust and gas. It grows larger and hotter, becoming the proto-Sun.

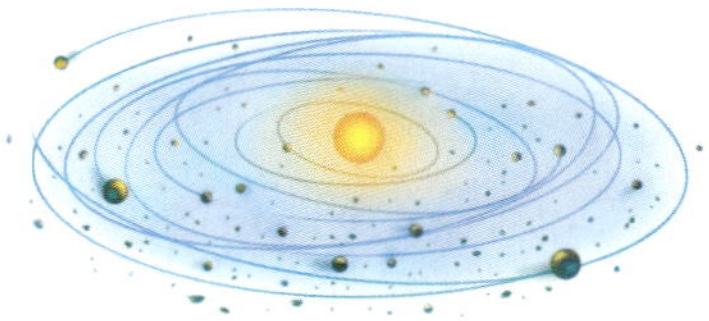

Particles of rock and ice stick together to become planetesimals—the building blocks of planets.

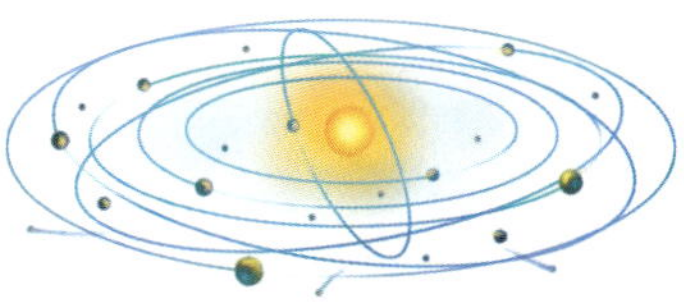

The planetesimals clump together to form larger bodies called proto-planets.

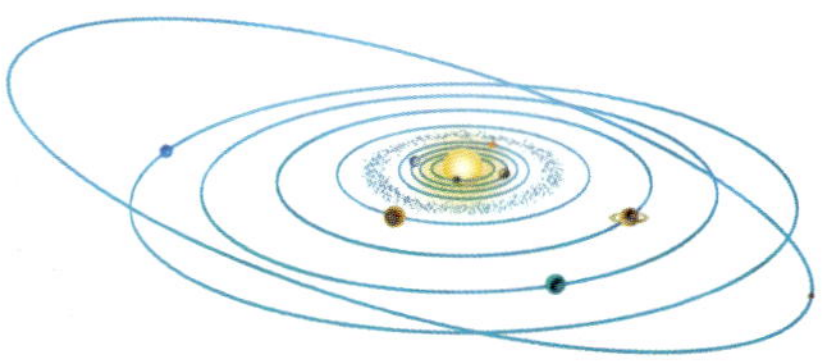

The Sun becomes a star and its radiation blows away leftover gas, leaving behind nine planets.

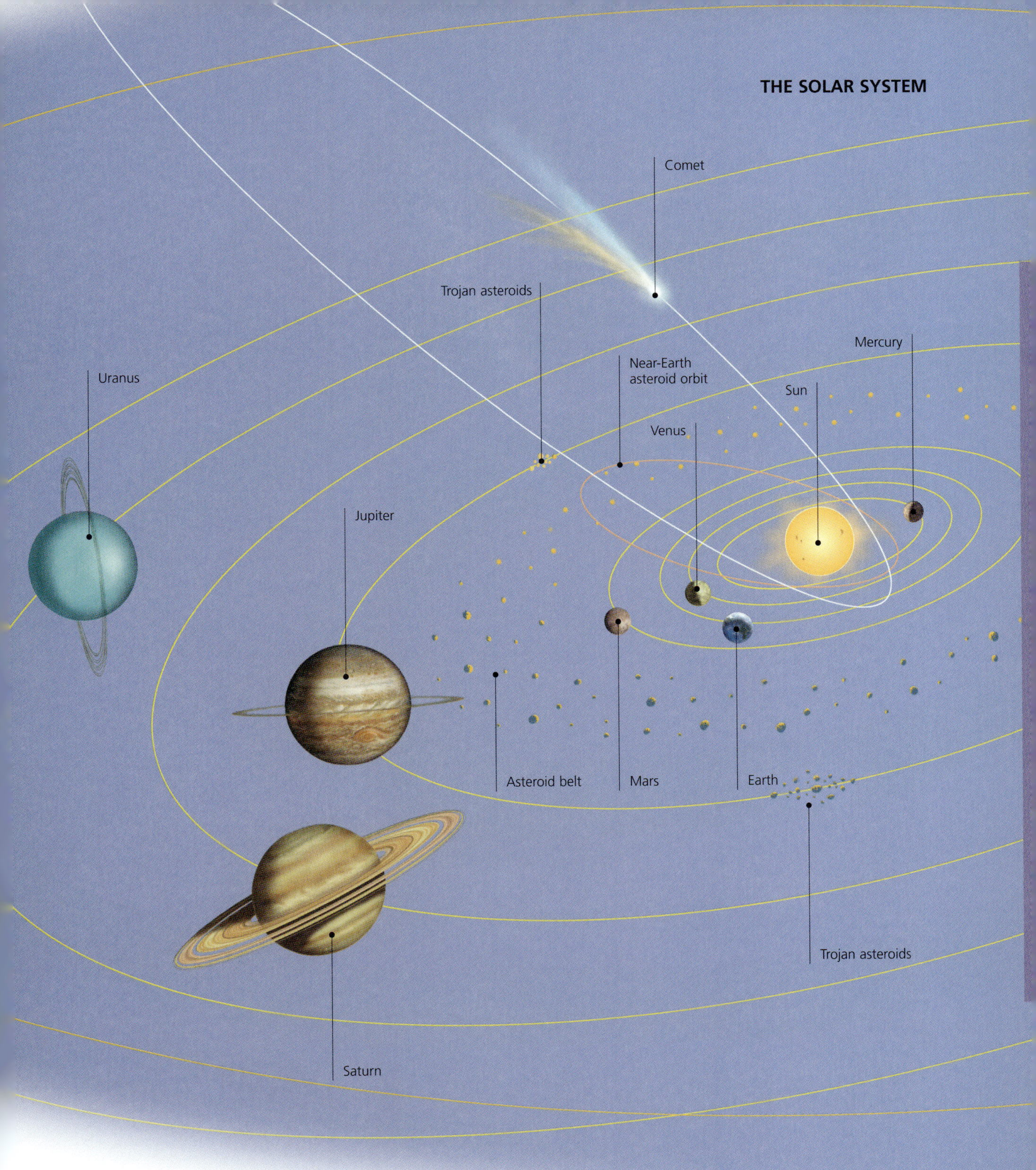
Comet
Trojan asteroids
Mercury
Near-Earth
asteroid orbit
Uranus
Sun
Venus
Jupiter
Asteroid belt
Mars
Earth
Trojan asteroids
Saturn

Mercury

MAP OF MERCURY

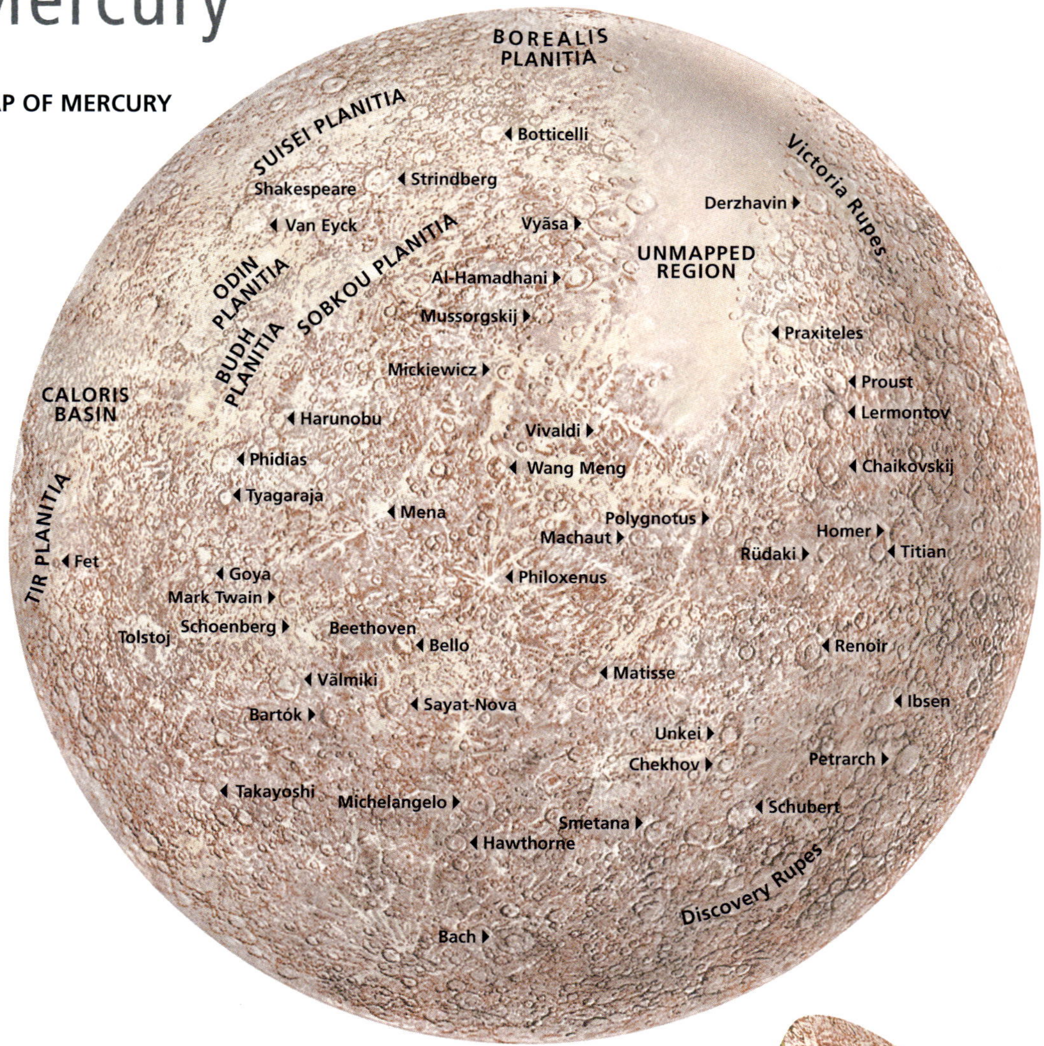

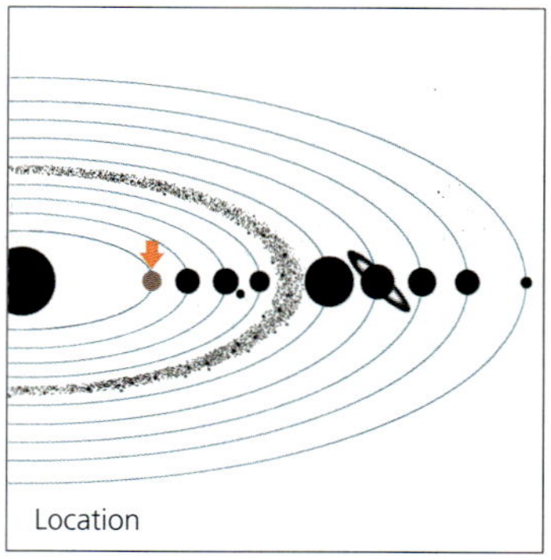

CROSS SECTION

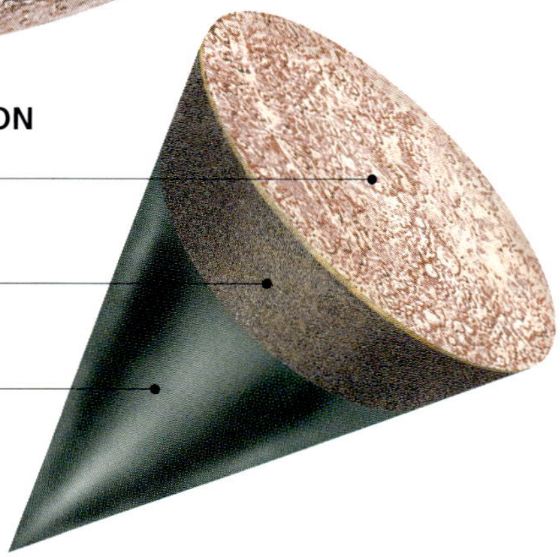

MERCURY'S ORBIT

Mercury has a year of 88 Earth days, while a full solar day from noon to noon lasts 176 Earth days.

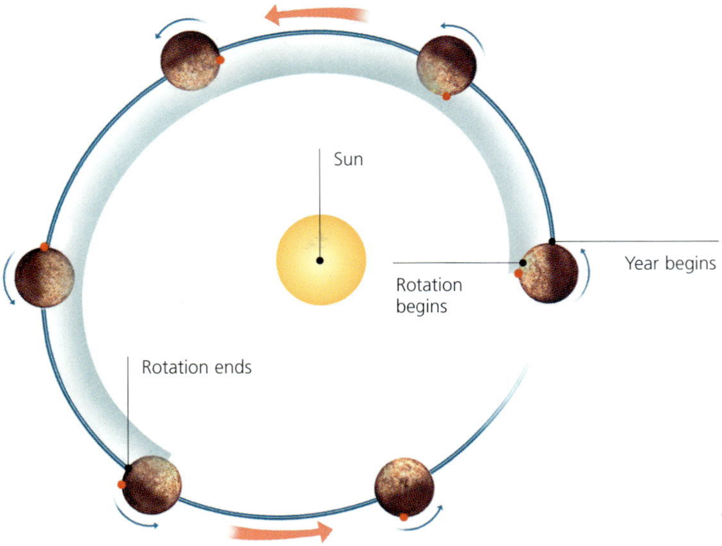

MERCURY'S SURFACE

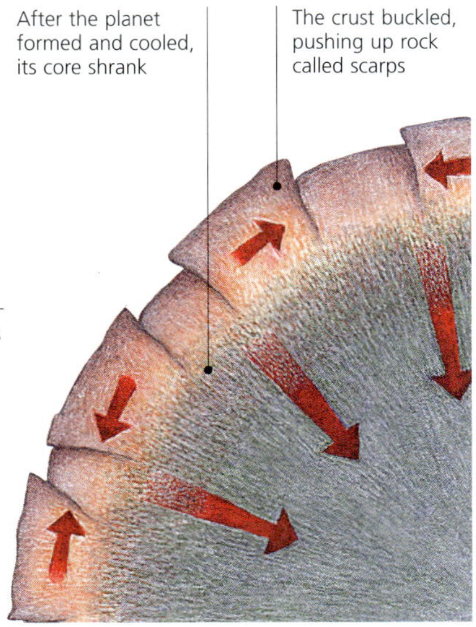

CALORIS BASIN

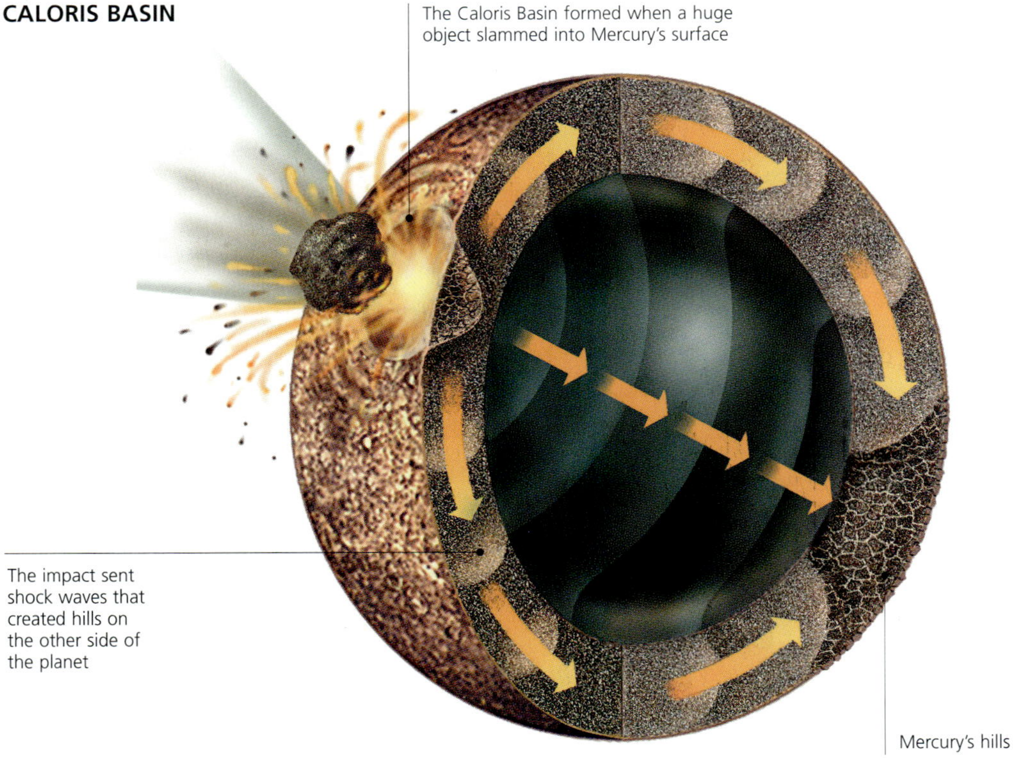

Venus

MAP OF VENUS
Aphrodite Terra hemisphere

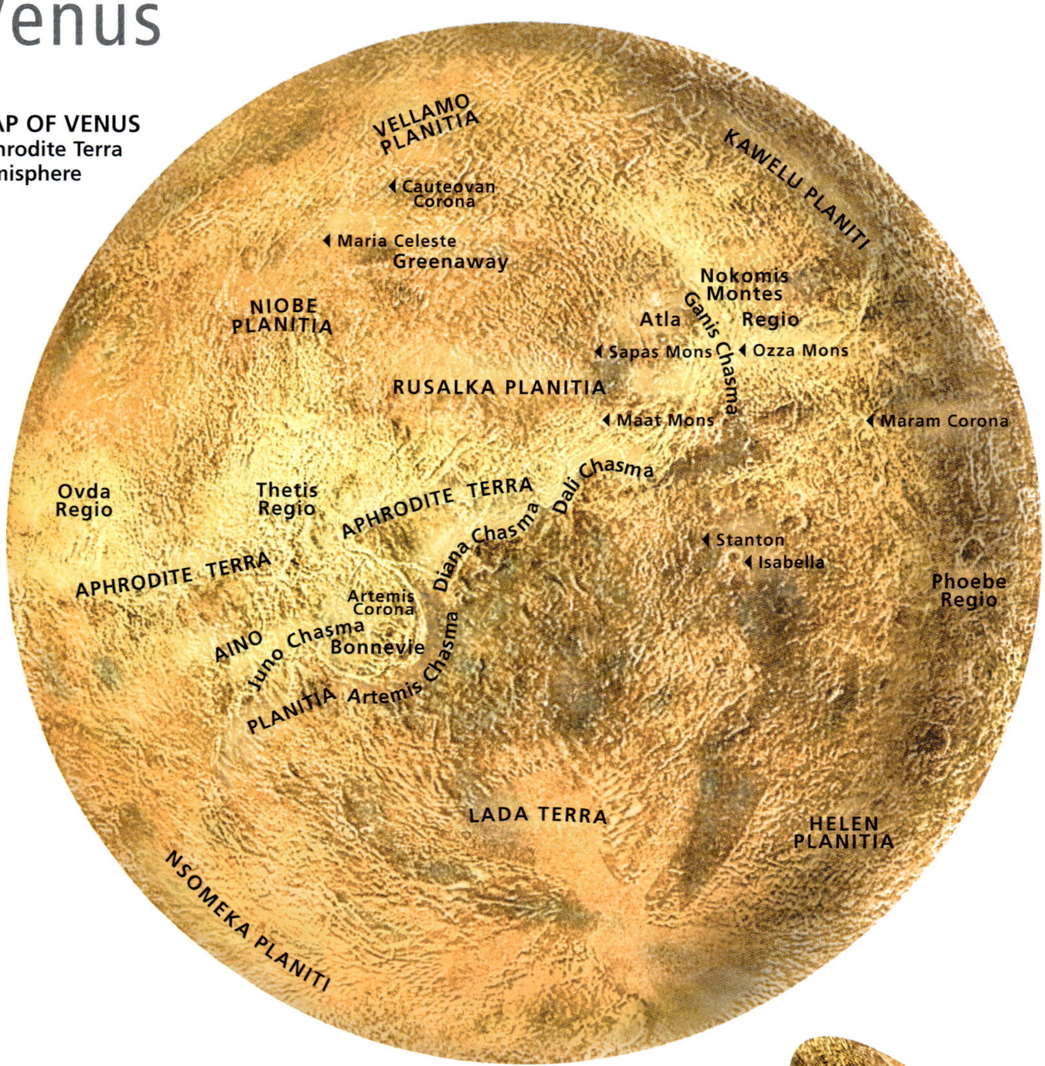

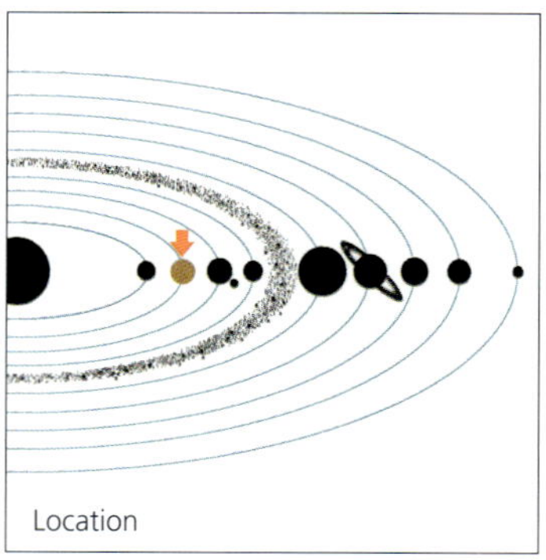

CROSS SECTION

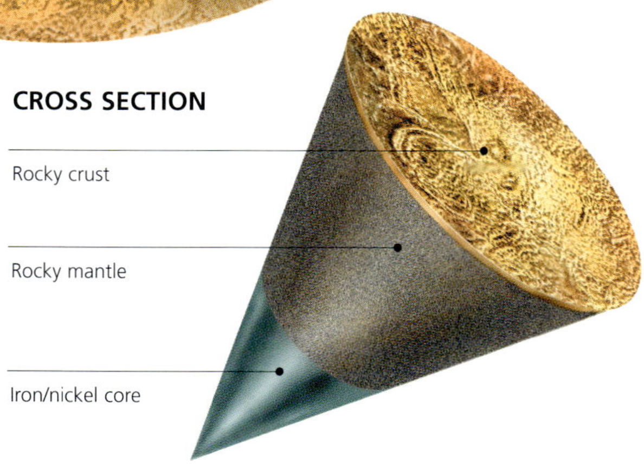

MAPPING VENUS

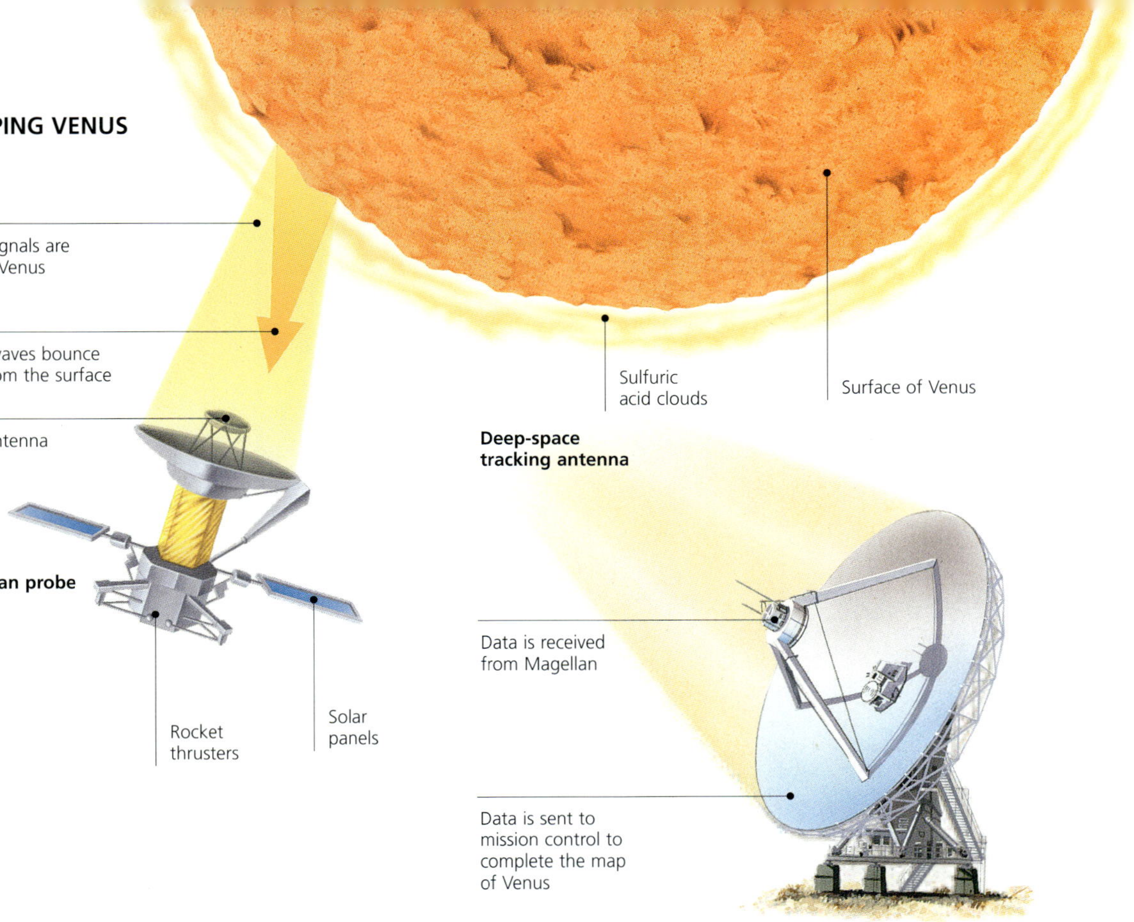

GREENHOUSE EFFECT

Venus suffers from a severe greenhouse effect.

VENERA
Venus spacecraft

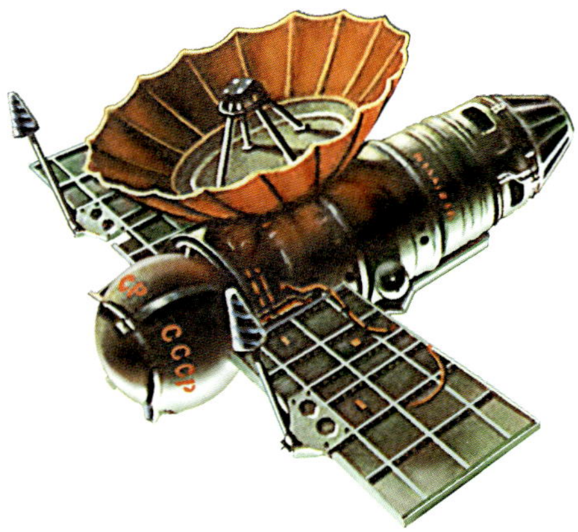

Earth

MAP OF EARTH
Western hemisphere

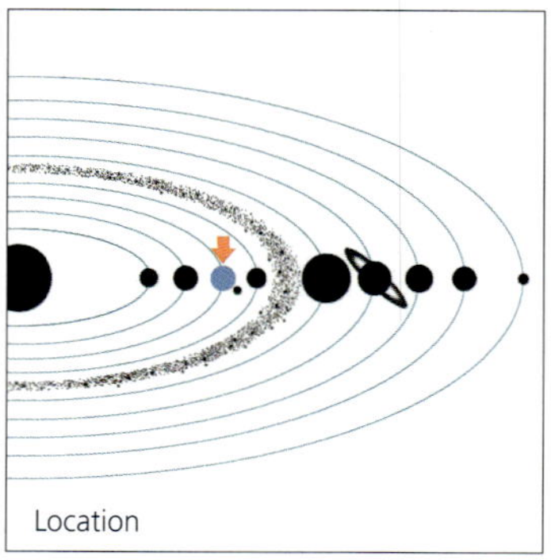

CROSS SECTION

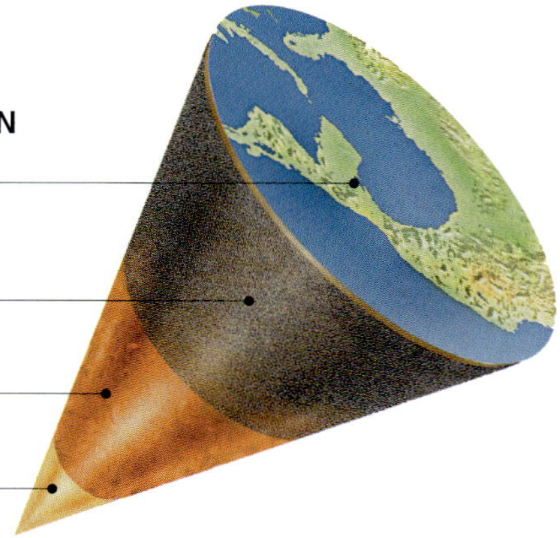

MAP OF EARTH
Eastern hemisphere

MARTIAN ROCKS ON EARTH

An asteroid smashes into Mars and blasts pieces of the planet into space.

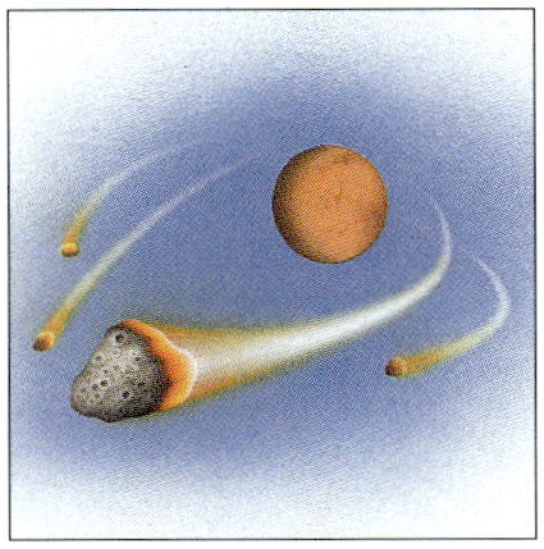

These Martian rocks go into orbit around the Sun for millions of years.

Some of the rocks collide with Earth and fall to the ground as meteorites.

Mars

MAP OF MARS
Western hemisphere

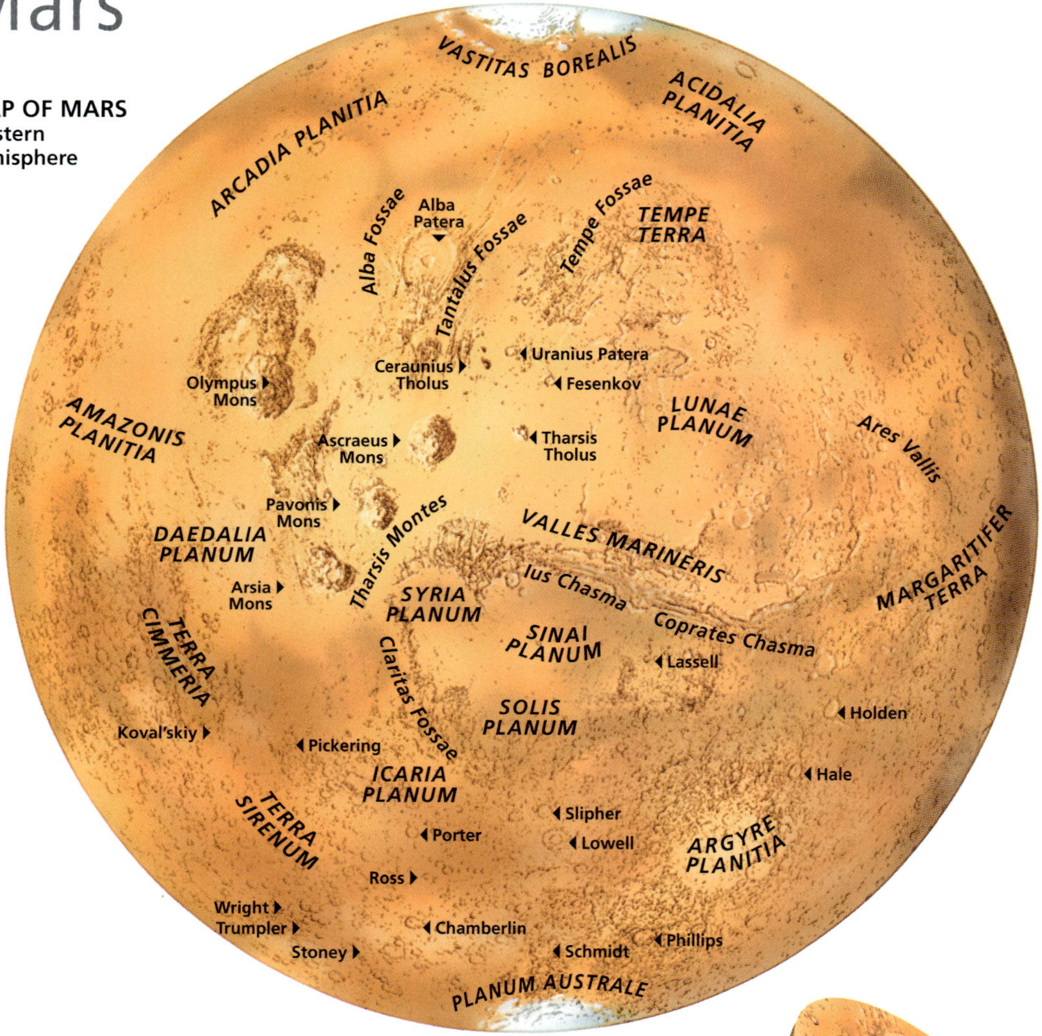

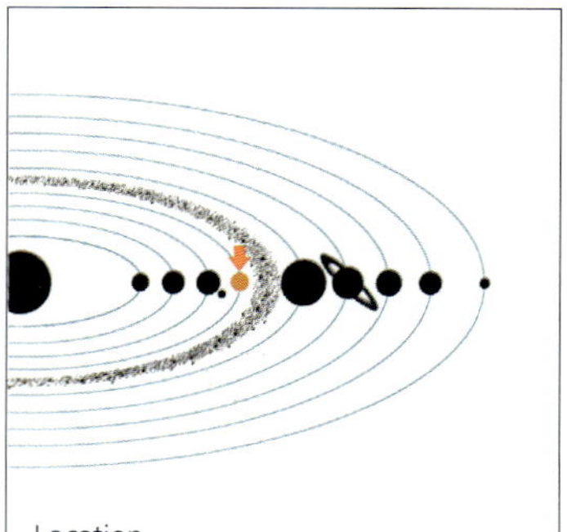
Location

CROSS SECTION

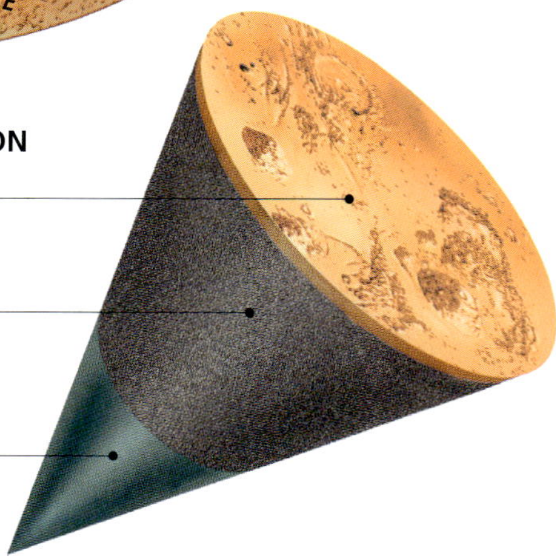

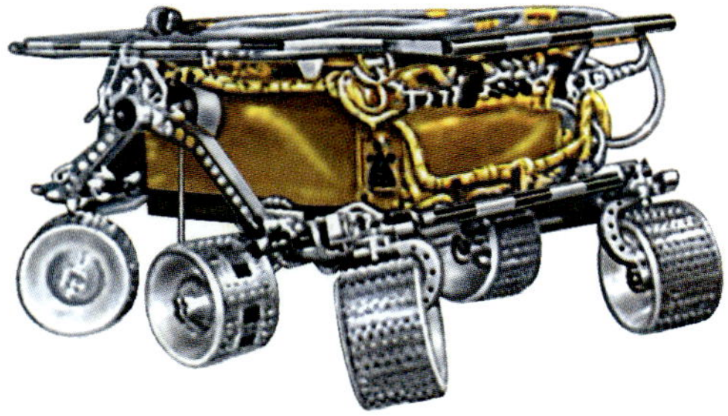

SOJOURNER ROVER

PATHFINDER MISSION TO MARS

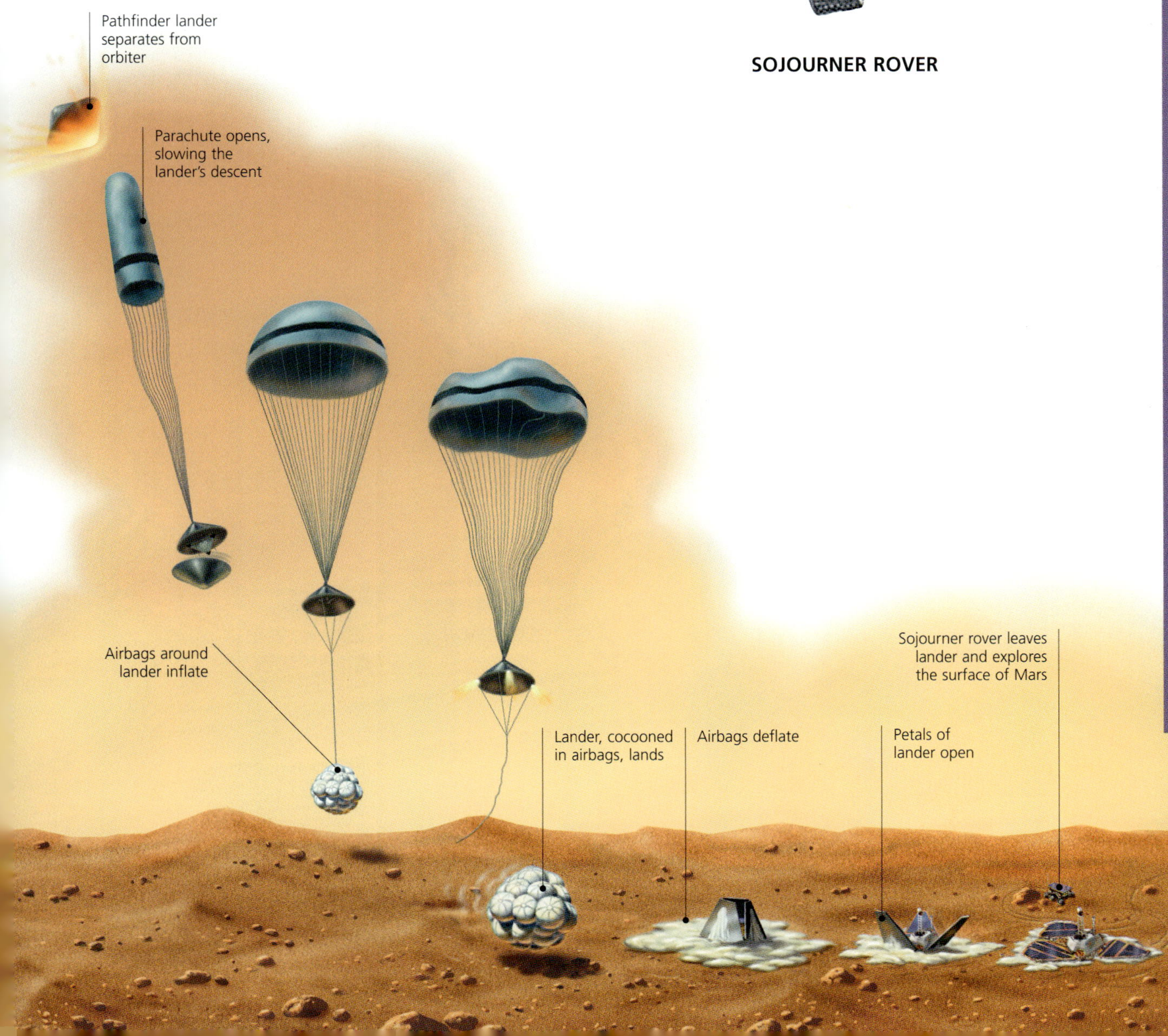

Jupiter

GALILEO ORBITER

In 1995, the Galileo orbiter shot an entry probe into Jupiter's atmosphere.

GALILEO PROBE

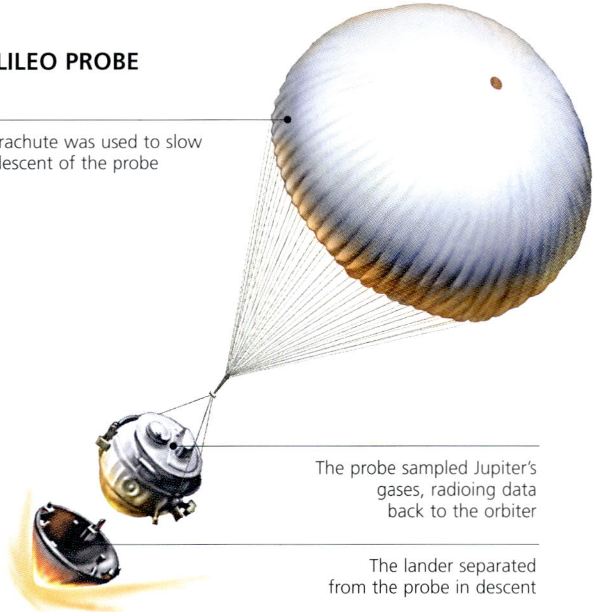

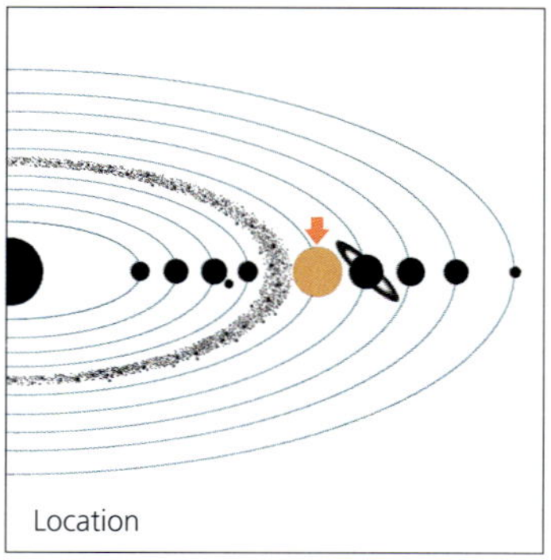

CROSS SECTION

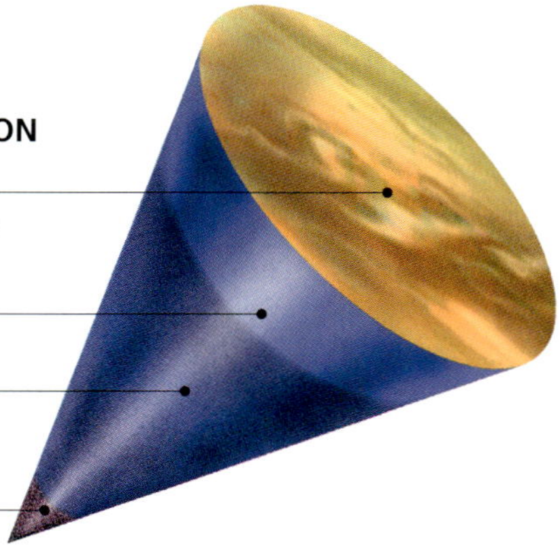

MAP OF JUPITER

Saturn

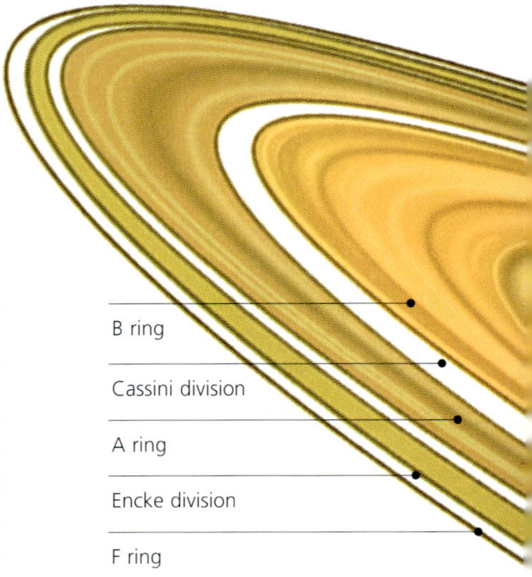

CREATING SATURN'S RINGS

1. A large comet or asteroid smashes into an icy moon orbiting Saturn.

2. The impact shatters the moon into a cloud of icy particles. These orbit Saturn.

3. Constant collisions among the icy particles grind them into smaller pieces.

4. Over years, these particles spread out to form a broad ring around the planet.

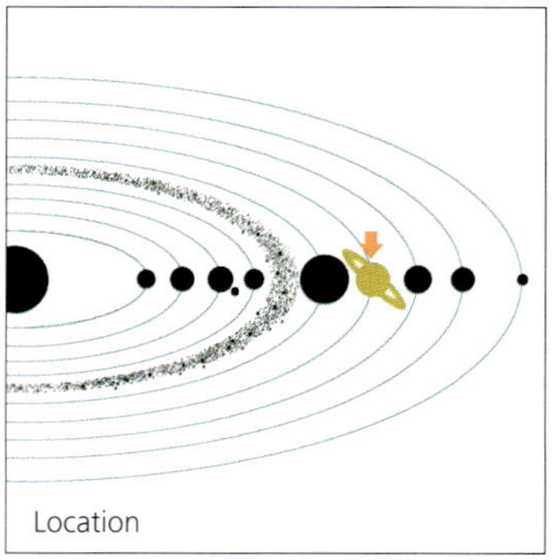

CROSS SECTION

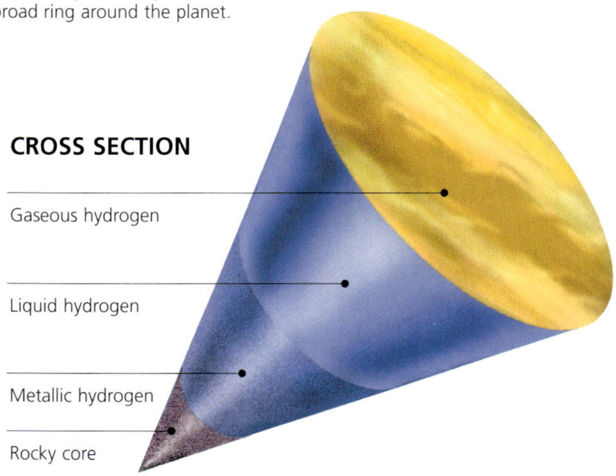

SPACE The Solar System

MAP OF SATURN

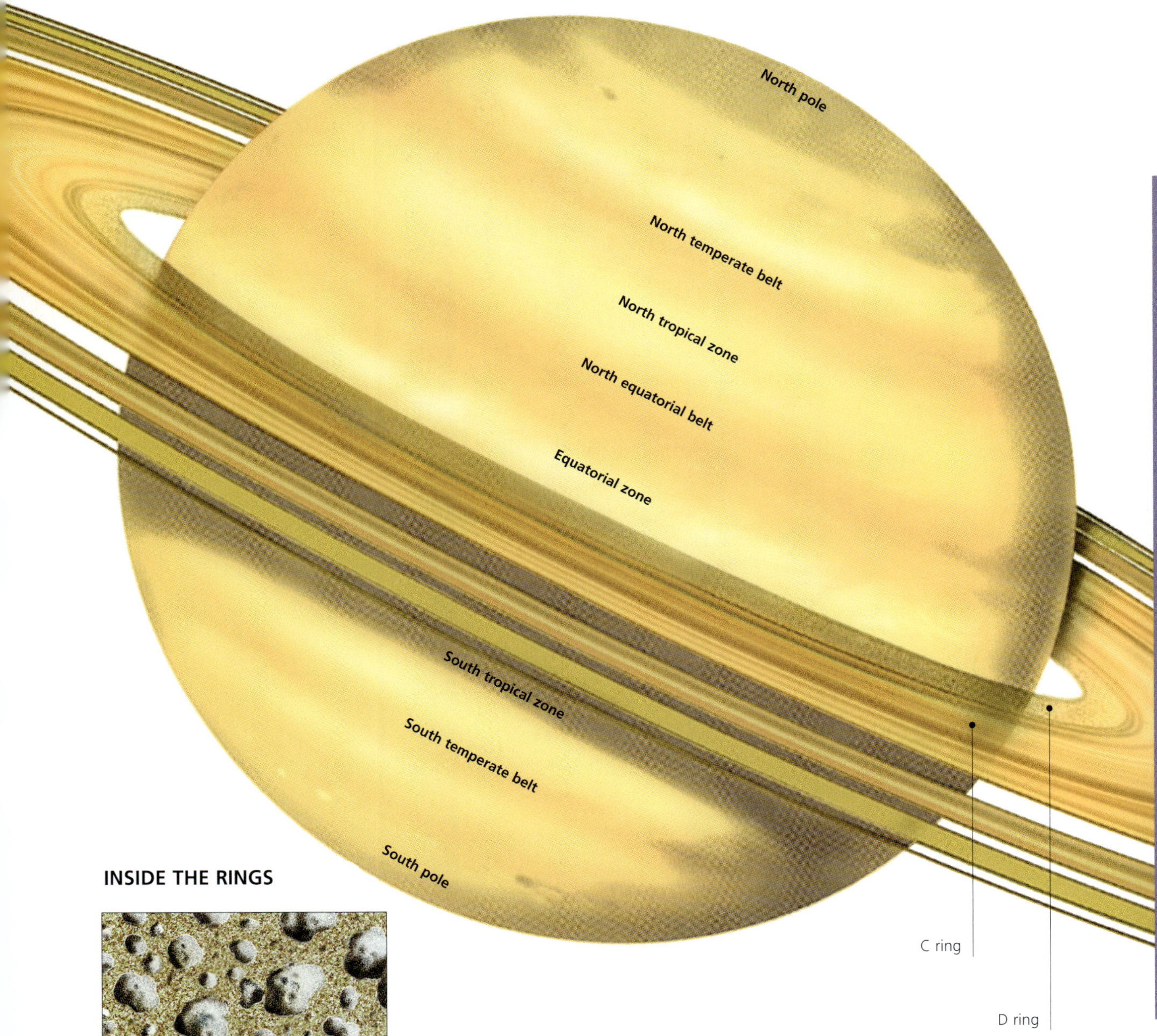

INSIDE THE RINGS

Uranus

SEASONS OF URANUS
Uranus's orbit takes 84 Earth years, so each pole receives a long period of constant sunlight followed by a long period of darkness.

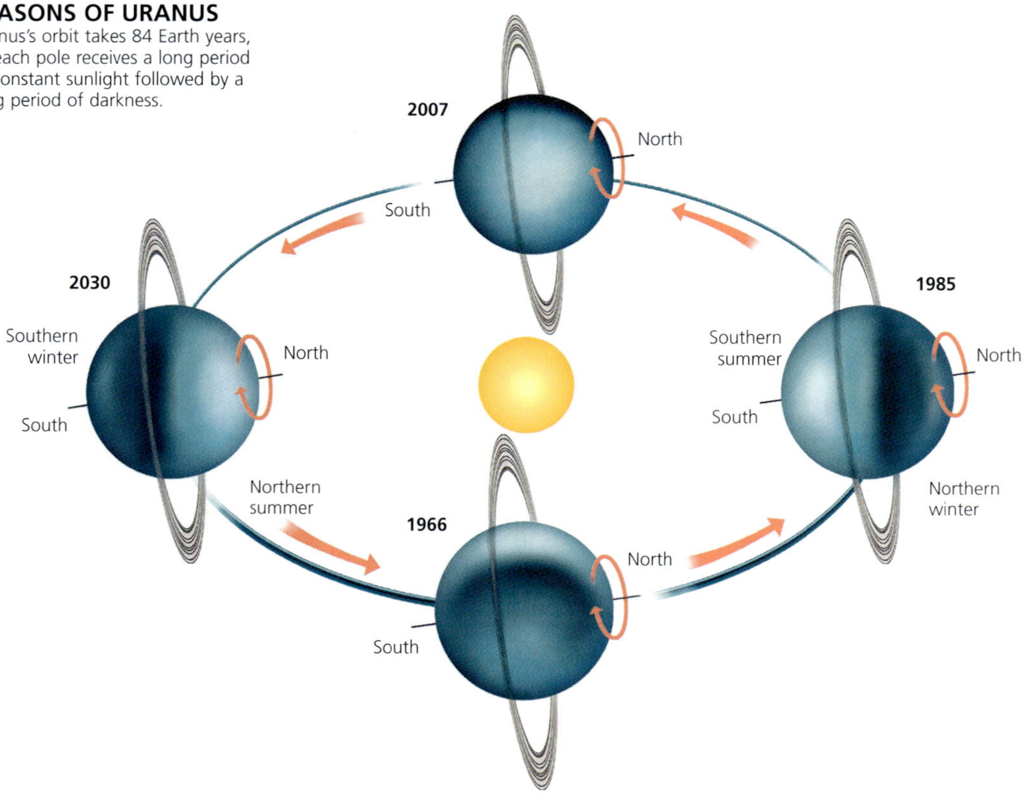

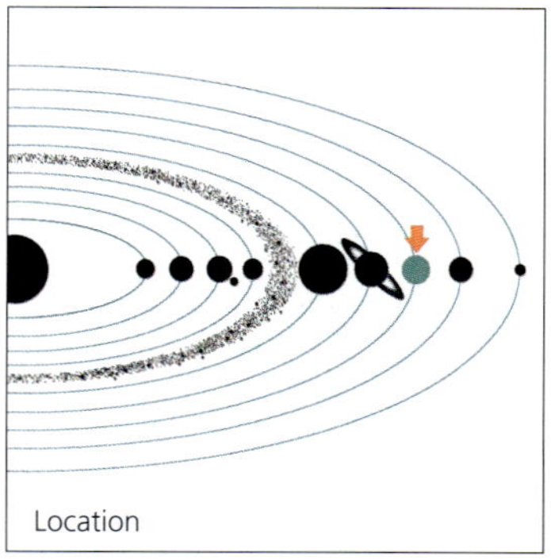

CROSS SECTION

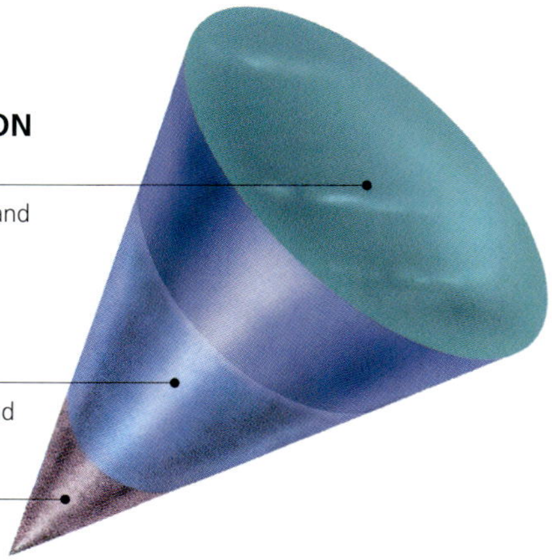

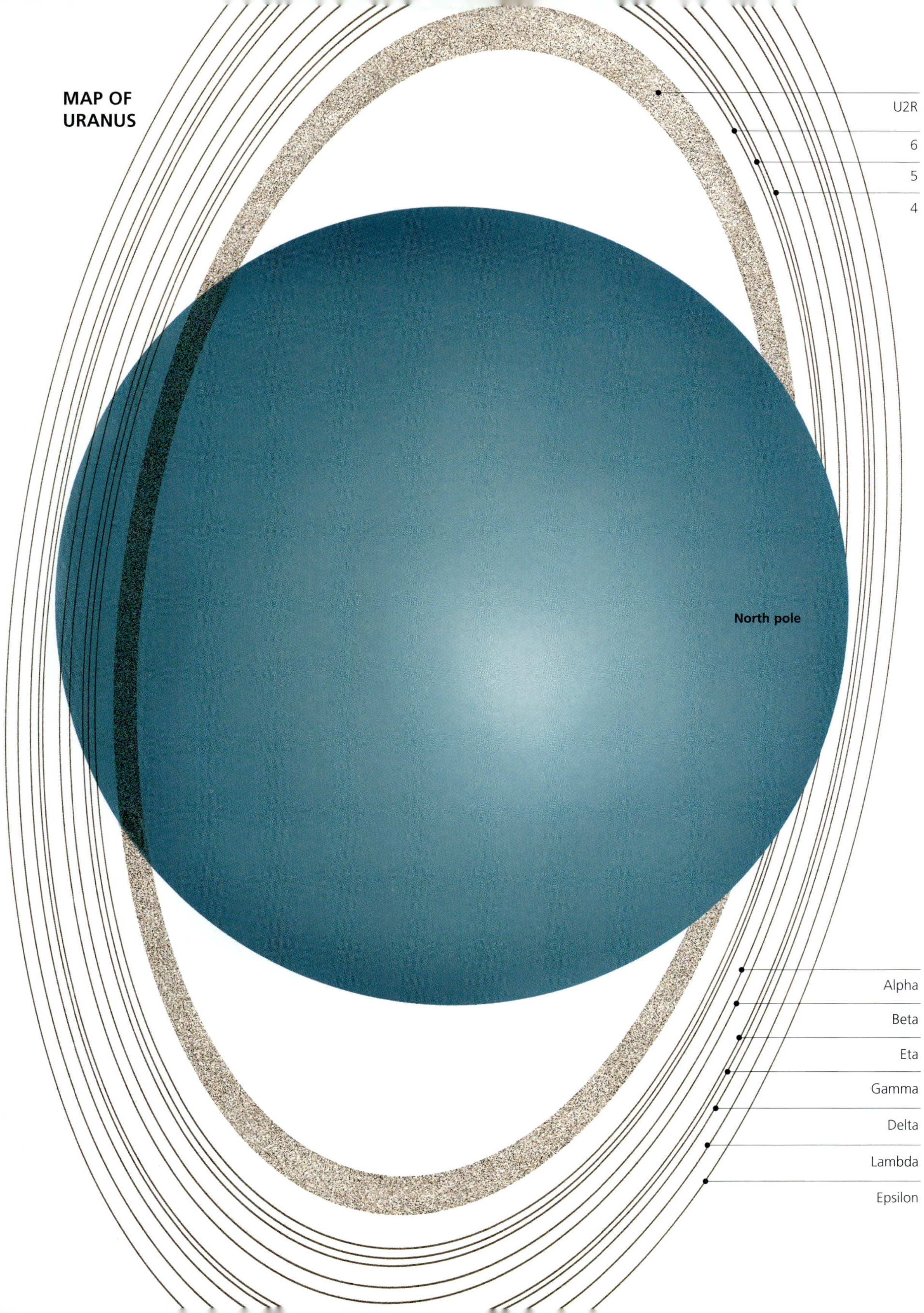
MAP OF
URANUS
U2R
6
5
4
North pole
Alpha
Beta
Eta
Gamma
Delta
Lambda
Epsilon

Neptune

VOYAGER 2

Voyager 2 flew past Neptune in 1986, relaying data to Earth.

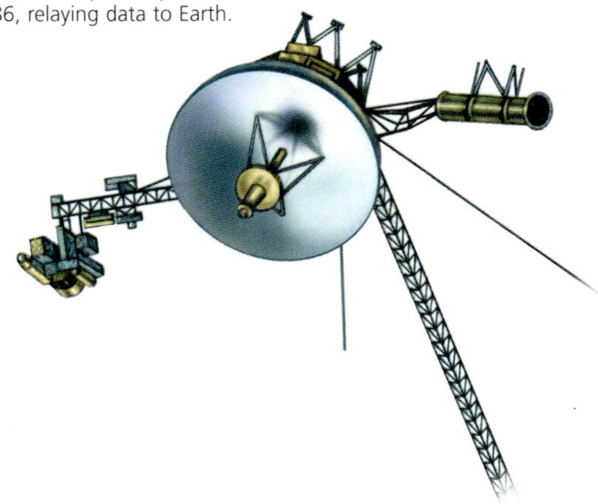

ORBIT

Neptune's orbit takes 165 Earth years. Since it was first seen in 1846, it has still not made a full orbit around the Sun.

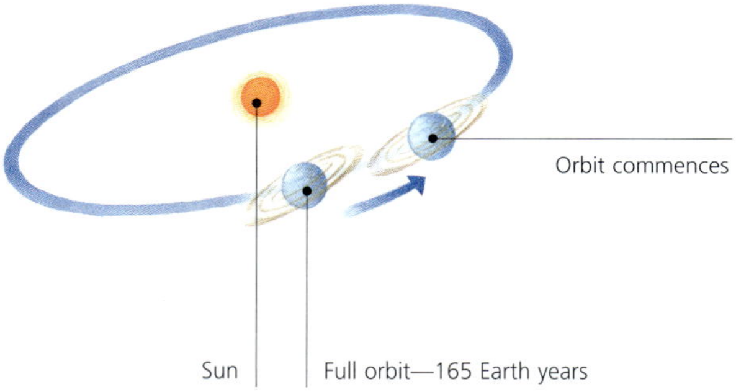

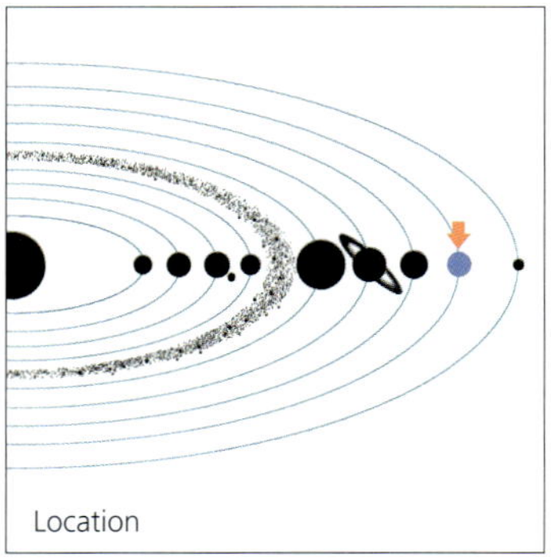

CROSS SECTION

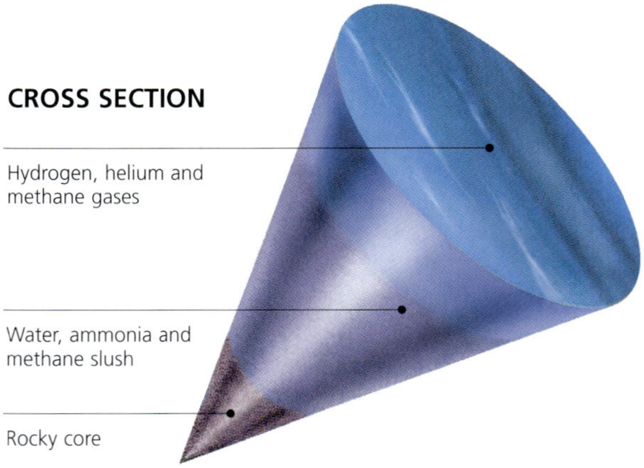

North pole
South pole
Leverrier
Lassell
Arago
Adams
Galle

Pluto

MAP OF PLUTO

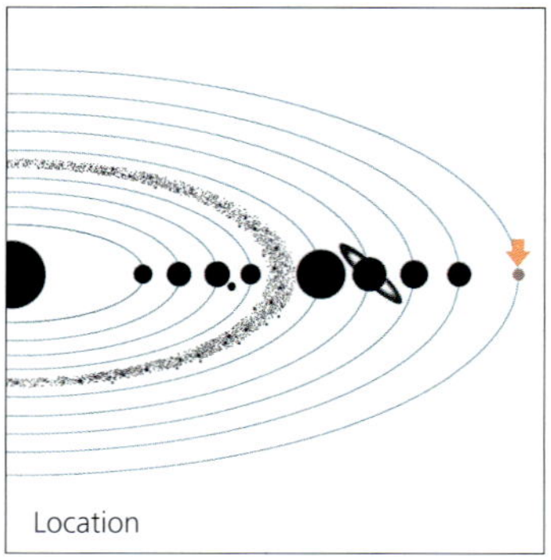

CROSS SECTION

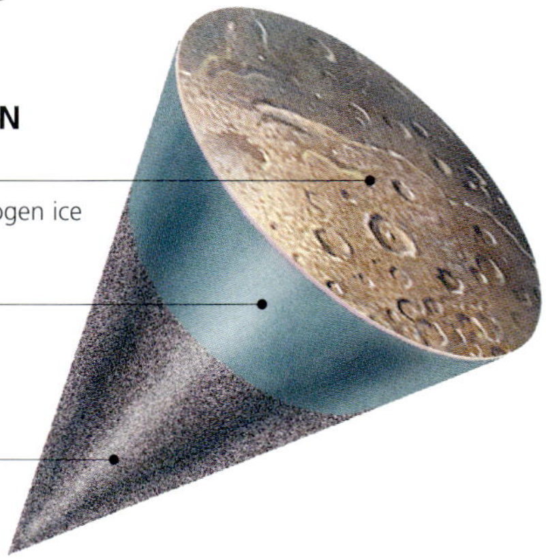

PLUTO'S DAY AND MONTH

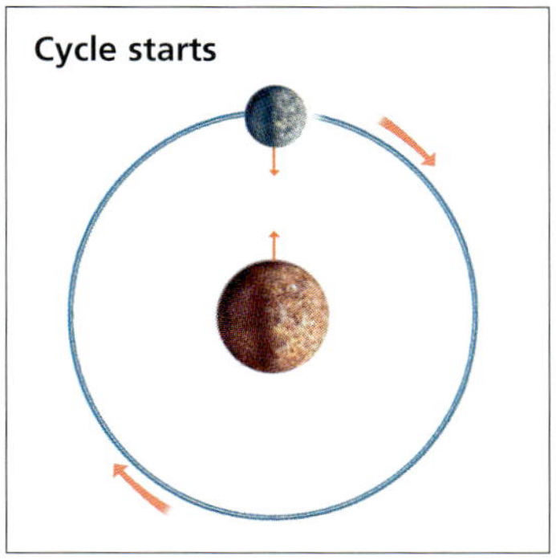

Due to the exact length of Pluto's rotation and its moon's orbit, Pluto's day and month are identical.

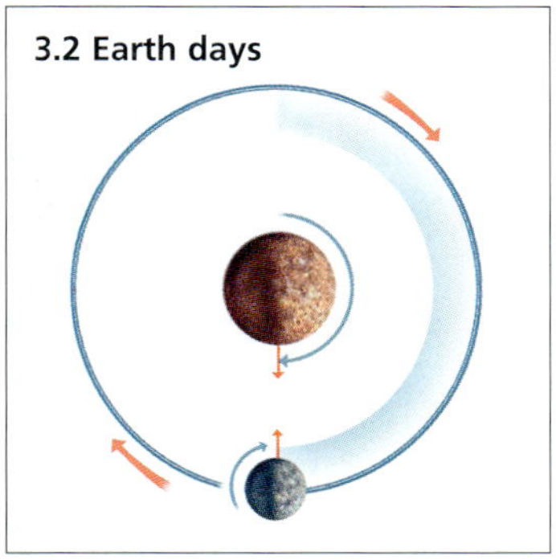

Pluto and its moon Charon keep the same faces turned toward each other.

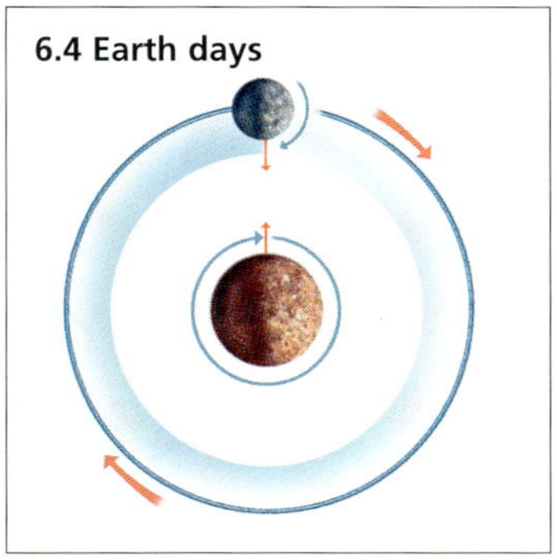

Pluto has completed its rotation and Charon has completed its orbit.

KUIPER BELT

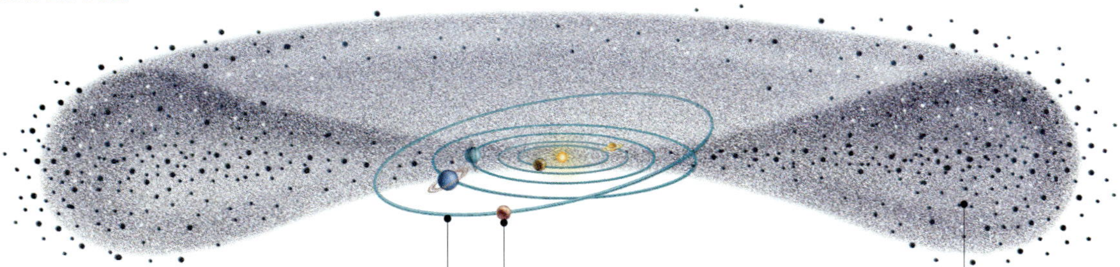

SIZE COMPARISON

Pluto

Earth's moon

Jupiter's moon—Ganymede

Size Comparison of Planets

RELATIVE SIZES

Uranus
Saturn
Neptune
Pluto

Asteroids and Meteoroids

TYPES OF METEORITES

Iron meteorite

Stony meteorite

Stony-iron meteorite

ASTEROID BELT

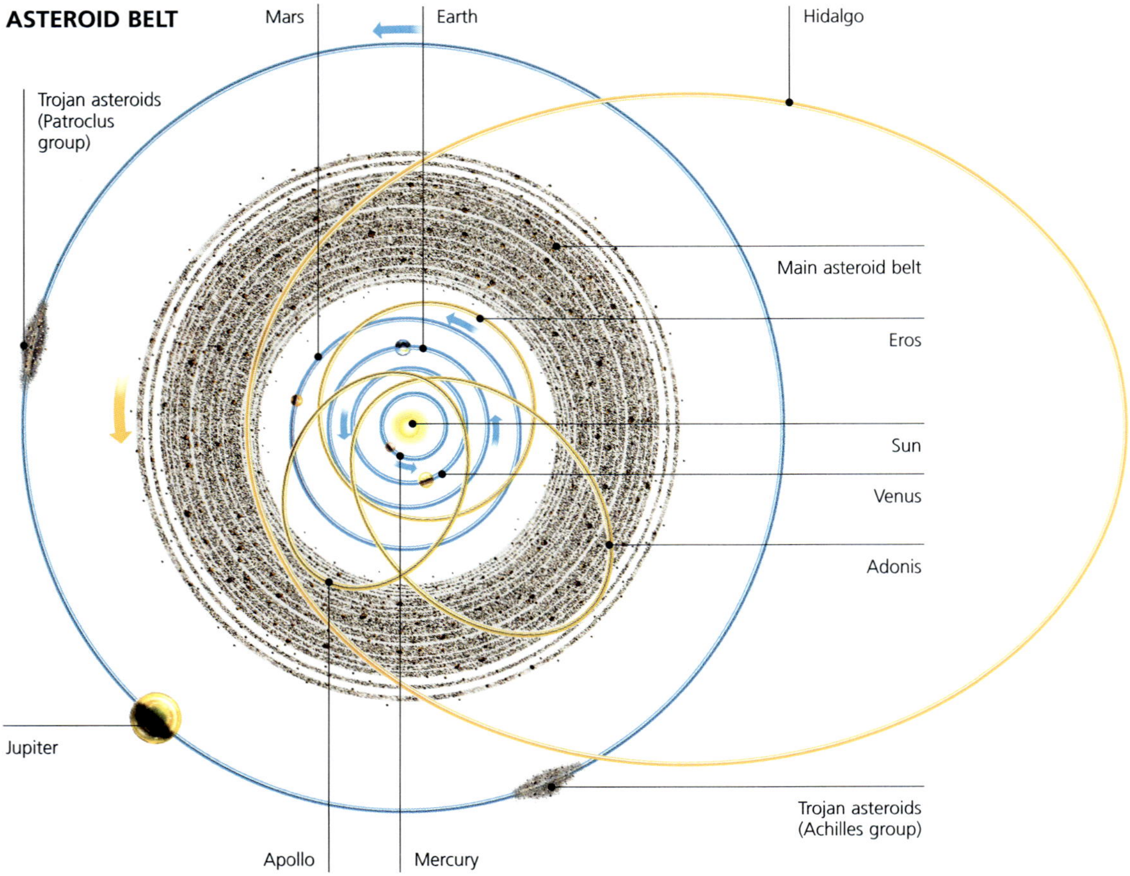

METEOR SHOWER
Although no large meteorite impact has occurred in human history, scientists believe it is just a matter of time.

Comets

COMET ORBITS

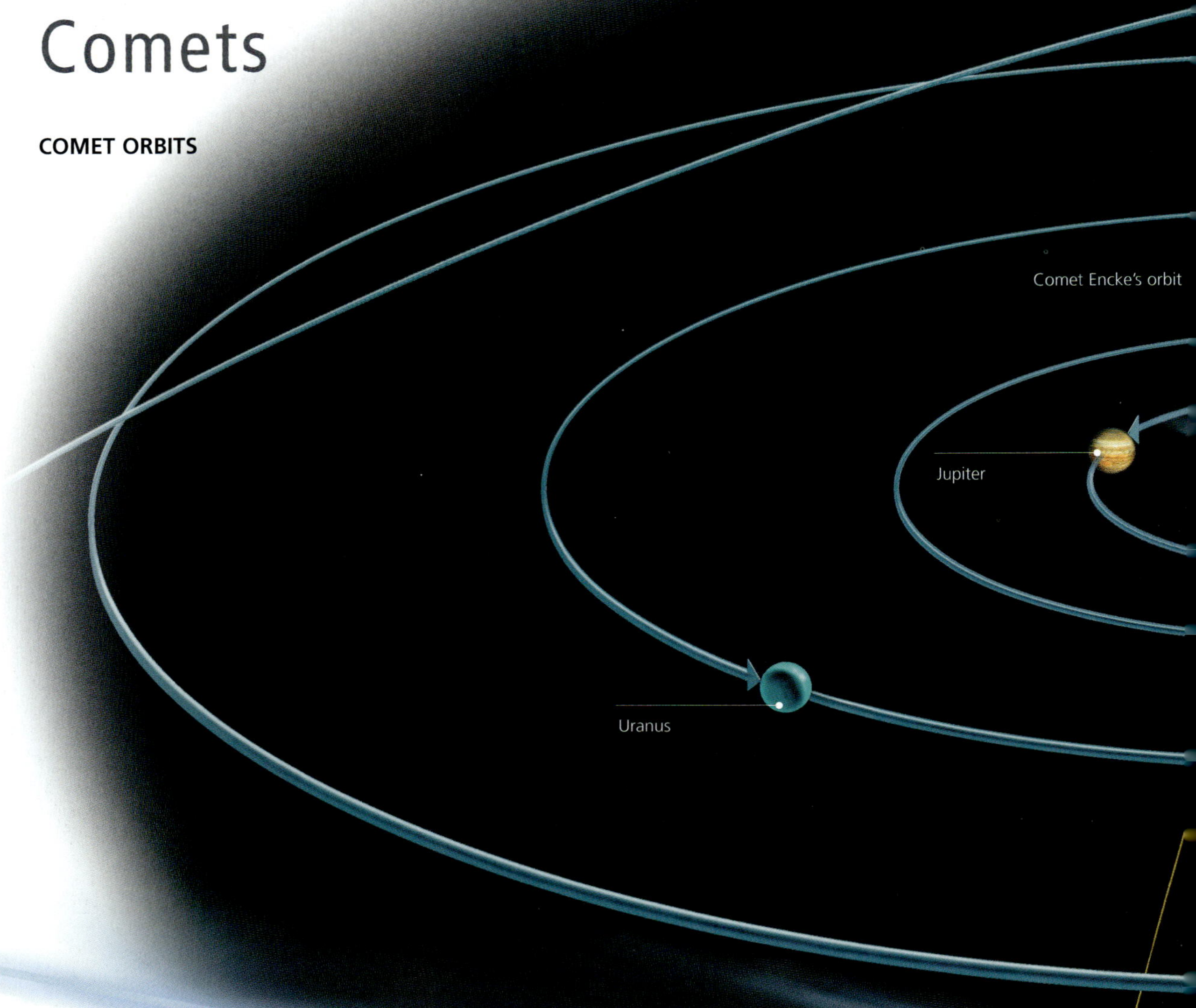

COMET CROSS SECTION

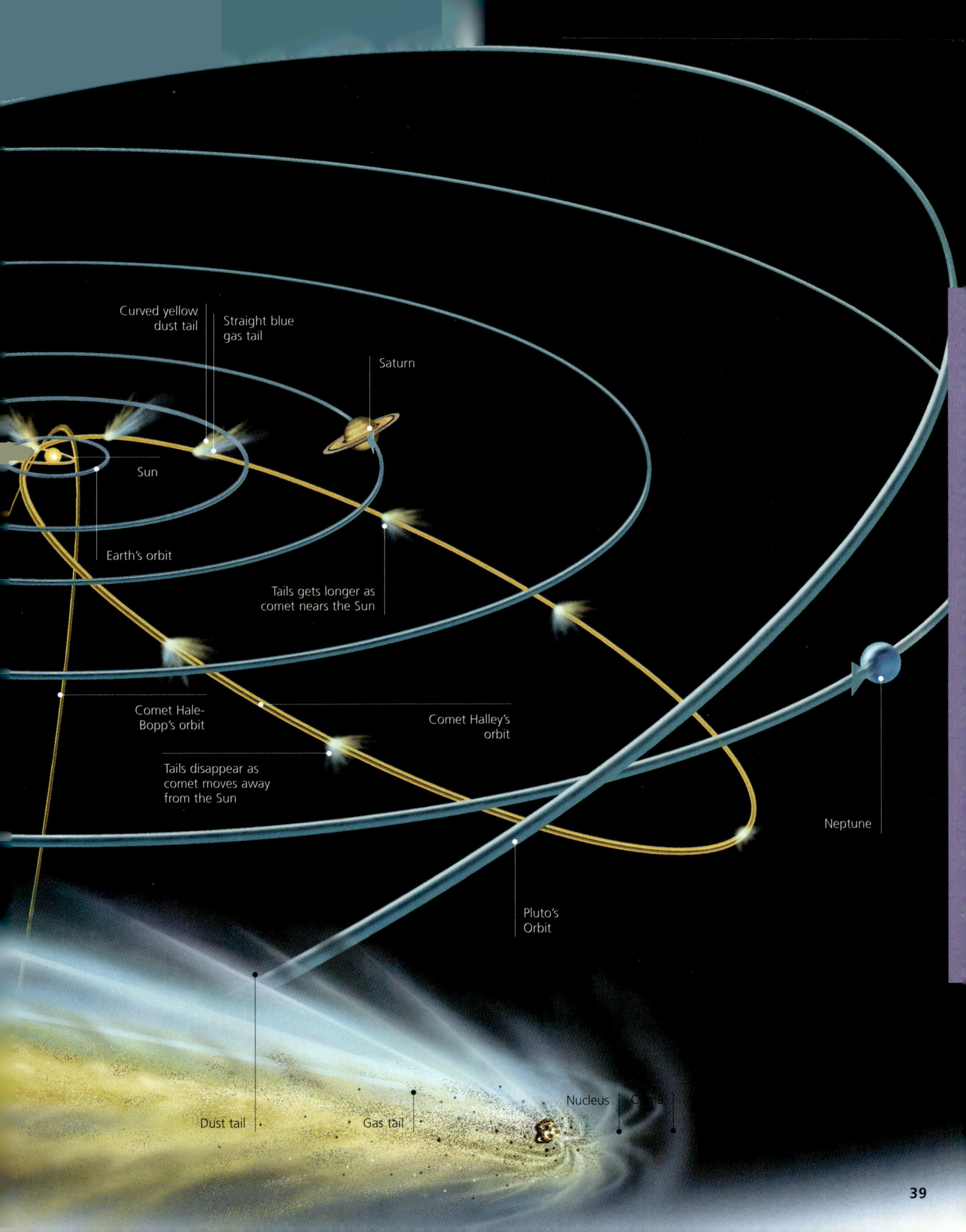
Curved yellow dust tail
Straight blue gas tail
Saturn
Sun
Earth's orbit
Tails gets longer as comet nears the Sun
Comet Hale-Bopp's orbit
Comet Halley's orbit
Tails disappear as comet moves away from the Sun
Neptune
Pluto's Orbit
Nucleus
Dust tail
Gas tail

Earth's Moon

MAP OF THE MOON
Farside hemisphere

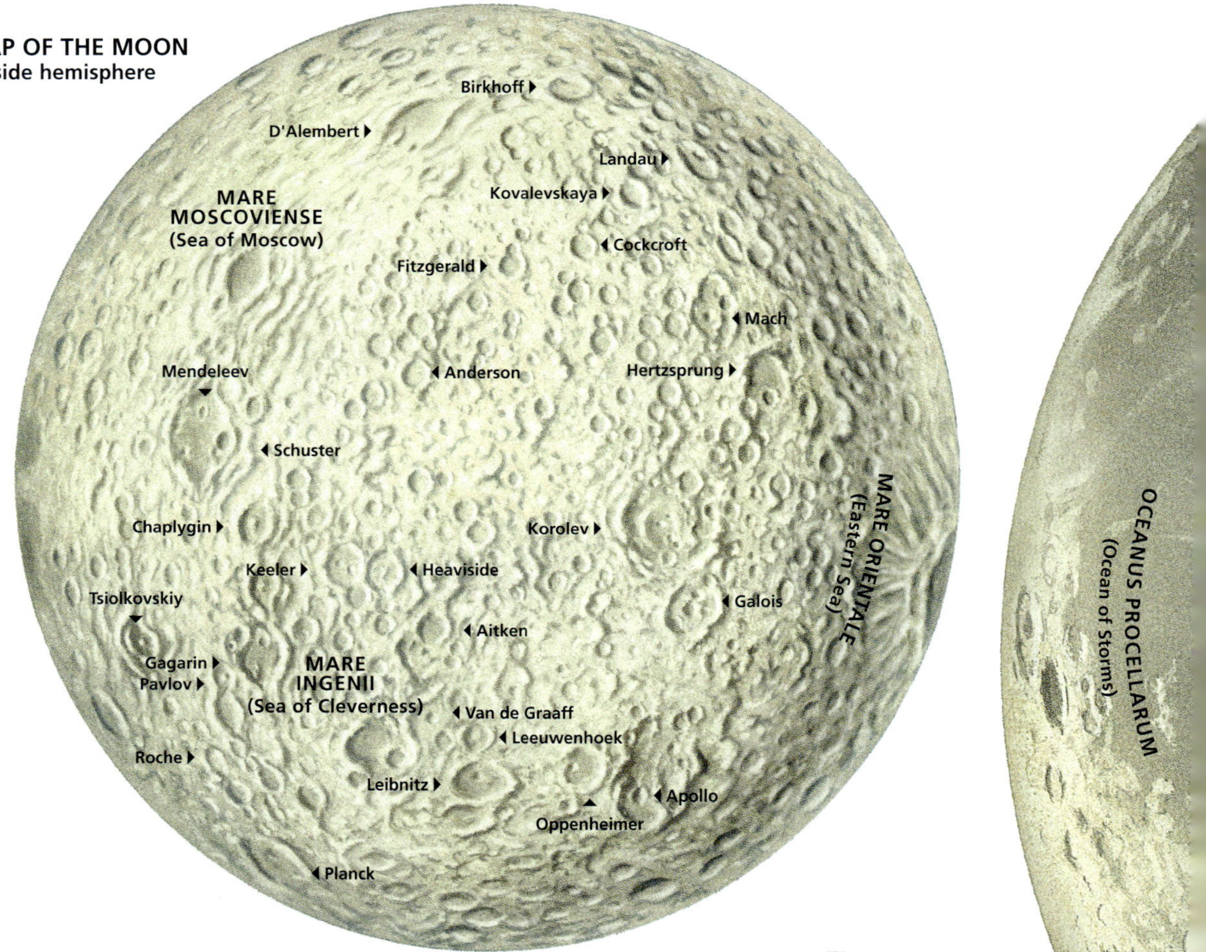

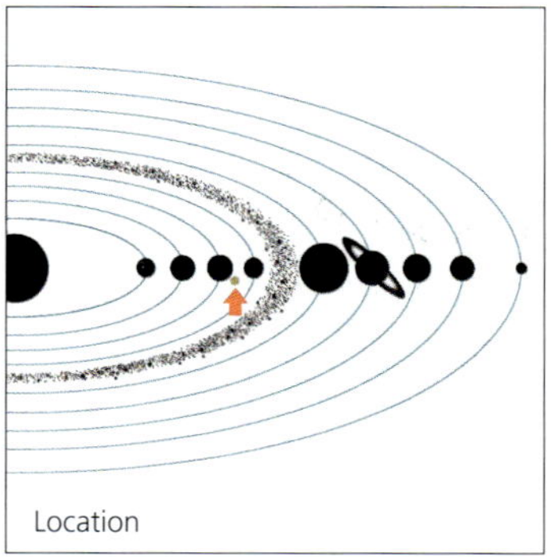

CROSS SECTION

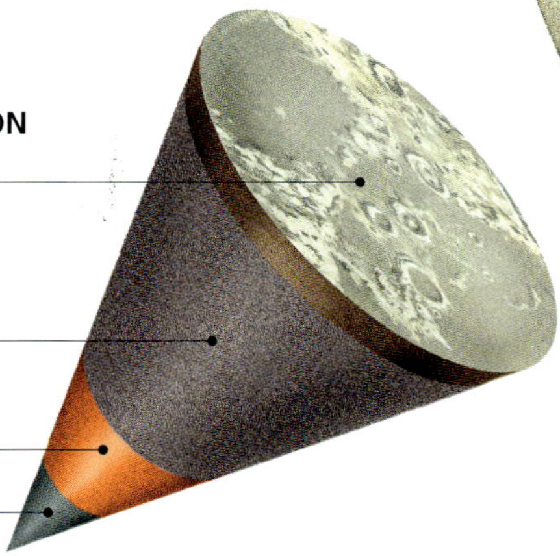

MAP OF THE MOON
Nearside hemisphere

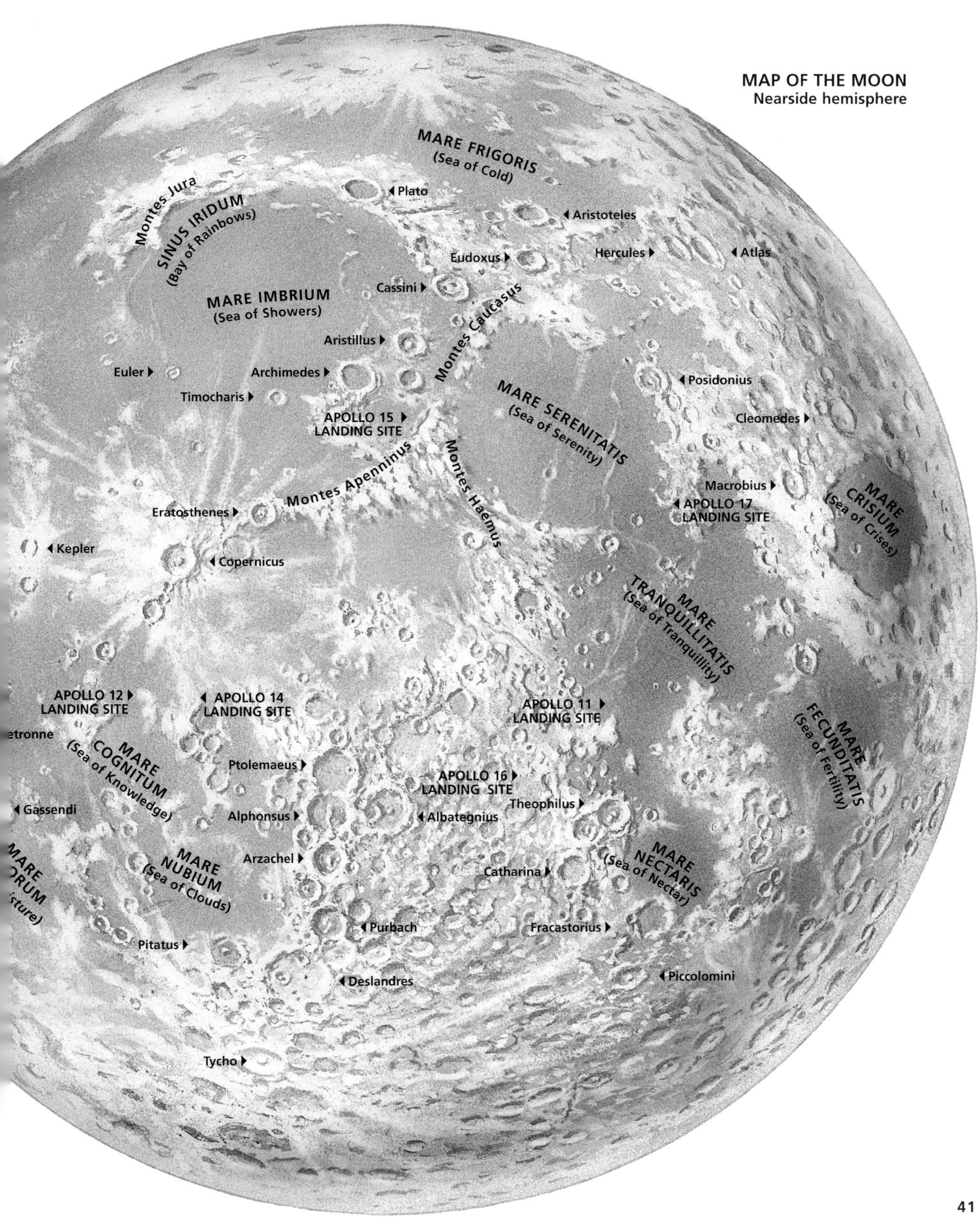

Earth's Moon

THE MOON'S FORMATION

Earth was struck by a large object.

The debris circled around Earth.

Eventually the debris clumped together.

LUNAR PROSPECTOR
This craft studied the Moon's composition, relaying data back to Earth.

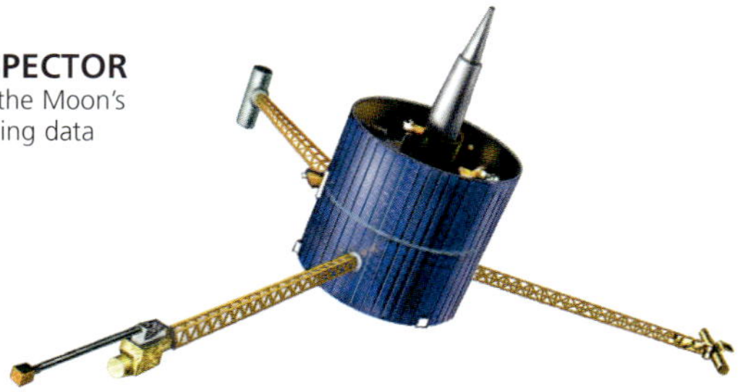

LUNA 16
This Soviet Union craft was the first to collect Moon rocks automatically.

LUNOKHOD 1
In 1970, this was the the first roving remote-controlled robot on the Moon.

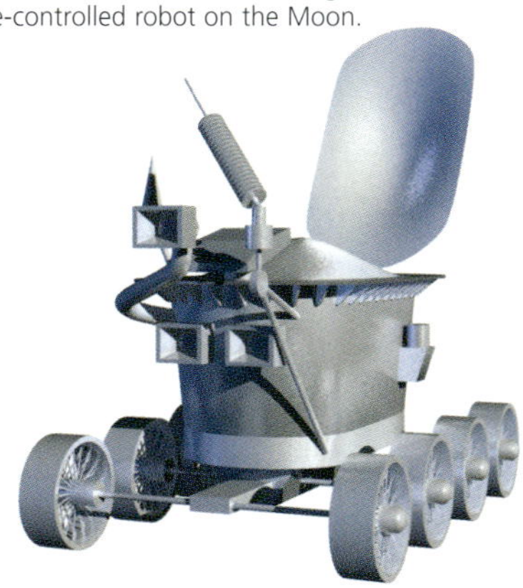

MISSION TO THE MOON

From 1968 to 1972, 27 astronauts visited the Moon in the Apollo spacecraft.

Solar and Lunar Eclipses

PHASES OF THE MOON

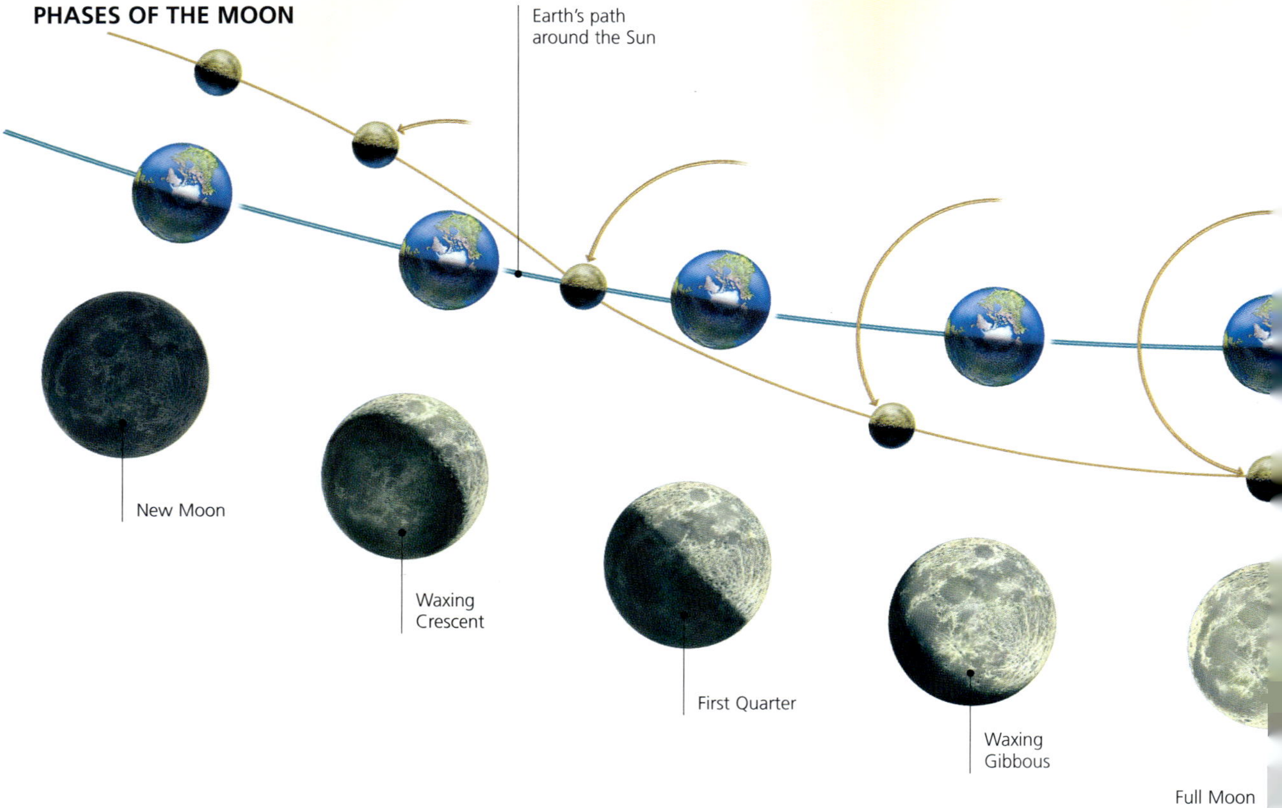

LUNAR ECLIPSE

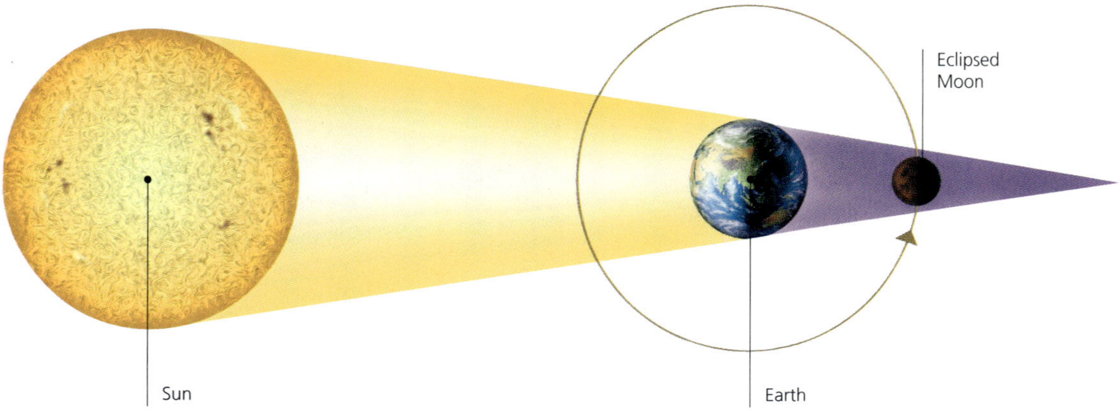

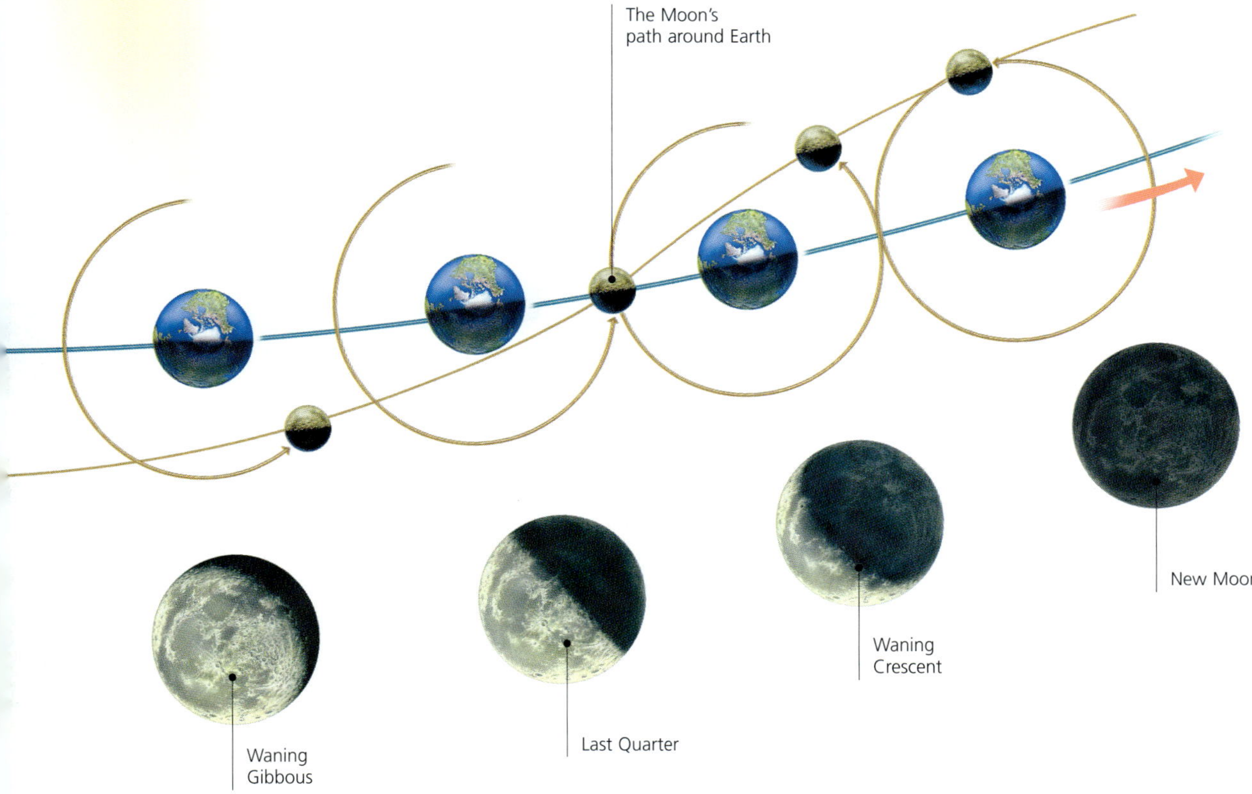

SOLAR ECLIPSE

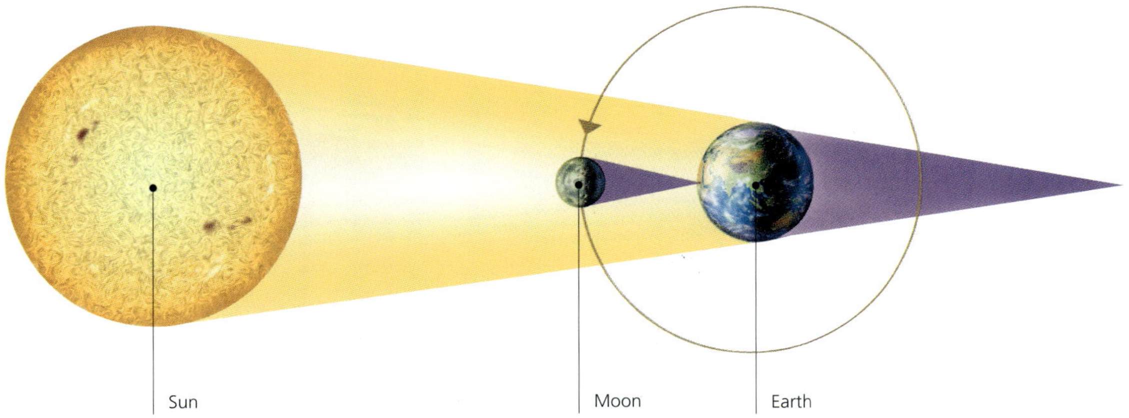

Moons

SATURN'S MAJOR MOONS

Mimas

Enceladus

Iapetus

Titan

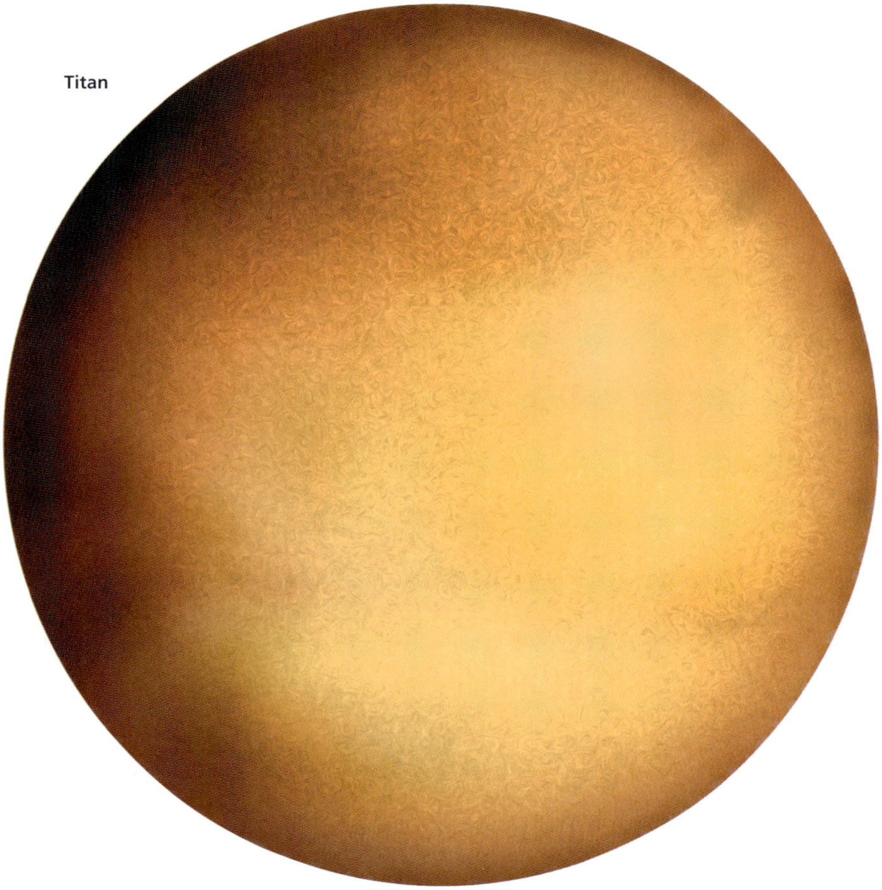

URANUS'S MAJOR MOONS

Miranda

Umbriel

Ariel

Titania

Oberon

Moons

NEPTUNE'S MAJOR MOONS

Nereid

Triton

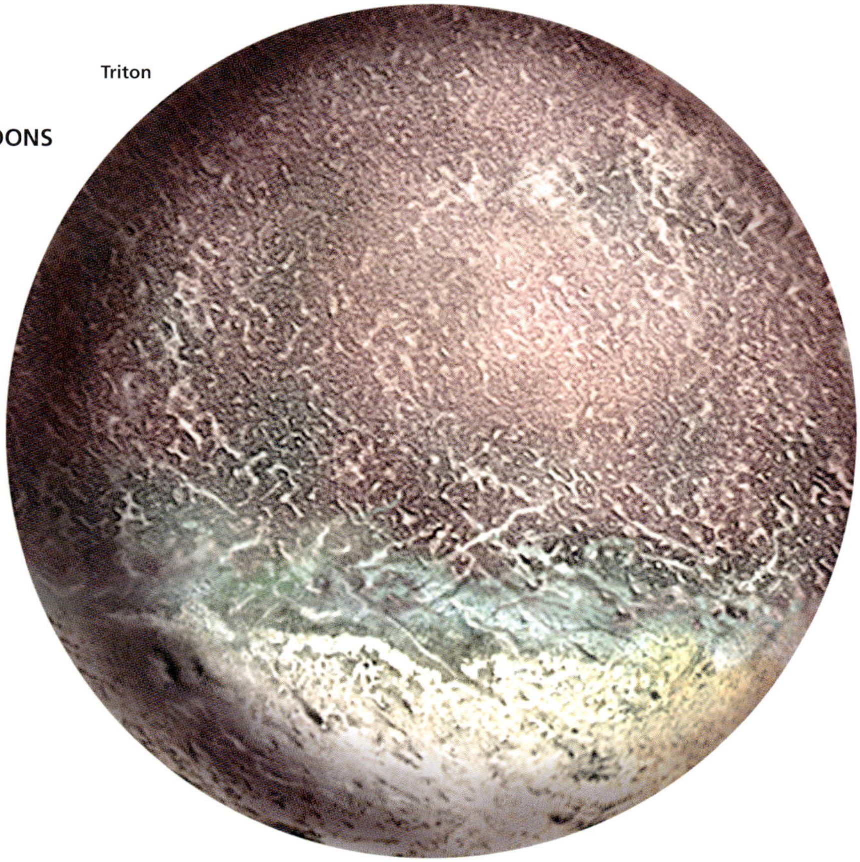

PLUTO'S MOON

Charon

MARS'S MOONS

Deimos

Phobos

JUPITER'S MAJOR MOONS

Ganymede

Europa

Io

Callisto

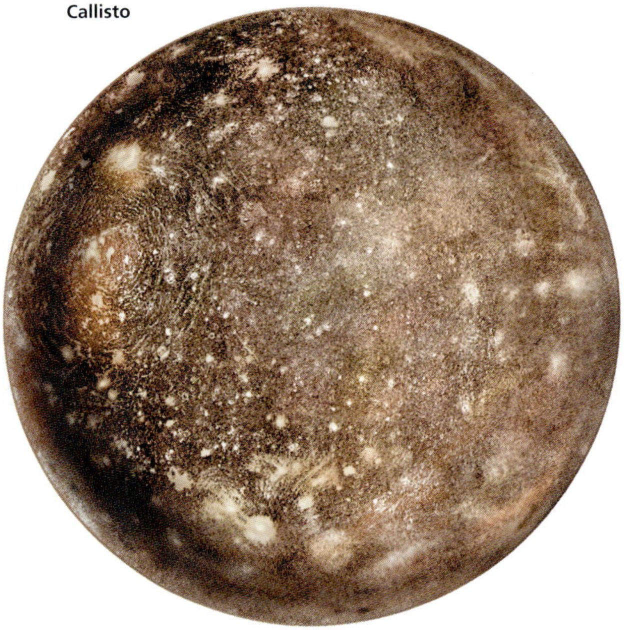

The Sun

MAP OF THE SUN

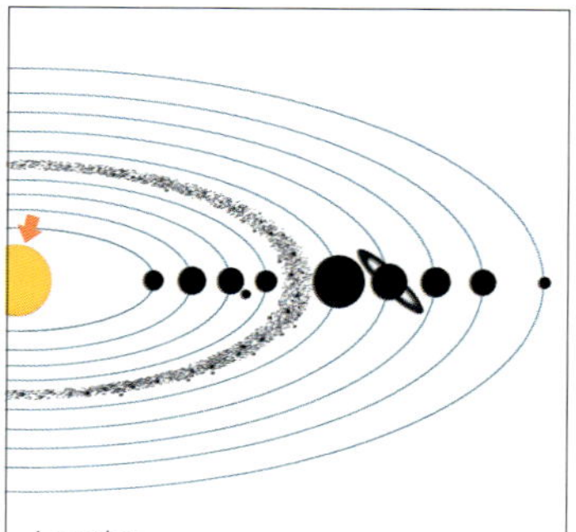

Location

CROSS SECTION

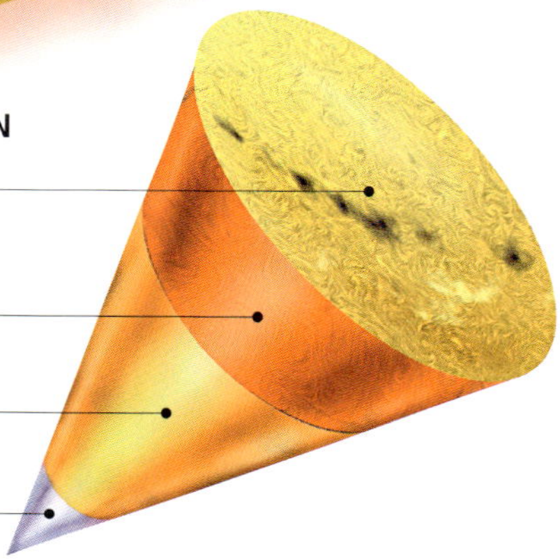

INSIDE THE SUN

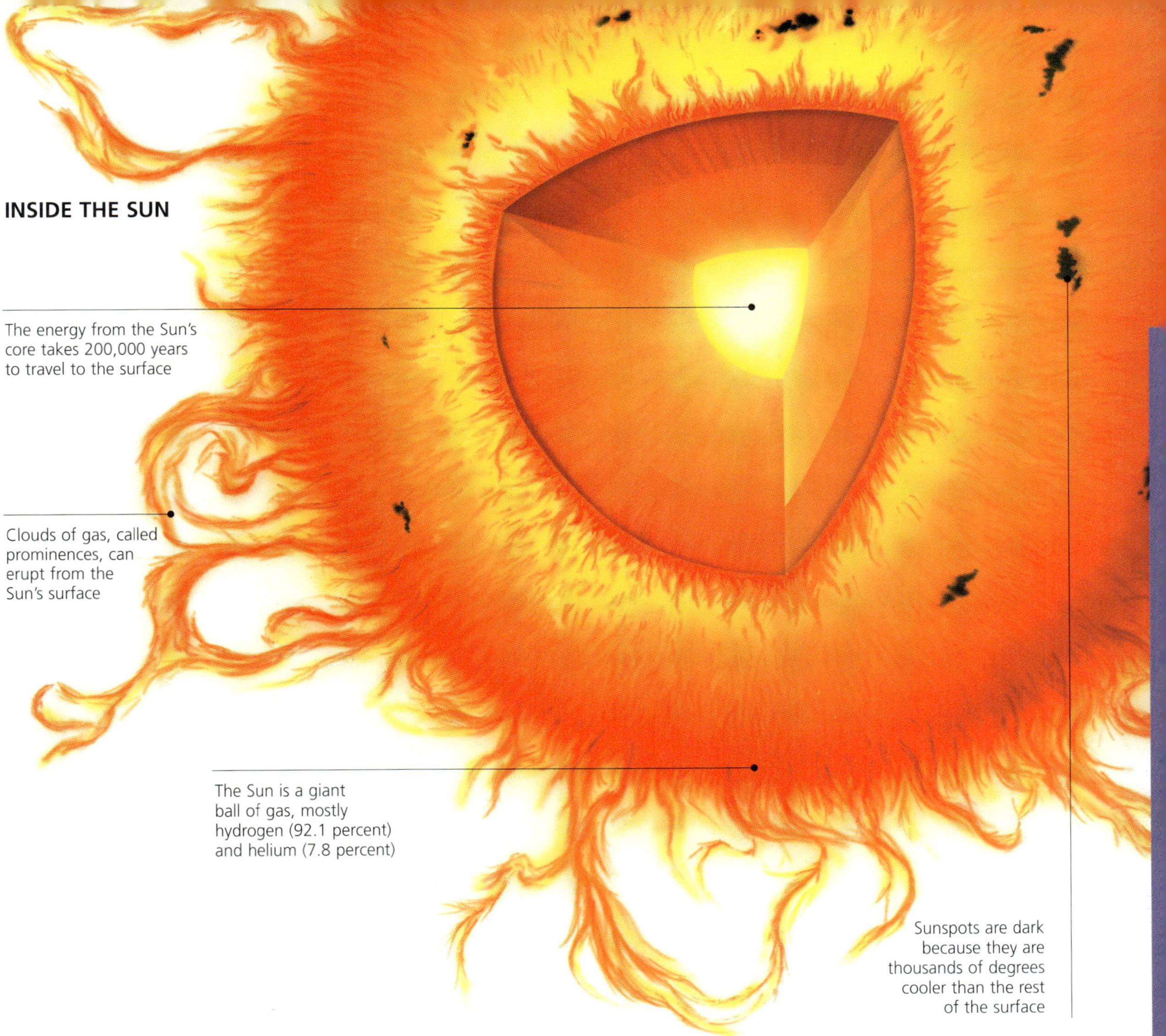

SUNSPOT CYCLE

Sunspots form where high magnetic force keeps heat from reaching the surface. The number of sunspots waxes and wanes every eleven years.

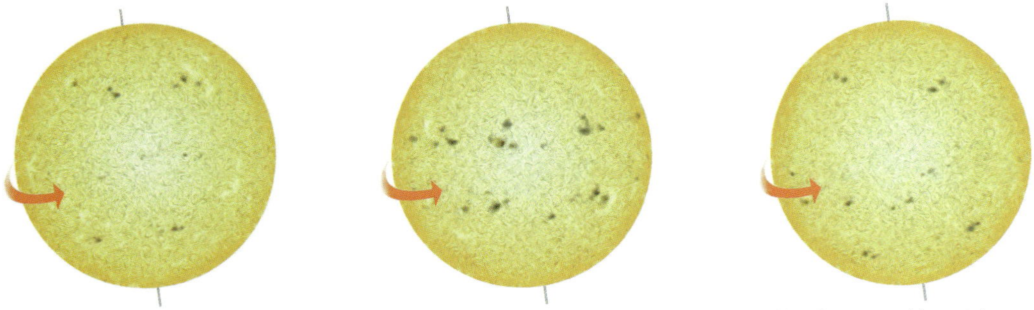

Year 1—sunspot minimum   Year 5—sunspot maximum   Year 9—approaching minimum

Life Cycle of a Star

LIFE CYCLE

1. Starbirth Nebula
An ordinary star is born in a nebula when a cloud of gas and dust starts to collapse and grow hotter.

2. Main Sequence Star
About 40 million years later, the star is fully formed.

3. Red Giant Star
After another 10 billion years, the star runs low on hydrogen fuel. It swells into a red giant that starts to pulsate.

4. Planetary Nebula
Three billion years later, the pulsations grow stronger and the bloated star sheds it outer layers.

5. White Dwarf Star
In less than 50,000 years, the planetary nebula disperses into space. It leaves behind a white dwarf, the star's white-hot core.

STAR SIZE COMPARISON

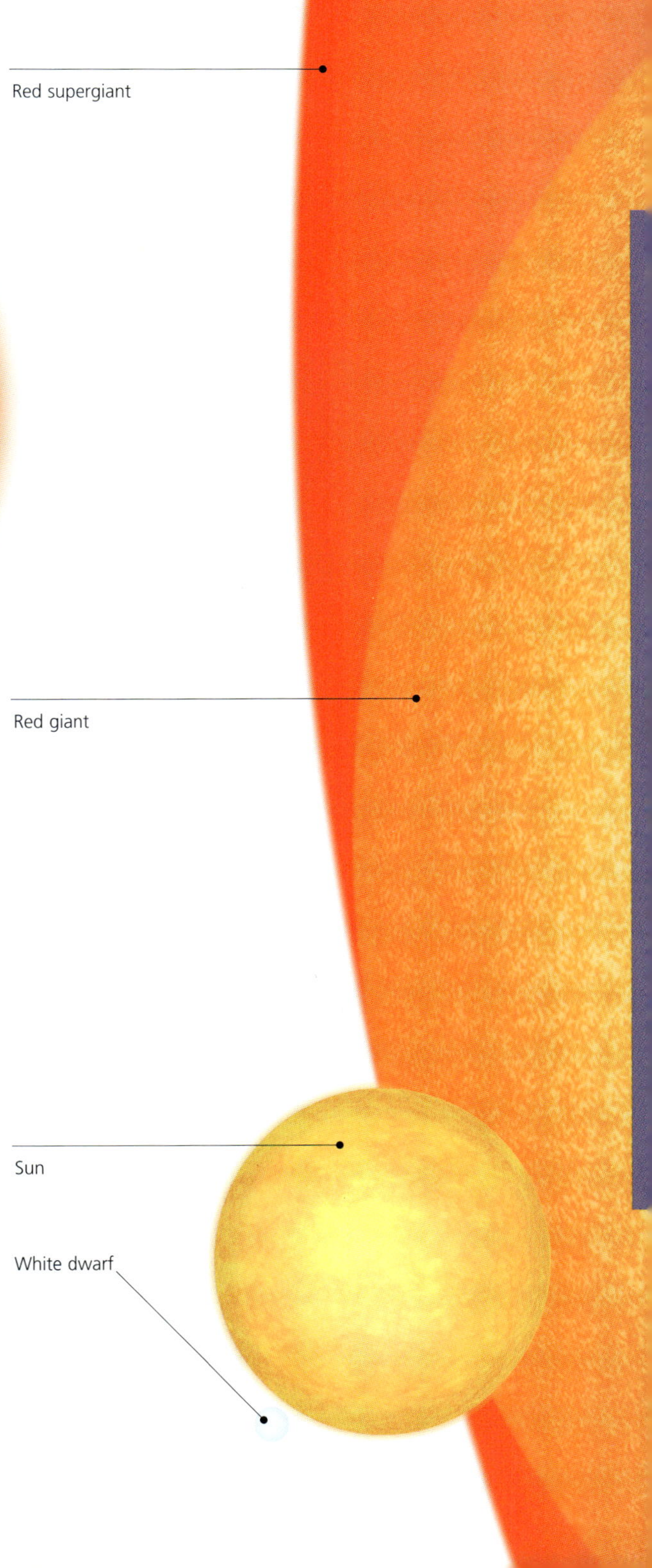

Stars and Supernovas

MASSIVE-STAR SUPERNOVA

This type of supernova signals the explosive death of a massive star.

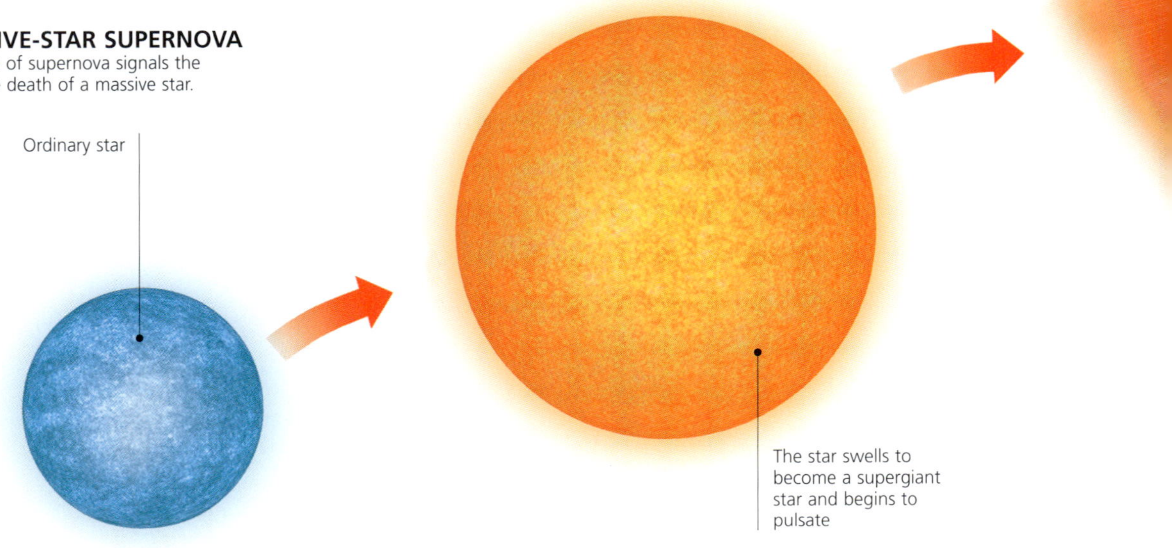

PULSARS

A neutron star is only a few miles across but it spins rapidly. If Earth lies in the beam of its energy, we see a repeating signal of light.

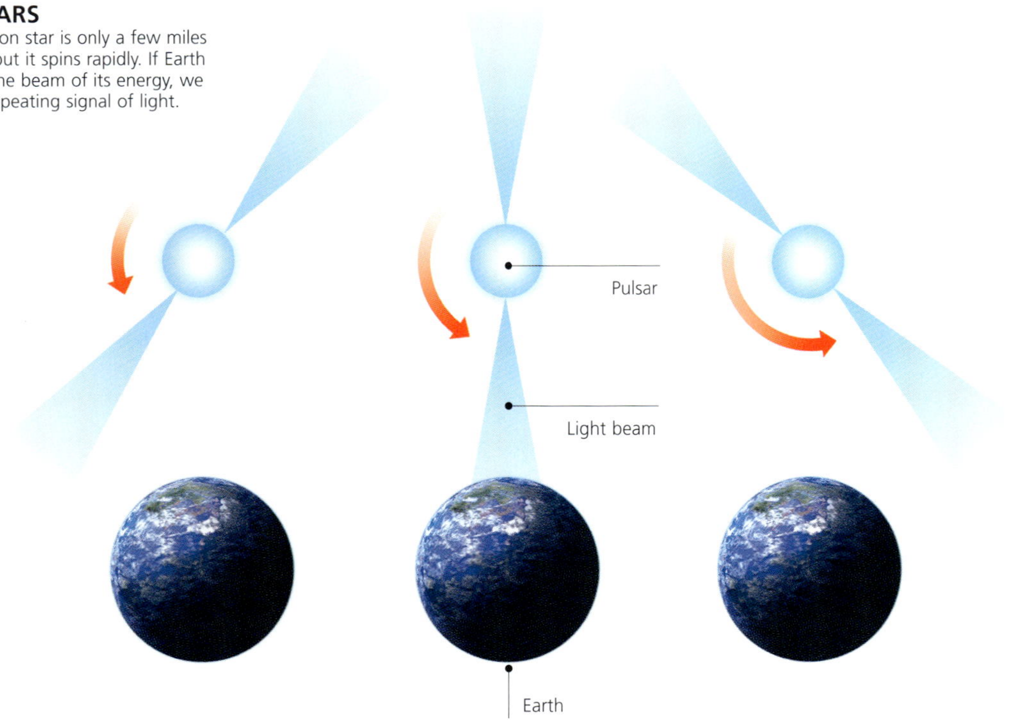

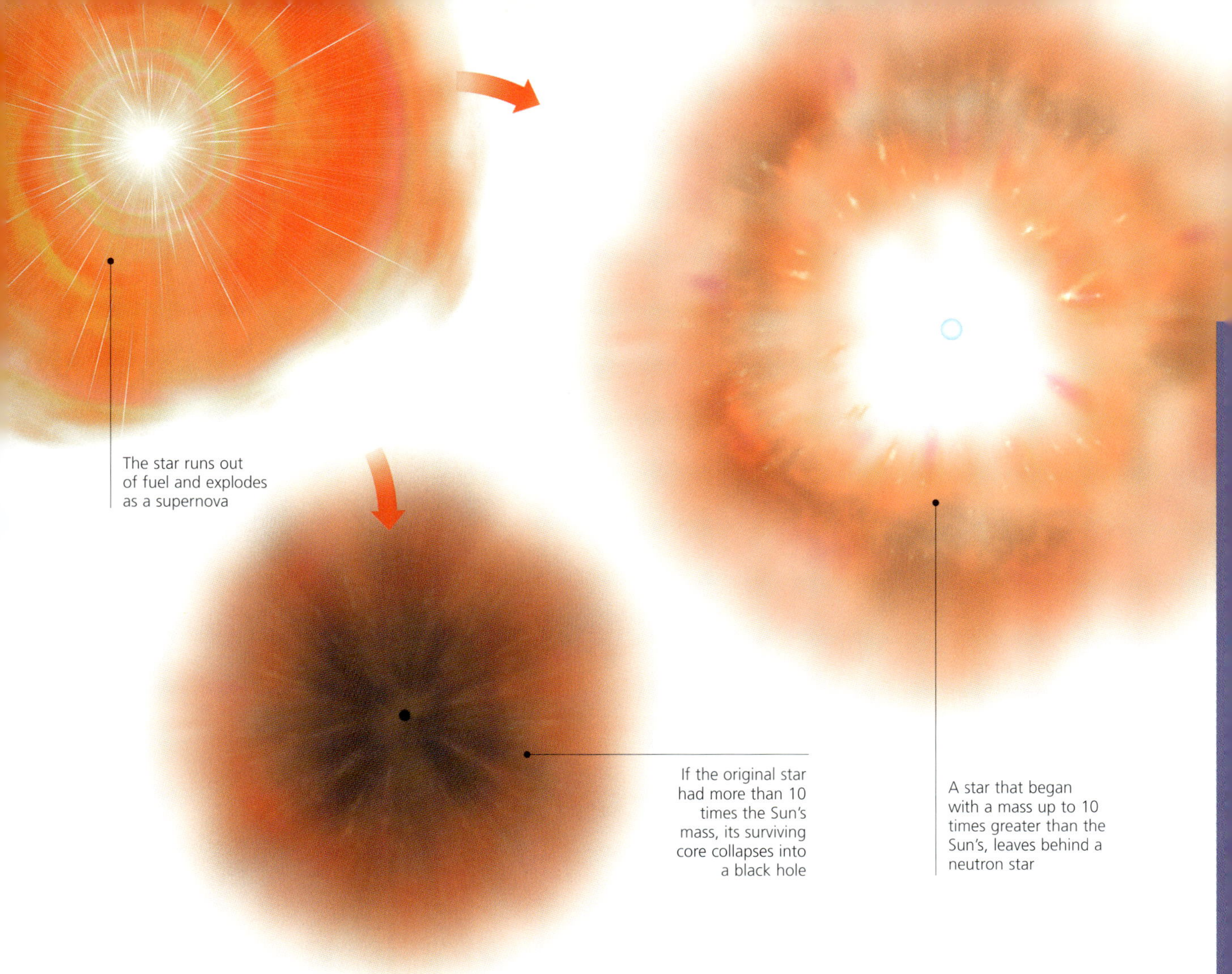

DOUBLE-STAR SUPERNOVA

A supernova can occur in double-star systems, where gas moves from one star to another.

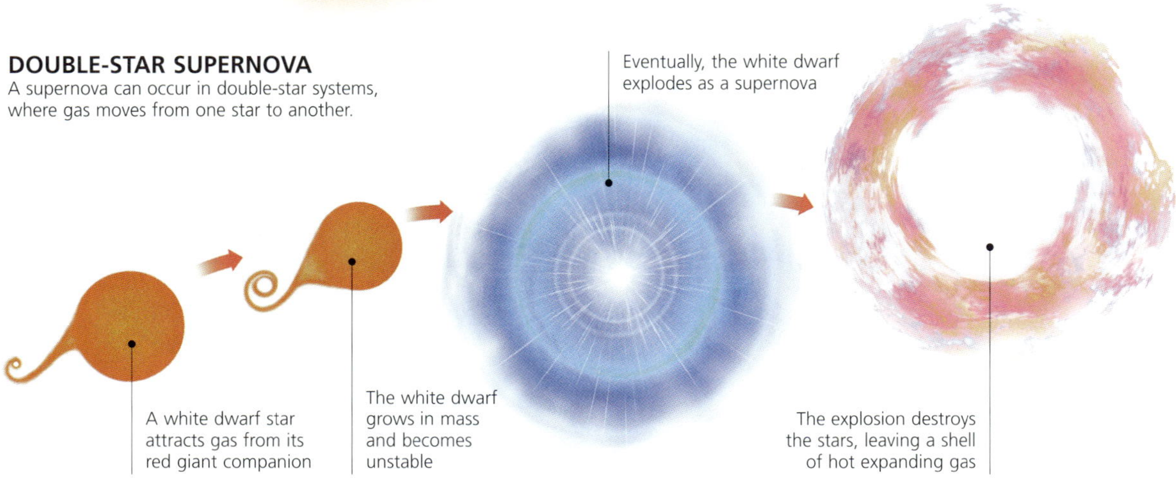

Clusters

MILKY WAY CLUSTERS

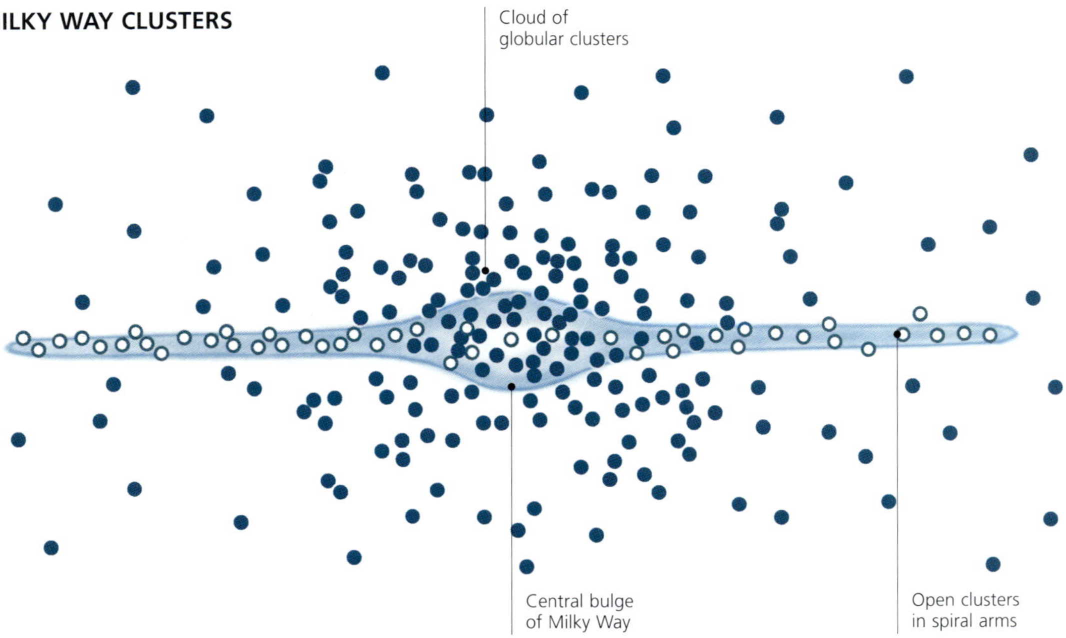

GLOBULAR CLUSTERS

Young

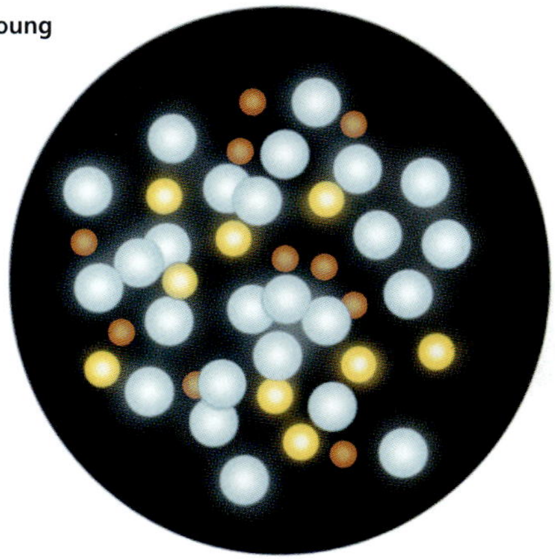

A young cluster has many white-hot stars, plus yellow stars like the Sun and dim red dwarfs.

Old

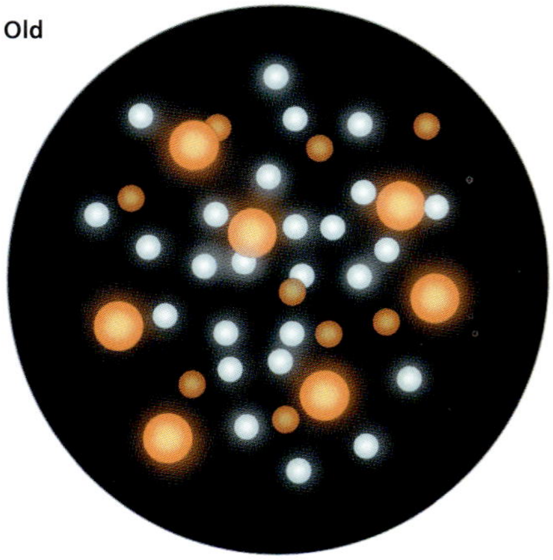

Stars in the original population have evolved, becoming red giants and white dwarfs.

OPEN CLUSTERS OVER TIME

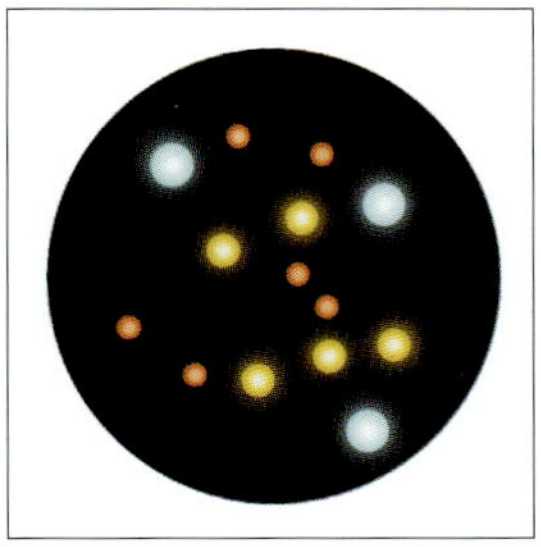

Members of the open cluster drift apart as the galaxy's gravity pulls.

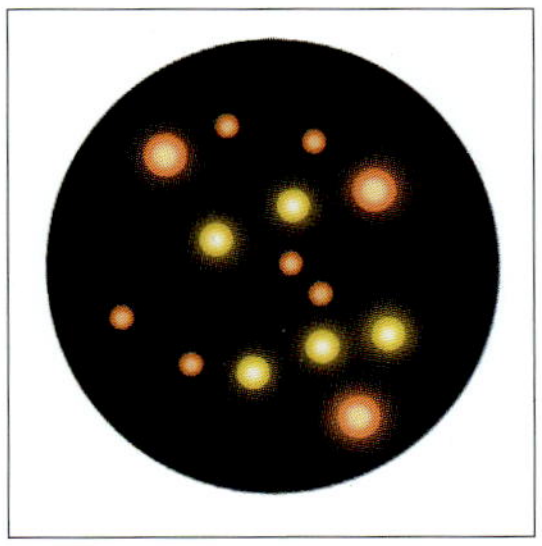

The cluster members evolve, with massive stars becoming red giants.

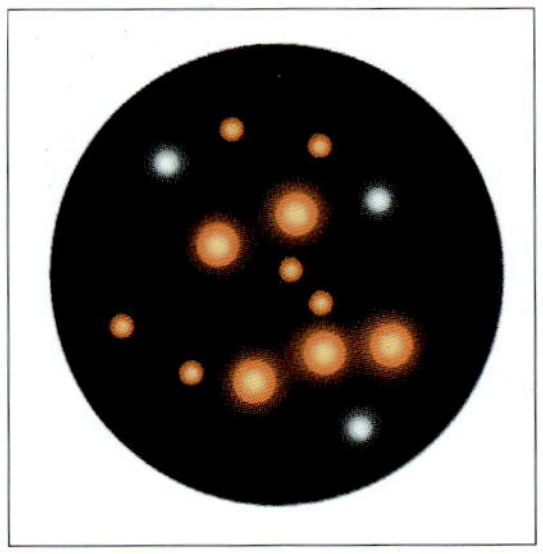

As the cluster becomes fainter, the red giants become white dwarfs.

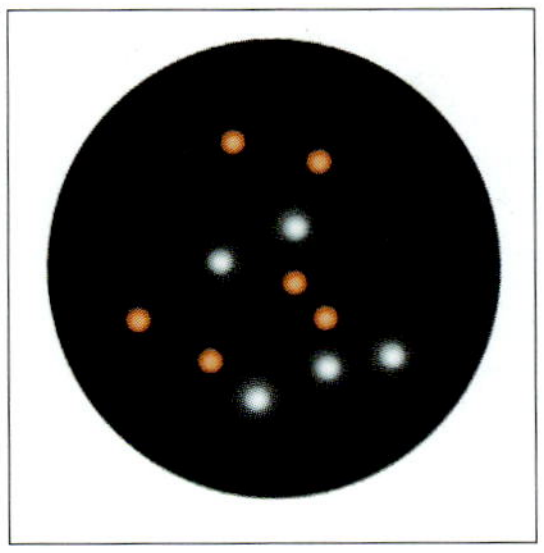

Eventually, the cluster becomes hard to tell apart from the rest of the galaxy.

THE PLEIADES

The Pleiades is an open cluster in the constellation of Taurus. It lies 375 light-years away from Earth

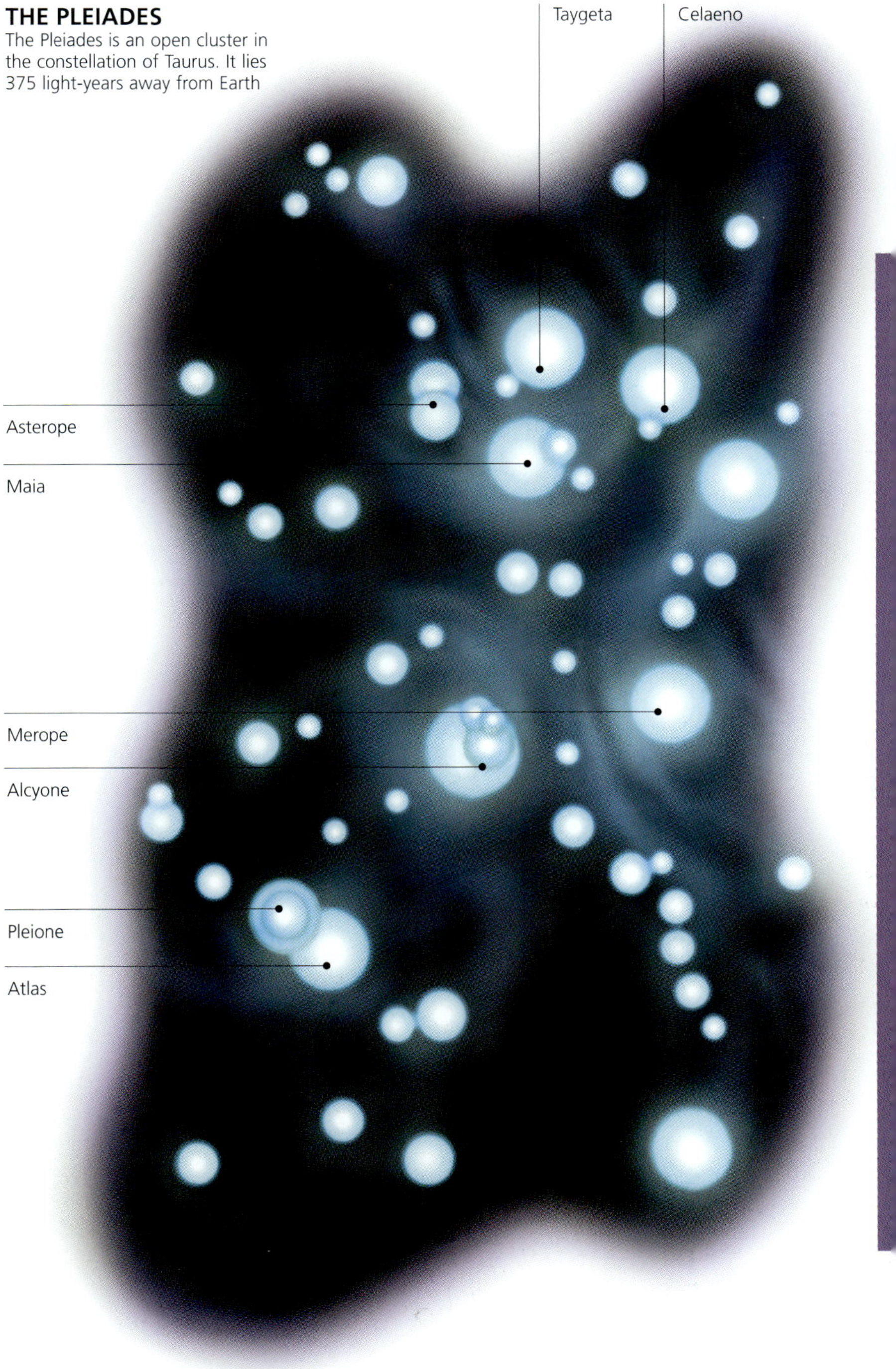

The Milky Way

SIDE VIEW

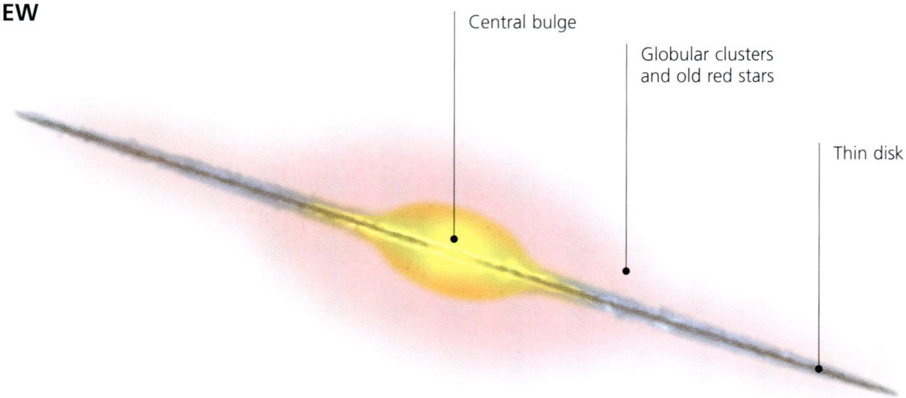

GALACTIC NEIGHBORS

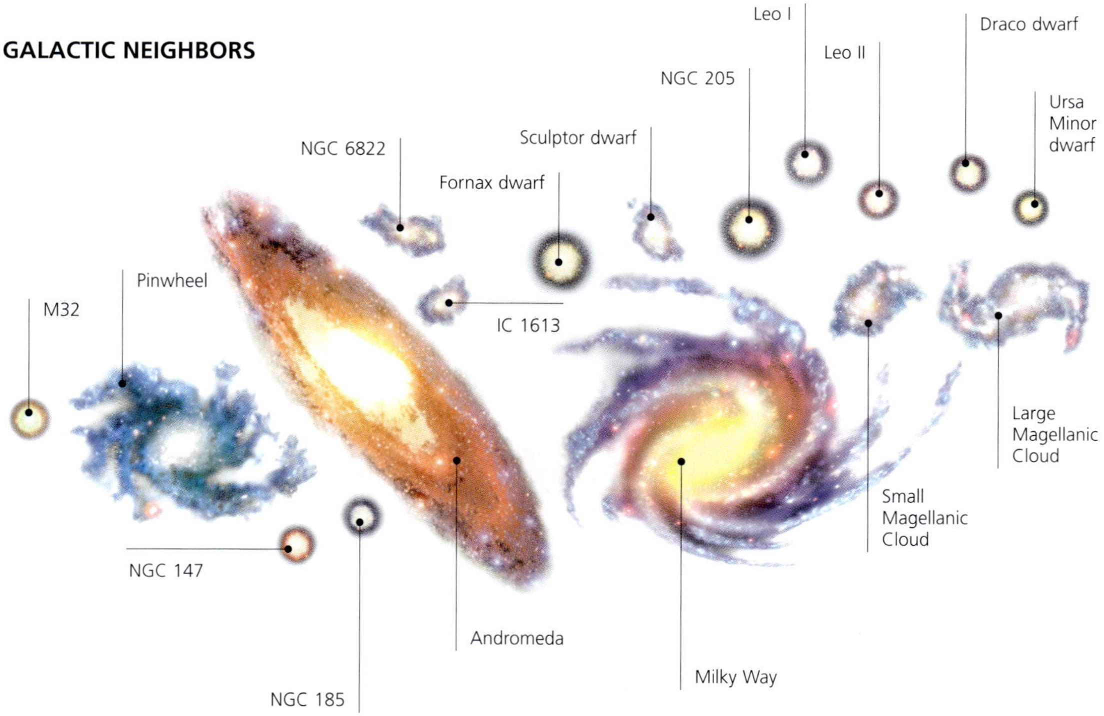

CROSS SECTION

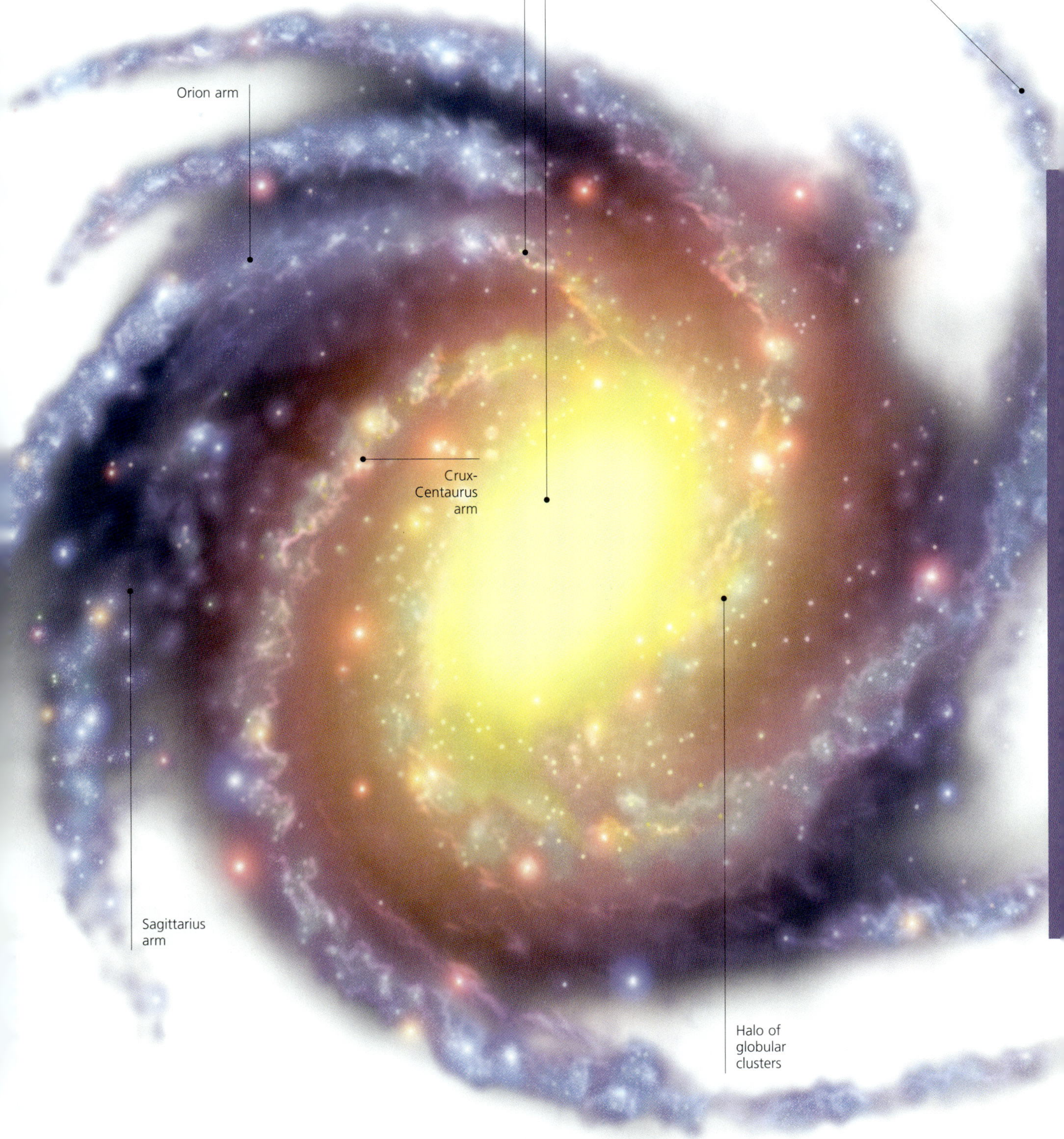

Galaxies and Black Holes

MULTIPLE IMAGES

A black hole is so powerful that it can bend light—creating the optical illusion of a double galaxy.

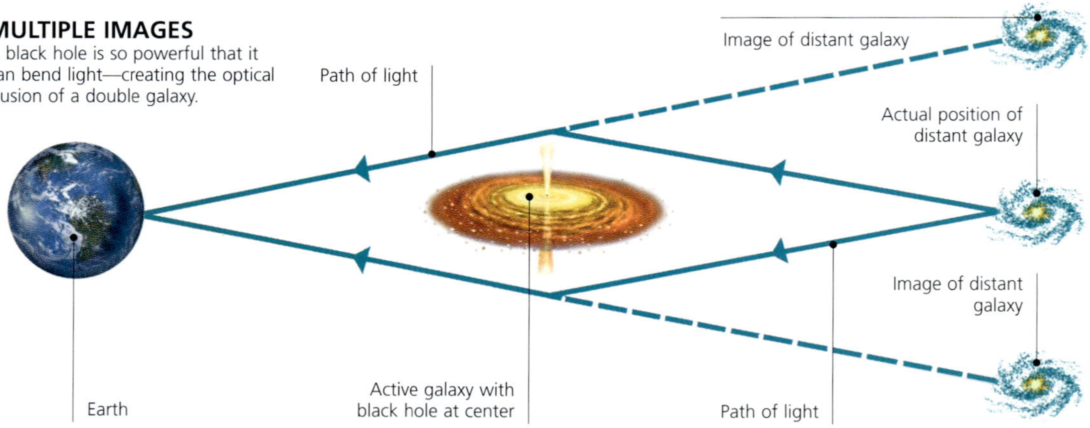

GALACTIC BLACK HOLE

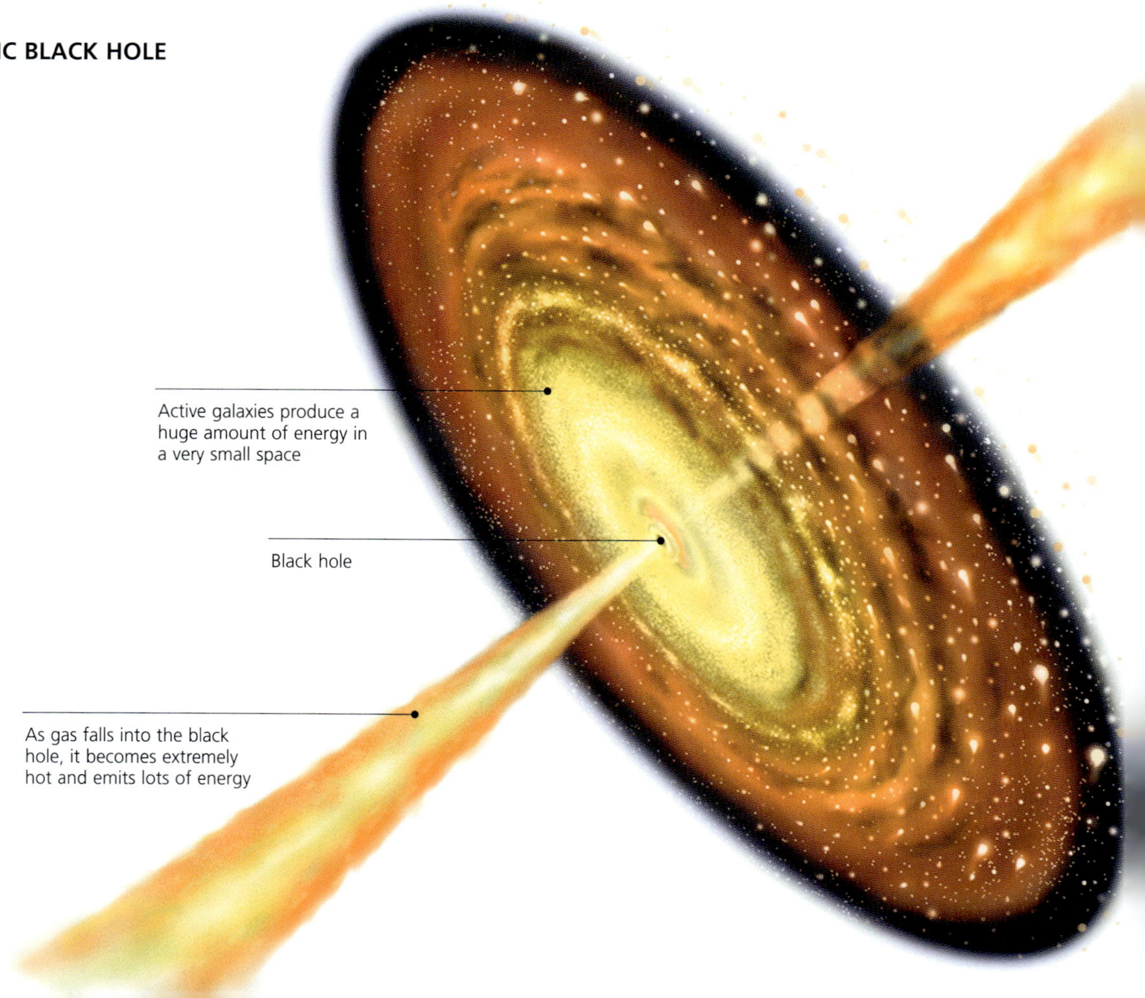

GALAXY CLASSIFICATION

Edwin Hubble developed this scheme for classifying galaxies by shape.

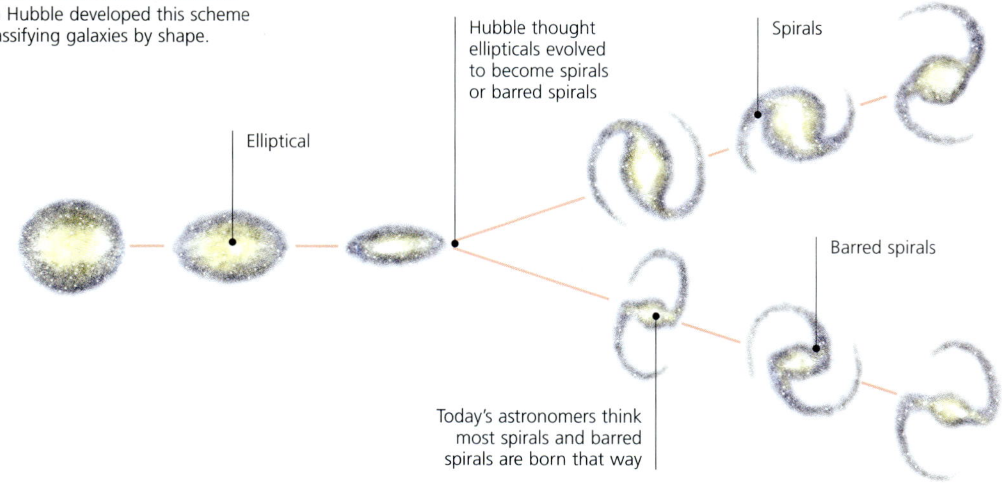

TYPES OF GALAXIES

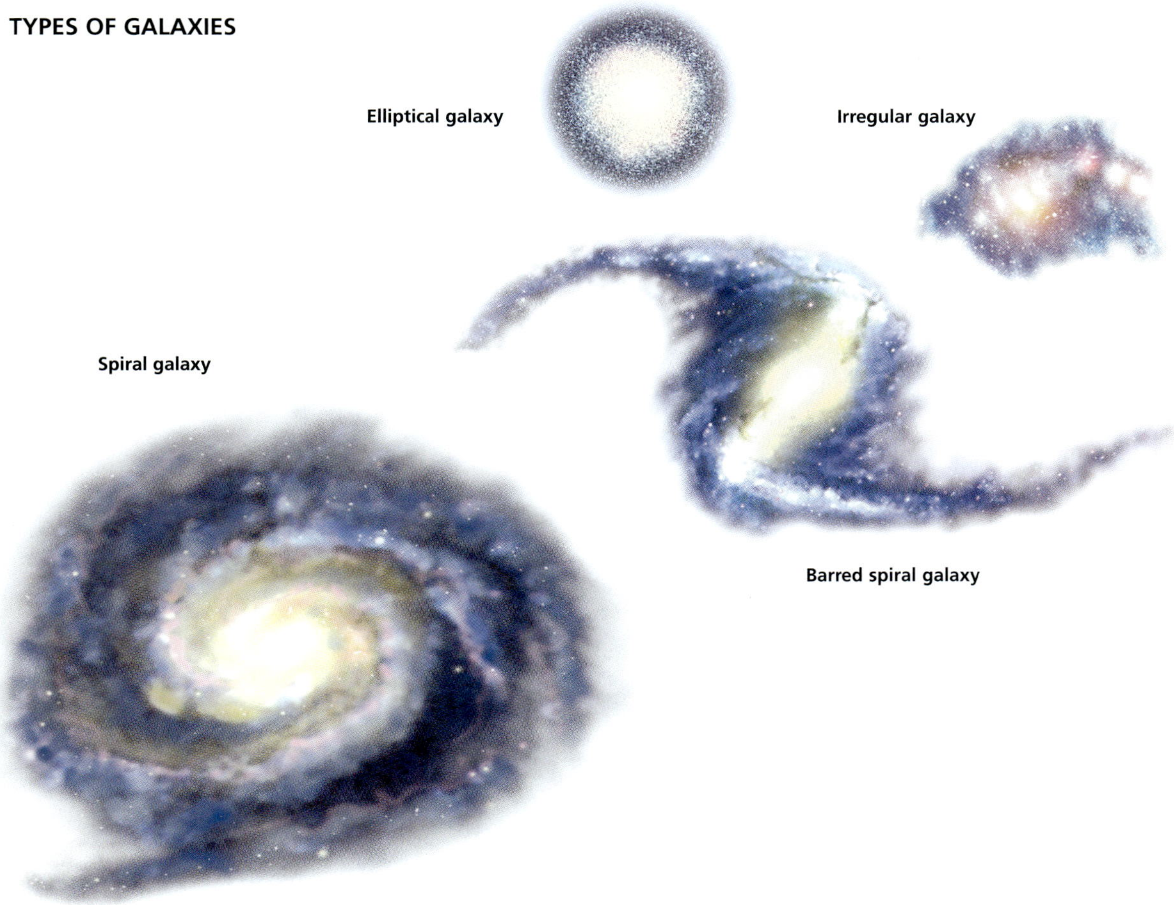

Using a Star Map

STAR MOVEMENT

The path of star movement depends on latitude.

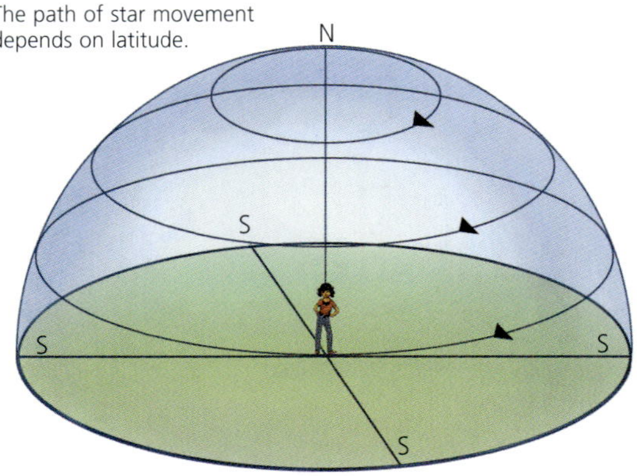

North Pole—90°N

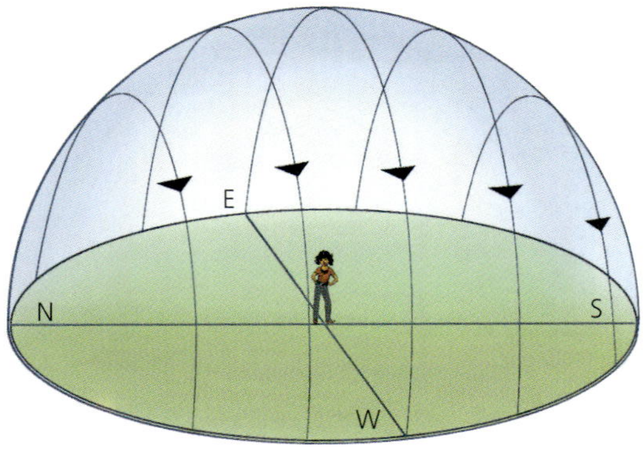

Equator—0°

FINDING THE POLES

Northern Hemisphere
First locate the Big Dipper using the correct map for your location and season. Then draw an imaginary line from the end of the Dipper's bowl to Polaris.

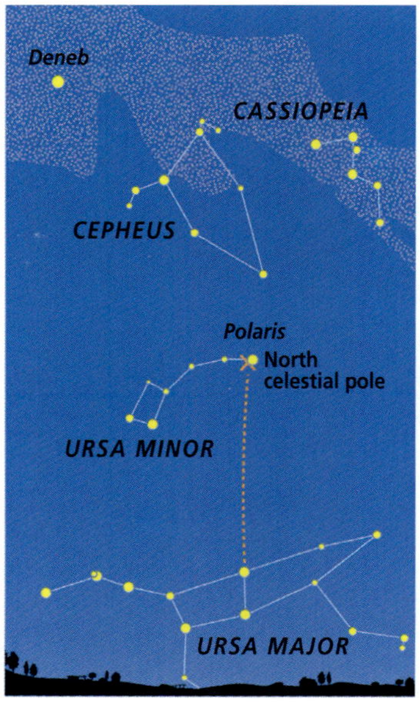

Southern Hemisphere
First locate Crux using the correct map for your location and season. Then draw imaginary lines between the other bright stars marked below, to find the pole.

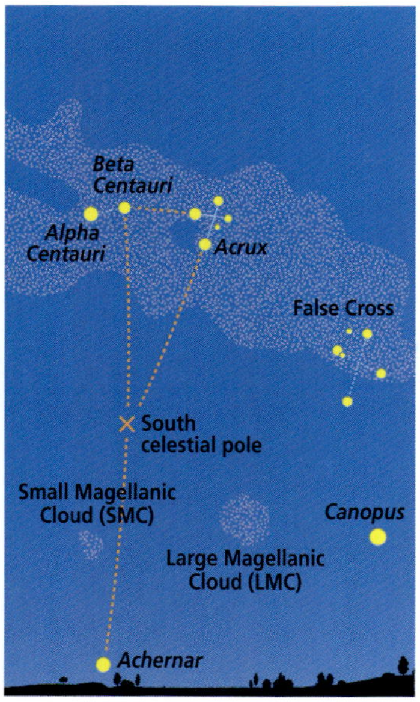

KEY TO MAP SYMBOLS

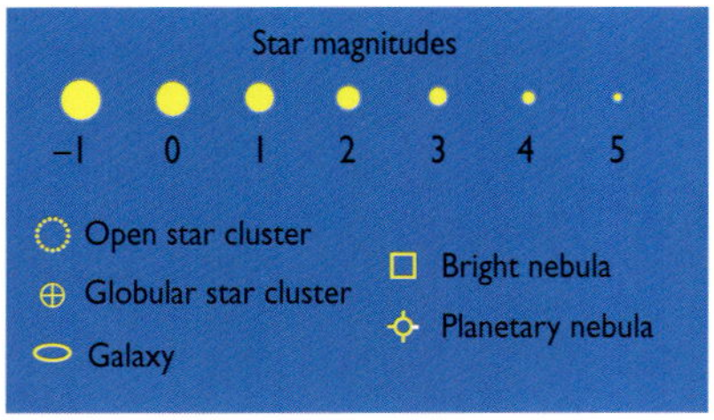

Sky maps show star brightness using dots sized according to their magnitude. Fainter stars have higher magnitude numbers, while the brightest stars have negative magnitudes.

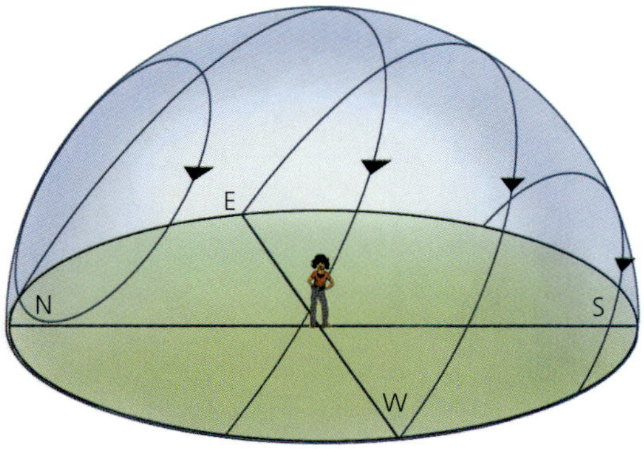

Northern middle latitudes—40°N

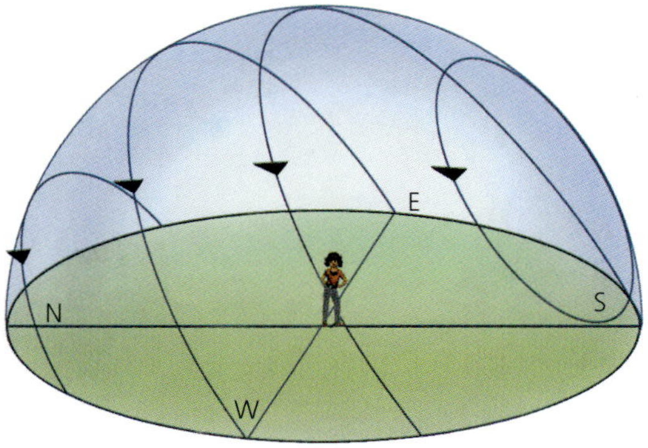

Southern middle latitudes—40°S

A GUIDE TO STAR MAPS

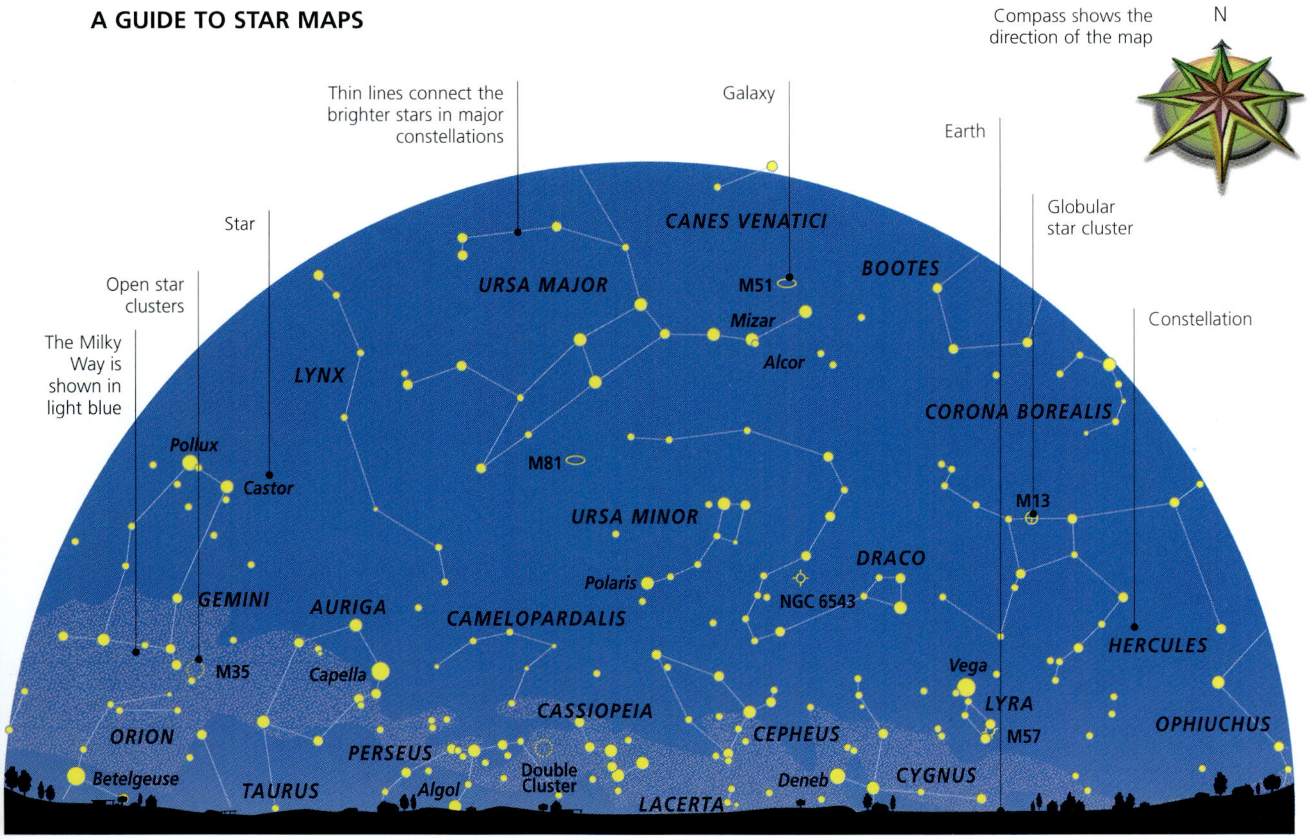

Winter Stars of the Northern Skies

PERSEUS THE HERO

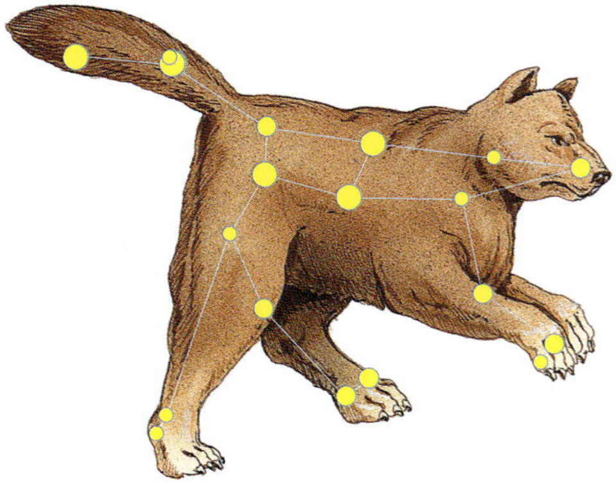

URSA MAJOR

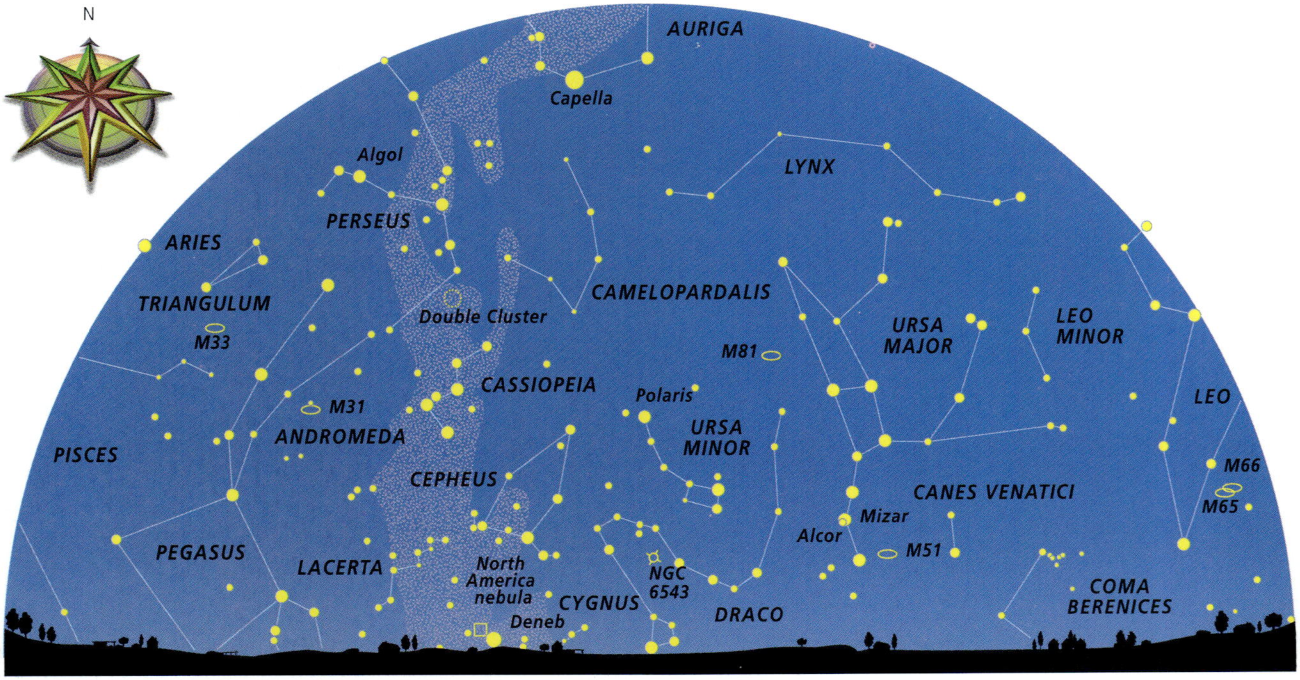

ORION THE HUNTER

CANIS MAJOR

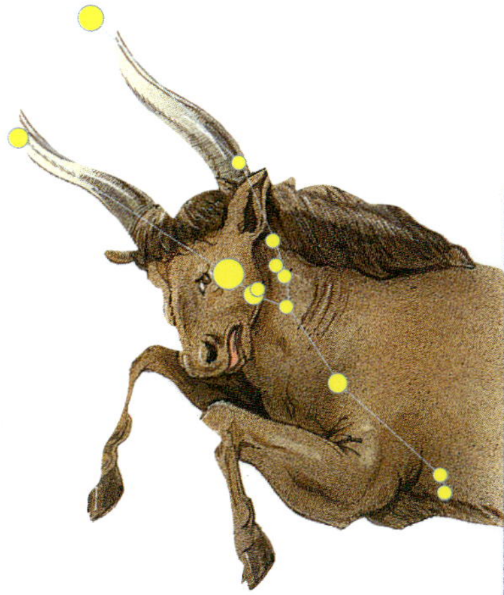

TAURUS THE BULL

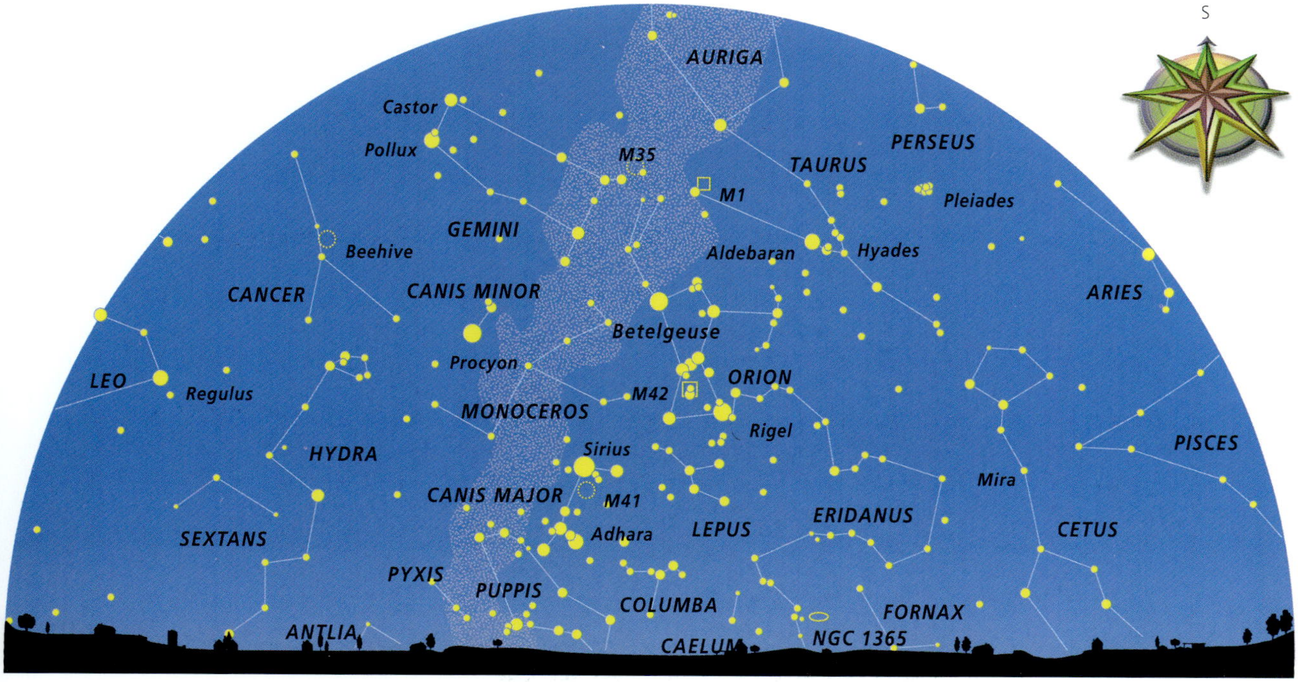

Spring Stars of the Northern Skies

HERCULES

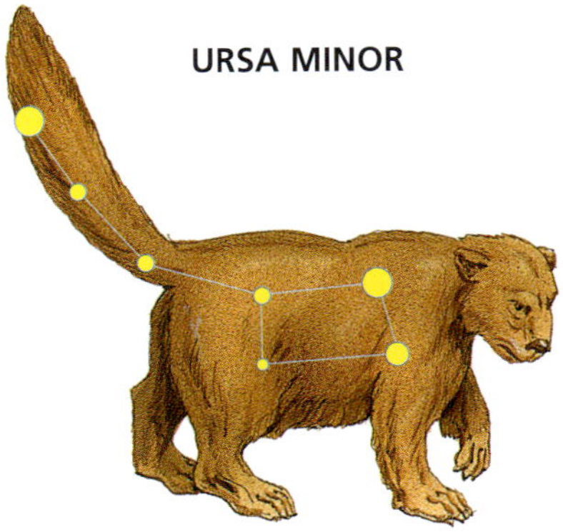

URSA MINOR

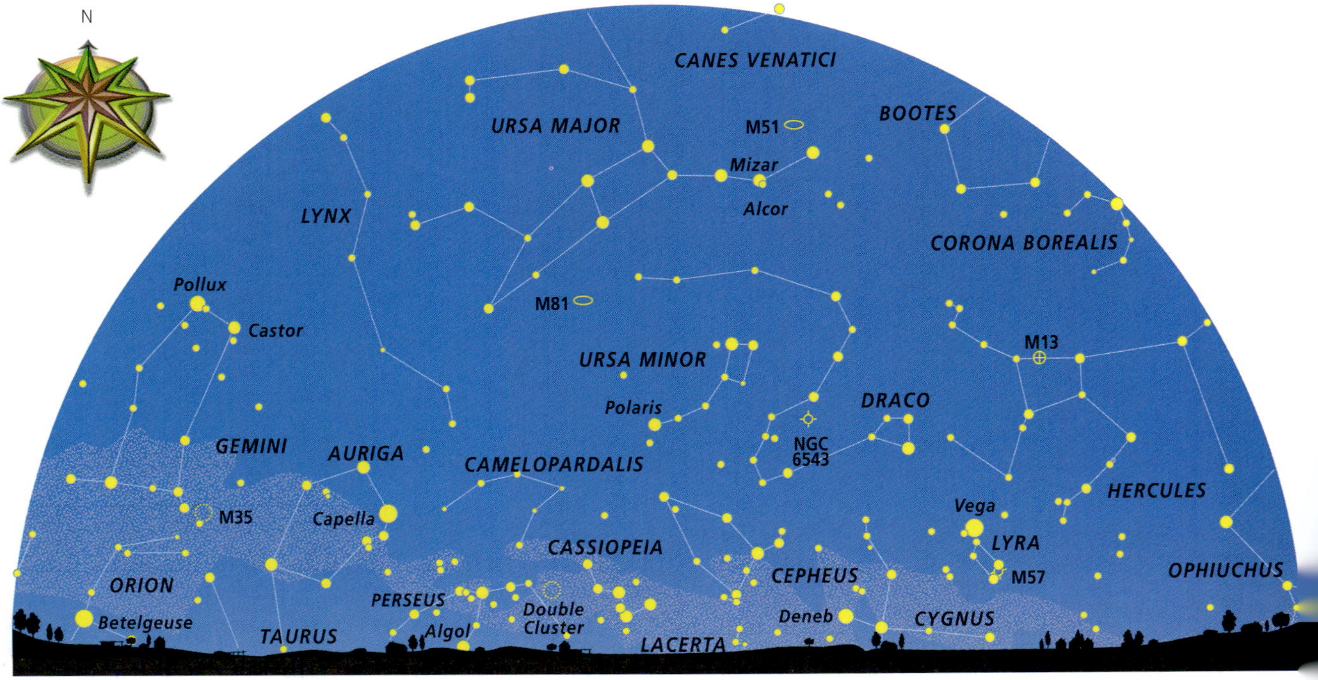

HYDRA

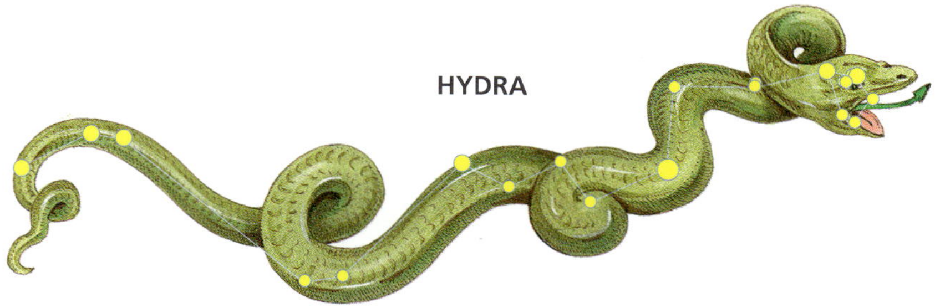

CANCER THE CRAB

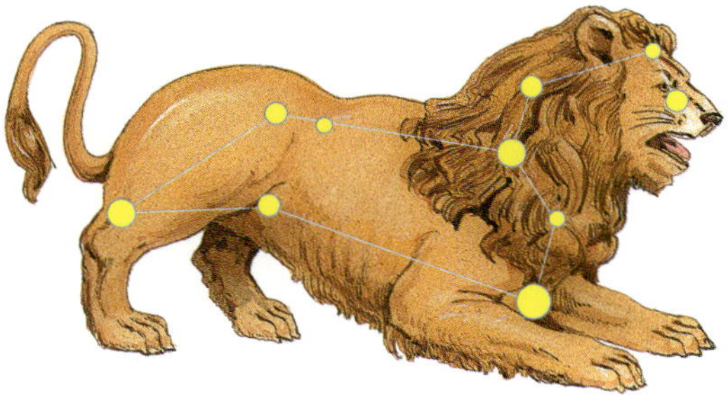

LEO THE LION

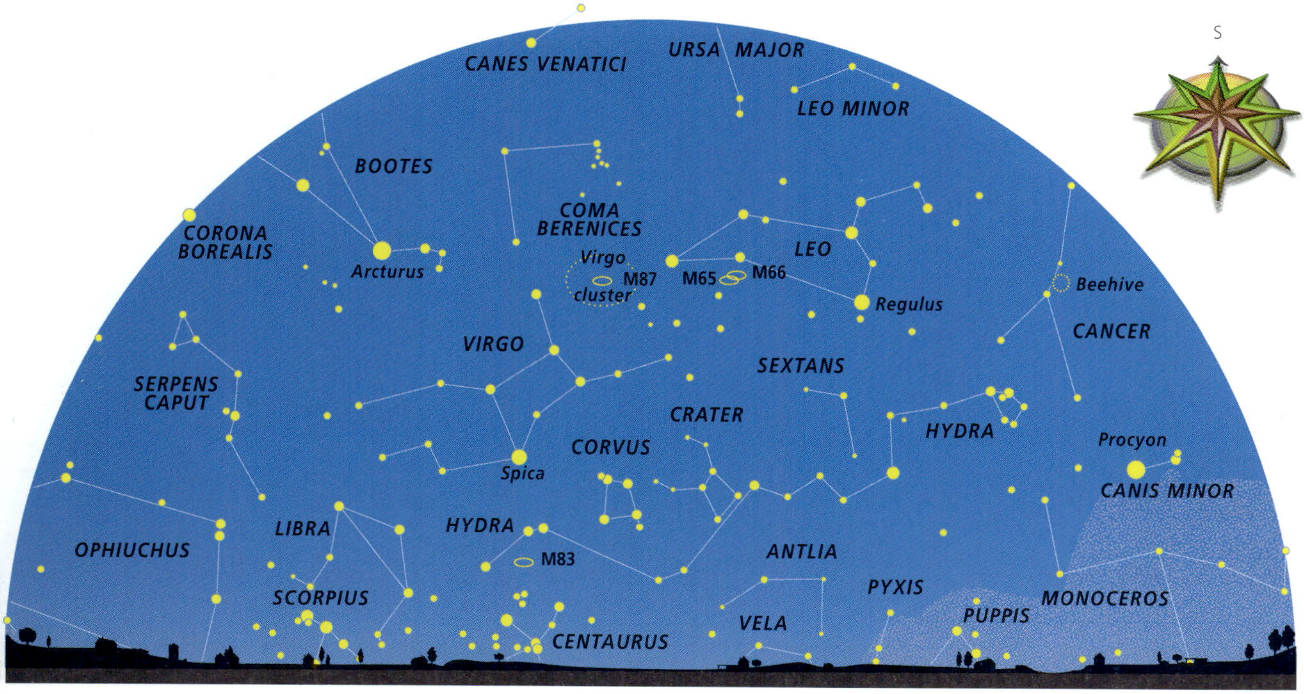

Summer Stars of the Northern Skies

CYGNUS THE SWAN

CEPHEUS THE KING

DRACO THE DRAGON

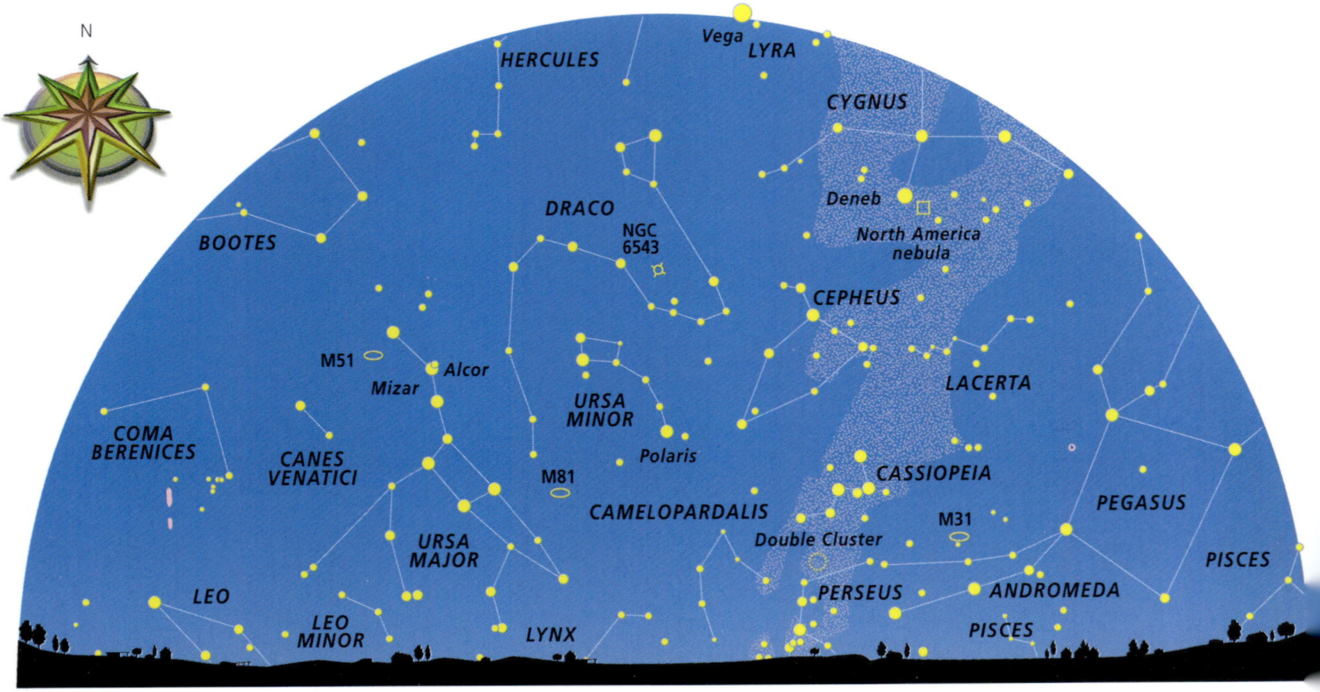

OPHIUCHUS

AQUILA THE EAGLE

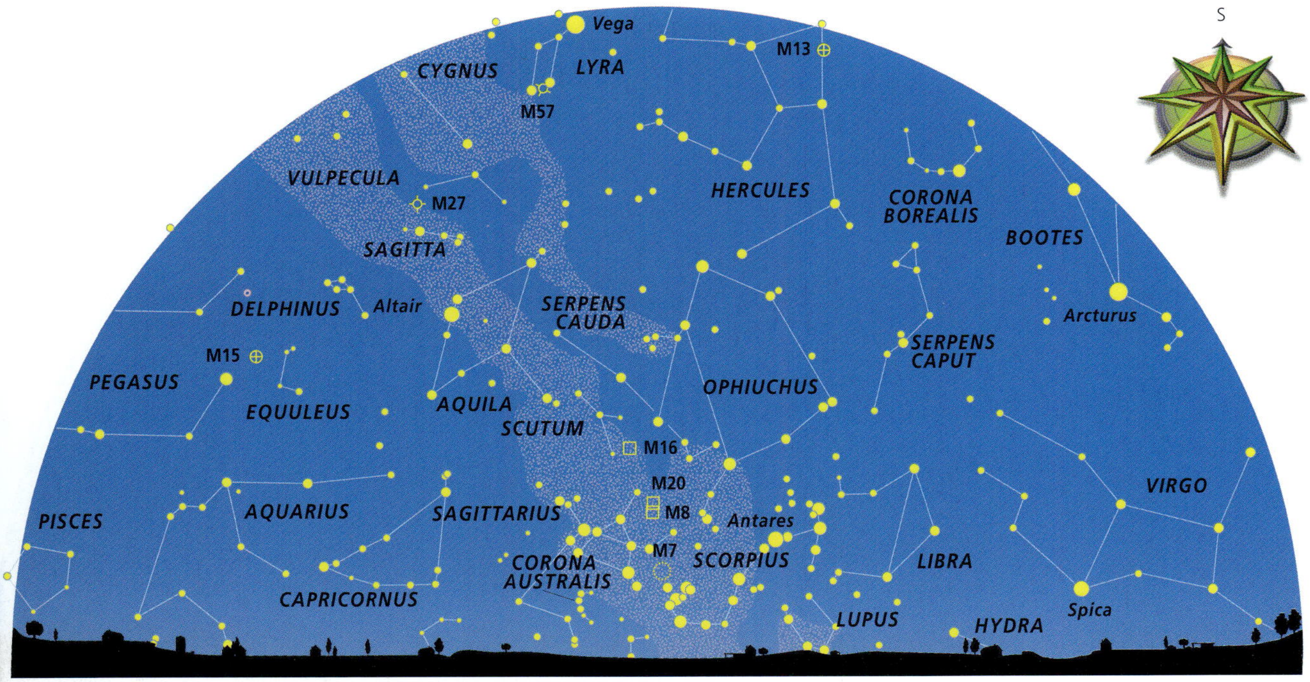

Autumn Stars of the Northern Skies

LYRA THE LYRE

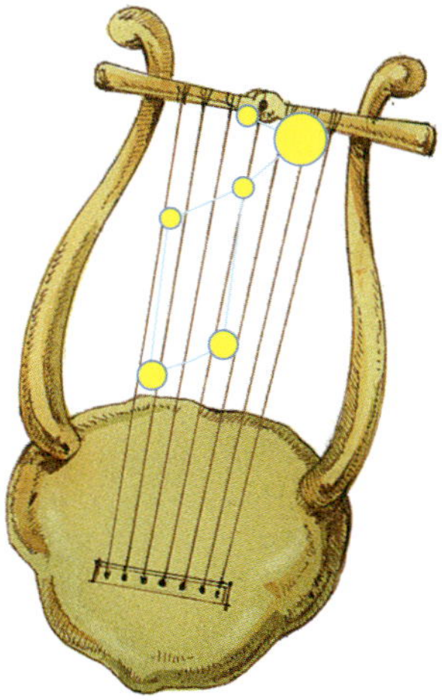

AURIGA THE CHARIOTEER

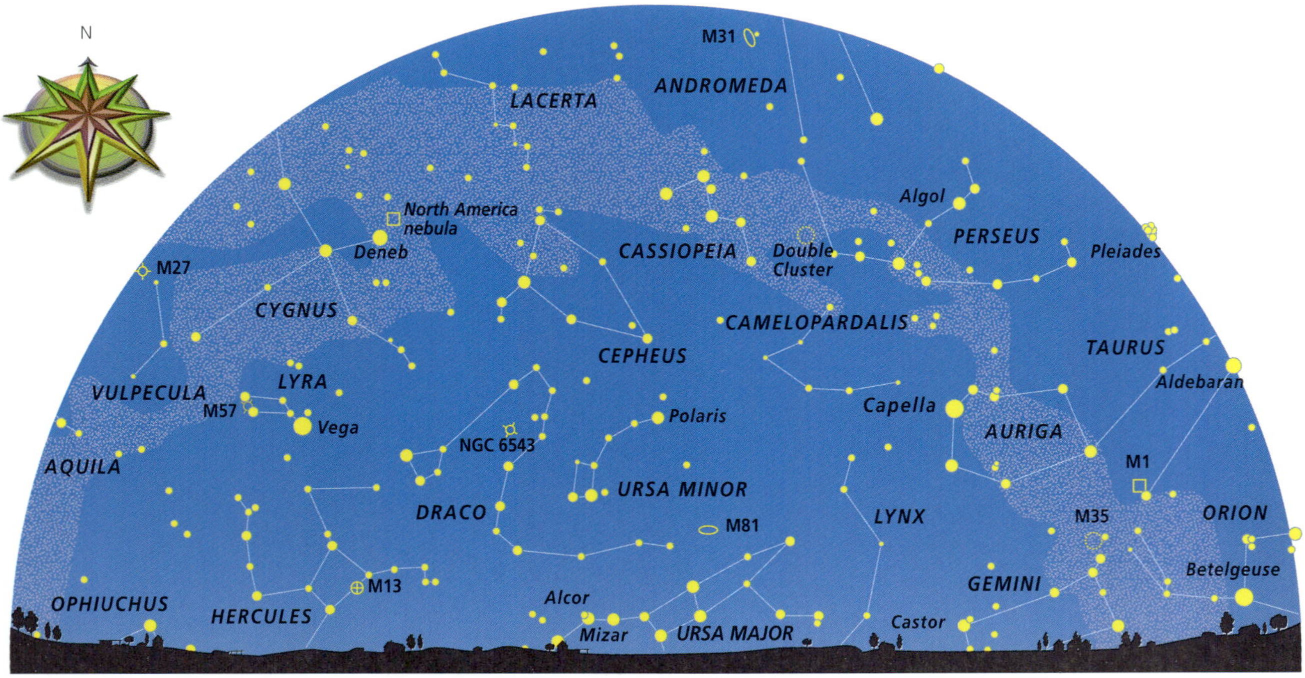

PISCES THE FISHES

AQUARIUS

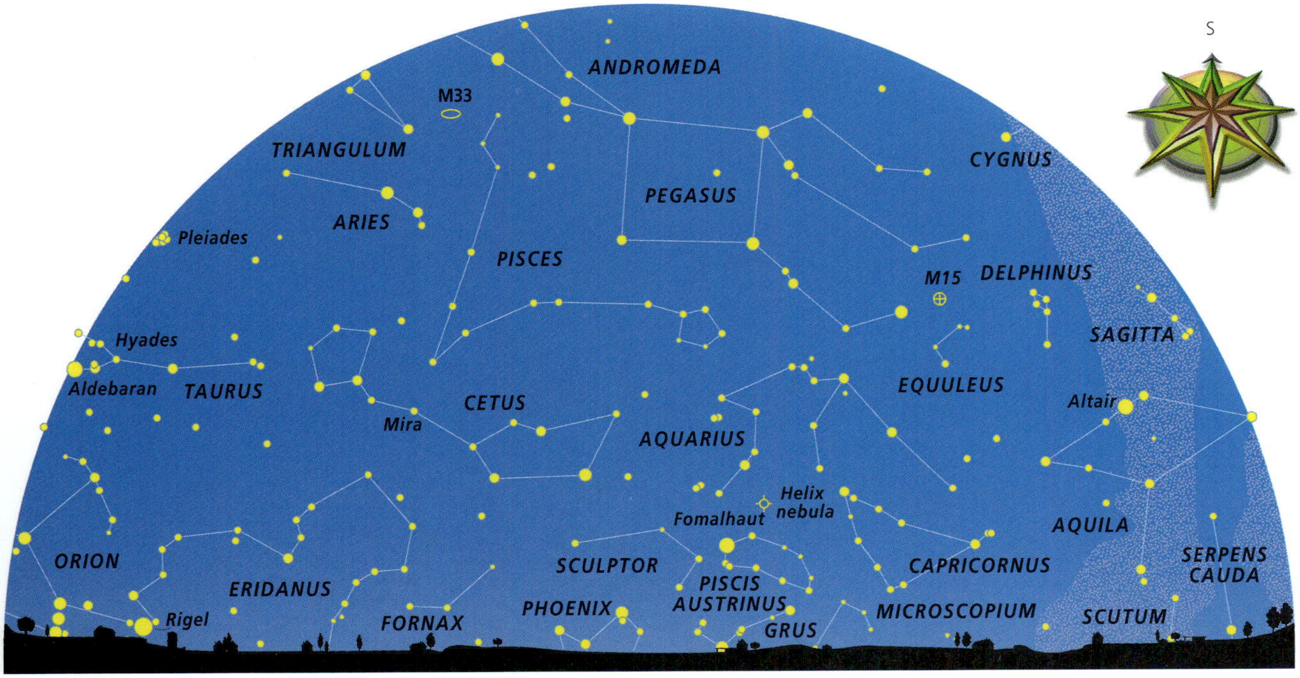

Winter Stars of the Southern Skies

SERPENS THE SERPENT

SAGITTARIUS THE ARCHER

LIBRA THE SCALES

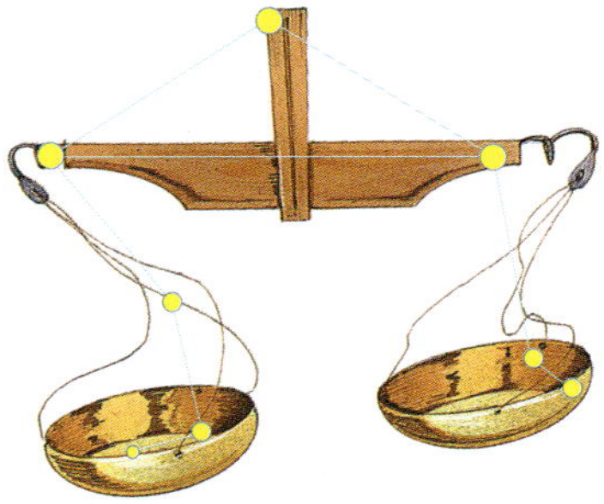

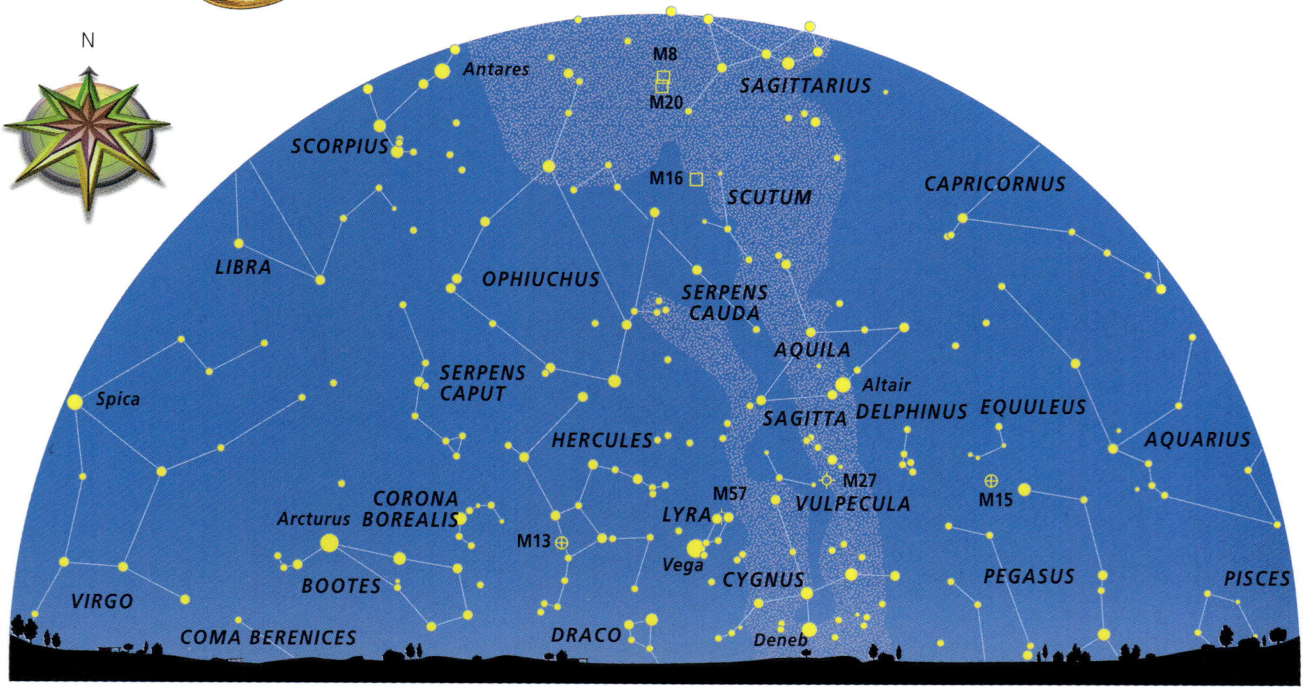

LUPUS THE WOLF

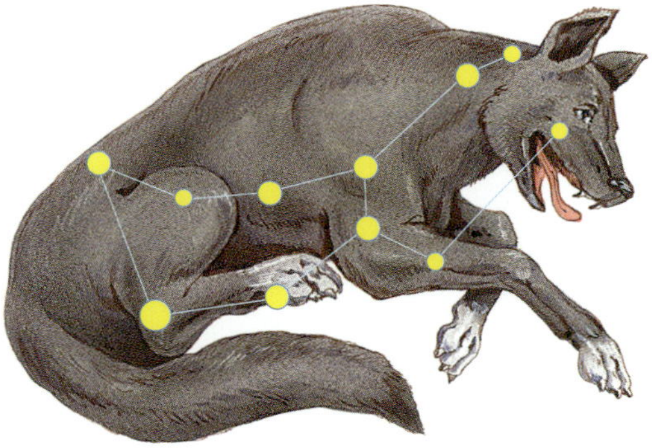

CORONA AUSTRALIS

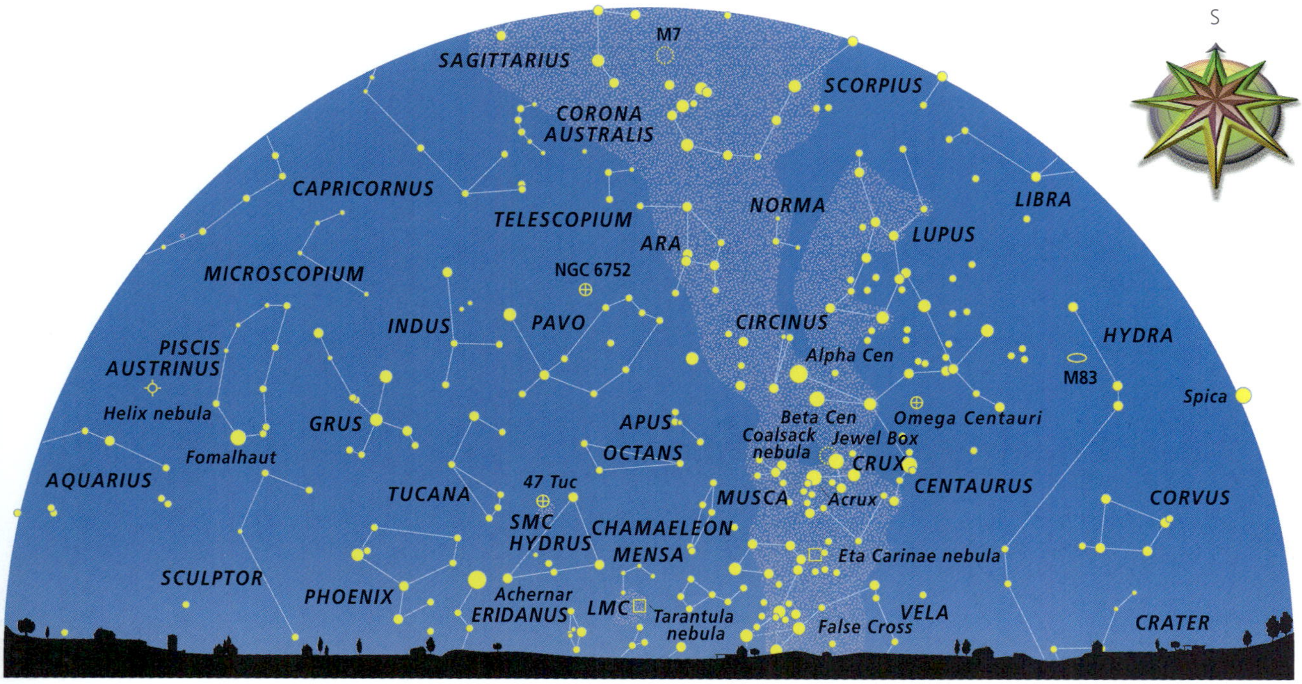

Spring Stars of the Southern Skies

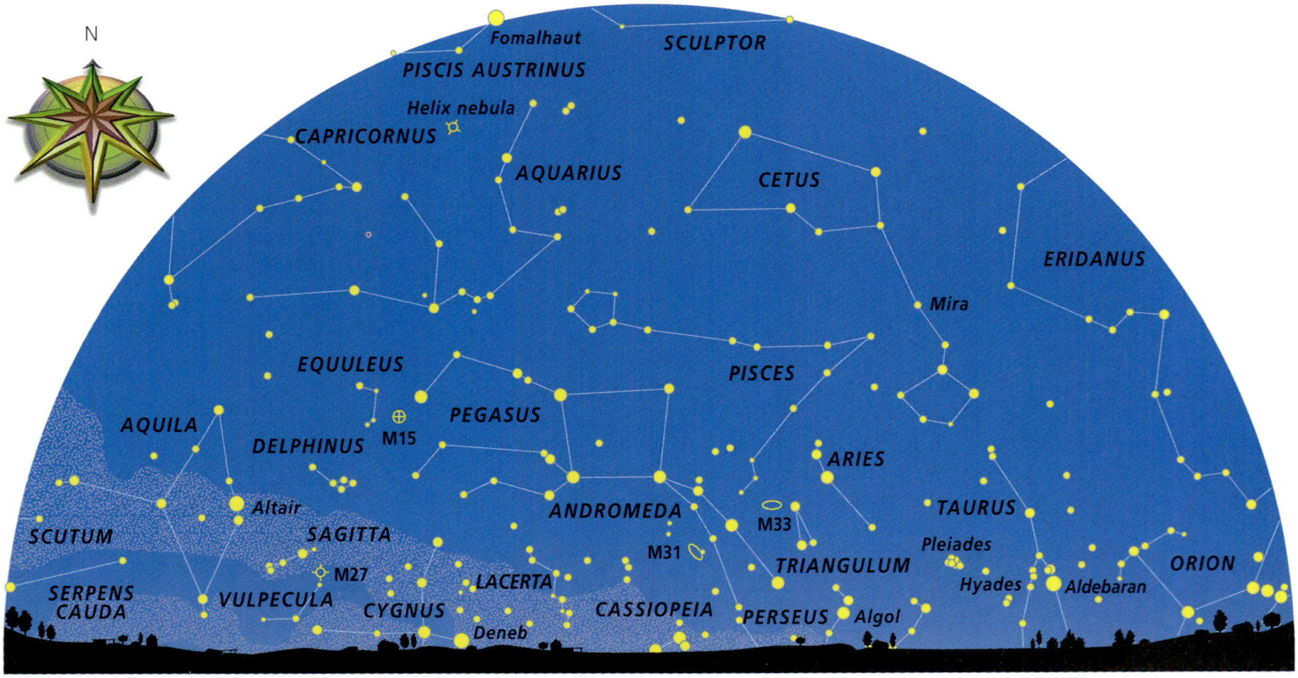

GRUS THE CRANE

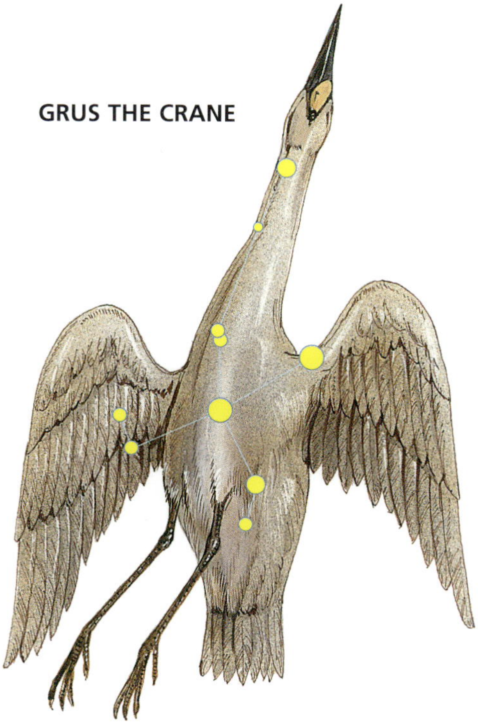

TUCANA THE TOUCAN

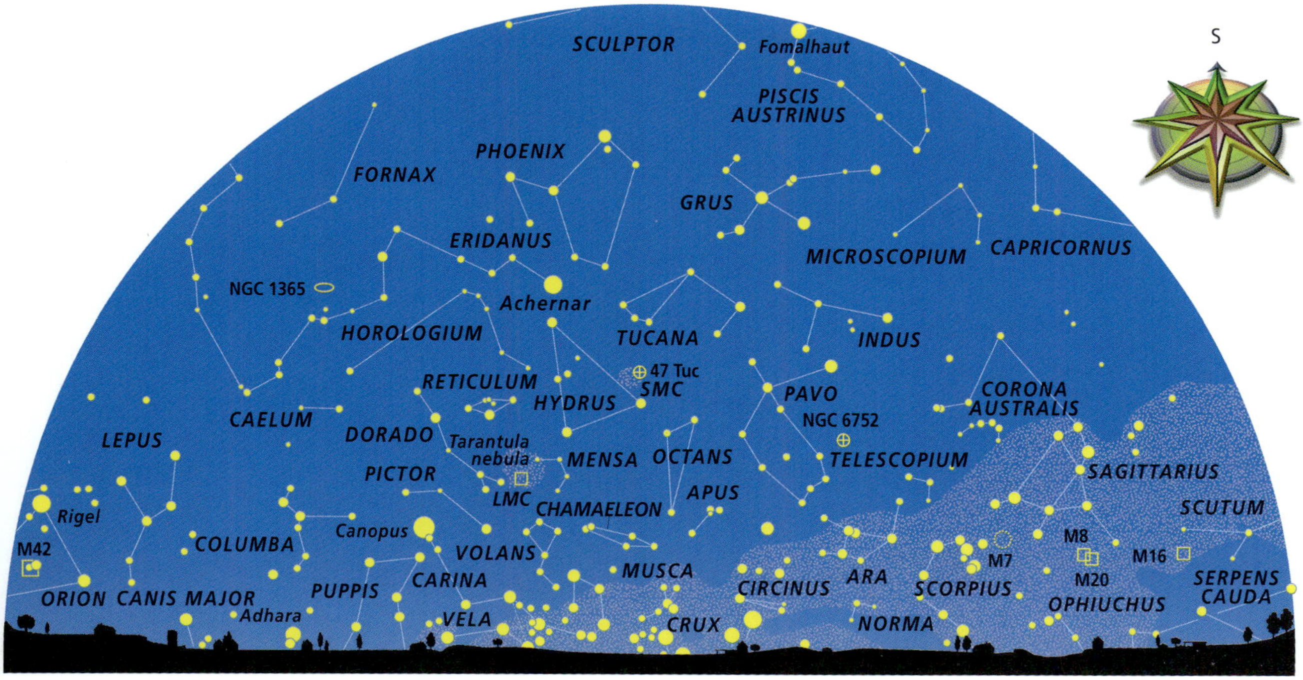

Summer Stars of the Southern Skies

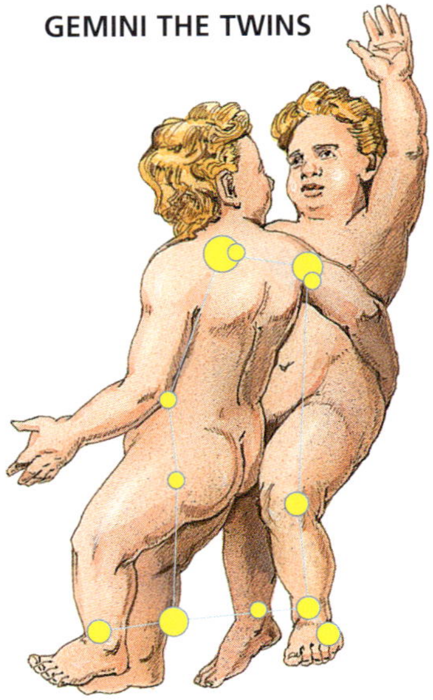

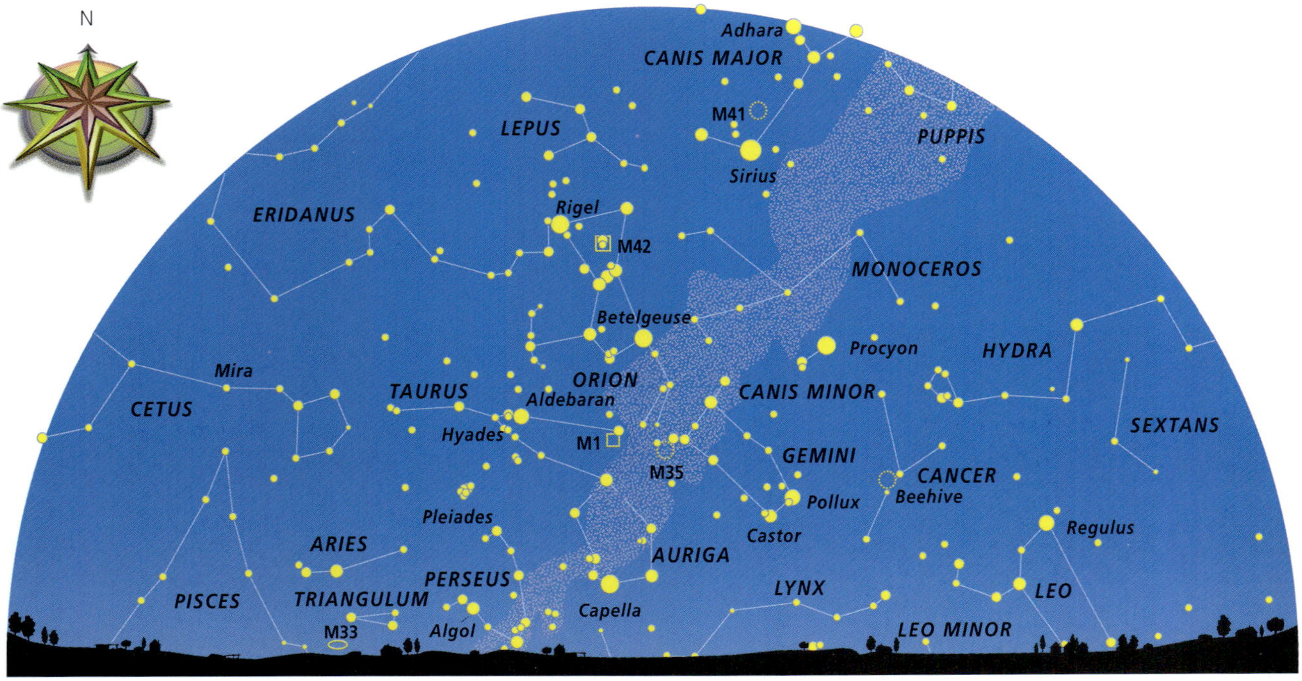

COLUMBA THE DOVE

ERIDANUS THE RIVER

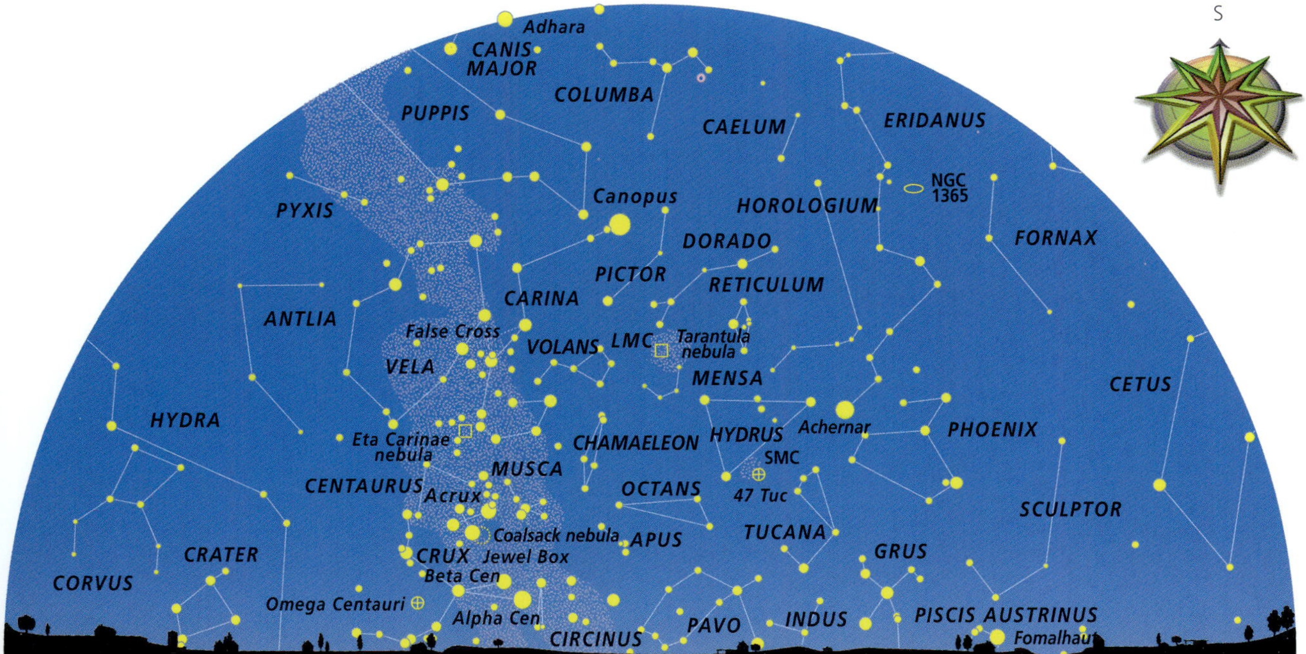

Autumn Stars of the Southern Skies

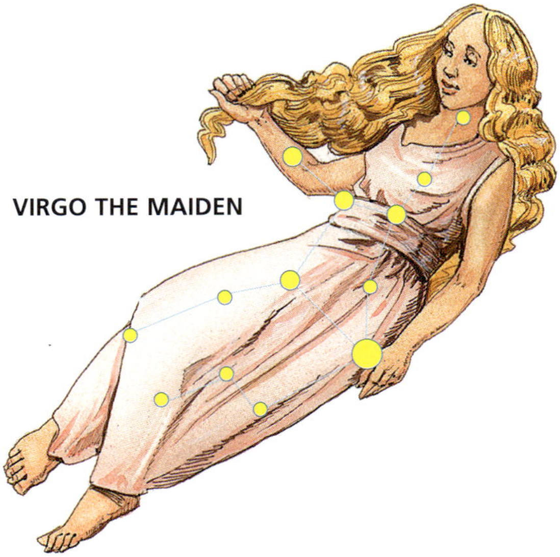

VIRGO THE MAIDEN

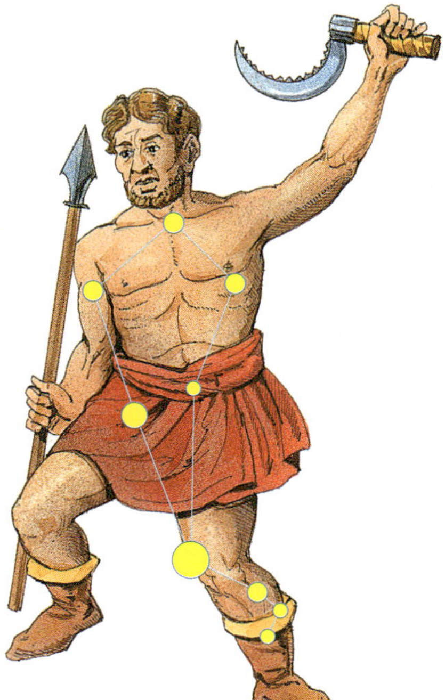

BOOTES THE HERDSMAN

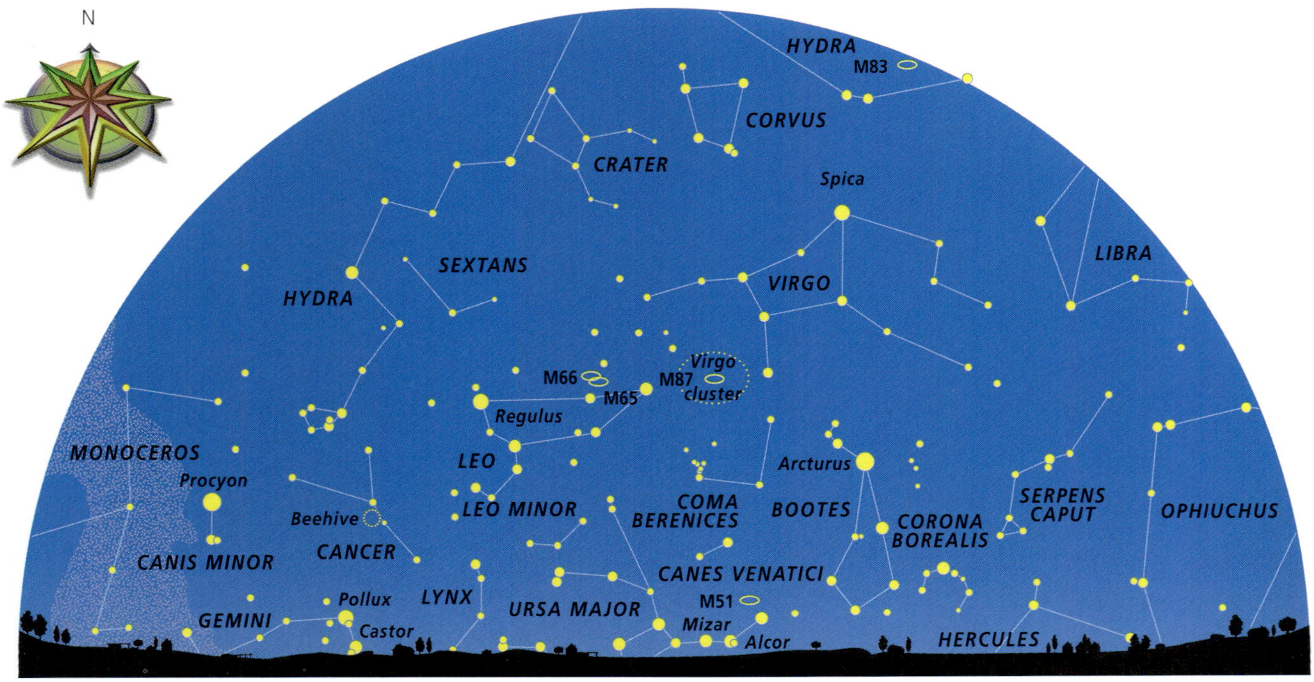

CRUX

SCORPIUS THE SCORPIAN

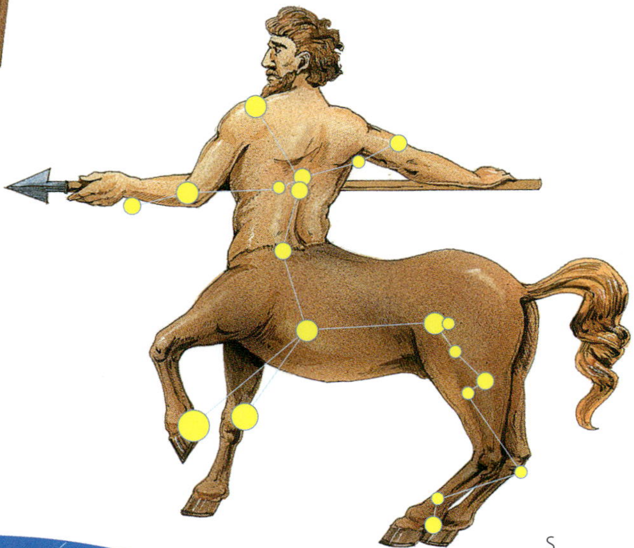

CENTAURUS THE CENTAUR

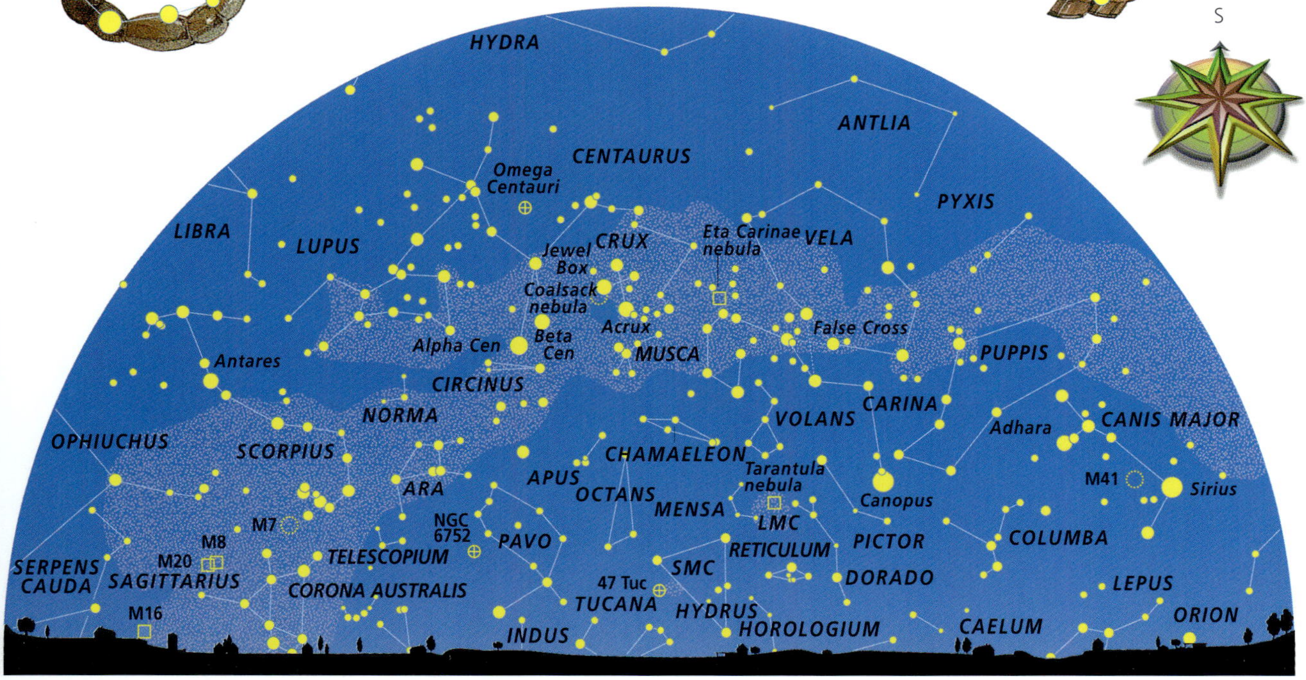

Our Place in Space

EARTH IN THE UNIVERSE

Solar System
The Solar System is a tiny speck in the millions of stars in the galaxy.

Spiral Arm of Milky Way
The Sun and Solar System lie near the edge of one of the Milky Way's spiral arms.

Local Group
With about 35 member galaxies, the Local Group is dominated by the Milky Way and two other large spiral galaxies.

Cosmic Structure
Galaxies seem to appear in groups, and groups gather in large clusters.

Milky Way
The Milky Way's nearest neighbors are two smaller galaxies called the Large and Small Magellanic Clouds.

Astronomy from Earth

TYPES OF TELESCOPES

Refractor

Reflector

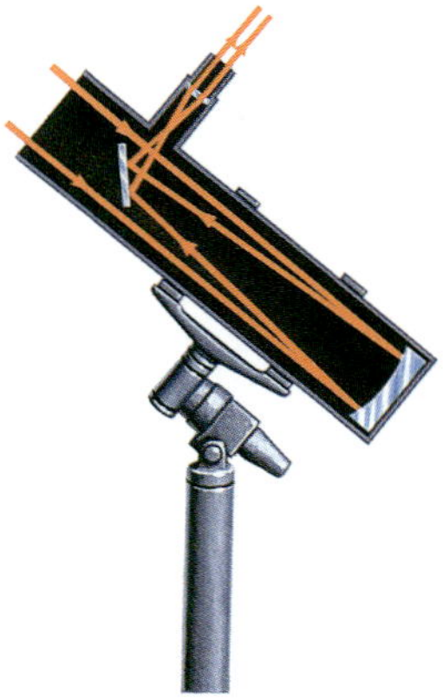

KECK TELESCOPES

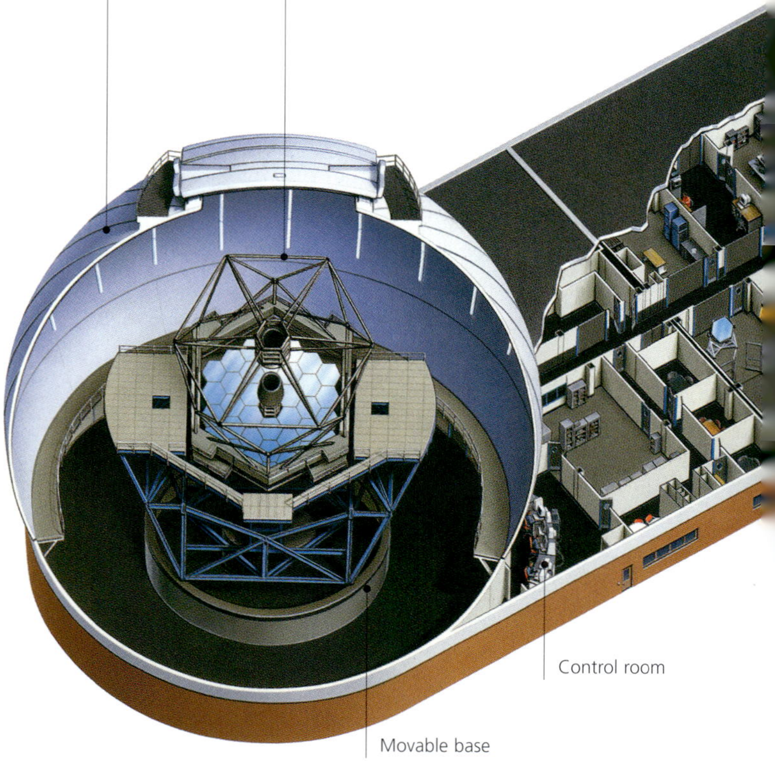

ASTRONOMY MILESTONES

Galileo's refractor, 1609

Isaac Newton's reflector, 1671

William Herschel's reflector, 1781

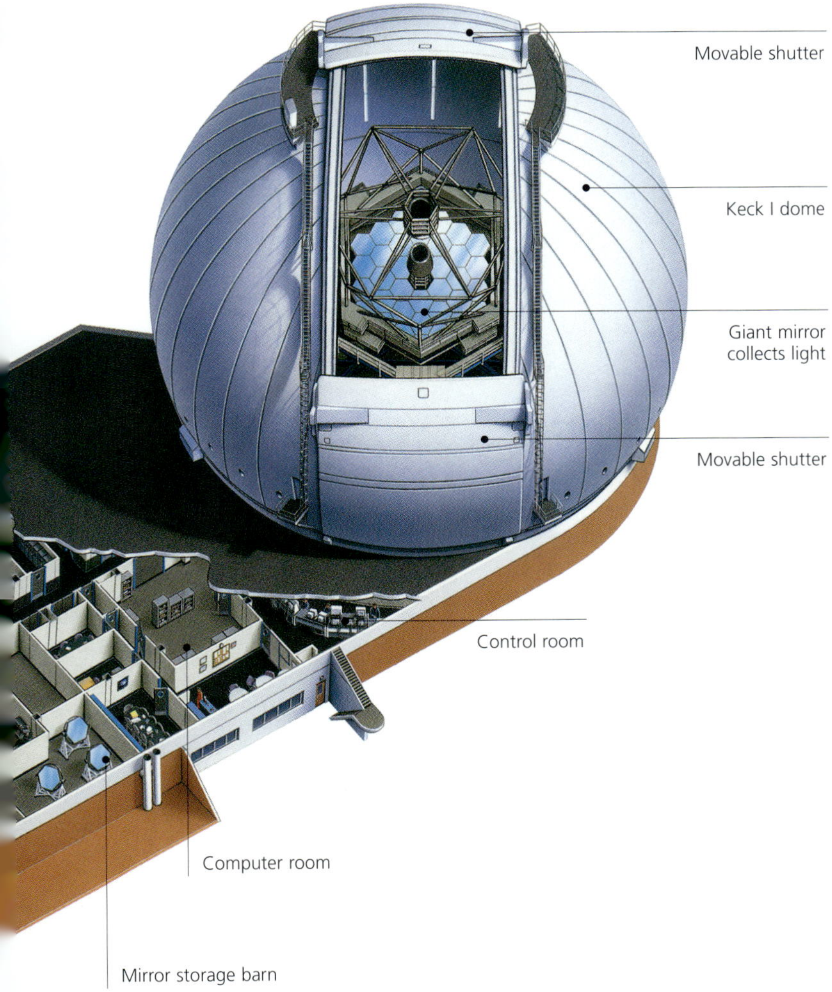

EYEPIECE FOCAL LENGTH

A telescope's main lens gathers incoming light, while the eyepiece magnifies the image.

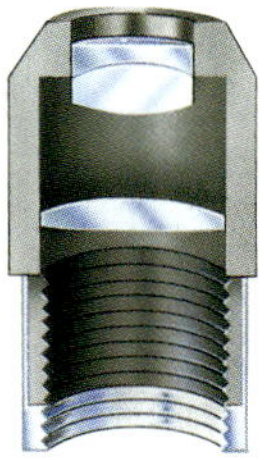

Kellner—3 lens elements

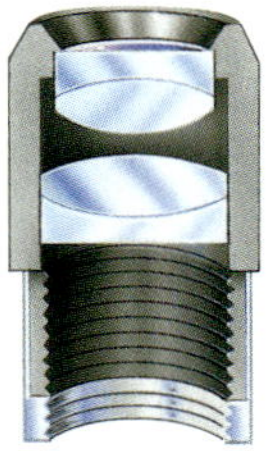

Plössl—4 lens elements

Nagler—8 lens elements

Green Bank telescope, 1965

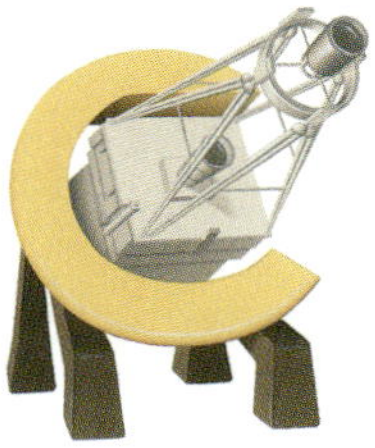

Anglo-Australian telescope, 1974

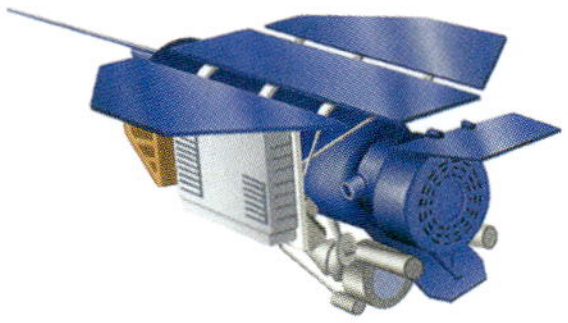

ROSAT X-ray telescope, 1990

Astronomy from Space

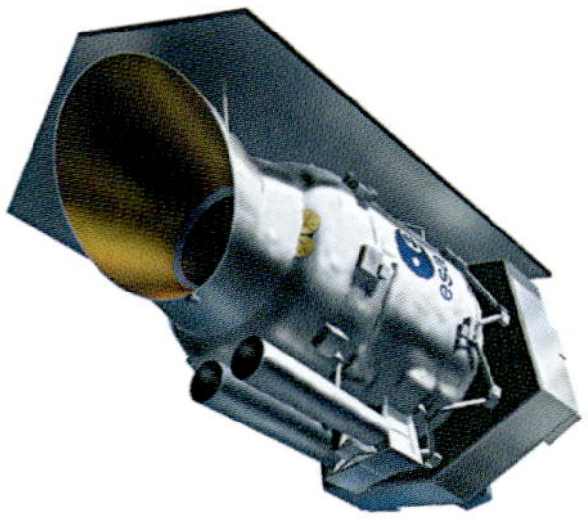

ISO SATELLITE OBSERVATORY

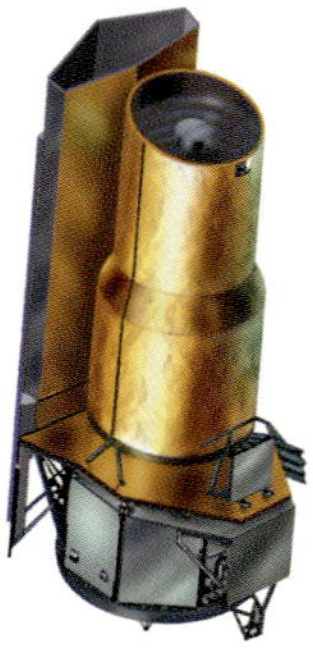

SITF SATELLITE

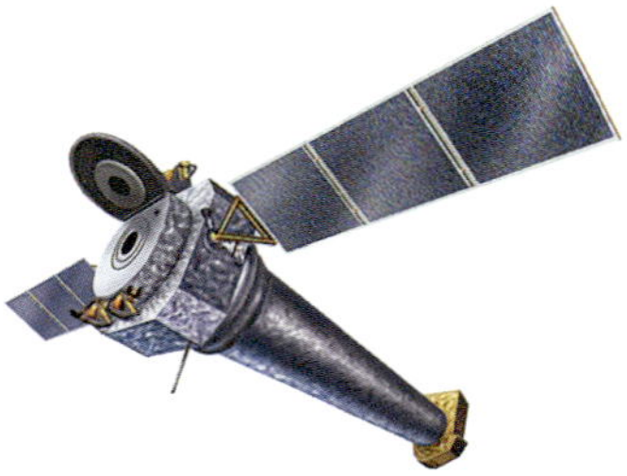

CHANDRA X-RAY OBSERVATORY

ROSAT SPACE TELESCOPE

COROT TELESCOPE

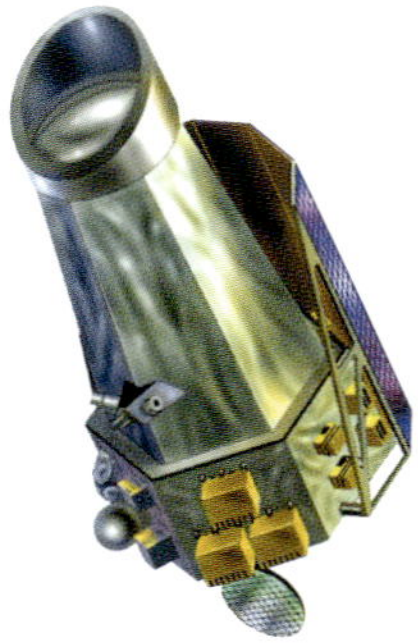

KEPLER SPACE TELESCOPE

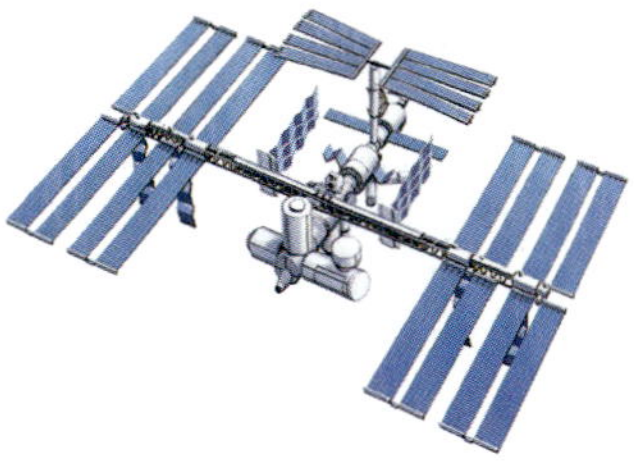

INTERNATIONAL SPACE STATION

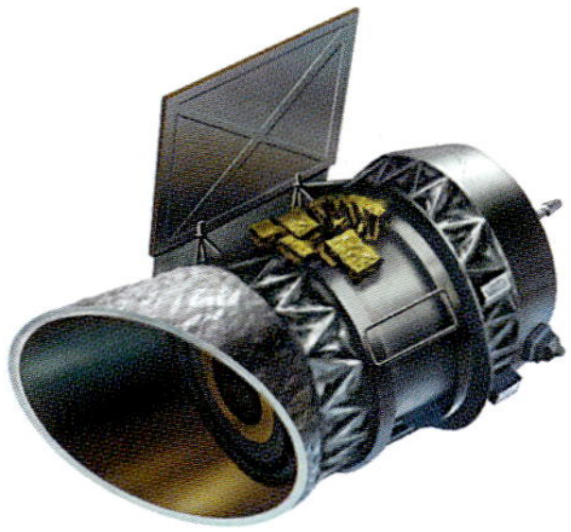

IRAS SPACE TELESCOPE

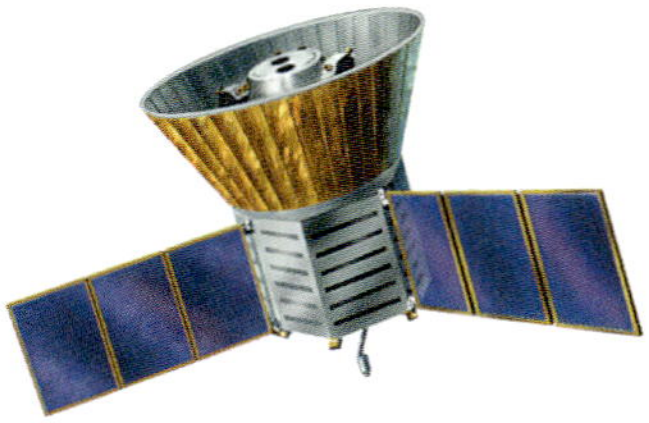

COBE SATELLITE

HUBBLE SPACE TELESCOPE

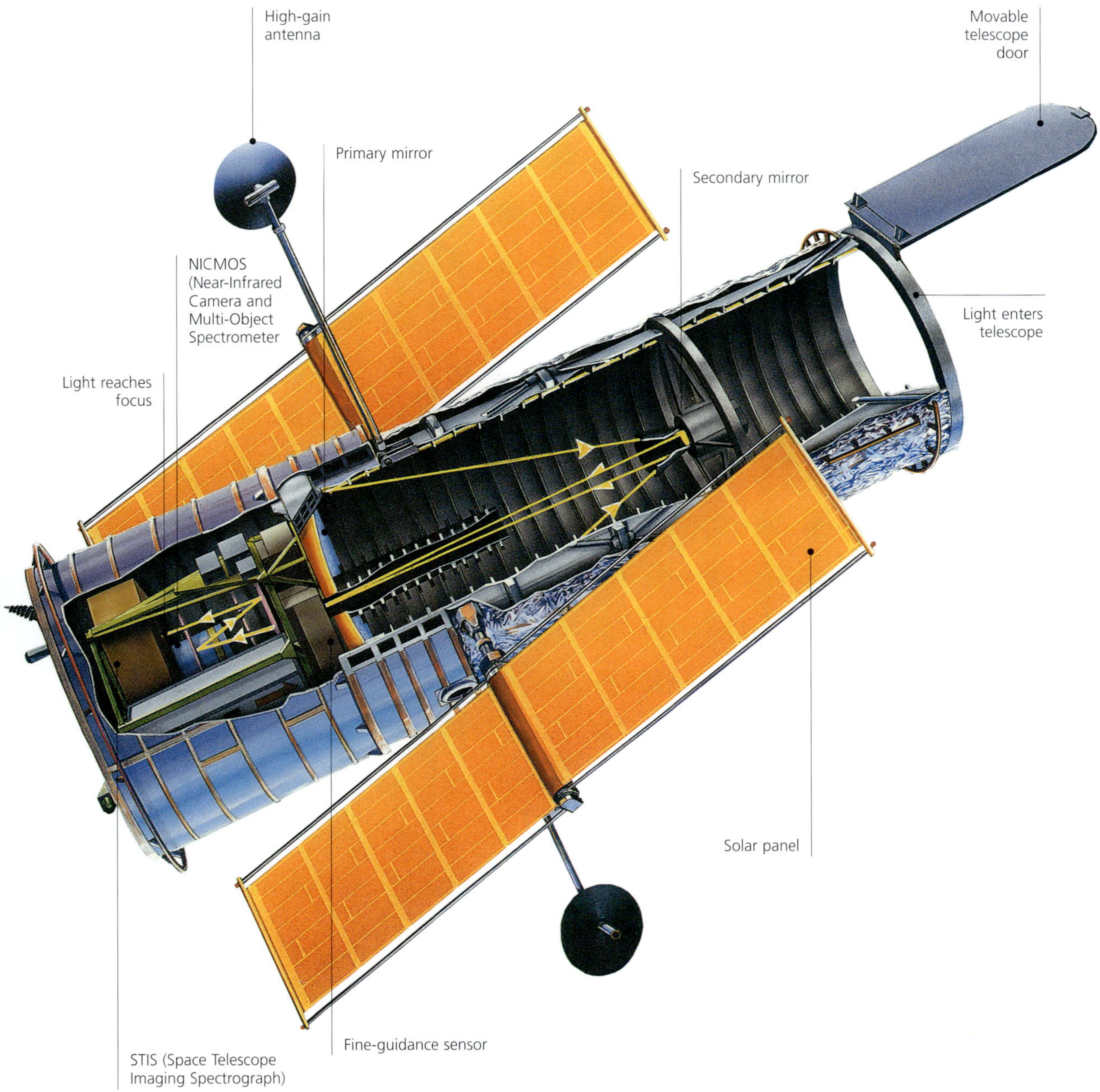

Robot Probes

EXPLORING VENUS

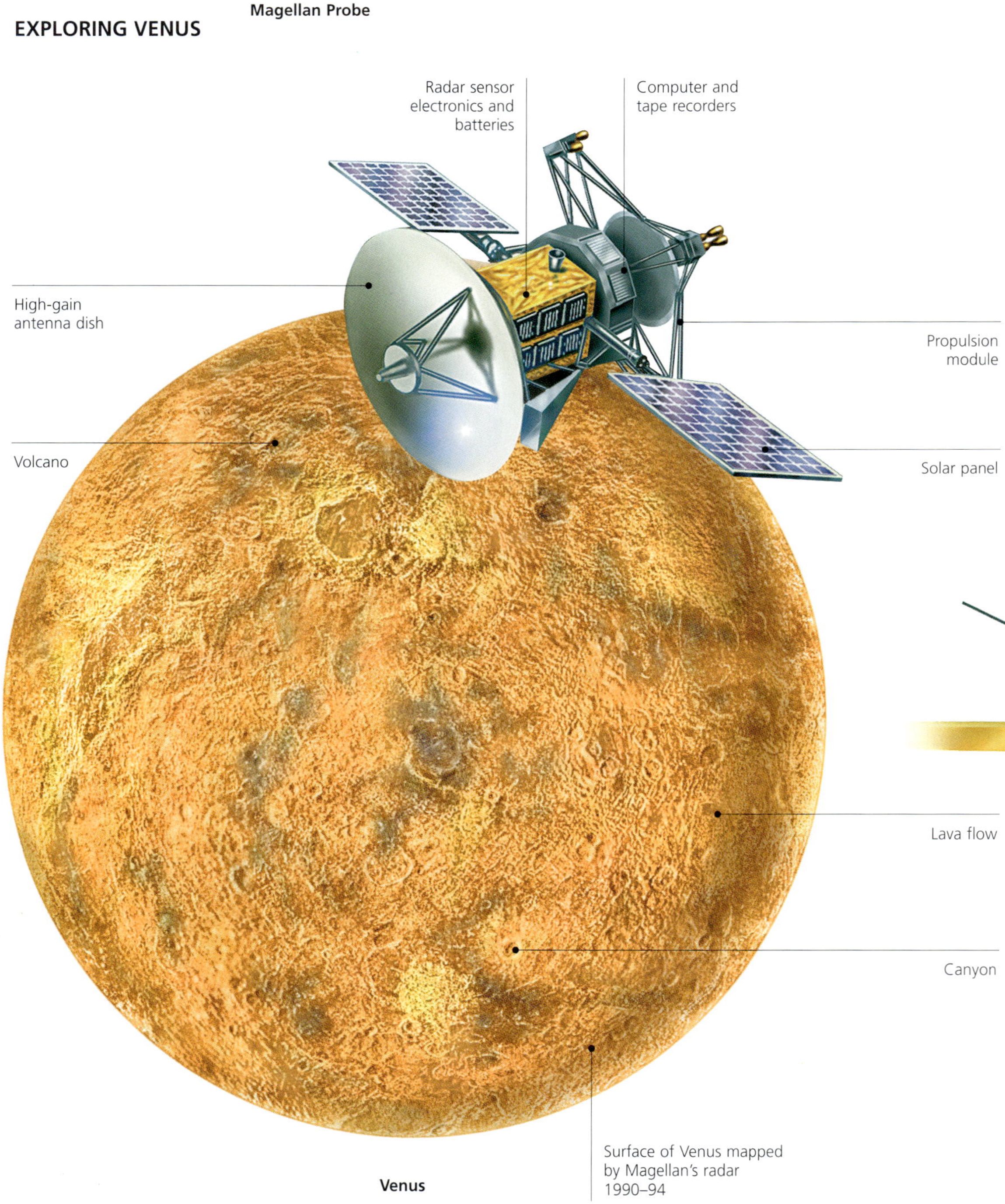

COMPTON GAMMA-RAY OBSERVATORY

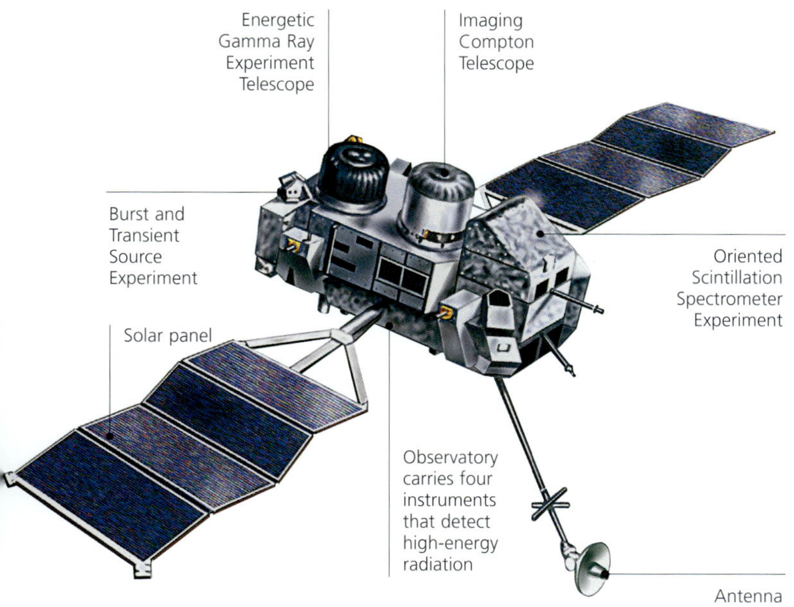

CASSINI

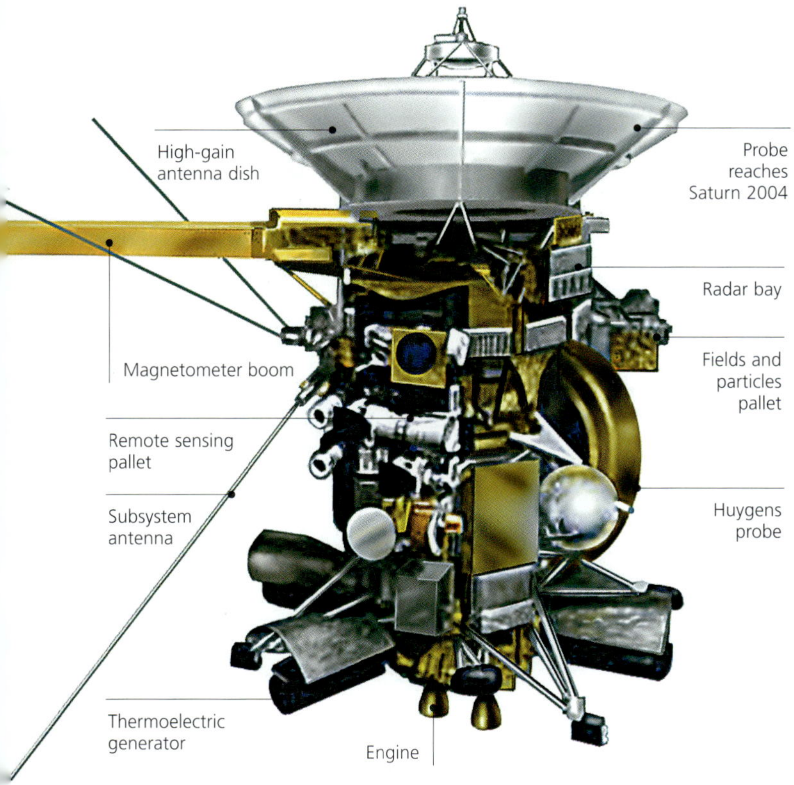

HUYGENS TO TITAN

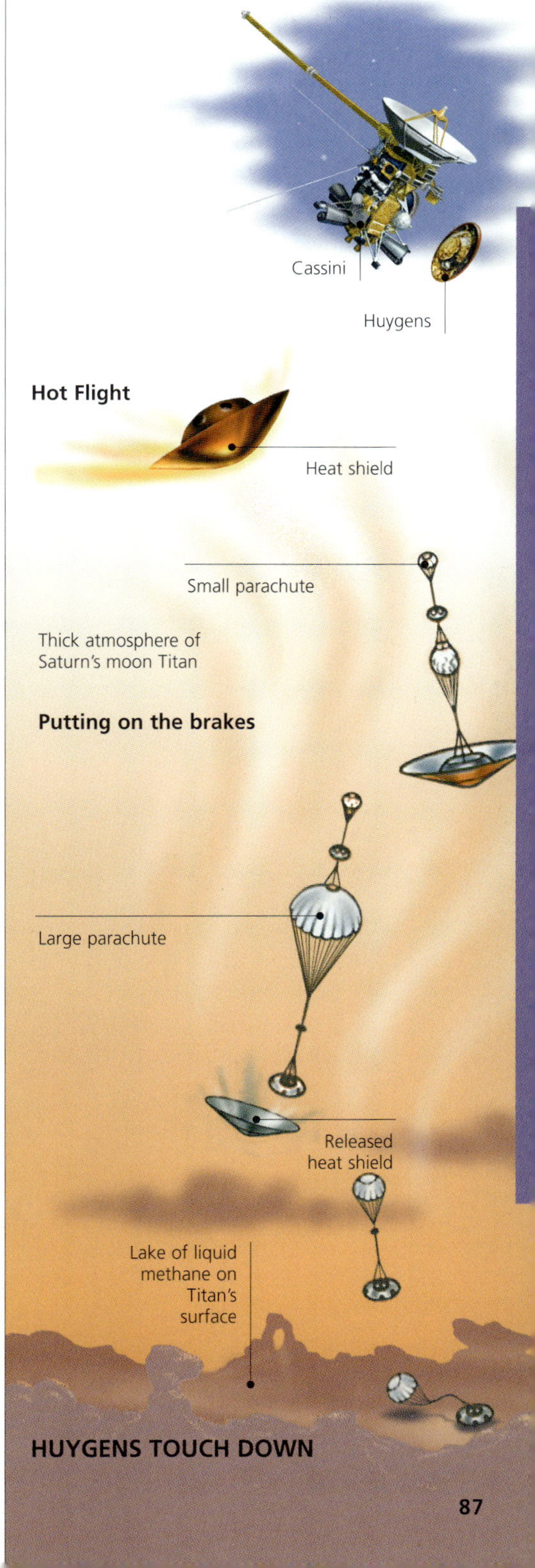

Spacecraft

GIOTTO PROBE

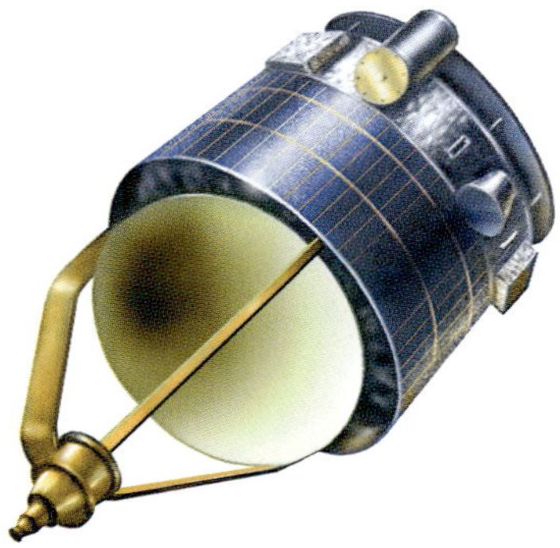

PLUTO—KUIPER EXPRESS

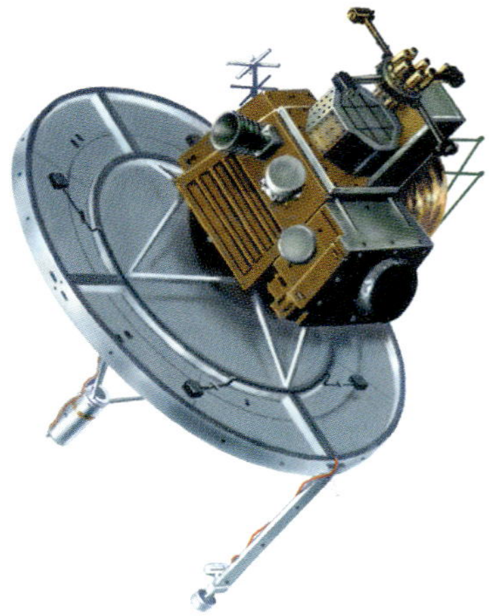

SPOT SATELLITE

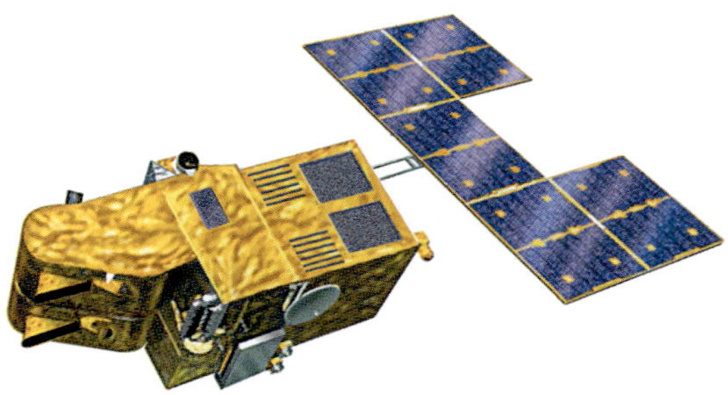

MARINER 10 MERCURY PROBE

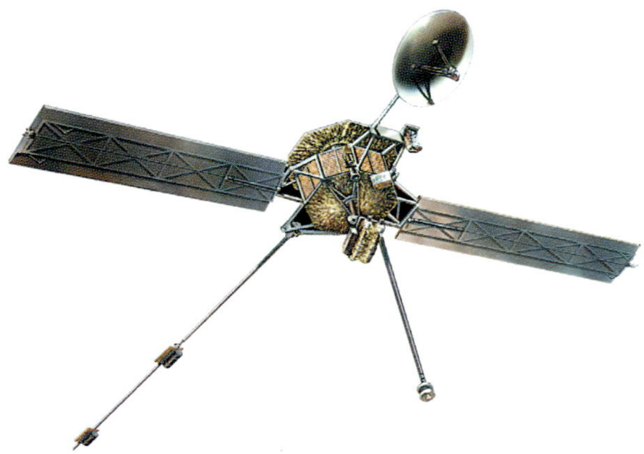

MARS SPACECRAFT

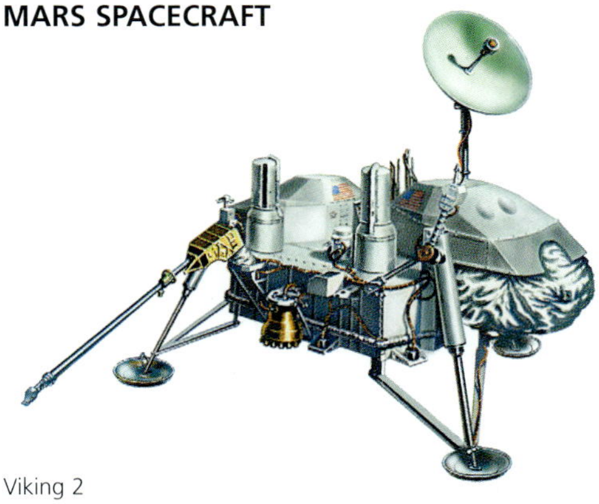

Viking 2

Mars Polar Lander

ASTEROID SPACECRAFT

Muses-C

NEAR (Near-Earth Asteroid Rendezvous) Spacecraft

SUN SPACECRAFT

SOHO (Solar and Heliospheric Observatory)

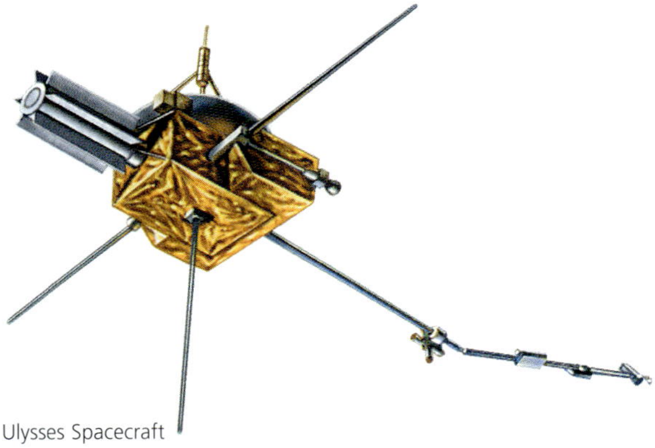

Ulysses Spacecraft

Space Travel

JOURNEY TO THE MOON

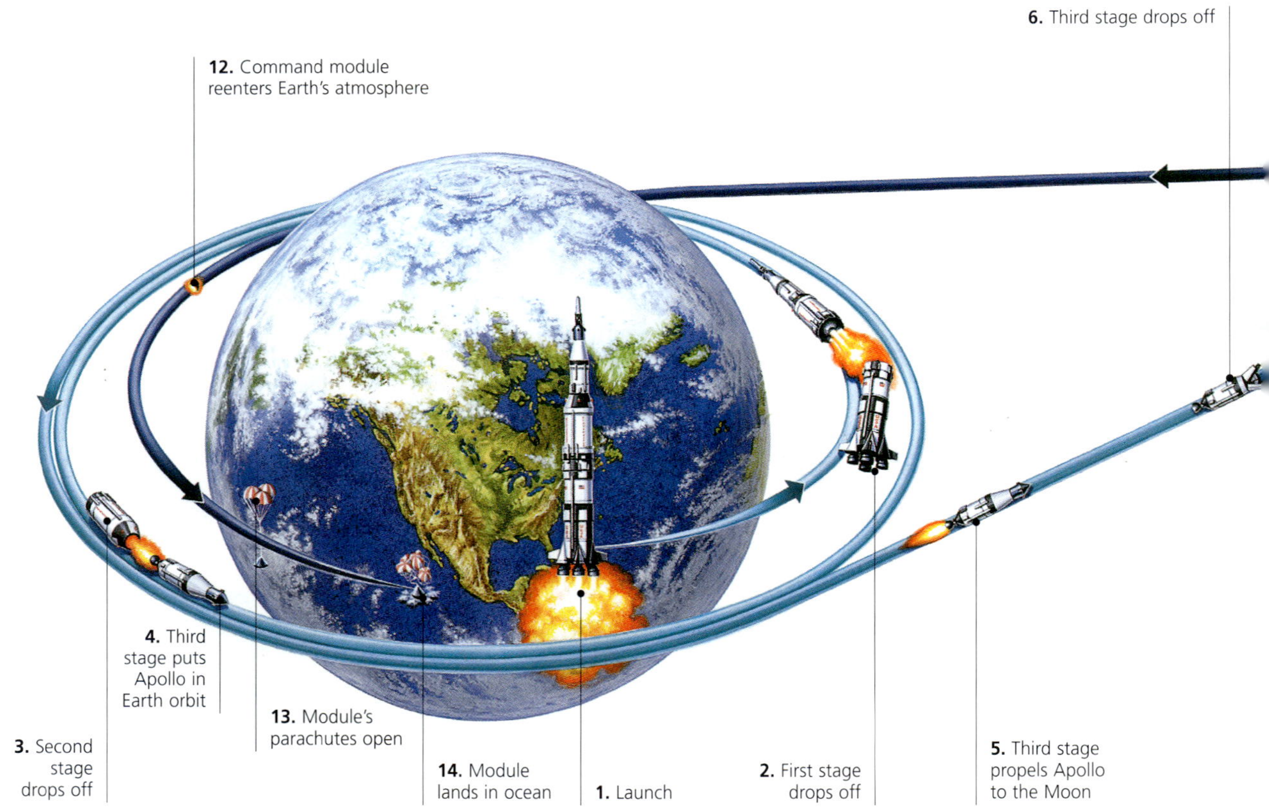

MISSIONS TO SPACE

Vostok, 1961

Gemini, 1965

Soyuz, 1967

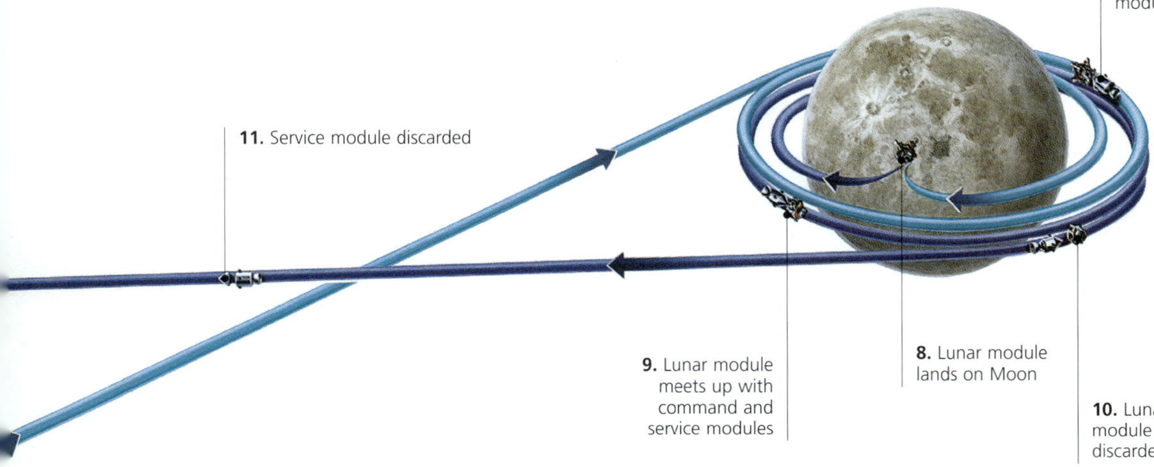

FLYING THE SPACE SHUTTLE

Liftoff

SRB separation

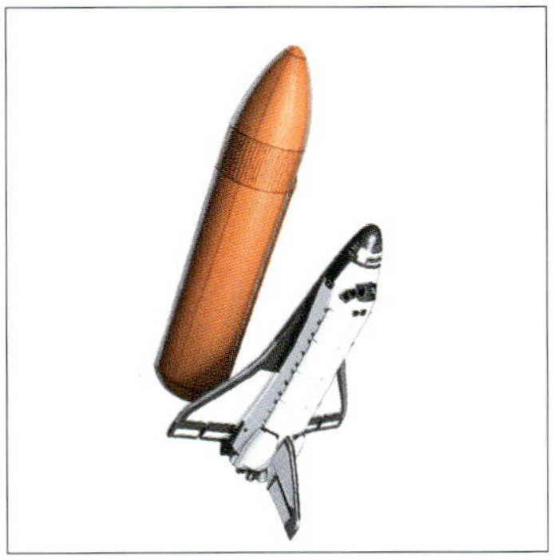

Tank falls away

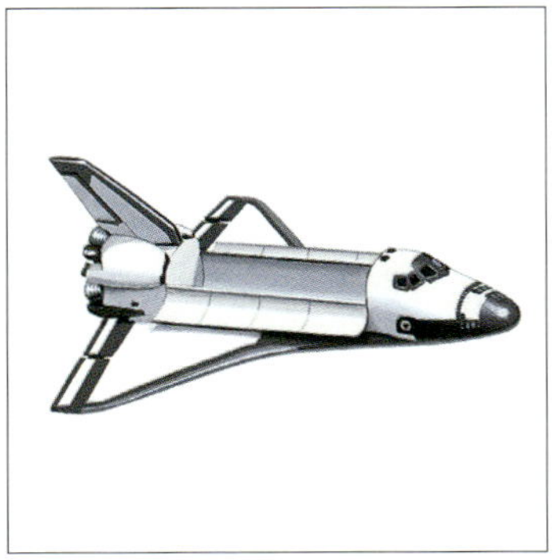

In orbit

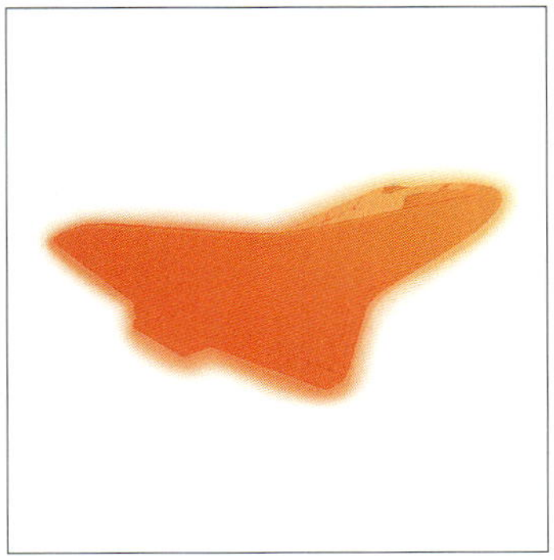

Reentry

Touchdown

THE SHIFTING EARTH

The Earth's Structure 96

Continental Drift 98

Shifting Surface 100

Fault Lines 102

ROCKS AND MINERALS

Types of Rocks 104

Types of Minerals 106

VOLCANOES AND EARTHQUAKES

Hotspot Volcanoes 108

Volcano Eruptions and Flows 110

Famous Volcanoes 112

Earthquakes 114

Tsunamis 116

The Earth's Structure

CROSS SECTION OF EARTH

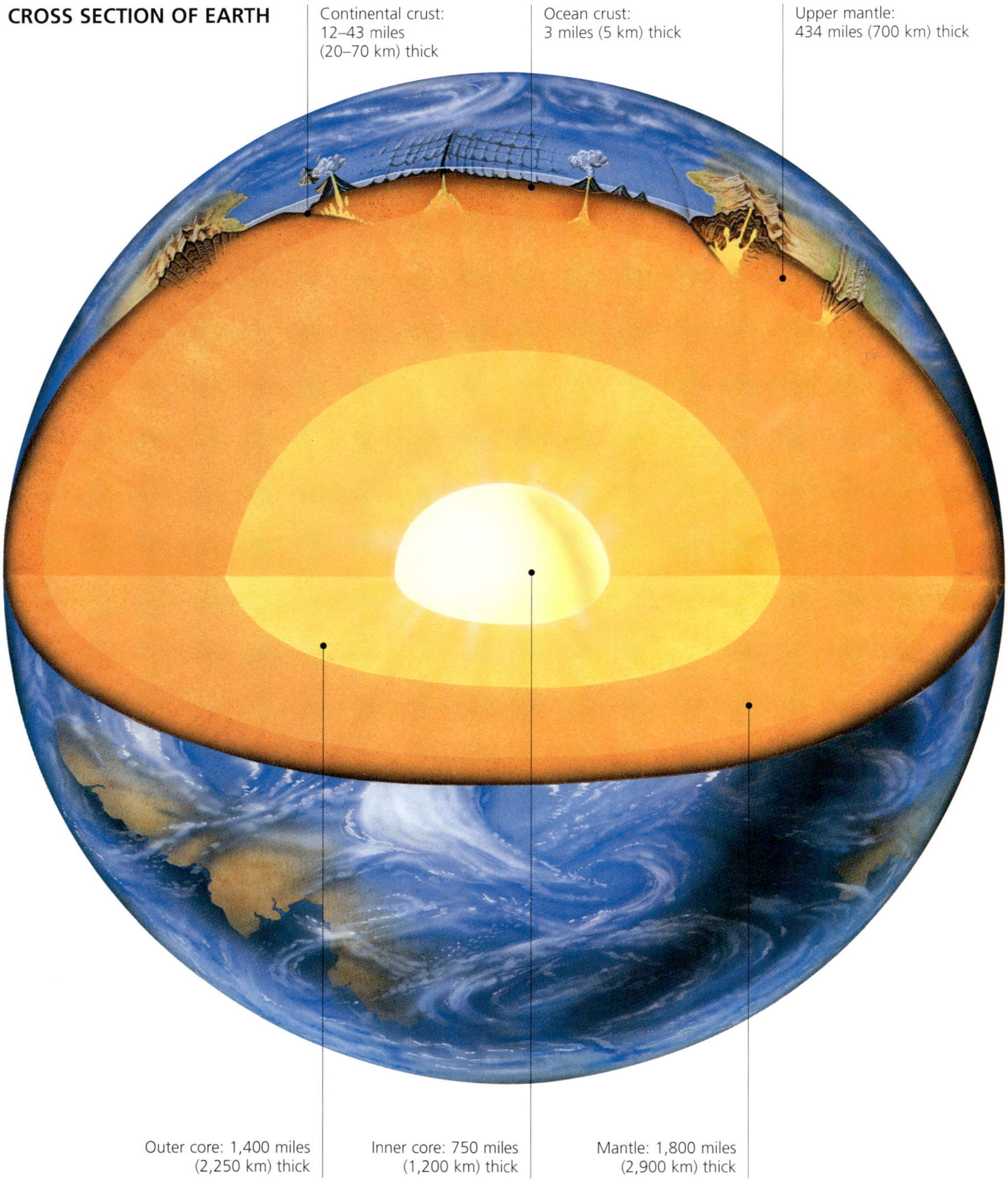

CROSS SECTION OF THE GRAND CANYON

By studying fossils and rocks in the walls of the Grand Canyon, geologists can paint a picture of the canyon's history—which dates back more than two billion years.

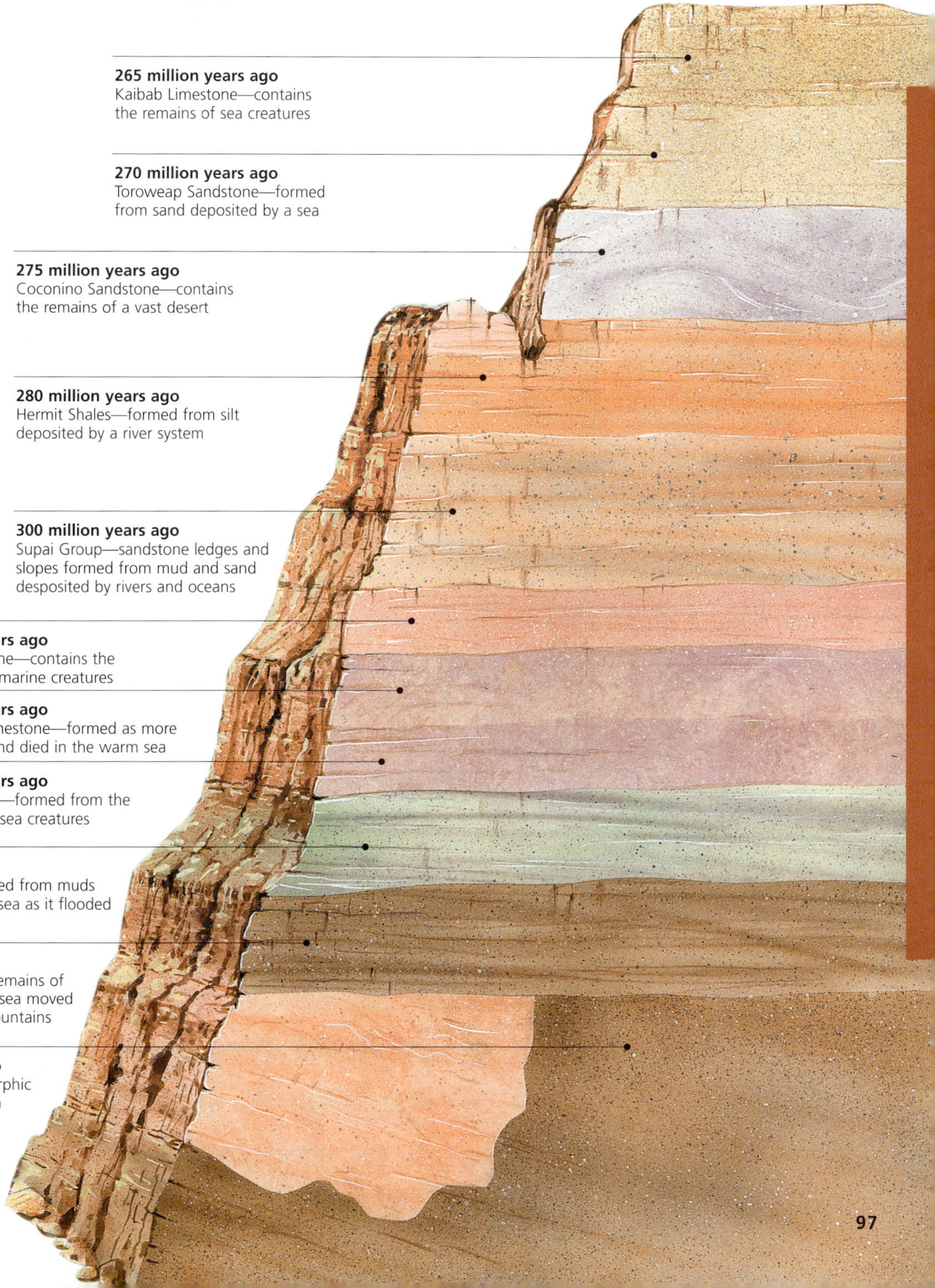

Continental Drift

SHIFTING PLATES

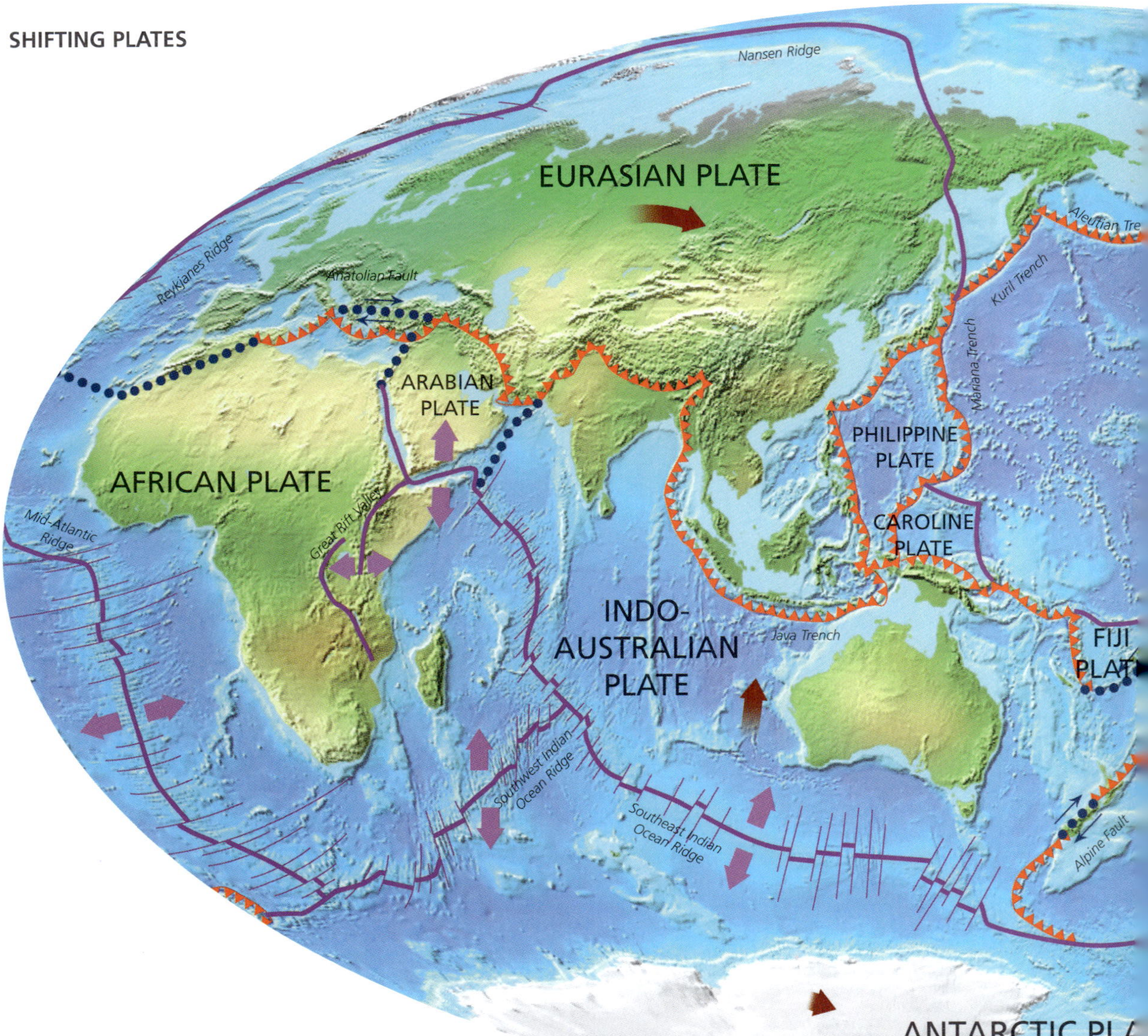

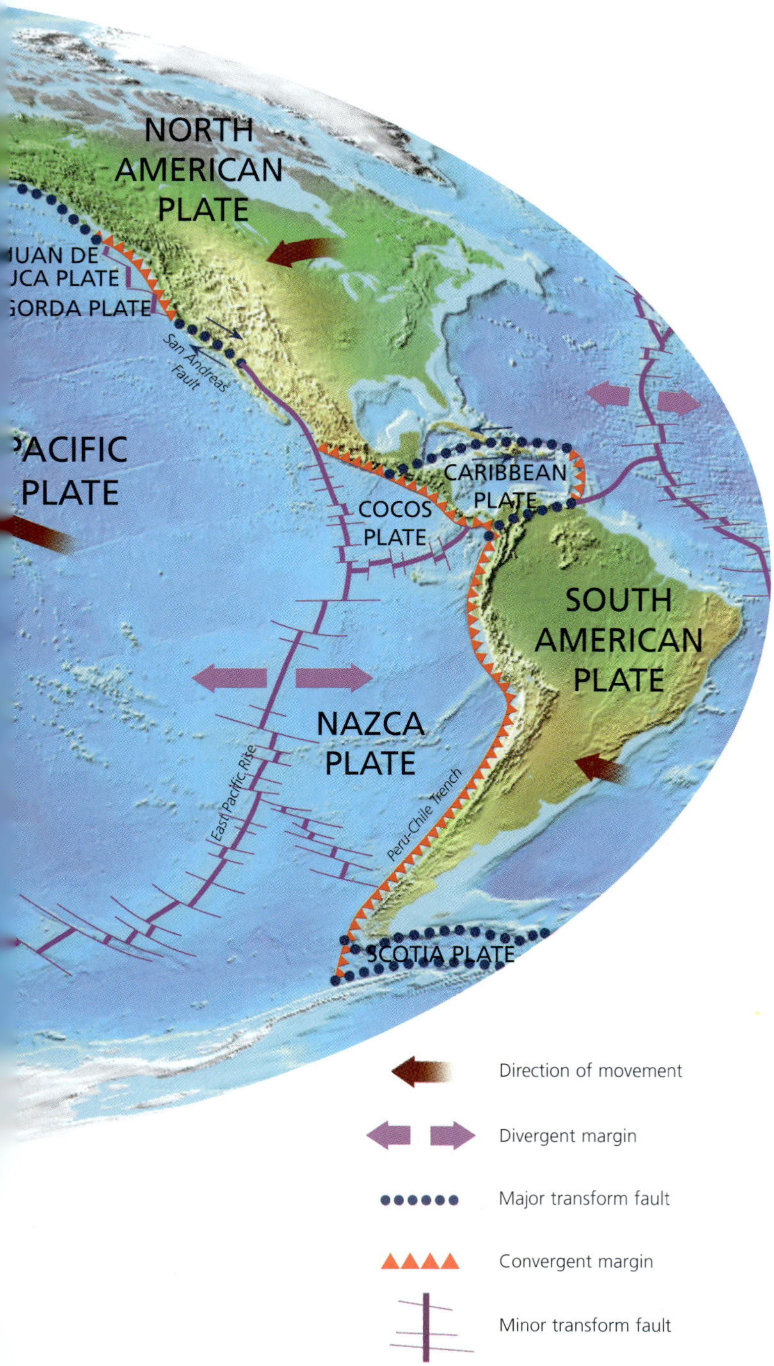

CONTINENTAL MOVEMENT

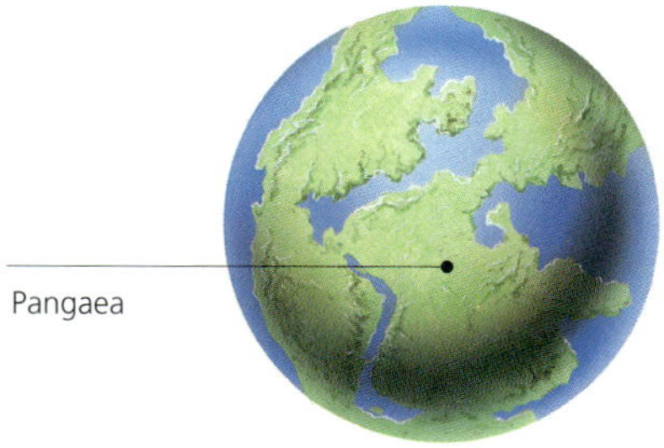

200 million years ago

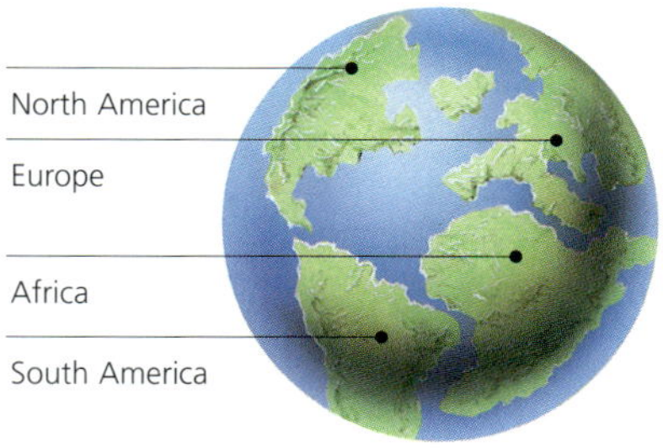

90 million years ago

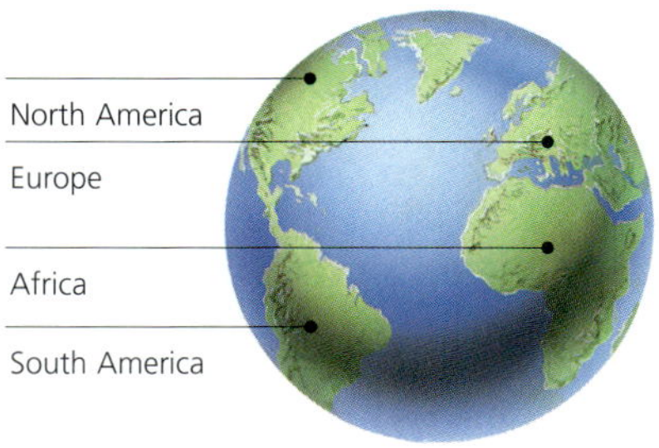

Present day

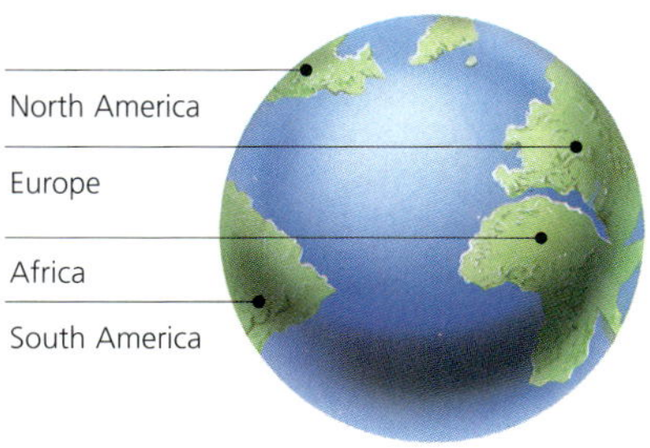

60 million years from now

Shifting Surface

SURFACE WEAR AND TEAR

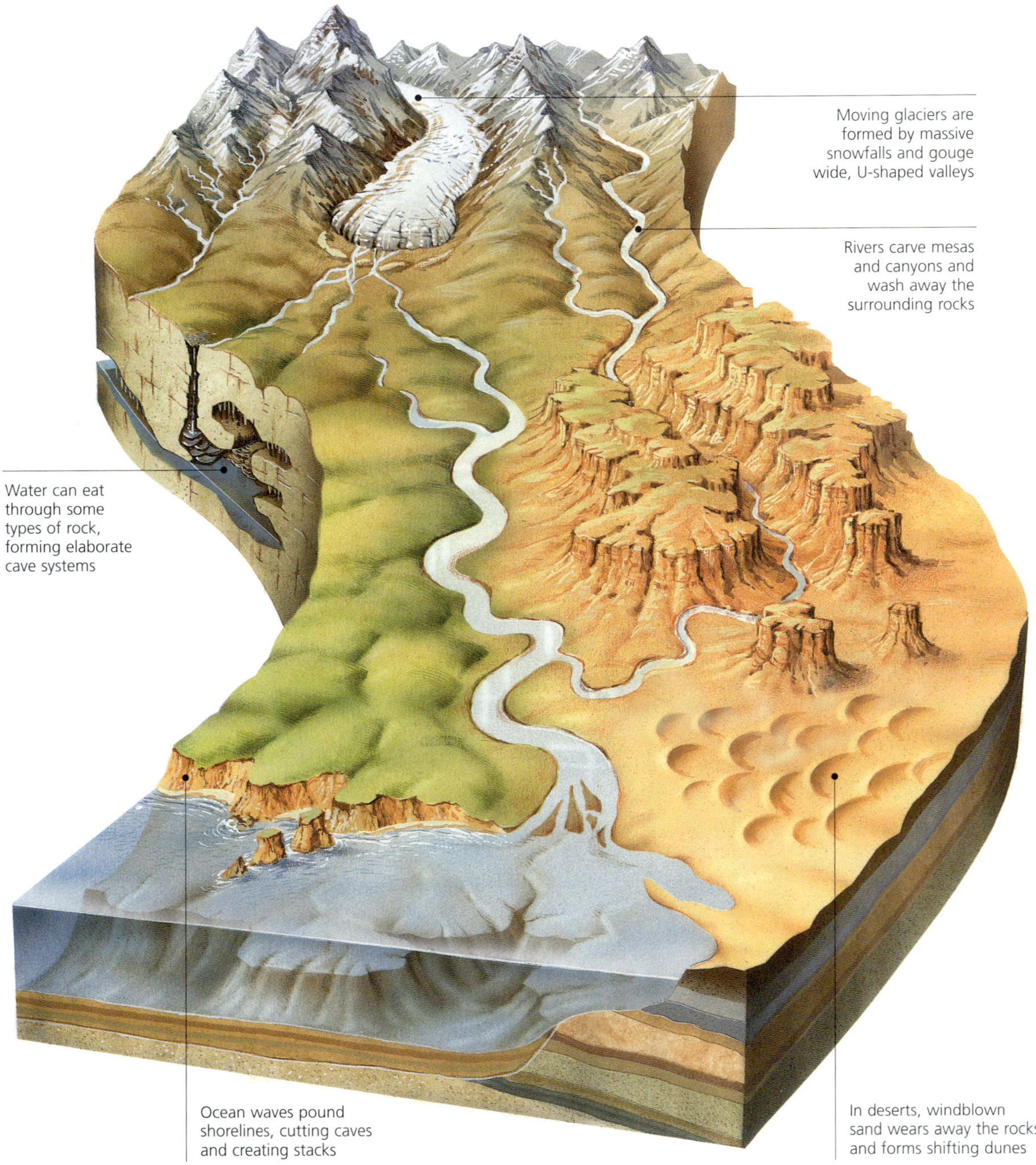

NATURAL SCULPTURE

Numbung Pinnacles, Australia

Devil's Tower, USA

Granite Tor, England

SPREADING SEA FLOOR

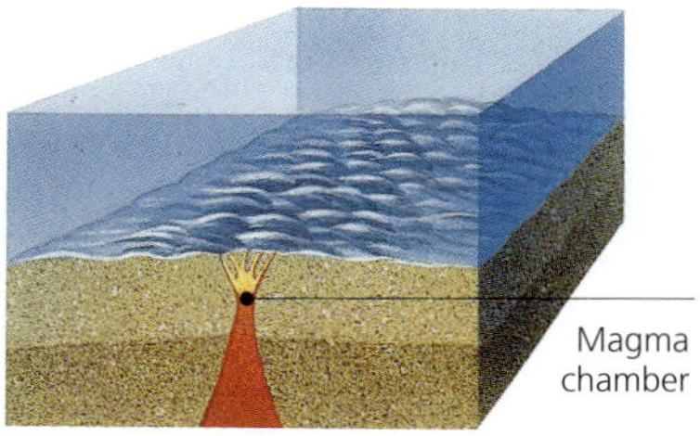

1. As two plates with ocean crust move apart, a crack or rift forms.

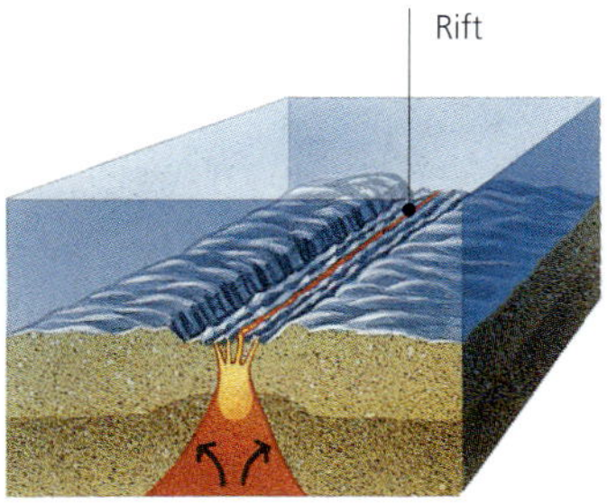

2. Magma from the mantle rises to fill the rift between the two plates.

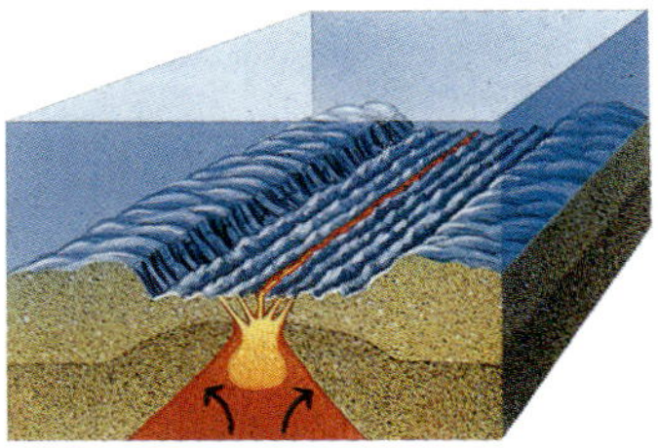

3. Magma cools and hardens and adds to the edges of the plates.

SPREADING CANYON

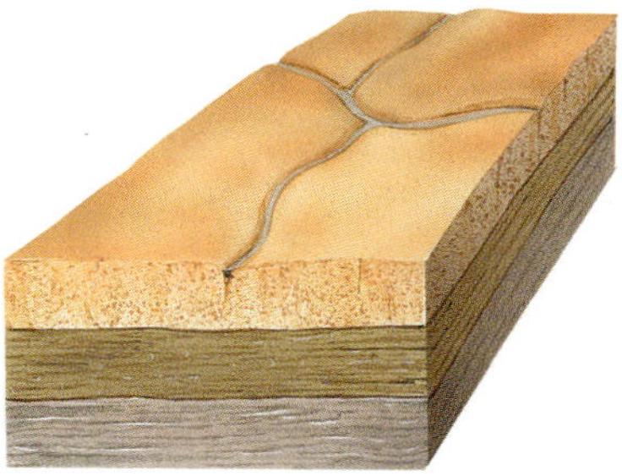

1. Sedimentary rocks are exposed when the sea level falls. Rivers cut deep into rocks, forming narrow pathways in the land.

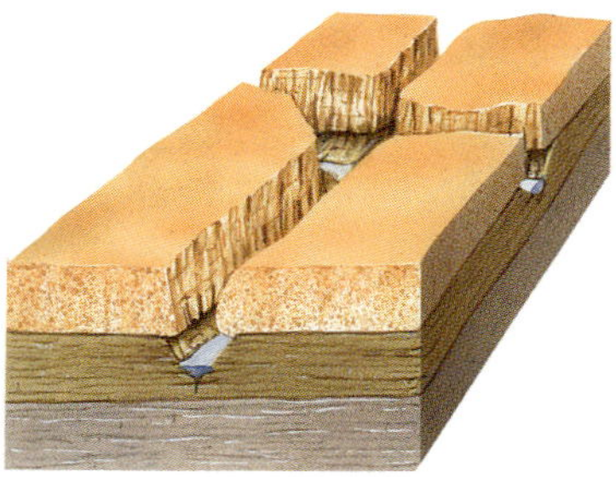

2. As the rivers cut deeper, they form steep-sided valleys. Reaching softer layers, the rivers start to dig under the hard rock.

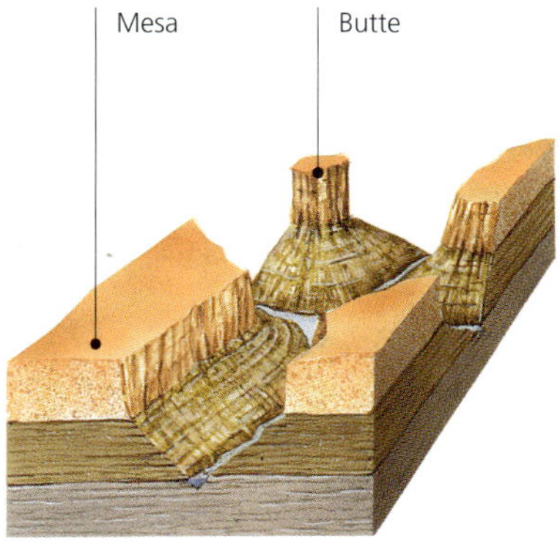

3. The undercutting causes the upper layers to collapse and the valley widens. This creates mesas and buttes in the landscape.

Fault Lines

FAMOUS FAULT LINES

Himalayas

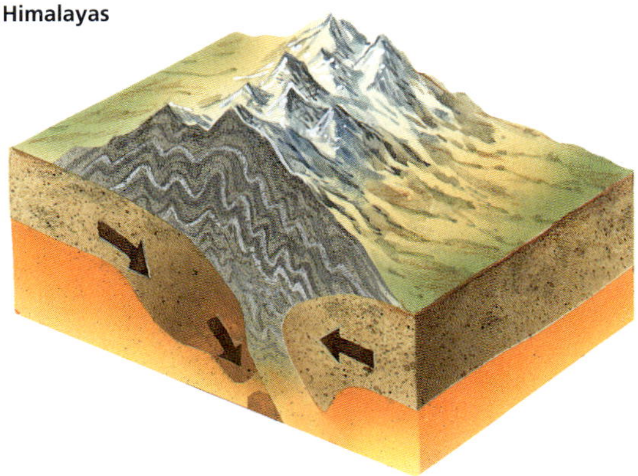

Formed at a convergent zone where two continental plates collided and squeezed together.

San Andreas

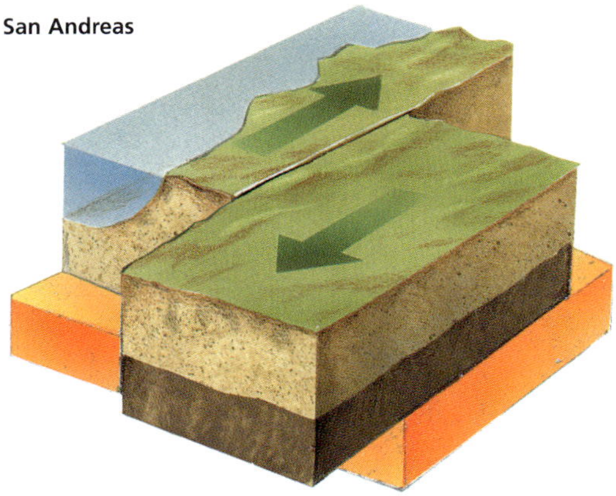

This fault line marks the transform boundary between the Pacific and North American plates.

TYPES OF FAULT LINES AND RIDGES

East African rift valley

This rift valley represents a continental divergent zone, where Africa will split and a new ocean will form.

Mid-Atlantic ridge

This ridge is a mid-ocean divergent zone, where oceanic crust is formed continually.

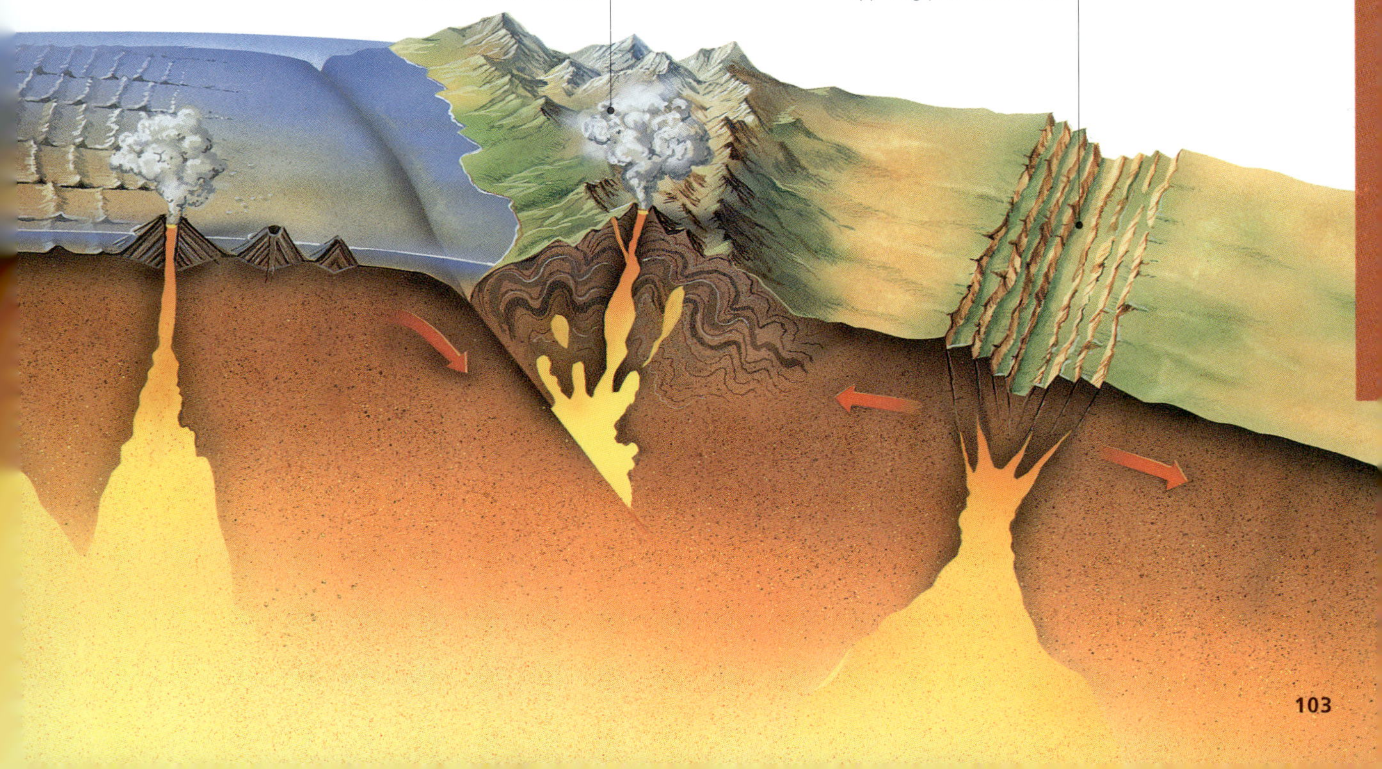

Types of Rocks

ROCK CYCLE

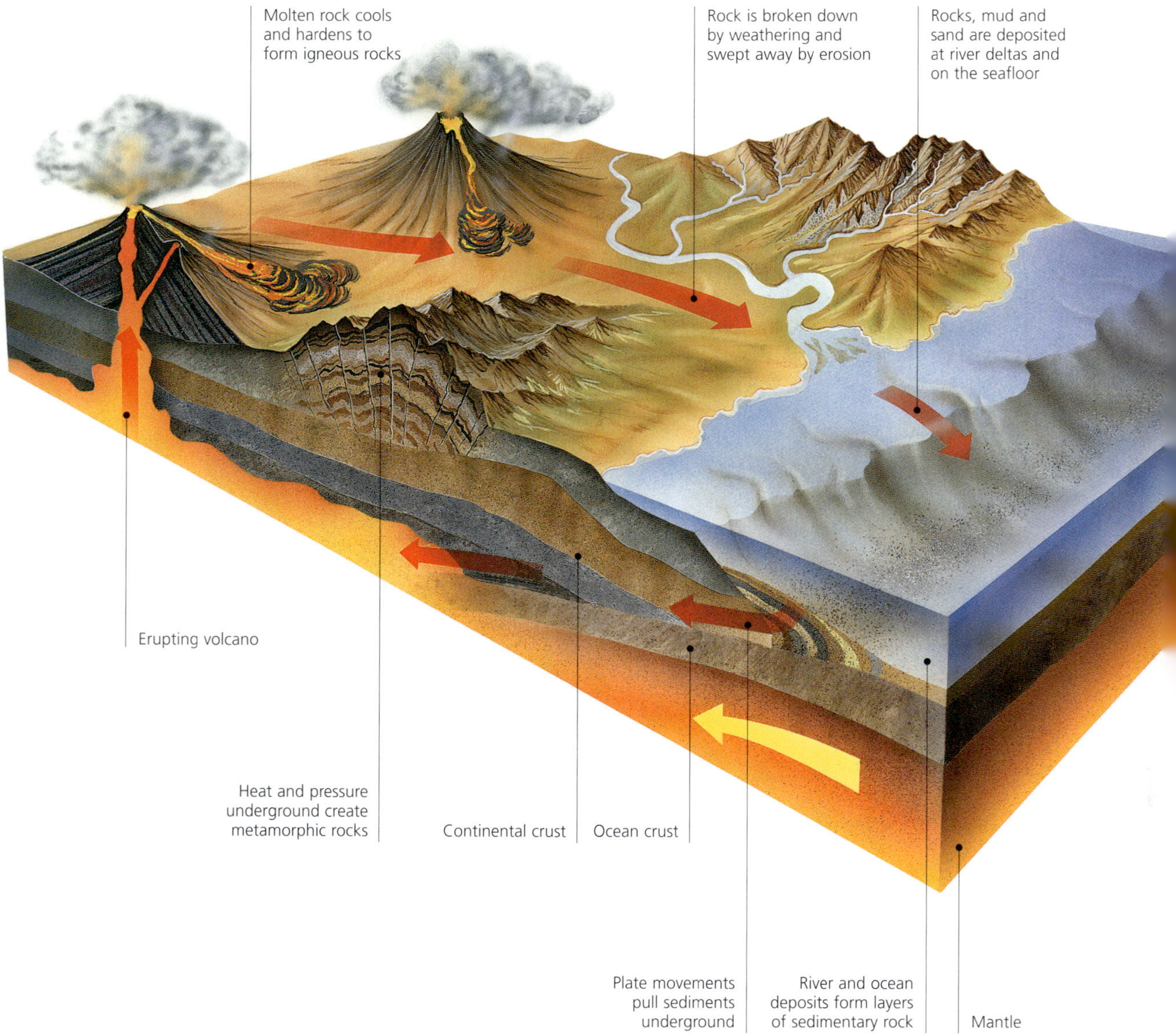

TYPES OF ROCKS

Igneous

Andesite

Gabbro

Obsidian

Sedimentary

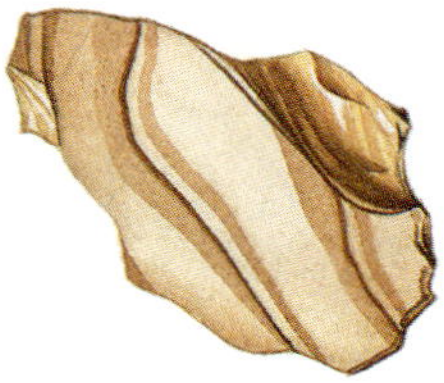
Chert

Conglomerate

Sandstone

Metamorphic

Banded gneiss

Quartzite

Folded schist

Unusual

Pyrite sand dollar

Pumice

Dumbbell micrometeorite

Types of Minerals

ROCK AND MINERAL ENVIRONMENT

MOHS SCALE OF HARDNESS
1 = softest, 10 = hardest

1. Talc

2. Gypsum

3. Calcite

4. Fluorite

5. Apatite

TYPES OF MINERAL STRUCTURE

Minerals are solid substances that occur naturally in Earth's crust. They may take on a variety of forms.

Dendritic (treelike)

Equant (equal-sided)

Massive (rocklike)

TYPES OF ORE

Minerals that are useful and can be mined economically are called ores. These minerals have been valued for thousands of years.

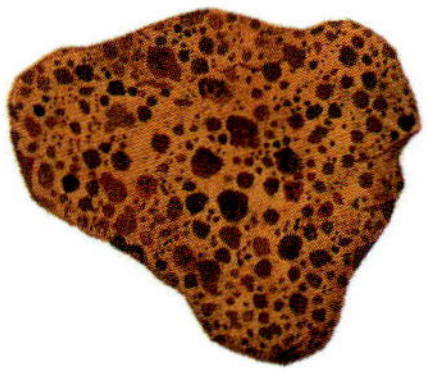
Bauxite—aluminum ore

Bornite—copper ore

Galena—lead ore

6. Orthoclase

7. Quartz

8. Topaz

9. Corundum

10. Diamond

Hotspot Volcanoes

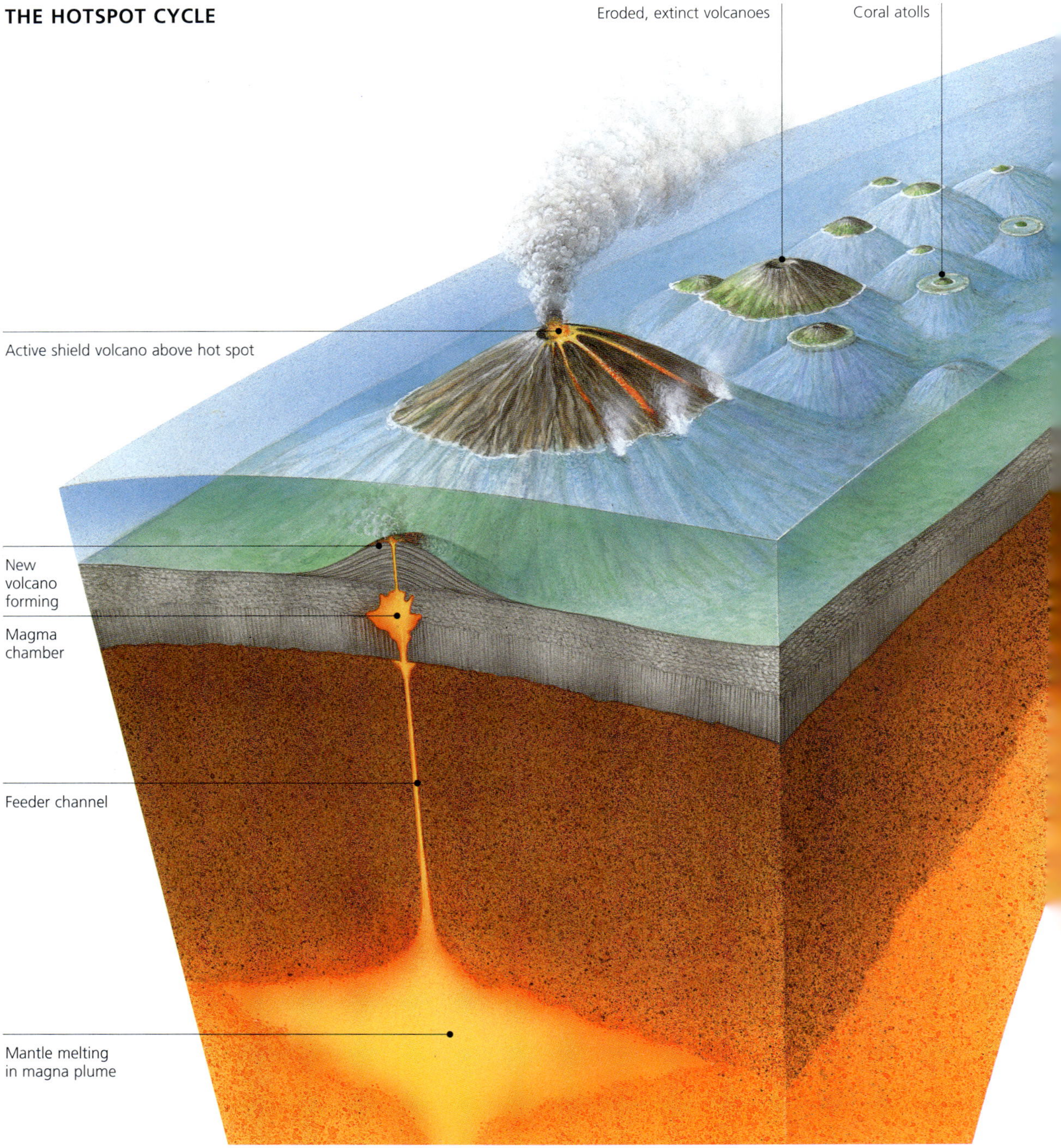

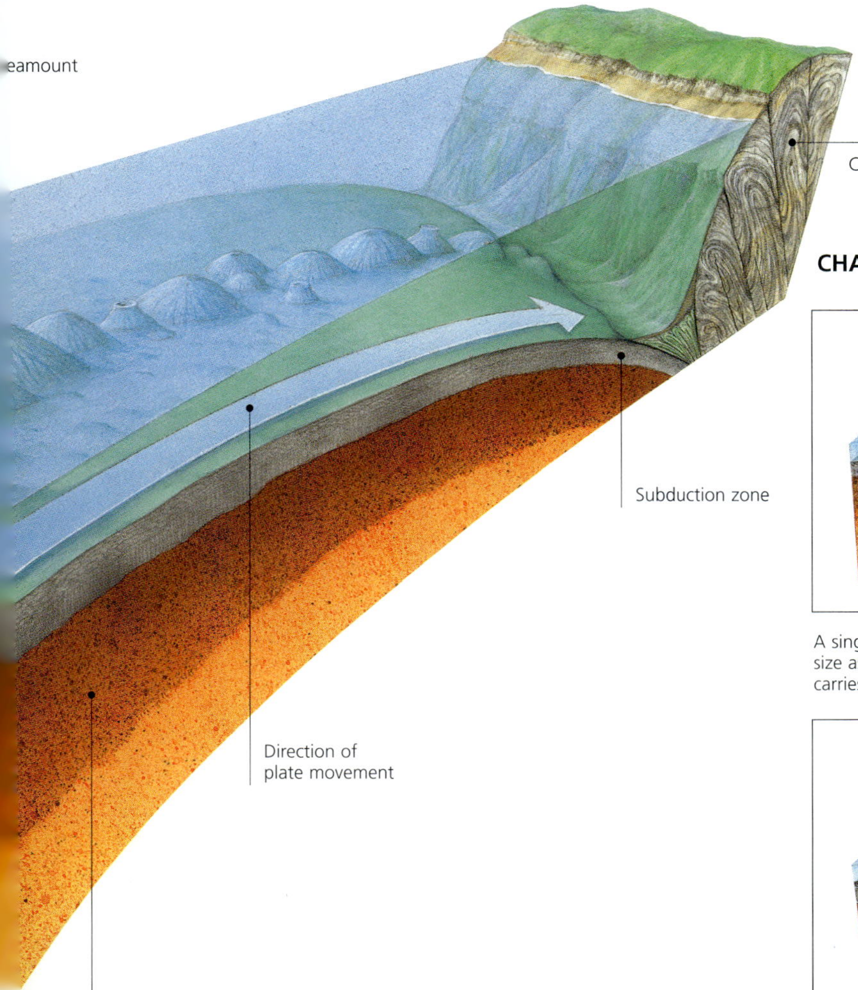

CHAIN FORMATION

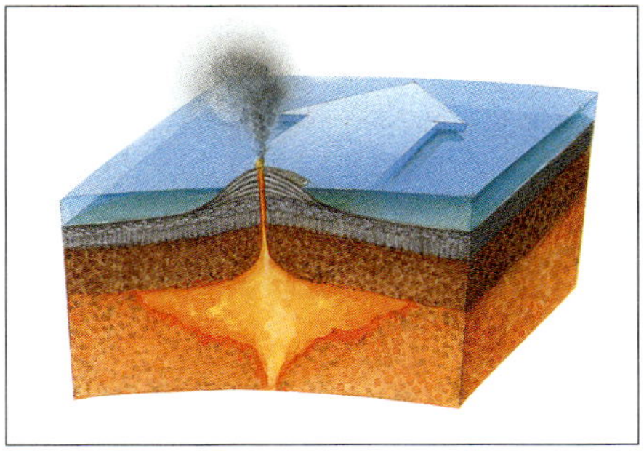

A single volcano forms above a hotspot, growing in size as the lava builds up. As the plate moves, it carries the volcano away from the hotspot.

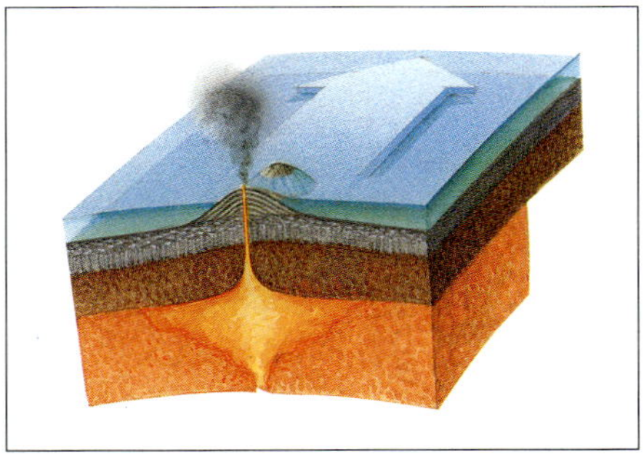

After millions of years, the volcano separates from the hotspot, its lava supply is cut off and it becomes extinct. A new volcano then forms above the hotspot.

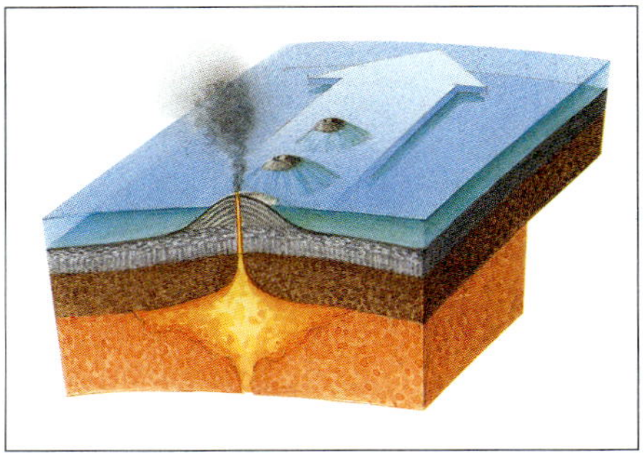

The chain of volcanoes continues to grow in the direction of the plate movement. If the hotspot fades, the chain of volcanoes stops growing.

Volcano Eruptions and Flows

TYPES OF ERUPTION

Hawaiian

Strombolian

Plinian

Vulcanian

Peléean

TYPES OF PYROCLASTIC FLOW

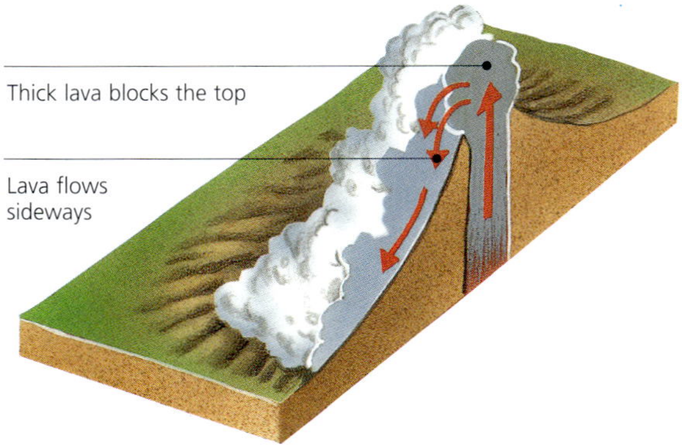

Dome collapse

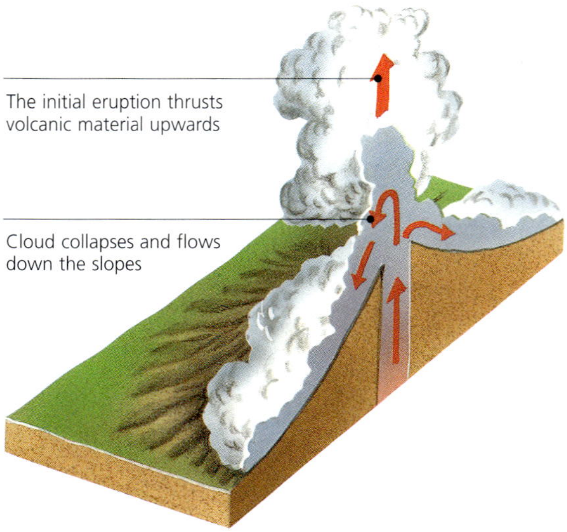

Collapsing vertical eruption

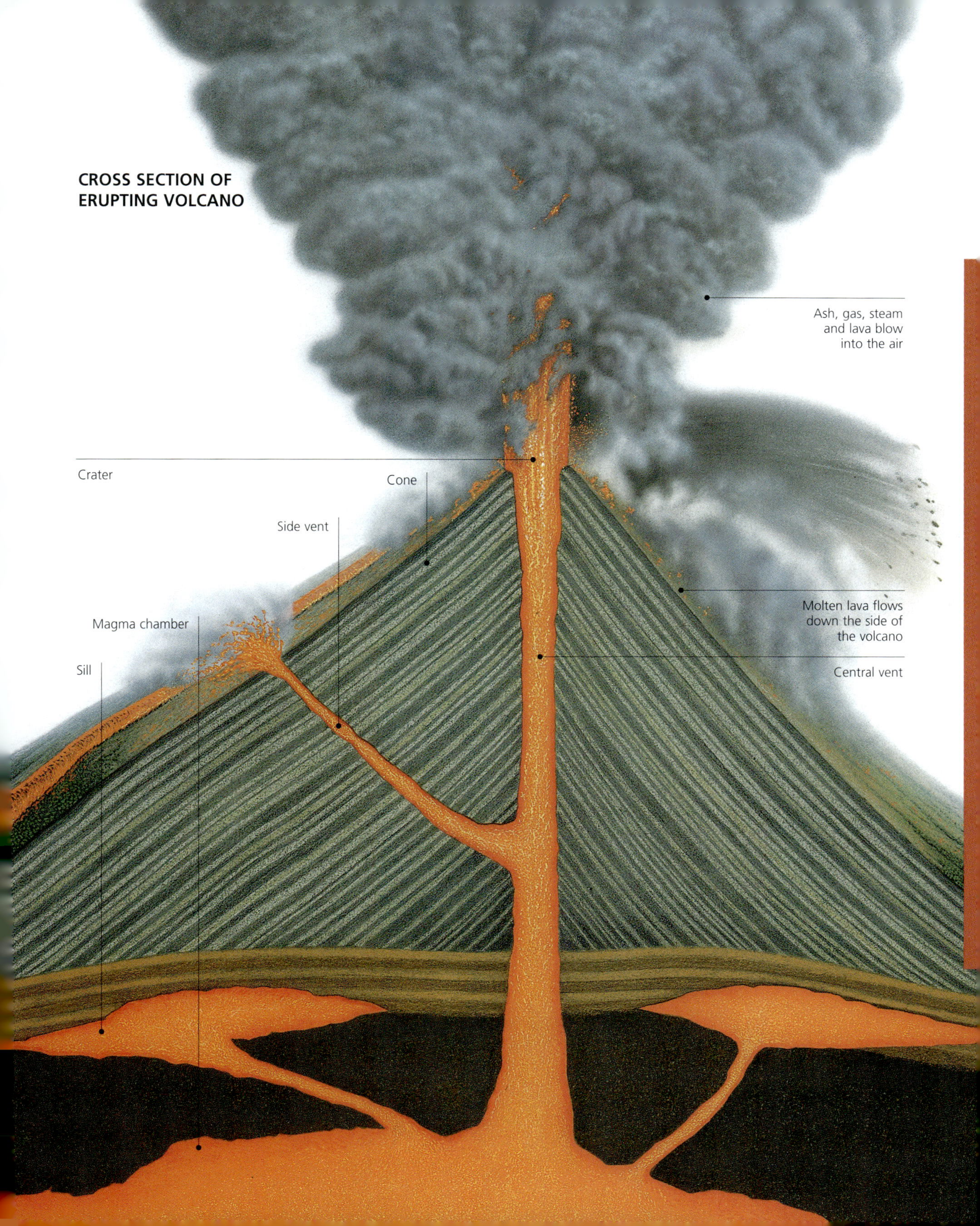
CROSS SECTION OF
ERUPTING VOLCANO
Ash, gas, steam
and lava blow
into the air
Crater
Cone
Side vent
Molten lava flows
down the side of
the volcano
Magma chamber
Sill
Central vent

Famous Volcanoes

WORLDWIDE VOLCANOES

COTOPAXI
Ecuador

MOUNT ST. HELENS
Washington, USA

TORRES DEL PAINE
Chile

MAYON
The Philippines

STROMBOLI
Italy

MOUNT FUJI
Japan

MOUNT ETNA
Italy

MOUNT AUGUSTINE
Alaska, USA

VILLARRICA
Chile

MOUNT RAINIER
Washington, USA

SANTORINI
Greece

MOUNT GARIBALDI
British Columbia, Canada

POMPEII ERUPTION
August 24, AD 79

Earthquakes

MAJOR EARTHQUAKES

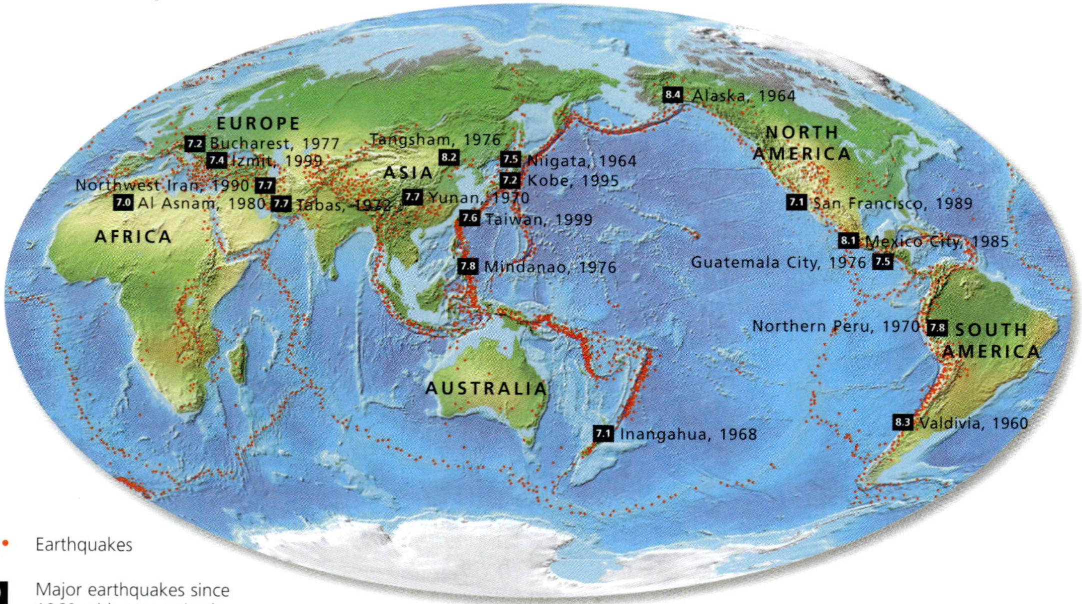

Earthquakes

7.0 Major earthquakes since 1960 with a magnitude of 7 or more (on the Richter Scale)

TYPES OF EARTHQUAKE WAVES

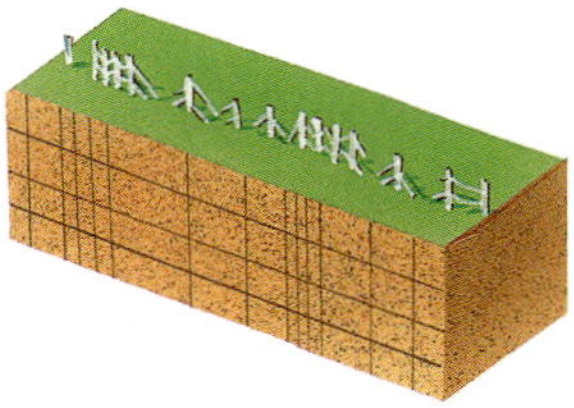

P-waves, or primary waves, are the first to arrive during an earthquake. They compress (push together) and dilate (pull apart) the rocks in the ground.

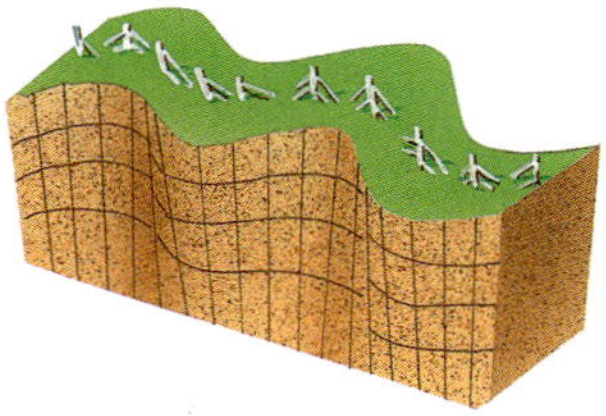

P- and S-waves are followed by surface waves, which only affect the Earth's surface. One type, Love waves, makes the surface move from side to side like a snake.

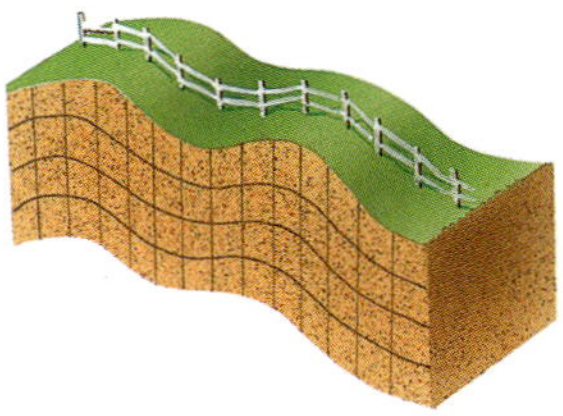

S-waves, or secondary waves, move more slowly than P-waves. They move rock layers up and down and from side to side.

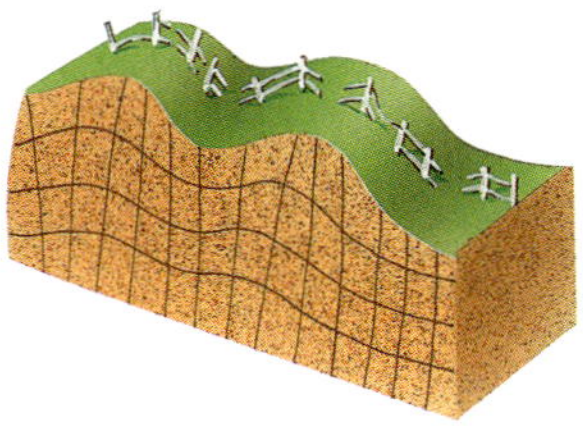

Rayleigh waves are the second type of surface waves and cause the ground to rise and fall.

AFTER AN EARTHQUAKE
Earthquakes strike suddenly and swiftly—often with devastating effect.

Tsunamis

EFFECTS OF AN EARTHQUAKE
Earthquakes that occur near the coast can trigger tsunamis—waves that spread across the ocean at great speed and rapidly grow in size as they near shore.

WAVE FORMATION

Unlike a surface wave, a tsunami is a whole column of water that reaches from the sea floor up.

Sometime after an earthquake, harbors can be drained dry as water is dragged out to the ocean to join the developing tsunami.

The power of the returning wave batters and floods the coast, causing enormous damage and loss of life. Tsunamis occur most often in the Pacific.

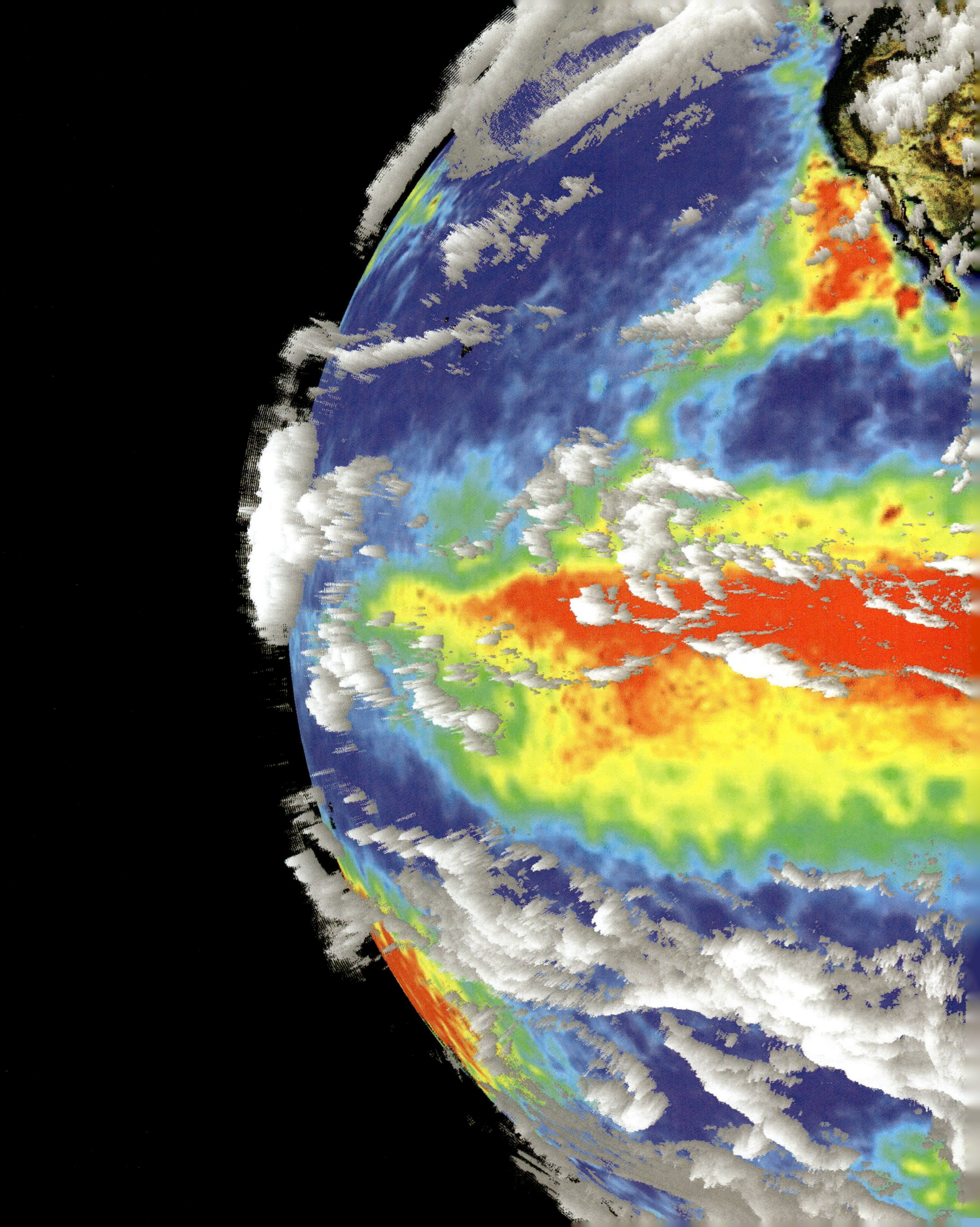

ATMOSPHERE AND OCEANS

WEATHER

Earth's Atmosphere 122

Water and Fog 124

Clouds 126

Precipitation 128

Storms 130

Mapping the Weather 132

Frontal Systems 134

SEASONS AND CLIMATE

The Seasons 136

Winds and Monsoons 138

Climate 140

EARTH'S OCEANS

Waves, Tides and Currents 142

The Sea Floor 144

The Shore 146

Earth's Atmosphere

OZONE LAYER

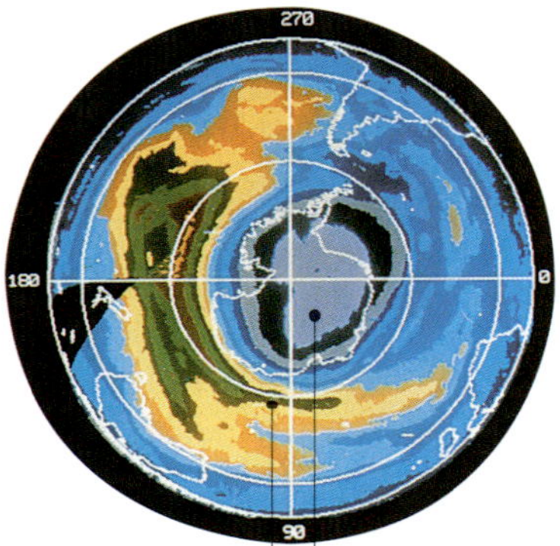

The ozone layer shields Earth from ultraviolet light

The light blue at the center of this picture shows a hole in the ozone layer situated over Antarctica

POLLUTION

The level of greenhouse gases in the atmosphere is increasing because of industrial pollution, deforestation, farming methods and the burning of fossil fuels.

Cows have a major effect on the atmosphere because they produce methane gas when they digest grass

More fossil fuels are being used each year. They provide power for transport and industry

SKY COLOR

Day
Blue rays scatter through the atmosphere.

Sunrise and sunset
Orange and red rays scatter through the atmosphere.

Water and Fog

MOVEMENT OF FOG

As the sun rises, it warms the edges of a bank of fog.

The fog bank gradually shrinks and rises as the sun rises higher.

By mid-morning, a thin deck of fog may remain suspended.

WATER CYCLE

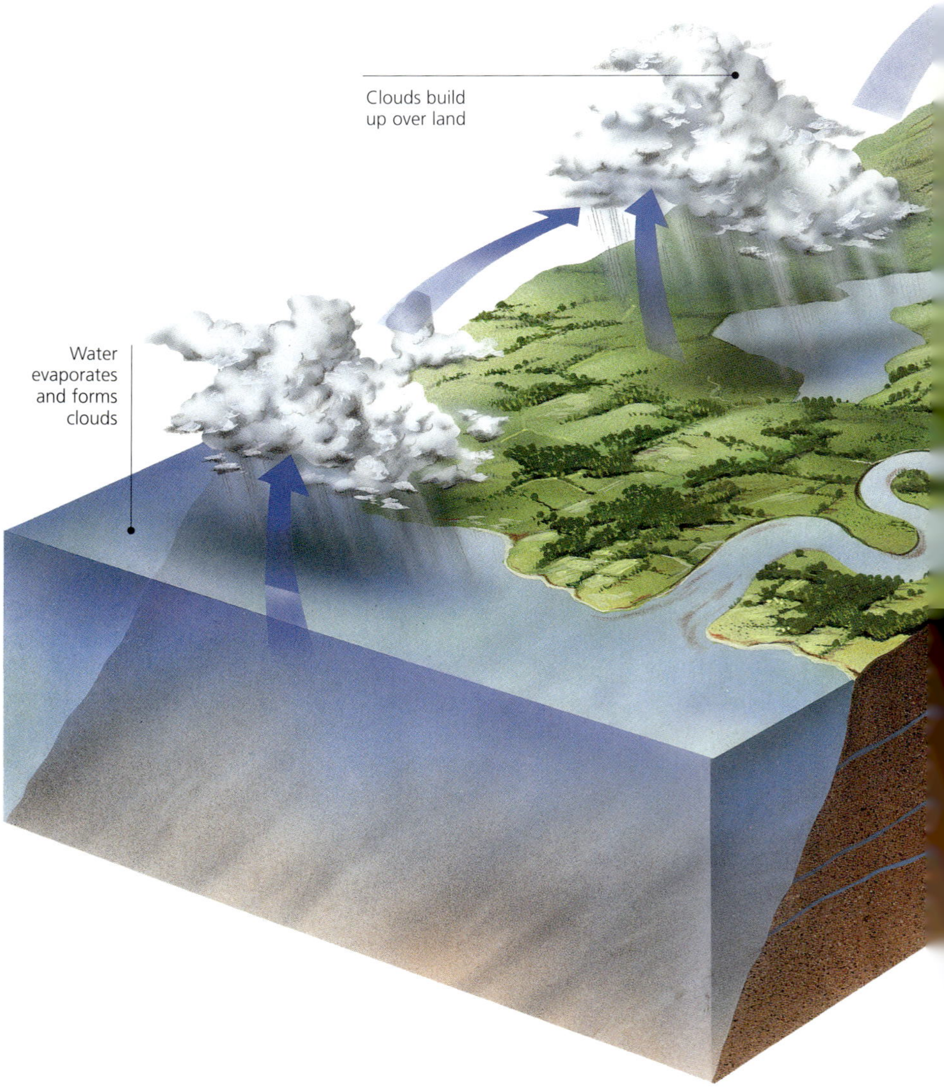

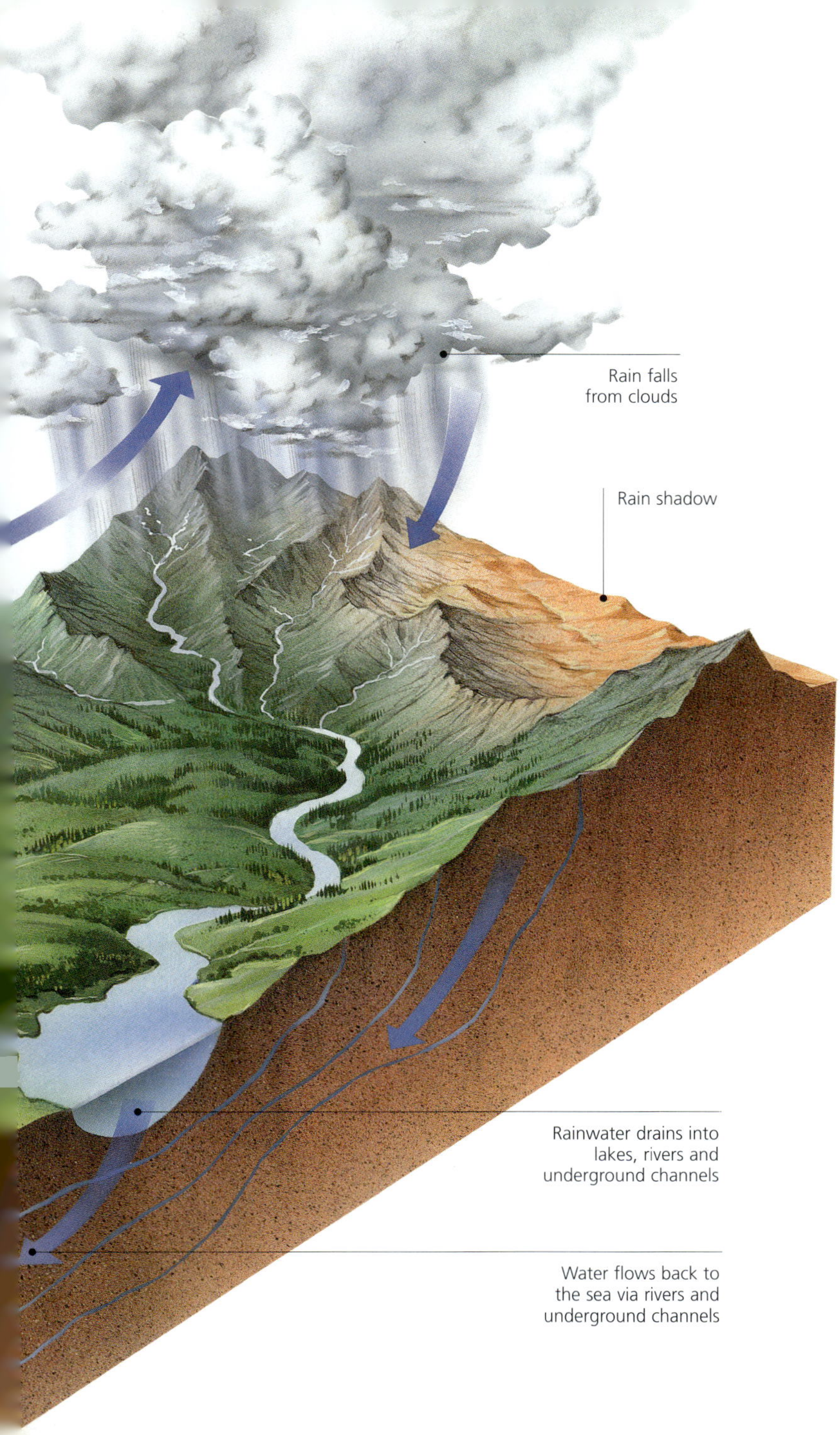

TYPES OF FOG

Advection

Fog forms when warm, humid air moves over a cold surface.

Radiation

When land cools rapidly, the air above is chilled, creating fog.

Stratus

Fog clears from the bottom up when the ground warms quickly.

Clouds

CLOUD COLOR

HOW CLOUDS LIFT

Convection
Ground heat causes air mass to rise.

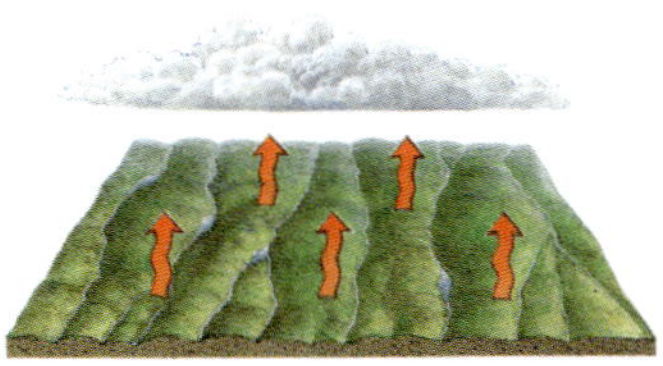

Frontal formation
Warm air rises when it meets cooler air.

Orographic lifting
Air is forced up at mountain ranges.

TYPES OF CLOUDS

Precipitation

AVALANCHE

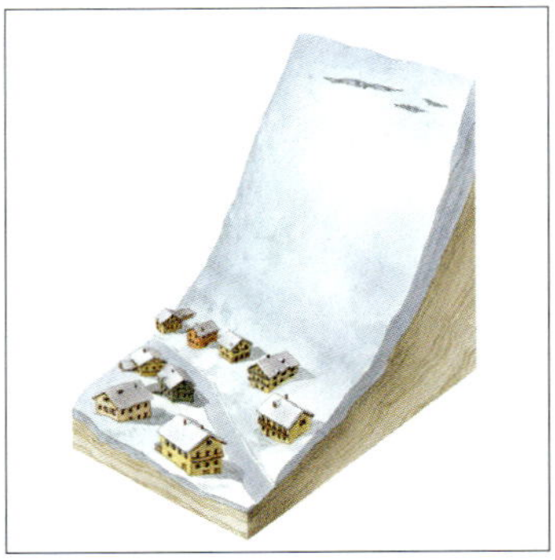

Avalanches can occur when a new fall of snow builds up on top of old snow.

Snow slides with increasing speed when it can no longer support its own weight.

Rescuers often use sniffer dogs to locate survivors buried under the snow.

TYPES OF PRECIPITATION

Snow
Snow forms if the freezing level is below a height of 1,000 feet (300 m) above the ground, and the ice crystals do not have time to melt before they reach the ground.

SNOWFLAKES

Snowflakes are loose clusters of ice crystals usually with a flat, six-sided (hexagonal) shape. The exact shape of a snowflake depends on the temperature of the air—no two snowflakes are the same.

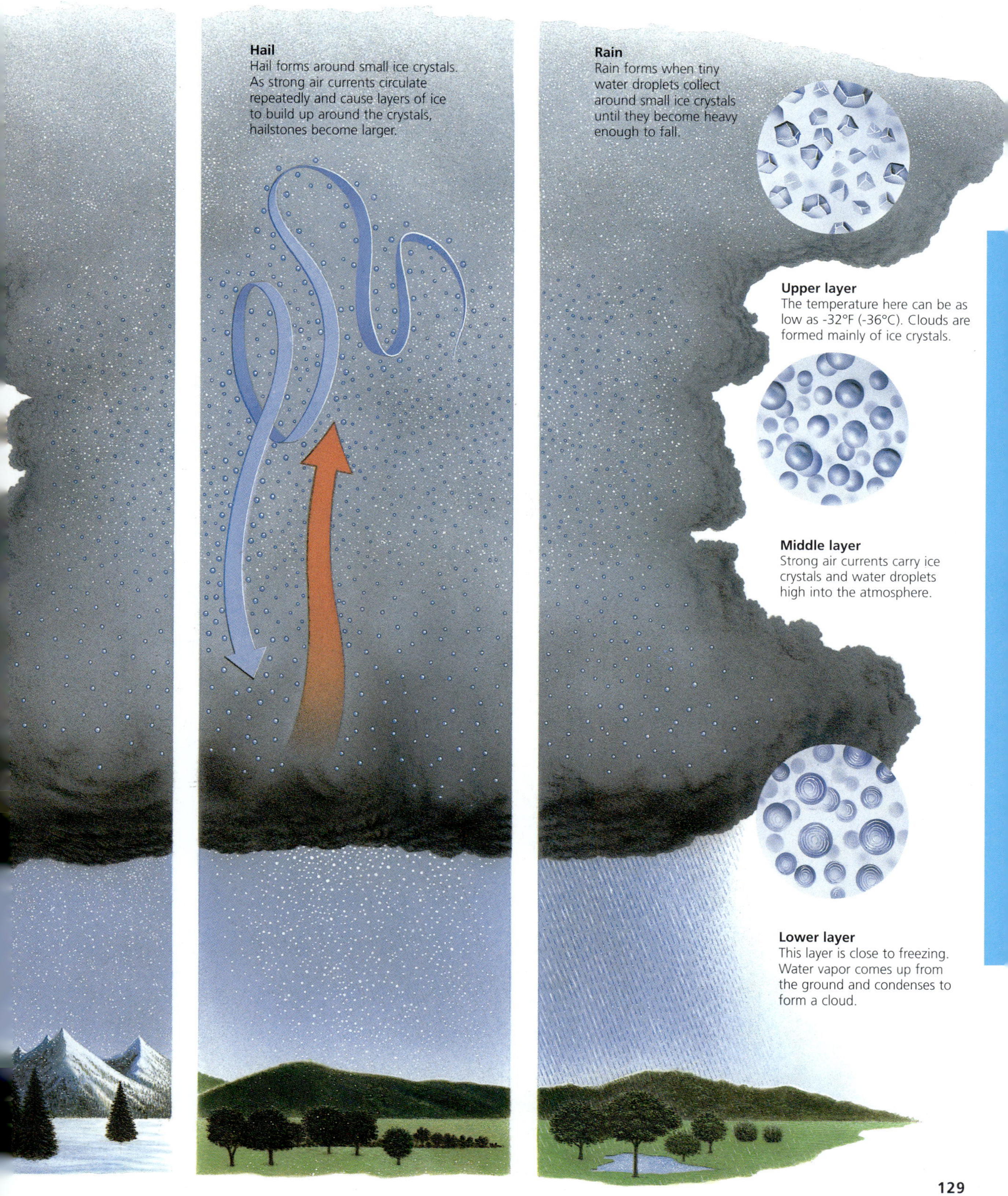
Hail
Hail forms around small ice crystals. As strong air currents circulate repeatedly and cause layers of ice to build up around the crystals, hailstones become larger.
Rain
Rain forms when tiny water droplets collect around small ice crystals until they become heavy enough to fall.
Upper layer
The temperature here can be as low as -32°F (-36°C). Clouds are formed mainly of ice crystals.
Middle layer
Strong air currents carry ice crystals and water droplets high into the atmosphere.
Lower layer
This layer is close to freezing. Water vapor comes up from the ground and condenses to form a cloud.

Storms

HURRICANE

Hurricanes start life as small thunderstorms over warm water.

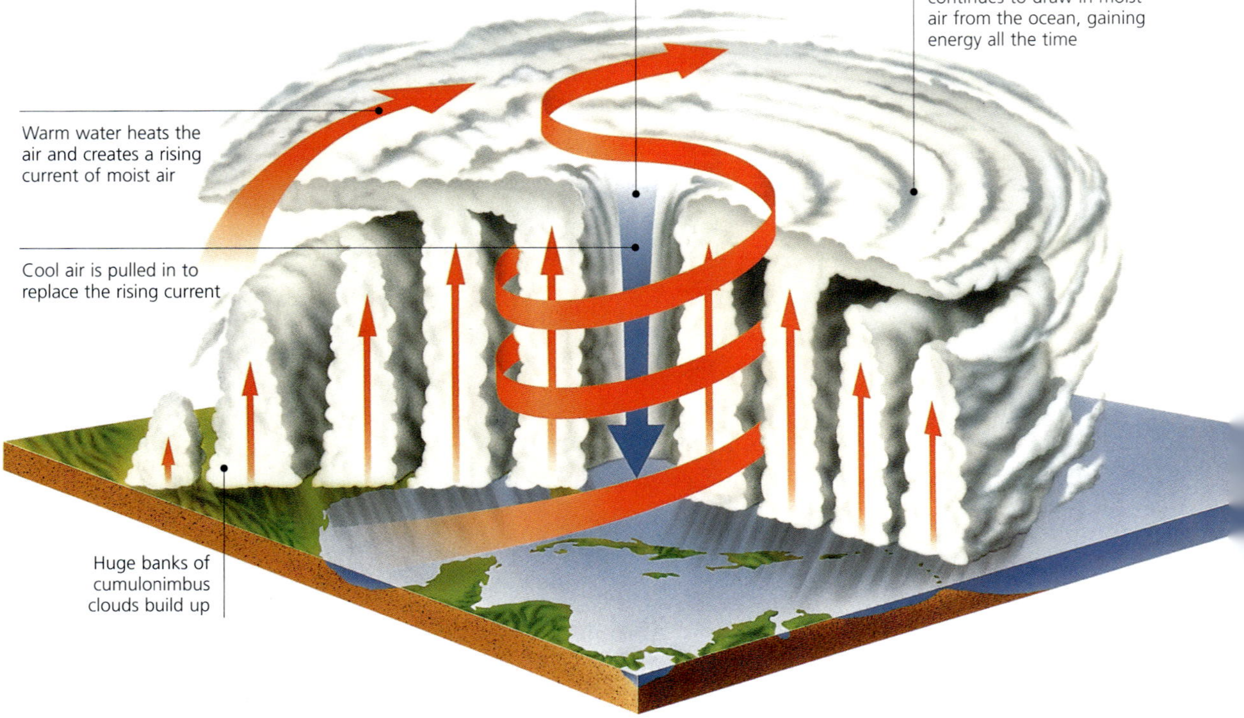

THE STORM CYCLE

Building up
Rising air currents carry water vapor upward into cooler air. Moisture condenses and cumulus cloud forms.

At its peak
Cumulonimbus grows to the tropopause and spreads to form an anvil. The air sinks, creating heavy downdrafts.

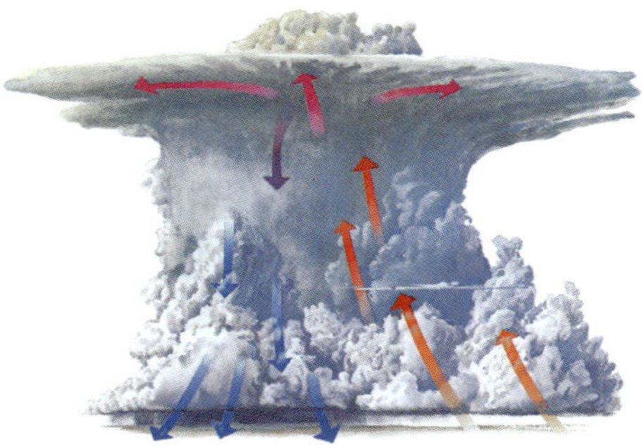

On the wane
The downdrafts begin to outnumber the updrafts. The storm's supply of warm air is cut off and the cloud slowly disintegrates.

TYPES OF LIGHTNING

Cloud-to-cloud lightning
Lightning may jump within one cloud or between opposite charges in adjacent clouds.

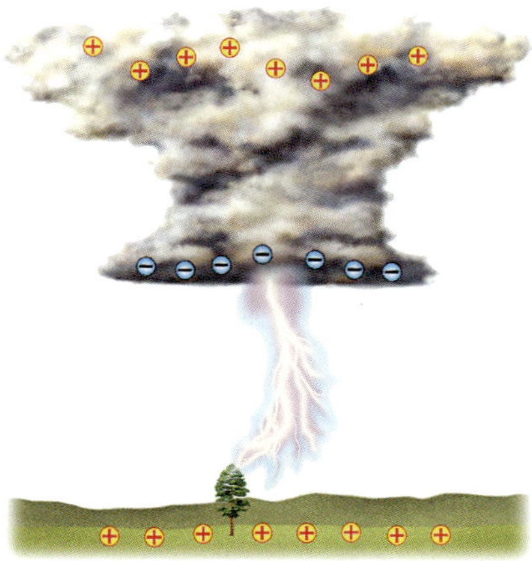

Cloud-to-ground lightning
If there is a positive charge on the ground, lightning may strike from the base of a cloud.

Cloud-to-air lightning
Electricity may move from the cloud to the surrounding, oppositely charged air.

HURRICANE LIFECYCLE

Day 1—a storm cluster forms

Day 2—storm starts to spin

Day 3—spiral shape develops

Day 6—eye emerges

Day 12—begins to fade

Mapping the Weather

Clear sky

Rain

Cloudy

Partly cloudy

Light wind

Moderate wind

H High pressure

L Low pressure

SYNOPTIC CHART

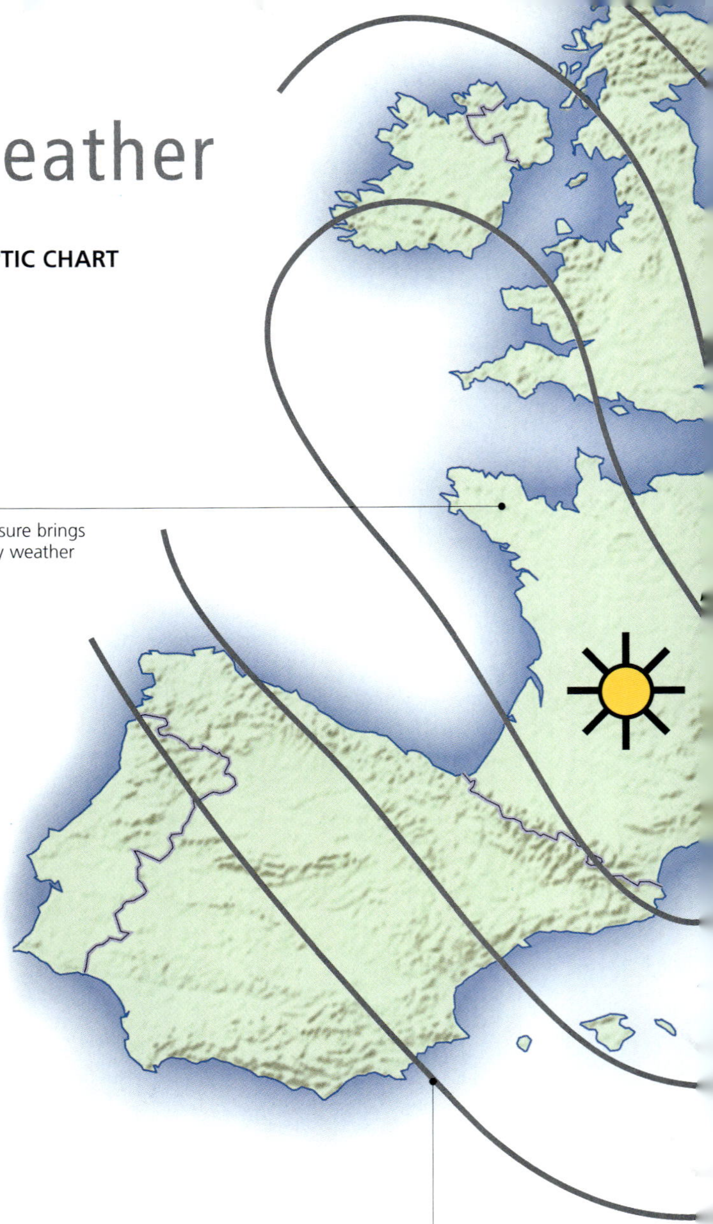

High pressure brings warm, dry weather

Isobars link points with the same air pressure and are measured in hectapascals

MAP SYMBOLS

Synoptic charts contain a wealth of information including air pressure, wind speed and direction, cloud cover, temperature and humidity.

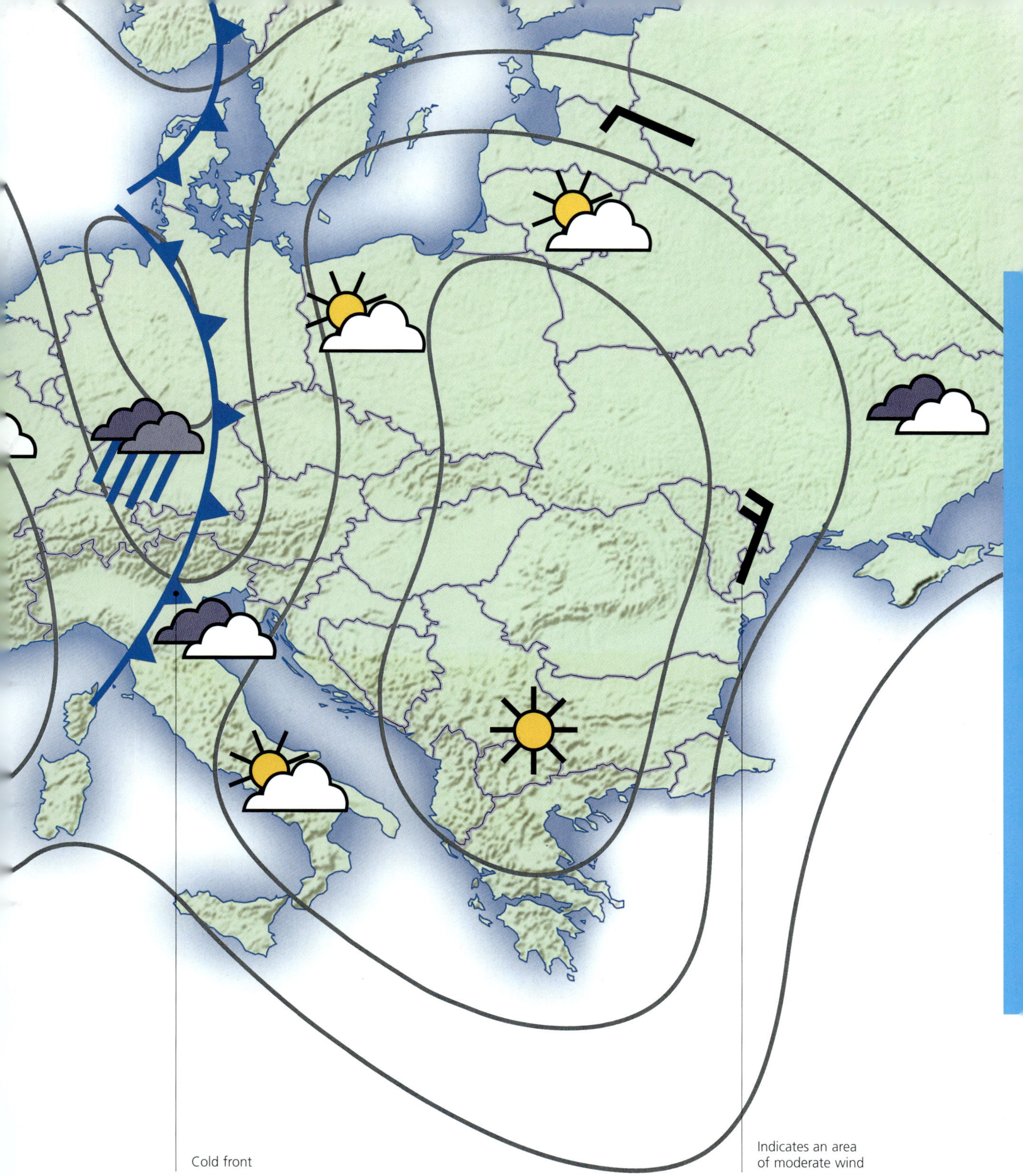
Cold front
Indicates an area
of moderate wind

Frontal Systems

LOW-PRESSURE SYSTEM

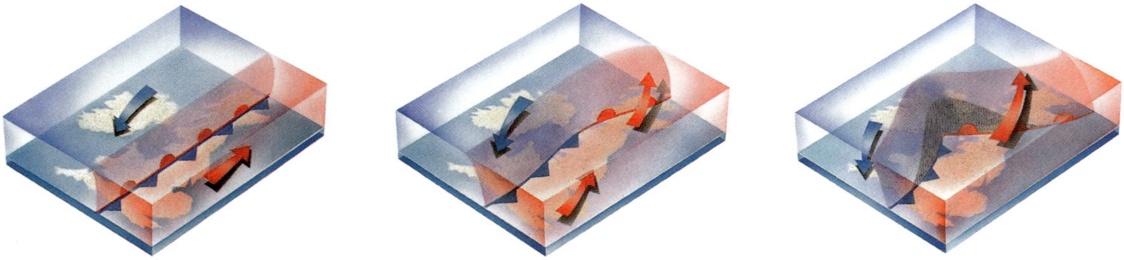

1. Low-pressure systems form when a cold air mass and a warm air mass meet.

2. Gradually, the warm air rises over the cold air. This creates an area of low pressure that the cold front moves into.

3. Rising air creates precipitation and clouds, and the fronts begin to rotate.

PRESSURE MOVEMENT

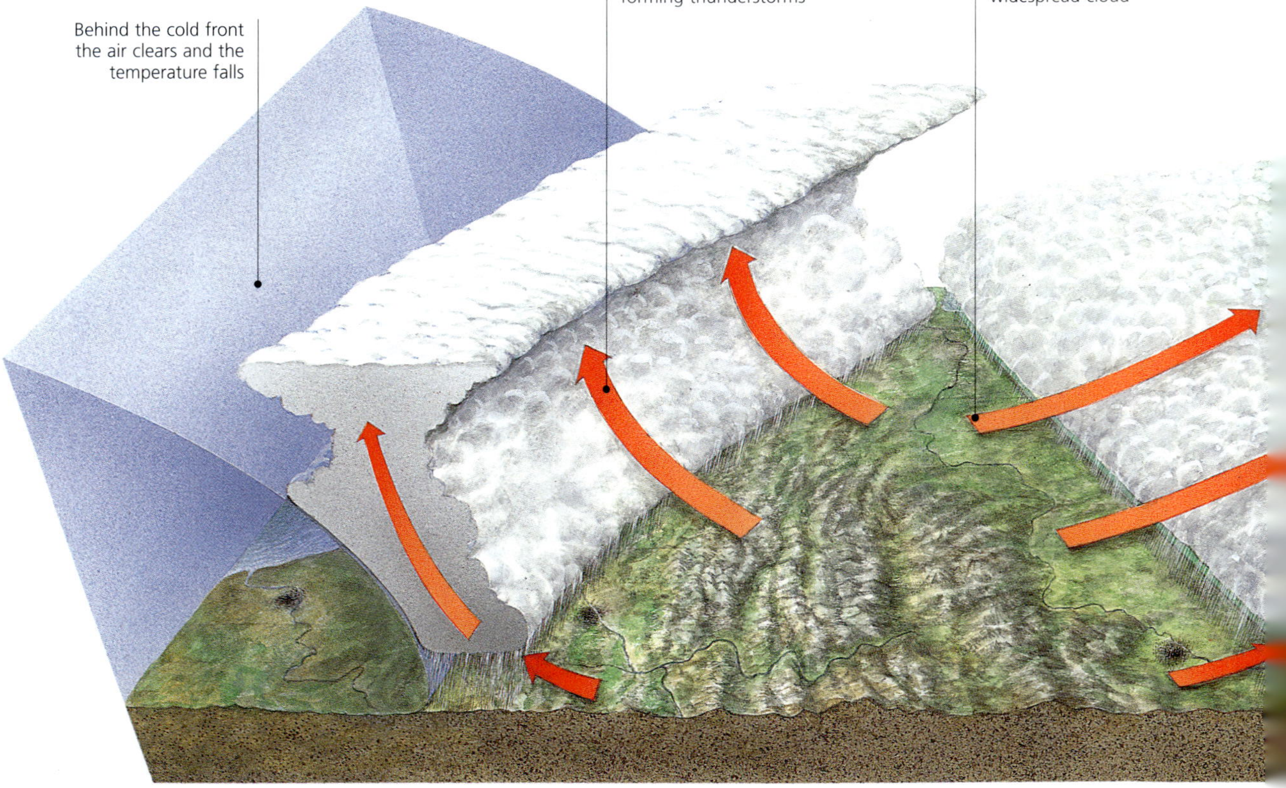

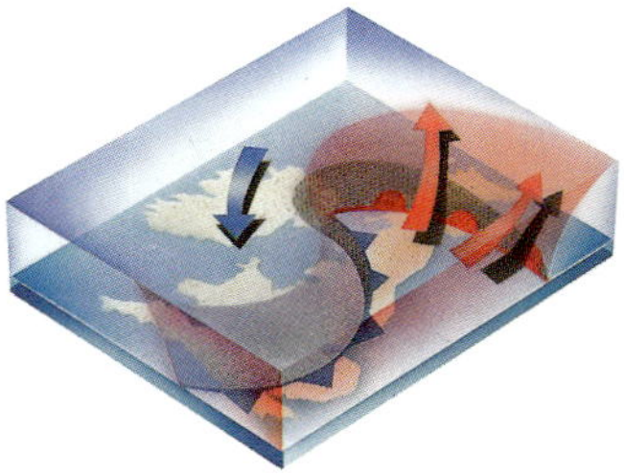

4. The faster-moving cold front starts to catch up with the warm front. Pressure decreases under the rising air, which intensifies precipitation.

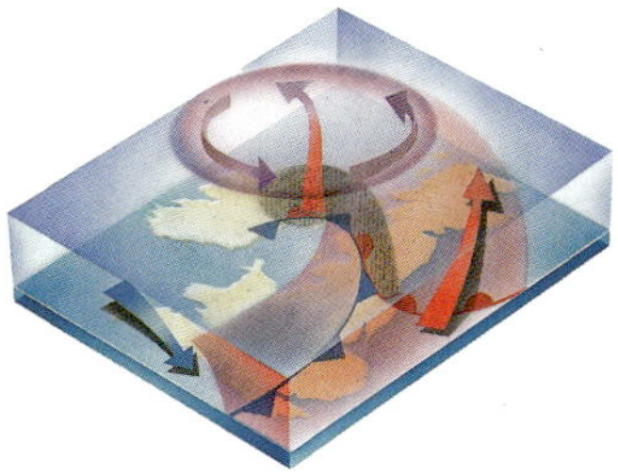

5. When the cold front catches up with the warm front, an occluded front forms. This creates windy, unsettled weather.

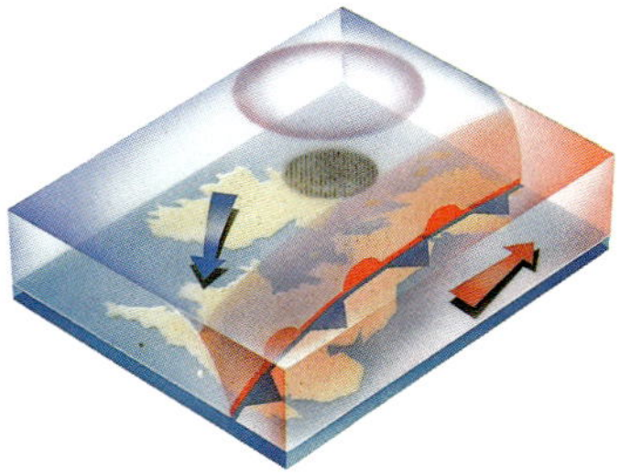

6. The fully formed occluded front cuts off the supply of warm air, and winds and precipitation subside.

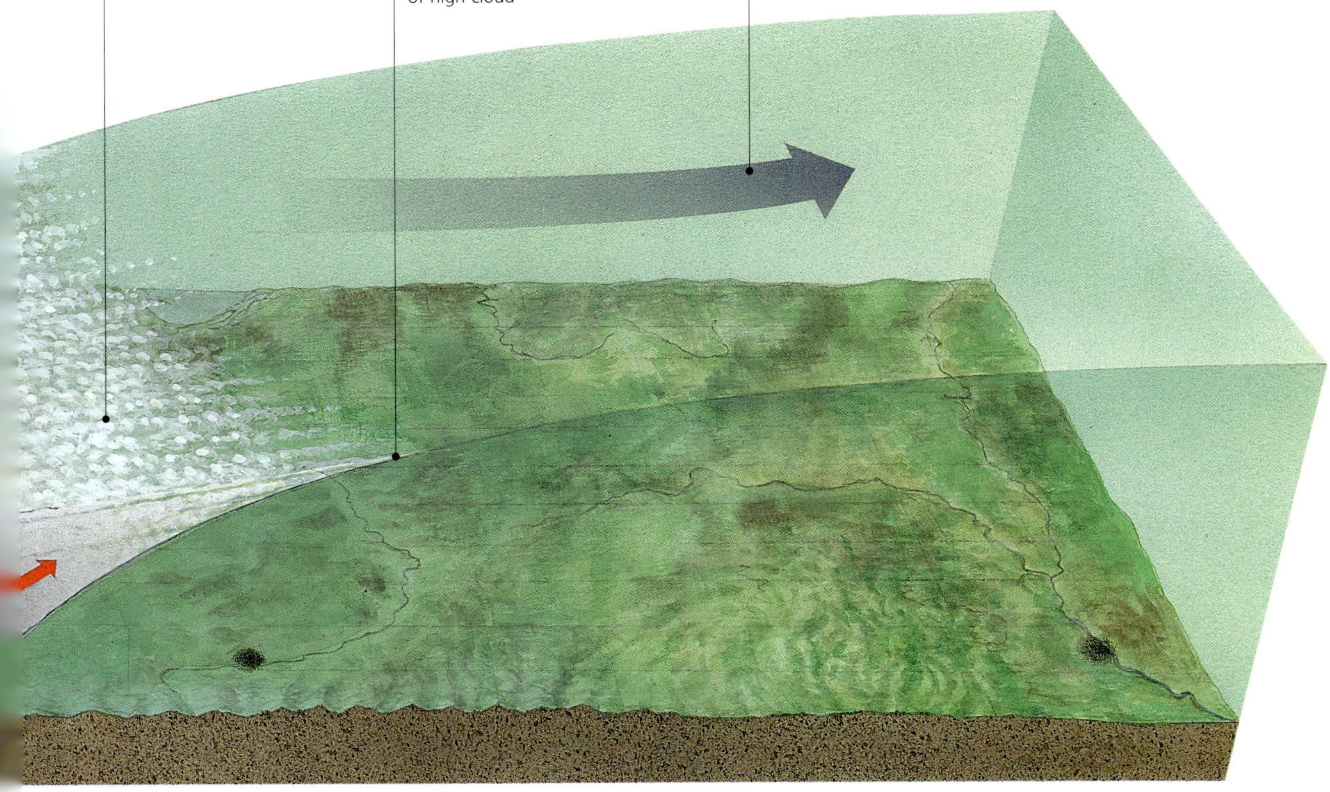

The Seasons

CLIMATE

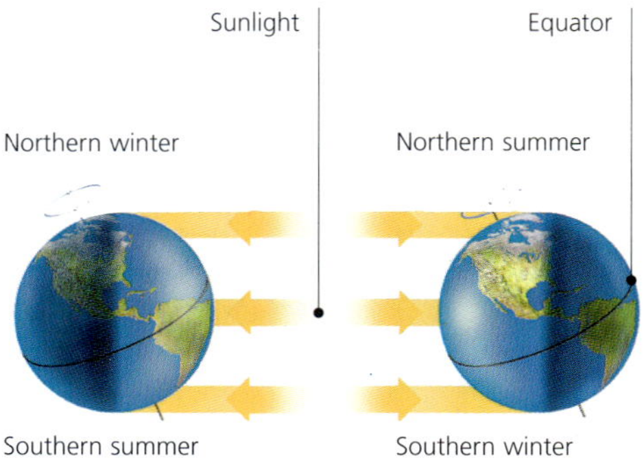

At the equator, the Sun's rays hit Earth almost directly all year long. This is the hottest zone on Earth. As you move farther away from the equator, the rays hit at more of an angle and the climate is cooler.

DAY AND NIGHT

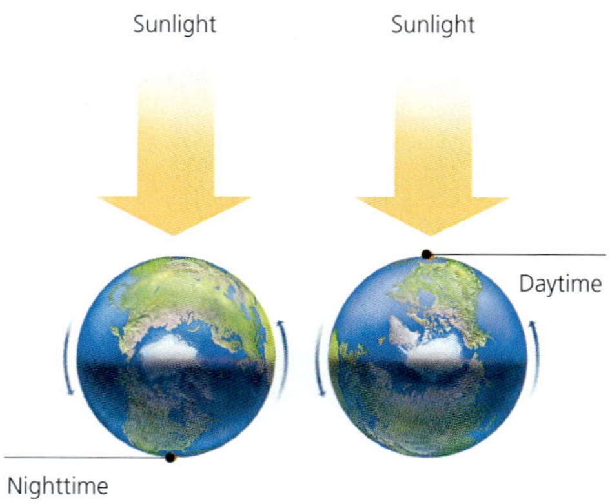

At any moment, parts of the world are experiencing sunrise and sunset, noon and midnight.

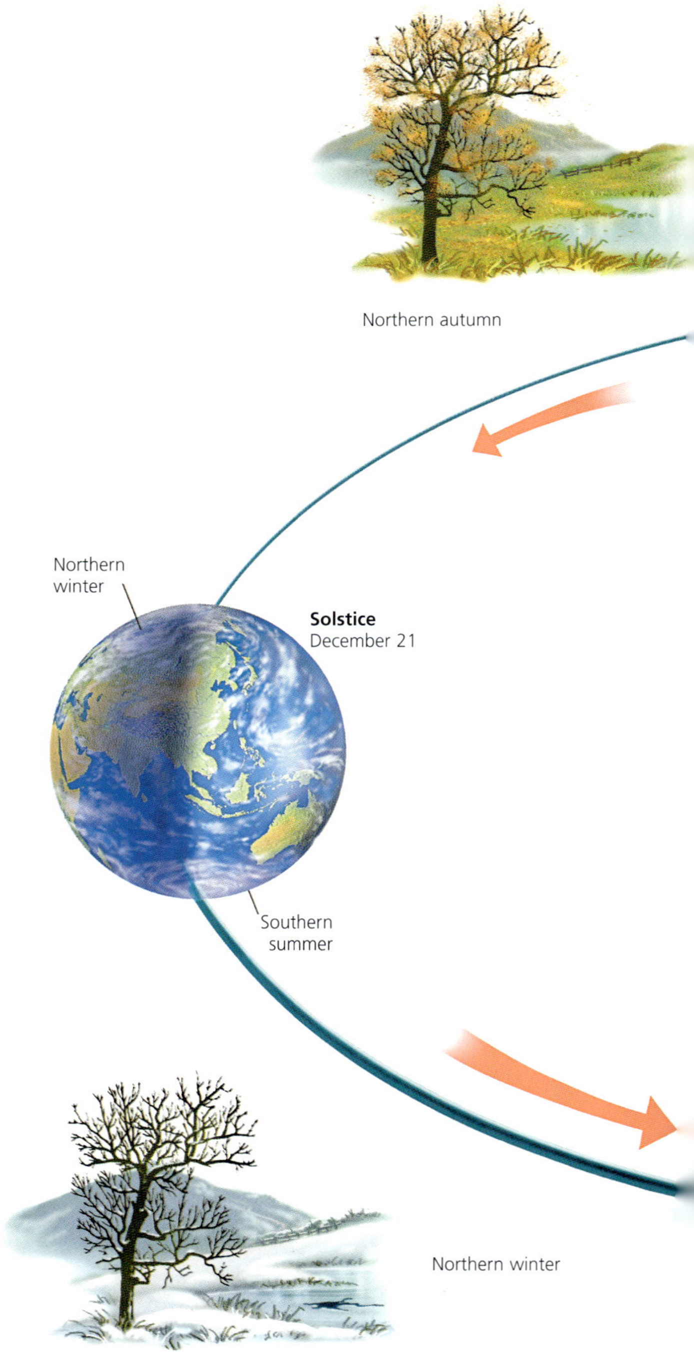

CYCLE OF SEASONS

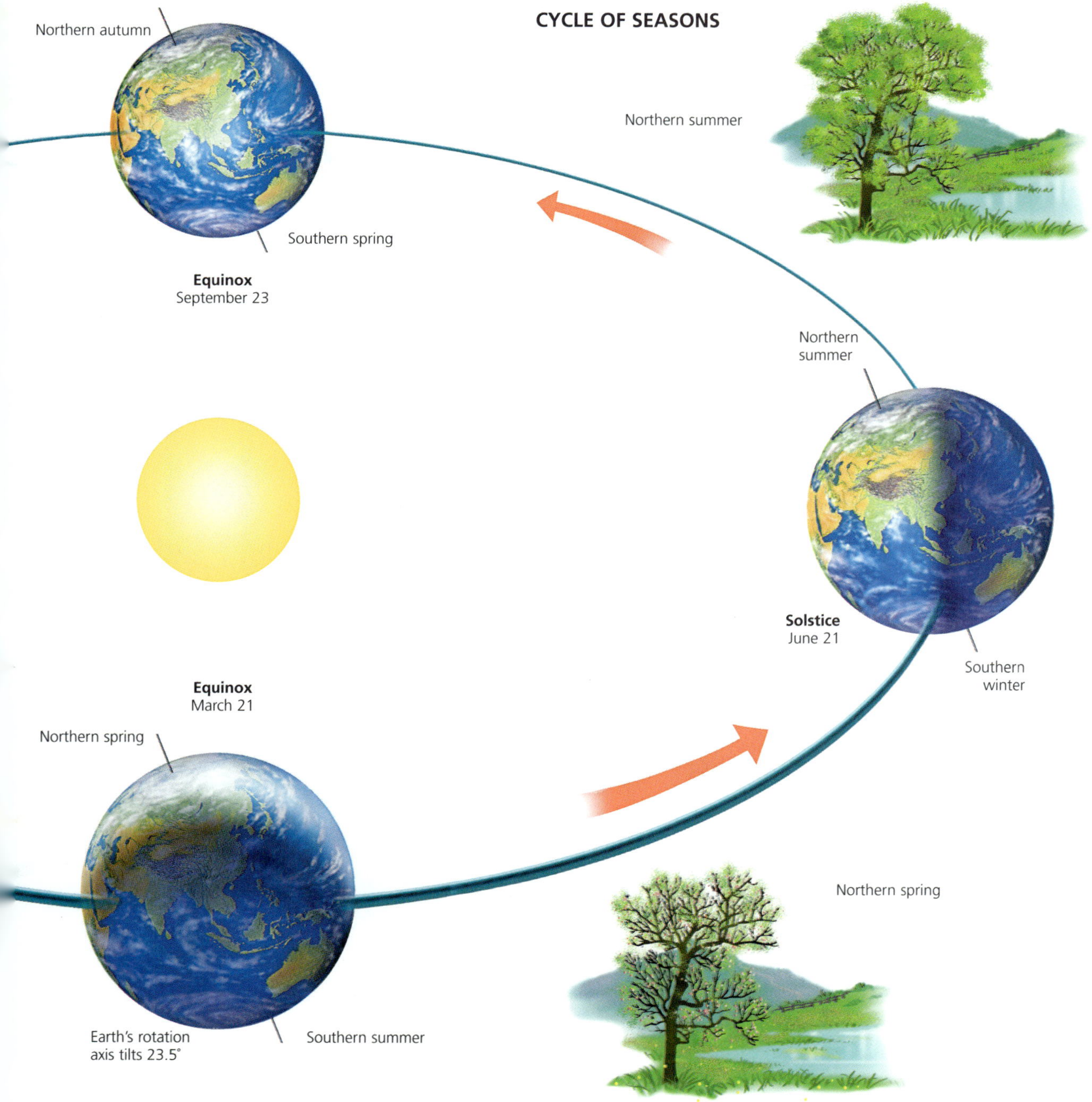

Winds and Monsoons

GLOBAL AIR FLOW

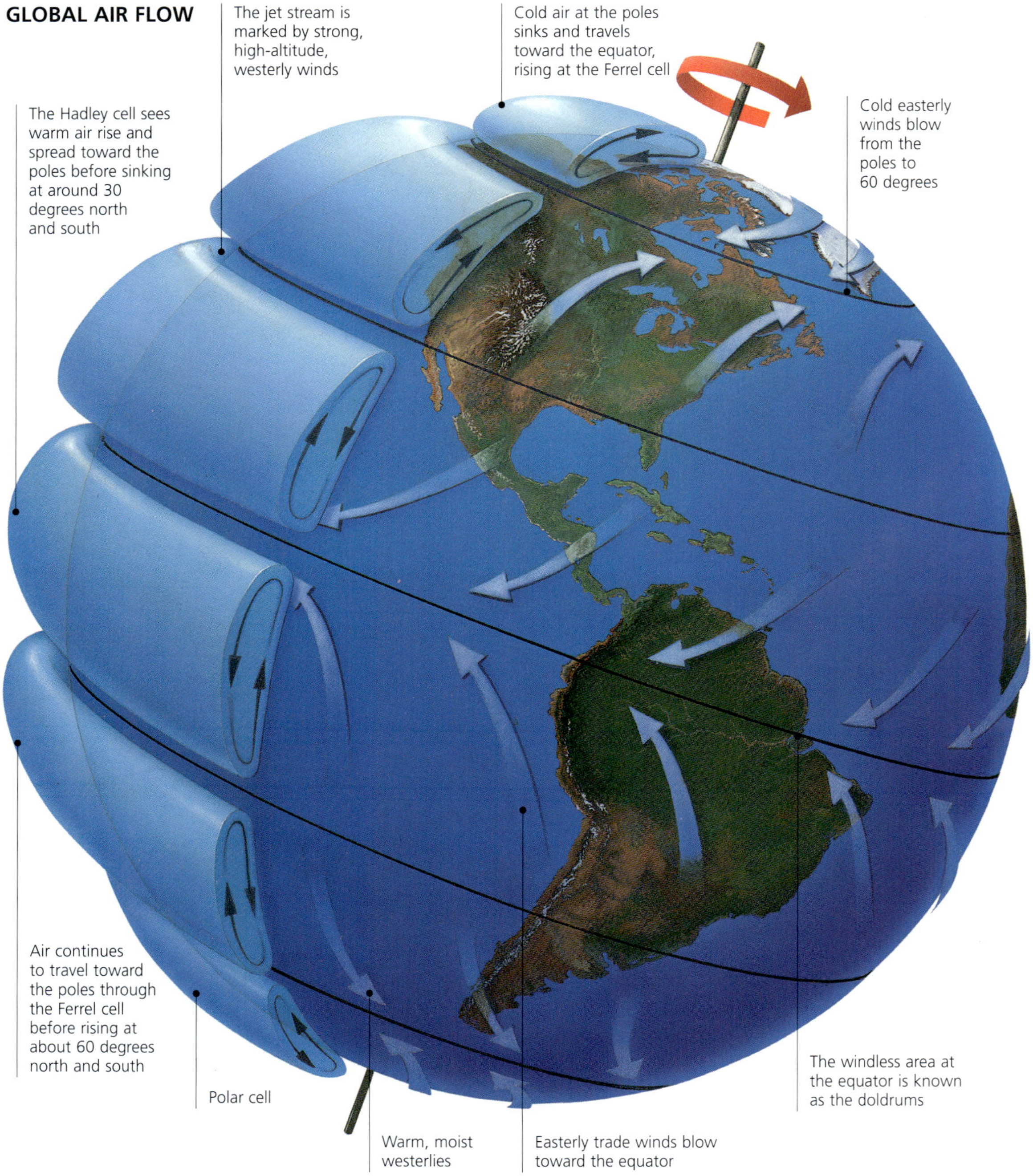

MOUNTAIN WIND

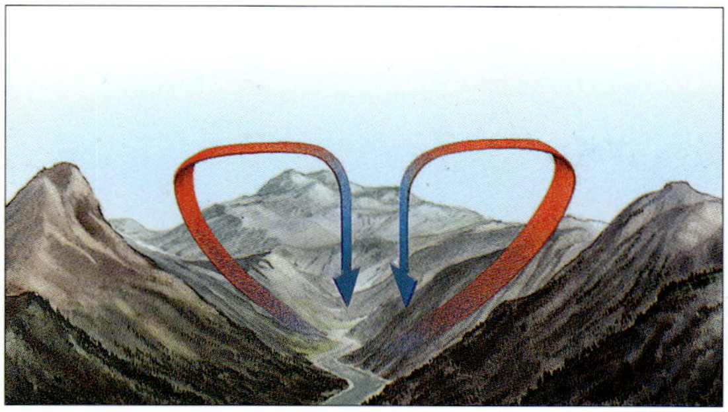

Warm air rises from mountain slopes. This cools and falls, creating a cool wind as it fills the space left by the rising warm air.

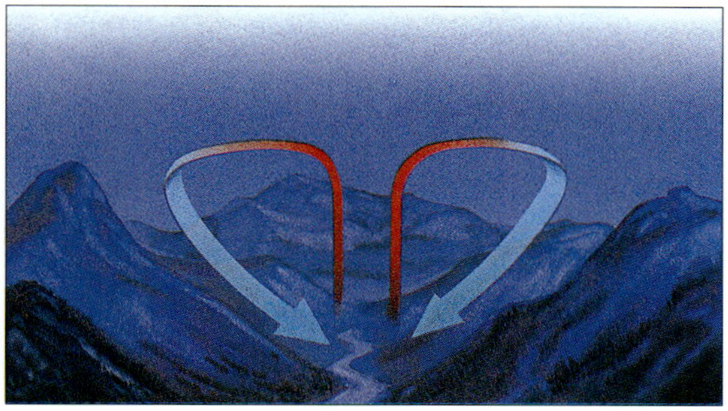

At night, warm mountain air cools and flows down the mountain slopes into the valley, creating a cool wind.

RAIN SHADOW

Most mountains experience dry wind which blows down the sheltered side. Moisture is deposited on the windward side.

CORIOLIS EFFECT

As a result of the Earth's shape, air in the northern hemisphere moves clockwise and down around high pressure and anticlockwise and up around low pressure. The opposite occurs in the southern hemisphere.

DRY SEASON

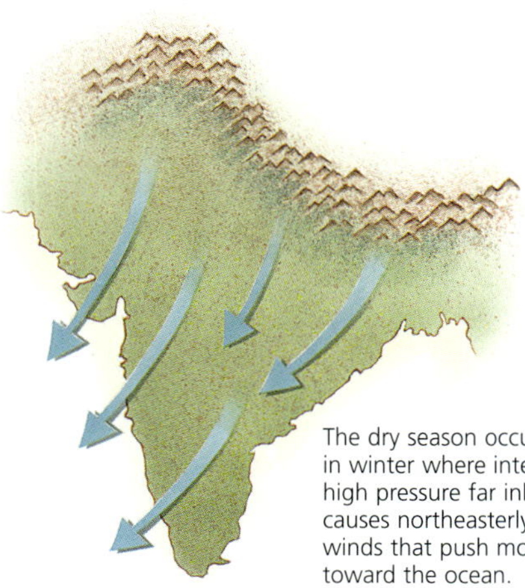

The dry season occurs in winter where intense high pressure far inland causes northeasterly winds that push moist air toward the ocean.

WET SEASON

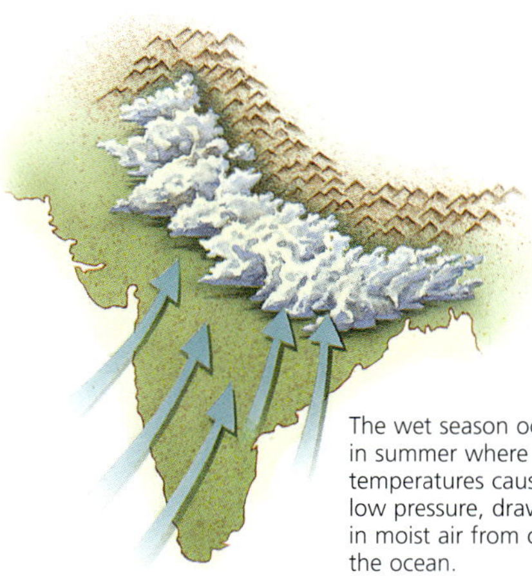

The wet season occurs in summer where higher temperatures cause low pressure, drawing in moist air from over the ocean.

Climate

WORLD CLIMATES

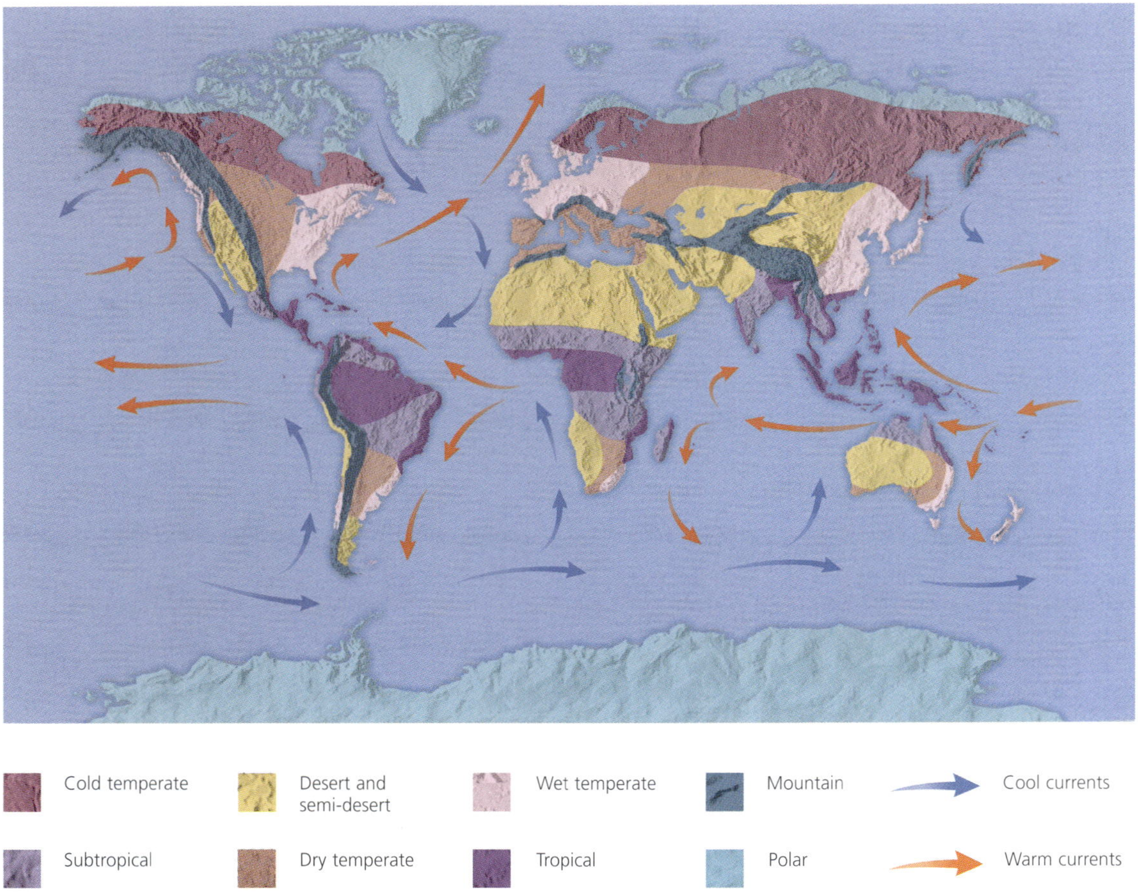

LANDSCAPES

MOUNTAIN ZONE

Nepal lies in the Himalayas. There is little flat land for villages, so houses are scattered. The warm, sunny, south-facing slopes are used for farming. The north-facing slopes are usually forested. As the steep slopes are difficult to farm, they have been gradually terraced to provide many small, level fields for farming. The higher pastures extend up to the permanent snow line.

EXTREME CLIMATES

High altitude

Desert

Arctic

Waves, Tides and Currents

OCEAN TIDES

Spring Tides
Strong tides occur when the Sun and Moon are lined up.

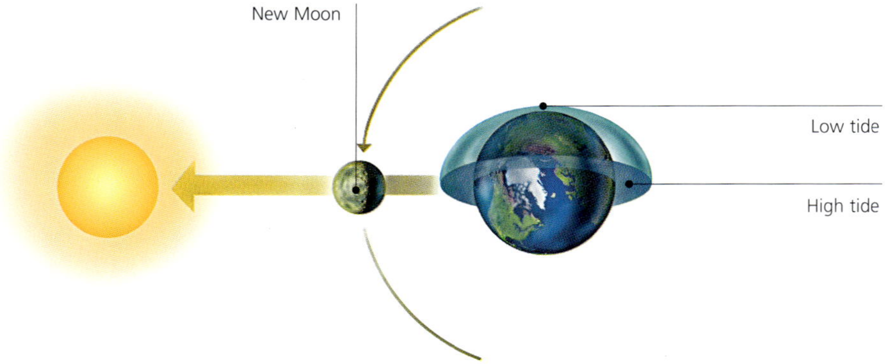

Neap Tides
Weak tides occur when the Sun and Moon are at right angles.

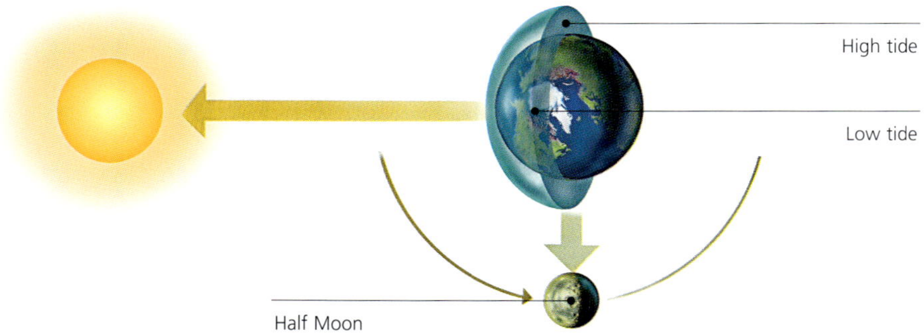

OCEAN CURRENTS

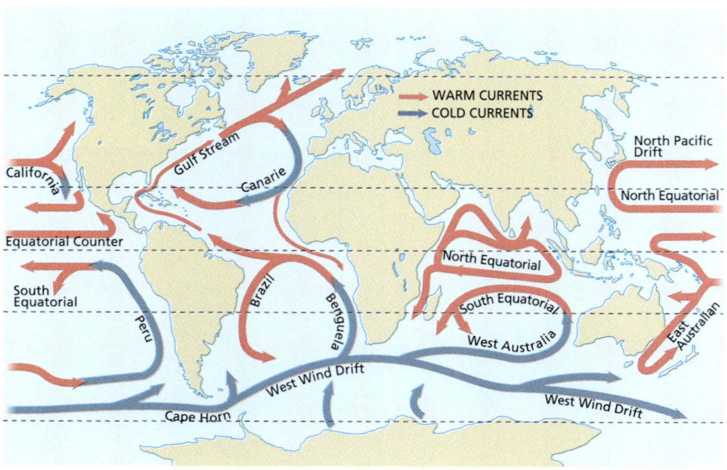

The thermocline is the ocean layer beneath the warm surface water and above deep sea

THE BEAUFORT SCALE

This scale uses the numbers 1 to 12 to indicate the strength of wind at sea.

WAVE FORMATION

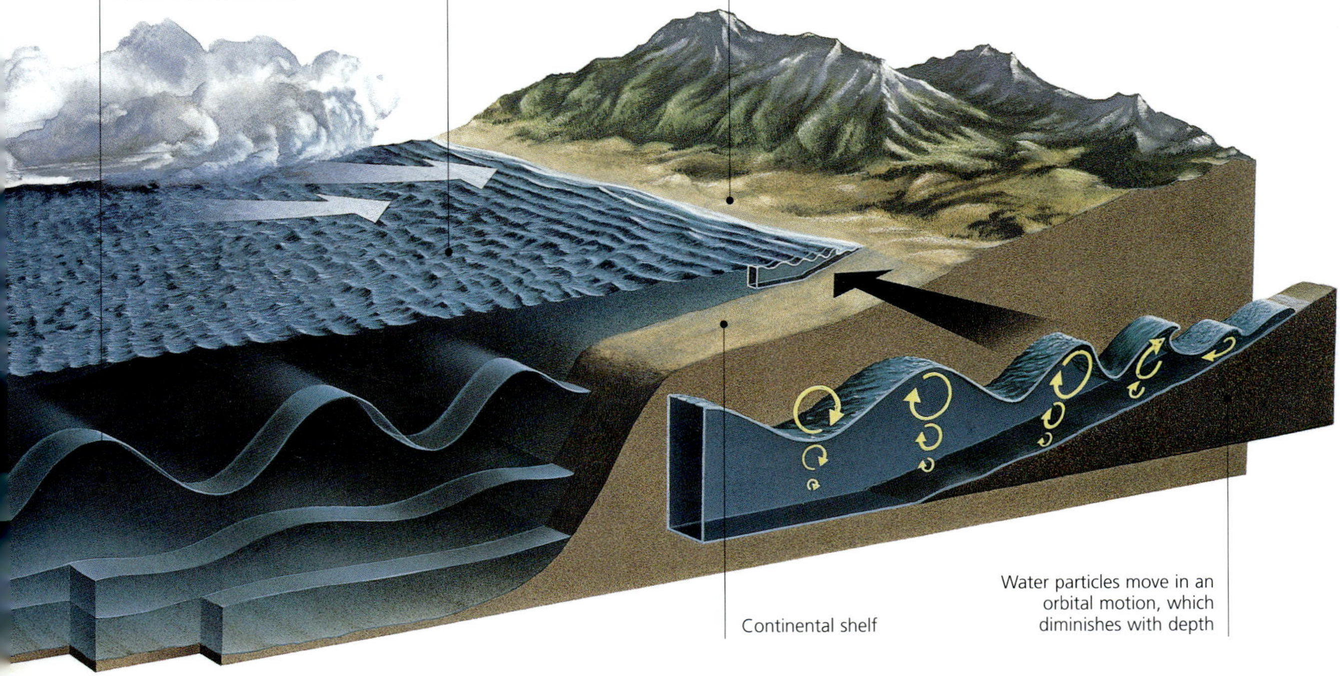

The Sea Floor

FOSSIL FUEL

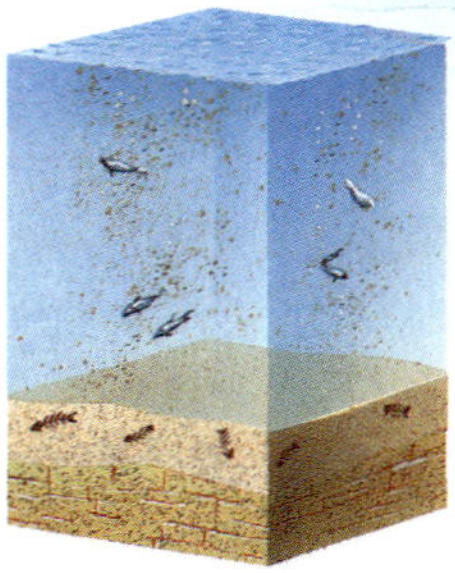

Microscopic sea creatures die and fall to the ocean floor. Over millions of years, layers of mud and silt slowly cover the sea creatures and turn into sedimentary rocks.

The rock layers continue to pile up on top of the dead sea creatures. As the pressure from the rocks increases, the sea creatures slowly turn into oil and gas.

The oil and gas rise through the rock layers. They pass through porous rocks, such as sandstone, but are blocked by impermeable (nonporous) rocks, such as shale.

Under the right conditions, the oil and gas collect in a reservoir under the impermeable rocks, with the gas on top of the oil. Reservoirs are drilled to remove the fuels.

UNDERWATER LANDSCAPE

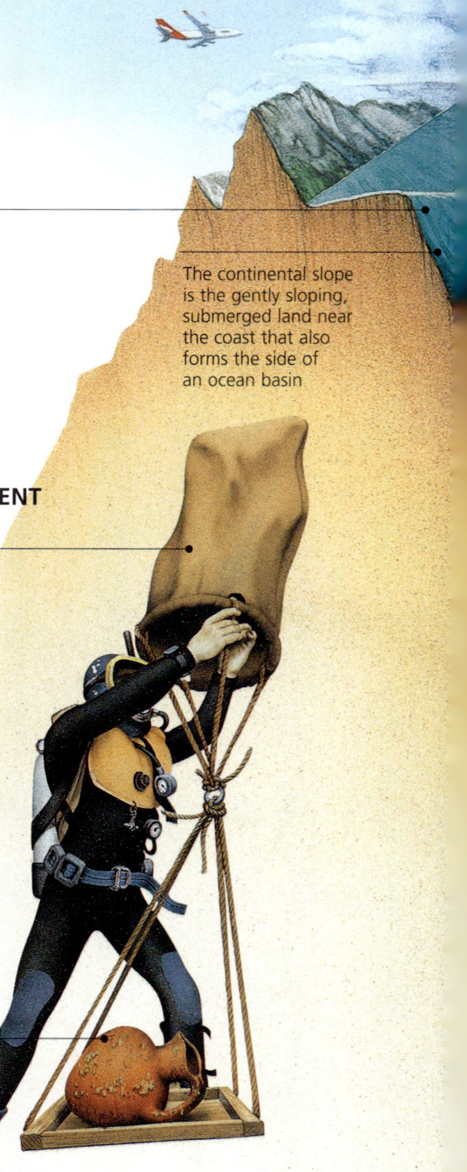

The continental shelf is a shallow extension of a continent, which is covered by water. This part of the ocean is rich in marine life. Oil exploration also takes place here

The continental slope is the gently sloping, submerged land near the coast that also forms the side of an ocean basin

LIFTING EQUIPMENT

Balloon-like bags, filled with air, slowly lift the diver's equipment to the water's surface

Artifacts found on the sea floor are placed on trays

Abyssal plains spread out flatly from the oceanic ridge to the edges of continents
Seamounts are underwater volcanoes. Those rising above the surface form islands
Guyots are flat-topped seamounts
Mapping the sea floor
An oceanic ridge rises when a new sea floor wells up from inside the Earth
A long, narrow valley, known as an oceanic trench, usually forms next to islands or beside coastal mountain ranges

The Shore

ROCKPOOL LIFE

SHORE EROSION

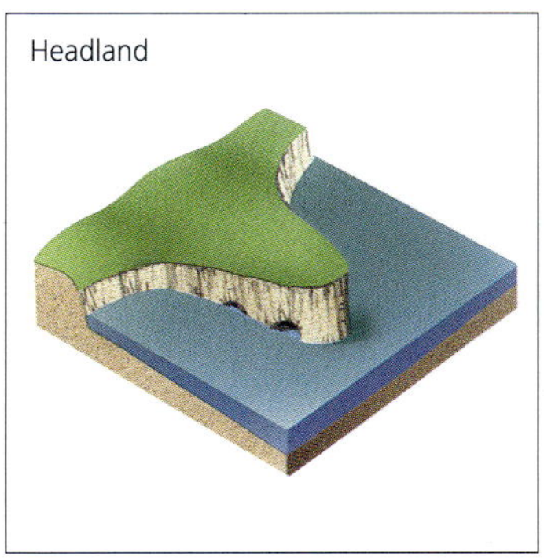

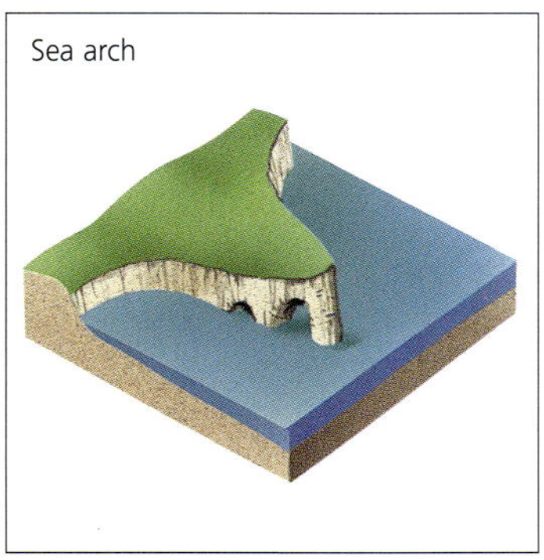

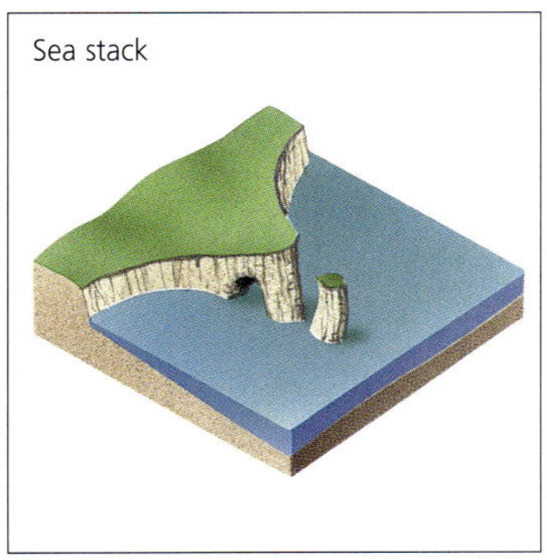

HOW THE SHORE FILTERS WATER

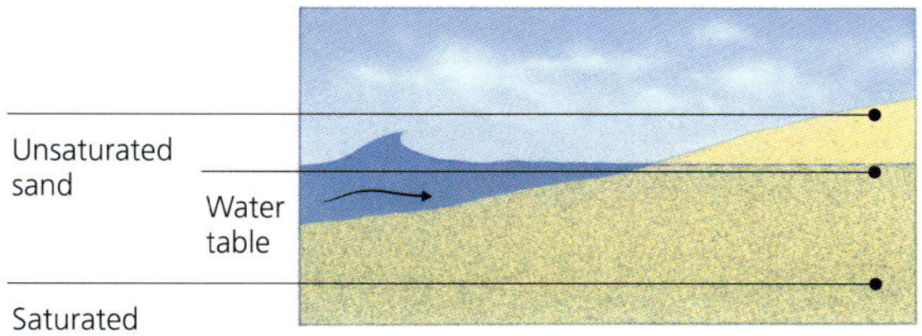

Advancing wave

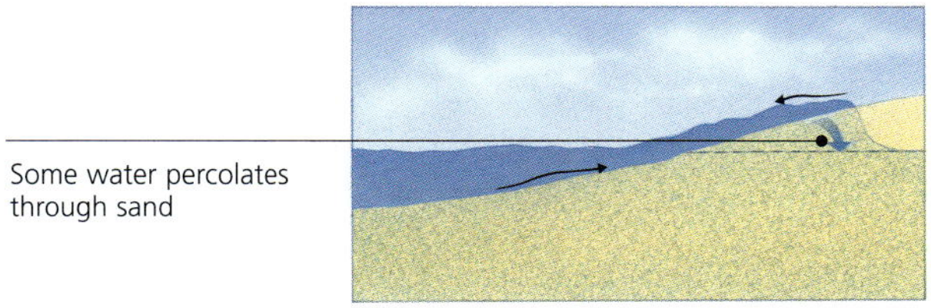

High wave

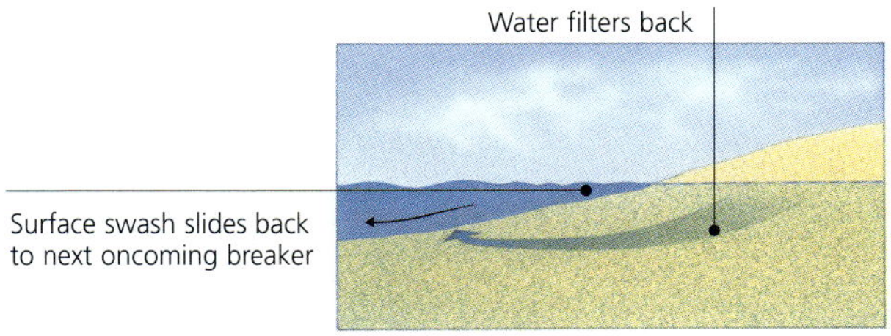

Receding wave

SHORELINE

PREHISTORIC LIFE

THE AGES OF PREHISTORY

Triassic Period 152

Jurassic Period 154

Cretaceous Period 156

TYPES OF DINOSAURS

Dinosaur Anatomy 158

Dinosaur Hips 160

Meat Eaters 162

Plant Eaters 164

Long-necked Dinosaurs 166

Armored Dinosaurs 168

Duckbilled Dinosaurs 170

AFTER THE DINOSAURS

Disappearance of the Dinosaurs 172

Fossils and Other Clues 174

Triassic Period

245–208 MILLION YEARS AGO

TRIASSIC ECOLOGY

DINOSAUR FOOD

Dragonfly

Haramiya

Tree fern

Wielandiella

TRIASSIC WORLD

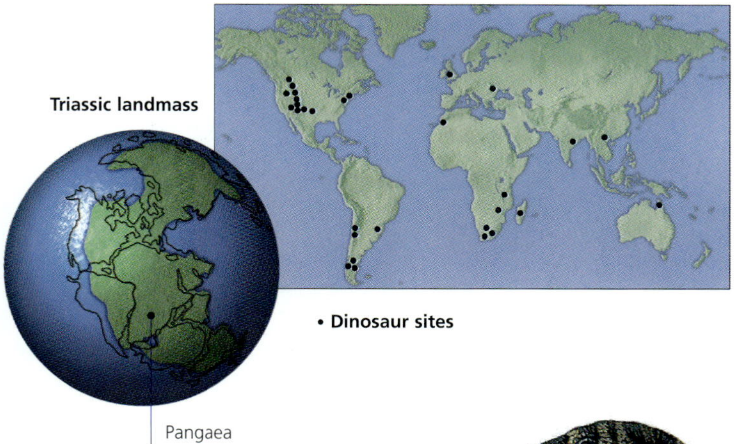

TRIASSIC LANDSCAPE

TRIASSIC ANIMALS

Synapsid
Kannemeyeria

Flying reptile
Eudimorphodon

TRIASSIC DINOSAURS

Zanclodon
Meat-eating carnosaur,
20 feet (6 m) long

Herrerasaurus
Meat-eating coelurosaur,
10 feet (3 m) long

Procompsognathus
Meat-eating coelurosaur,
4 feet (1.2 m) long

Saltopus
Meat-eating carnosaur,
2 feet (0.6 m) long

Jurassic Period

208–145 MILLION YEARS AGO

JURASSIC DINOSAURS

JURASSIC WORLD

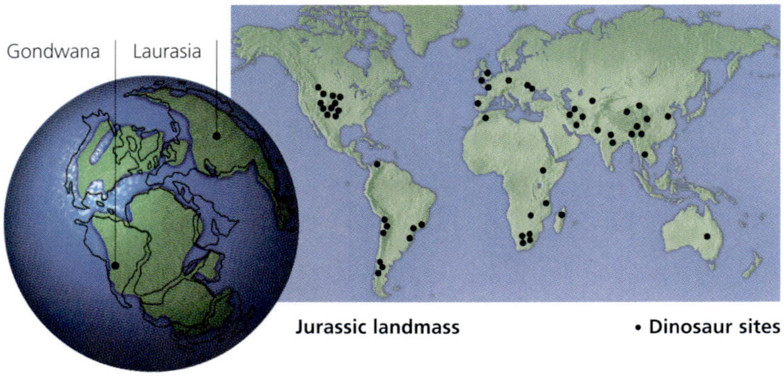

Jurassic landmass

• Dinosaur sites

JURASSIC PLANTS

Cycad

Horsetail

Jurassic landscape

DINOSAUR FOOD

Ginkgo

Cockroach

Turtle (*Pleisochelys*)

Dragonfly

JURASSIC ECOLOGY

Cretaceous Period

145–65 MILLION YEARS AGO

CRETACEOUS ANIMALS

Early lizard
Polyglyphanodon

Marine reptile
Kronosaurus

Snake
Pachyrhachis

CRETACEOUS WORLD

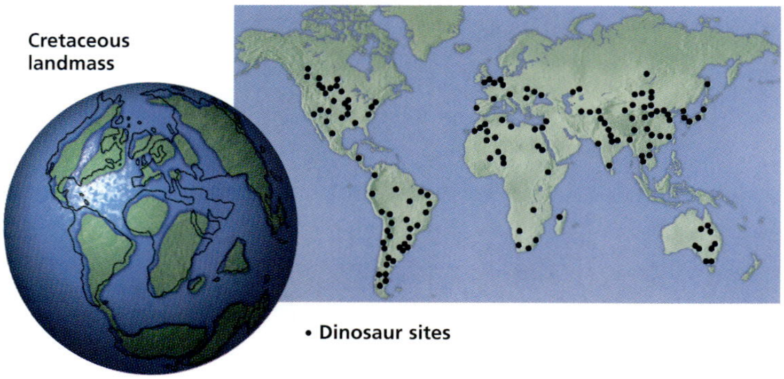

Ancient mammal
Crusafontia

CRETACEOUS DINOSAURS

Conifer forest
CRETACEOUS LANDSCAPE
Prenocephale
Magnolias
Protoceratops
Velociraptor

Dinosaur Anatomy

INSIDE *APATOSAURUS*

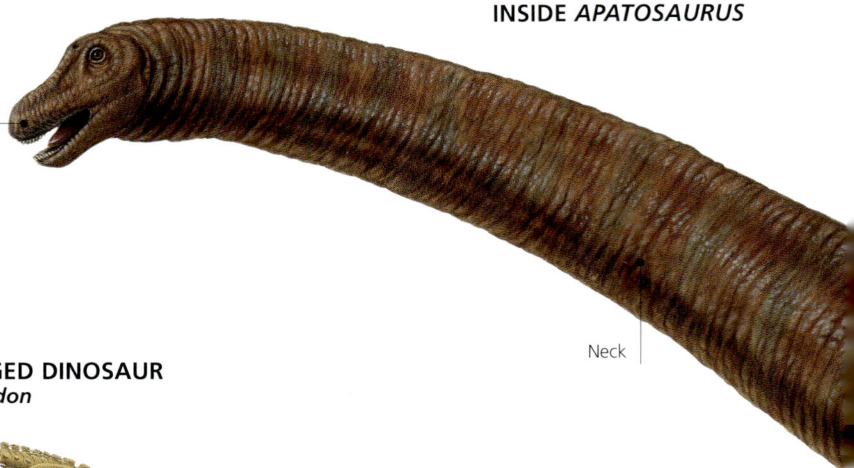

TWO-LEGGED DINOSAUR
Hypsilophodon

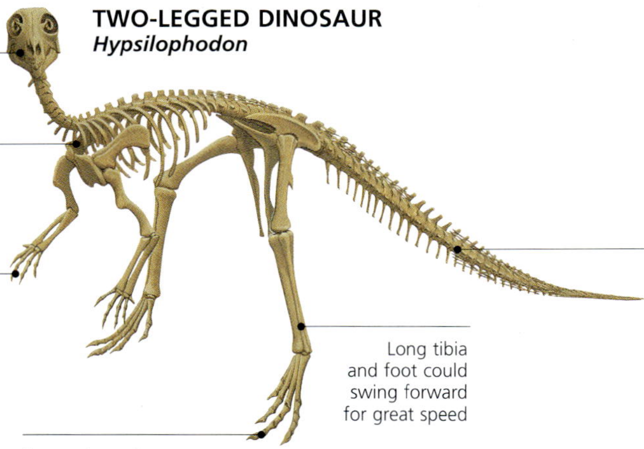

FOUR-LEGGED DINOSAUR
Camarasaurus

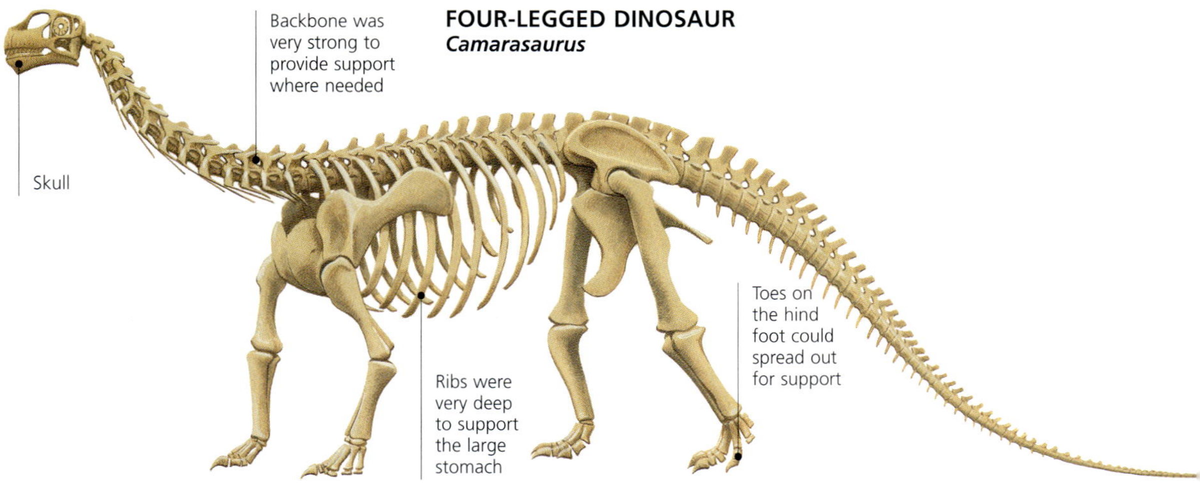

JAWS

Ceratosaurus,
Meat eater

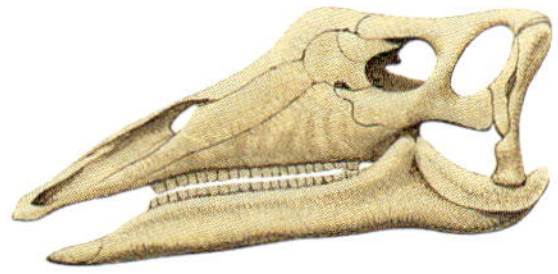

Ouranosaurus,
Plant eater

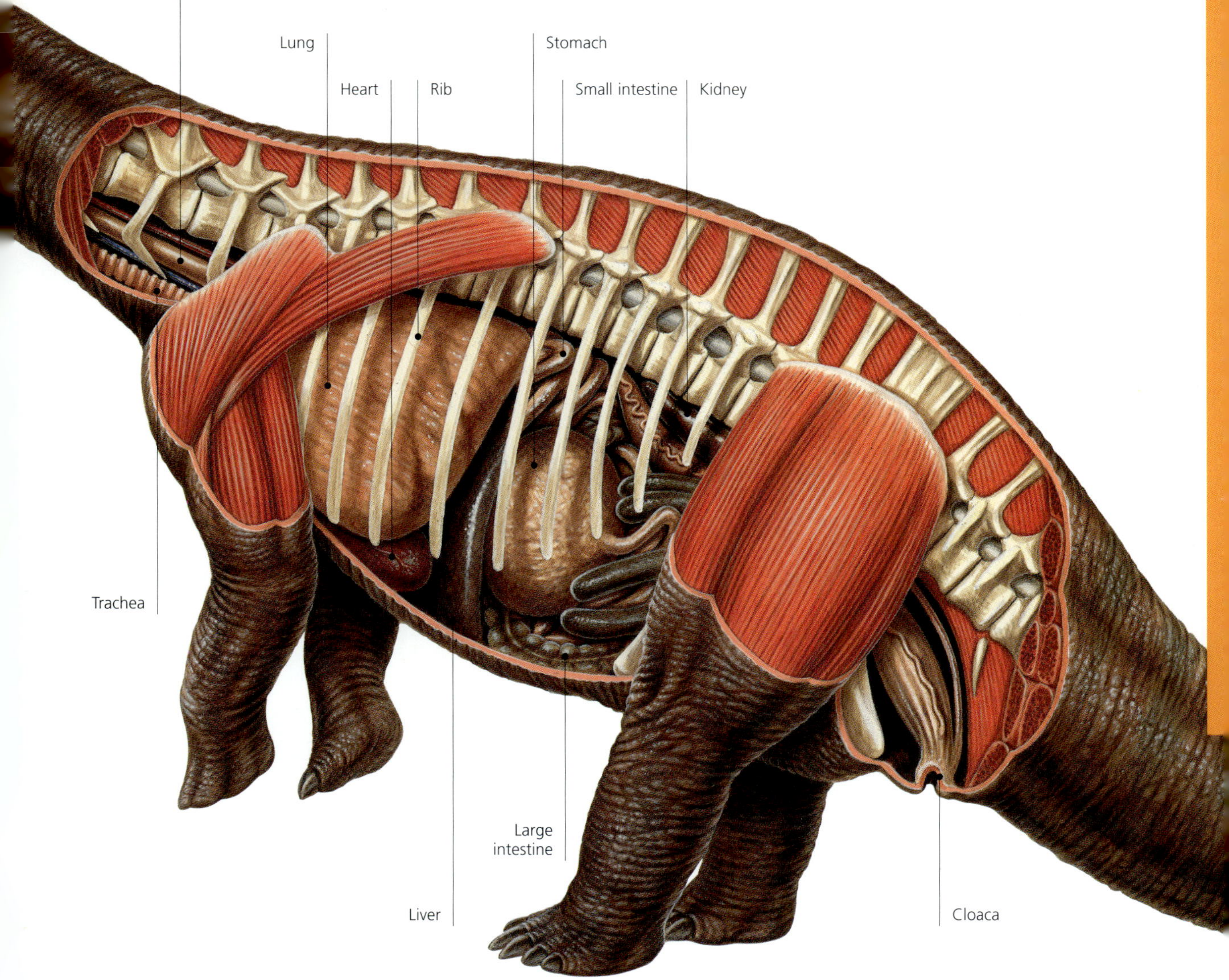

Dinosaur Hips

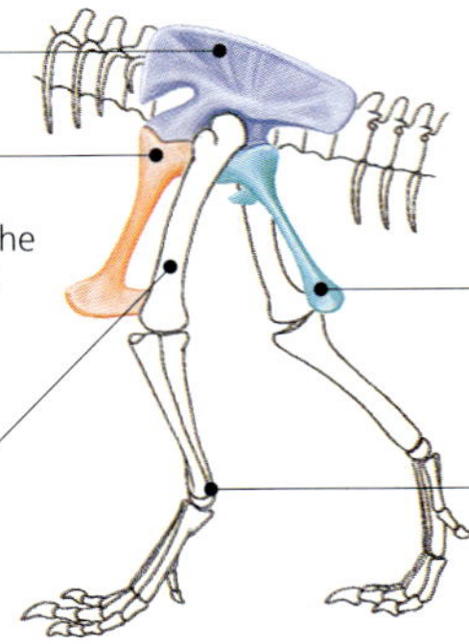

FAST-MOVING HUNTER
The pubis bone of *Allosaurus* pointed forward between the legs and with the other pelvic bones formed a rigid triangle to support the leg muscles for fast running.

TWO-LEGGED PLANT EATER

The pubis bone of *Edmontosaurus* pointed backward to allow space for the large intestines these plant-eating ornithischians (bird-hipped dinosaurs) needed to digest their food. Conversely, in plant-eating saurischians (lizard-hipped dinosaurs) the intestines were slung forward. This meant the pubis bone did not get in the way of these four-legged dinosaurs.

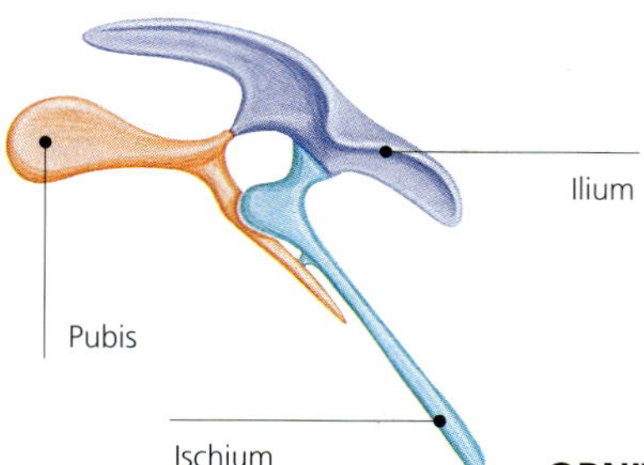

ORNITHISCHIAN HIP
Bird-hipped dinosaurs

Meat Eaters

SKULL TYPES

Deinonychus

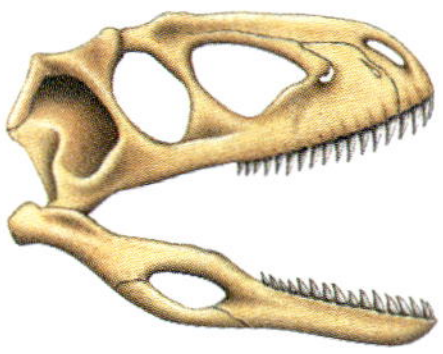

Allosaurus

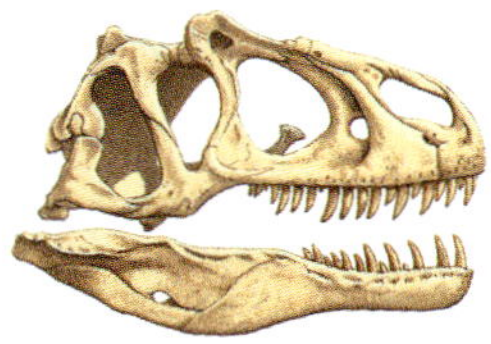

Tyrannosaurus

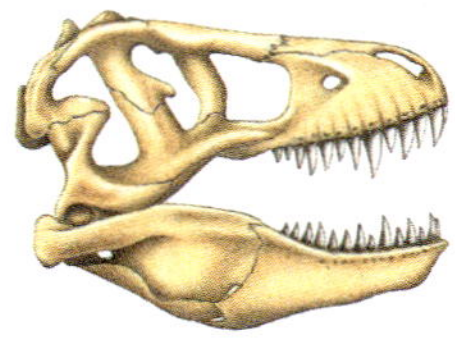

DEINONYCHUS

BYRONOSAURUS

HAND VARIETIES

Velociraptor

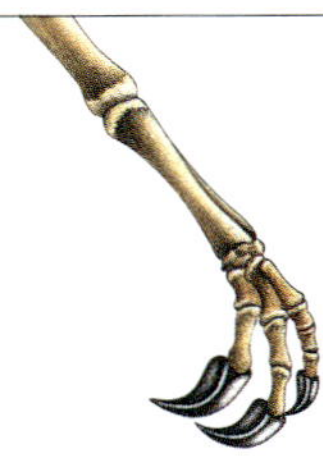

Allosaurus

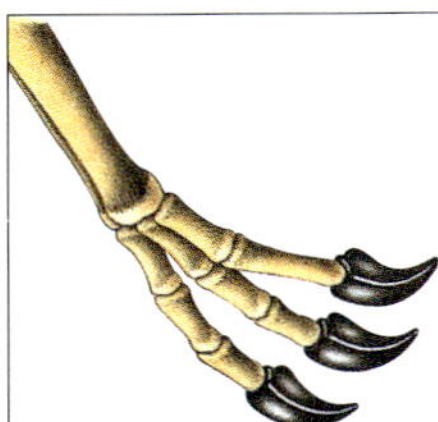

Deinocheirus

Tyrannosaurus

OVIRAPTOR

SCIPIONYX

MAJUNGATHOLUS

IRRITATOR

EATING TOOLS

Compsognathus used its hands to catch and eat lizards.

Baryonyx used the huge hook on its hand to spear its prey.

Albertosaurus used its powerful jaws to tear off pieces of meat.

Gallimimus used its beak to catch insects and small animals.

Plant Eaters

BRACHIOSAURUS

SALTASAURUS

EATING ACTION

When *Iguanodon's* mouth closed the upper and lower teeth ground against one another, shredding food.

KINDS OF FOOD

Pine cone

Flowering magnolia plant

Ginkgo

Tree fern

OTHNIELIA

This dinosaur used its five-fingered hands to push aside and hold down a fern while eating.

TEETH VARIATIONS

Brachiosaurus stripped leaves from tall trees.

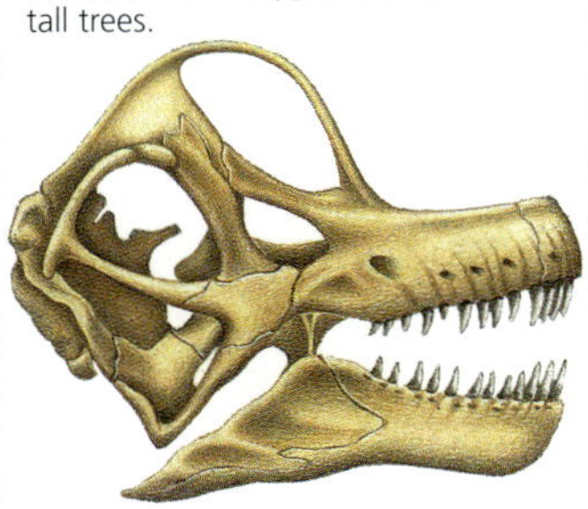

Heterodontosaurus had cutting teeth in front, fanglike teeth in the middle and chopping teeth in the back of its mouth.

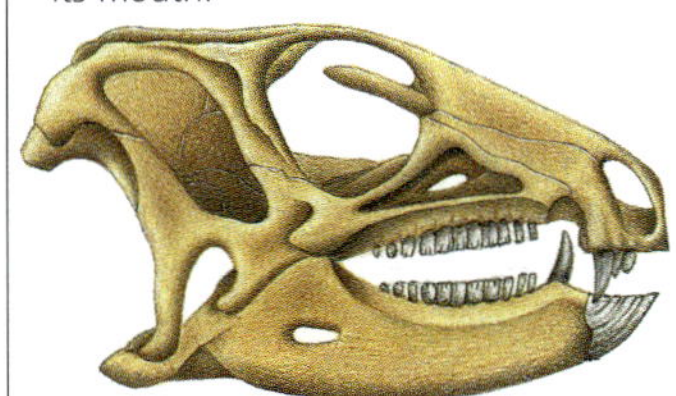

Protoceratops had a parrot-like beak and slicing teeth.

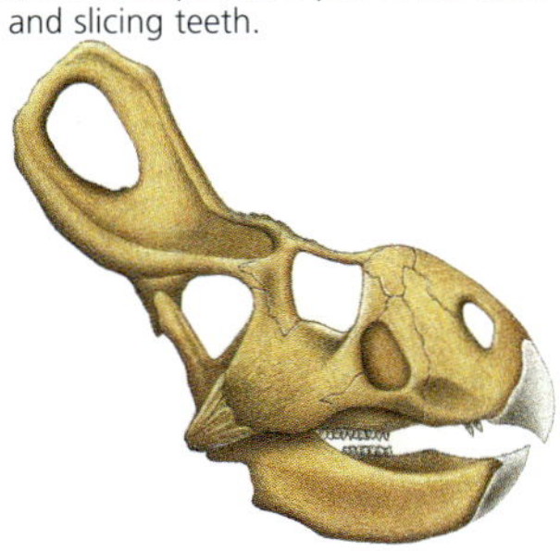

Lambeosaurus had a horny beak and grinding teeth.

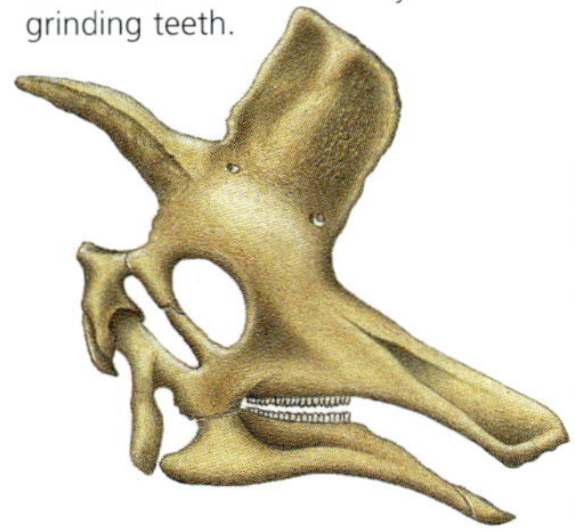

Long-necked Dinosaurs

BAROSAURUS SKELETON

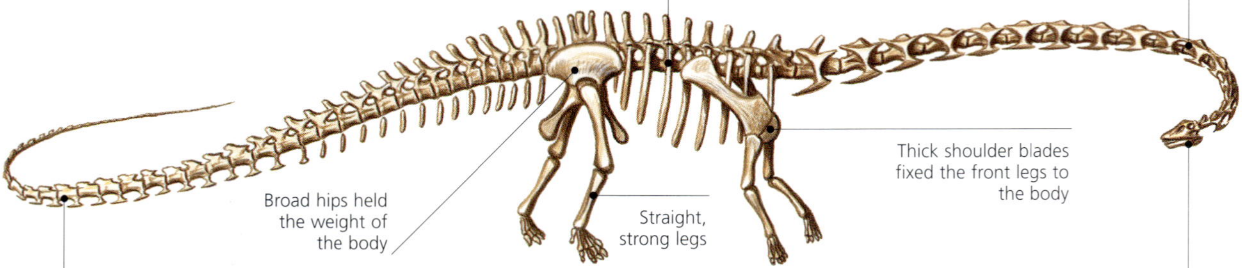

JUVENILE *BAROSAURUS*

CAMARASAURUS

SAUROPOD FEATURES

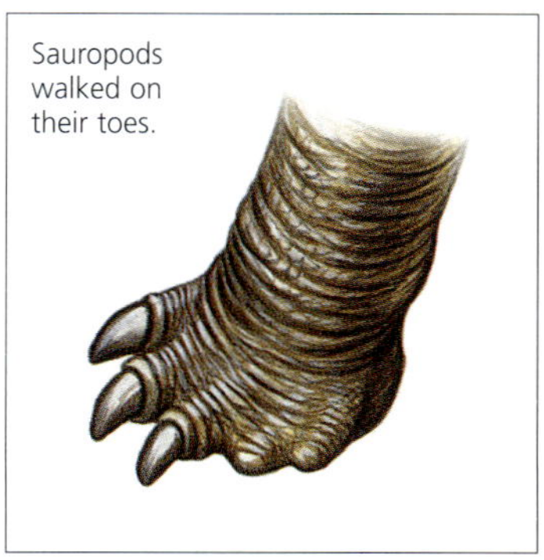

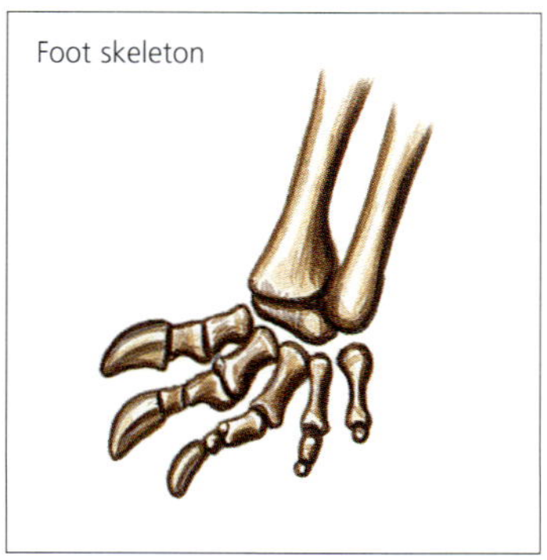

LONGEST NECK
Mamenchisaurus had the longest neck of any animal—36 feet (11 m).

COMPACT BODY
Barosaurus had a relatively compact body that supported a long neck and tail.

MAMENCHISAURUS

SALTASAURUS

APATOSAURUS

Armored Dinosaurs

HEAD PROTECTION

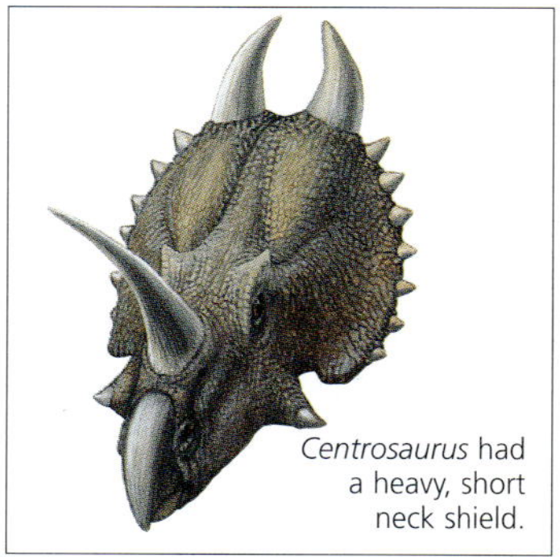

Centrosaurus had a heavy, short neck shield.

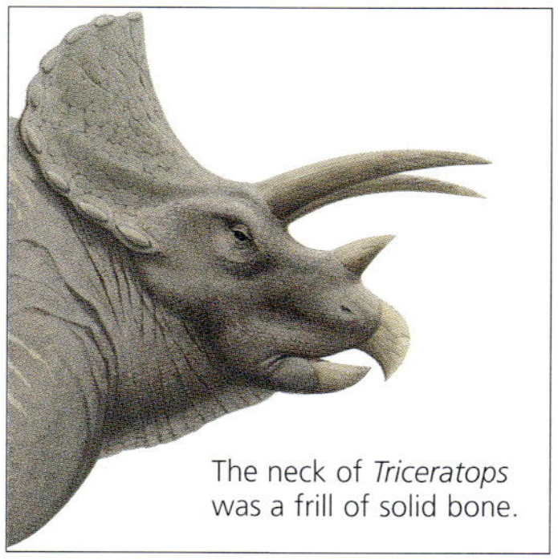

The neck of *Triceratops* was a frill of solid bone.

Chasmosaurus had a light head shield.

KENTROSAURUS

EUOPLOCEPHALUS
This heavily armored dinosaur had several defense mechanisms including bony eyelids and a club tail.

STEGOSAURUS

SCUTELLOSAURUS

POLACANTHUS

SAUROPELTA

CHASMOSAURUS

EDMONTONIA

DEFENSIVE FEATURES

Triceratops horn

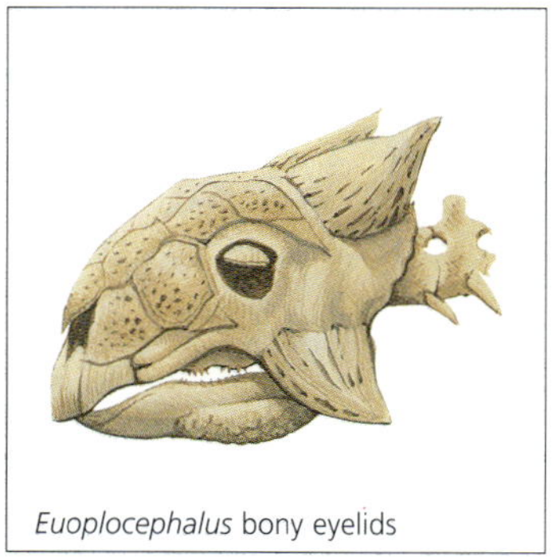

Euoplocephalus bony eyelids

Euoplocephalus club tail

Duckbilled Dinosaurs

PARASAUROLOPHUS HEADS

Adult male

Adult female

Juvenile

DUCKBILLED COMMUNICATION

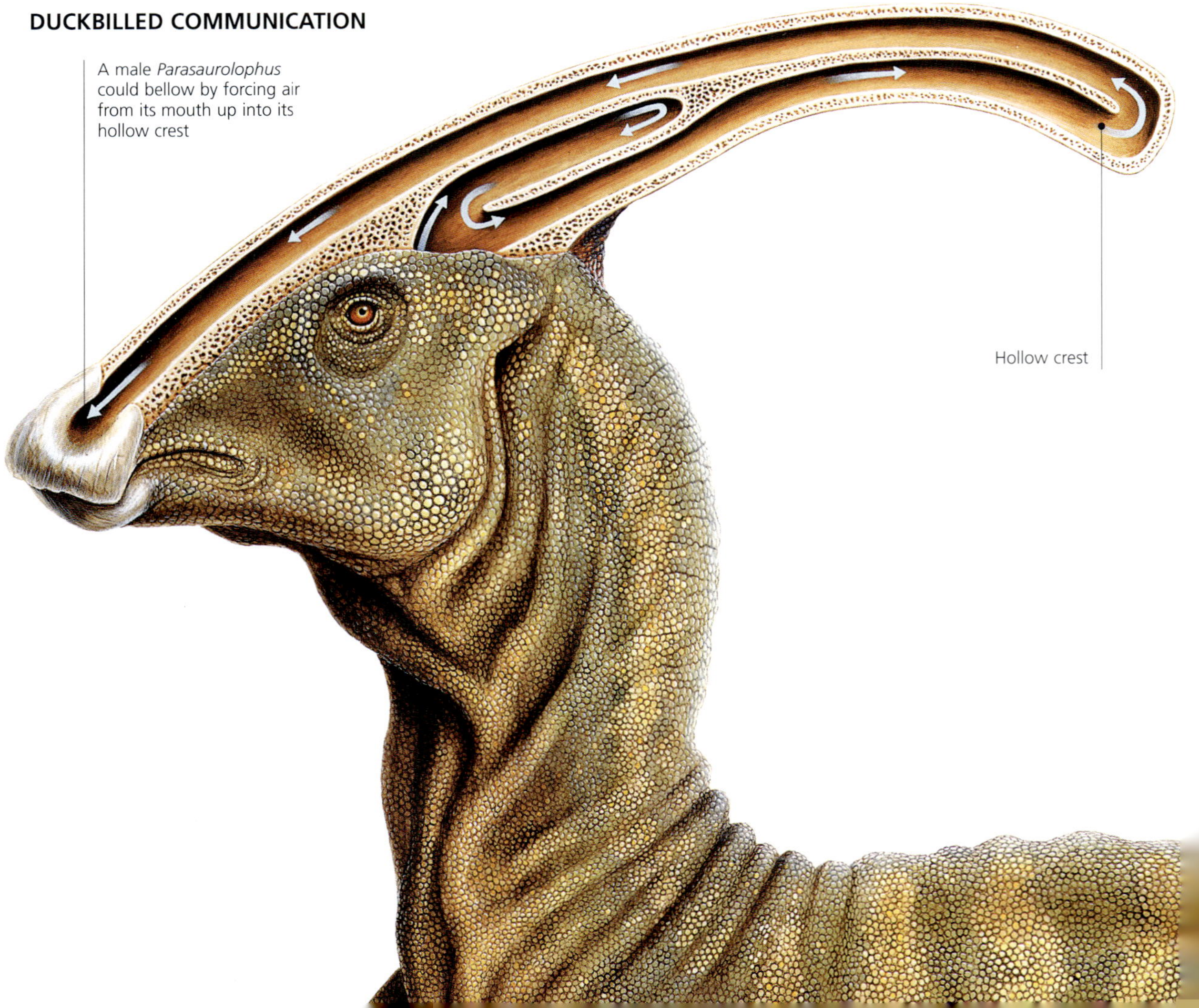

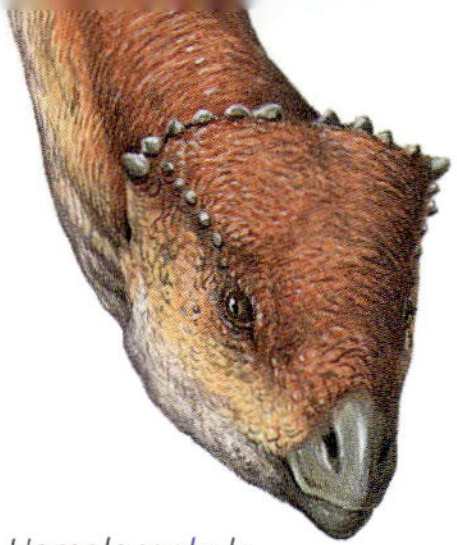

Homalocephale

Kritosaurus

Shantungosaurus

HEAD VARIETIES

DILOPHOSAURUS

SAUROLOPHUS

EDMONTOSAURUS

CORYTHOSAURUS

HEAD FEATURES

Edmontosaurus had a flat head and an inflatable sac of skin on the front of its face, which enabled it to make sounds.

Stegoceras had a dome of solid bone on its head.

Saurolophus had head spike and possibly an inflatable nose sac.

Lambeosaurus had a hollow crest on its head.

Disappearance of the Dinosaurs

EXTINCTION THEORIES

Cold climate change

Hot climate change

Volcanic eruptions

Baryonyx

Crocodile

DISTANT RELATIVES

Baryonyx had a head very similar to a crocodile. Their jaws look alike because they probably did the same job—catch fish.

DINOSAUR EXTINCTION

Dinosaurs suddenly vanished 65 million years ago. Scientists have several theories about what caused this. Some believe there were major weather changes or a volcanic disaster. The main theory is that a huge meteorite hit Earth causing environmental chaos.

Late Cretaceous mammals were small but evolved rapidly into thousands of new species

FROM DINOSAUR TO BIRD

Compsognathus

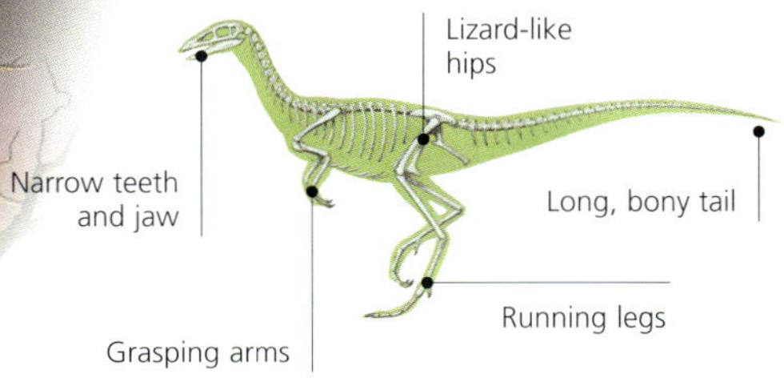

Archaeopteryx

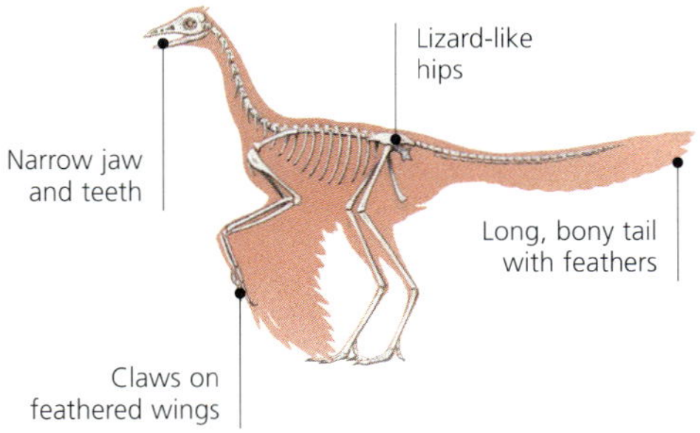

Modern bird

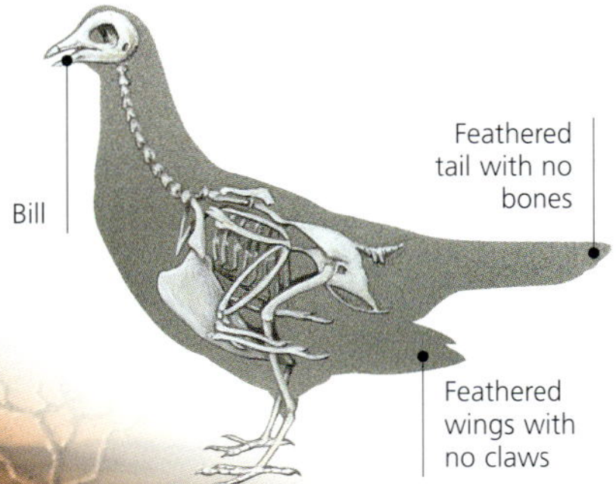

Fossils and Other Clues

KINDS OF FOSSILS

Conifer pine

Cycad

Gingko

Limulus

RECONSTRUCTING *BARYONYX*

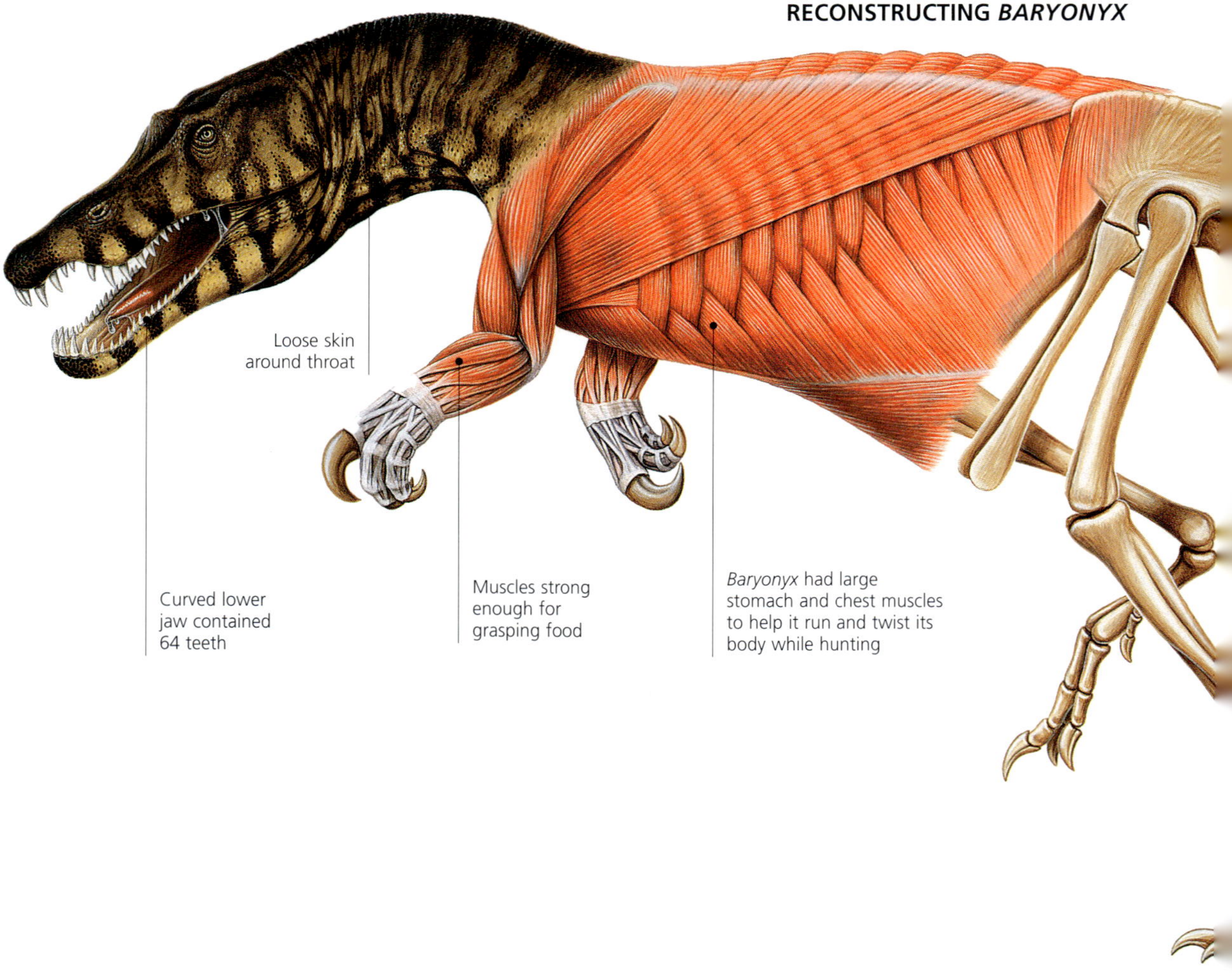

HOW A FOSSIL FORMS

1. Beneath the surface of a lake, a dead dinosaur is safe from scavengers. Its flesh rots but the skeleton remains intact.

2. Layers of sand cover the bones.

3. Bones are gradually replaced by minerals that are harder than the rocks around them.

4. Millions of years later movements in Earth's crust return the fossilized skeleton to the surface.

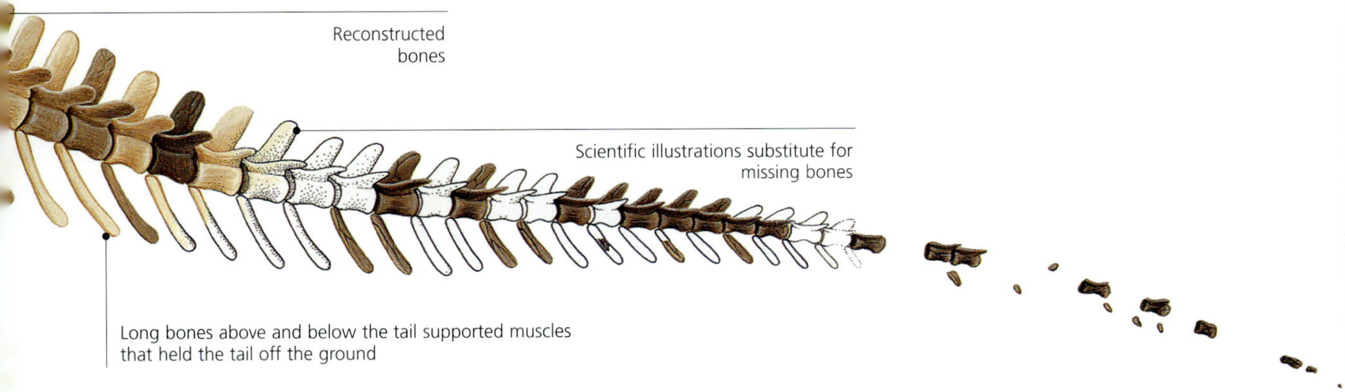

FOSSILIZED FOOTPRINTS

Small theropod tracks

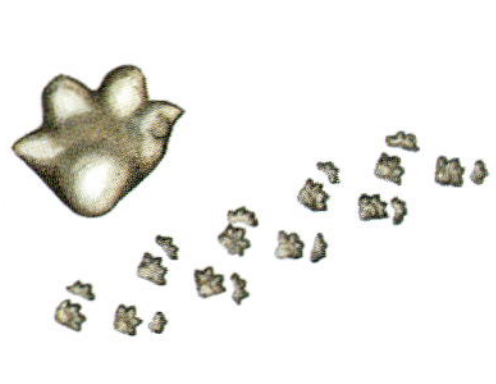

Ceratopsian tracks

Large theropod tracks

Sauropod tracks

PLANTS

CHARACTERISTICS

Plant Parts 180

Plant Processes 182

FERNS AND TREES

Ferns and Mosses 184

Tree Types 186

Conifers 188

FLOWERS AND FOOD PLANTS

Flowering Plants 190

Flowering Plant Cycles 192

Types of Flowering Plants 194

Food and Medicinal Plants 196

PLANT HABITATS

Forests and Rainforests 198

Rainforest Life 200

Plant Parts

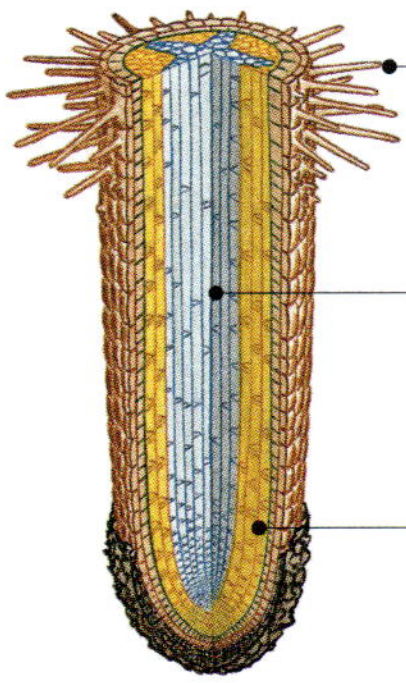

INSIDE A ROOT

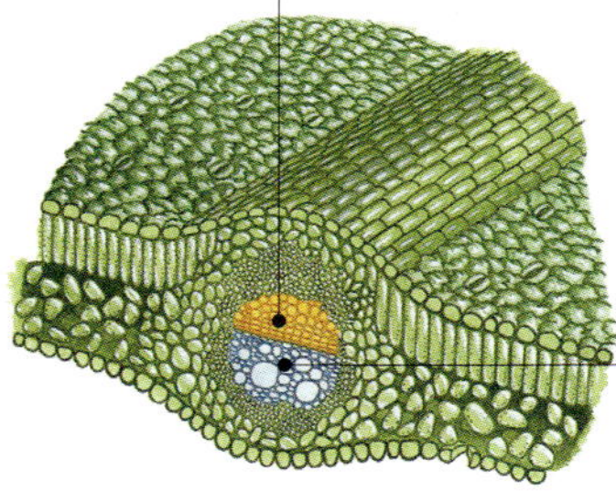

LEAF CROSS-SECTION

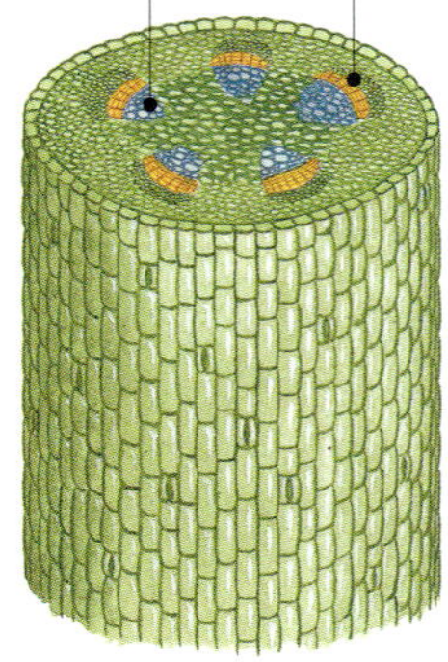

STEM SUPPORT

ROOT SYSTEMS

AERIAL ROOTS

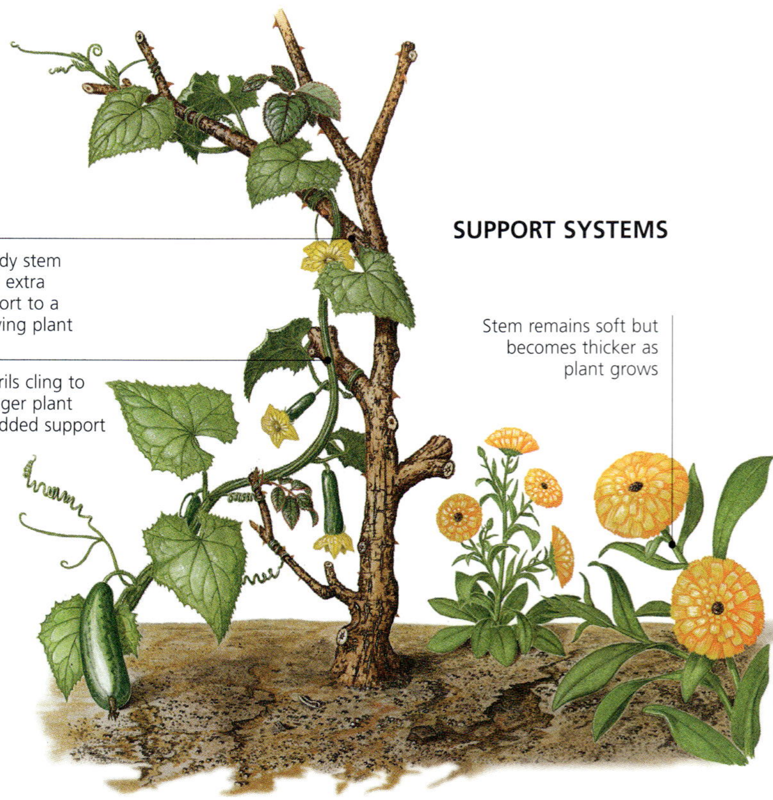

SUPPORT SYSTEMS

ROSE PLANT PARTS

Plant Processes

SAVING WATER

Plants lose water through their leaves. Some trees shed their leaves in the cold or dry season to save water.

LEAF VARIATIONS

PHOTOSYNTHESIS

Carbon dioxide from the air enters the leaves through the stomata

Oxygen, a by-product of photosynthesis, and excess water are released into the air

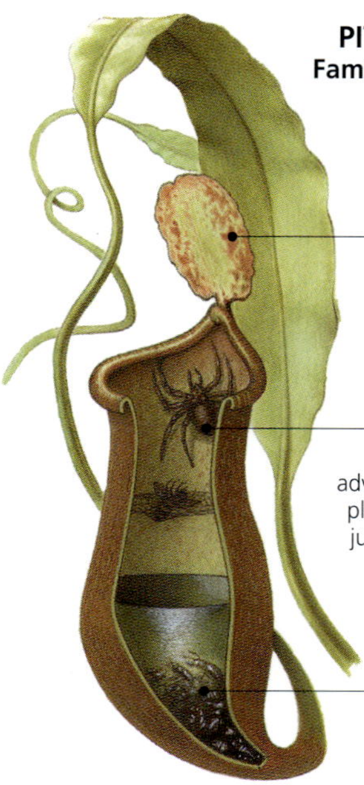

PITCHER PLANT
Family *Nepenthaceae*

Lid acts as a colorful and fragrant lure to insects

Certain spiders take advantage of the pitcher plants by building webs just above the water to catch prey

Insects drown in the water and are digested by the plant

STORING FOOD

Daffodil bulb stores food to use when it rests between growing and reproducing

The flower needs energy from the plant's sugars to grow
Phloem cells transport the sugars from leaves to other parts of the plant
Green chlorophyll in the leaf cells absorbs sunlight
Rainwater lands on the soil where the roots collect it
Xylem cells transport water and mineral salts from the roots to the leaves
Phosphates, nitrates and other mineral salts are absorbed by the roots

Ferns and Mosses

HORSETAIL

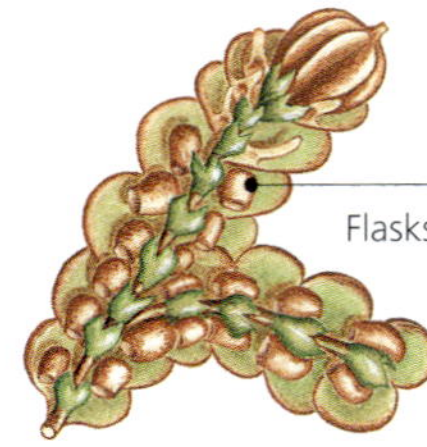

***FRULLANIA* LIVERWORT**

REPRODUCTION

FERN FROND

A FERN SELECTION

FERN LIFECYCLE

Ferns have a unique lifecycle. The first generation produces asexual spores. The seond generation produces sex cells (or gametes) and these grow into the third generation of spore producers.

Tree Types

MORETON BAY FIG
Ficus macrophylla

COMMON BEECH
Fagus sylvatica

COASTAL SHE-OAK
Casuarina equisetifolia

ENGLISH OAK
Quercus robur

AMERICAN ELM
Ulmus americana

BATSWING CORAL-TREE
Erythrina vespertilio

MONTEREY PINE
Pinus radiata

SILVER BIRCH
Betula pendula

SUGAR MAPLE
Acer saccharum

LAWSON CYPRESS
Chamaecyparis lawsoniana

BALSAM FIR
Abies balsamea

SENEGAL DATE PALM
Pheonix reclinata

SOUTHERN BLUE GUM
Eucalyptus bicostata

ATLAS CEDAR
Cedrus atlantica

Conifers

PINE REPRODUCTION

UNUSUAL CONIFER

Larches have green leaves in spring and summer. These leaves change color in autumn and drop off in winter, which is unusual for a conifer.

INSIDE A TREE TRUNK

GINGKO
Female gingko trees have fleshy, foul-smelling cones and fan-shaped leaves.

YEW
Yew trees are narrow and flat. Female yew seeds are a fleshy red.

SCOTS PINE
Scots pines have egg-shaped cones and paired, blue-green leaves.

ARIZONA CYPRESS
Cypresses have dark green overlapping leaves and small round cones.

CYCAD
Cycad cones are the largest in the world.

PLUM PINE
Plum pines have berry-like cones.

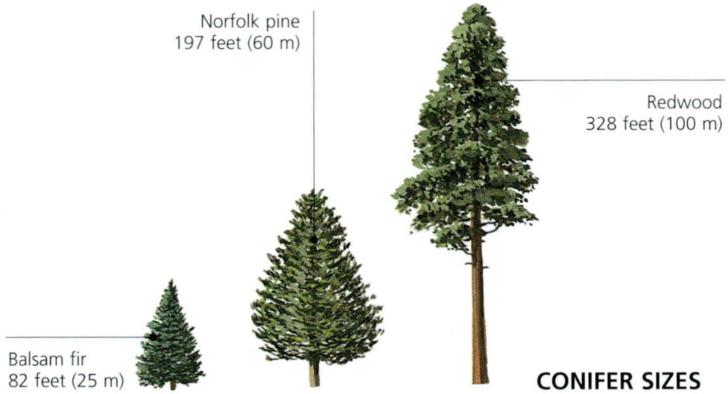

CONIFER SIZES

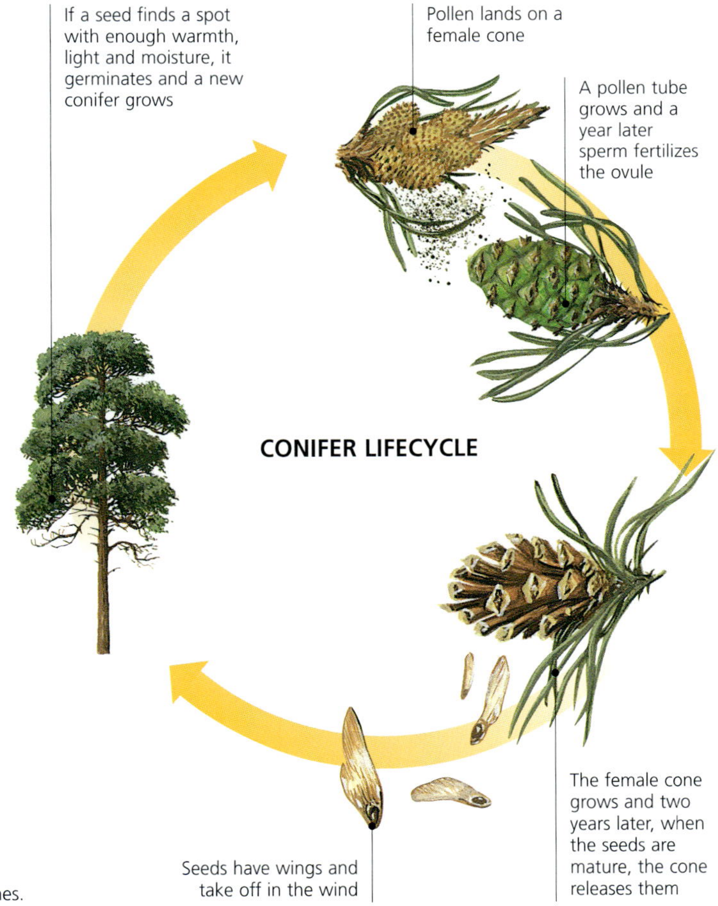

CONIFER LIFECYCLE

Flowering Plants

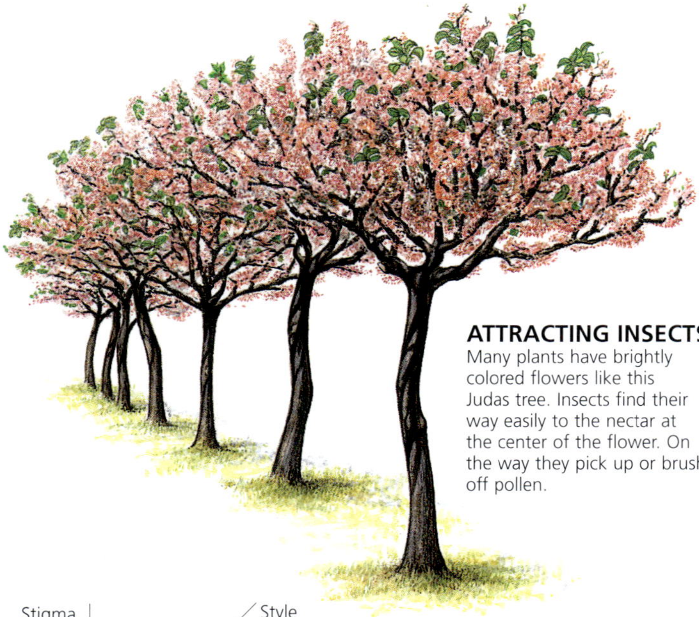

ATTRACTING INSECTS

Many plants have brightly colored flowers like this Judas tree. Insects find their way easily to the nectar at the center of the flower. On the way they pick up or brush off pollen.

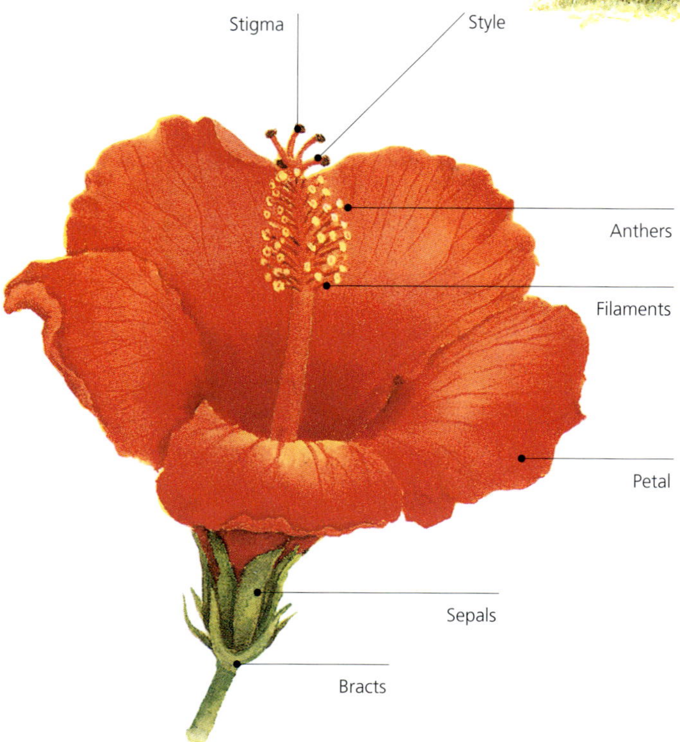

HIBISCUS

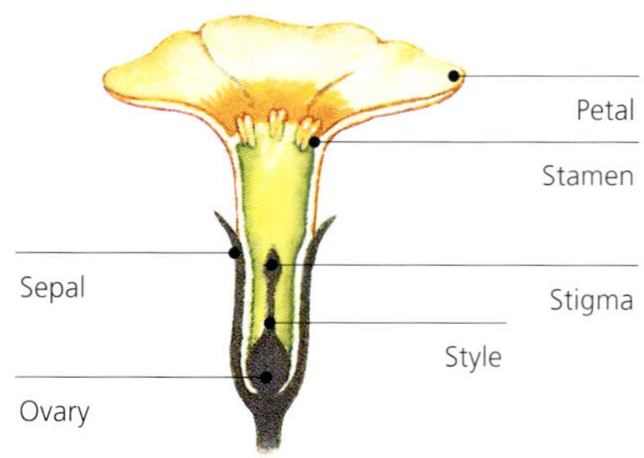

THRUM-EYED PRIMROSE

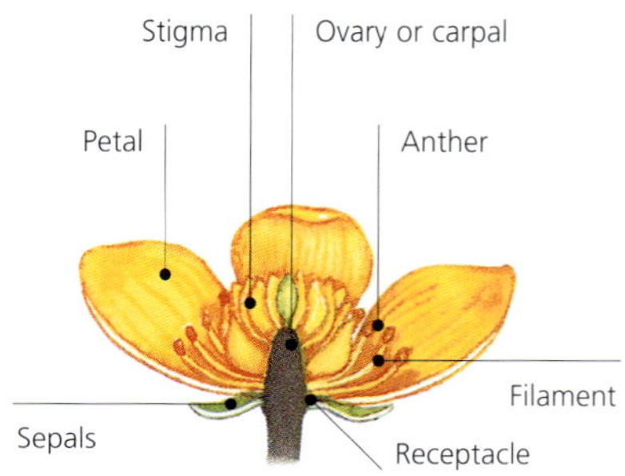

BUTTERCUP

EUCALYPTUS FLOWERS

Eucalpypts are evergreen, flowering trees. They are the dominant trees in Australia.

BULB REPRODUCTION

Daffodil bulbs split and grow new bulbs on the side of the parent bulb.

PUMPKIN REPRODUCTION

The male and female pumpkin flowers grow on the same vine. A male can pollinate its sister female flower—this is called self-pollination. To avoid this, the male and female flowers mature at different times.

Male pumpkin flower

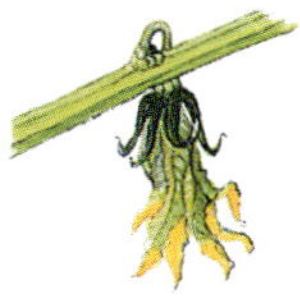

Female pumpkin flower

KINDS OF INFLORESCENCE

Flowering Plant Cycles

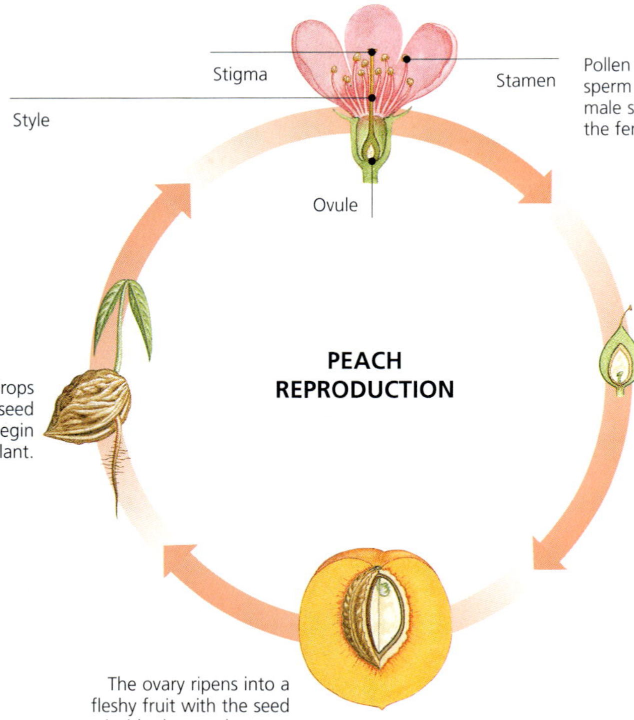

Pollen containing the male sperm is released from the male stamen and carried to the female stigma.

The pollen develops a tube that grows down the style to the ovule. The sperm fertilizes the female cell and the ovule starts to develop into a seed inside the ovary.

The ovary ripens into a fleshy fruit with the seed inside the peach stone.

When the ripe fruit drops to the ground, the seed can germinate and begin to form a new plant.

FOUR SEASONS

The London plane tree has four very different stages in its yearly cycle.

Spring
Yellow male and red female flowers hang in separate clusters on the same tree. Once fertilized, the female flower begins to grow fruit.

Summer
The clusters of tightly packed green fruits grow larger and protect the seeds inside.

Autumn
As the leaves change color, the hairy fruits also change to a brown color. They are dispersed with the wind.

Winter
The leaves and their stalks drop off the branches. The sticky buds on the end of bare twigs protect the young leaves, which emerge in the spring.

A TREE'S YEAR

Types of Flowering Plants

ROSE
Family *Rosaceae*

POPPY
Family *Papaveraceae*

STURT'S DESERT PEA
Swainsona formosa

LILAC
Family *Oleaceae*

SUNFLOWER
Family *Compositae*

MADONNA LILY
Family *Liliaceae*

IMPERIAL CRIMSON LILY
Family *Liliaceae*

DAYLILY
Family *Liliaceae*

FOXGLOVE
Family *Scorphulariaceae*

MARIGOLD
Family *Compositae*

EDELWEISS
Leontopodium alpinum

Food and Medicinal Plants

CHIVE
Allium schoenoprasum

ANISE
Pimpinella anisum

BASIL
Ocimum basilicum

MEADOWSWEET
Filipendula ulmaria

ECHINACEA
Echinacea purpurea

FRUIT AND VEGETABLES

A strawberry is a fruit with many ovaries, each with one seed.

An orange is the fruit of an evergreen tree.

A carrot is an orange-colored tap root.

A potato is the thick part of an underground stem called a tuber.

A tomato is a fruit originally from the Americas.

An onion is an underground bulb.

A pumpkin is a fruit grown on a vine.

Ginger is an underground stem.

Lettuce is a plant with crisp, green leaves usually eaten raw.

Asparagus is a green stem with reduced leaves, or bracts.

CABBAGE FAMILY

GARLIC CLOVE

NUT VARIATIONS

Forests and Rainforests

ROOT SYSTEMS

LIFE IN A TANK BROMELIAD

The leaves of a tank bromeliad form a watertight bowl that accumulates rainwater. Bromeliads are non-parasitic epiphytic plants. They gain their nutrients from the animal matter that filters to the bottom of the pool.

Rainforest Life

RAINFOREST CANOPY

High above the ground the leaves of the tall trees almost meet to form a roof or canopy. Tropical rainforests are home to a wider range of plants and animals than any other habitat.

STRANGLER FIG

This epiphyte grows from a bird-borne seed high in a host tree. It grows roots into the soil and forms a woody "corset" around the trunk. Because the host tree cannot grow outward, it rots and dies. The strangler fig then stands alone.

ANT HOUSE

Ants live inside the cavities of this epiphytic ant plant.

ENERGY FLOW

Dead plant and animal matter are raw materials for the rainforest nutrient cycle. These cells must be broken down by fungi and bacteria before nutrients can be released into the soil.

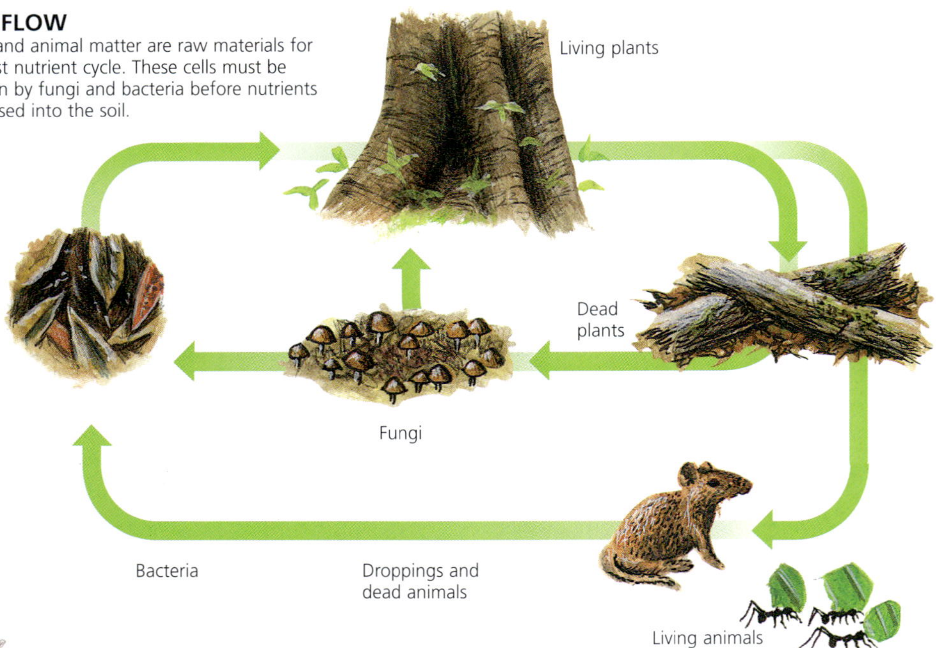

ANIMALS

BIRDS

Bird Characteristics 206
Bird Anatomy 208
Feathers and Flight 210
Waterbirds 212
Seabirds and Shorebirds 214
Penguins 216
Flightless Birds 218
Raptor Characteristics 220
Raptors 222
Hawks and Eagles 224
Pigeons and Parrots 226
Hummingbirds 228
Kingfishers and their Allies 230
Woodpeckers and Barbets 232
Land Birds 234
Songbirds 236
Finches and Starlings 238

MAMMALS

Monotremes and Marsupials 240
Marsupials 242
Insect-eating Mammals 244
Bats 246
Primates 248
Old World Monkeys 250
New World Monkeys 252
Dogs 254
Cat Characteristics 256
Great Cats 258
Small Cats 260
Bears 262

REPTILES

Turtle and Tortoise Anatomy 280
Turtles and Tortoises 282
Crocodiles and Alligators 284
Amphisbaenians and Tuataras 286
Iguanas, Chameleons and Agamids 288
Geckos 290
Lizards 292
Snake Anatomy 294
Snakes 296

AMPHIBIANS

Salamanders, Newts and Caecilians 298
Frogs and Toads 300

FISHES

Shark Anatomy 306
Shark Variations 308
Rays and Chimaeras 310
Bony Fishes 312
Freshwater Fishes 316
Ocean Fishes 320

INSECTS AND SPIDERS

Insect Anatomy 326
Beetles and Bugs 328
Butterflies and Moths 330
Bees, Wasps and Ants 332
Flies and Dragonflies 334
Grasshoppers and Crickets 336
Spider Anatomy 338
Spider Varieties 340

Bird Characteristics

BIRD SIZES

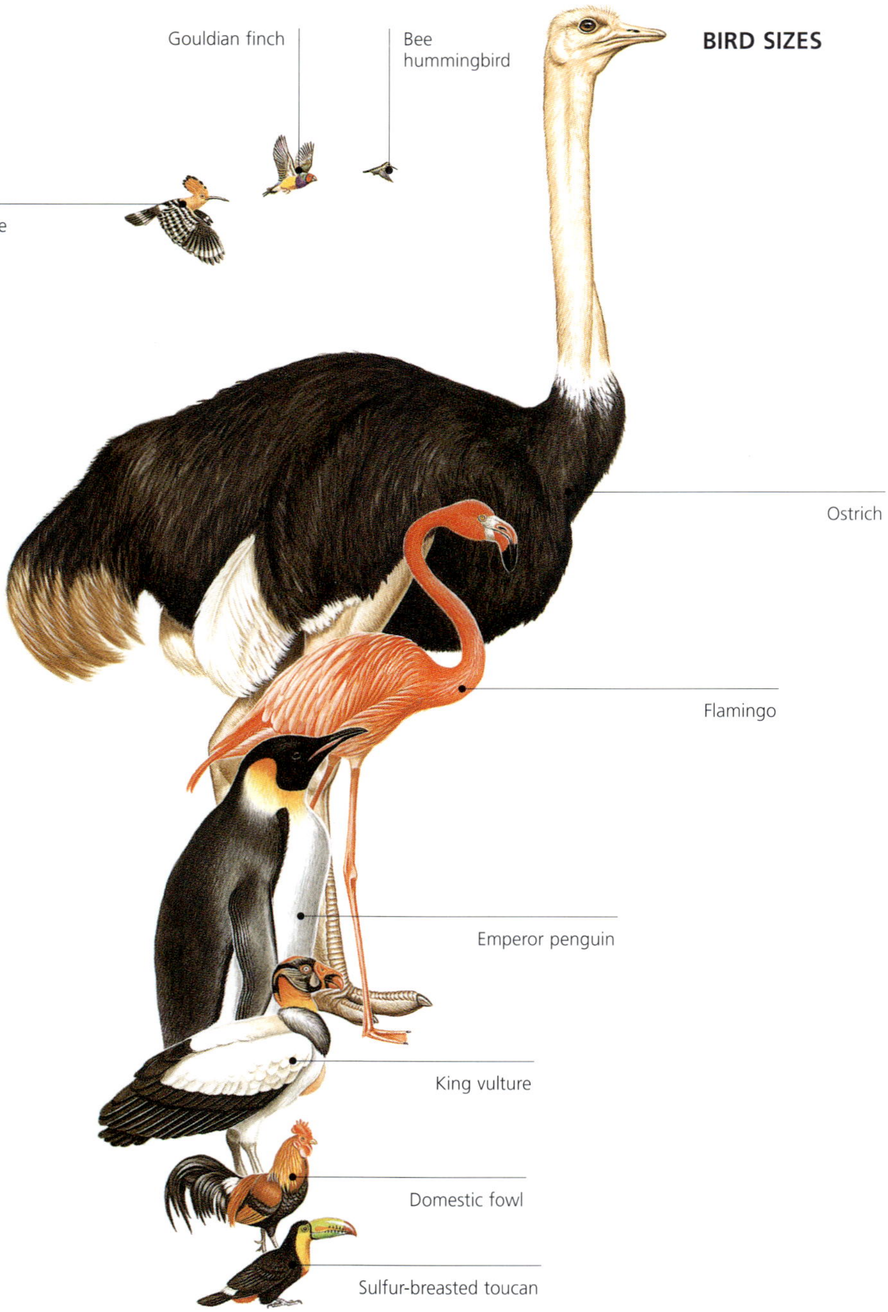

BILL VARIETIES

African spoonbill

Pileated woodpecker

Palm cockatoo

Far eastern curlew

Bald eagle

Ring-necked pheasant

Ring-necked pheasant skeleton

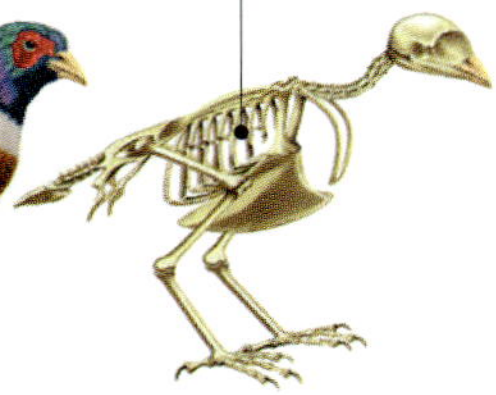

Wire-tailed manakin

Wire-tailed manakin skeleton

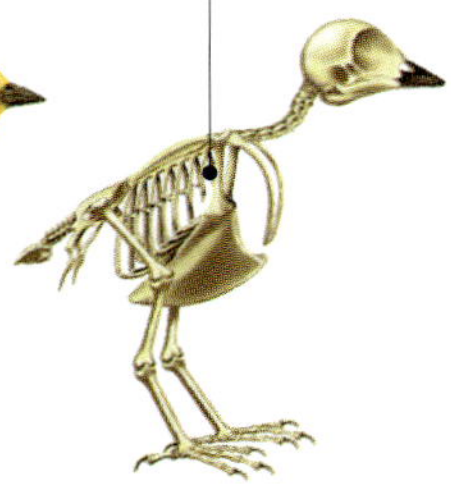

Scarlet ibis

Scarlet ibis skeleton

FEET VARIETIES

Black-capped lorikeet

Mallard

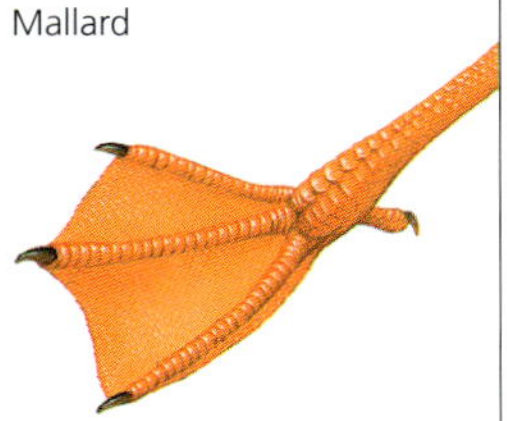

Northern jacana

Rhea

Bird Anatomy

BIRD SKELETON

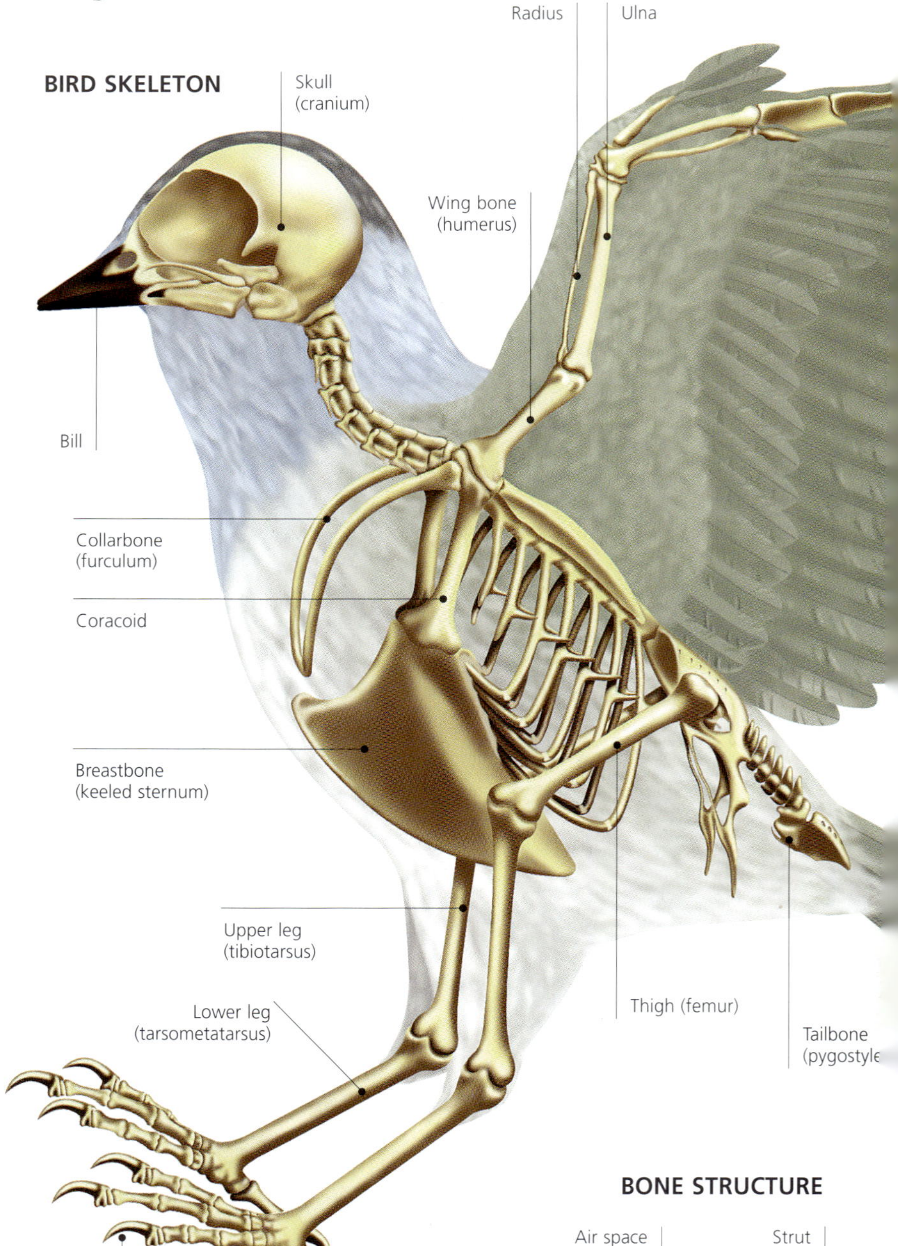

INSIDE THE HEART

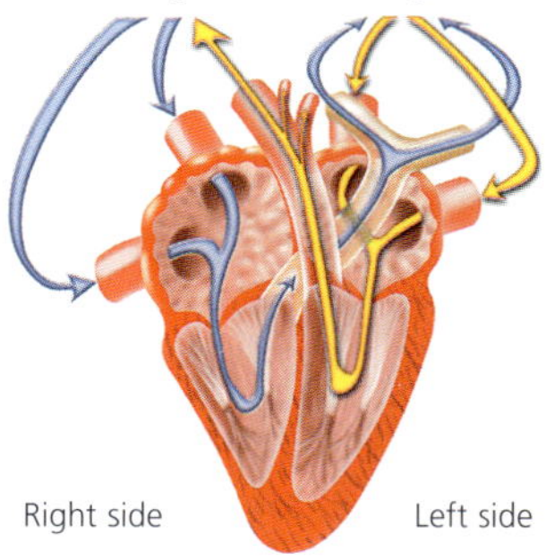

BONE STRUCTURE

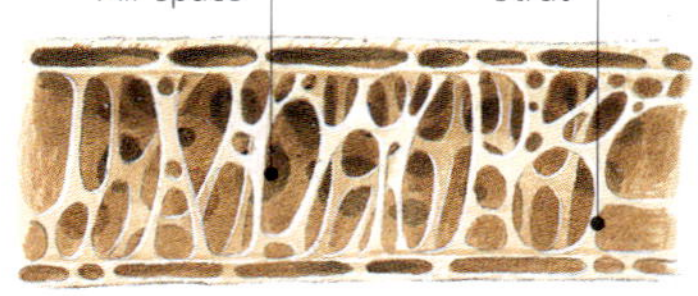

LEG MUSCLES

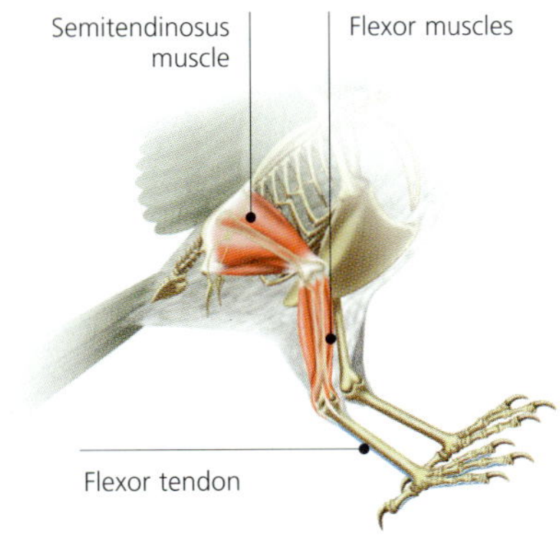

LUNGS

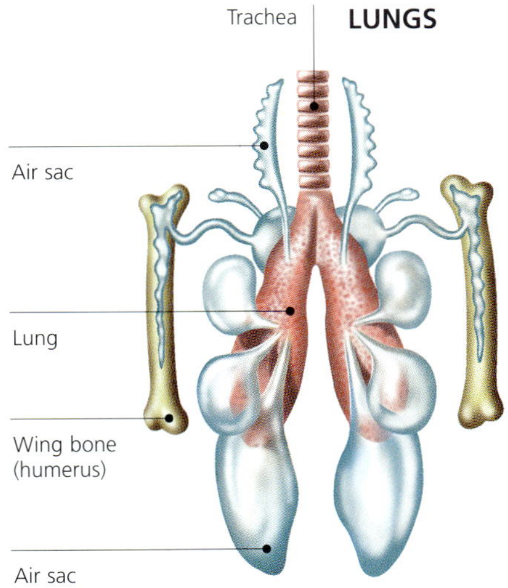

WINGS

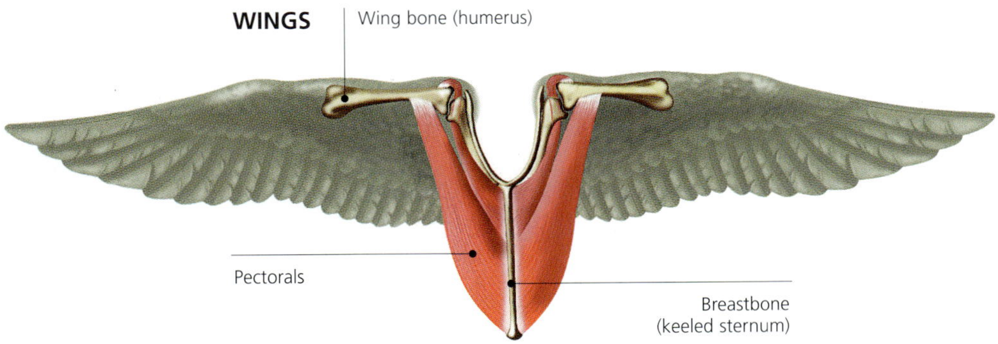

DIGESTIVE SYSTEM

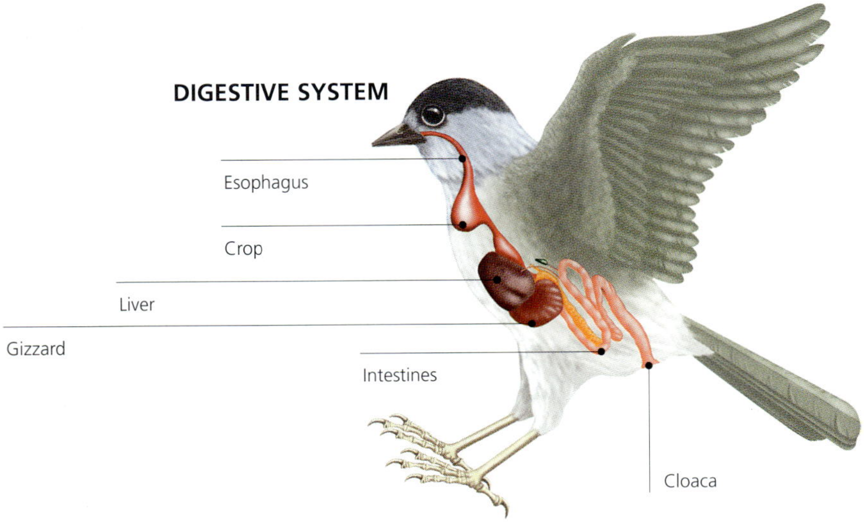

Feathers and Flight

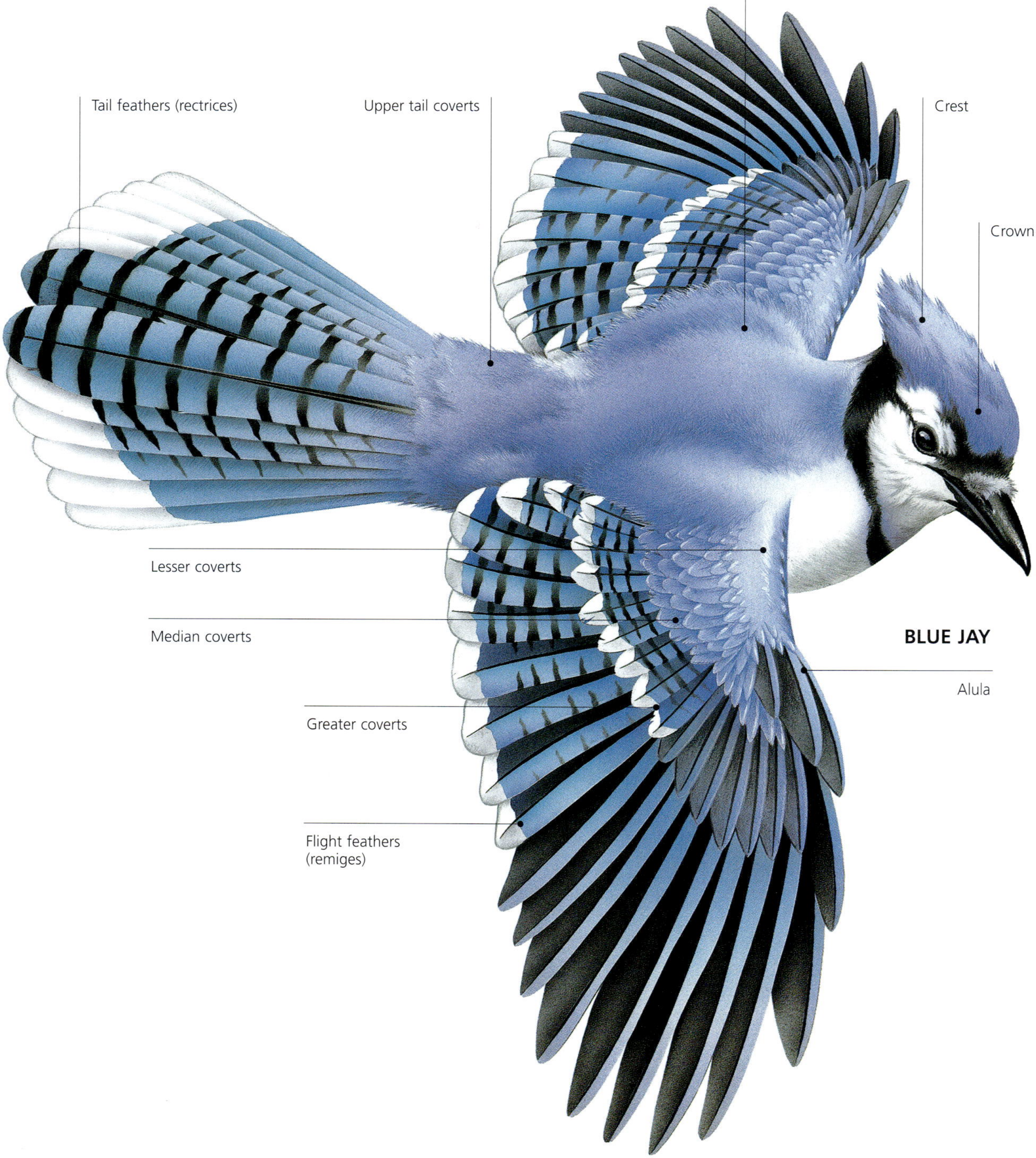

AMERICAN CROW FLIGHT

SCARLET MINIVET FLIGHT

PEACOCK PLUMAGE

FLIGHT OR CONTOUR FEATHER

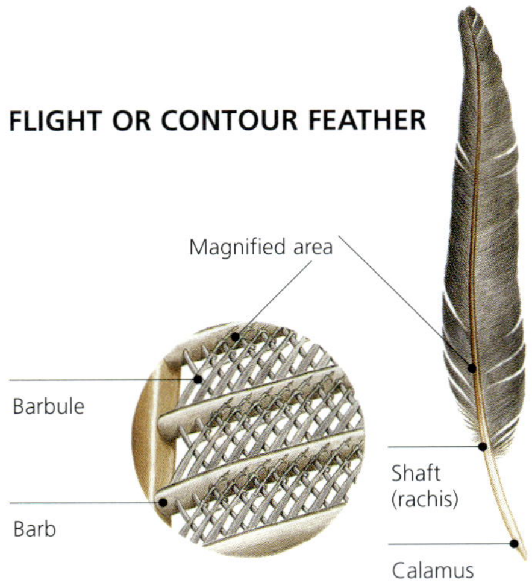

SEMI PLUME OR DOWN FEATHER

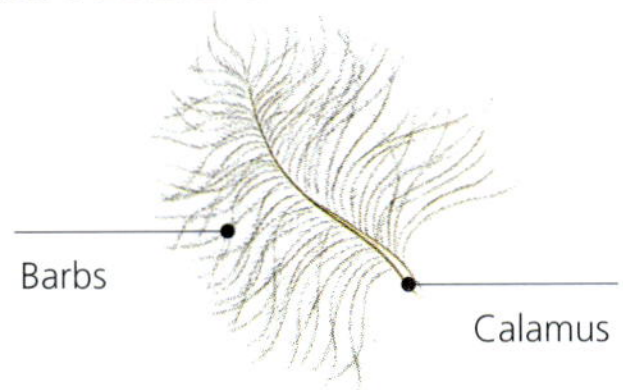

FEATHER GROWTH

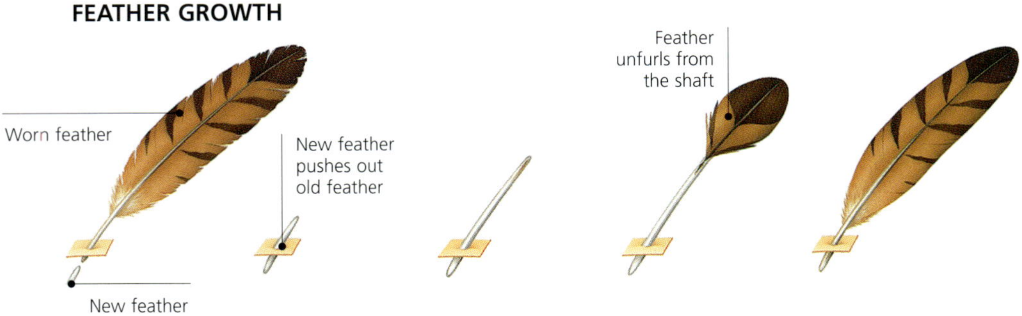

Waterbirds

MUTE SWAN
Cygnus olor

GEESE FLYING IN “V” FORMATION

KING EIDER
Somateria spectabilis

WOOD DUCK
Aix sponsa

RED-BREASTED GOOSE
Branta ruficollis

PURPLE GALLINULE
Porphyrio martinica

WALDRAPP
Geronticus eremita

PAINTED STORK
Mycteria leucocephala

PURPLE HERON
Ardea purpurea

NORTHERN SCREAMER
Chauna chavaria

CROWNED CRANE
Balearica pavonina

Seabirds and Shorebirds

BROWN PELICAN
Pelecanus occidentalis

LESSER GOLDEN PLOVER
Pluvialis dominica

BANDED LAPWING
Vanellus tricolor

BLUE-FOOTED BOOBY
Sula nebouxii

GREAT AUK
Pinguinus impennis

ATLANTIC PUFFIN
Fratercula arctica

BLACK SKIMMER
Rhynchops niger

Penguins

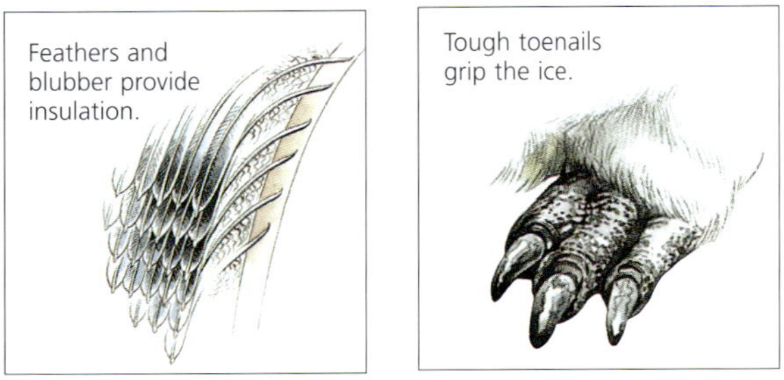

EMPEROR PENGUIN ANATOMY

EMPEROR PENGUIN
Aptenodytes forsteri

CHINSTRAP PENGUIN
Pygoscelis antarctica

YELLOW-EYED PENGUIN
Megadyptes antipodes

KING PENGUIN
Aptenodytes patagonicus

ROCKHOPPER PENGUIN
Eudyptes chrysocome

FIORDLAND PENGUIN
Eudyptes pachyrhynchus

MAGELLANIC PENGUIN
Spheniscus magellanicus

FAIRY PENGUIN
Eudyptula minor

Flightless Birds

REEVE'S PHEASANT
Syrmaticus reevesii

WEKA
Gallirallus australis

BROWN KIWI
Apteryx australis

BLACK KORHAAN
Eupodotis afra

CALIFORNIA QUAIL
Callipepla californica

VULTURINE GUINEA FOWL
Acryllium vulturinun

KAKAPO
Strigops habroptilus

TAKAHE
Porphyrio mantelli

EMU
Dromaius novaehollandiae

Raptor Characteristics

RAPTOR TALONS

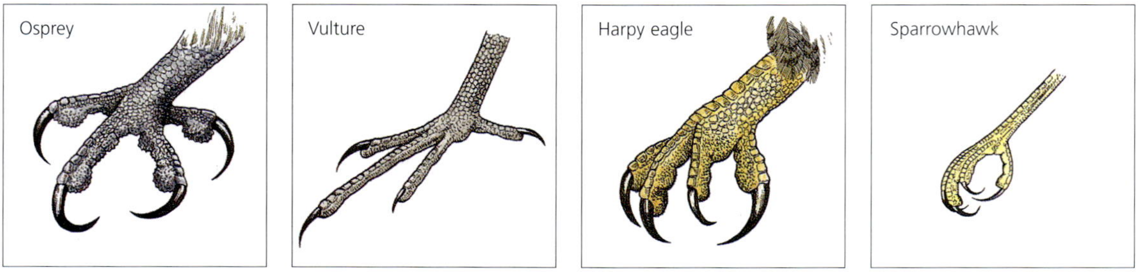

RAPTOR ANATOMY

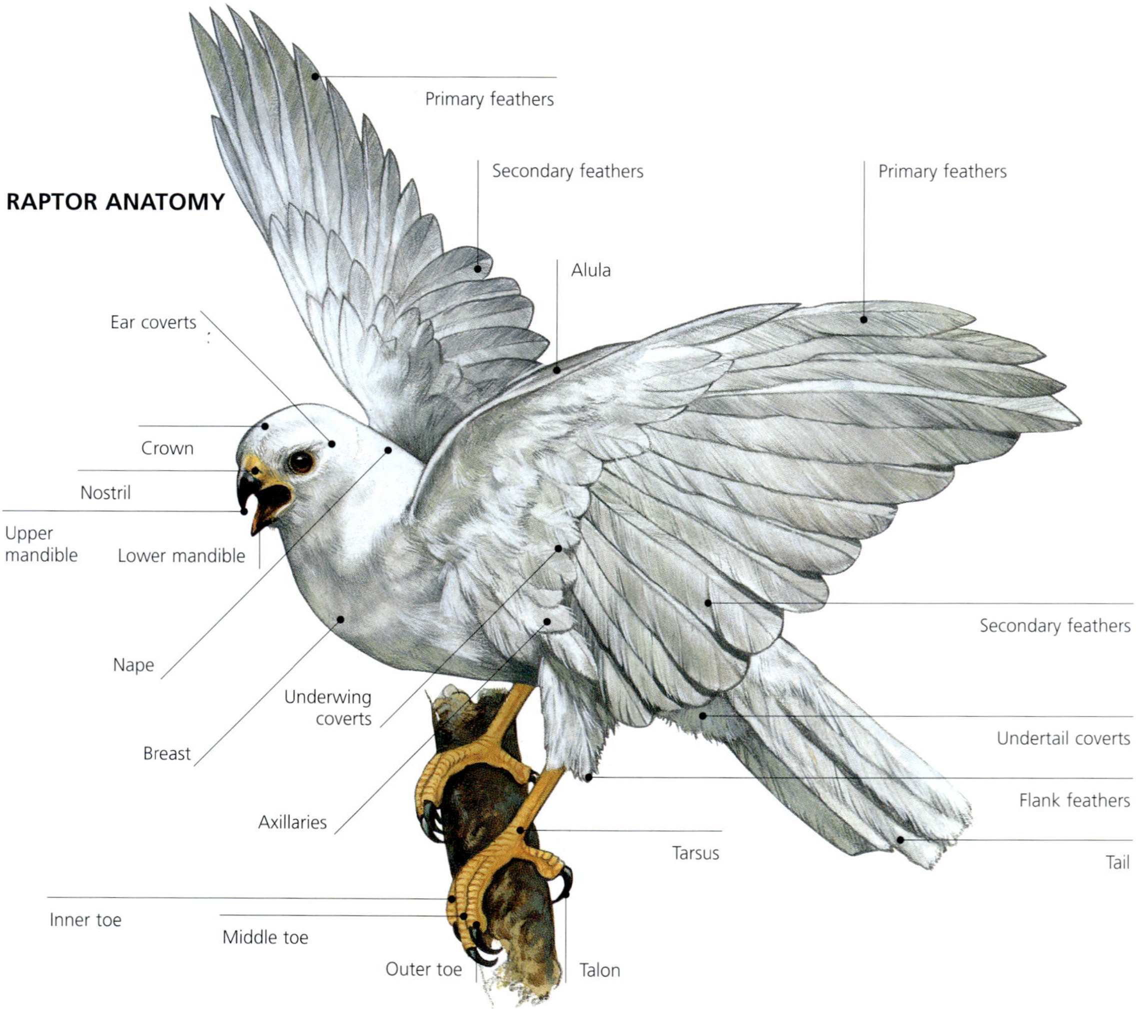

SNAIL KITE
Rostrhamus sociabilis

BLACK-SHOULDERED KITE
Elanus caeruleus

PEARL KITE
Gampsonyx swainsonii

BRAHMINY KITE
Haliastur indus

BEARDED VULTURE
Gypaetus barbatus

RAPTOR WINGSPANS

Andean condor
9 ½ feet (2.9 m)

Bearded vulture
8 feet (2.5 m)

Secretarybird
6 ¾ feet (2.1 m)

White-bellied sea eagle
6 ½ feet (2.0 m)

Rough-legged buzzard
4 ½ feet (1.5 m)

Peregrine falcon
3 ¼ feet (1.0 m)

Lesser kestrel
2 ¾ feet (0.7 m)

Little sparrowhawk
1 ¼ feet (0.4 m)

Raptors

BATELEUR
Terathopius ecaudatus

BLACK KITE
Milvus migrans

CRESTED CARACARA
Polyborus plancus

AMERICAN KESTREL
Falco sparverius

BARN OWL AND SKULL
Tyto alba

Asymmetrical ears enhance the owl's "stereo" hearing

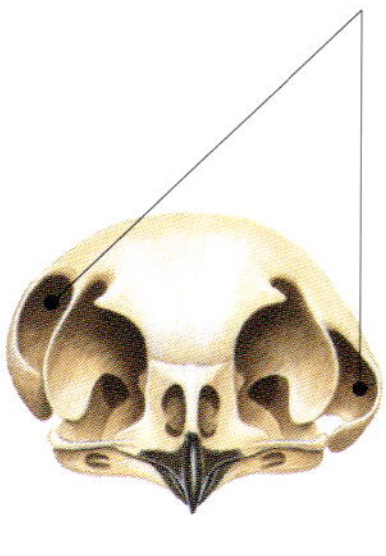

AFRICAN PYGMY FALCON
Polihierax semitorquatus

WHITE-EYED KESTREL
Falco rupicoloides

EURASIAN GRIFFON
Gyps fulvus

PALMNUT VULTURE
Gypohierax angolensis

Hawks and Eagles

BONELLI'S EAGLE
Hieraaetus fasciatus

ORNATE HAWK EAGLE
Spizaetus ornatus

CRESTED SERPENT EAGLE
Spilornis cheela

GREAT PHILIPPINE EAGLE
Pithecophaga jefferyi

WHITE-BELLIED SEA EAGLE
Haliaeetus leucogaster

ROUGH-LEGGED HAWK
Buteo lagopus

SLATE-COLORED HAWK
Leucopternis schistacea

Pigeons and Parrots

PESQUET'S PARROT
Psittrichas fulgidus

EASTERN ROSELLA
Platycercus eximius

BLACK-CAPPED LORY
Lorius lory

NICOBAR PIGEON
Caloenas nicobarica

SUPERB FRUIT DOVE
Ptilinopus superbus

HAWK-HEADED PARROT
Deroptyus accipitrinus

PIN-TAILED SANDGROUSE
Pterocles alchata

Hummingbirds

BLACK-CHINNED HUMMINGBIRD
Archilochus alexandri

ANNA'S HUMMINGBIRD
Clypte anna

RUBY-THROATED HUMMINGBIRD
Archilochus colubris

EXTRACTING NECTAR
This male ruby-throated hummingbird (*Archilochus colubris*) hovers in front of a flower and inserts its bill to extract the nectar. Hummingbirds also eat insects, which form a large part of their diet.

HUMMINGBIRD FLIGHT

Flying forward
Hummingbirds flap their wings up and down to move forward.

Hovering
Hummingbirds move their wings in a rapid figure-of-eight motion to hover in place.

Flying backward
Hummingbirds flap their wings above and behind their heads to move backward.

BROAD-BILLED HUMMINGBIRD
Cynanthus latirostris

CALLIOPE HUMMINGBIRD
Stellula calliope

RUFOUS HUMMINGBIRD
Selasphorus rufus

Kingfishers and their Allies

SPANGLED KOOKABURRA
Dacelo tyro

DIVING FOR FISH
This belted kingfisher (*Ceryle alcyon*) plunges head-first into water to catch fish.

YELLOW-BILLED HORNBILL
Tockus flavirostris

RAINBOW BEE-EATER
Merops ornatus

WHITE-THROATED KINGFISHER
Halcyon smyrnensis

BLUE-CROWNED MOTMOT
Momotus momota

MALACHITE KINGFISHER
Alcedo cristata

LILAC-BREASTED ROLLER
Coracias caudata

Woodpeckers and Barbets

RUFOUS-TAILED JACAMAR
Galbula ruficauda

RED-AND-YELLOW BARBET
Trachyphonus erythrocephalus

HAIRY WOODPECKER
Picoides villosus

ACORN WOODPECKER
Melanerpes formicivorus

DOWNY WOODPECKER
Picoides pubescens

SULFUR-BREASTED TOUCAN
Ramphastos sulfuratus

NORTHERN FLICKER
Colaptes auratus

WOODPECKER TAILS

Hairy woodpecker   Downy woodpecker

WOODPECKER'S TONGUE

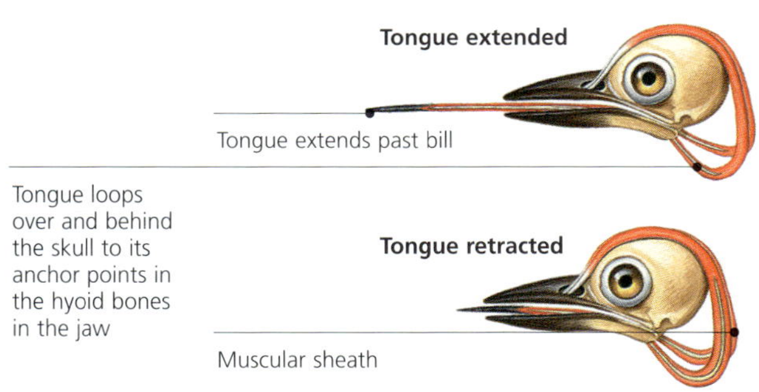

Land Birds

WHITE-CHEEKED TURACO
Tauraco leucotis

CHANNEL-BILLED CUCKOO
Scythrops novaehollandia

GREAT KISKADEE
Pitangus sulphuratus

GREATER ROADRUNNER
Geococcyx californianus

WIRE-TAILED MANAKIN
Pipra filicauda

RESPLENDENT QUETZAL
Pharomachrus mocinno

GUIANA COCK-OF-THE-ROCK
Rupicola rupicola

GREEN BROADBILL
Calyptomena viridis

BANDED PITTA
Pitta guajana

VIOLACEOUS TROGON
Trogon violaceus

Songbirds

BARRED CUCKOOSHRIKE
Coracina lineata

GOLDEN-FRONTED LEAFBIRD
Chloropsis aurifrons

RED-BILLED LEIOTHRIX
Leiothrix lutea

GOLDEN-CROWNED KINGLET
Regulus satrapa

RUFOUS-BELLIED NILTAVA
Niltava sundara

SHRIKE-TIT
Falcunculus frontatus

SPECTACLED MONARCH
Monarcha trivirgatus

REGAL SUNBIRD
Nectarinia regia

RUFOUS-BACKED SHRIKE
Lanius schach

WHITE'S THRUSH
Zoothera dauma

WHITE-RUMPED SHAMA
Copsychus malabaricus

ORANGE CHAT
Epthianura aurifrons

SPLENDID FAIRY-WREN
Malurus splendens

RED-CAPPED ROBIN
Petroica goodenovii

SPOTTED PARDALOTE
Pardalotus punctatus

EASTERN SPINEBILL
Acanthorhynchus tenuirostris

REGENT HONEYEATER
Xanthomyza phrygia

PAINTED BUNTING
Passerina ciris

RED-LEGGED HONEYCREEPER
Cyanerpes cyaneus

SUPERB TANAGER
Tangara fastuosa

Finches and Starlings

EURASIAN GOLDFINCH
Carduelis carduelis

CHAFFINCH
Fringilla coelebs

JAVA SPARROW
Padda oryzivora

GOULDIAN FINCH
Chloebia gouldiae

RED BISHOP
Euplectes orix

MELBA FINCH
Pytilia melba

GREEN FIGBIRD
Sphecotheres viridis

SUPERB GLOSSY STARLING
Spreo superbus

GREATER RAQUET-TAILED DRONGO
Dicrurus paradiseus

GALAPAGOS FINCHES

These finches evolved from a single ancestral species which probably looked like the bird in the center. The birds vary in bill shape and diet throughout the Galápagos Islands.

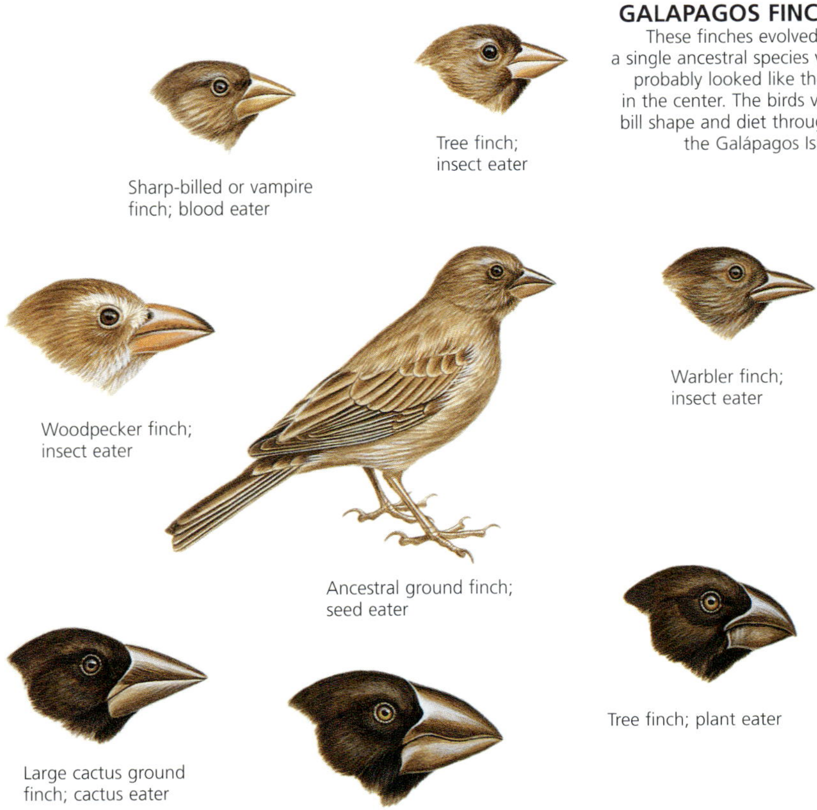

Monotremes and Marsupials

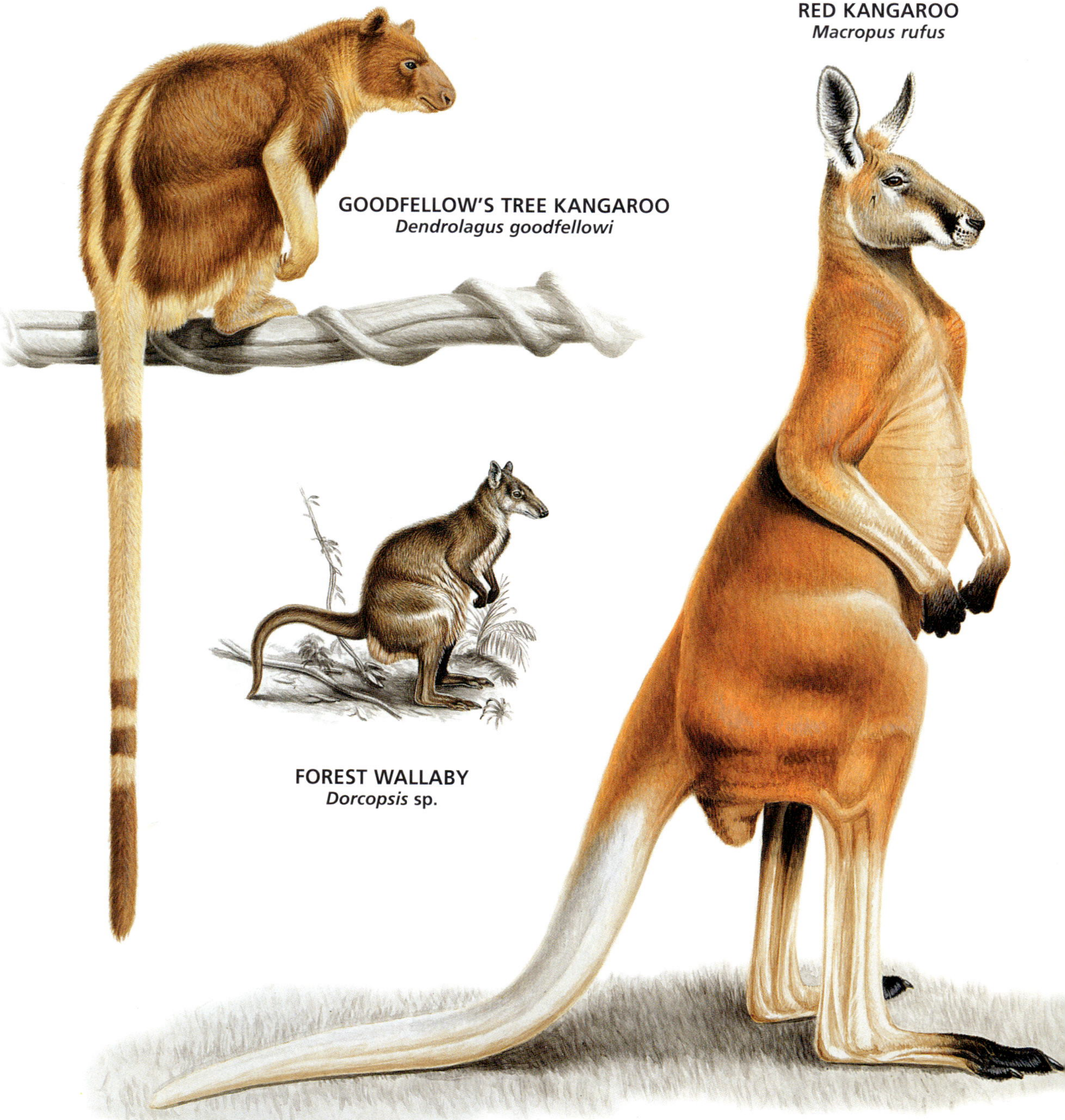

GOODFELLOW'S TREE KANGAROO
Dendrolagus goodfellowi

RED KANGAROO
Macropus rufus

FOREST WALLABY
Dorcopsis sp.

PLATYPUS ANATOMY

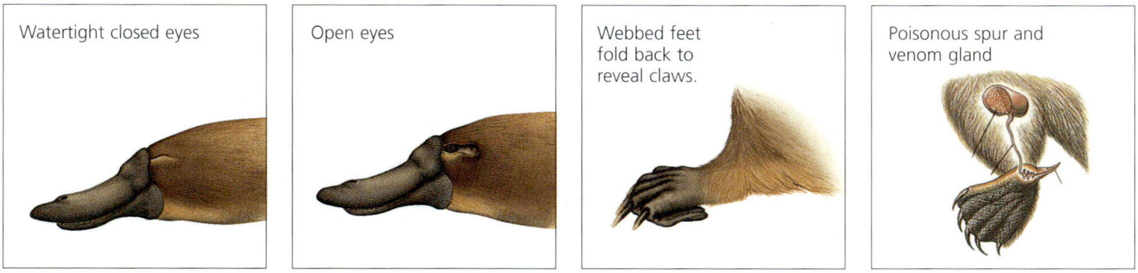

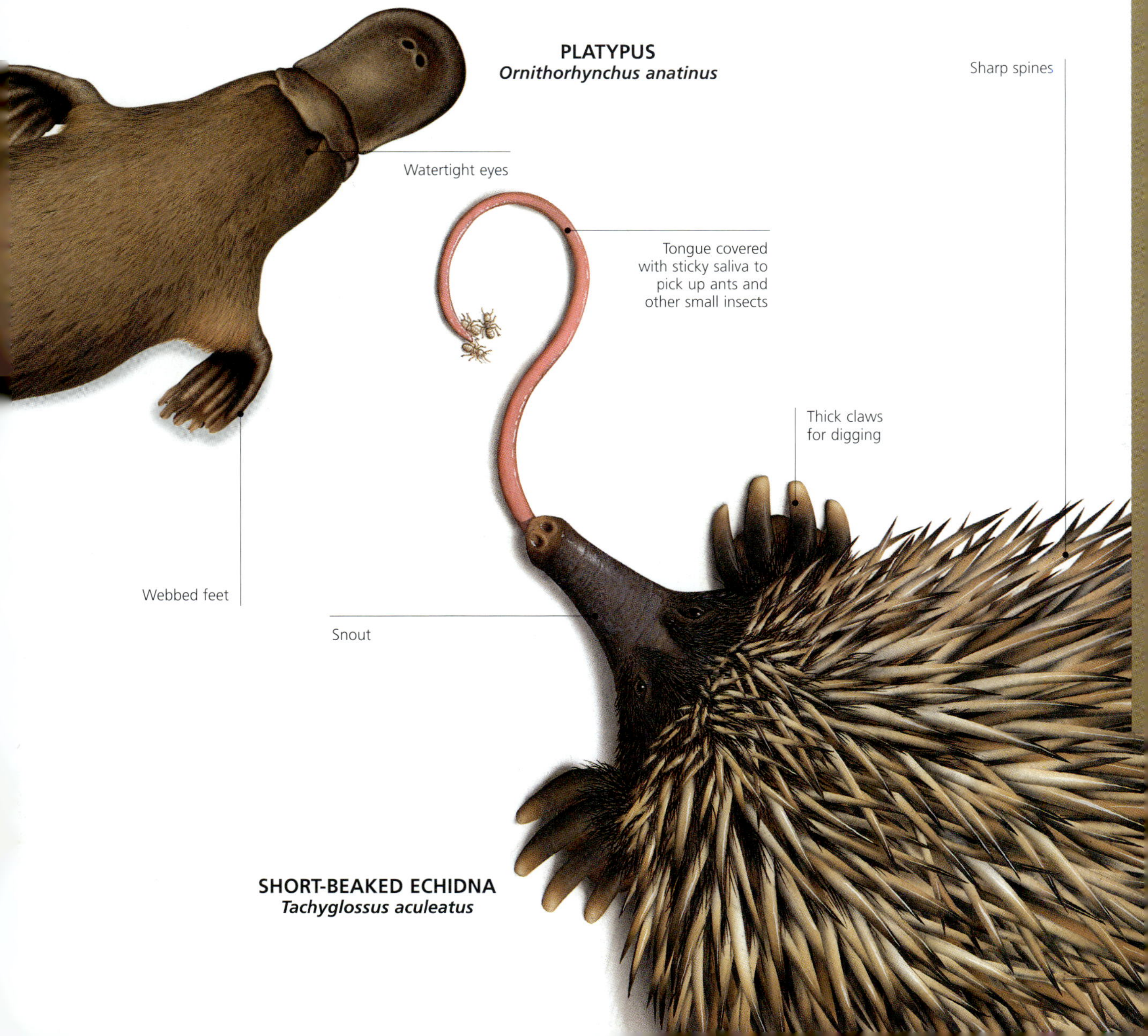

Marsupials

BILBY
Macrotis lagotis

KOALA
Phascolarctos cinereus

SQUIRREL GLIDER
Petaurus norfolcensis

MUSKY RAT-KANGAROO
Hypsiprymnodon moschatus

NUMBAT
Myrmecobius fasciatus

COMMON SPOTTED CUSCUS
Spilocuscus maculatus

WOOLLY OPOSSUM
Caluromys sp.

SPOTTED-TAILED QUOLL
Dasyurus maculatus

WATER OPOSSUM
Chironectes minimus

STRIPED POSSUM
Dactylopsila trivirgata

Insect-eating Mammals

GREATER MOONRAT
Echinosorex gymnura

PYRENEAN DESMAN
Galemys pyranaicus

PANGOLIN
Manis sp.

NOSE VARIETIES

Algerian hedgehog

European mole

African aardvark

Pyreanean desman

THREE-BANDED ARMADILLO
Tolypeutes tricinctus

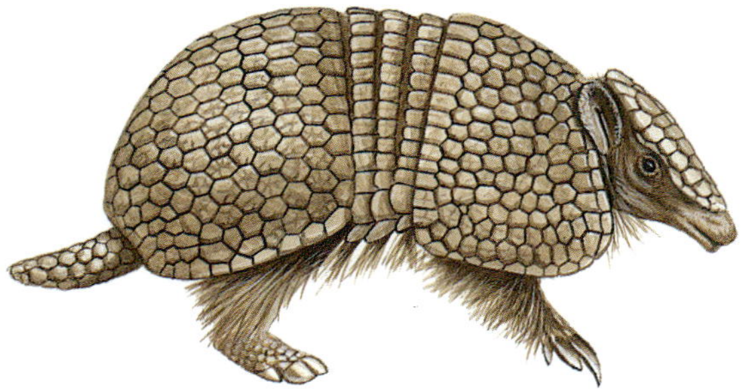

To defend itself from predators the three-banded armadillo rolls into a tight ball using its thick bony plating like armor

TAMANDUA
***Tamandua* sp.**

Bats

LONG-EARED BAT
Family *Vespertilionidae*

ORANGE HORSESHOE BAT
Rhinonicteris aurantius

TENT-BUILDING BAT
Uroderma bilobatum

SWORD-NOSED BAT
Lonchorhina sp.

GAMBIAN EPAULETTED FRUIT BAT
Epomorphorus gambianus

LESSER BARE-BACKED FRUIT BAT
Dobsonia minor

COMMON VAMPIRE BAT
Desmodus rotundus

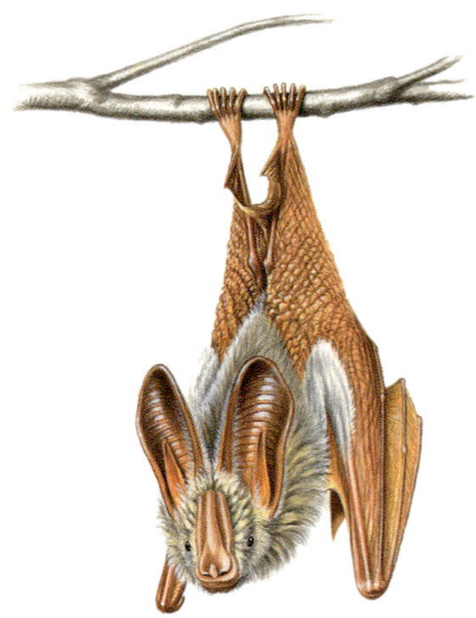

AFRICAN YELLOW-WINGED
FALSE VAMPIRE BAT
Lavia frons

HAMMER-HEADED FRUIT BAT
Hypisgnathus monstrosus

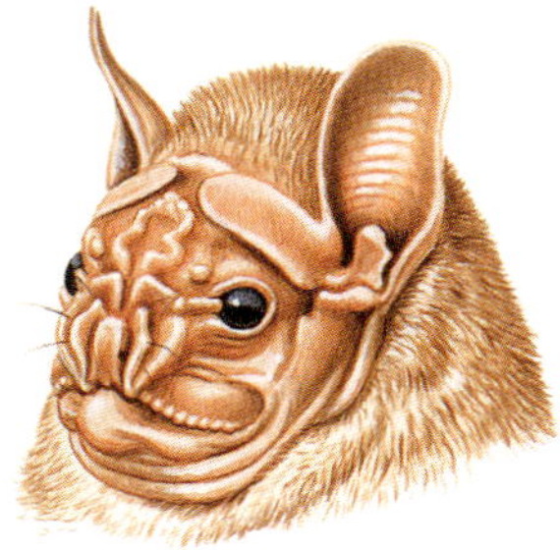

WRINKLE-FACED BAT
Centurio senex

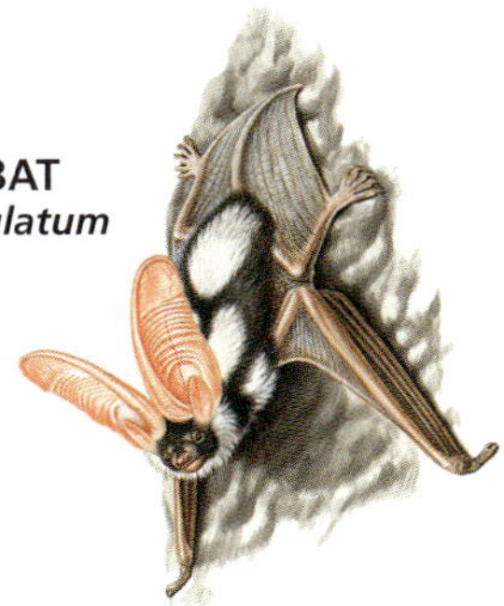

SPOTTED BAT
Euderma maculatum

ECHOLOCATION

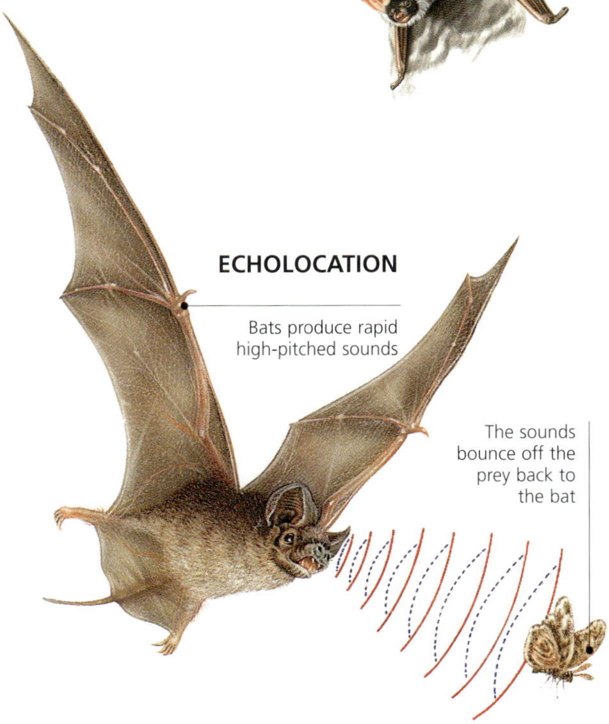

GRAY-HEADED FLYING FOX
Pteropus poliocephalus

Primates

GRAY MOUSE LEMUR
Microcebus murinus

LAR GIBBON
Hylobates lar

PRIMATE FEET AND HANDS

Indri foot and hand

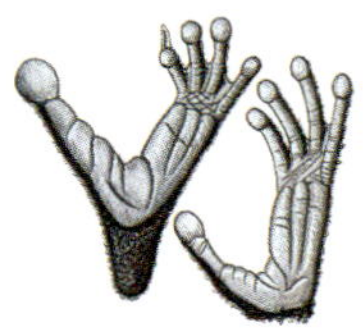

Aye-aye foot and hand

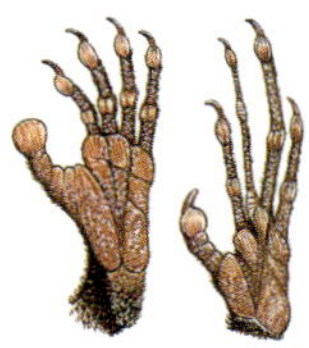

Tarsier foot and hand

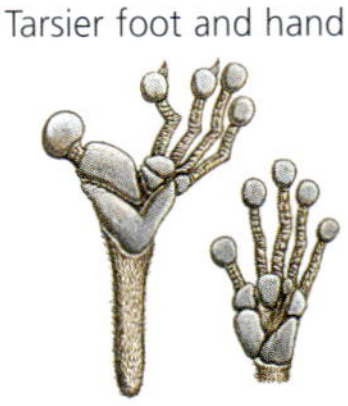

Gorilla foot and hand

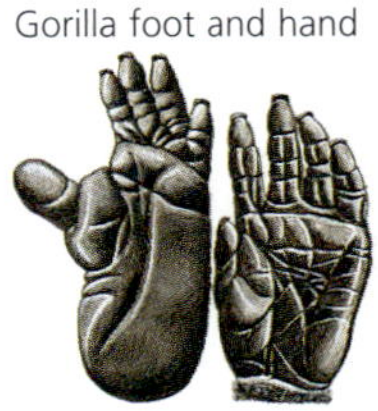

RED RUFFED LEMUR
Varecia variegata rubra

GOLDEN POTTO
Arctocebus aureus

BRACHIATION
The orang-utan (*Pongo pygmaeus*) moves through the trees primarily via brachiation—swinging hand over hand from branch to branch.

PHILIPPINES TARSIER
Tarsius syrichta

INDRI
Indri indri

AYE-AYE
Daubentonia madagascariensis

Old World Monkeys

Old World monkeys
Monkeys from Africa and Asia have prominent noses with narrow nostrils that face forward.

BLACK AND WHITE COLOBUS
Colobus guereza

CELEBES MACAQUE
Macaca nigra

DUSKY LEAF MONKEY
Trachypithecus obscurus

MANDRILL
Mandrillus sphinx

DIANA GUENON
Cercopithecus diana

GELADA
Theropithecus gelada

PROBOSCIS MONKEY
Nasalis larvatus

GOLDEN SNUB-NOSED MONKEY
Rhinopithecus roxellana

New World Monkeys

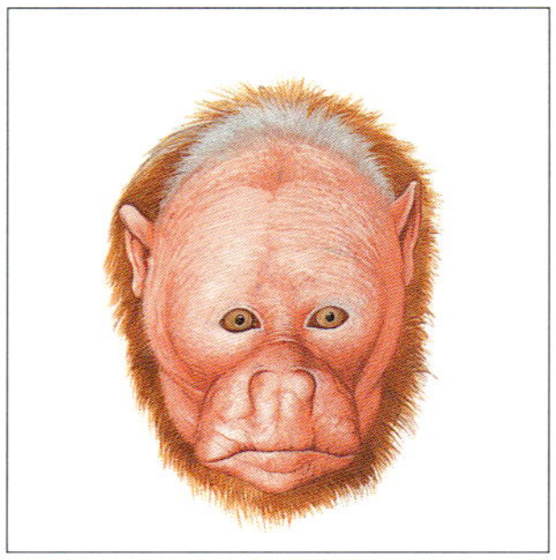

New World monkeys
Monkeys from Central and South America have flattened noses with nostrils that face sideways.

NIGHT MONKEY
Aotus trivirgatus

BLACK HOWLER MONKEY
Alouatta caraya

RED UAKARI
Cacajao calvus

RED HOWLER MONKEY
Aloutta seniculus

SPIDER MONKEYS
Family *Cebidae*

SOUTH AMERICAN SPIDER MONKEYS
Aletes sp.

Dogs

TAIL COMMUNICATION

RED WOLF
Canis rufus

RACOON DOG
Nyctereutes procyonoides

MANED WOLF
Chrysocyon brachyurus

COYOTE
Canis latrans

BUSH DOG
Speothos venaticus

BAT-EARED FOX
Octocyon megalotis

AFRICAN HUNTING DOG
Lycaon pictus

GRAY FOX
Urocyon cinereoargenteus

COYOTE FACIAL EXPRESSIONS

Attacking

Defending

Submissive

Playful

Friendly

Cat Characteristics

CAT SKELETON

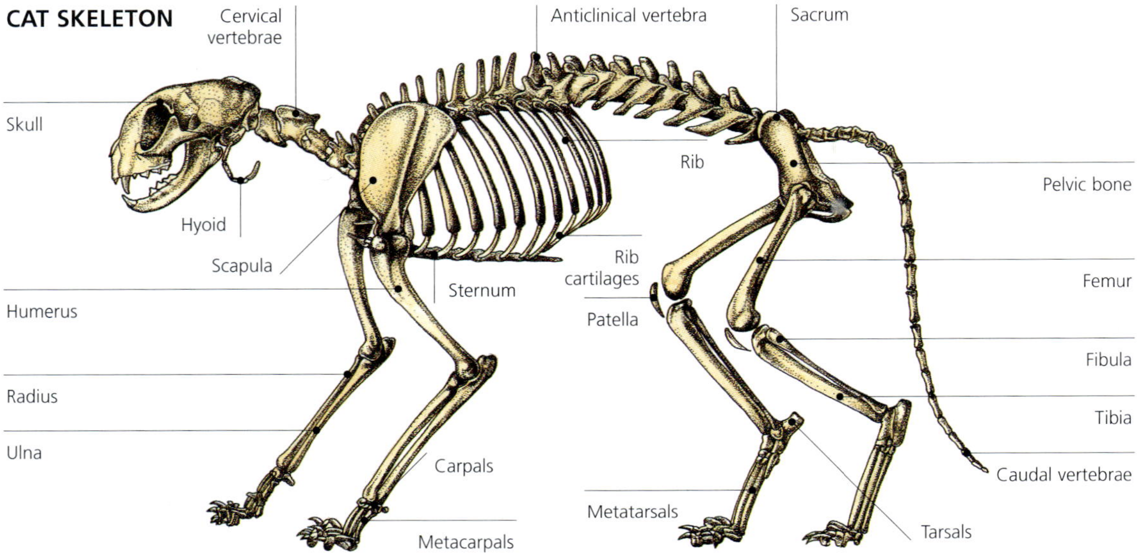

CAT CLAWS

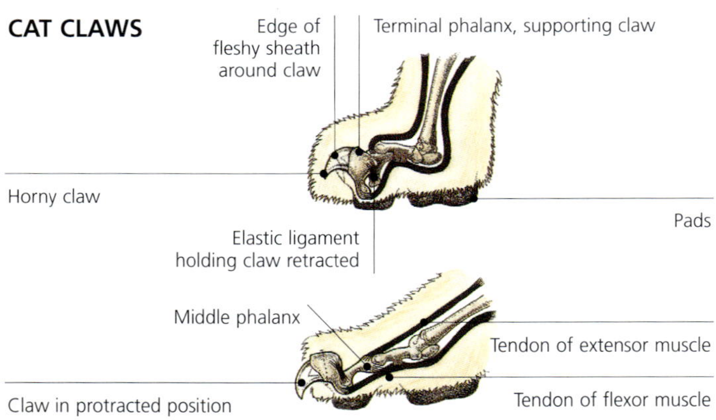

FACIAL EXPRESSIONS

Attacking

Defending

LEOPARD
Panthera pardus

SNOW LEOPARD
Panthera uncia

PUMA
Felis concolor

FASTEST ANIMAL

Cheetahs are the fastest land animal. They reach speeds of 70 miles (110 km) per hour. The cheetah's long tail acts as a rudder.

CHEETAH
Acinonyx jubatus

Great Cats

BOBCAT
Lynx rufus

NORTH AMERICAN LYNX
Lynx canadensis

CARACAL
Lynx caracal

EURASIAN LYNX
Lynx lynx

JAGUAR
Panthera onca

SPANISH LYNX
Lynx pardinus

TIGER
Panthera tigris

LION
Panthera leo

CLOUDED LEOPARD
Neofelis nebulosa

Small Cats

FISHING CAT
Felis viverrina

SERVAL
Felis serval

ASIAN GOLDEN CAT
Felis temminckii

MARGAY
Felis wiedii

ONCILLA
Felis tigrina

LEOPARD CAT
Felis bengalensis

PALLAS' CAT
Felis manul

WILD CAT
Felis silvestris

JUNGLE CAT
Felis chaus

AFRICAN GOLDEN CAT
Felis aurata

KODKOD
Felis guigna

OCELOT
Felis pardalis

ANDEAN MOUNTAIN CAT
Felis jacobita

GEOFFROY'S CAT
Felis geoffroyi

BLACK-FOOTED CAT
Felis nigripes

CHINESE DESERT CAT
Felis bieti

SAND CAT
Felis margarita

Bears

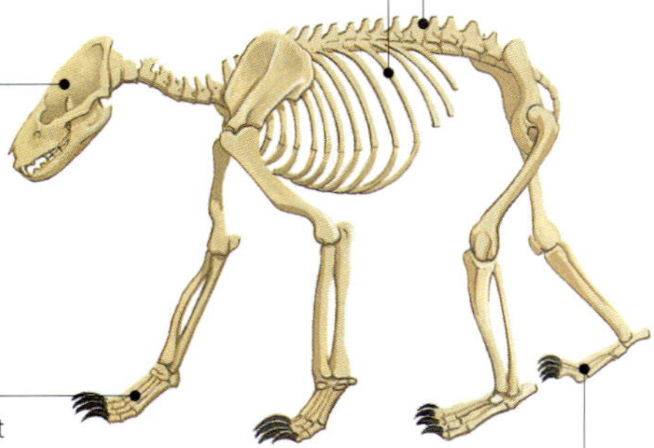

BEAR POSTURE

The skeleton of this brown bear shows its posture when standing on all four feet. The bear's hindfeet are flat to the ground and the forefeet are partly flat to ground.

CLAW SKELETONS

Brown bear

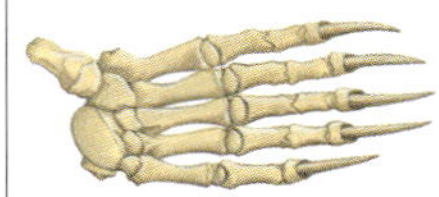

Giant panda

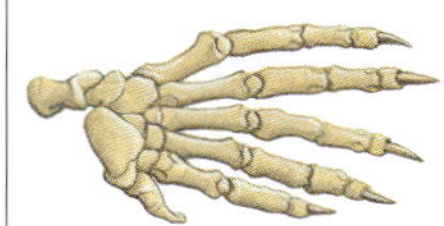

BEAR SIZES

BROWN BEAR
Ursus arctos

BEAR FEET

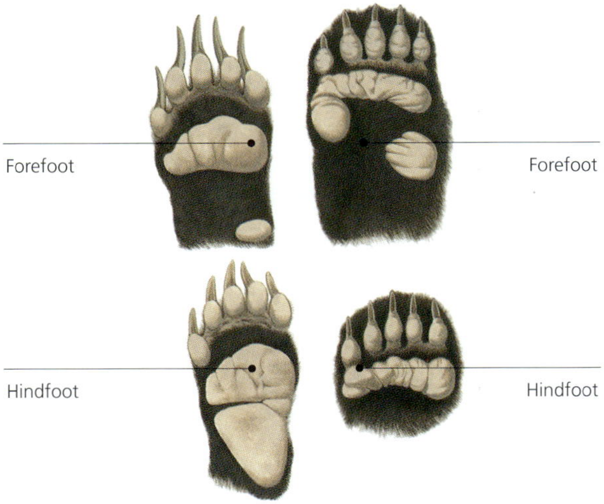

American black bear
(Ursus americanus)

Giant panda
(Ailuropoda melanoleuca)

ASIATIC BLACK BEAR
Ursus thibetanus

SUN BEAR
Ursus malayanus

SLOTH BEAR
Ursus ursinus

Bears

TREE CLIMBERS
American black bears are excellent tree climbers and often sleep in tree-tops.

GIANT PANDA
Ailuropoda melanoleuca

SPECTACLED BEAR
Tremarctos ornatus

Cinnamon color

Black color

AMERICAN BLACK BEAR
Ursus americanus

RED PANDA
Ailurus fulgens

POLAR BEAR
Ursus maritimus

Whales, Dolphins and Porpoises

WHALE TAILS

Humpback whale

Blue whale

Southern right whale

Gray whale

DOLPHIN ANATOMY

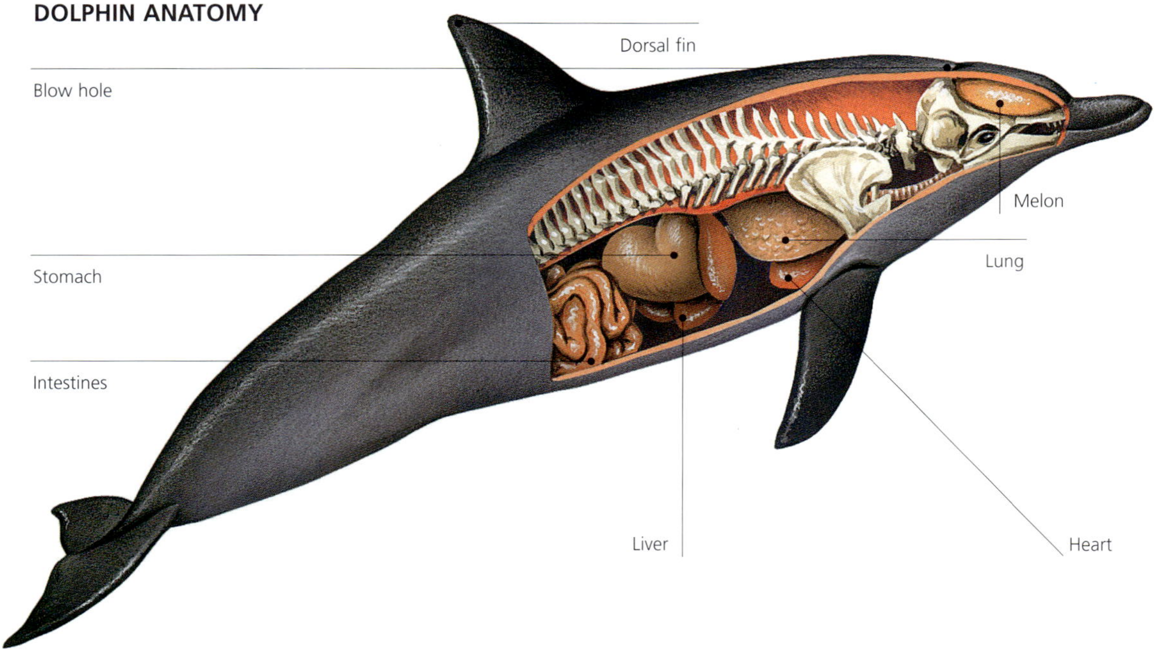

HEAD TYPES

Minke whale

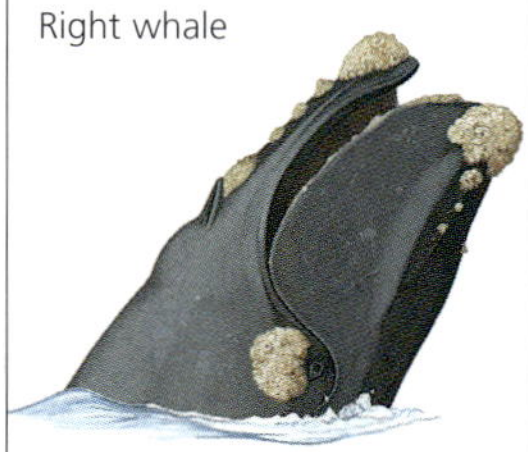
Right whale

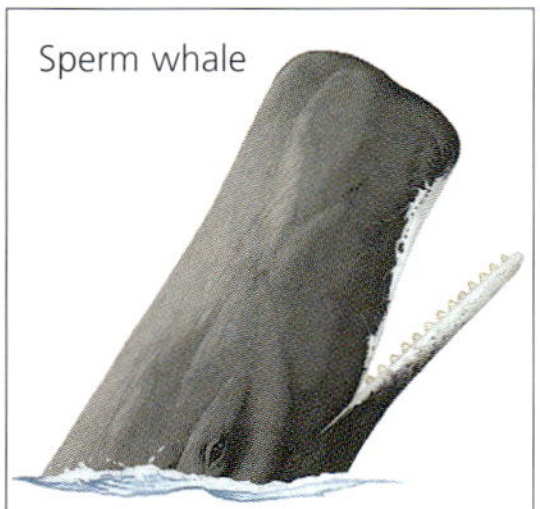
Sperm whale

Bottlenose dolphin

BALEEN WHALE
Pygmy right whale (*Caperea marginata*)

TOOTHED WHALE
Atlantic white-sided dolphin (*Lagenorhynchus acutus*)

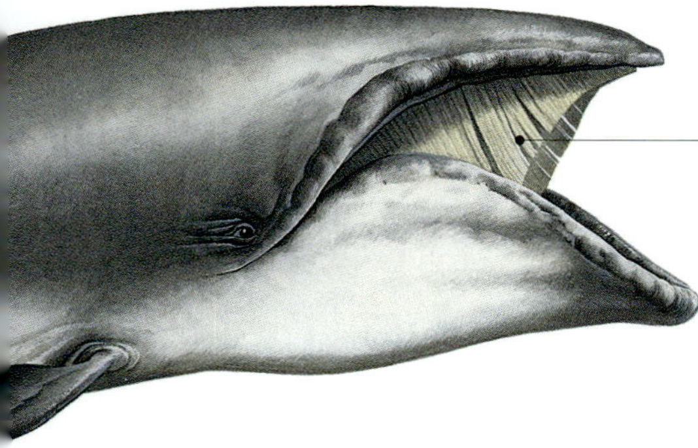

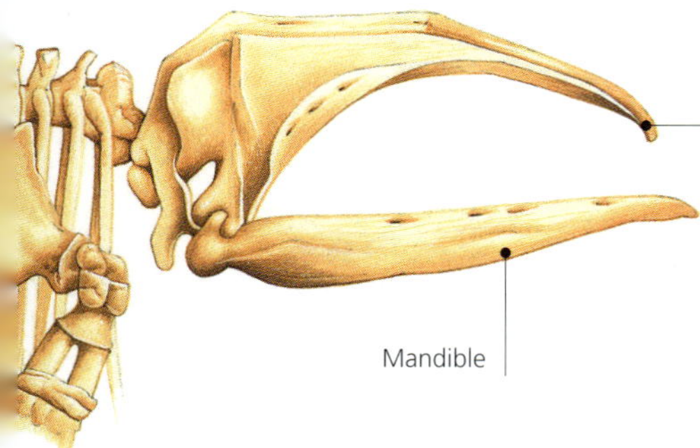

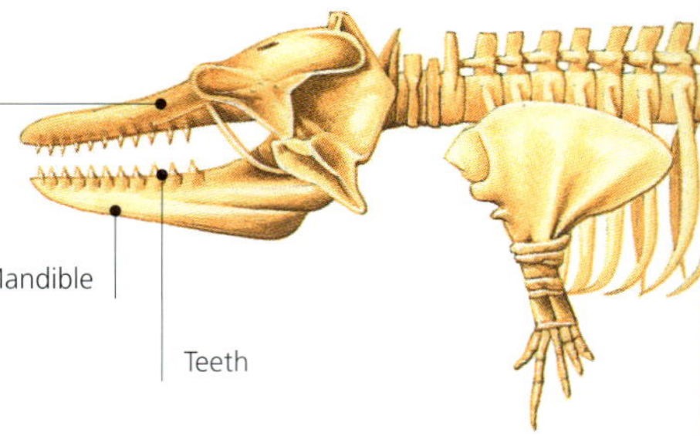

DIFFERENCES BETWEEN BALEEN AND TOOTHED WHALES

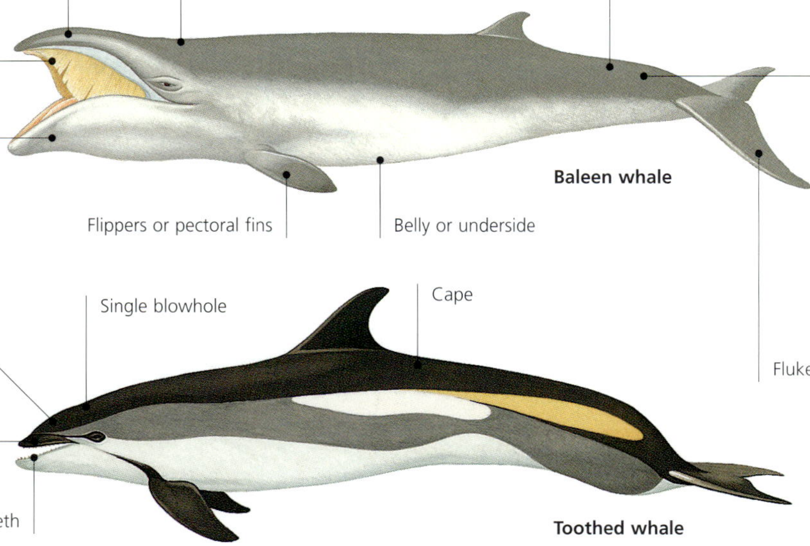

Whales, Dolphins and Porpoises

SPERM WHALE
Physeter macrocephalus

Newborn

6 to 10 years old

18 to 19 years old

27 years old

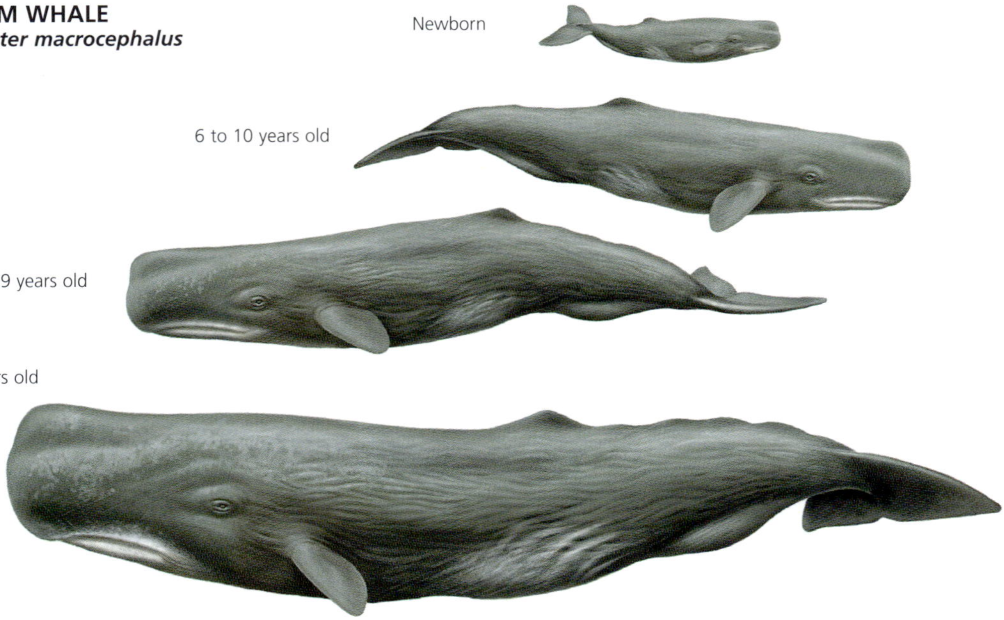

GROUP DEFENSE
Sperm whales form a circle around calves or injured adults to protect them from attack from predators such as these orcas.

NARWHAL
Monodon monoceros

NORTHERN RIGHT WHALE
Eubalaena glacialis

MINKE WHALE
Balaenoptera acutorostrata

DIVE SEQUENCES

Minke whale

Humpback whale

Southern right whale

Sperm whale

HUMPBACK WHALE
Megaptera novaeangliae

BOWHEAD WHALE
Balaena mysticetus

Whales, Dolphins and Porpoises

ENDANGERED SPECIES

Vaquita
Phocoena sinus

Indus River dolphin
Platanista minor

Baiji
Lipotes vexillifer

FINLESS PORPOISE
Neophocaena phocaenoides

HARBOR PORPOISE
Phocoena phocoena

TOOTH VARIATIONS

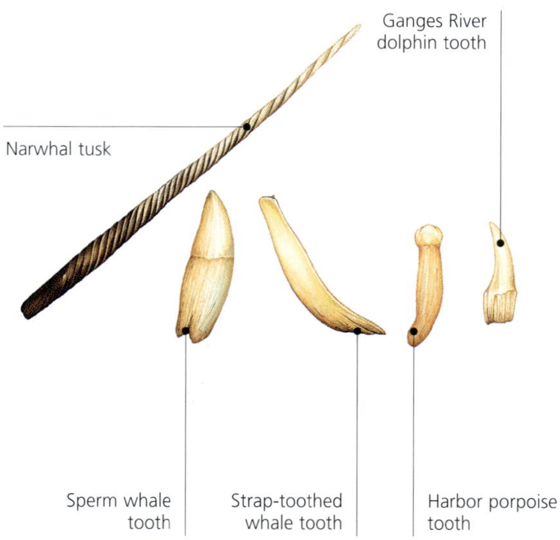

SOUND PRODUCTION

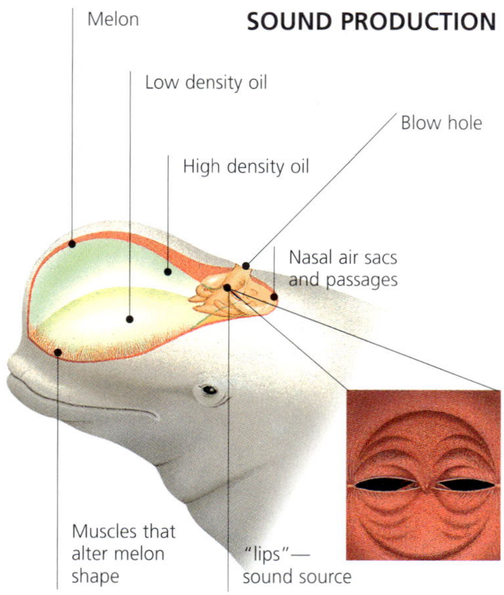

DALL'S PORPOISE
Phocoenoides dalli

ORCA
Orcinus orca

DOLPHIN PROPULSION

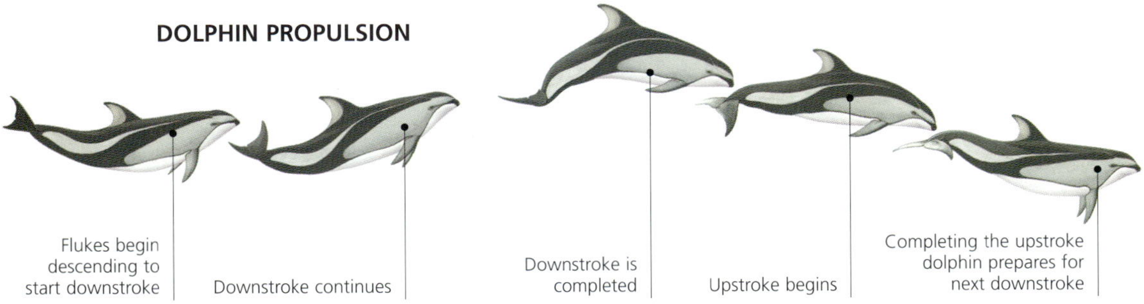

PACIFIC WHITE-SIDED DOLPHIN
Lagenorhynchus obliquidens

Elephants

FOREST AFRICAN ELEPHANT
Loxodonta cyclotis

MAINLAND ASIAN ELEPHANT
Elephas maximus indicus

SUMATRAN ASIAN ELEPHANT
Elephas maximus sumatranus

SRI LANKAN ASIAN ELEPHANT
Elephas maximus maximus

AFRICAN AND ASIAN ELEPHANT DIFFERENCES

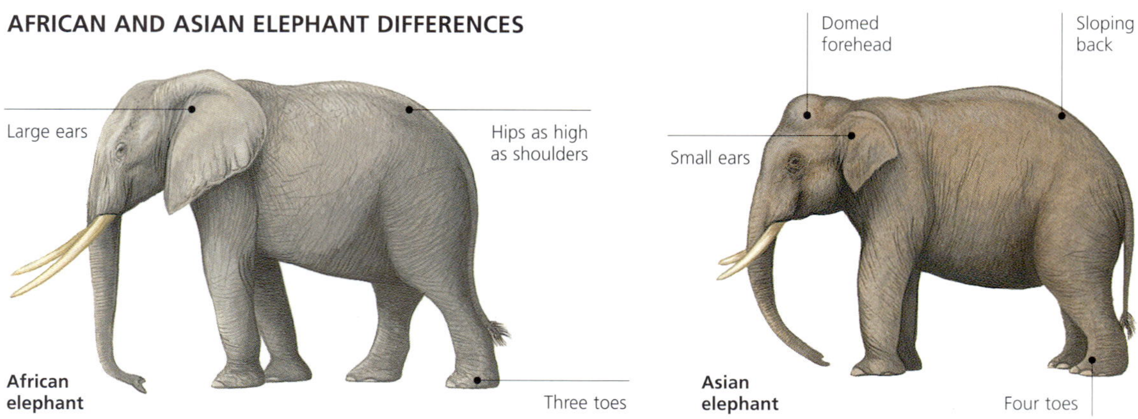

ELEPHANT TUSK

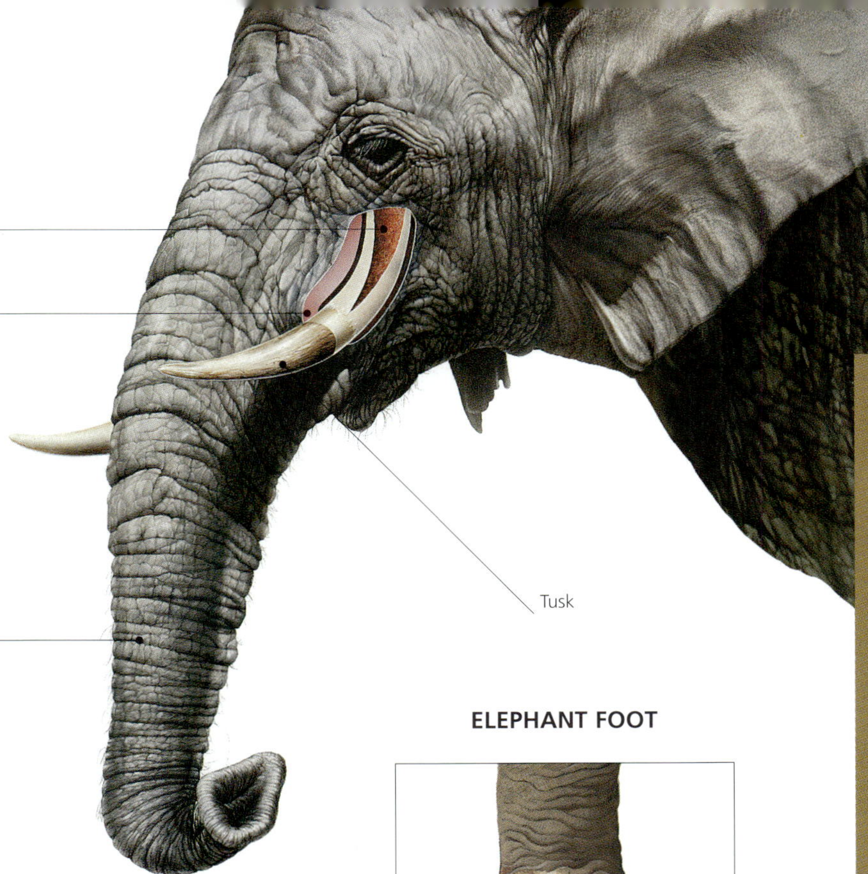

ELEPHANT FOOT

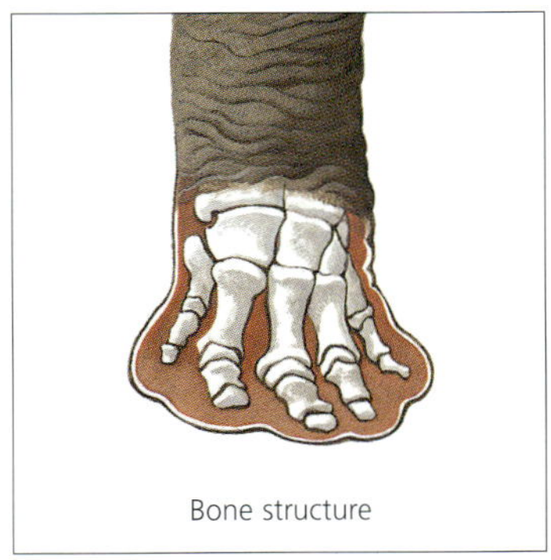

BUSH AFRICAN ELEPHANT
Loxodonta africana

Hoofed Mammals

DROMEDARY CAMEL
Camelus dromedarius

ZEBRA
Equus burchelli

WHITE RHINOCEROS
Ceratotherium simum

BLACK RHINOCEROS
Diceros bicornis

GAUR
Bos gaurus

MOUNTAIN ANOA
Bubalus quarlesi

BARBARY SHEEP
Ammotragus lervia

BIGHORN SHEEP
Ovis canadensis

HIMALAYAN TAHR
Hemitragus jemlahicus

MUSK OX
Ovibos moschatus

WILD GOAT
Capra aegragus

Deer, Gazelles and Antelopes

GROWING ANTLERS

BLUE WILDEBEEST
Connochaetes taurinus

WAPITI
Cervus elaphus

MOOSE
Alces alces

FOUR-HORNED ANTELOPE
Tetracerus quadricornus

GERENUK
Litocranius walleri

INDIAN ANTELOPE
Antilope cervicapra

BONTEBOK
Damaliscus dorcas

FALLOW DEER
Dama dama

THOMPSON'S GAZELLE
Gazella thompsonii

PUDU
Pudu puda

BANDED DUIKER
Cephalophus zebra

BONGO
Tragelaphus euryceros

SAIGA
Saiga tatarica

INDIAN MUNTJAC
Muntiacus muntjac

KLIPSPRINGER
Oreotragus oreotragus

REINDEER
Rangifer tarandus

GEMSBOK
Oryx gazella

GIANT SABLE ANTELOPE
Hippotragus niger variani

Rodents

GERBIL
Family *Muridae*

GIANT BLACK SQUIRREL
Ratufa bicolor

SOUTHERN FLYING SQUIRREL
Glaucomys volans

LEAST CHIPMUNK
Tamias minimus

COLUMBIAN GROUND SQUIRREL
Spermophilus columbianus

HOARY MARMOT
Marmota caligata

CAPYBARA
Hydrochaerus hydrochaeris

PATAGONIAN MARA
Dolichotis patagonum

CRESTED PORCUPINE
Hystrix cristata

GOLDEN AGOUTI
Dasyprocta leporina

PLAINS VISCACHA
Lagostomus maximus

EURASIAN RED SQUIRREL
Sciurus vulgaris

BLACK RAT
Rattus rattus

PREHENSILE-TAILED PORCUPINE
Coendou prehensilis

SPINY RAT
Proechimys sp.

Turtle and Tortoise Anatomy

TORTOISE SKELETON

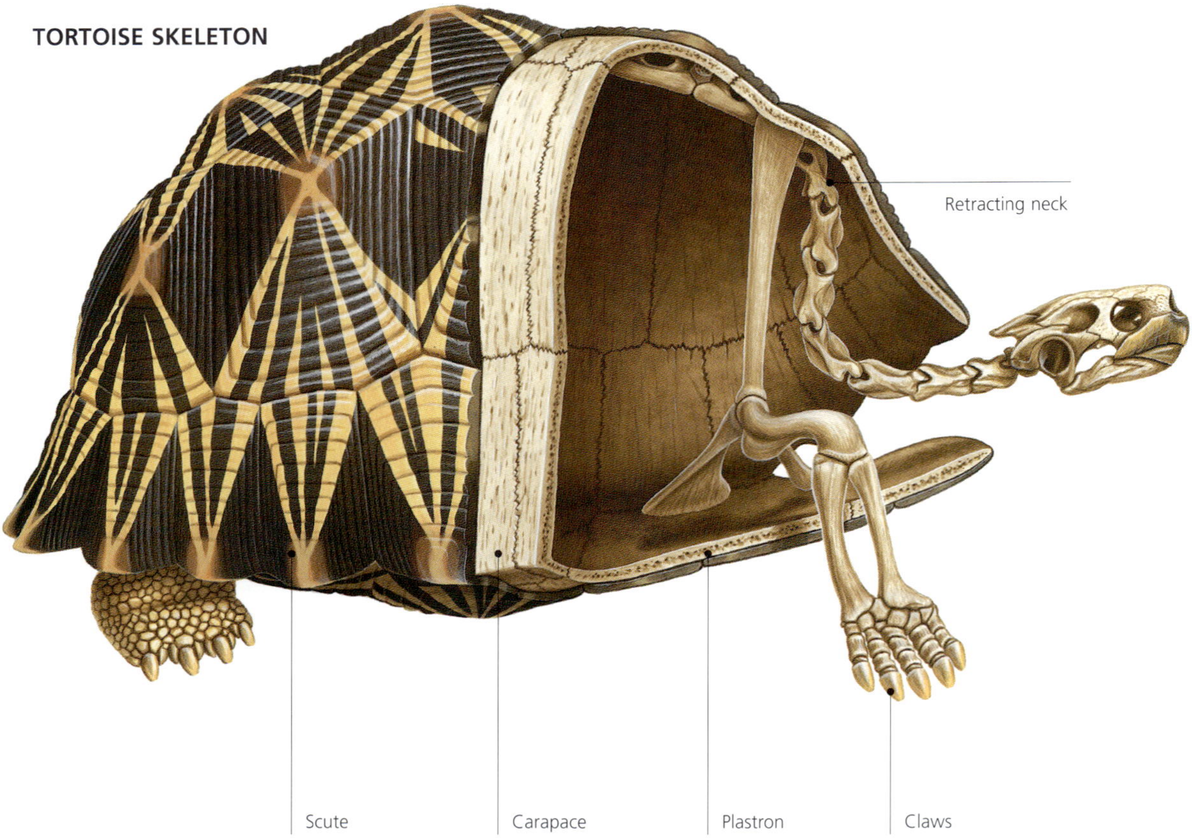

LEG TYPES

Sea turtle

Land tortoise

Pond turtle

MUSK TURTLE
Sternotherus odoratus

Musk turtles produce a strong, unpleasant smell when picked up

ORNATE BOX TURTLE
Terrapene ornata

The box turtle pulls its legs and head inside its shell for protection

LOGGERHEAD SEA TURTLE
Caretta caretta

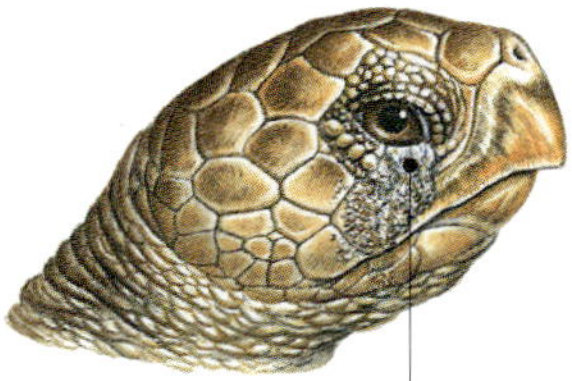

Sea turtles "cry" to remove salt from their eyes

LAND TORTOISE SHELL
Domed shell, slow moving

SEMI-TERRESTRIAL TURTLE SHELL
Flattened shell for land and water

SEA TURTLE SHELL
Streamlined shell for swimming

POND TURTLE SHELL
Small flattened shell

Turtles and Tortoises

GREEN TURTLE
Chelonia mydas

TURTLE'S CARAPACE

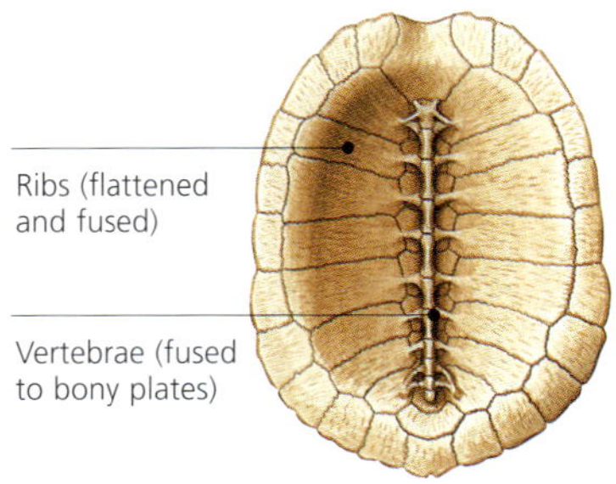

View from below

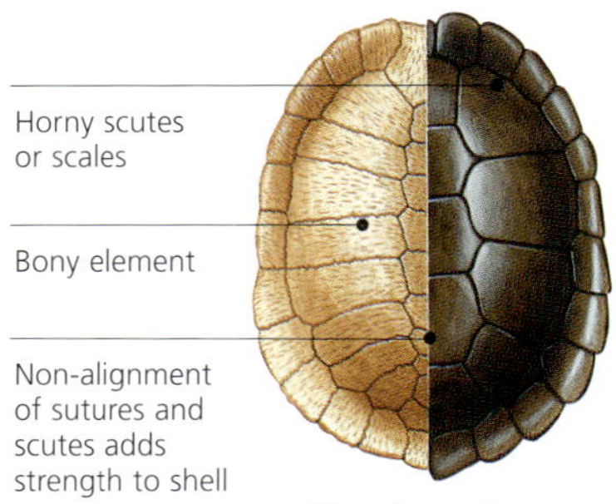

View from above

EASTERN SPINY SOFTSHELL TURTLE
Apalone spinifera spinifera

SEA TURTLE
Family *Cheloniidae*

TURTLE REPRODUCTION
Female green turtles (*Chelonia mydas*) leave the sea to lay their eggs on specific nesting beaches.

YELLOW-SPOTTED AMAZON RIVER TURTLE
Podocnemis unifilis

TWIST-NECKED TURTLE
Platemys platycephala platycephala

PACIFIC HAWKSBILL TURTLE
Eretmochelys imbricata bissa

SOUTHERN LOGGERHEAD MUSK TURTLE
Sternotherus minor minor

EASTERN BOX TURTLE
Terrapene carolina carolina

PANCAKE TORTOISE
Malacochersus tornieri

VIETNAMESE BIG-HEADED TURTLE
Platysternon megacephalum shiui

PAINTED TURTLE
Chrysemys picta belli

DESERT TORTOISE
Gopherus agassizii

RADIATED TORTOISE
Asterochelys radiata

MALAYAN SNAIL-EATING TURTLE
Malayemys subtrijuga

SPINED TURTLE
Heosemys spinosa

Crocodiles and Alligators

FLOTATION
Crocodiles and alligators have buoyant bodies and can conserve energy by floating in water.

FALSE GHARIAL
Tomistoma schlegelii

CUVIER'S DWARF CAIMAN
Paleosuchus palpebrosus

SNOUT VARIETIES

American crocodile, side view

American crocodile, top view

Gharial, side view

Gharial, top view

Black caiman, side view

Black caiman, top view

AQUATIC ADAPTATIONS

Crocodiles and alligators can breathe while almost totally submerged as they have nostrils on the top of their snouts that remain above the water.

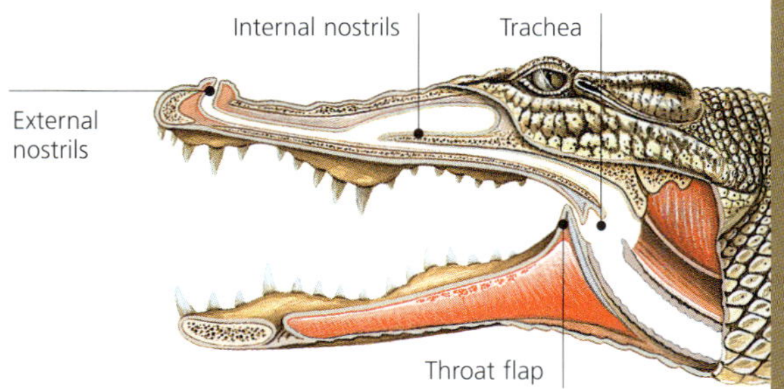

GHARIAL ANATOMY

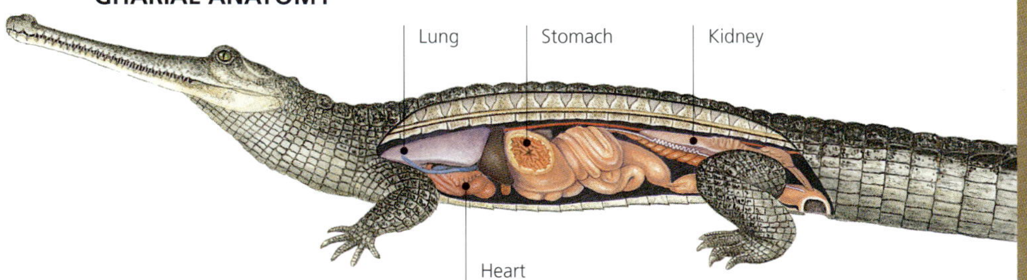

NILE CROCODILE

Crocodylus niloticus

Amphisbaenians and Tuataras

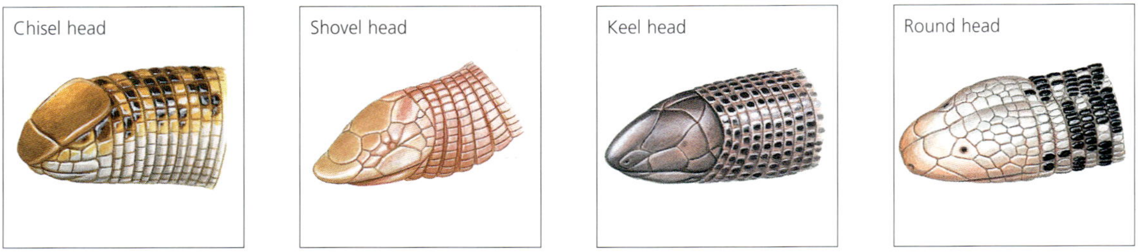

AMPHISBAENIAN HEAD TYPES

SHOVEL-SNOUTED WORM LIZARD
Family *Amphisbaenidae*

KEEL-SNOUTED WORM LIZARD
Keel-snouted worm lizards occur in South America and Africa.

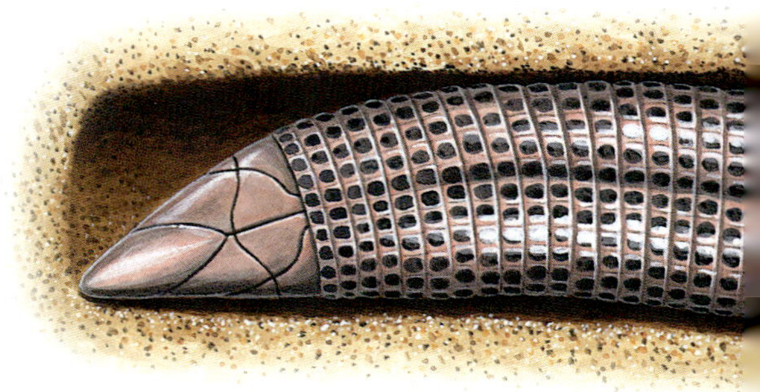

SHOVEL-SNOUTED WORM LIZARD
This worm lizard grows up to 30 inches (75 cm) long. It uses its hard head to push soil upwards and compact it into the top of the tunnel.

TUATARA

***Sphenodon* sp.**

These ancient reptiles are found only in New Zealand.

NIGHT HUNTERS

Tuataras spend the day sleeping or basking in the sun at the entrance to their burrows. They hunt insects and other prey at night.

Female tuataras weigh about half as much as males and are about 6 inches (15 cm) shorter

GENDER DIFFERENCES

Male tuataras weigh up to 2.2 pounds (1 kg) and can grow up to 2 feet (60 cm) long

Male tuataras have larger spines on their necks and backs

Iguanas, Chameleons and Agamids

CUBAN BROWN ANOLE
Anolis sagrei sagrei

BASILISK LIZARD
Basiliscus basiliscus

FIJIAN CRESTED IGUANA
Brachylophus vitiensis

COLLARED LIZARD
Croptaphytus collaris

BEARDED DRAGON LIZARD
Family *Agamidae*

MILITARY DRAGON
Ctenophorus isolepis gularis

MALAGASY CHAMELEON
Furcifer lateralis

FRILL-NECKED LIZARD
Chlamydosaurus kingii

KNYSNA DWARF CHAMELEON
Bradypodion damaranum

SAIL-TAILED WATER LIZARD
Hydrosaurus ambionensis

CHAMELEON TAIL

TREE DRAGON
Diporiphora superba

MARINE IGUANA
Amblyrhynchus cristatus

Geckos

FLYING GECKO
The flying gecko of Southeast Asia (*Ptychozoon* sp.) has flaps of skin along its sides, and glides from tree to tree to escape predators.

LEOPARD GECKO
Eublepharis macularius

BLUE-TAILED DAY GECKO
Phelsuma cepediana

SPOTTED VELVET GECKO
Oedura tryoni

GECKO CHARACTERISTICS

Leaf-tailed gecko tail

Desert gecko's foot

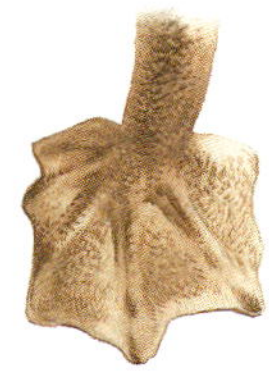

RING-TAILED GECKO
Cyrtodactylus louisiadensis

YELLOW-HEADED GECKO
Gonatodes albogularis fuscus

Lizards

FLAP-FOOTED LIZARD
Delma tincta

GOULD'S MONITOR LIZARD
Varanus gouldii

CHECKERED WHIPTAIL LIZARD
Cnemidophorus tesselatus

GRANITE NIGHT LIZARD
Xantusia henshawi

KOMODO DRAGON
Varanus komodoensis

ITALIAN WALL LIZARD
Podarcis sicula

DWARF FLAT LIZARD
Platysaurus guttatus

JUNGLE RUNNER
Ameiva ameiva

LIZARD TAILS

PERENTIE GOANNA
Varanus giganteus

RED-TAILED SKINK
Morethia ruficauda exquisita

PINK-TONGUED SKINK
Cyclodomorphus gerrardii

FIVE-LINED SKINK
Eumeces fasciatus

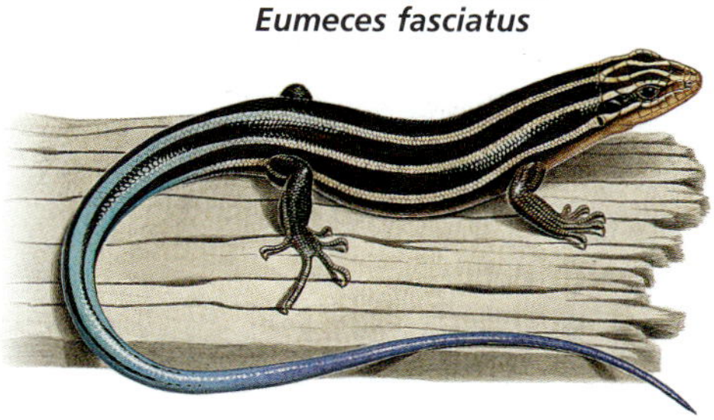

LIZARD SENSES

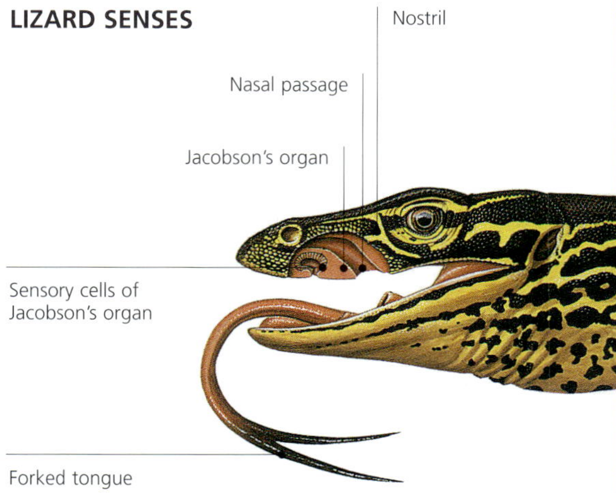

TONGUE TYPES

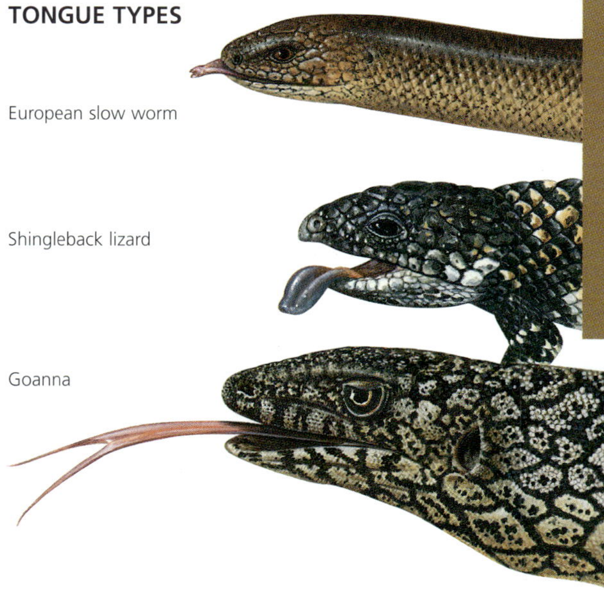

Snake Anatomy

Vine snake

SNAKE SKIN TYPES

Keeled scales

Granular scales

Smooth scales

FANG VARIETIES

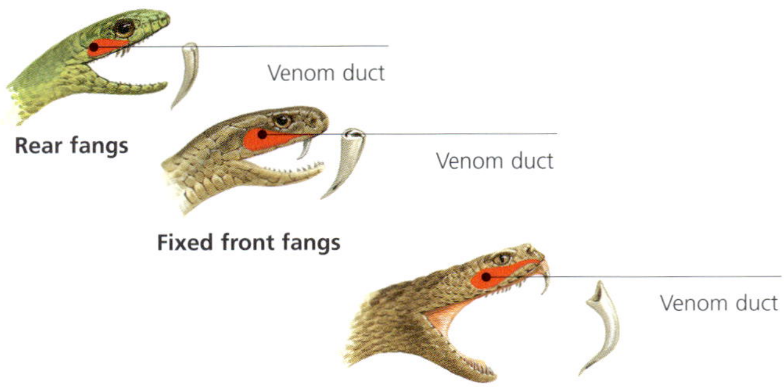

SNAKE EYES

Nocturnal snake

Diurnal snake

RATTLESNAKE ANATOMY

SNAKE HEAD TYPES

SNAKE SIZES

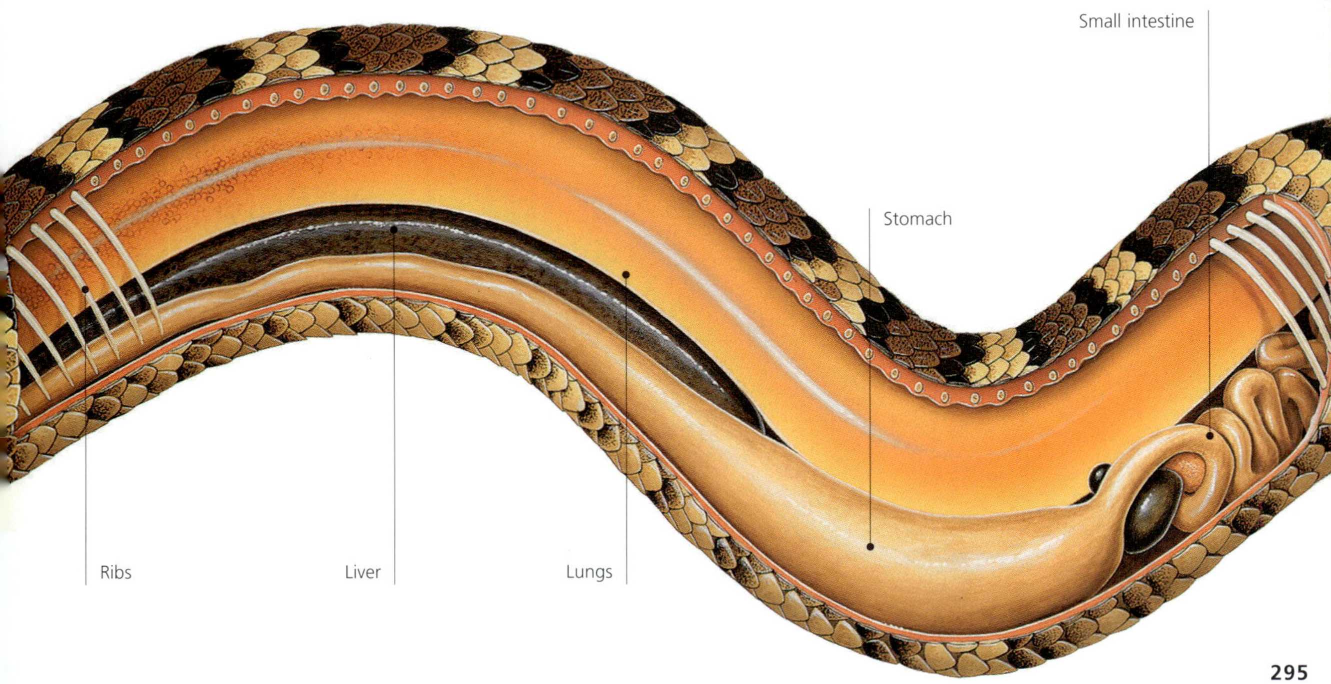

Snakes

LANCE-HEADED RATTLESNAKE
Crotalus polystictus

RHINOCEROS VIPER
Bitis nasicornis

SOUTH AMERICAN CORAL PIPE SNAKE
Anilius scytale

BLOOD PYTHON
Python curtus

BRAZILIAN RAINBOW BOA
Epicrates cenchria cenchria

KENYAN SAND BOA
Eryx colubrinus loveridgei

URUTU
Bothrops alternatus

SPITTING COBRA
Spitting cobras (Family *Elapidae*) spray venom at the eyes of their attackers. They can hit targets nearly 10 feet (3 m) away.

BLUNT-HEADED TREE SNAKE
Imantodes cenchoa

ARIZONA CORAL SNAKE
Micruroides euryxanthus

EASTERN RIBBON SNAKE
Thamnophis sauritus

CARPET PYTHON
Morelia spilota

YELLOW-LIPPED SEA KRAIT
Laticauda colubrina

BLOTCHED PIPE SNAKE
Cylindrophus maculatus

IMITATION COLORS

Some harmless snakes avoid predators by copying the colors and patterns of venomous snakes. The false coral snake imitates the dangerous Mayan coral snake.

SPOTTED HARLEQUIN SNAKE
Homoroselaps lacteus

MANDARIN RATSNAKE
Elaphe mandarina

Salamanders, Newts and Caecilians

CAECILIAN ANATOMY

The caecilian skull is powerfully built with a pointed snout and a recessed mouth, both of which are ideal for burrowing. Caecilians are the only vertebrates with an extra set of jaw-closing muscles.

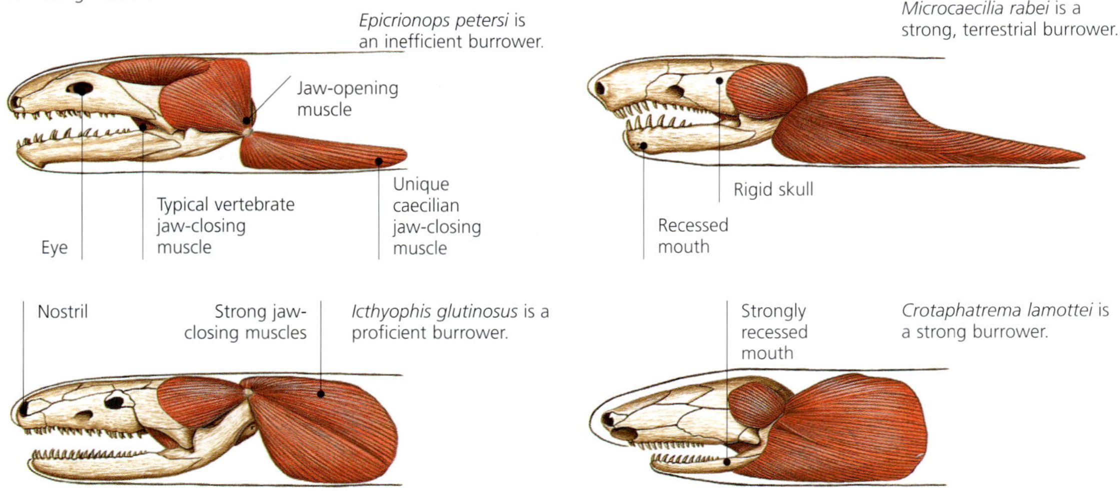

AQUATIC CAECILIAN
Typhlonectes natans

TERRESTRIAL CAECILIAN
Dermophis mexicanus

SOUTHEAST ASIAN CAECILIAN
Ichthyophis kohtaoensis

MARBLED NEWT
Triturus marmoratus

CONGO EEL
Amphiuma means

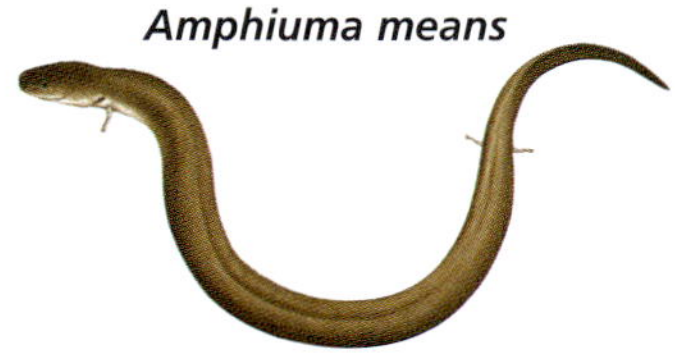

ALPINE NEWT
Triturus alpestris

TWO-LINED SALAMANDER
Eurycea bislineata cirrigera

RED SALAMANDER
Pseudotriton ruber

DWARF SIREN
Pseudobranchus striatus

MUDPUPPY
Necturus maculosus

TIGER SALAMANDER
Ambystoma tigrinum mavortium

PACIFIC GIANT SALAMANDER
Dicamptodon ensatus

LIFECYCLE OF AN AMPHIBIOUS SALAMANDER

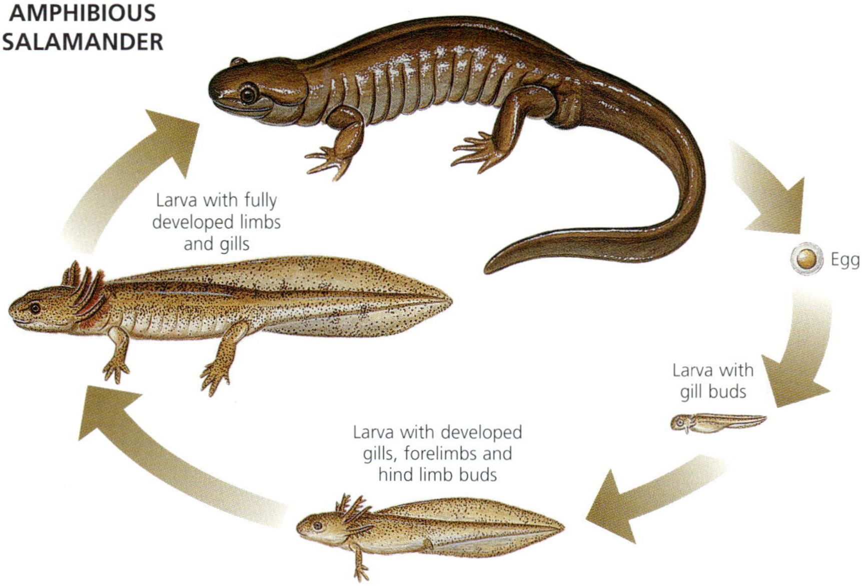

Frogs and Toads

COUCH'S SPADEFOOT
Scaphiopus couchii

MEXICAN BURROWING TOAD
Rhinophrynus dorsalis

SOUTH AMERICAN BULLFROG
Leptodactylus pentadactylus

LIFECYCLE OF A FROG

At six weeks the metamorphosis is complete. The young frog leaves the water and switches from a vegetarian diet to one of mainly insects.

The male clasps the female under the arms and hangs on until she lays the eggs.

On contact with the water, the jelly surrounding the eggs swells. The eggs float in large masses near the surface.

The lungs become functional and the gills disappear after about three weeks. After four weeks the tail begins to shrink as the limbs begin to appear.

The eggs hatch after about two weeks. The tadpoles feed on weeds and algae and breathe through external gills.

ORNATE HORNED TOAD
Ceratophrys ornata

TAILED FROG
Ascaphus truei

WESTERN BARKING FROG
Eleutherodactylus augusti cactorum

EUROPEAN PAINTED FROG
Discoglossus pictus

CAPE CLAWED FROG
Xenopus gilli

ASIAN HORNED TOAD
Megophyrus nasuta

Frogs and Toads

AMPHIBIOUS ANIMAL

Frogs are well suited to life on land and in the water.

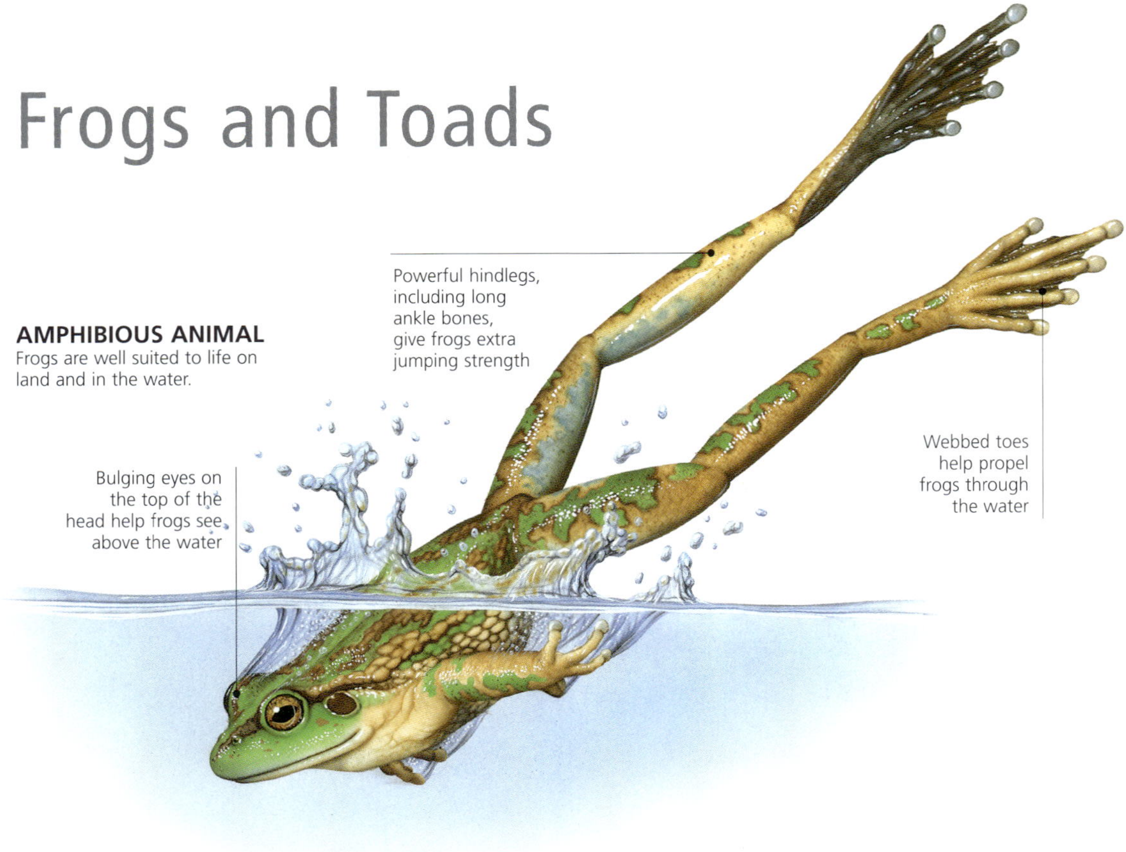

SPOTTED GRASS FROG
Limnodynastes tasmaniensis

CRUCIFIX TOAD
Notaden bennettii

LEOPARD TOAD
Bufo pardalis

CORROBOREE FROG
Pseudophyrne corroboree

BURROWING TREEFROG
Pternohyla fodiens

GREEN AND GOLDEN BELL FROG
Litoria aurea

FUNEREAL POISON FROG
Phyllobates lugubris

ORANGE AND BLACK POISON FROG
Dendrobates leucomelas

VARIABLE HARLEQUIN FROG
Atelopus varius

ASIATIC CLIMBING TOAD
Pedostibes hosii

STRAWBERRY POISON FROG
Dendrobates pumilio

RED-EYED TREEFROG
Agalychnis callidryas

Frogs and Toads

ORNATE BURROWING FROG
Hildebrandtia ornata

PICKEREL FROG
Rana palustris

SOLOMON ISLANDS TREEFROG
Platymantis guppyi

ASIAN PAINTED FROG
Kaloula pulchra

EASTERN NARROW-MOUTHED TOAD
Gastrophryne carolinensis

RED-BANDED CREVICE CREEPER
Phrynomerus bifasciatus

CAPE GHOST FROG
Heleophryne purcelli

PARADOX FROG
Pseudis paradoxa

DARWIN'S FROG
Rhinoderma darwinii

WALLACE'S FLYING FROG
Racophorus nigropalmatus

GOLD FROG
Brachycephalus ephippium

PAINTED REED FROG
Hyperolius marmoratus

SENEGAL RUNNING FROG
Kassina senegalensis

Shark Anatomy

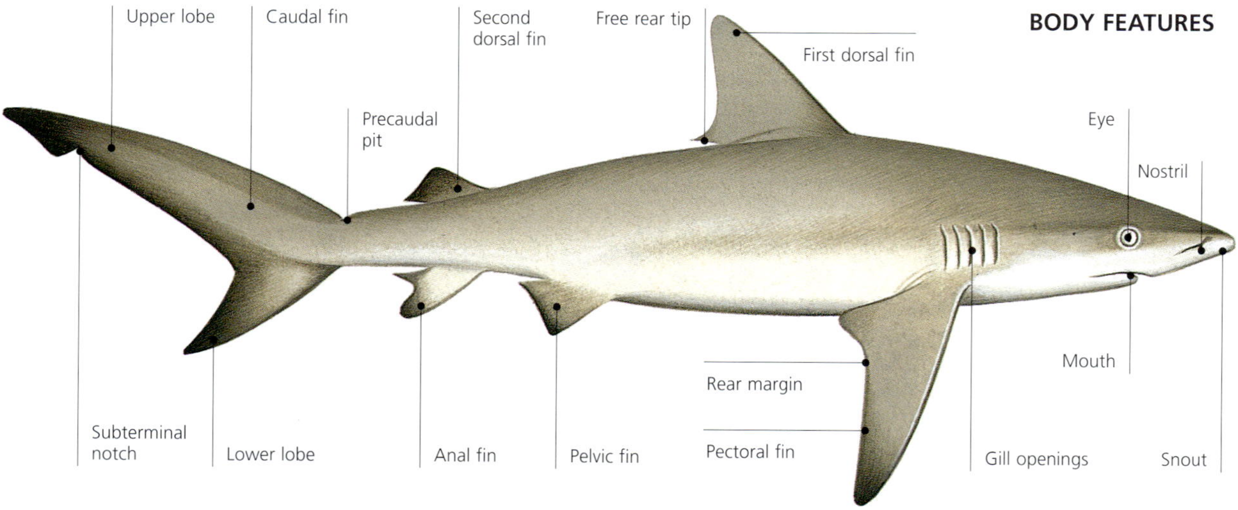

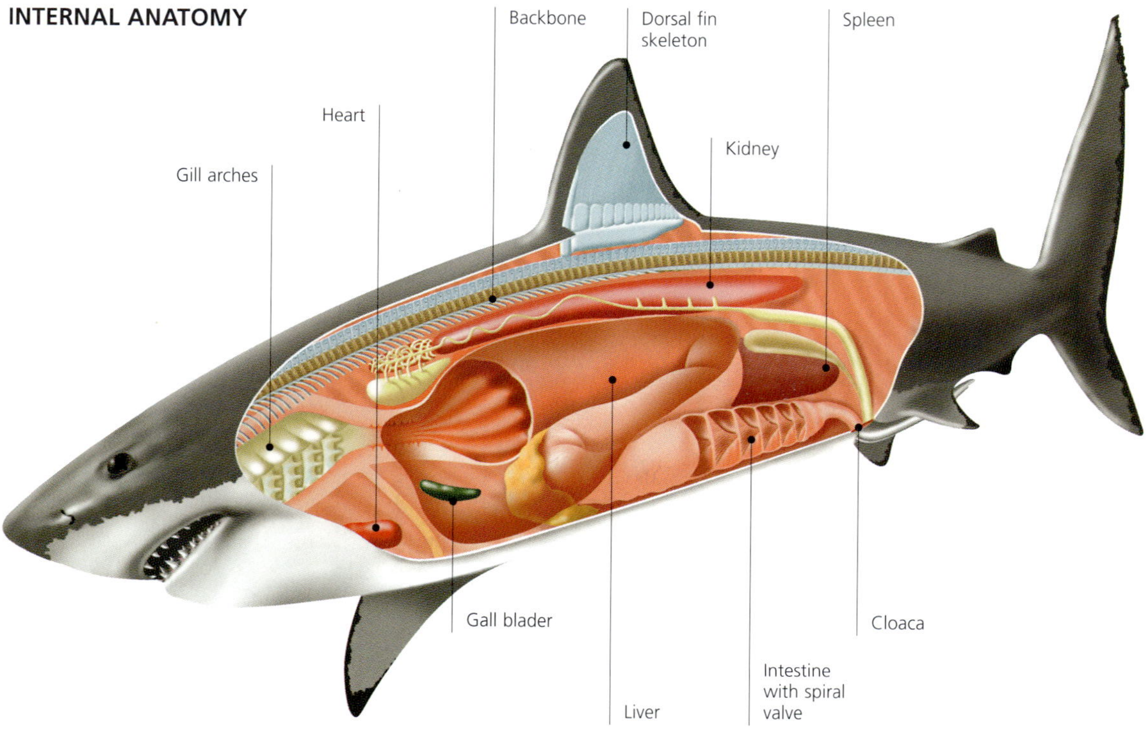

VARIETIES OF TAILS

Cookiecutter shark

Thresher shark

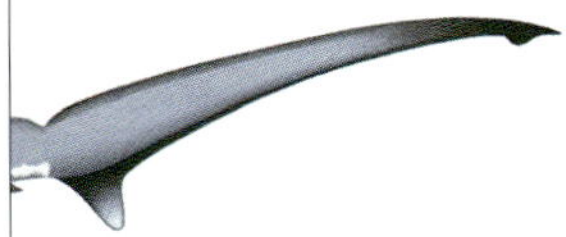

Porbeagle shark

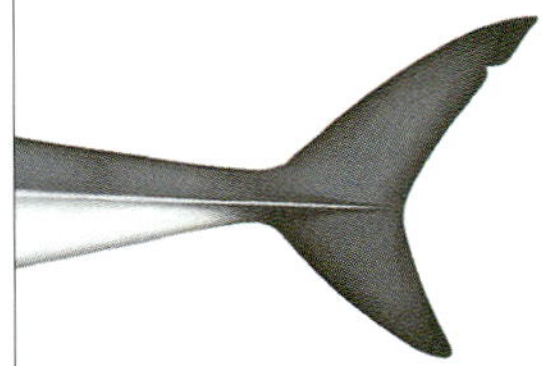

Mako shark

Nurse shark

Tiger shark

SHARK SENSES

Vibration-sensitive nerve cells, arranged in a series called the lateral line, run along a shark's sides. They help the shark to "feel" objects some distance away.

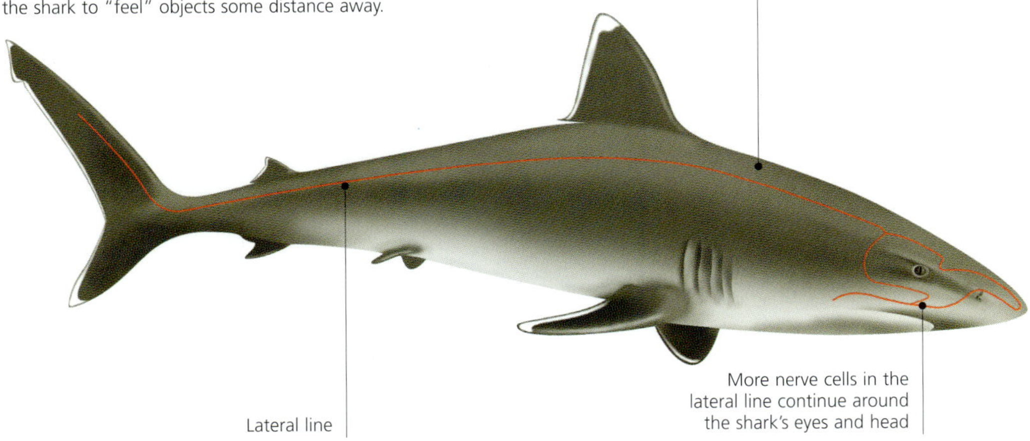

Shark Variations

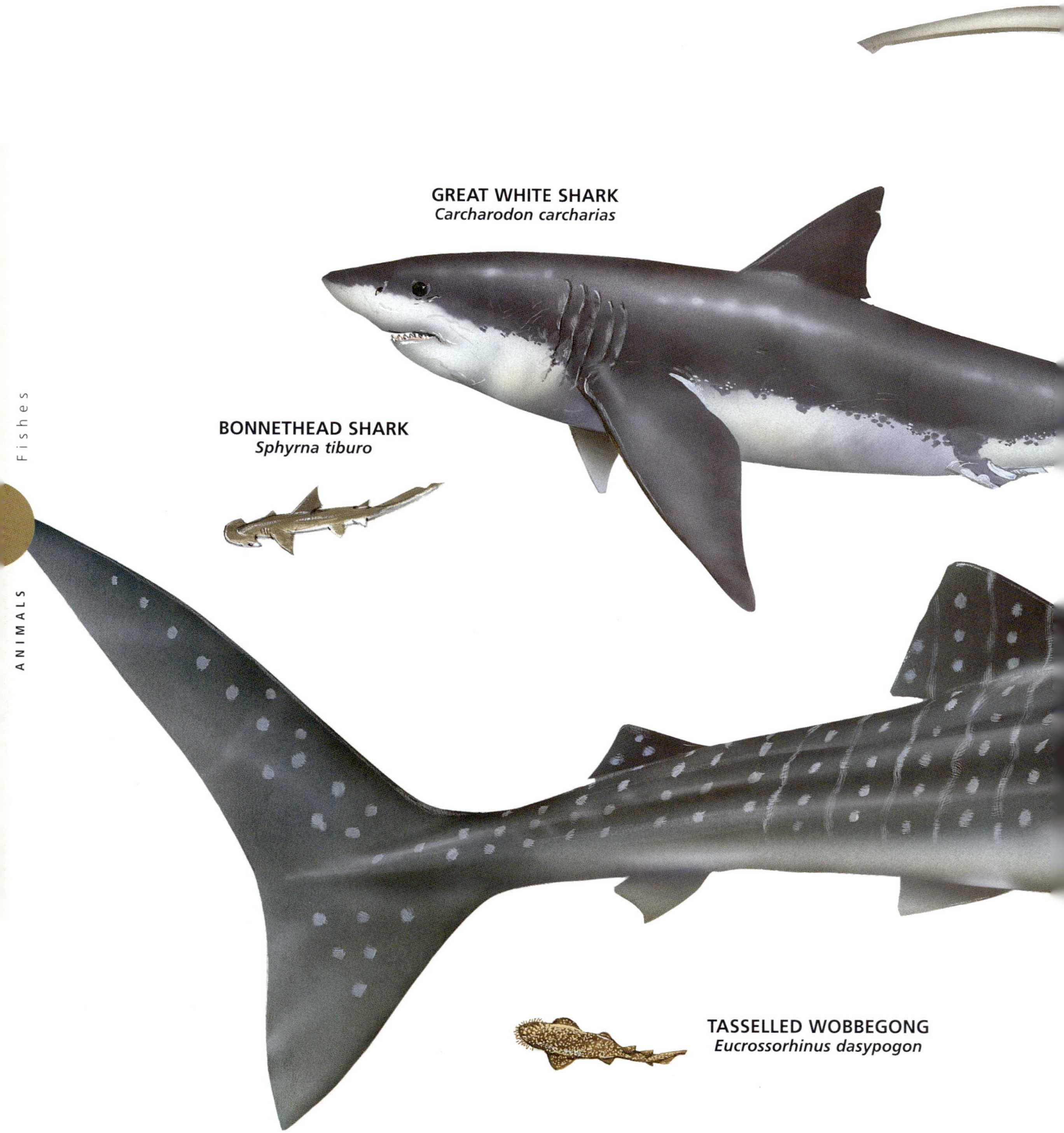

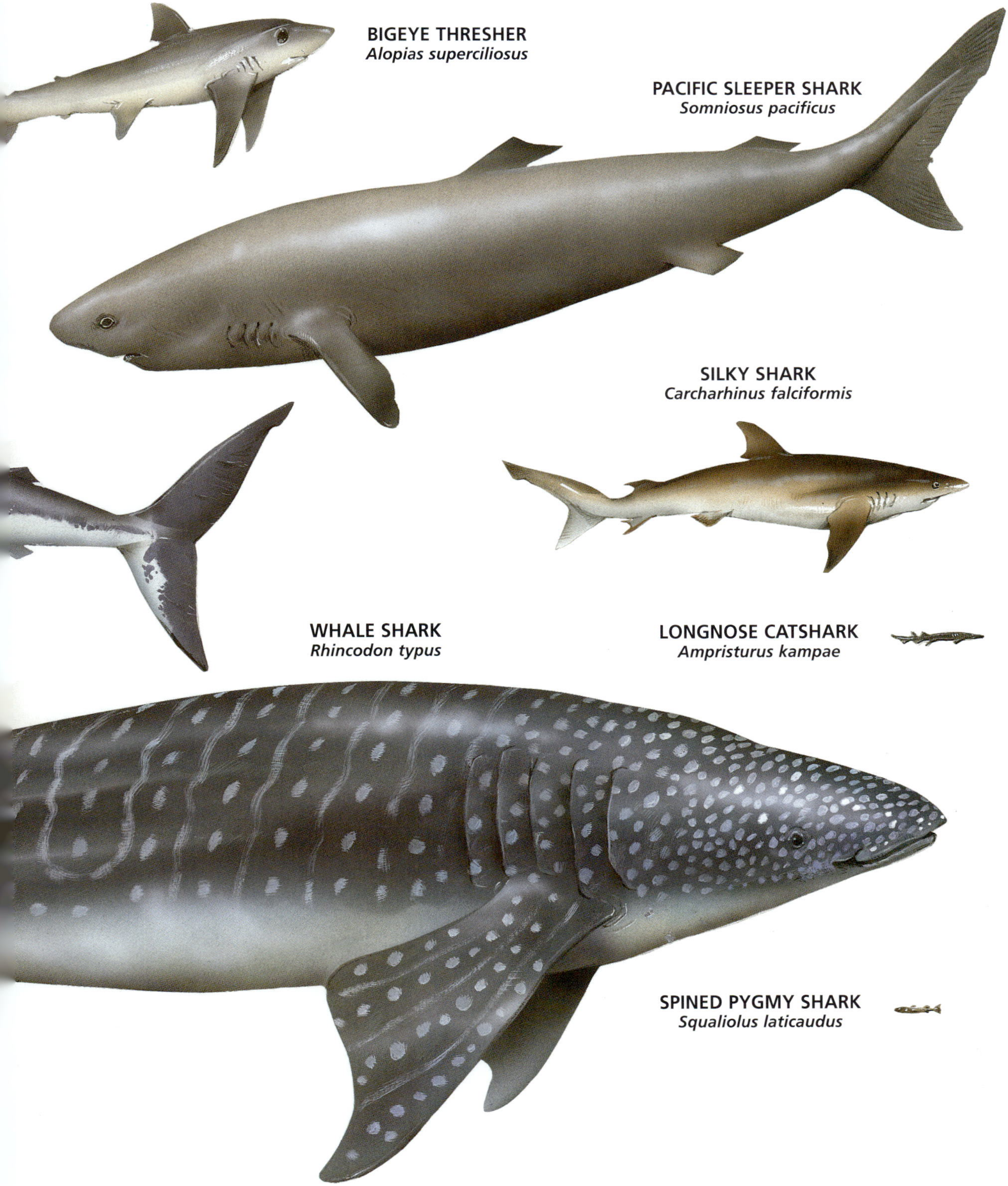

BIGEYE THRESHER
Alopias superciliosus

PACIFIC SLEEPER SHARK
Somniosus pacificus

SILKY SHARK
Carcharhinus falciformis

WHALE SHARK
Rhincodon typus

LONGNOSE CATSHARK
Apristurus kampae

SPINED PYGMY SHARK
Squaliolus laticaudus

Rays and Chimaeras

RAY FEATURES

Upperside view

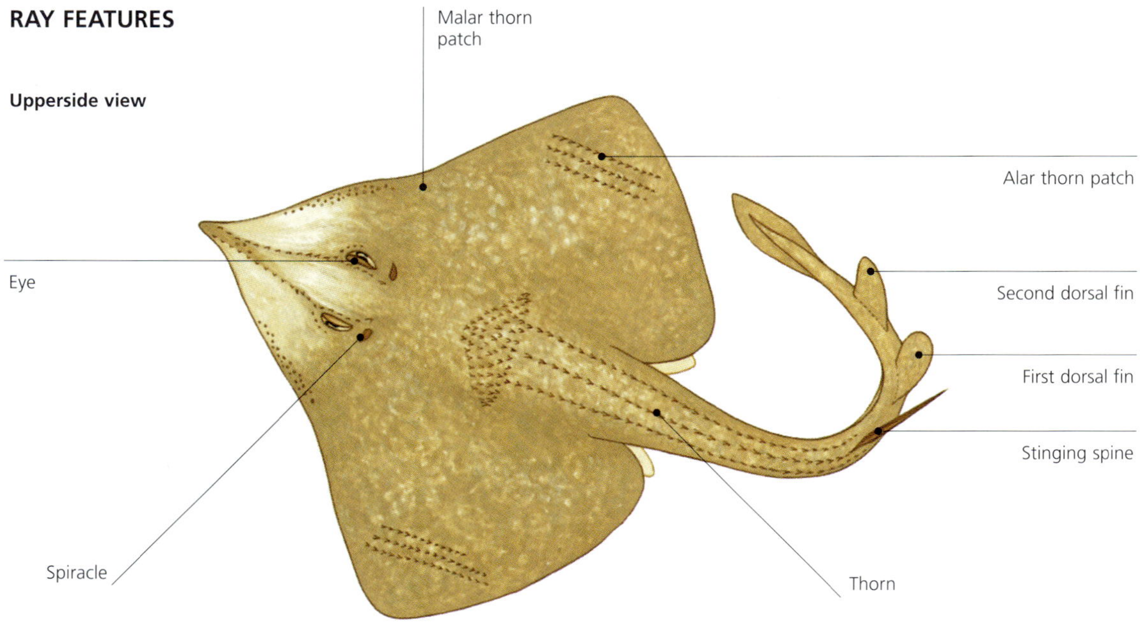

Underside view

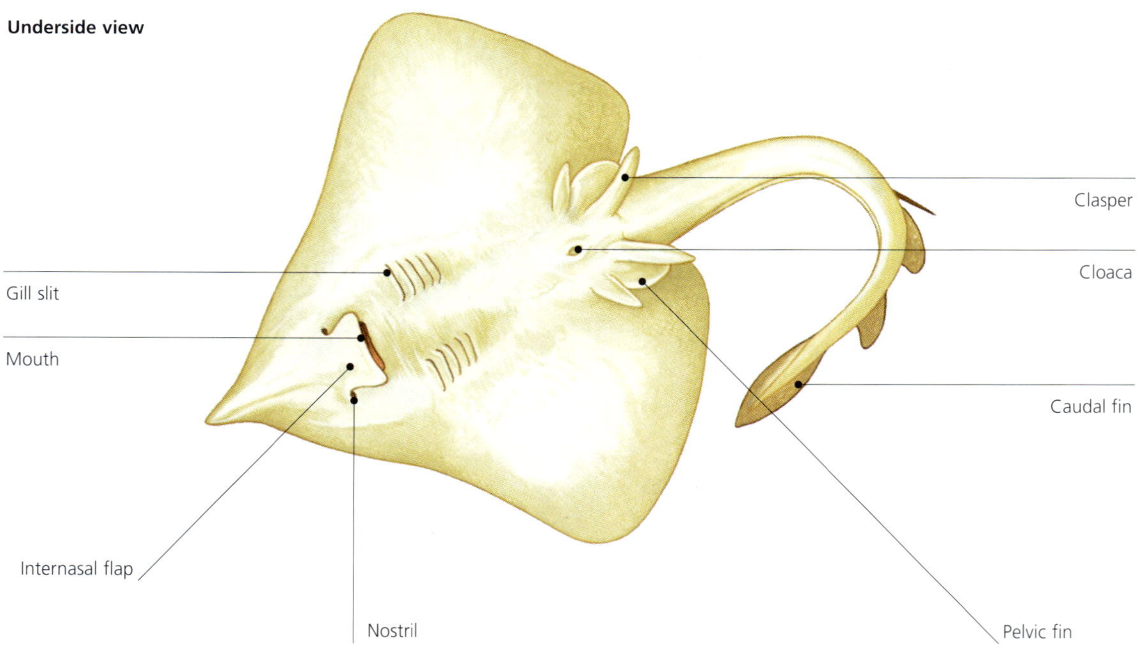

PORT DAVEY SKATE
Raja sp.

LEG SKATE
Anacanthobatis sp.

BLUE SKATE
Notoraja sp.

GUITARFISH
Family *Rhinobatidae*

OCELLATED FRESHWATER STINGRAY
Potamotrygon motoro

BLUNT-NOSED CHIMAERA
Hydrolagus colliei

SIXGILL STINGRAY
Hexatrygon bickelli

BLIND ELECTRIC RAY
Typhlonarke aysoni

SKATE
Family *Rajidae*

ELEPHANTFISH
Family *Callorhynchidae*

SPOOKFISH
Family *Rhinochimaeridae*

SHORTNOSE CHIMAERA
Family *Chimaeridae*

Bony Fishes

BUTTERFLYFISH
Pantodon buchholzi

COELACANTH
Latimeria chalumnae

ELEPHANTNOSE
Gnathonemus petersi

SOUTH AMERICAN LUNGFISH
Lepidosiren paradoxa

STERLET
Acipenser ruthenus

SPOTTED GAR
Lepisosteus oculatus

RIBBON EEL
Rhinomuraena quaesita

SPOTTED AFRICAN LUNGFISH
Protopterus dolloi

BLACK-SPOTTED MORAY EEL
Gymnothorax favagineus

AUSTRALIAN LUNGFISH
Neoceratodus forsteri

CLOWN KNIFEFISH
Chitala chitala

Bony Fishes

STRIPED JULIE
Julidochromis regani

MEYER'S BUTTERFLYFISH
Chaetodon meyeri

MOORISH IDOL
Zanclus cornutus

PURPLEQUEEN
Pseudanthis tuka

LAKE MALAWI ZEBRA CICHLID
Pseudotropheus zebra

LICORICE GOURAMI
Paraosphromenus dreissneri

GIANT GROUPER
Epinephalus lanceolatus

SIXLINE SOAPFISH
Grammistes sexlineatus

VELVET CICHLID
Astronotus ocellatus

SOUTHEAST ASIAN PIKEHEAD
Luciocephalus pulcher

Freshwater Fishes

RED-BELLIED PIRANHA
Pygocentrus nattereri

ELECTRIC CATFISH
Malapterurus electricus

ZEBRA DANIO
Brachydanio rerio

MARBLED HATCHETFISH
Carnegiella strigata

STRIPED HEADSTANTER
Anostomus anostomus

SADDLED HILLSTREAM LOACH
Homaloptera orthogoniata

SAILFIN PIMELODID
Genus Leiarius

SLIMY LOACH
Acantophthalmus myersi

WHITE-SPOTTED SPINY EEL
Mastacembelus armatus

Freshwater Fishes

STEEL-BLUE KILLIFISH
Aphyosemion gardneri

CLOWN KILLIFISH
Aplocheilus annulatus

MALAYAN HALFBEAK
Dermogenys pusilla

PIRATE PERCH
Aphredoderus sayanus

AUSTRALIAN RAINBOWFISH
Melanotaenia boesemani

CUATRO OJOS
Anableps anableps

MADAGASCAR RAINBOWFISH
Bedotia geayi

JAVANESE RICEFISH
Oryzias javaniaus

SWORDTAIL
Xiphophorus helleri

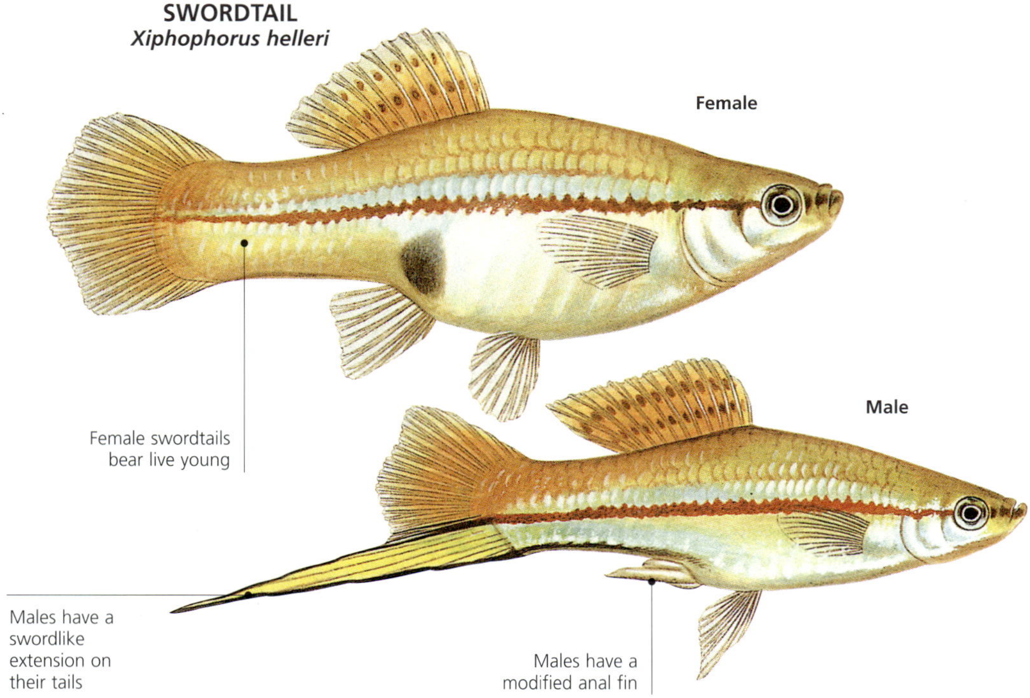

Ocean Fishes

VARIEGATED LIZARDFISH
Synodus variegatus

LANTERNFISH
Family *Myctophidae*

BRISTLEMOUTH
Family *Gonostomatidae*

Larval stage

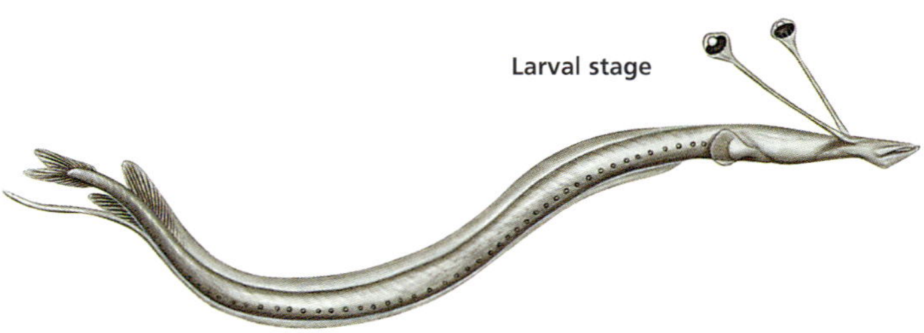

BLACK DRAGONFISH
Idiacanthus fasciola

Adult

ARTHUR'S PARAGALAXIAS
Paragalaxias mesotes

ALASKA BLACKFISH
Dallia pectoralis

CIRCUMPOLAR BURBOT
Lota lota

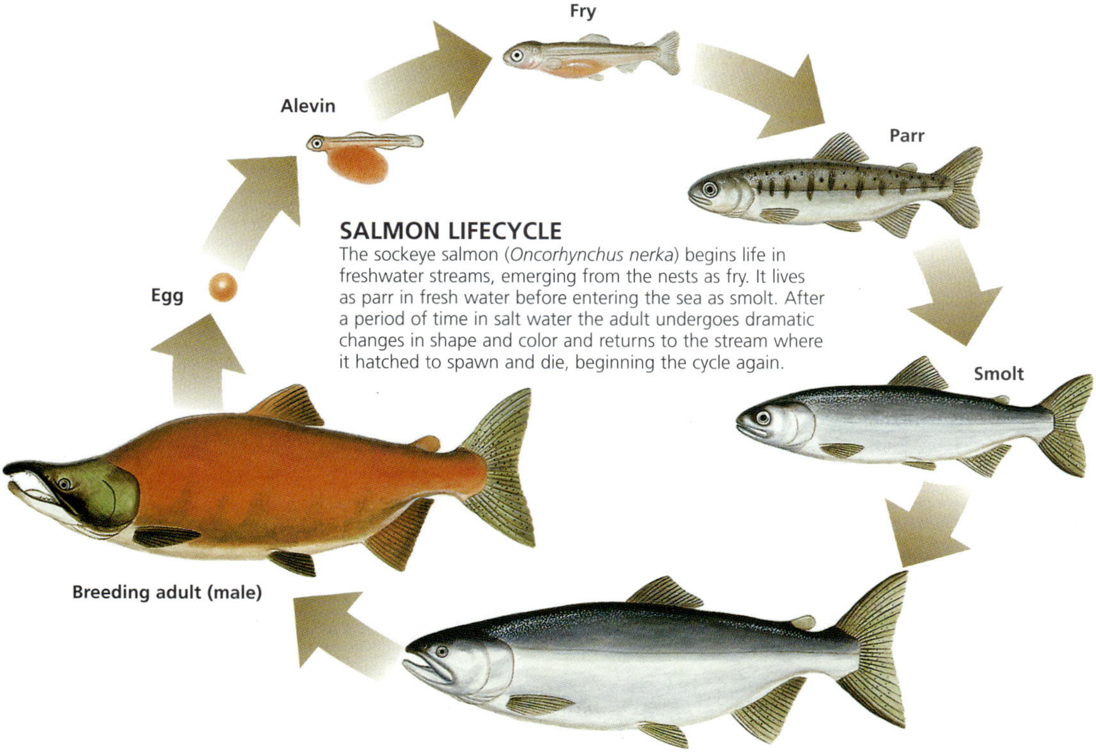

SALMON LIFECYCLE
The sockeye salmon (*Oncorhynchus nerka*) begins life in freshwater streams, emerging from the nests as fry. It lives as parr in fresh water before entering the sea as smolt. After a period of time in salt water the adult undergoes dramatic changes in shape and color and returns to the stream where it hatched to spawn and die, beginning the cycle again.

Ocean Fishes

BANDED PIPEFISH
Doryrhamphus dactyliophorus

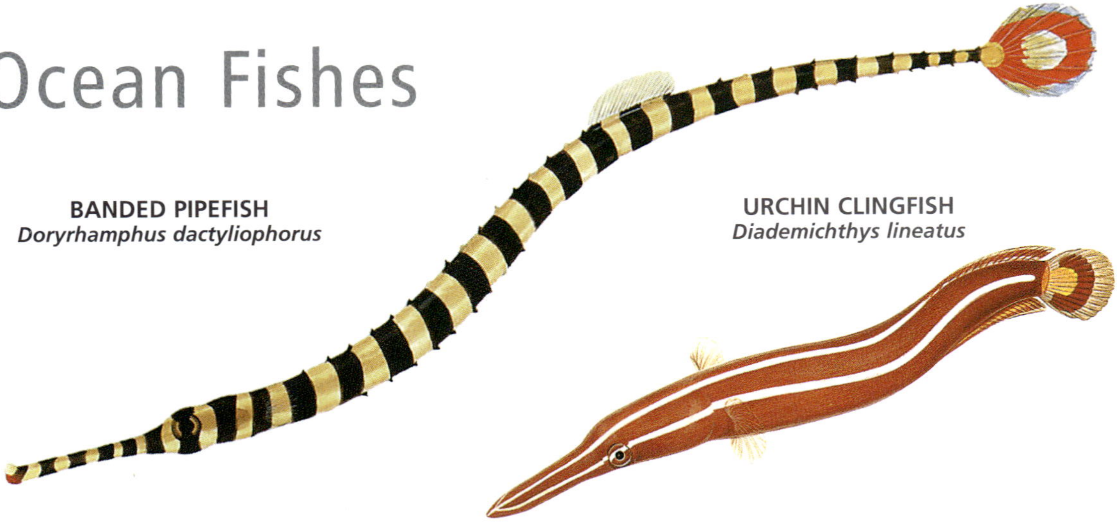

URCHIN CLINGFISH
Diademichthys lineatus

CARIBBEAN TRUMPETFISH
Aulostomus maculatus

POT-BELLIED SEAHORSE
Hippocampus abdominalis

SPLENDID TOADFISH
Sanopus splendidus

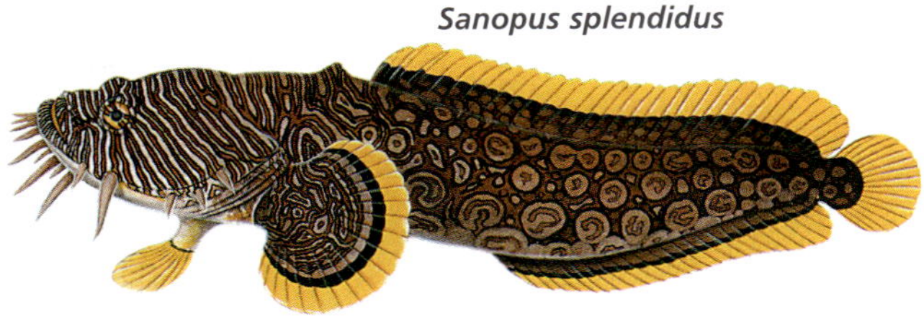

RIBBONFISH
Trachipterus altivelis

OPAH
Lampris guttatus

AUSTRALIAN PINEAPPLEFISH
Cleidopus gloriamaris

SPOTTED OREO
Pseudocyttus maculatus

FLASHLIGHT FISH
Photoblepharon palpebratus

SOUTHERN ROUGHY
Trachichthys australis

TIGER ROCKFISH
Sebastes nigrocinctus

COCKATOO WASPFISH
Ablabys taenionotus

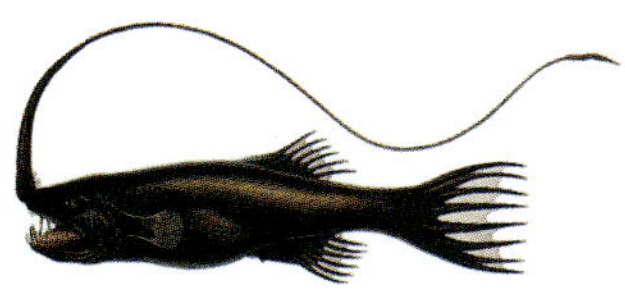

PAXTON'S WHIPNOSE ANGLER
Gigantactis paxtoni

LUMPSUCKER
Cyclopterus lumpus

MANDARIN FISH
Synchiropus splendidus

Ocean Fishes

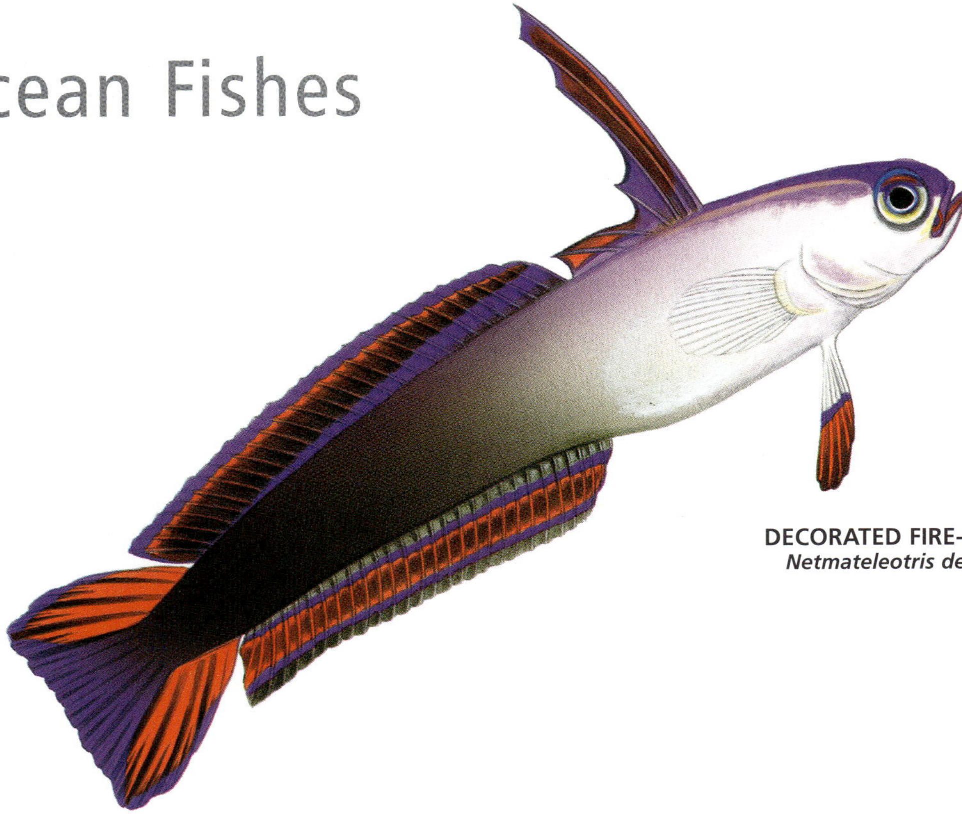

DECORATED FIRE-GOBY
Netmateleotris decora

SEX REVERSAL IN PARROTFISHES

In its lifetime the highfin parrotfish (*Scarus altipinnis*) travels through three color phases as well as gender change.

Juvenile—usually female, not sexually active

Initial phase—usually female

Terminal phase—always a mature male

SPINE-CHEEK ANEMONEFISH
Premnas biaculeatus

HARLEQUIN TUSKFISH
Choerodon fasciatus

DORIA'S BUMBLEBEE GOBY
Brachygobius doriae

BLACK-HEADED BLENNY
Lipophrys nigriceps

BLUEBANDED GOBY
Lythrypnus dalli

FIGURE-EIGHT PUFFER
Tetraodon biocellatus

IMITATION PUFFERFISH

As a defense mechanism the mimic filefish (*Paraluteres prionurus*) has evolved to look almost exactly like the highly toxic black-saddled puffer (*Canthigaster valentini*).

Toxic black-saddled puffer

Non-toxic mimic filefish

CLOWN TRIGGERFISH
Balistoides conspicillum

Insect Anatomy

INSECT CHARACTERISTICS

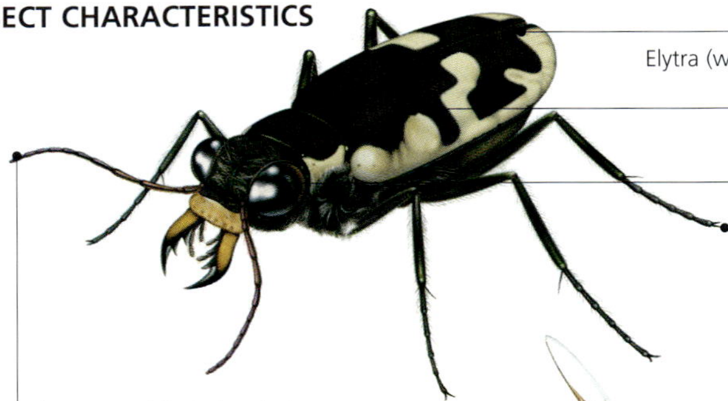

WASP INTERNAL ANATOMY

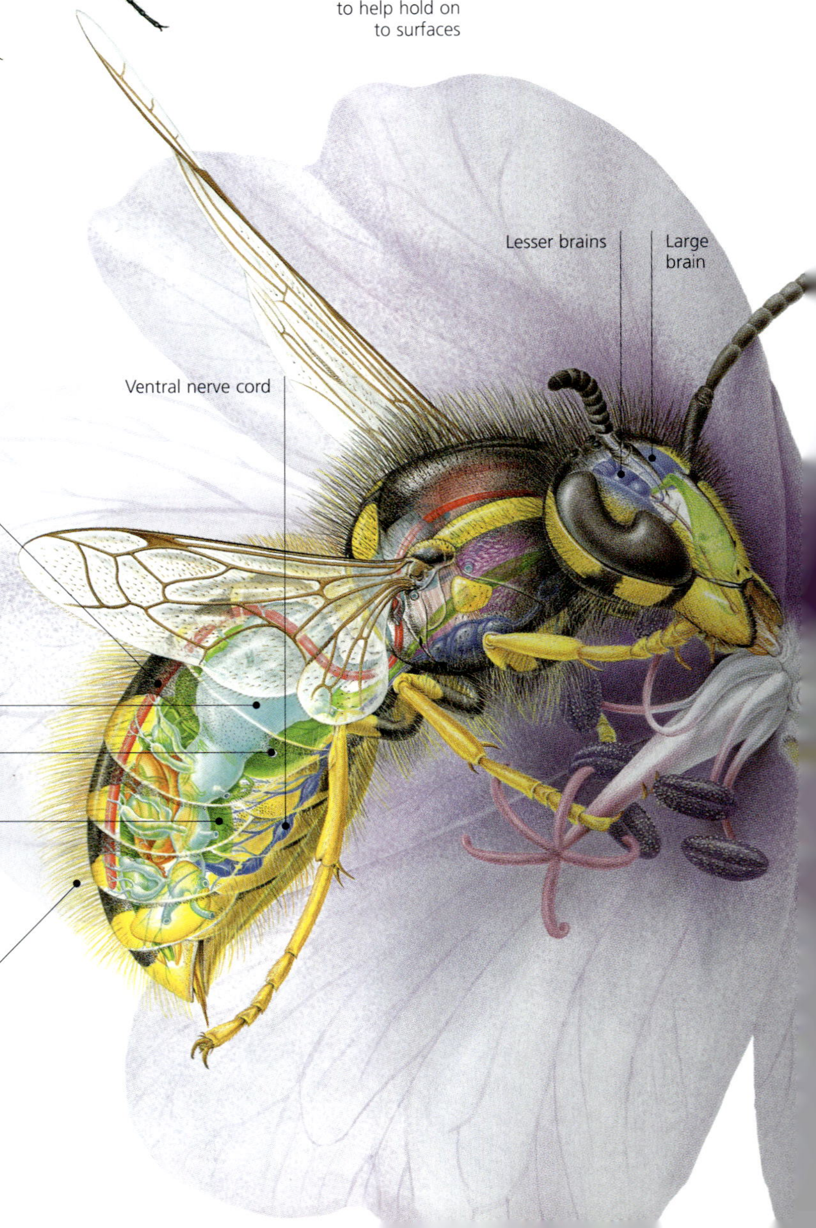

WING VARIETIES

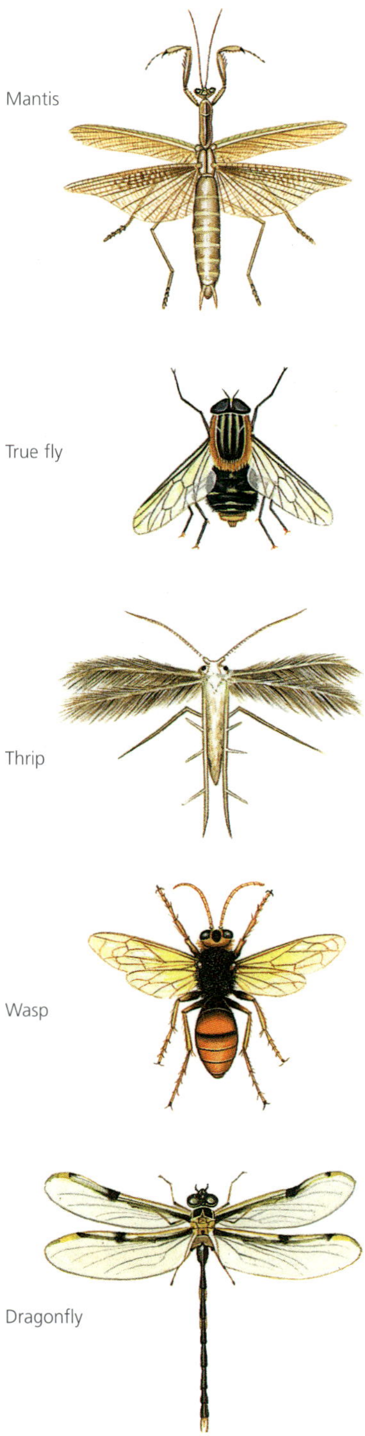

ANTENNAE VARIETIES

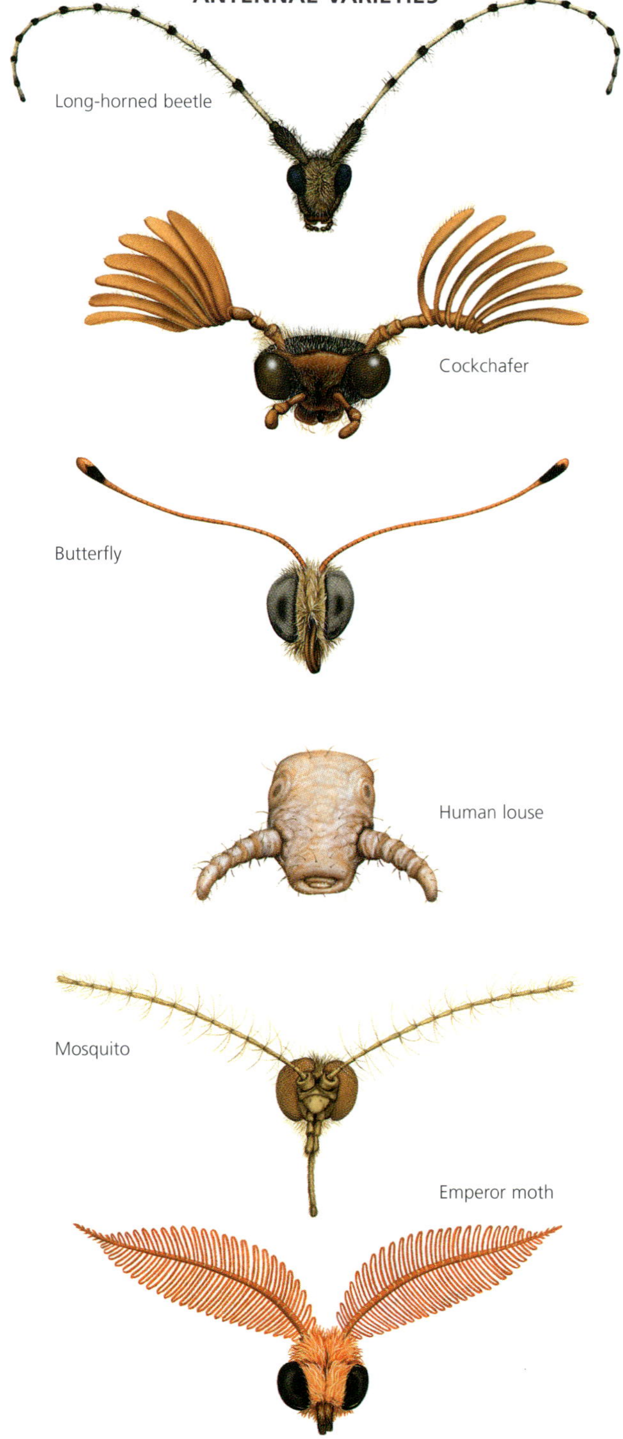

Beetles and Bugs

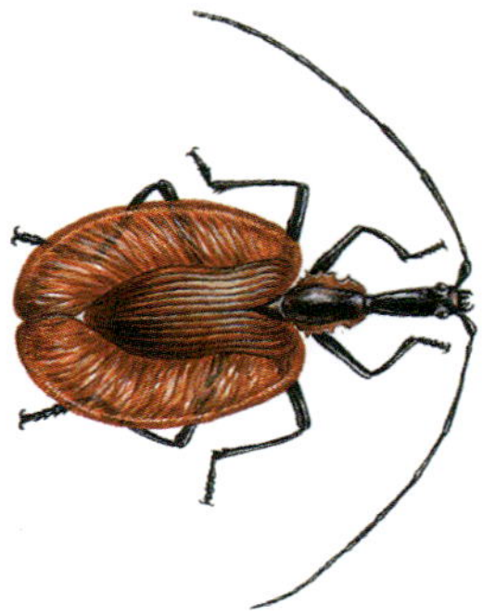

VIOLIN BEETLE
Family *Buprestidae*

WEEVIL
Family *Curculionidae*

GIRAFFE WEEVIL
Family *Brentidae*

FIVE-SPOTTED LADYBIRD
Family *Coccinellidae*

TEN-SPOTTED LADYBIRD
Family *Coccinellidae*

TORTOISE BEETLE
Family *Chrysomelidae*

STINK BUG
Family *Pentatomidae*

SOUTH AMERICAN LONGHORN BEETLE
Family *Cerambycidae*

LONG-HORNED BEETLE
Family *Cerambycidae*

LADYBIRD IN FLIGHT

BOX ELDER BUG
Family *Rhopalidae*

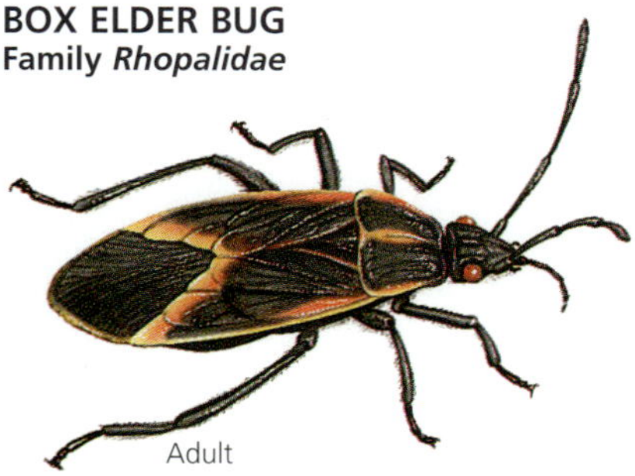

Adult

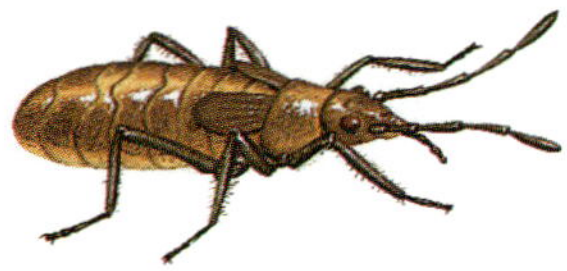

Nymph

BEE-EATING BEETLE
Family *Cleridae*

BLISTER BEETLE
Family *Meloidae*

HARLEQUIN BEETLE
Family *Cerambycidae*

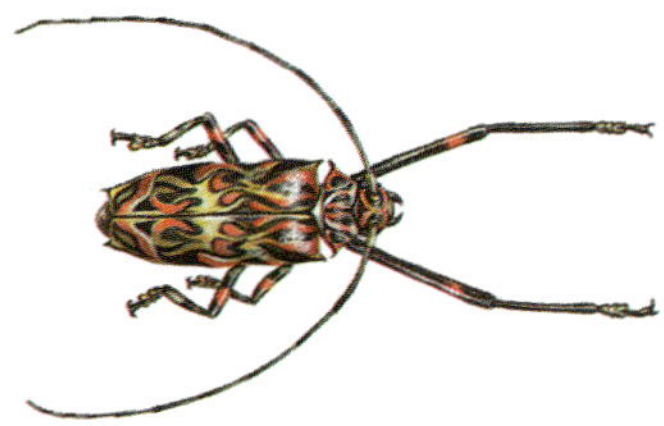

ROVE BEETLE
Family *Staphylinidae*

CARDINAL BEETLE FLIGHT
Family *Pyrochroidae*

Takeoff

In flight

Butterflies and Moths

SWALLOWTAIL BUTTERFLY
Family *Papilionidae*

HELICONIID MIMIC BUTTERFLY
Family *Nymphalidae*

ORCHARD BUTTERFLY CATERPILLAR
Family *Papilionidae*

SILK MOTH CATERPILLAR
Family *Bombycidae*

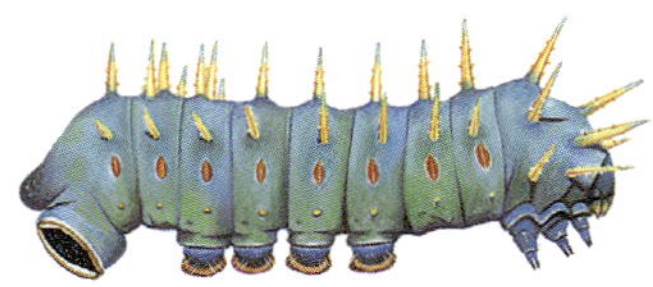

HERCULES MOTH CATERPILLAR
Family *Saturniidae*

MALAY LACEWING BUTTERFLY
Cethosia hypsea hypsina

88 BUTTERFLY
Family *Nymphalidae*

PAINTED LADY BUTTERFLY
Family *Nymphalidae*

MADAGASCAN SUNSET MOTH
Uraniidae Chrysiridia riphearia

INDIAN MOON MOTH
Family *Saturniidae*

BUTTERFLY AND MOTH DIFFERENCES

Butterflies and moths can be distinguished from each other by looking at antennae. Butterflies have threadlike antennae whereas moths have feathery antennae.

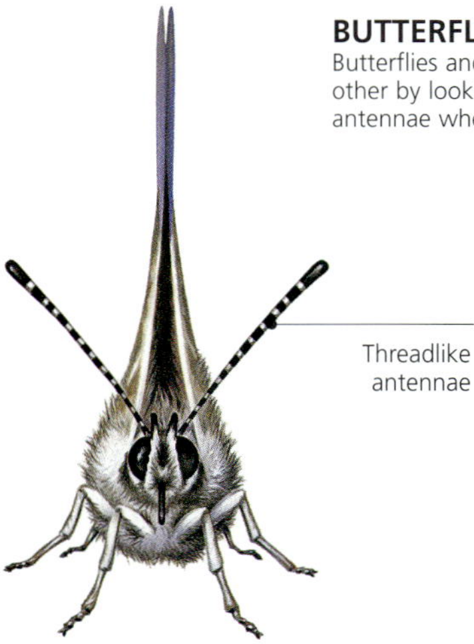

Butterfly

Moth

SHEEP MOTH
Family *Saturniidae*

YELLOW EMPEROR MOTH
Family *Saturniidae*

FIVE-SPOTTED BURNET MOTH
Family *Sphingidae*

Bees, Wasps and Ants

POLLINATION

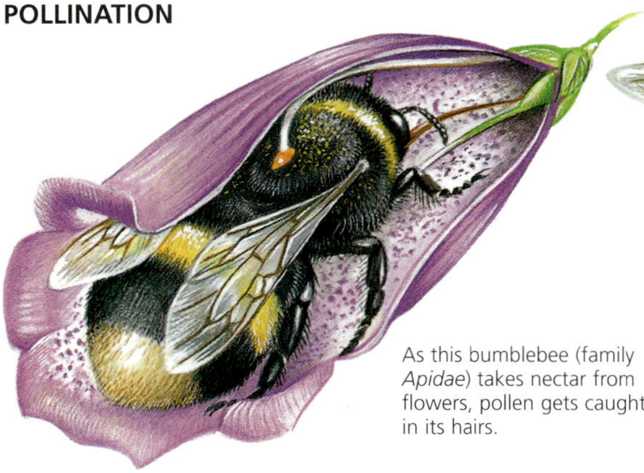

As this bumblebee (family *Apidae*) takes nectar from flowers, pollen gets caught in its hairs.

The bumblebee covered in pollen visits other flowers. Some of the pollen will rub off in these flowers thus fertilizing them. This is called pollination.

MUD DAUBER
Family *Sphecidae*

TORYMID WASP
Family *Torymidae*

HAIRY-LEGGED MINING BEE
Family *Andrenidae*

HORNET
Family *Vespidae*

SPIDER WASP
Family *Pompilidae*

COW KILLER WASP
Family *Mutillidae*

BEE HIVE

Larva

Cell

Larva in a capped cell spins a cocoon and pupates for several weeks

A worker bee caps the cell of a mature larva with a wax seal

BIG-HEADED ANT
Family *Formicidae*

ANT
Family *Formicidae*

VELVET ANT
Family *Mutillidae*

BULLDOG ANT
***Myrmecia* sp.**

Flies and Dragonflies

DEER FLY IN MOTION
Family *Tabanidae*

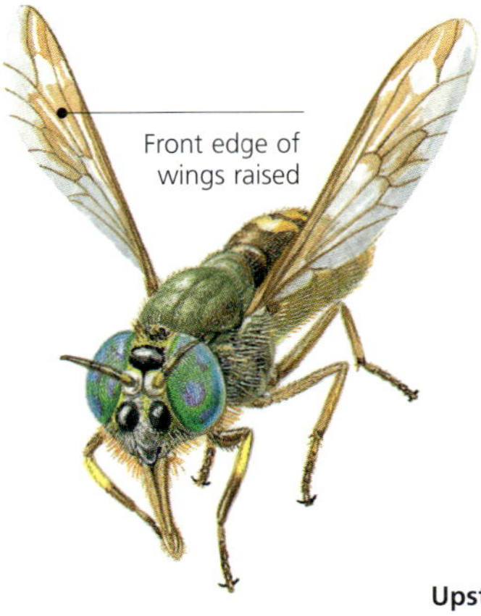

Upstroke

Downstroke begins

Downstroke completed

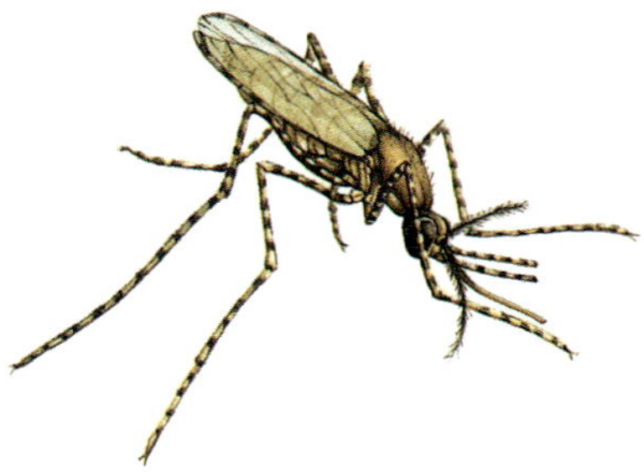

MOSQUITO
Family *Culicidae*

GREEN BOTTLE FLY
Family *Calliphoridae*

HOVER FLY
Family *Syrphidae*

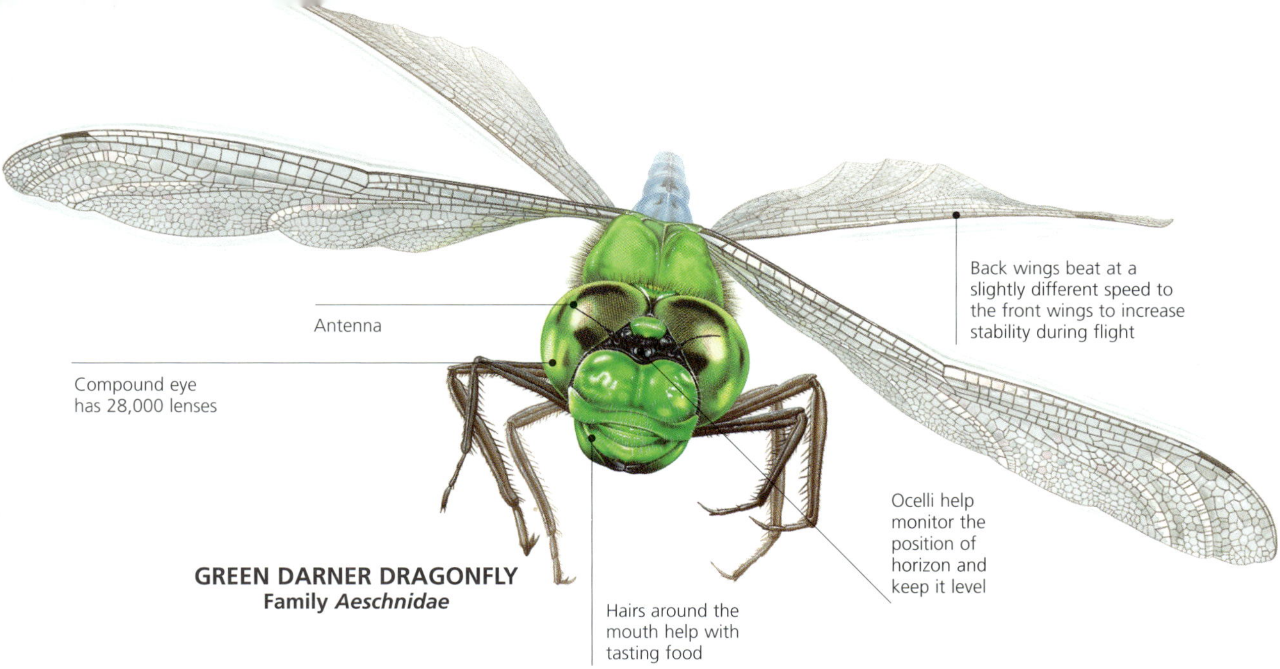

GREEN DARNER DRAGONFLY
Family *Aeschnidae*

SOLDIER FLY
Family *Stratiomyidae*

HAIRY BEE FLY
Family *Bombyliidae*

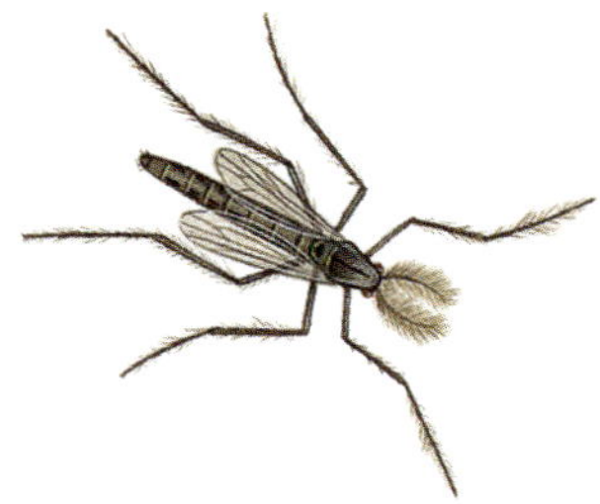

MIDGE
Family *Chironomidae*

FLY FOOD

House flies eat most organic matter.

Tsetse flies feed on human and animal blood.

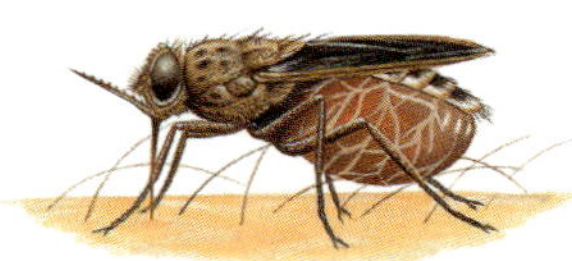

Fruit flies feed on rotting fruit.

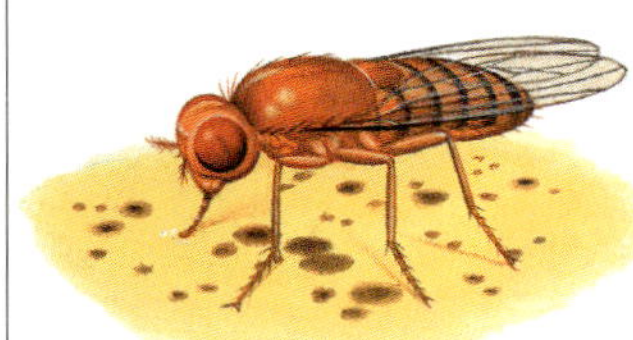

Grasshoppers and Crickets

GREEN BUSH CRICKET
Family *Eneopterinae*

GRASSHOPPER FLIGHT
Grasshoppers leap to become airborne. They then unfold large fanlike hindwings to glide long distances.

GRASSHOPPER LOCOMOTION
Grasshoppers jump to avoid predators and to launch themselves into flight. Their back legs flick backward and push them into the air.

FIELD CRICKET
Family *Gryllidae*

JERUSALEM CRICKET
Family *Stenopelmatidae*

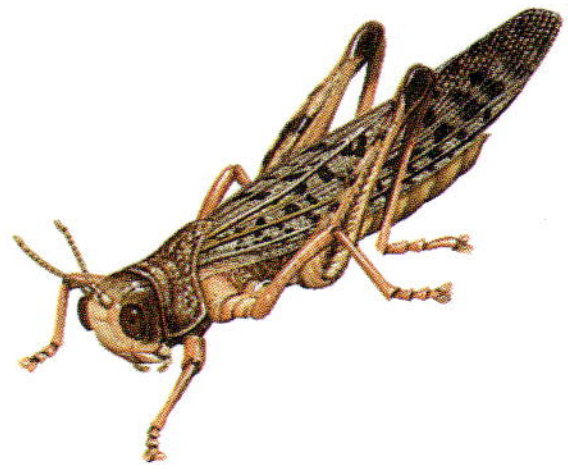

GRASSHOPPER SENSES

Grasshoppers and locusts have ears on their abdomen. They are particularly sensitive to calls from their own species.

DESERT LOCUST
Family *Acrididae*

Adult

Nymph

COMMUNICATION

This painted grasshopper rapidly rubs small pegs on the back of its legs against the hard ridges along its wings. The wings vibrate and make a loud rasping noise. Male grasshoppers use this call to attract females.

Spider Anatomy

ORB-WEB SPIDER
Family *Araneidae*

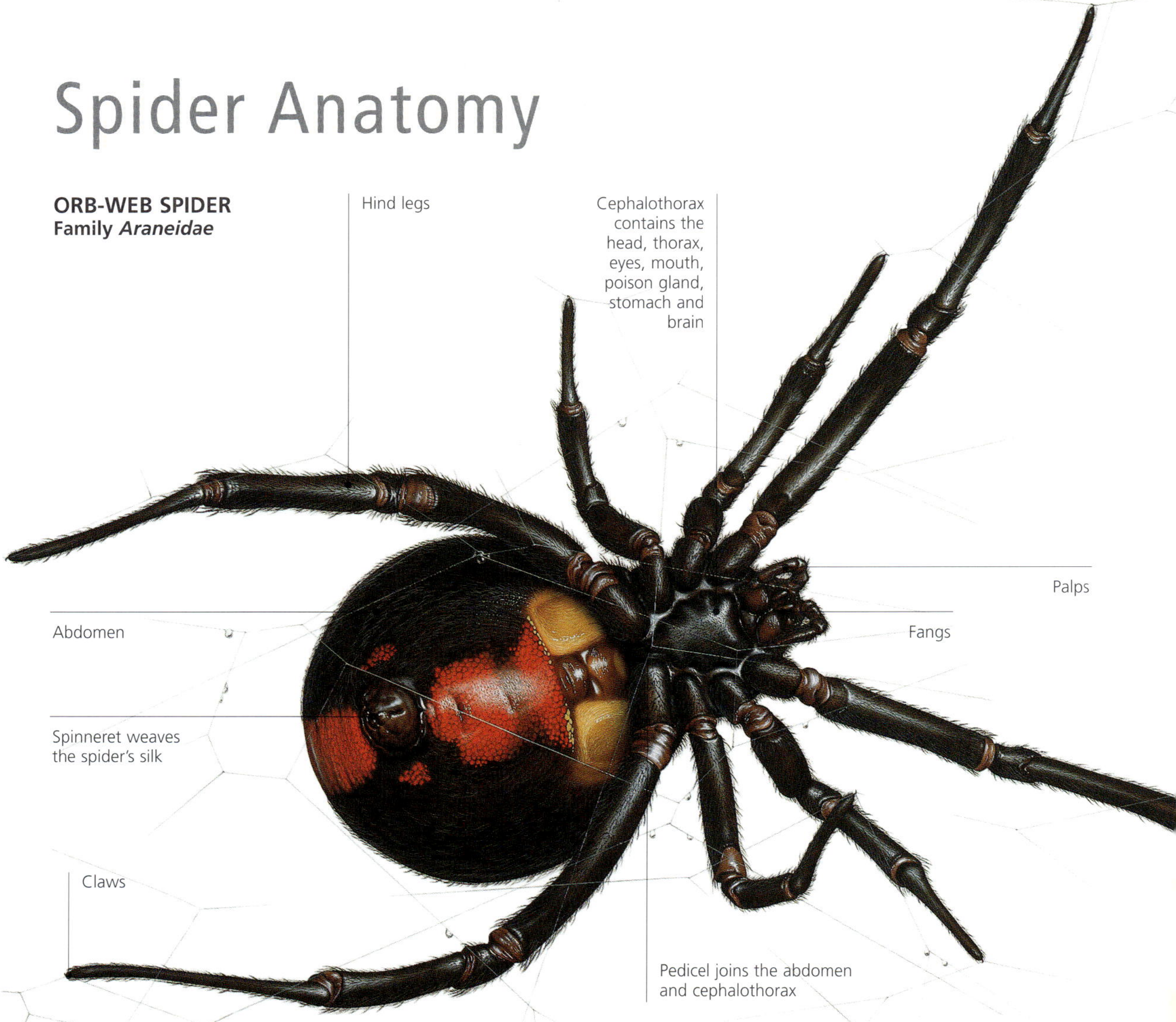

SPIDER FANGS

SPIDER EYES

Huntsman spider

Woodlouse-eating spider

Crab spider

Ogre-faced spider

HUNTSMAN SPIDER
Family *Heteropodidae*

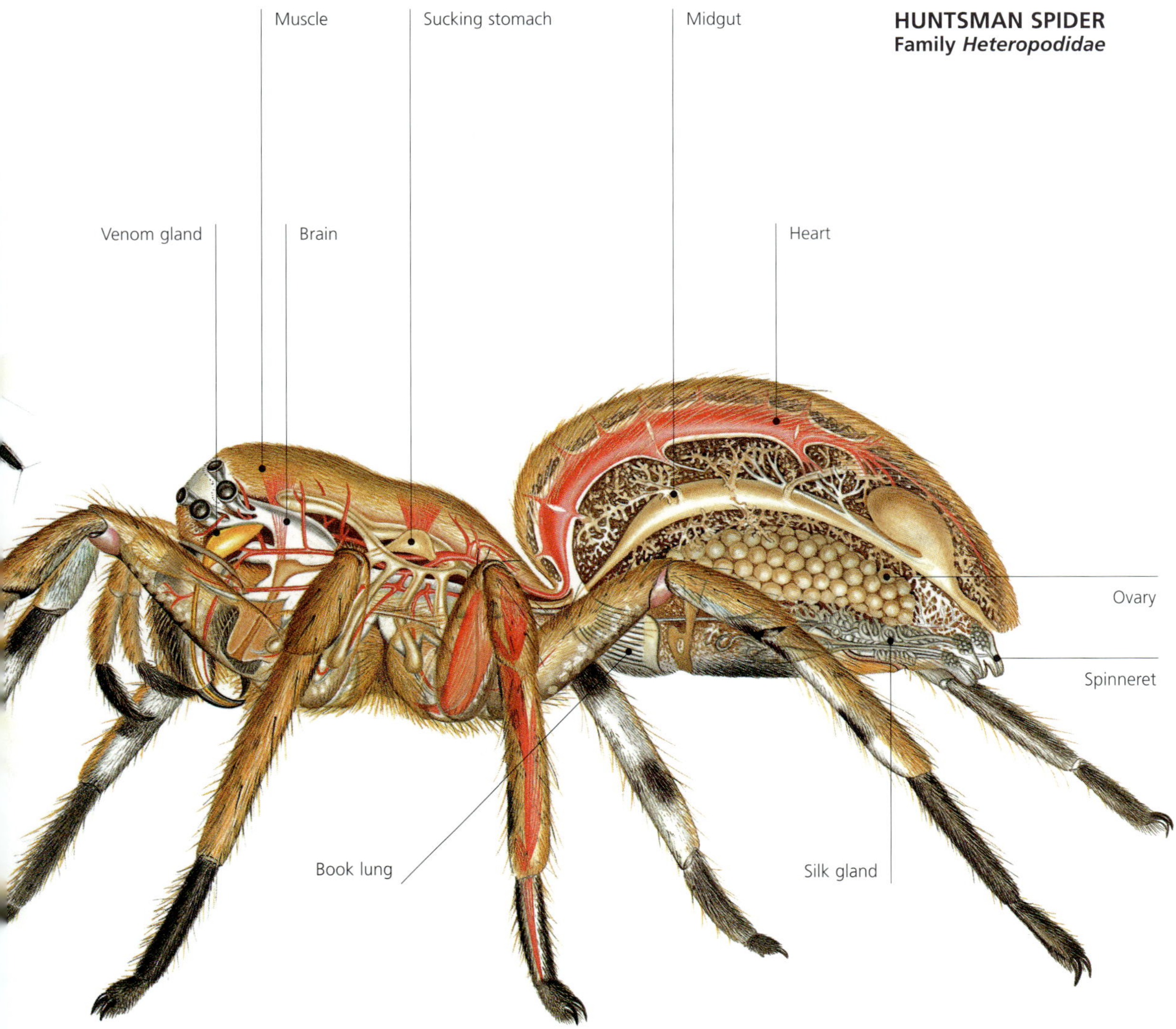

Spider Varieties

JUMPING SPIDER
Family *Salticidae*

WHITE LADY SPIDER
Family *Sparassidae*

TRAPDOOR SPIDER
Family *Ctenizidae*

HUNTSMAN SPIDER
Family *Heteropodidae*

TARANTULA
Family *Theraphosidae*

COMB-FOOTED SPIDER
Family *Theridiidae*

LYNX SPIDER
Family *Oxyopidae*

RED WIDOW SPIDER
Family *Theridiidae*

HUNTSMAN SPIDER LIFECYCLE

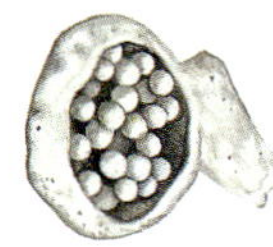

Eggs and egg sac

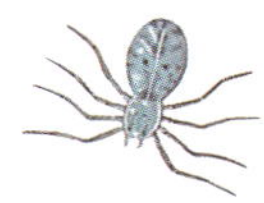

Spiderling

Juvenile

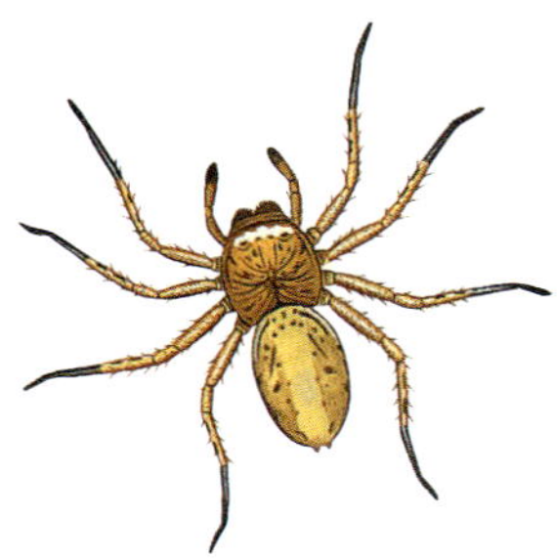

Adult

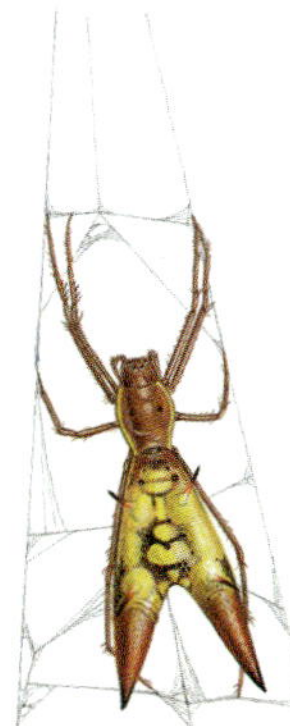

SPINY ORB WEAVER
Family *Araneidae*

MARBLED ORB WEAVER
Family *Araneidae*

LONG-JAWED ORB WEAVER
Family *Araneidae*

CLOSE RELATIVES

Northern black widow spider
Family *Theridiidae*

Redback spider
Family *Theridiidae*

MOUSE SPIDER
***Missulena* sp.**

CRAB SPIDER
Family *Thomisidae*

Spider Behavior

SPIDER WEB VARIETIES

Orb web

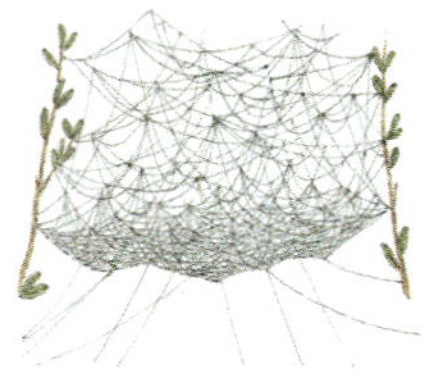
Sheet web

Lace-sheet web

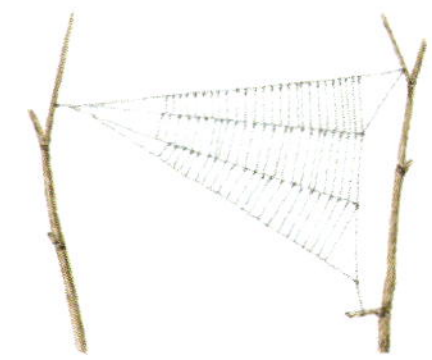
Triangle web

VENOMOUS SPIDERS

Brazilian wandering spider
Family *Ctenidae*

Violin spider
Family *Loxoscelidae*

Southern black widow spider
Family *Theridiidae*

Funnel-web spider
Family *Dipluridae*

SHEDDING SKIN

Old exoskeleton splits on edge of the cephalothorax.

Old skin on abdomen comes away.

Spider pulls legs clear.

New exoskeleton hardens.

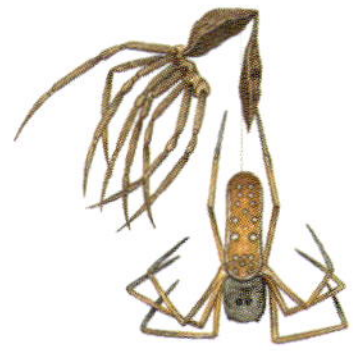

SPIDER DISGUISES

Scorpion spiders (family *Araneidae*) hang in the air imitating a dead leaf to discourage predators.

This Brazilian ant-mimicking spider (family *Araneidae*) uses its disguise to get up close to ants and eat them.

As a defense mechanism this jumping spider from Borneo (family *Salticidae*) imitates the dangerous Asian multillid wasp.

JUMPING SPIDER COURTSHIP DISPLAY

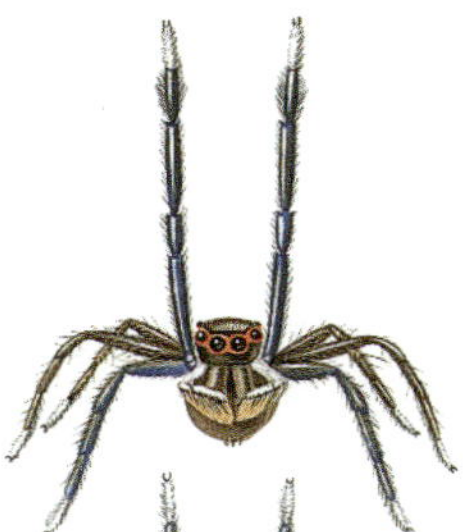

ATTACKING SPIDER

The funnel-web spider (family *Dipluridae*) has large fangs and highly potent venom. The spider raises its head to attack and stabs its prey by moving its head down.

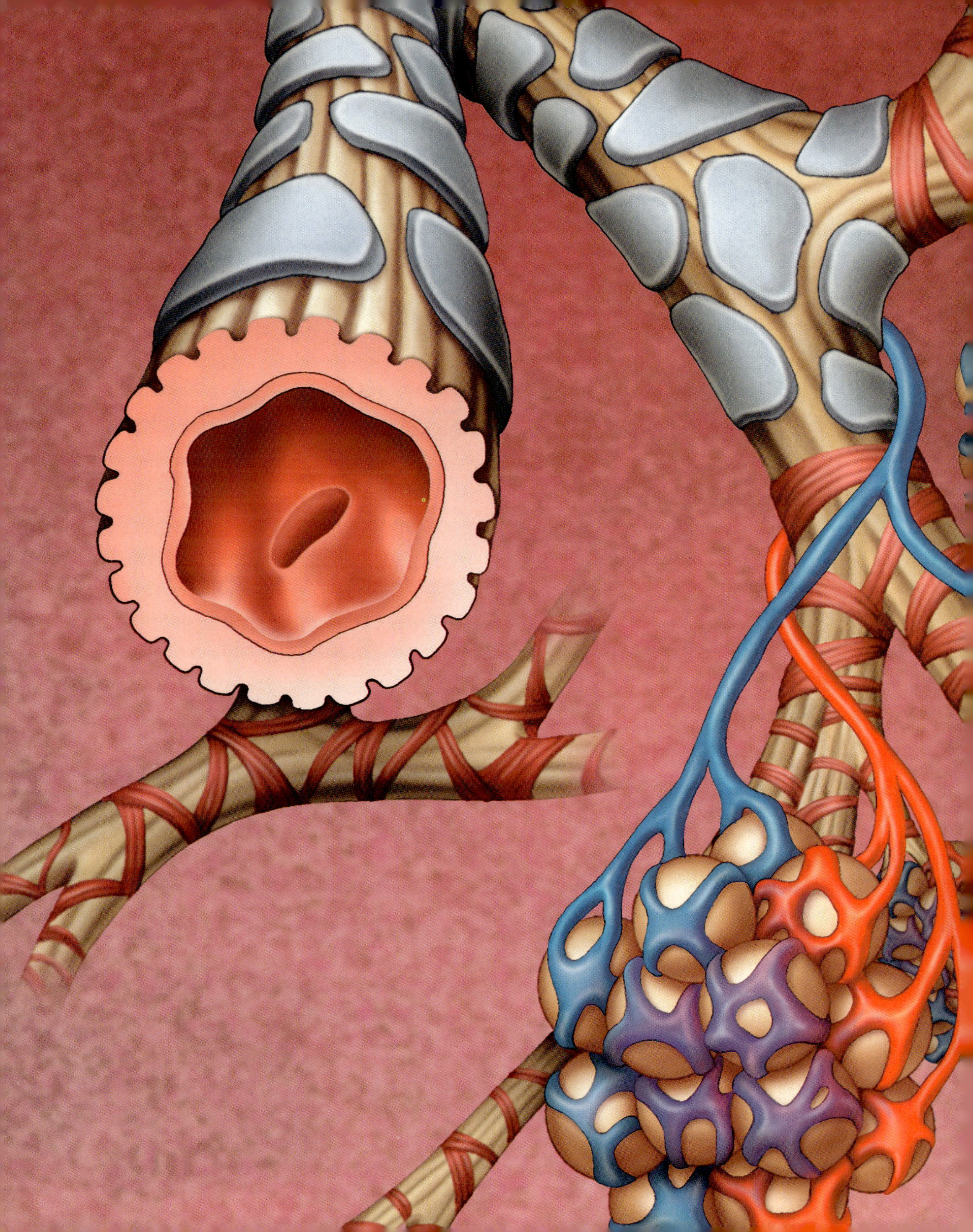

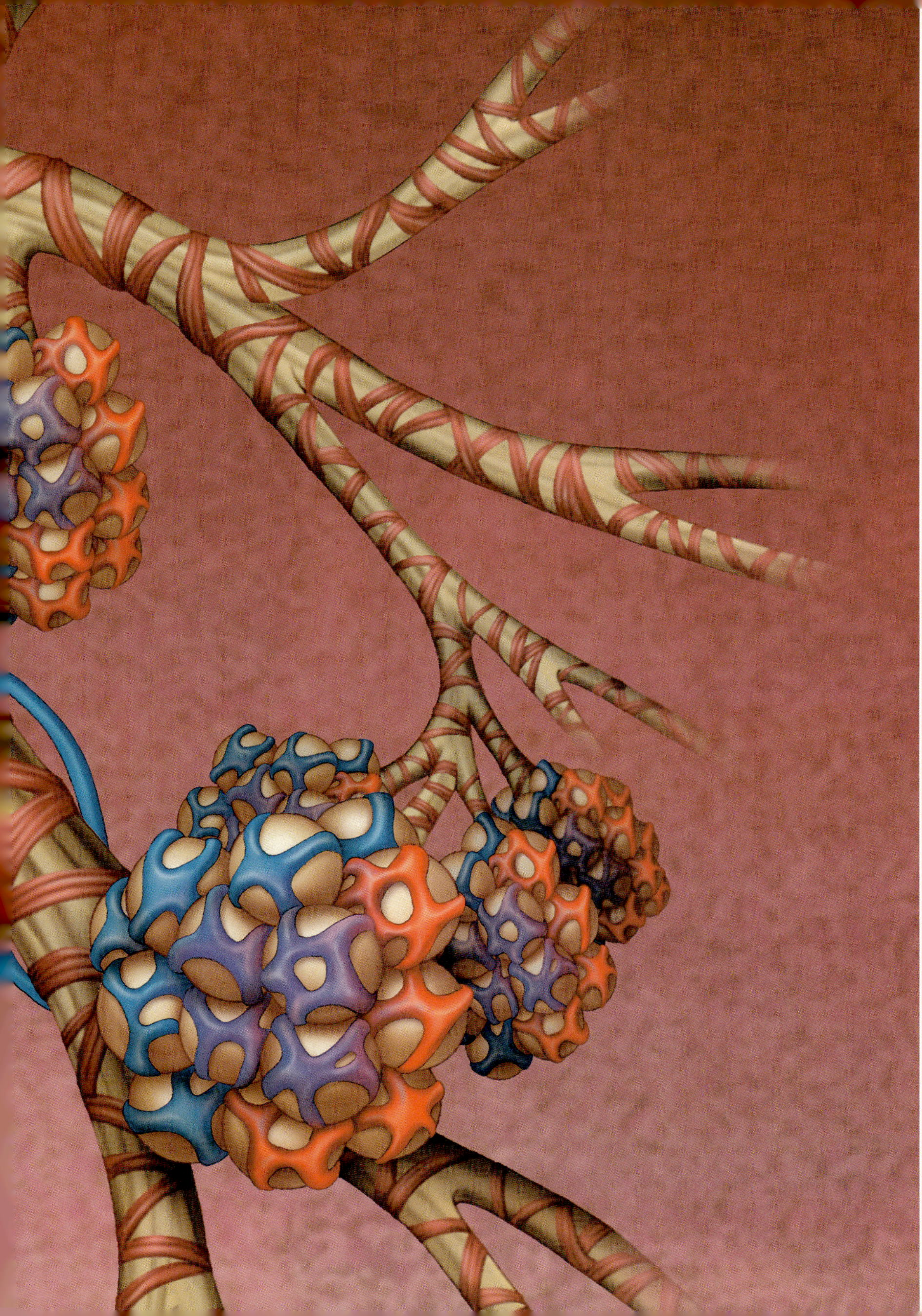

THE HUMAN BODY

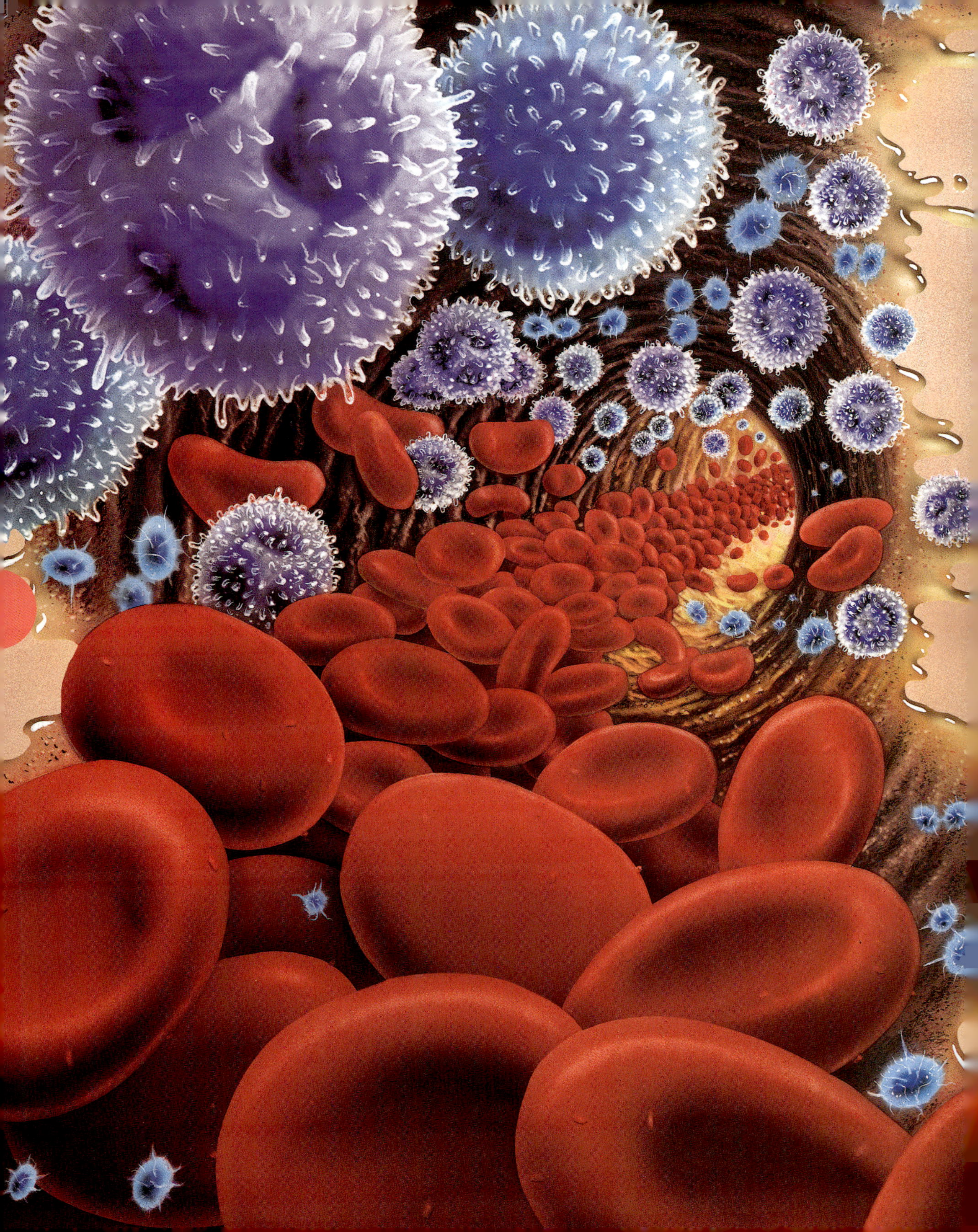

THE VITAL SYSTEMS

Cells 348

Blood 350

The Heart 352

The Respiratory System 354

Digestion 356

Kidneys and Liver 358

Reproductive Systems 360

BONES, MUSCLES AND SKIN

The Skeleton 362

Bones and Joints 366

Muscles 368

Skin and Nails 370

SENSES AND NERVES

The Brain 372

Sight 374

Hearing and Speaking 376

Taste and Smell 378

Nerves and Hormones 380

Cells

INSIDE A CELL

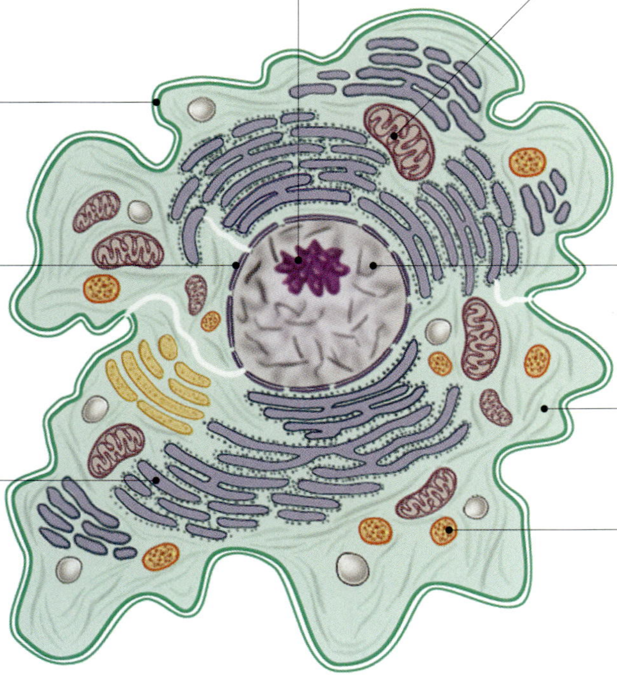

CELL CLONING

Cells form when a parent cell divides in two.This is called mitosis.

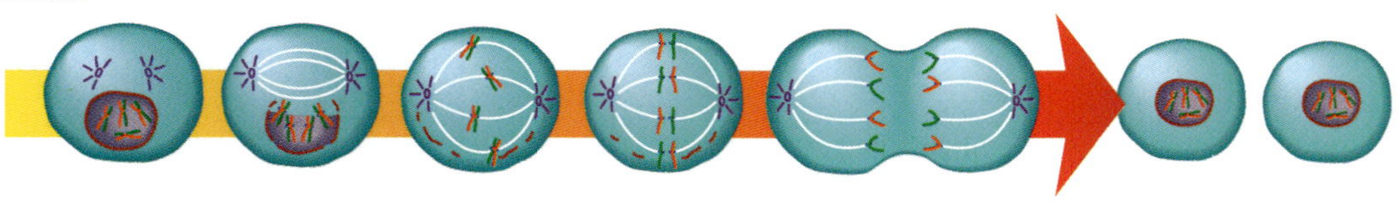

HELPFUL BACTERIA

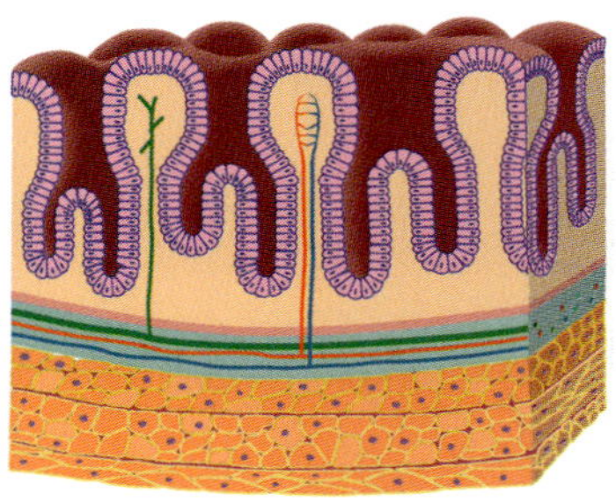

Some bacteria can destroy healthy tissue. Bacteria in the lining of the stomach, however, help the body use vitamins from food.

VIRUSES

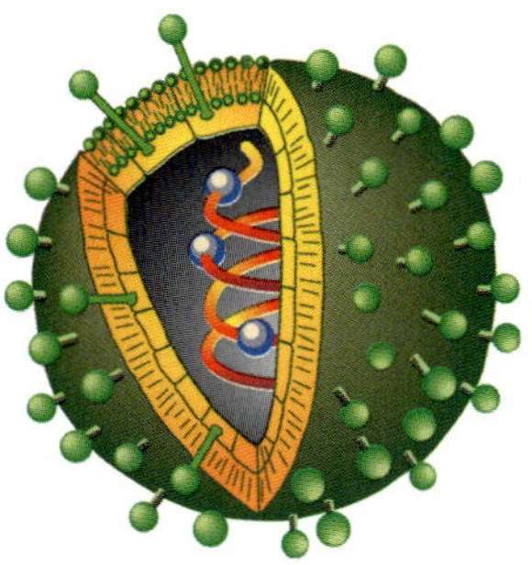

Viruses invade cells and trick them into making more viruses. This process changes the cells chemically. They are damaged or they die.

TYPES OF CELLS

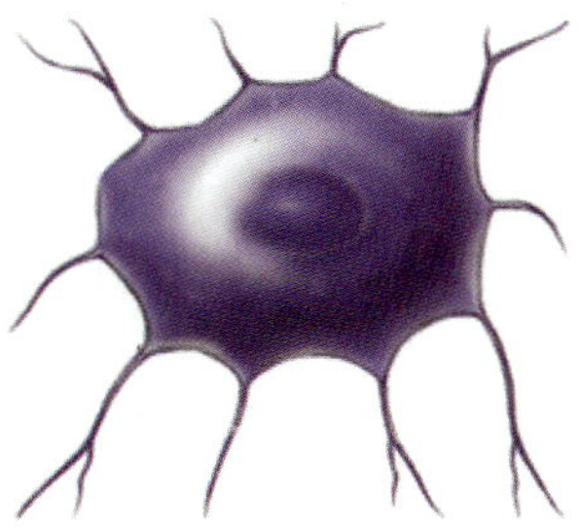

Bone cell

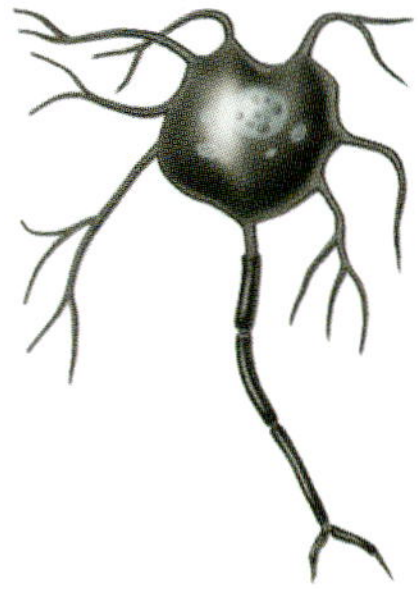

Nerve cell

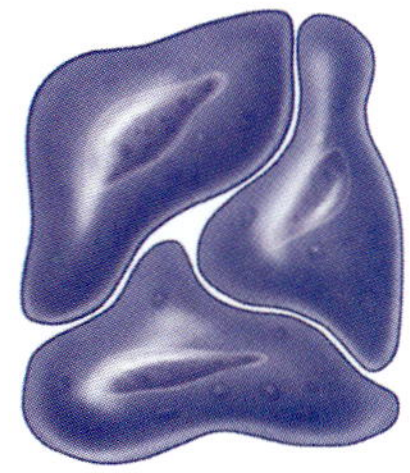

Skin cells

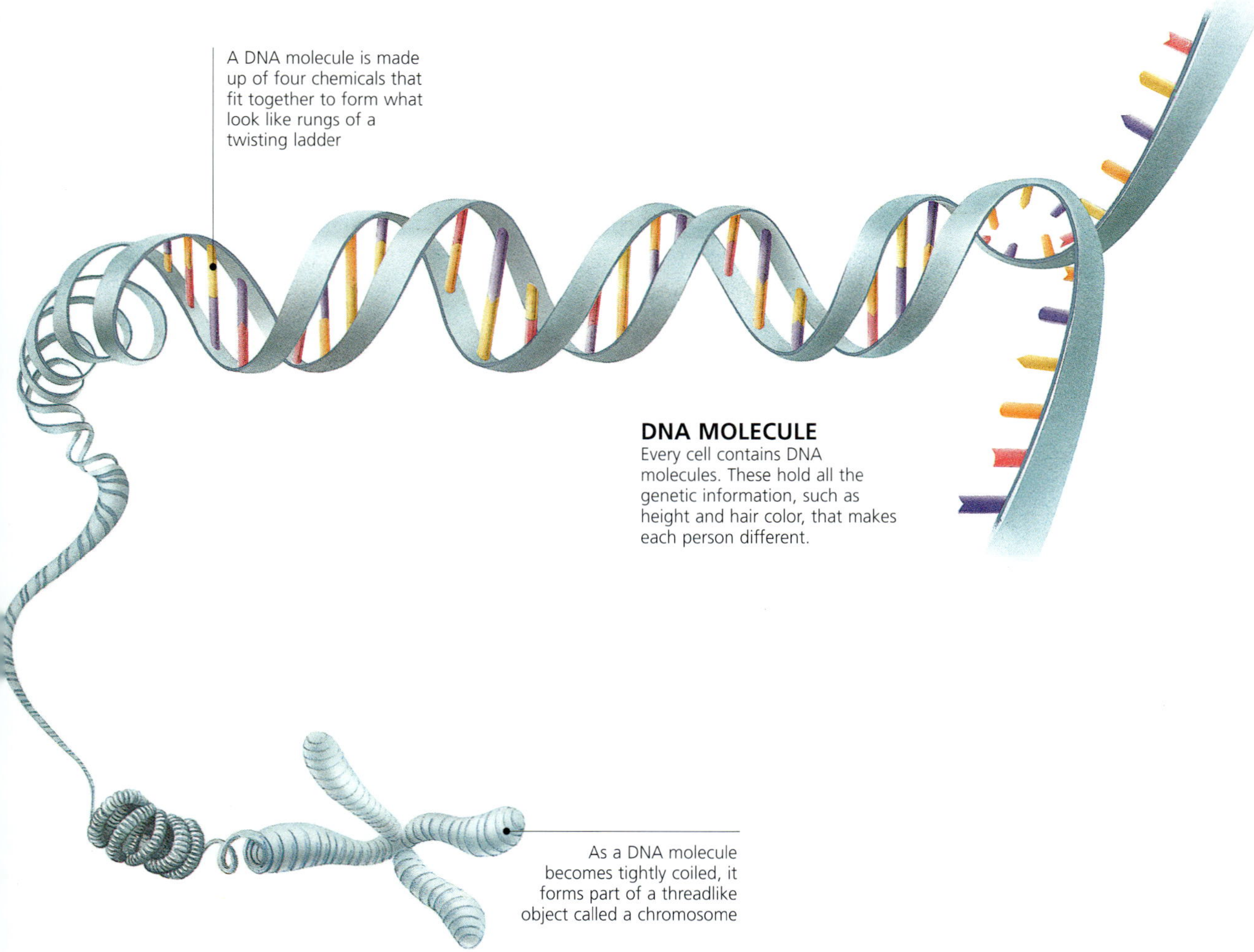

DNA MOLECULE

Every cell contains DNA molecules. These hold all the genetic information, such as height and hair color, that makes each person different.

Blood

BLOOD CLOTTING

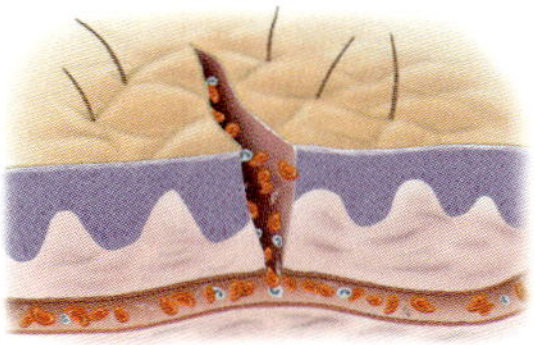

At a wound, platelets and sticky fibers trap red cells, white cells and germs. A clot is formed that seals the leak.

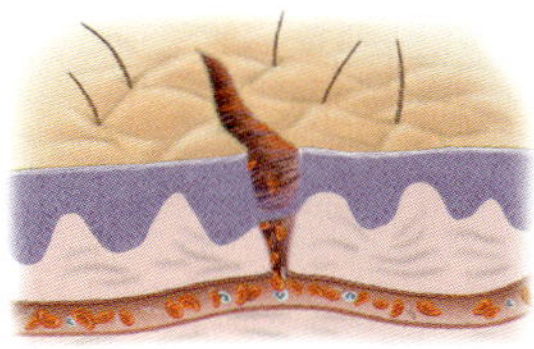

Cells at the wound's edge multiply to make new skin as healing begins. The clot hardens into a protective scab.

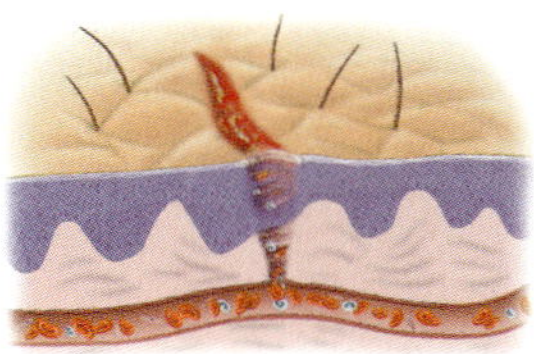

Capillaries under the skin reseal, and new cells grow together. Eventually the scab falls off and the wound is healed.

BLOOD TYPES

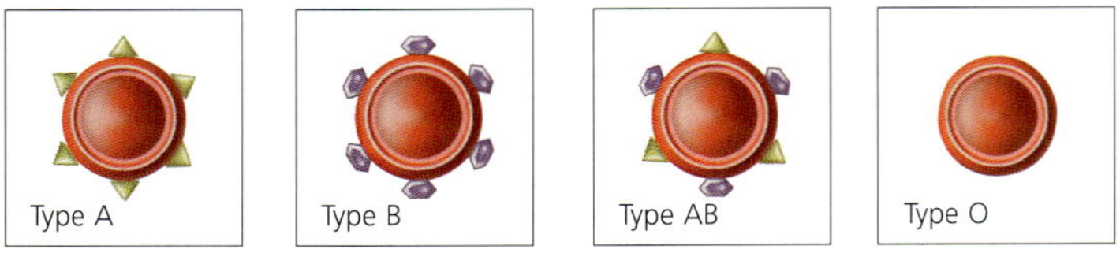

ARTERY

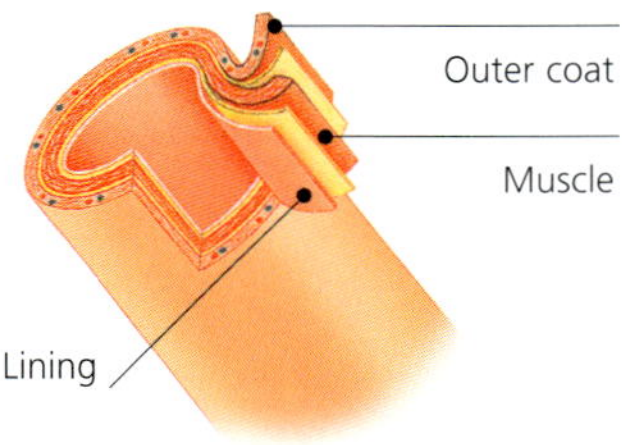

VEIN

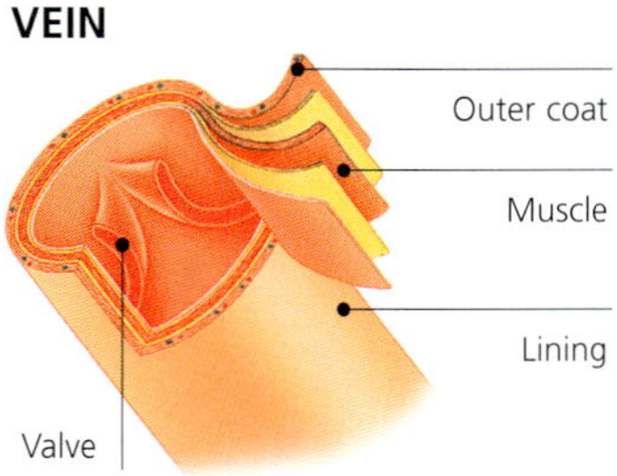

CAPILLARY

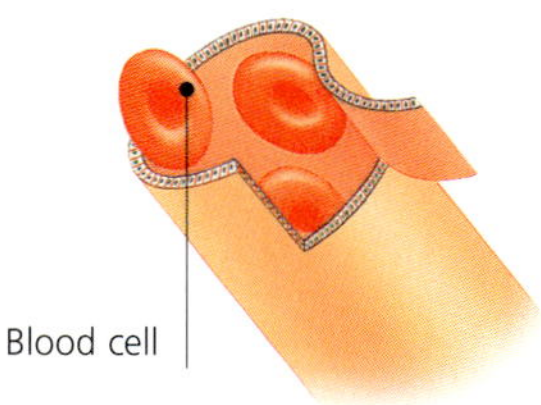

BLOOD CIRCULATION

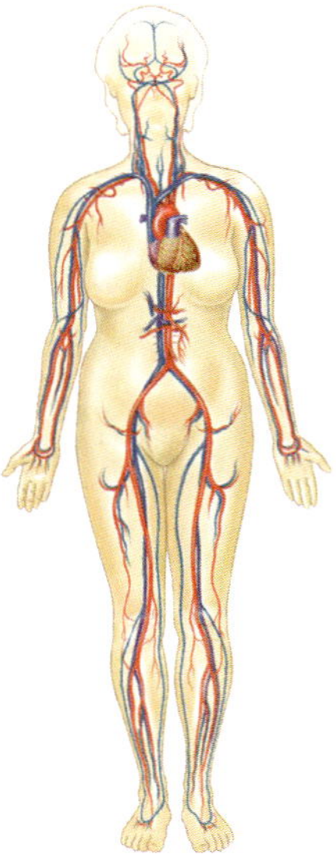

BLOOD COMPOSITION

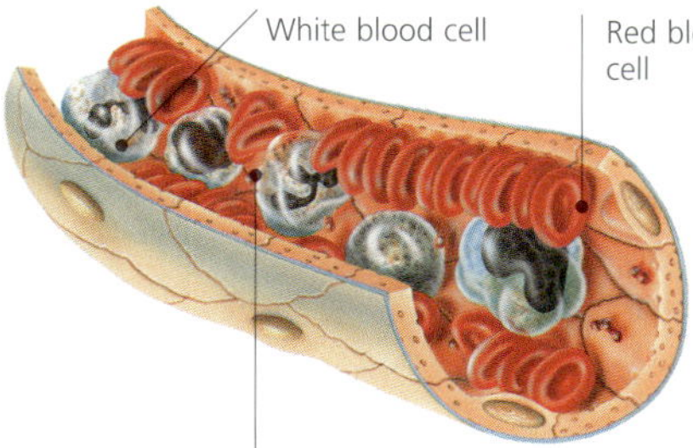

FIGHTING GERMS

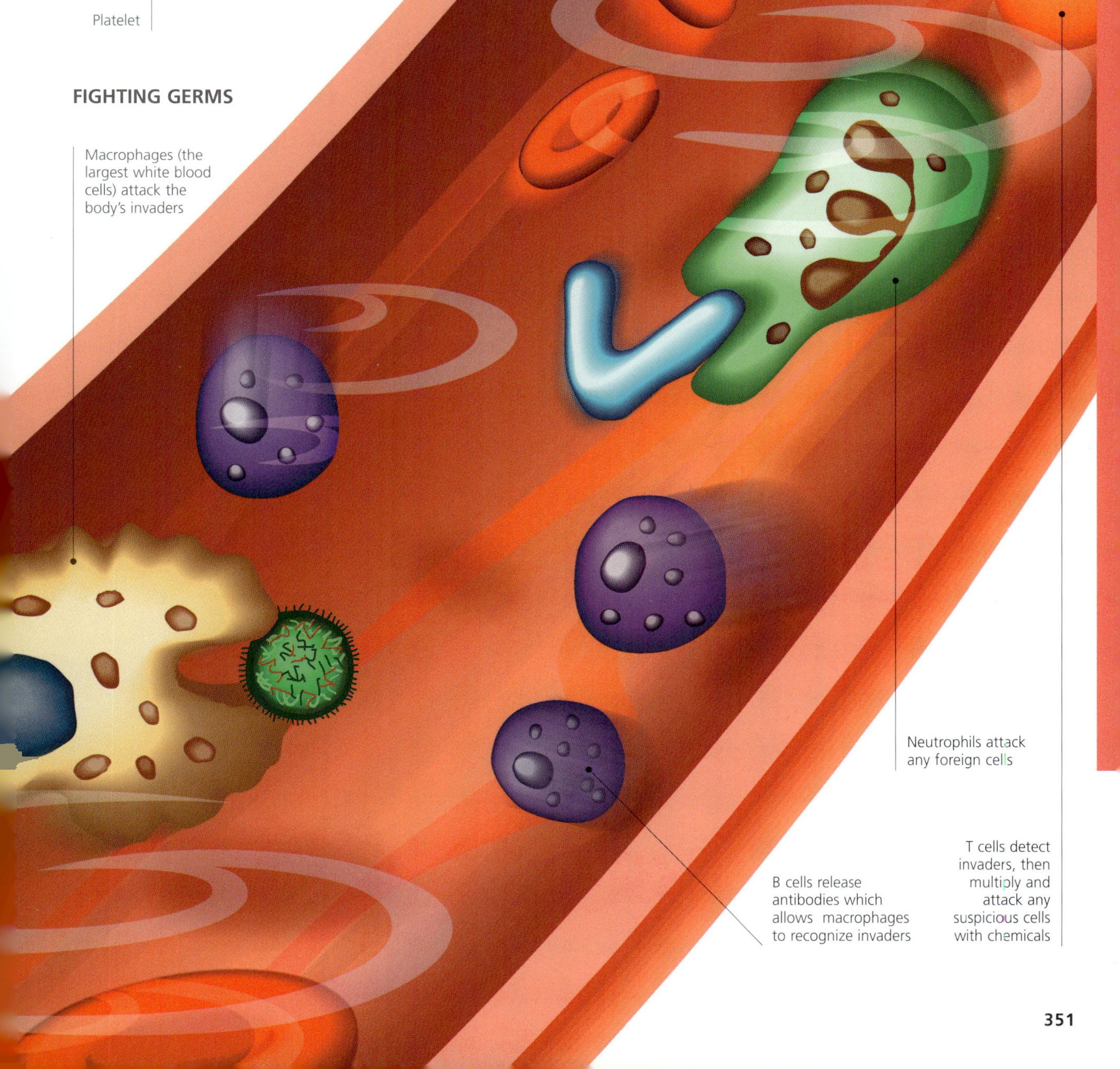

The Heart

INSIDE THE HEART

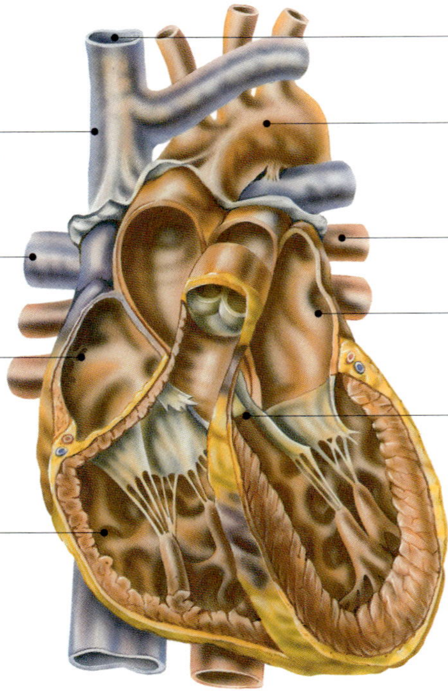

HEART FRONT

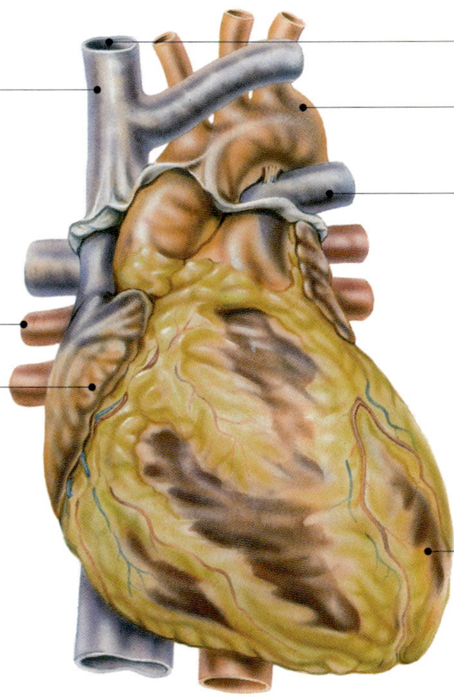

HEART CYCLE

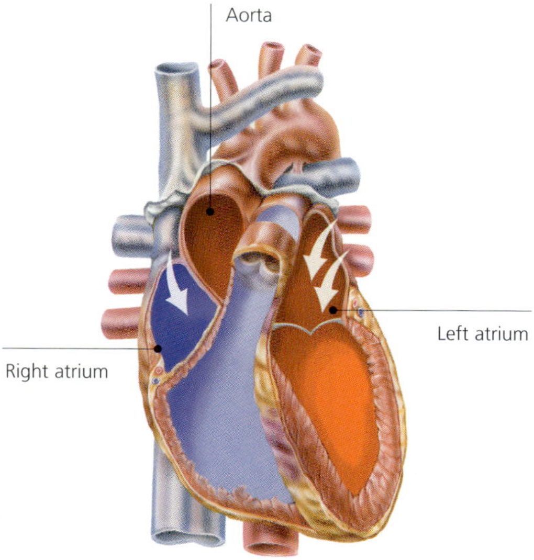

Deoxygenated blood from the body pours into the right atrium. Oxygen-rich blood from the lungs fills the left atrium.

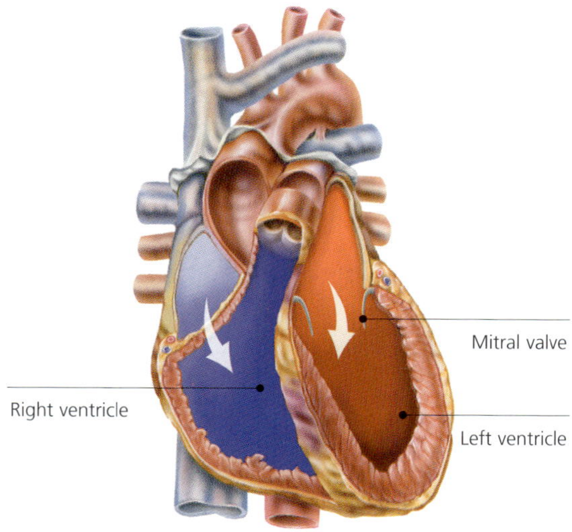

The atria contract. Blood pushes open the valves leading to the heart's pumping chambers. The ventricles fill with blood.

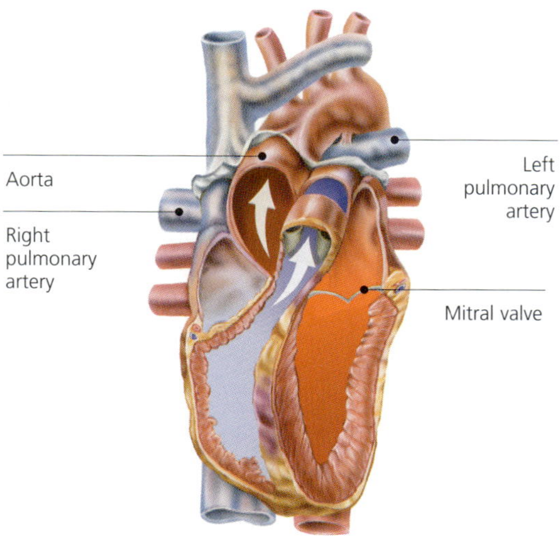

The ventricles contract, forcing open the valves to the aorta and pulmonary arteries. These fill with blood.

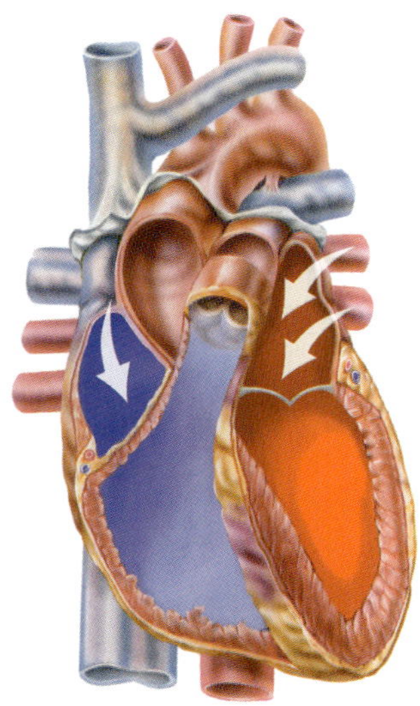

As the ventricles relax, the cycle begins again.

The Respiratory System

INSIDE THE LUNGS

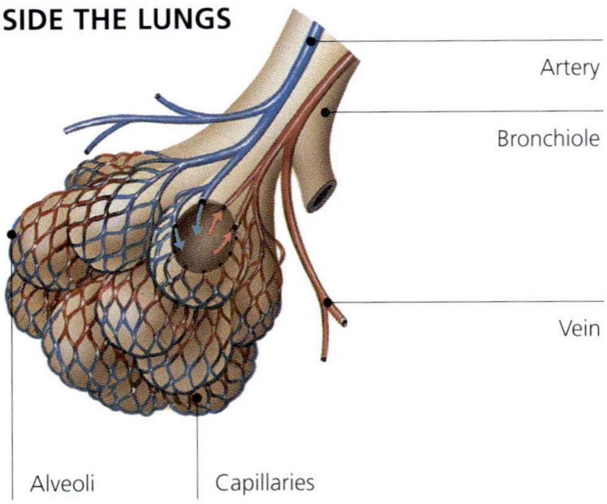

BREATHING

Breathing In
The curved diaphragm under the lungs is the main breathing muscle. It contracts and flattens to stretch the lungs and suck in air.

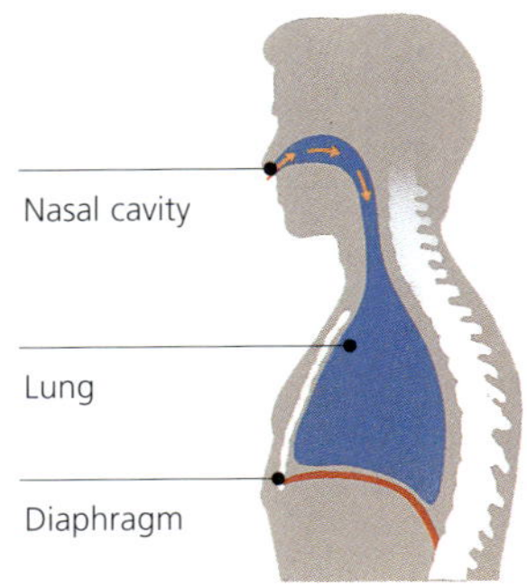

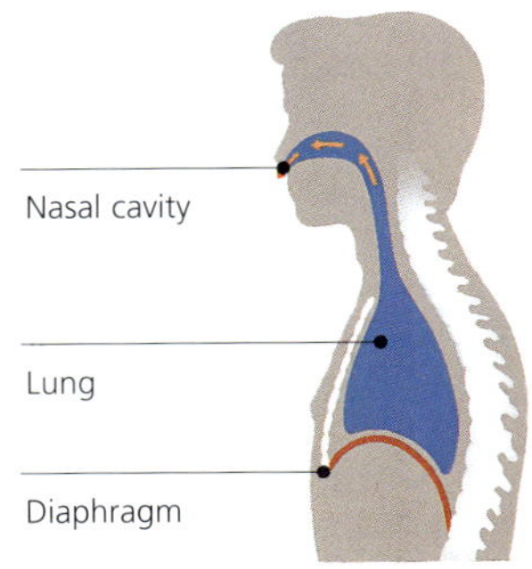

Breathing Out
The diaphragm relaxes as we breathe out. The stretched elastic lungs spring back to their natural smaller size, and blow out air.

RESPIRATORY SYSTEM

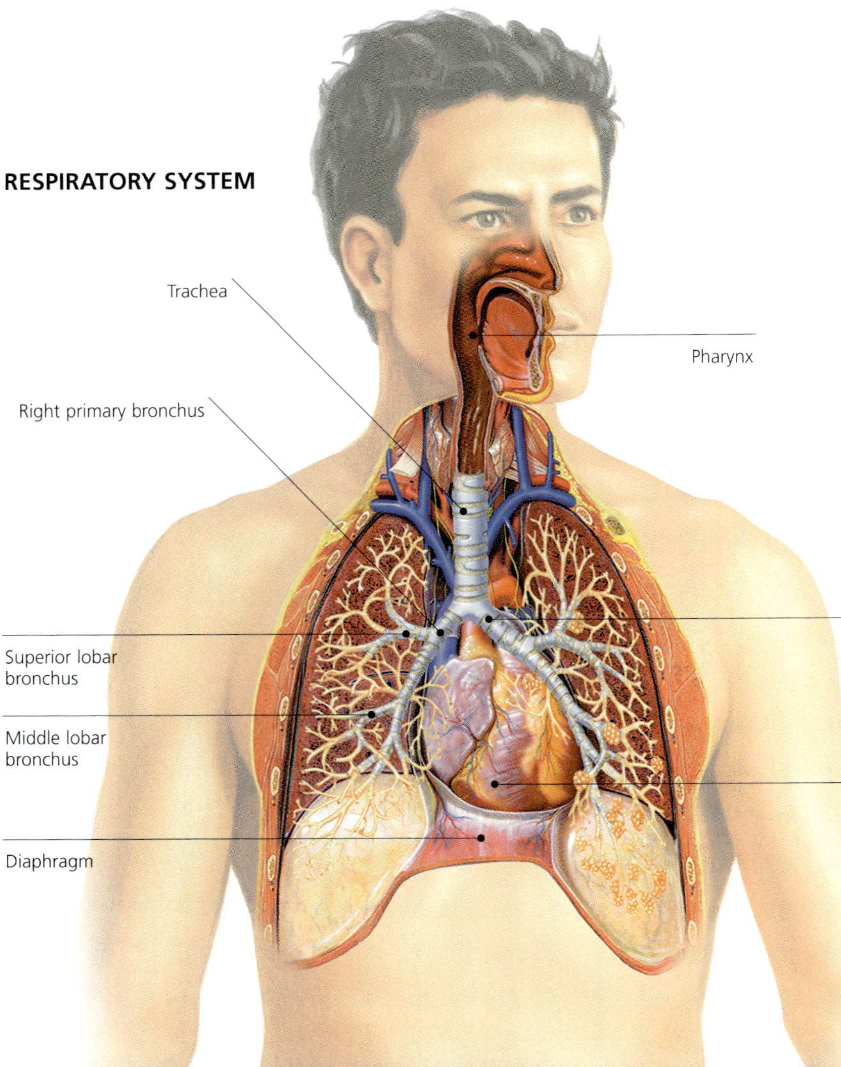

BRONCHIAL TREE

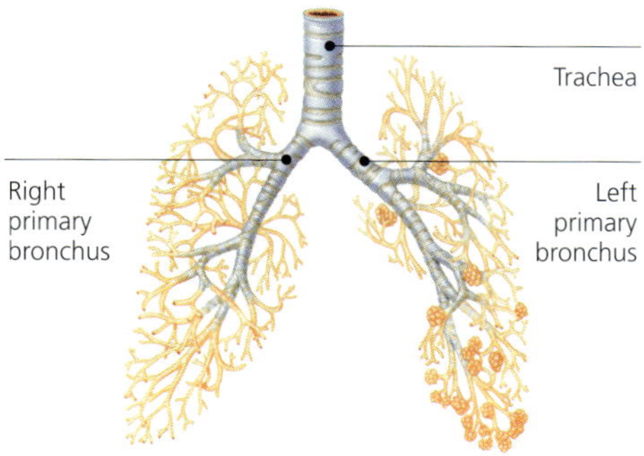

TRACHEA

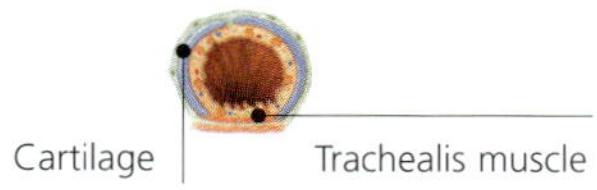

LUNGS

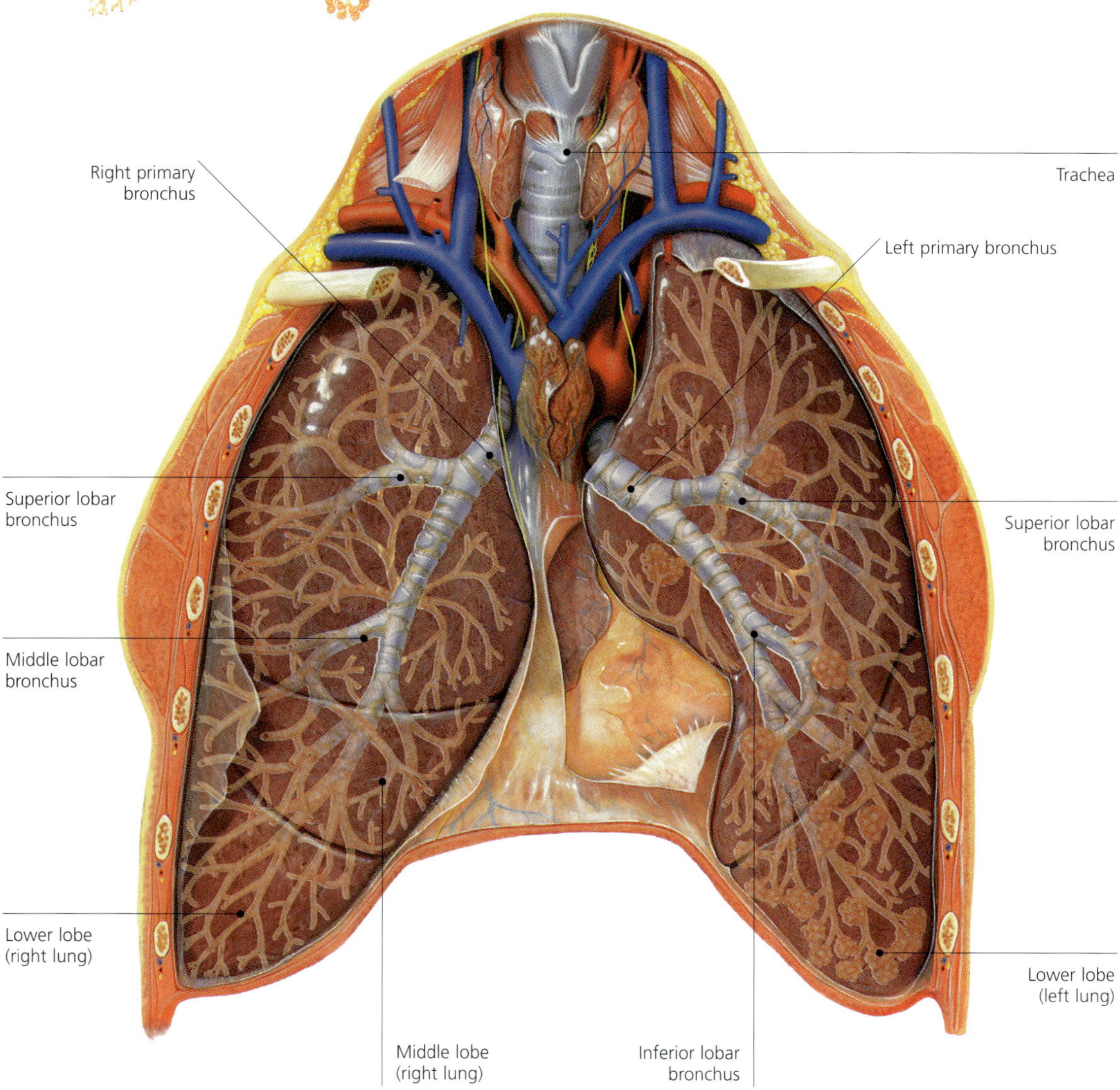

Digestion

STOMACH STRUCTURE

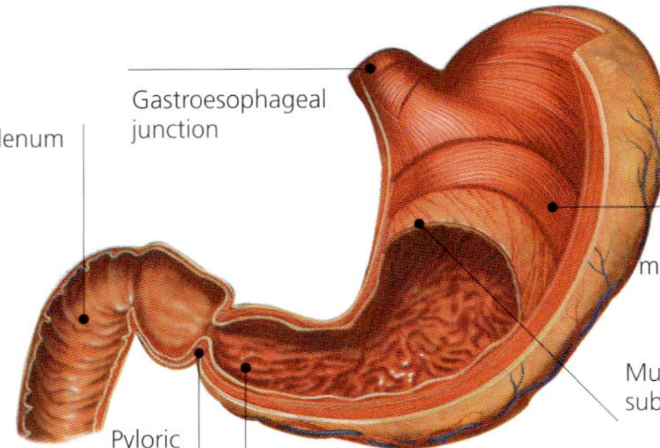

STOMACH FUNCTION

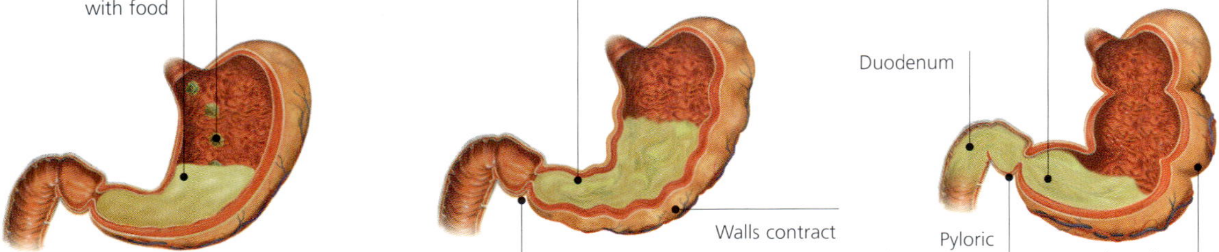

DIGESTIVE ORGANS

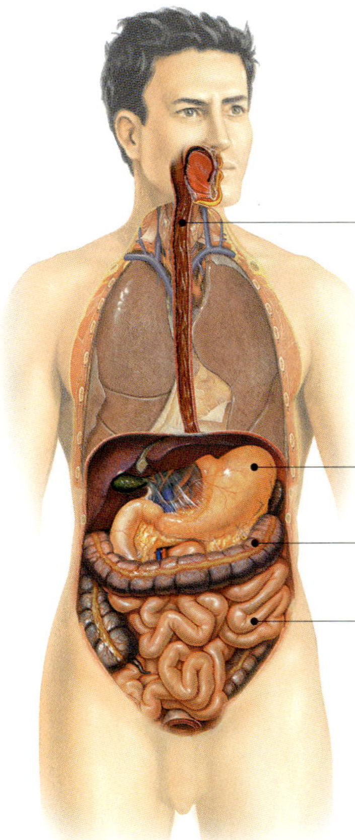

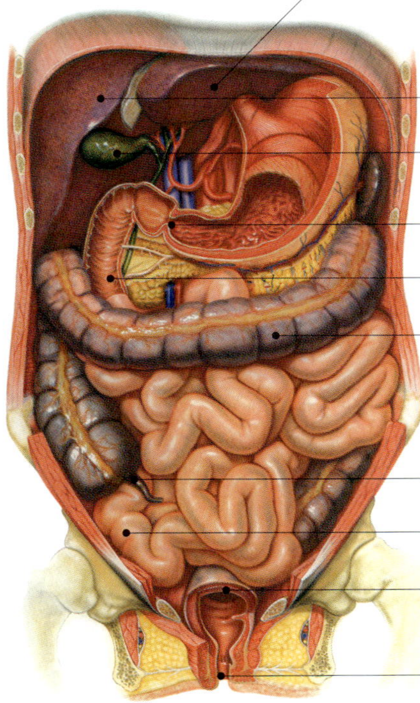

SALIVARY GLANDS

Salivary glands make watery spit, or saliva. Saliva makes food soft and easier to swallow. It also contains enzymes that start to digest food.

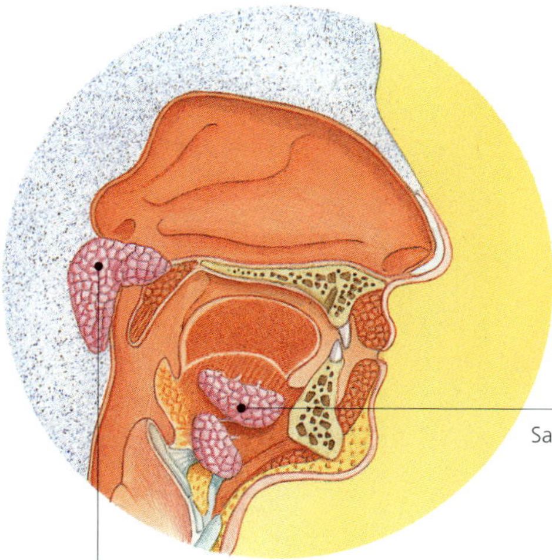

SMALL INTESTINE

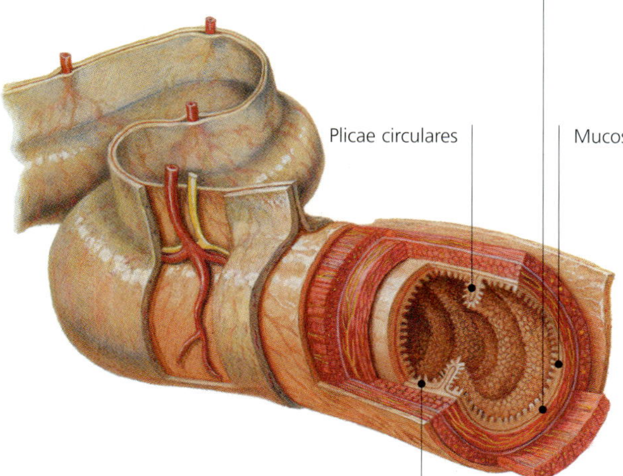

EATING

The tongue separates a small portion of the food in the mouth. It presses this against the mouth's roof, or hard palate, to shape it into a soft lump.

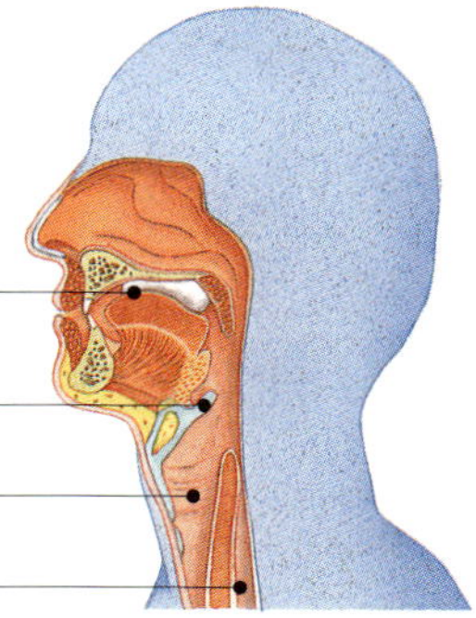

The tongue pushes the food into the upper throat. The epiglottis closes over the trachea to stop food going down it.

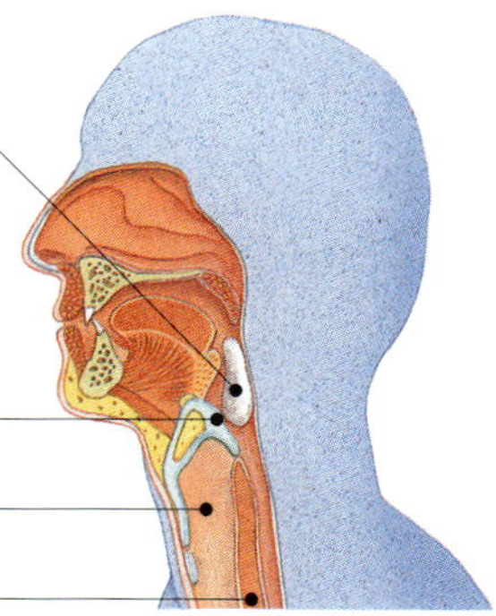

Muscles in the walls of the lower throat and esophagus contract in waves. They force the food down the esophagus into the stomach.

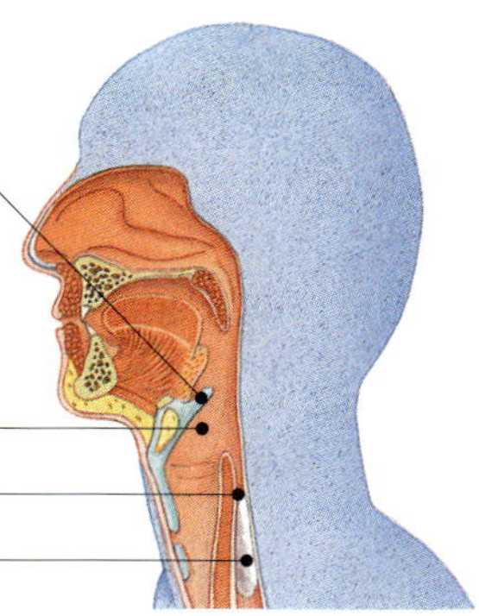

Kidneys and Liver

KIDNEY CROSS-SECTION

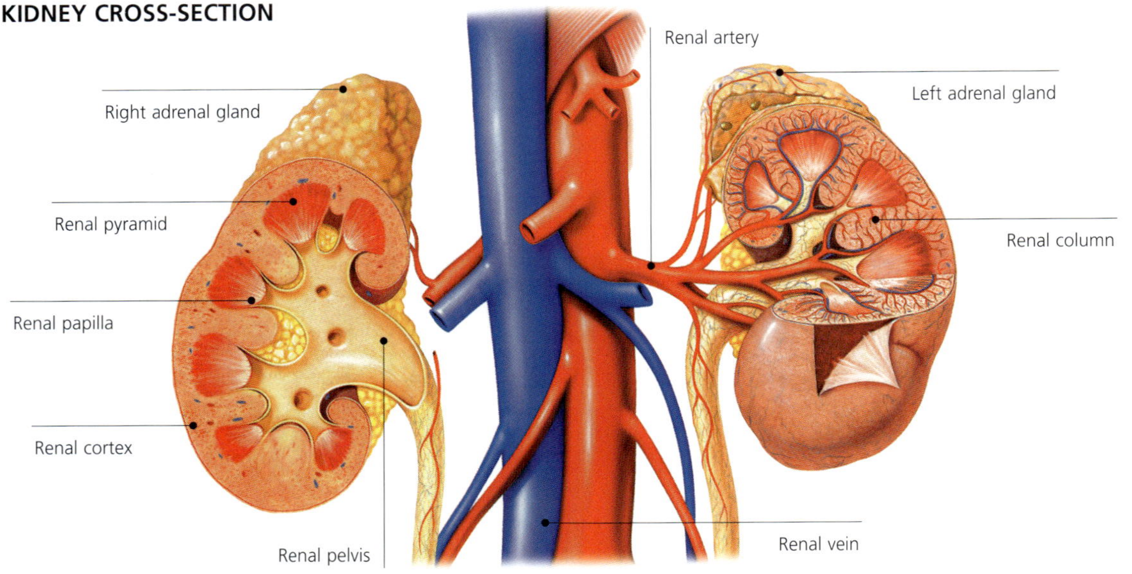

URINARY SYSTEM

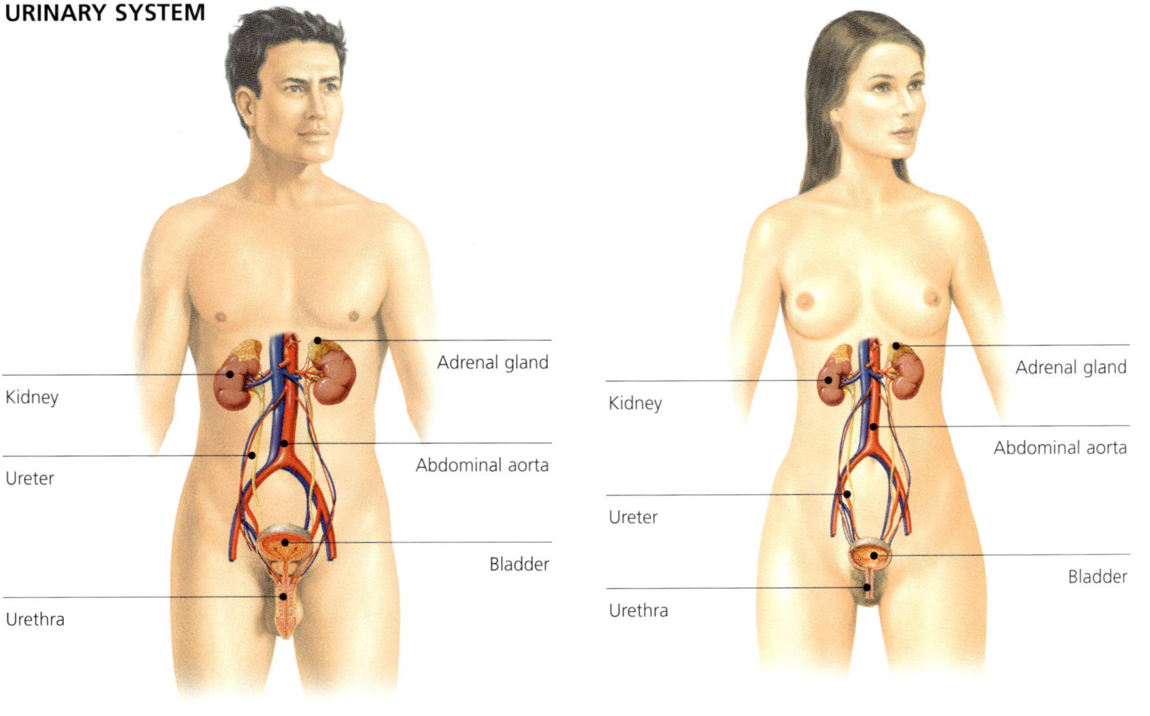

AROUND THE LIVER

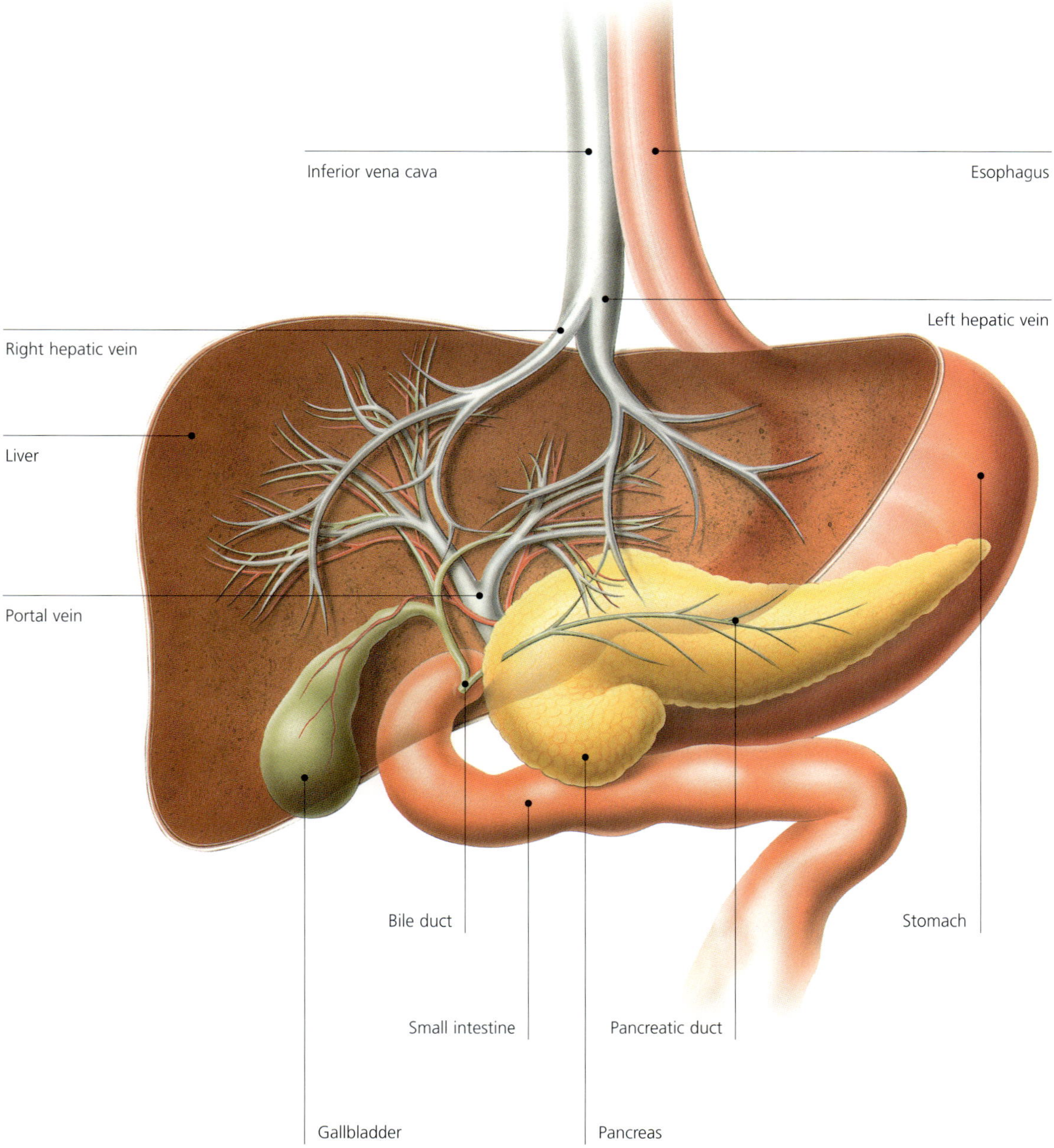

Reproductive Systems

BIRTH

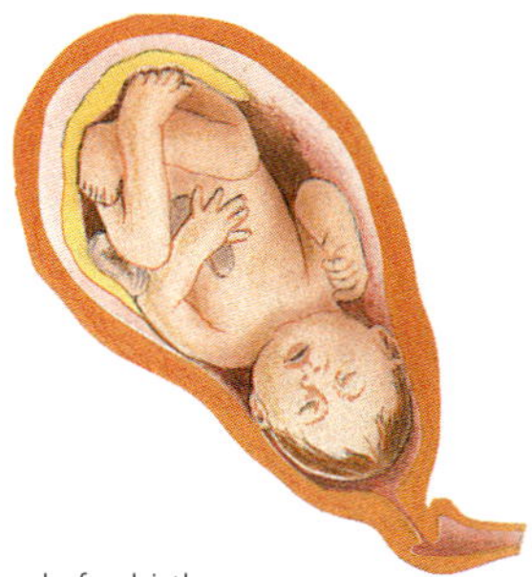

Ready for birth

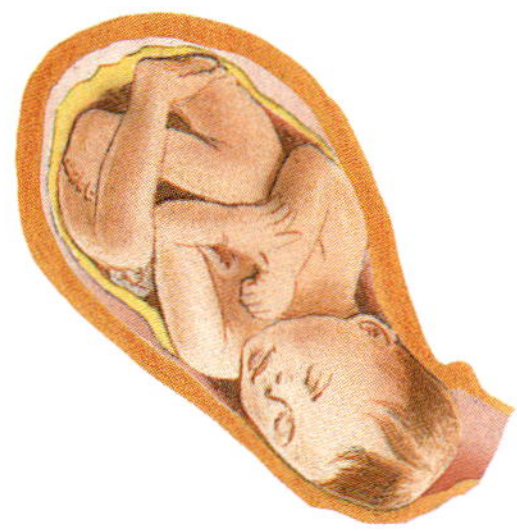

Delivery

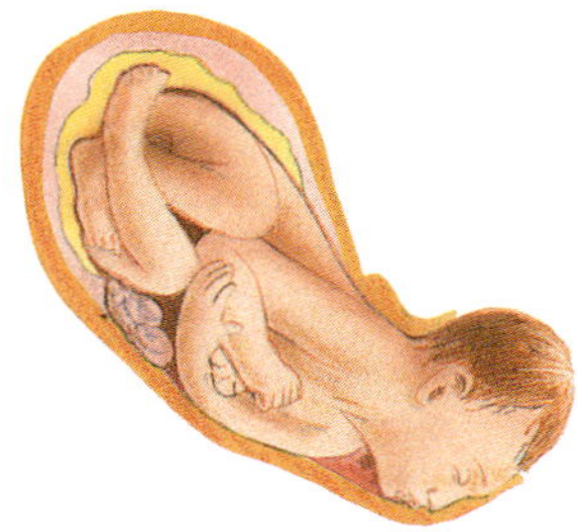

Leaving the womb

MALE REPRODUCTIVE ORGANS

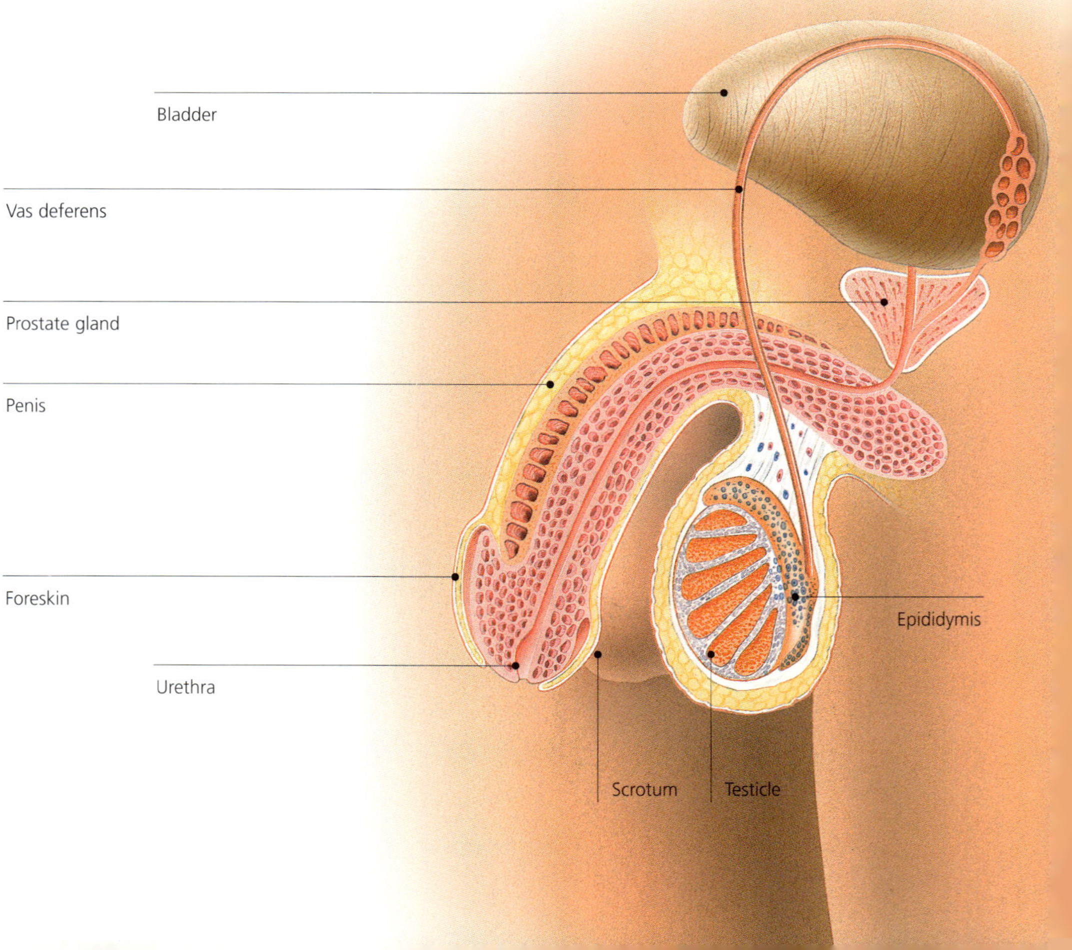

BEGINNING LIFE

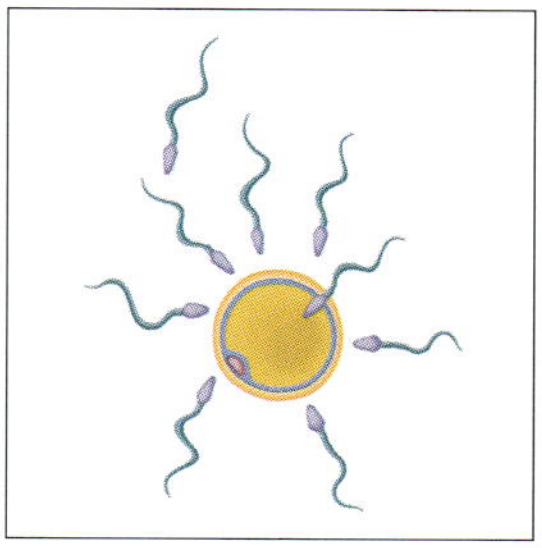

Fertilization
A sperm penetrates and fertilizes the egg. The egg is now called a zygote.

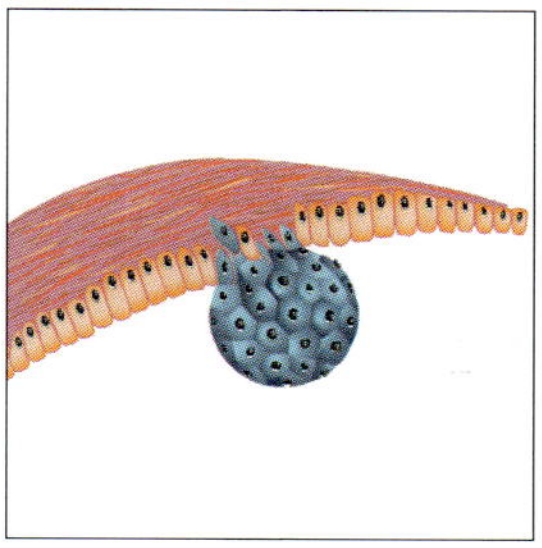

Implantation
The fertilized egg divides many times and attaches to the wall of the uterus.

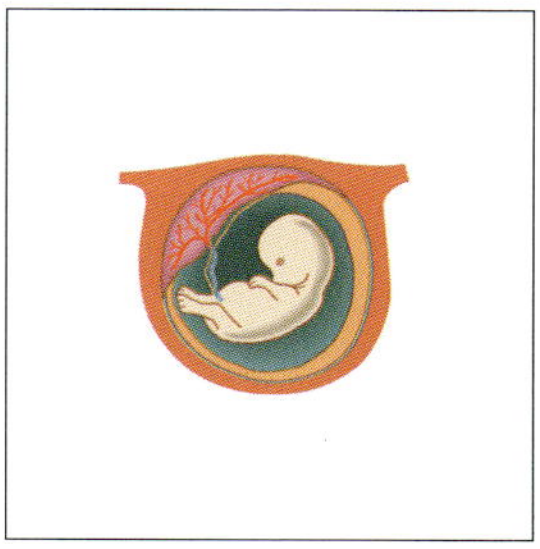

Embryo
At seven weeks the unborn child is called an embyro.

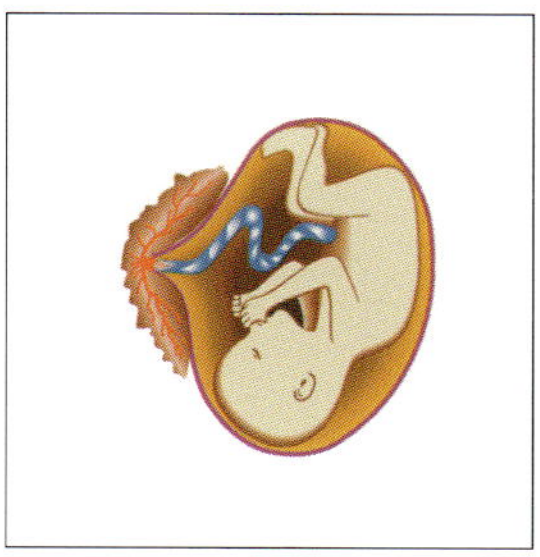

Fetus
At two months the embryo becomes a fetus. It is not much larger than a walnut.

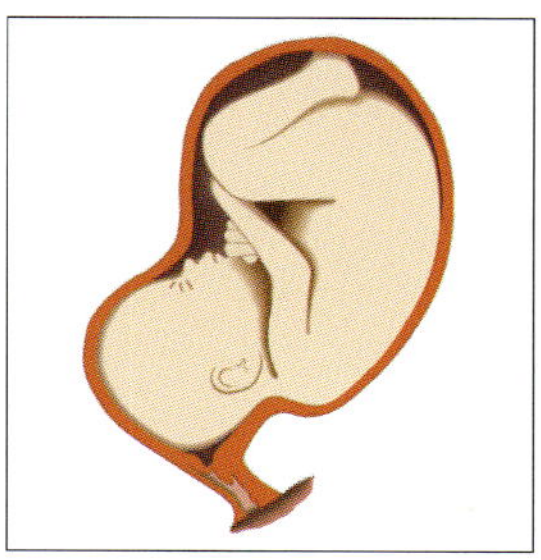

Birth
At nine months, strong uterine movements push the baby through the vagina into the world.

REPRODUCTIVE SYSTEM LOCATION

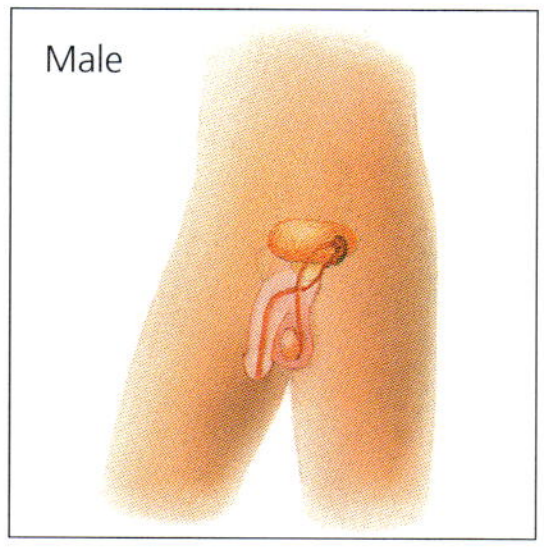

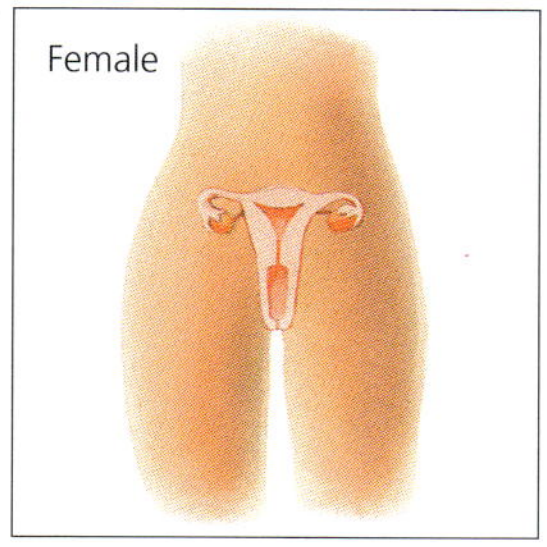

FEMALE REPRODUCTIVE ORGANS

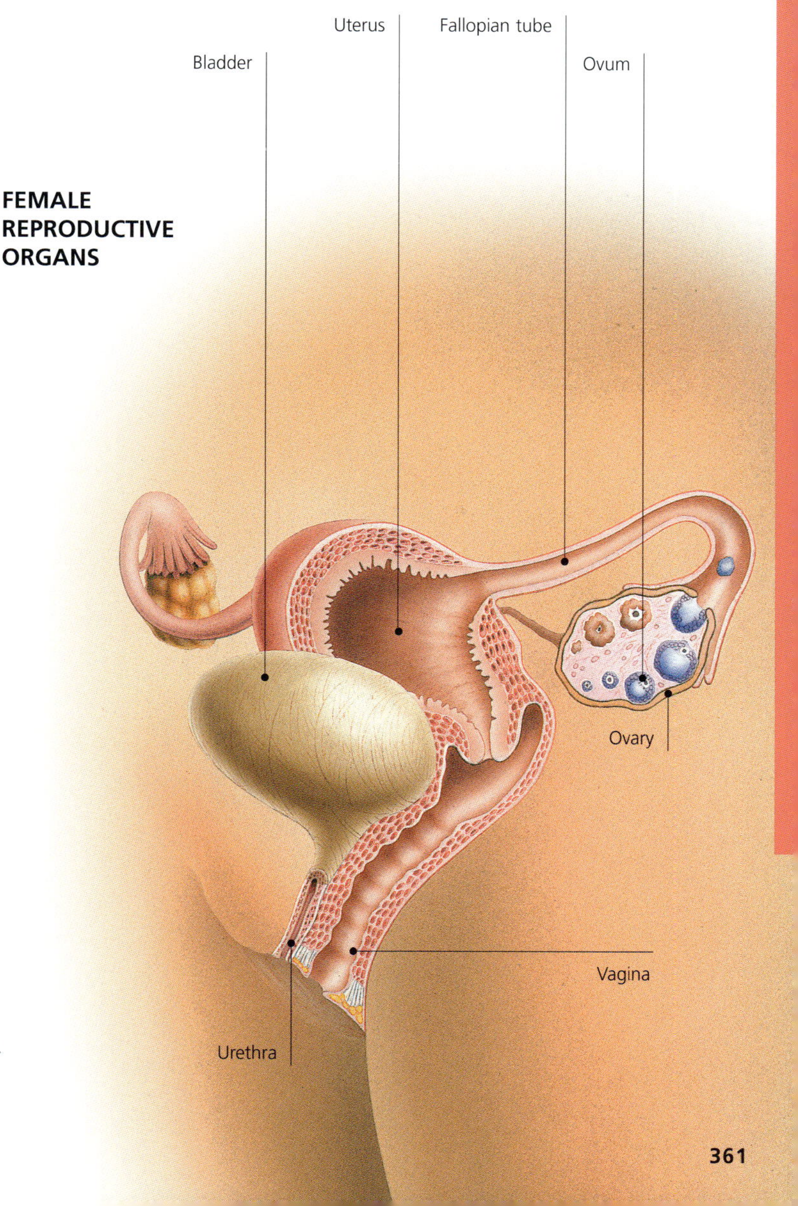

The Skeleton

FRONT VIEW

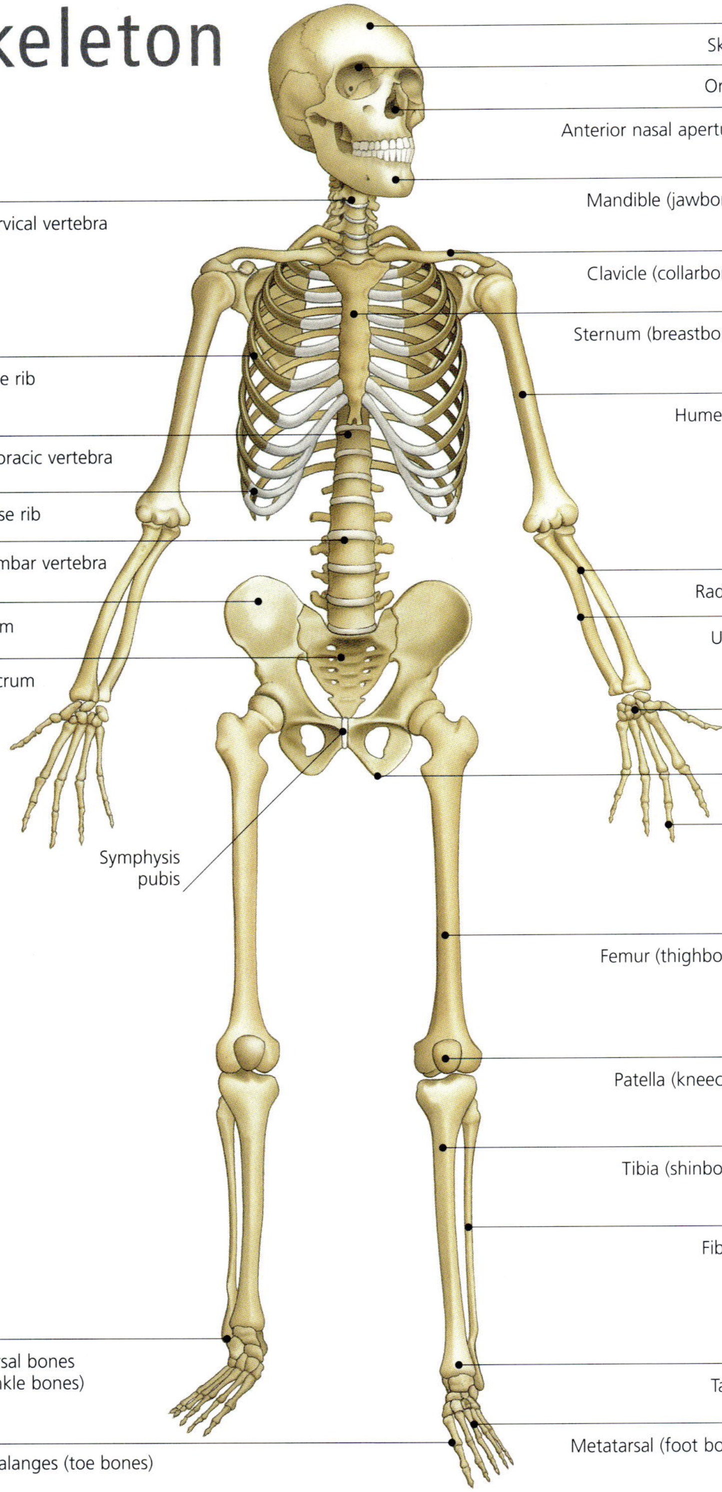

BACK VIEW

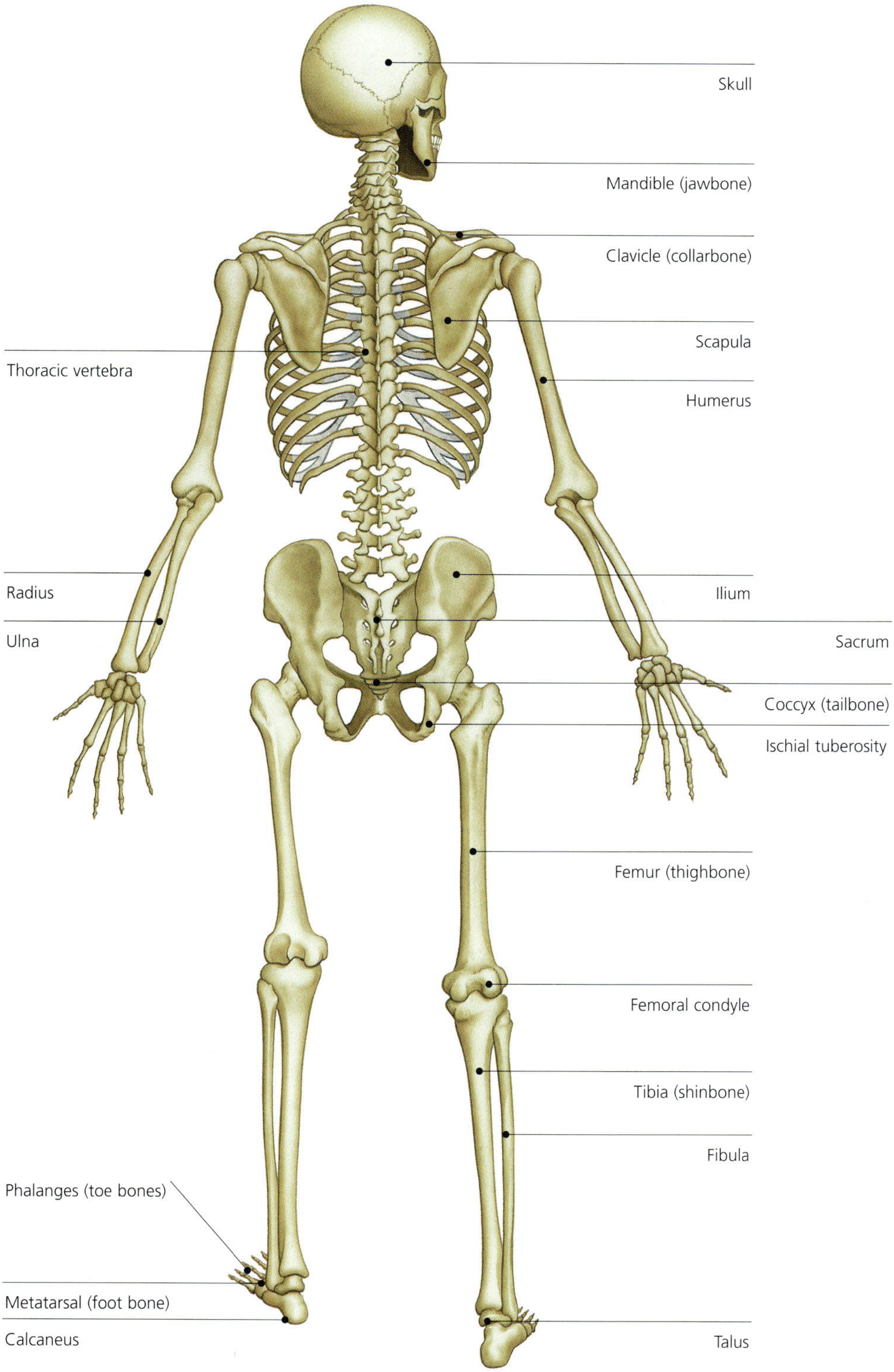

Skull
Mandible (jawbone)
Clavicle (collarbone)
Scapula
Humerus
Thoracic vertebra
Radius
Ulna
Ilium
Sacrum
Coccyx (tailbone)
Ischial tuberosity
Femur (thighbone)
Femoral condyle
Tibia (shinbone)
Fibula
Phalanges (toe bones)
Metatarsal (foot bone)
Calcaneus
Talus

The Skeleton

TEETH TYPES

SIDE VIEW

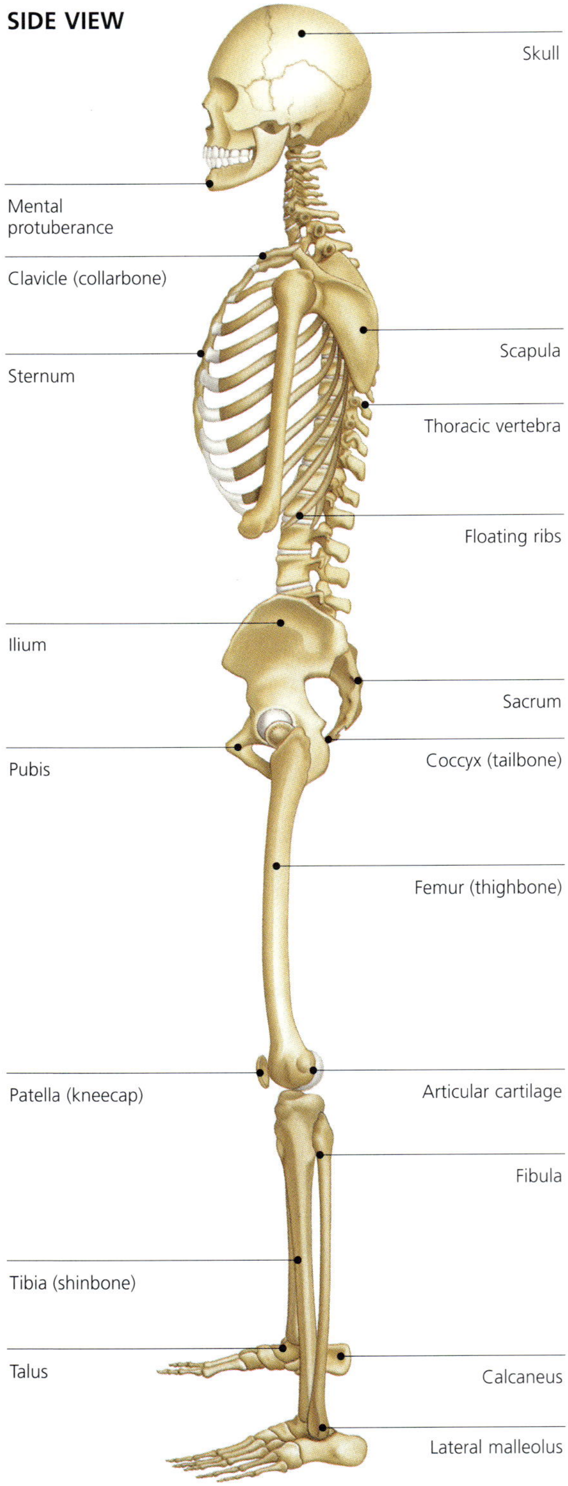

SKULL SIDE VIEW

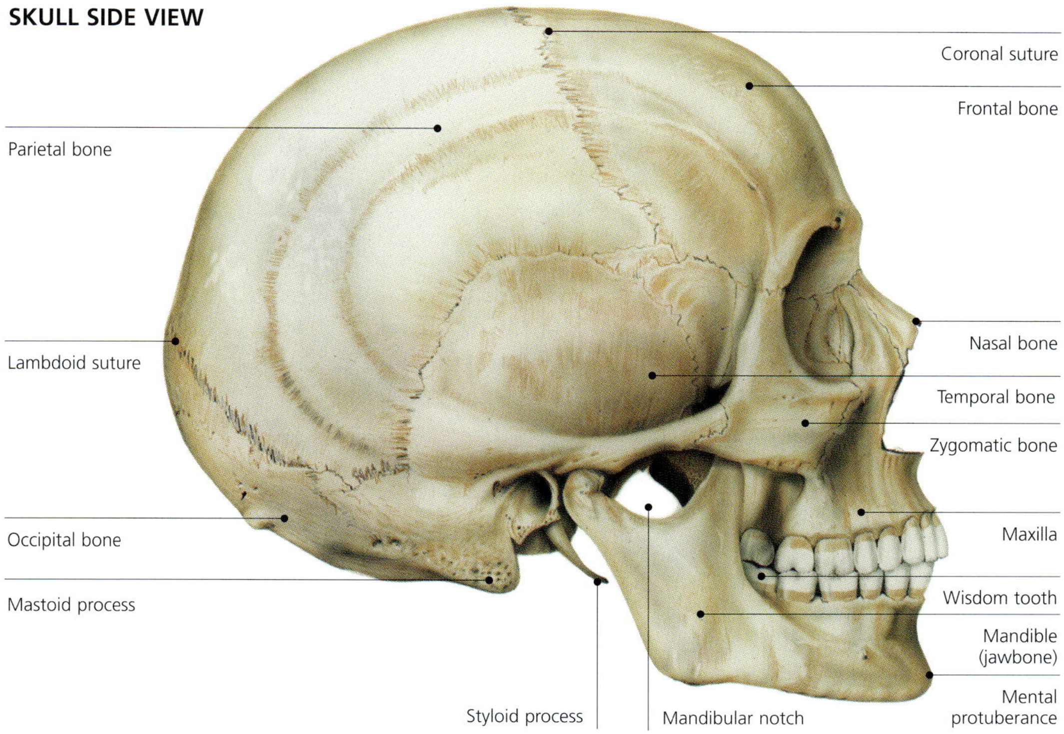

INSIDE THE SKULL

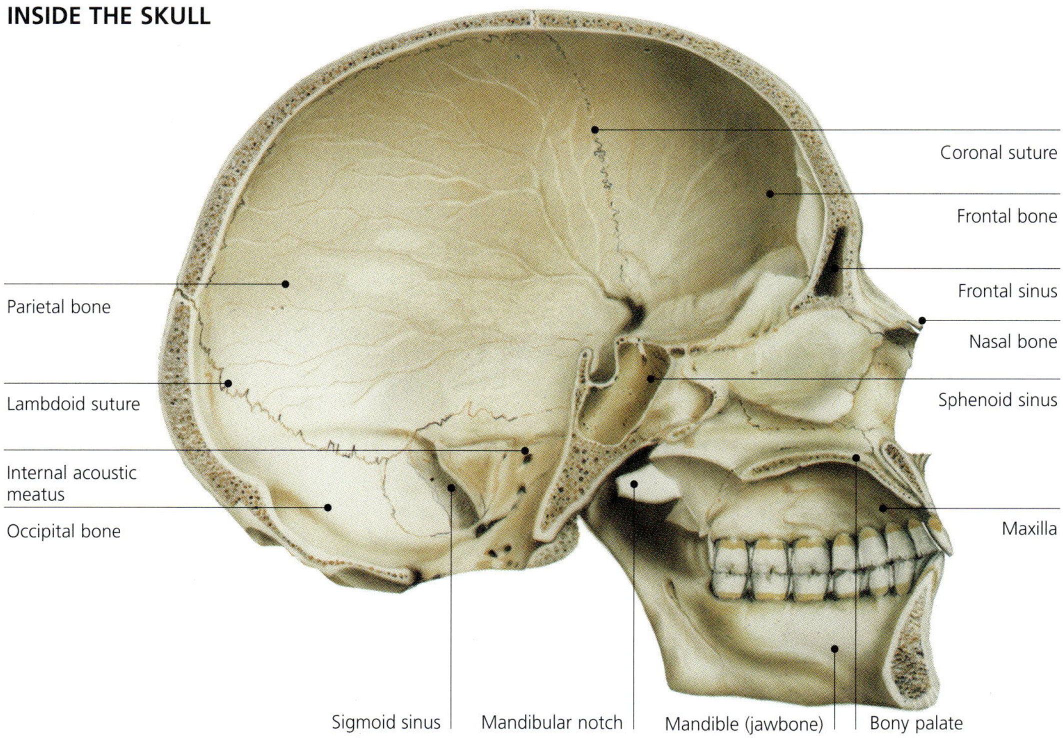

Bones and Joints

HEALING BROKEN BONES

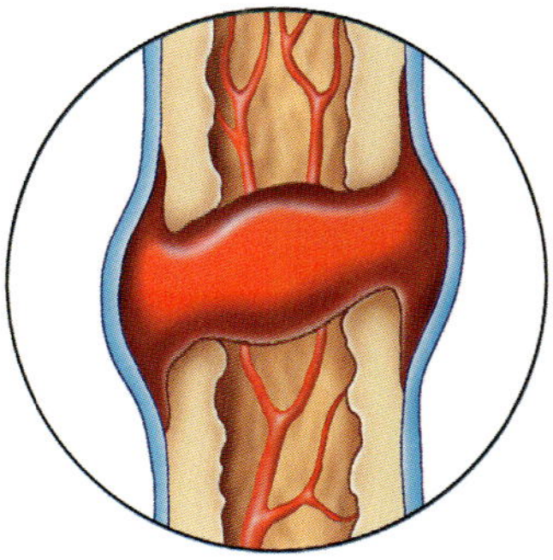

1. When a bone breaks, so do blood vessels. Blood flows into the fracture.

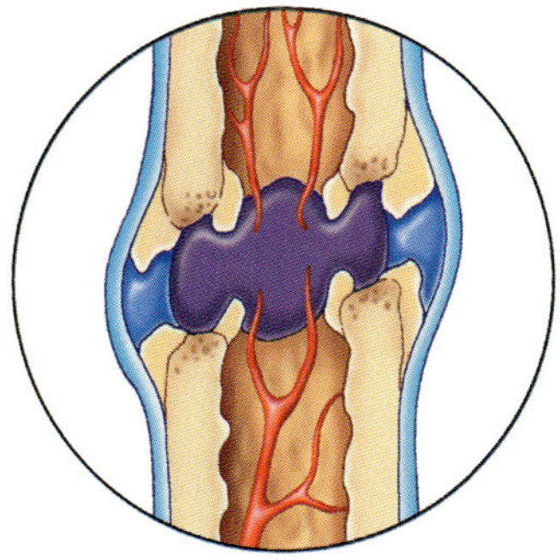

2. The blood grows sticky and thickens, forming a clot. The clot hardens. It will provide the platform on which the new bone will form.

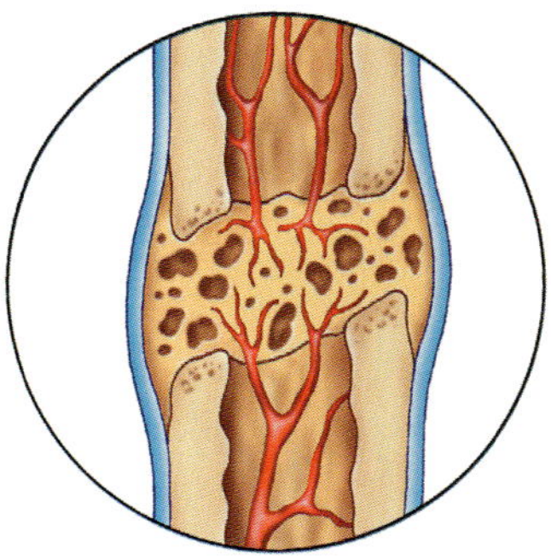

3. Cells from the broken ends rush to the clot. They quickly form a dense web of support tissue called a callus.

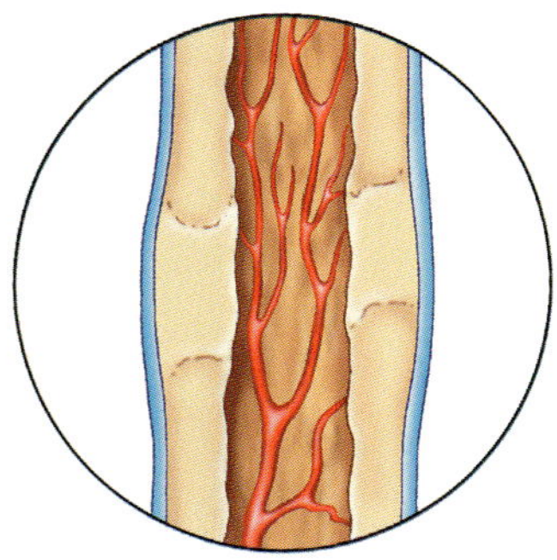

4. Over time the callus hardens into bone. At first, the bone bulges slightly but special cells reshape the bone, returning it to its original shape.

JOINTS

Joints are where two bones meet. Smooth cartilage coats the end of each bone. Synovial fluid moistens the joint. Ligaments lash the joint together and keep it from moving too much.

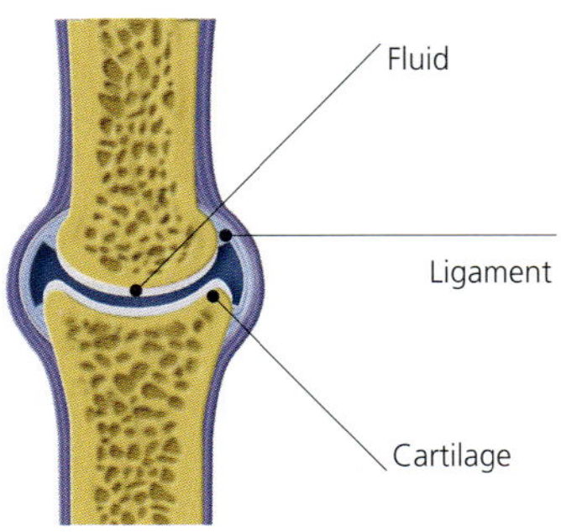

TYPES OF BROKEN BONE

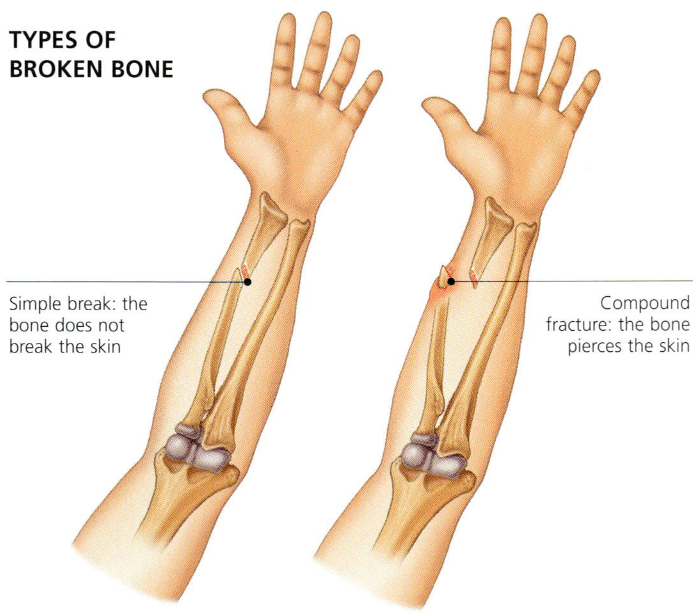

AT THE JOINT

Ball-and-socket joint

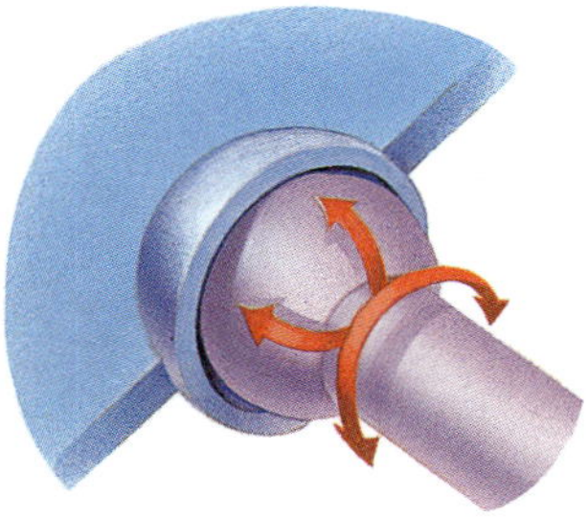

Hip joint

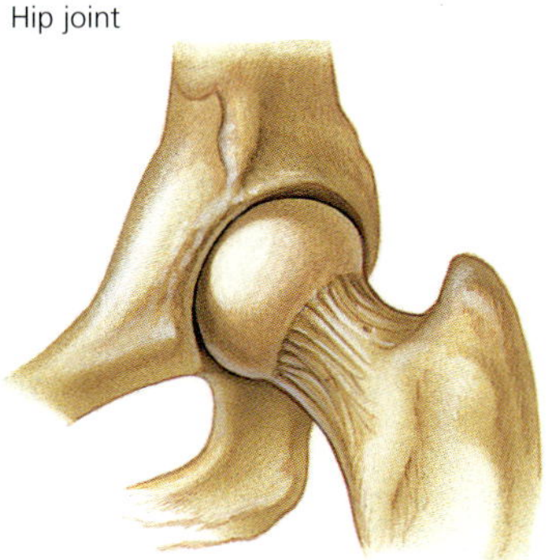

Hinge joint

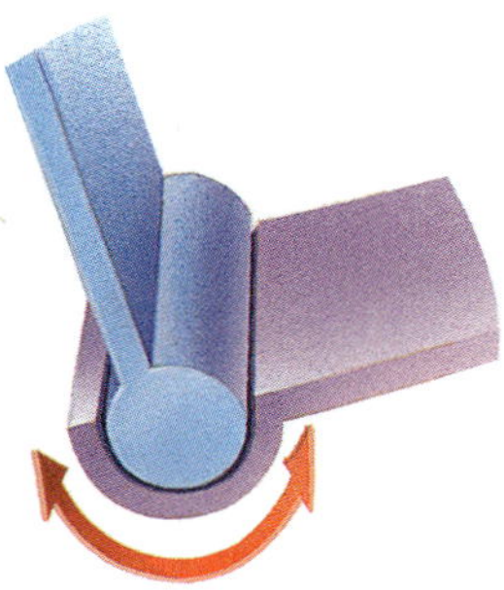

Elbow joint

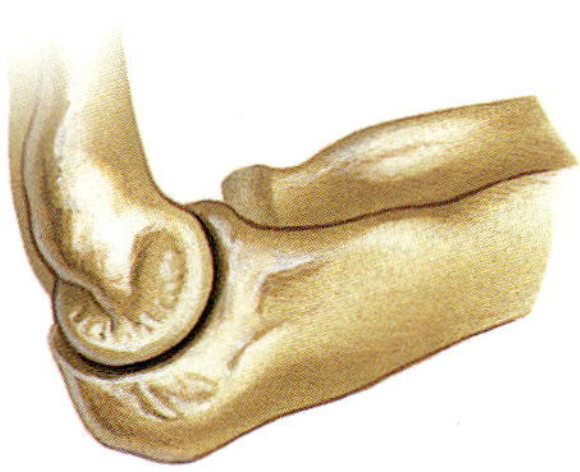

INSIDE A BONE

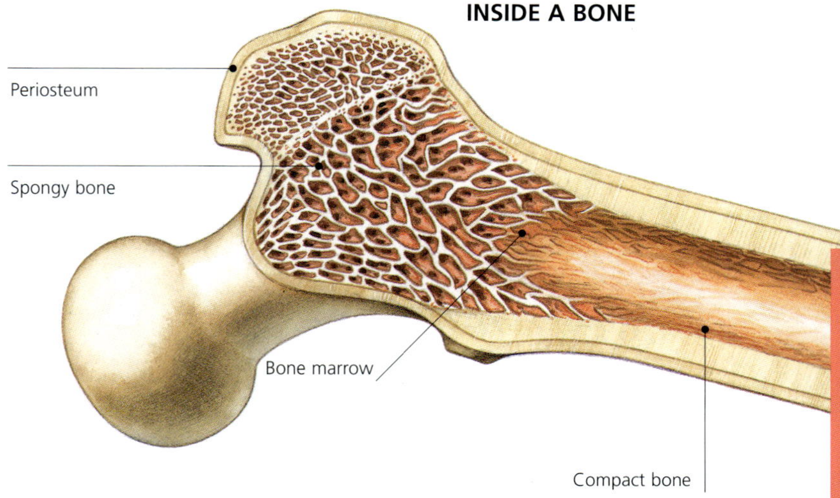

SPINE

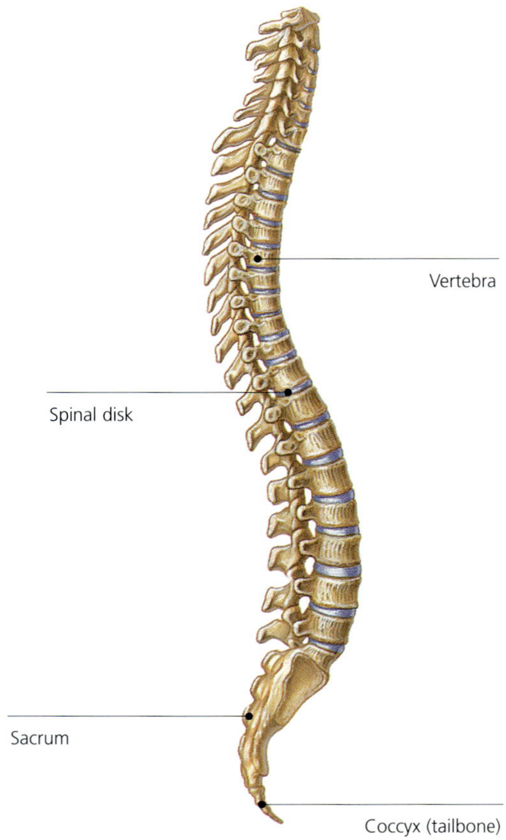

Muscles

TYPES OF MUSCLES

Skeletal muscle

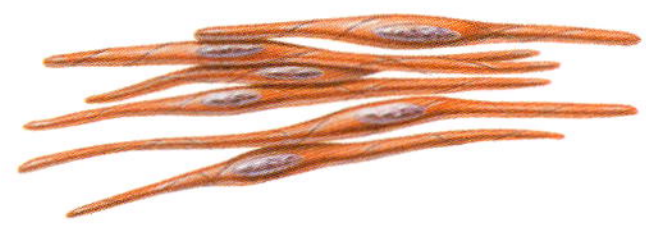

Smooth muscle

Cardiac muscle

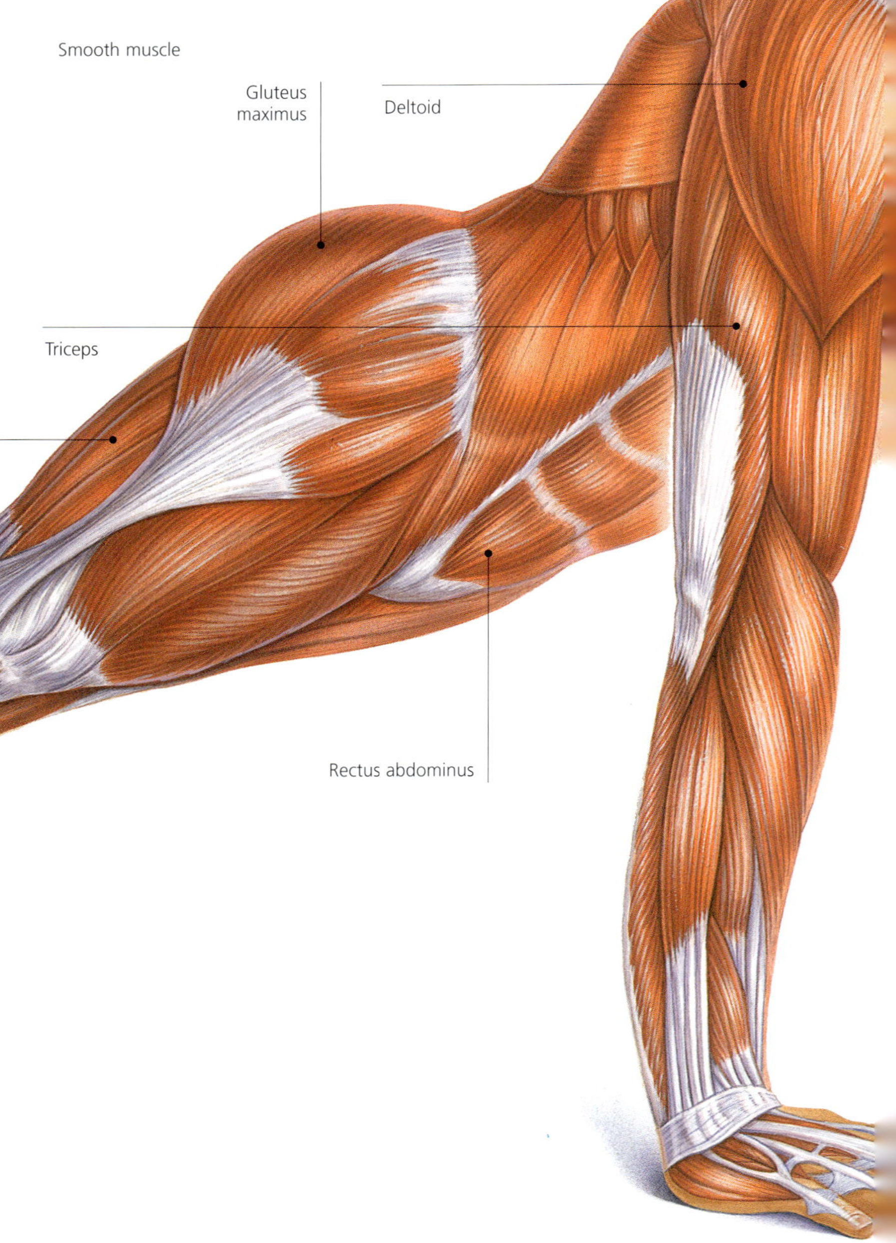

MUSCLE LAYERS

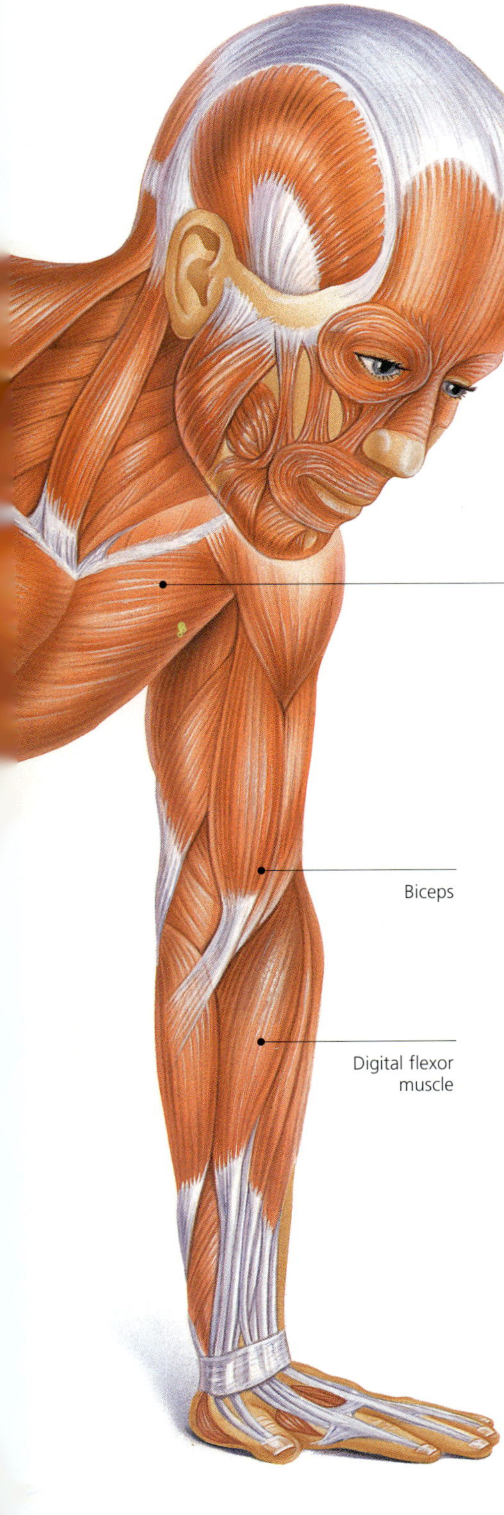

MUSCLES IN ACTION

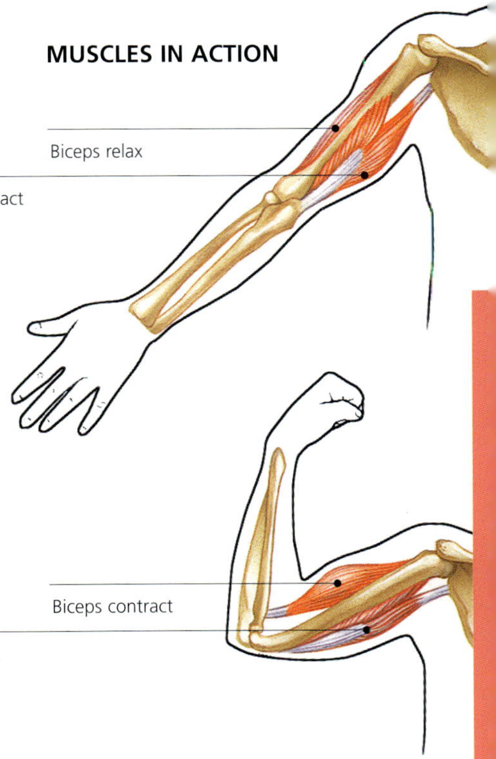

FRONT VIEW

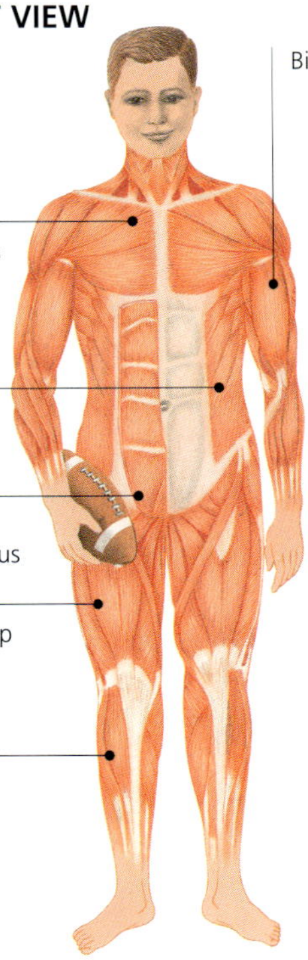

BACK VIEW

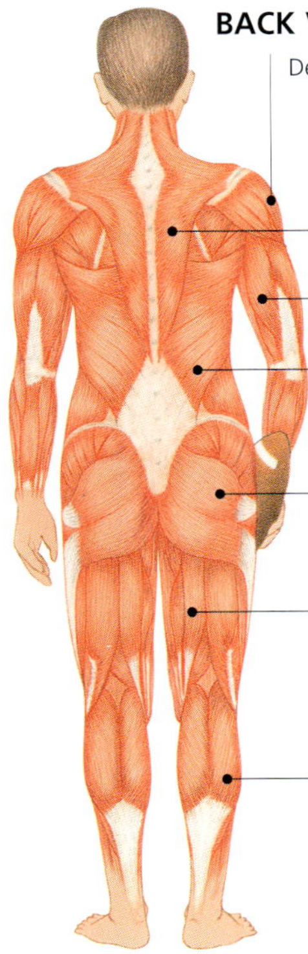

Skin and Nails

SKIN COLOR

Dark skin contains high levels of the pigment melanin which determines skin color.

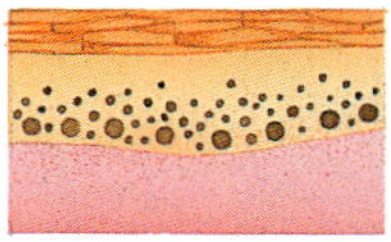

Olive skin contains medium levels of melanin.

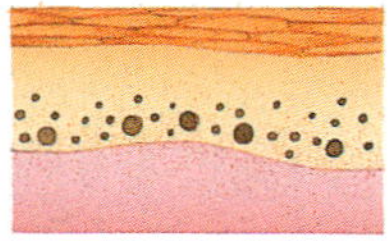

Fair skin has low levels of the pigment.

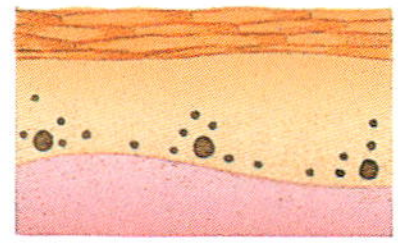

UNDER THE SKIN

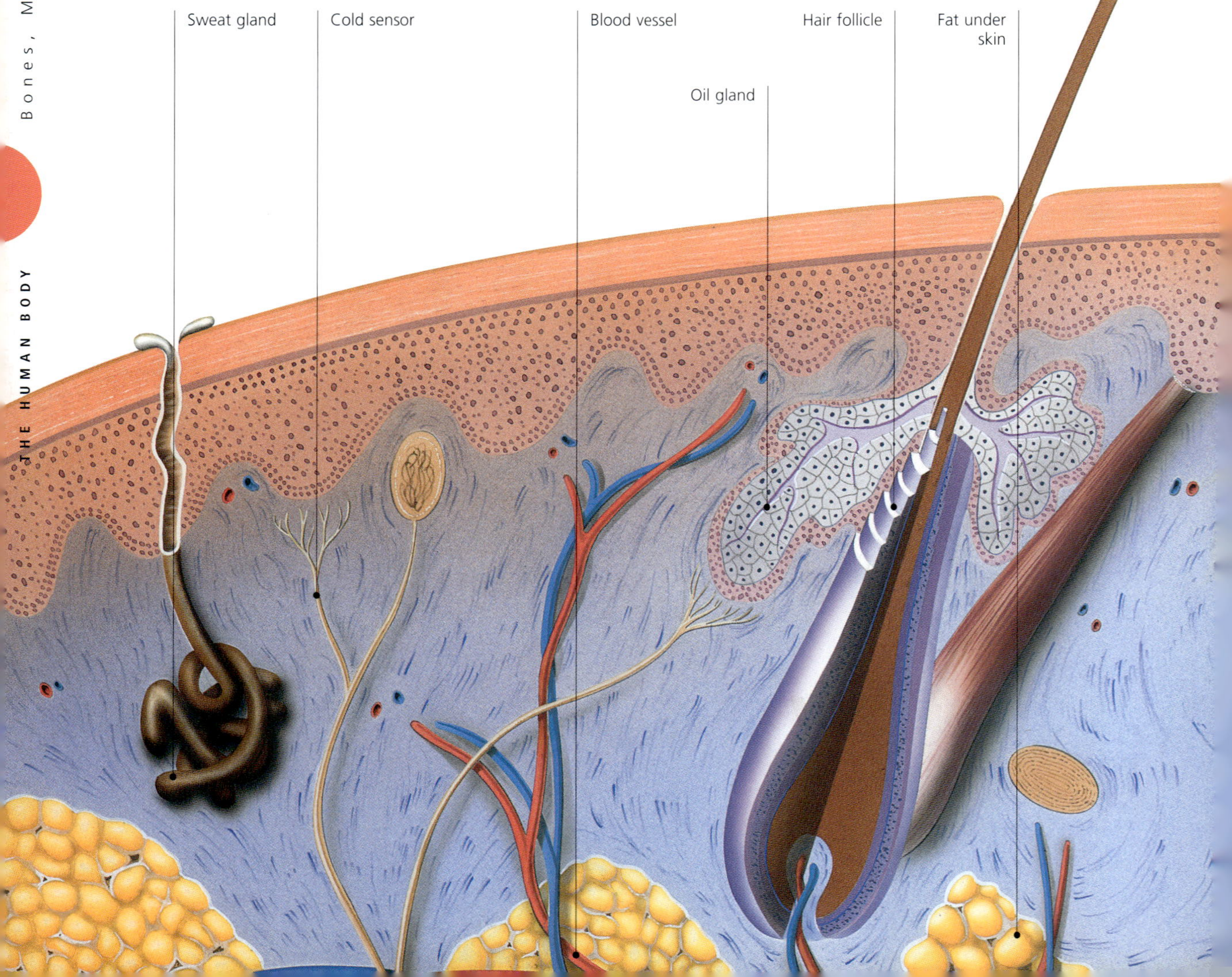

FINGER TIP

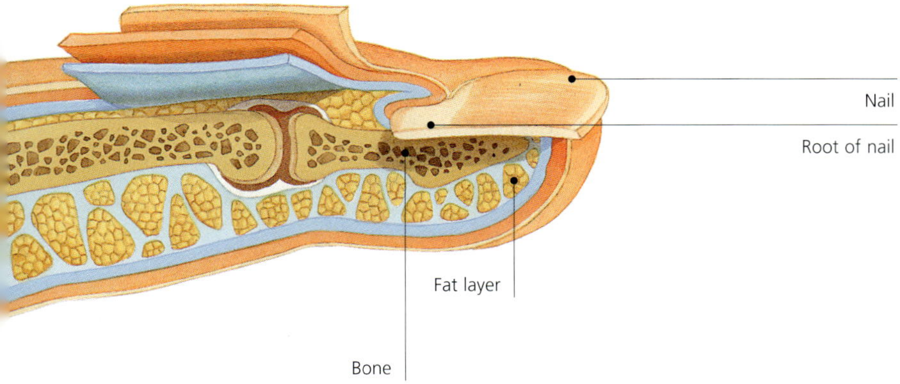

FINGER NAILS

Heart or lung disease can cause the fingers to swell, which makes the nails bulge.

Frequent use of chemicals can cause the nails to curve.

A bang can cause harmless white spots in the nail.

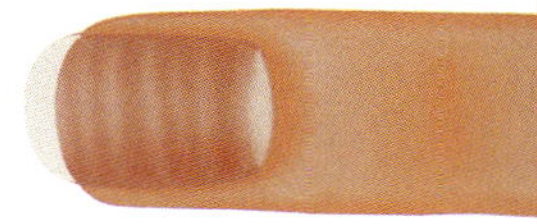

Illness can cause the nails to grow poorly.

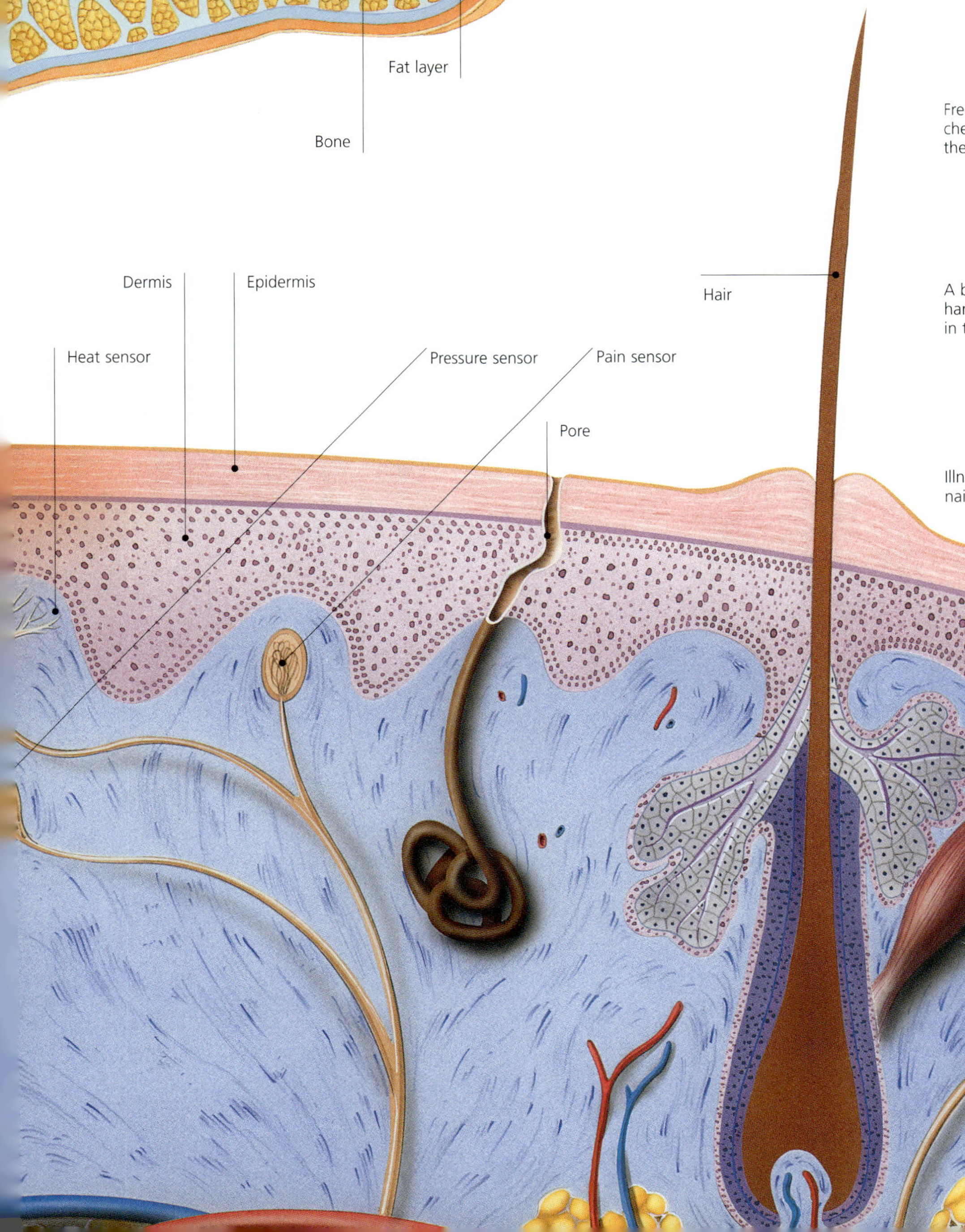

The Brain

BRAIN FUNCTIONS

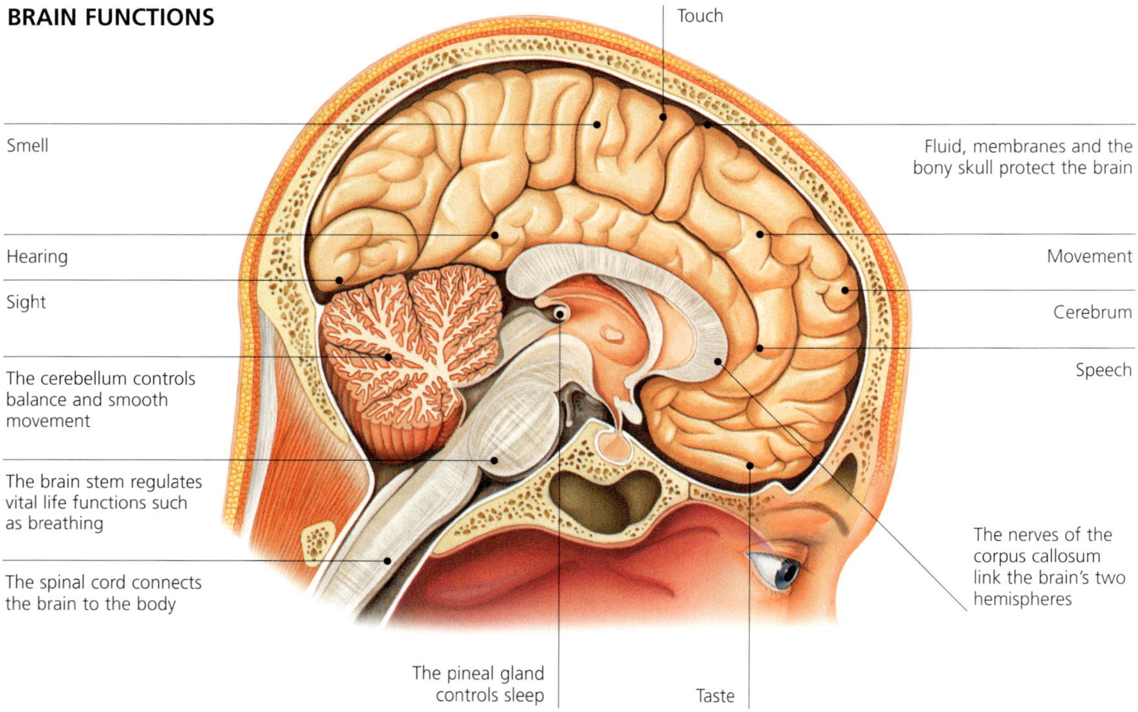

BRAIN LOBES

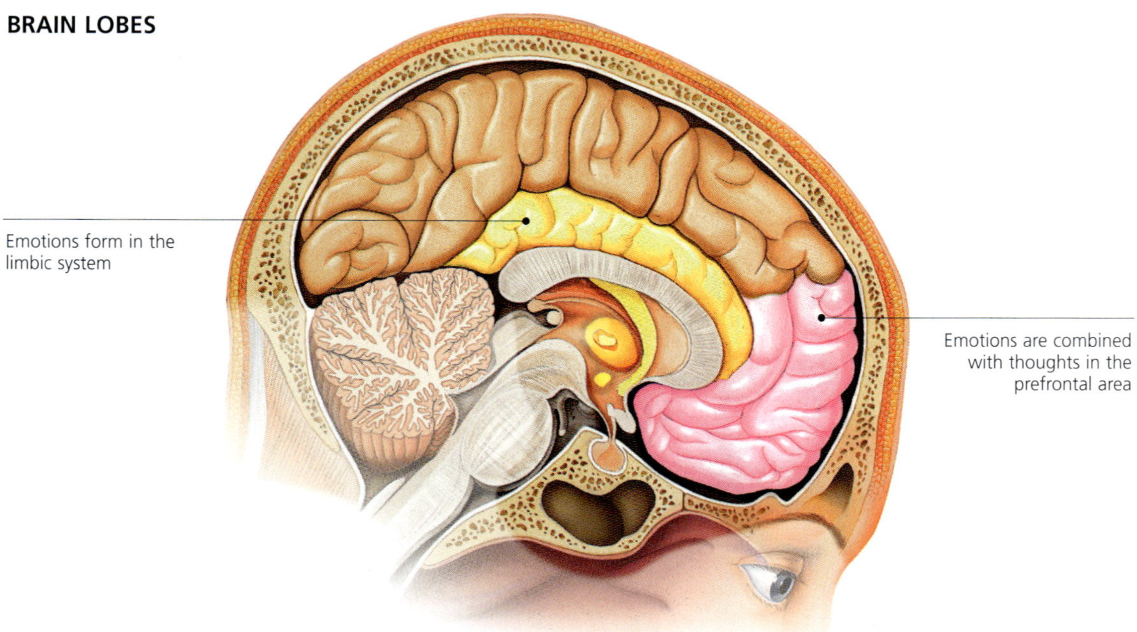

BRAIN CROSS SECTION

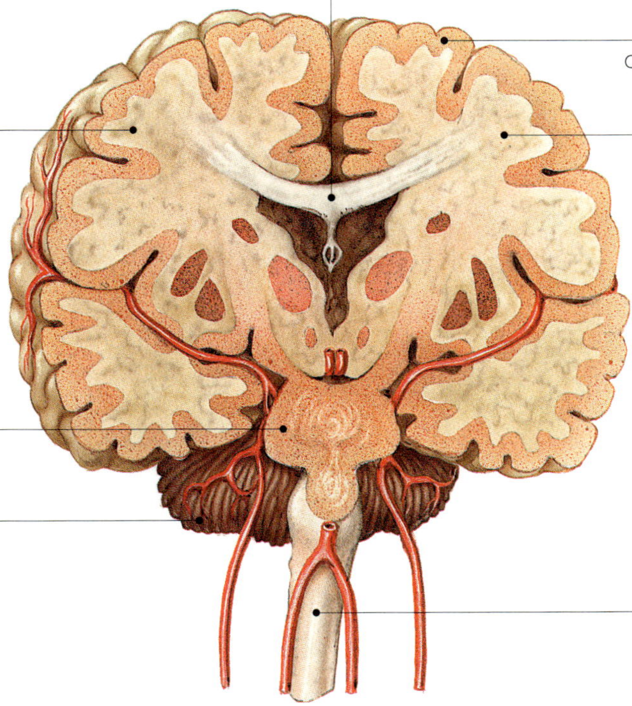

BRAIN STEM LATERAL VIEW

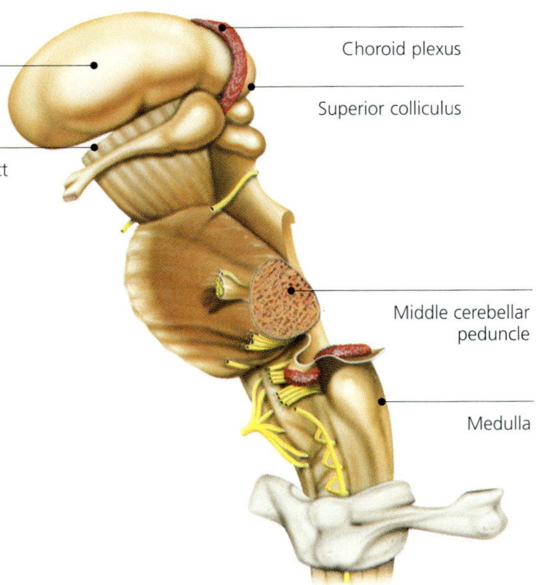

BRAIN STEM FRONT VIEW

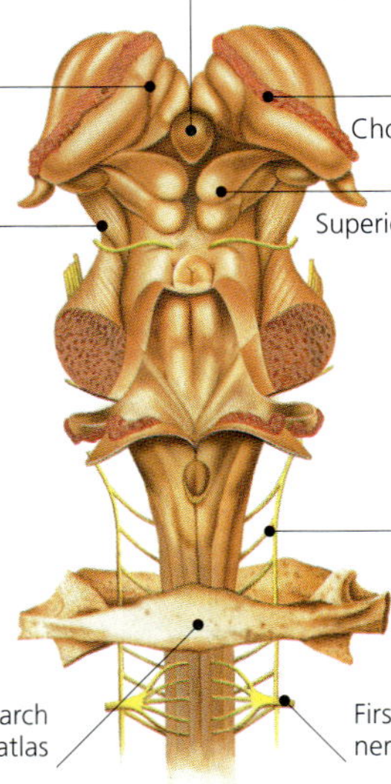

Sight

TEARS

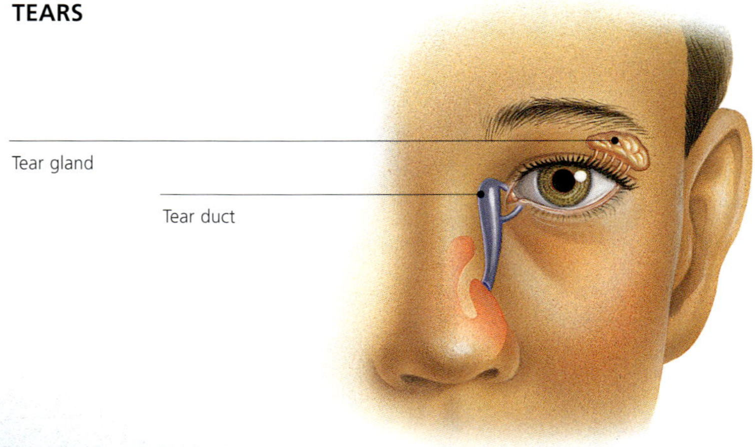

Tear gland
Tear duct

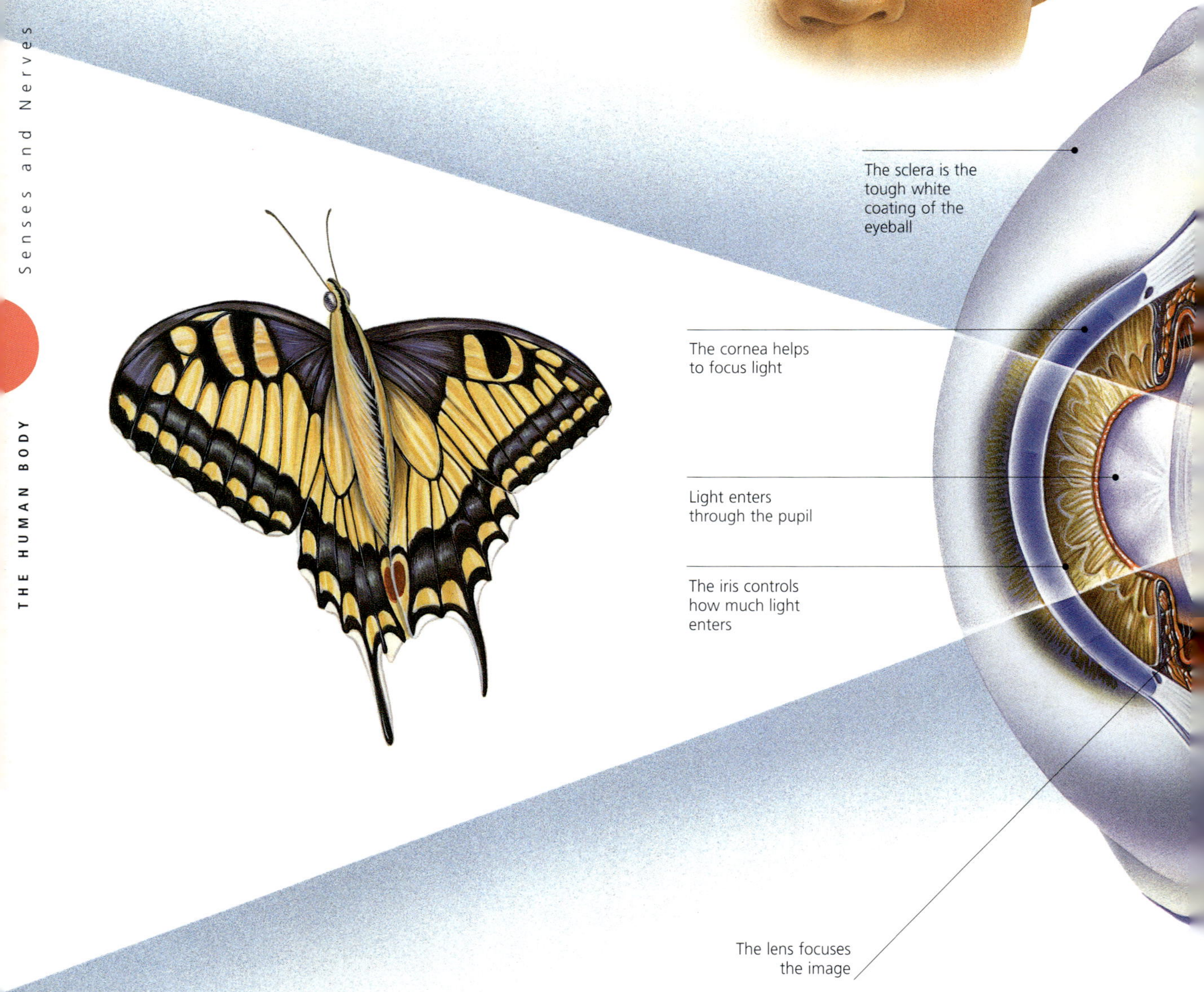

The sclera is the tough white coating of the eyeball
The cornea helps to focus light
Light enters through the pupil
The iris controls how much light enters
The lens focuses the image

HOW EYES FUNCTION

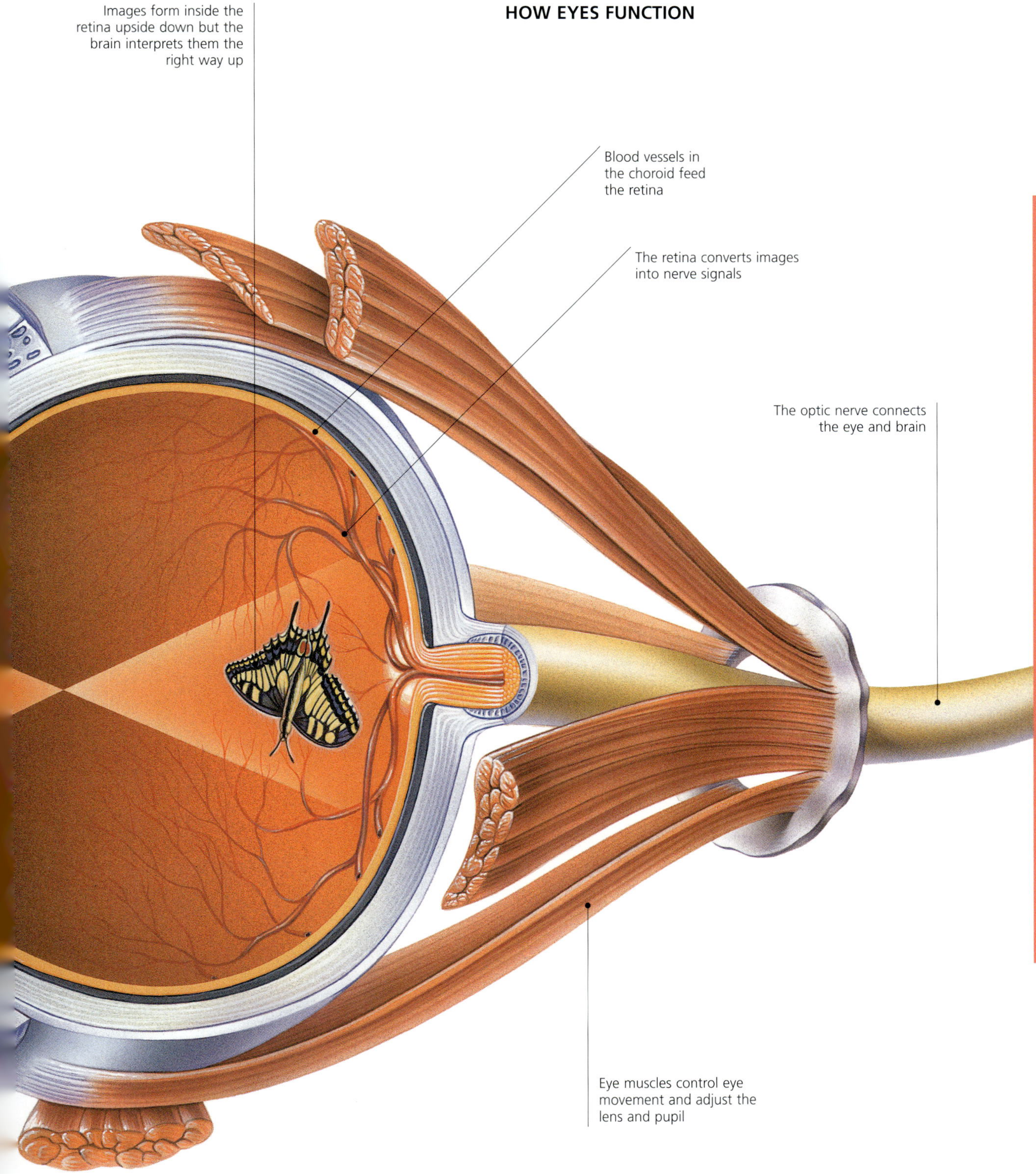

Hearing and Speaking

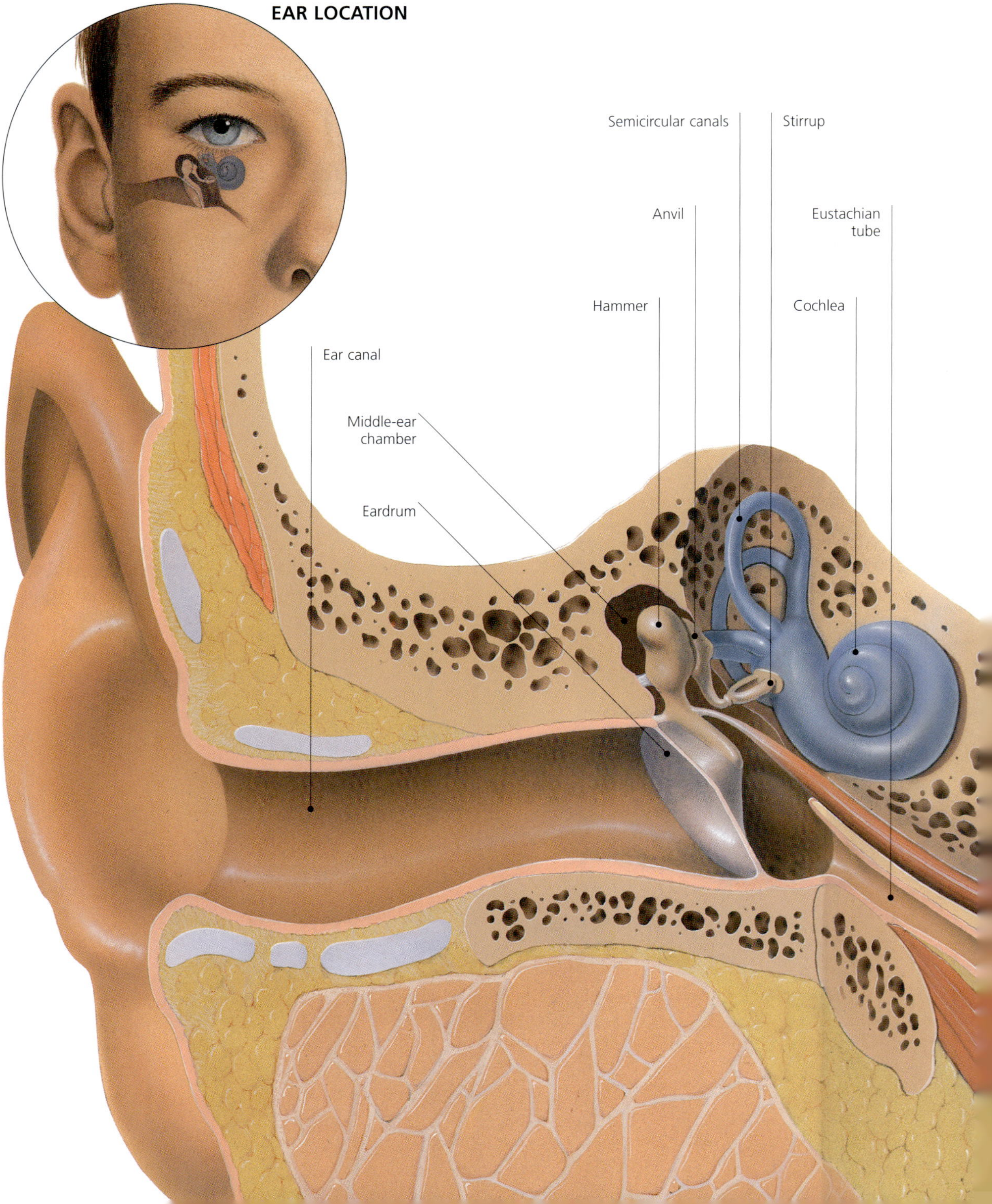

EAR PRESSURE

The middle-ear chamber is a tiny air pocket behind the eardrum. The Eustachian tube links it to the throat and so to the outside air.

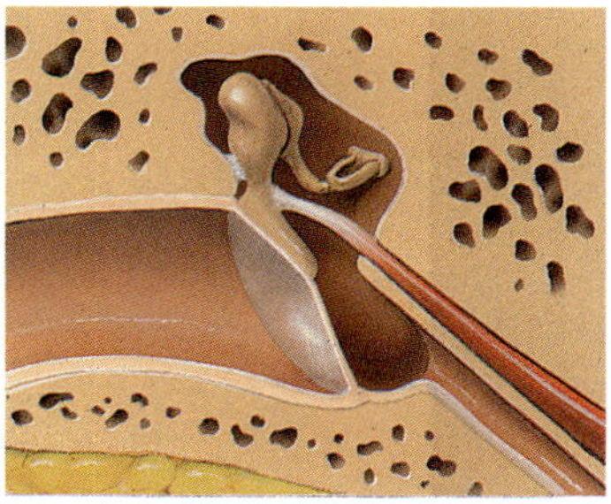

Outside pressure is less at altitude. Because the middle-ear pressure remains the same the ear drum bulges and hearing fades.

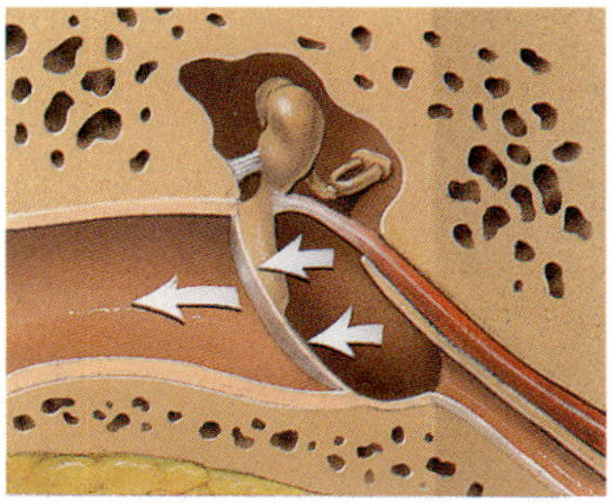

If you swallow hard the Eustachian tube opens. Air rushes out of the middle ear to relieve the pressure.

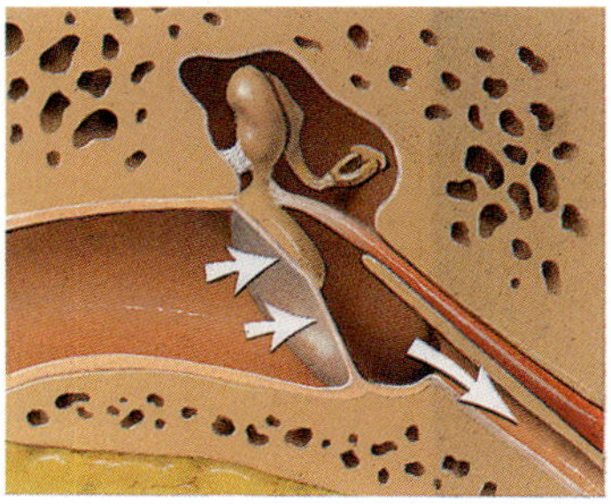

SPEECH

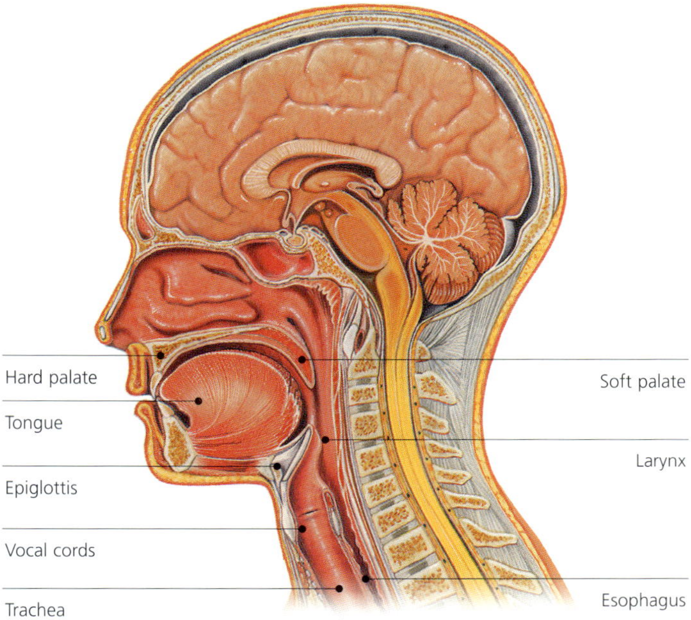

VOICEBOX

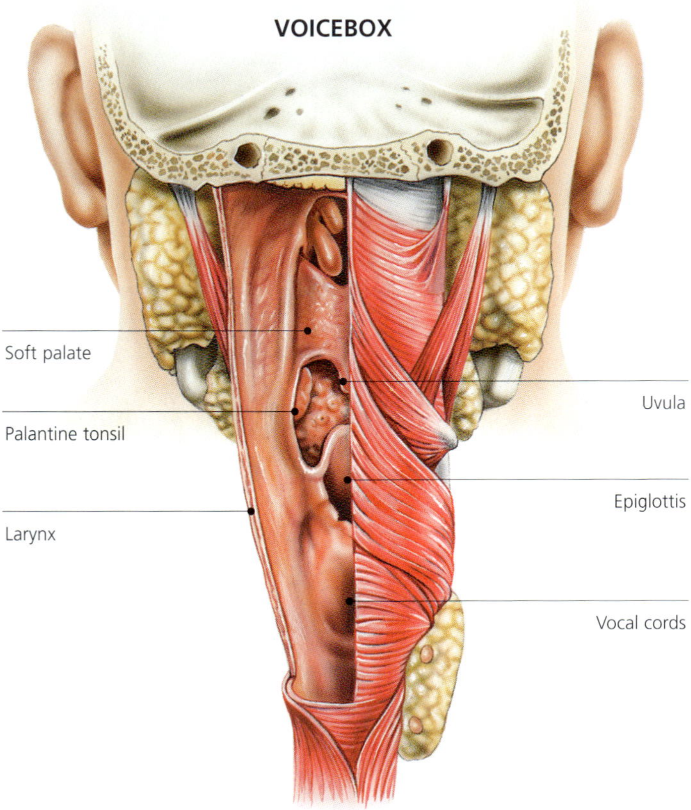

Taste and Smell

SNEEZING

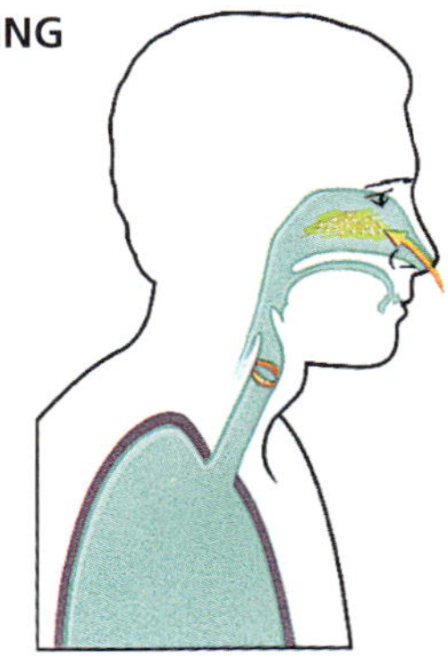

Dust, animal fur or pollen irritate the sensitive lining of the nose.

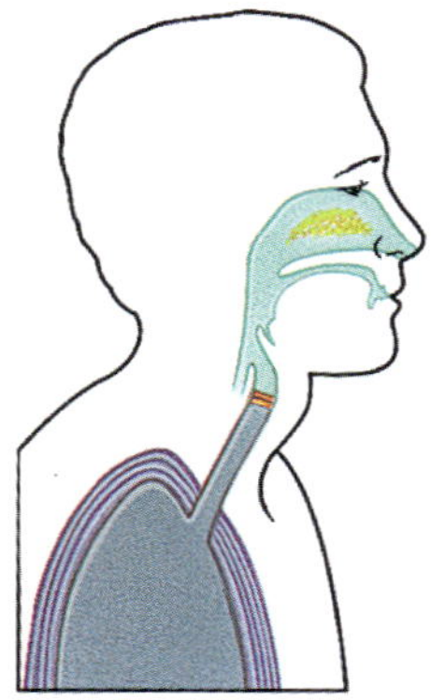

The throat and windpipe close. Muscles in the chest and abdomen press the lungs and squash the air inside.

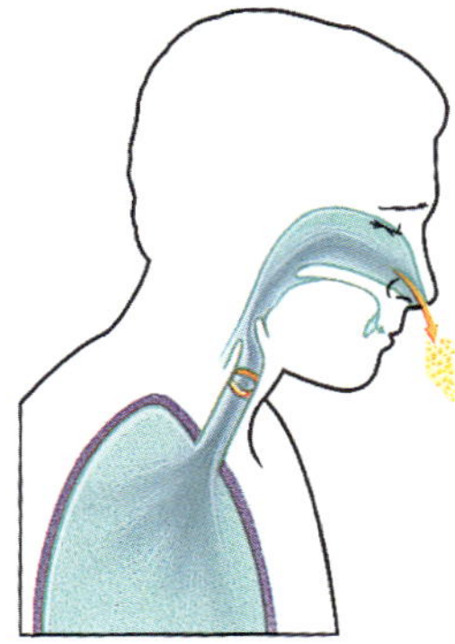

When the windpipe and throat open again, high-pressure air blasts through the nose to blow away the irritants.

TASTE

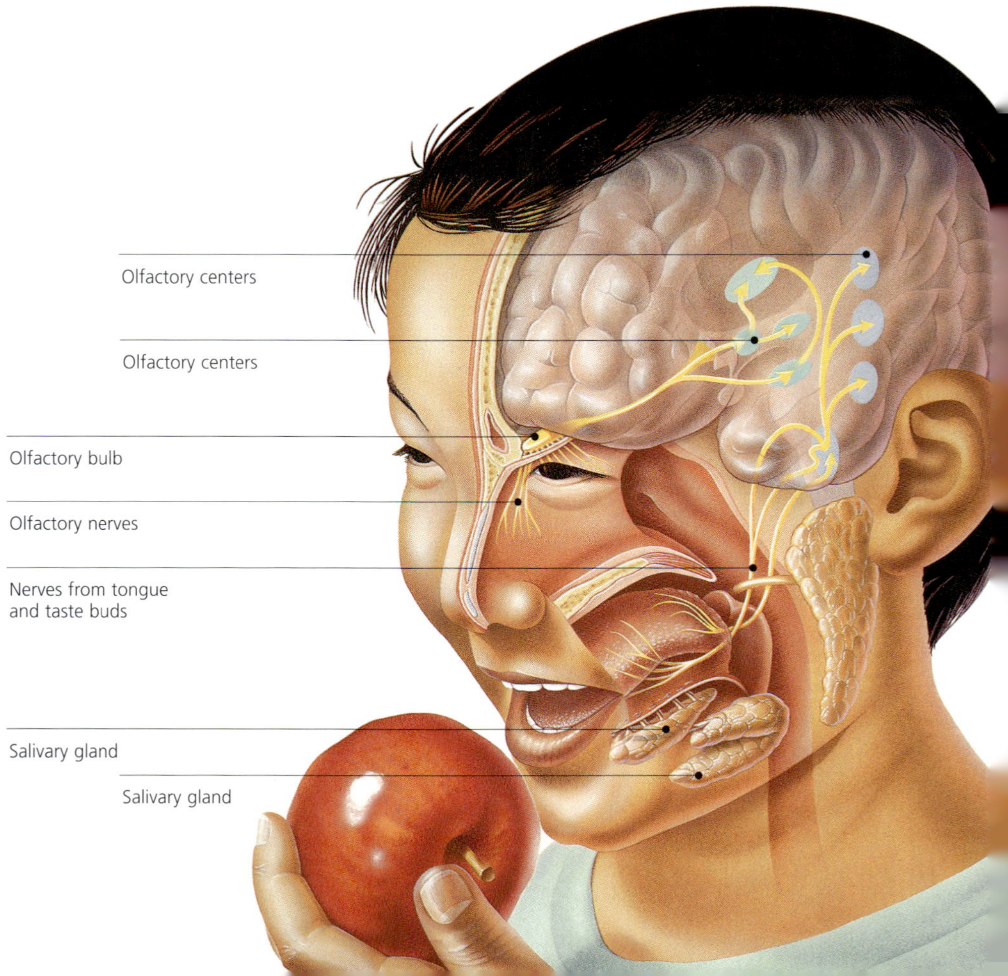

SMELL

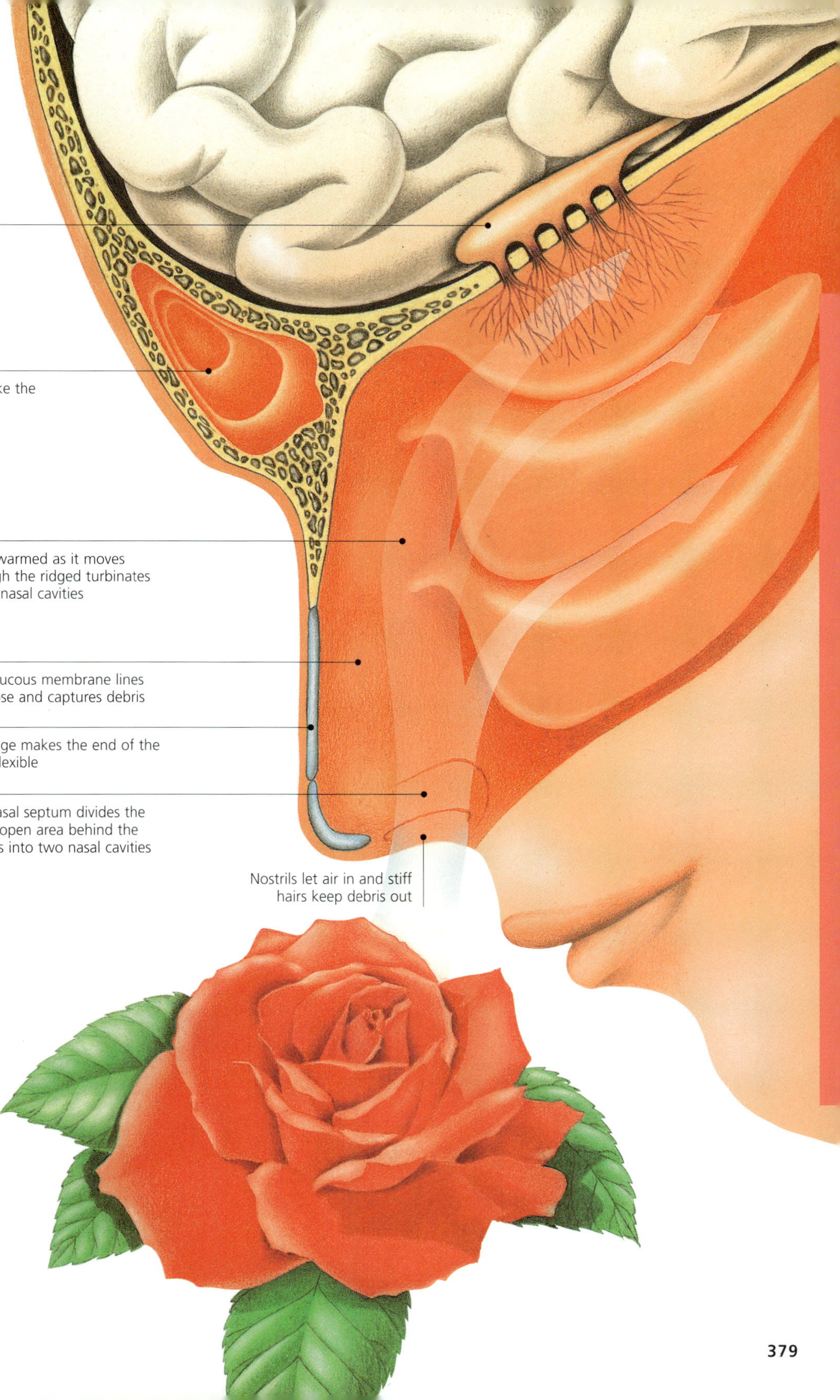

The olfactory bulbs contain the smell cells which relay messages between the nose and the brain
The sinuses make the skull lighter
Air is warmed as it moves through the ridged turbinates in the nasal cavities
The mucous membrane lines the nose and captures debris
Cartilage makes the end of the nose flexible
The nasal septum divides the large, open area behind the nostrils into two nasal cavities
Nostrils let air in and stiff hairs keep debris out

Nerves and Hormones

NERVES

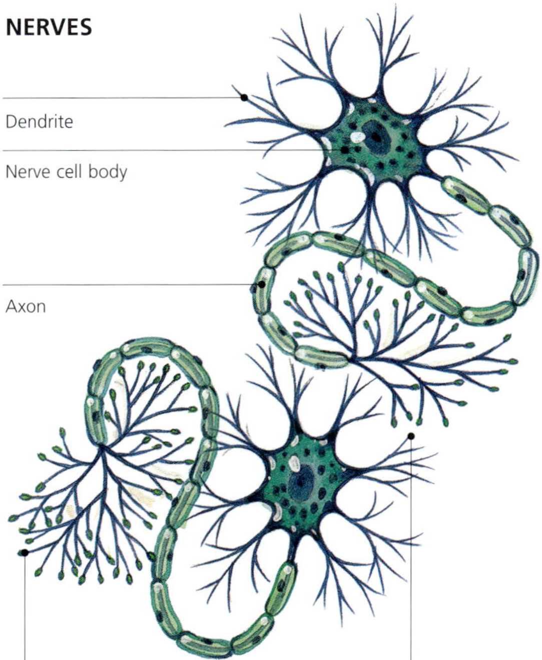

INSIDE THE SPINE

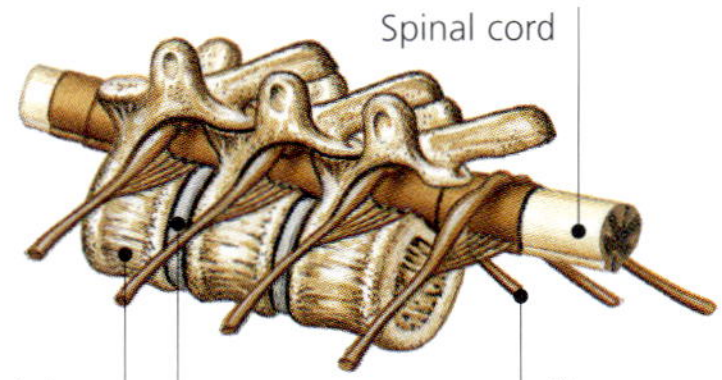

SYNAPSE

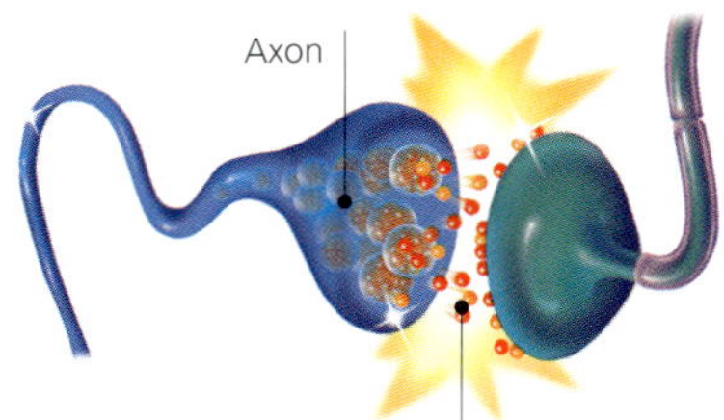

HORMONE GLANDS

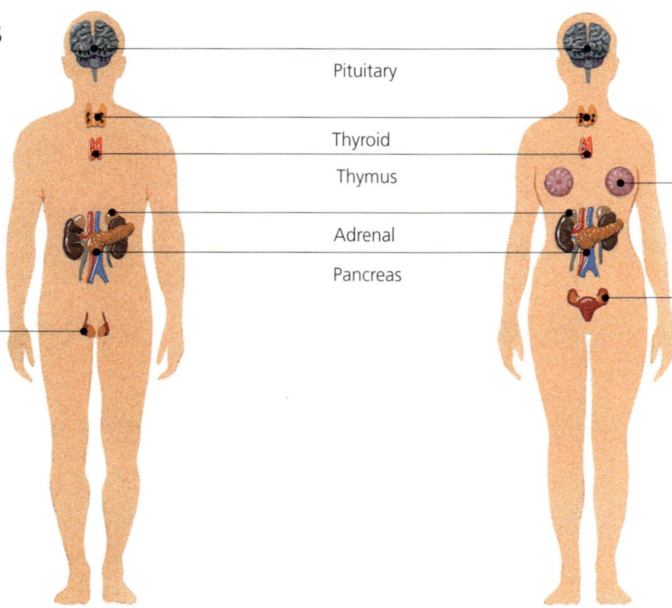

NERVOUS SYSTEM

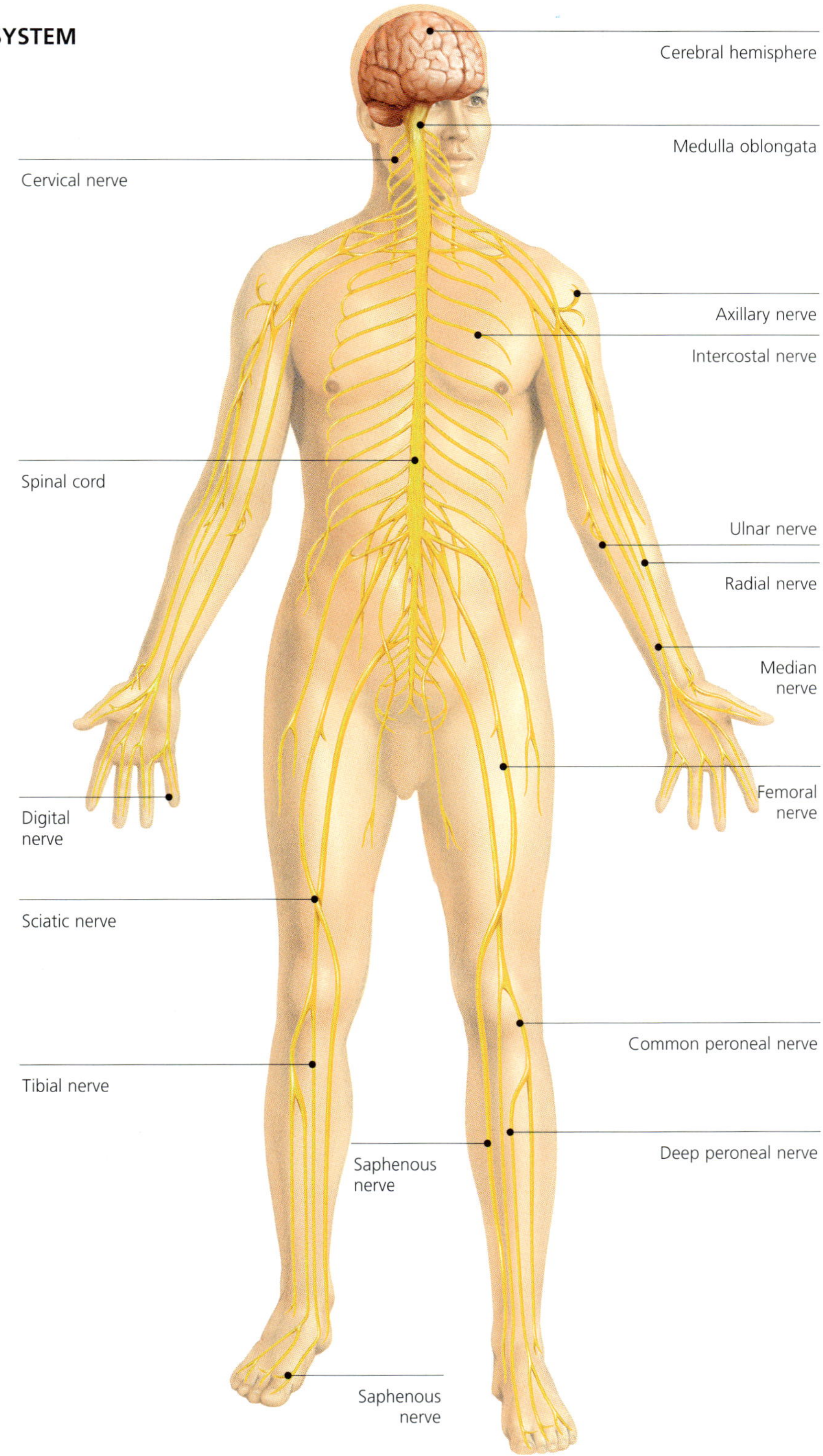

ANCIENT EGYPT

The Egyptian Empire 386
Worshiping the Gods 388
Burial and the Afterlife 390
Writing and Art 392

ANCIENT CHINA

Empire and Emperors 394
Society and Culture 396
Science and Communication 398
Craft and Trade 400

ANCIENT GREECE

The Greek World 402
Society and Culture 404
Daily Life 406
War and Warfare 408

ANCIENT ROME

The Roman World 410
Engineering and Science 412
Into Battle 414
Roman Baths 416

NATIVE AMERICANS

Village Life 418
Travel and Hunting 420
Culture and Ceremonies 422

The Egyptian Empire

CROWNS OF THE PHAROAH

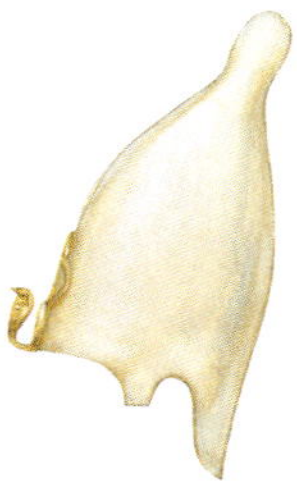

White crown of Upper Egypt

Red crown of Lower Egypt

Double crown of united Egypt

Blue crown

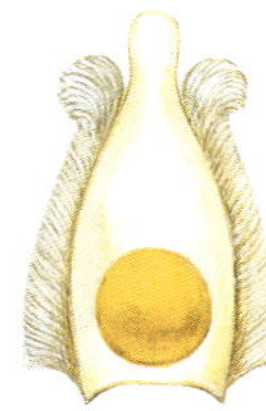

Atef crown of Osiris

QUEEN HATSHEPSUT

When Queen Hatshepsut's husband died she took over the government and held power for about 20 years—statues show her wearing the false beard of kingship

LAND OF THE LOTUS

People in modern times likened ancient Egypt to a lotus plant, with its valley as the stem and its delta as the flower

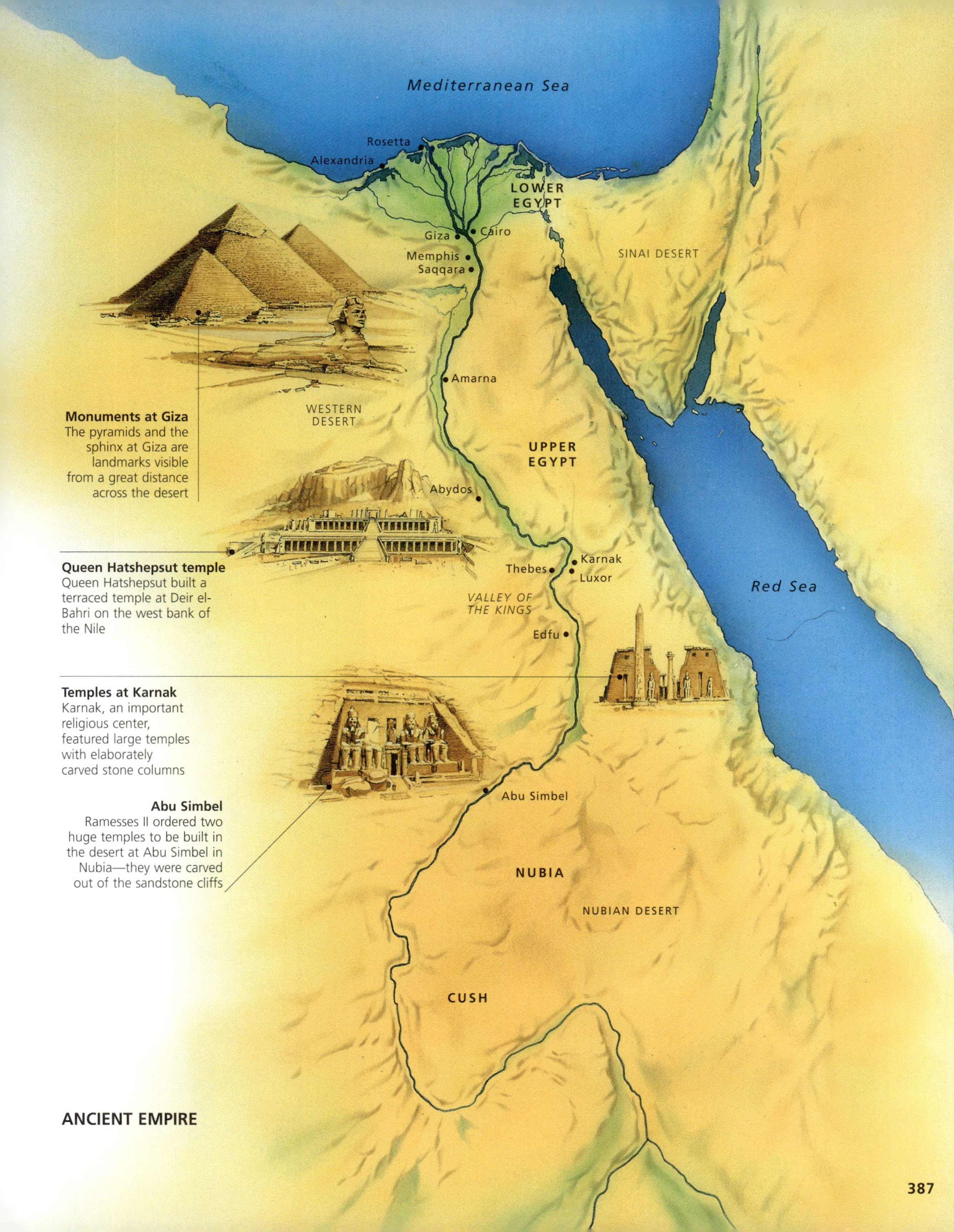

Monuments at Giza
The pyramids and the sphinx at Giza are landmarks visible from a great distance across the desert

Queen Hatshepsut temple
Queen Hatshepsut built a terraced temple at Deir el-Bahri on the west bank of the Nile

Temples at Karnak
Karnak, an important religious center, featured large temples with elaborately carved stone columns

Abu Simbel
Ramesses II ordered two huge temples to be built in the desert at Abu Simbel in Nubia—they were carved out of the sandstone cliffs

ANCIENT EMPIRE

Worshiping the Gods

FESTIVAL DAYS
The priests placed the god's statue in a shrine and carried it in procession around the outside of the temple.

SISTRUM
A sistum was a rattle used in temple rituals.

A PARADE OF GODS

Thoth
God of knowledge

Re
The sun god

Hathor
Goddess of the dead

ENTERTAINING THE GODS

In temple courtyards, women sang, danced and put on acrobatic displays for the gods.

Burial and the Afterlife

PREPARING THE MUMMY

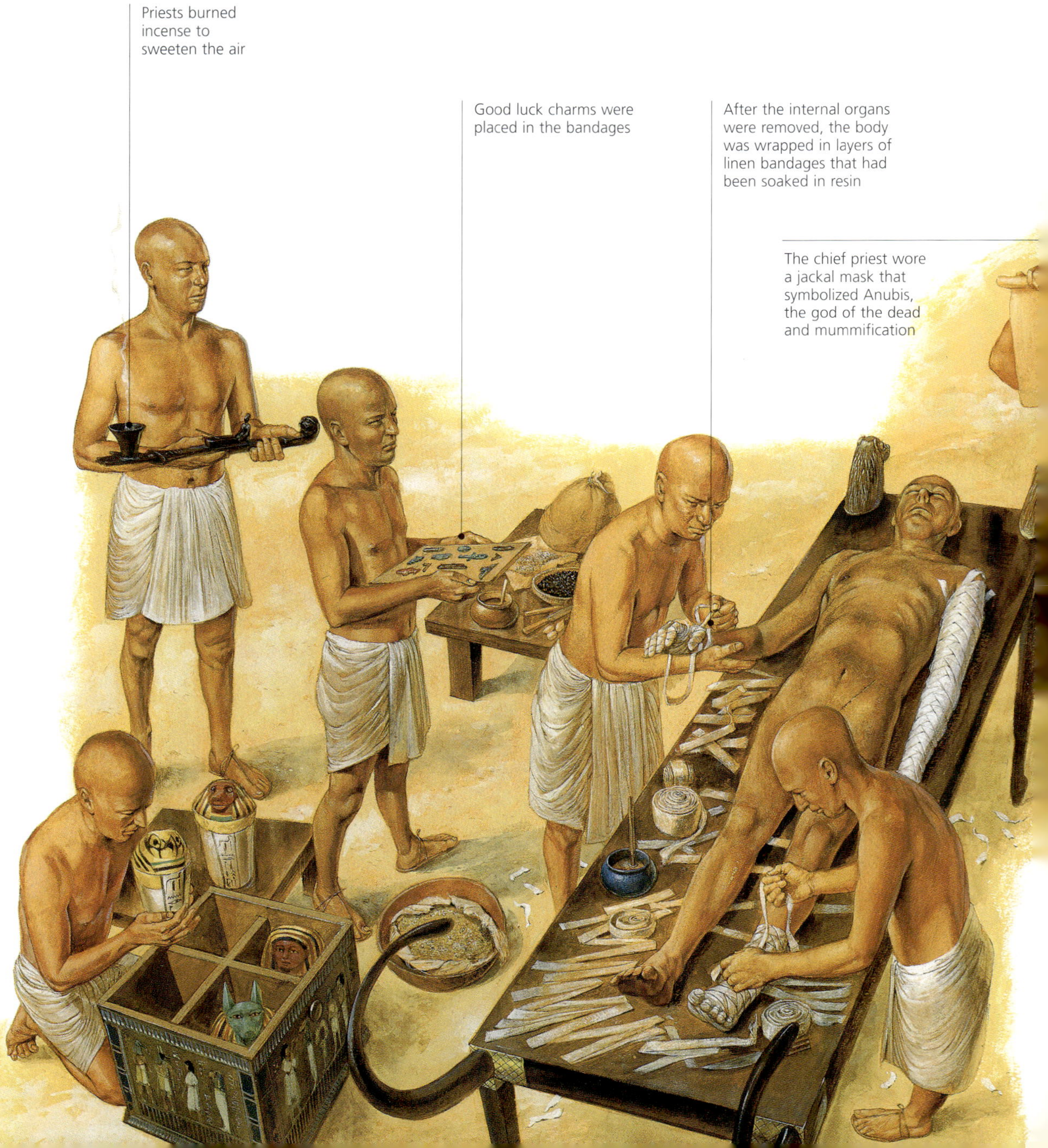

MUMMY CASES

Coffins were made of wood or cartonnage, which was a kind of papier-mâché

Lid of outer mummy case

Lid of inner mummy case

Linen wrappings

Wrapped mummy with mask

Two coffins for protection from animals and tomb robbers

Paintings of gods, spells, and hieroglyphs

Bottom of inner mummy case

Bottom of outer mummy case

Writing and Art

A stonemason smoothed the wall and covered it with a layer of thin plaster

HIEROGLYPHS

Owl

Water

Bread

Man

Arm

Reed

Mouth

Flax

Basket

WRITING KIT

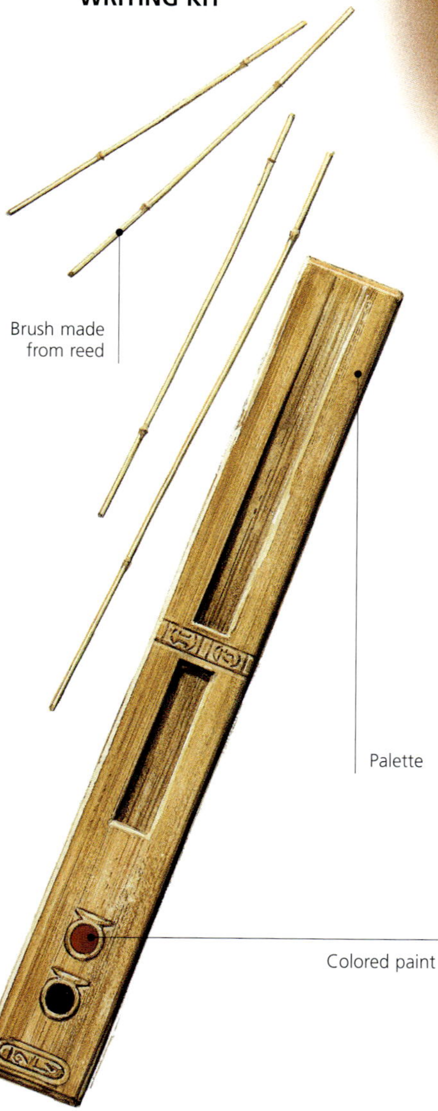

TRAVELING SYMBOLS

Traveling north

Traveling south

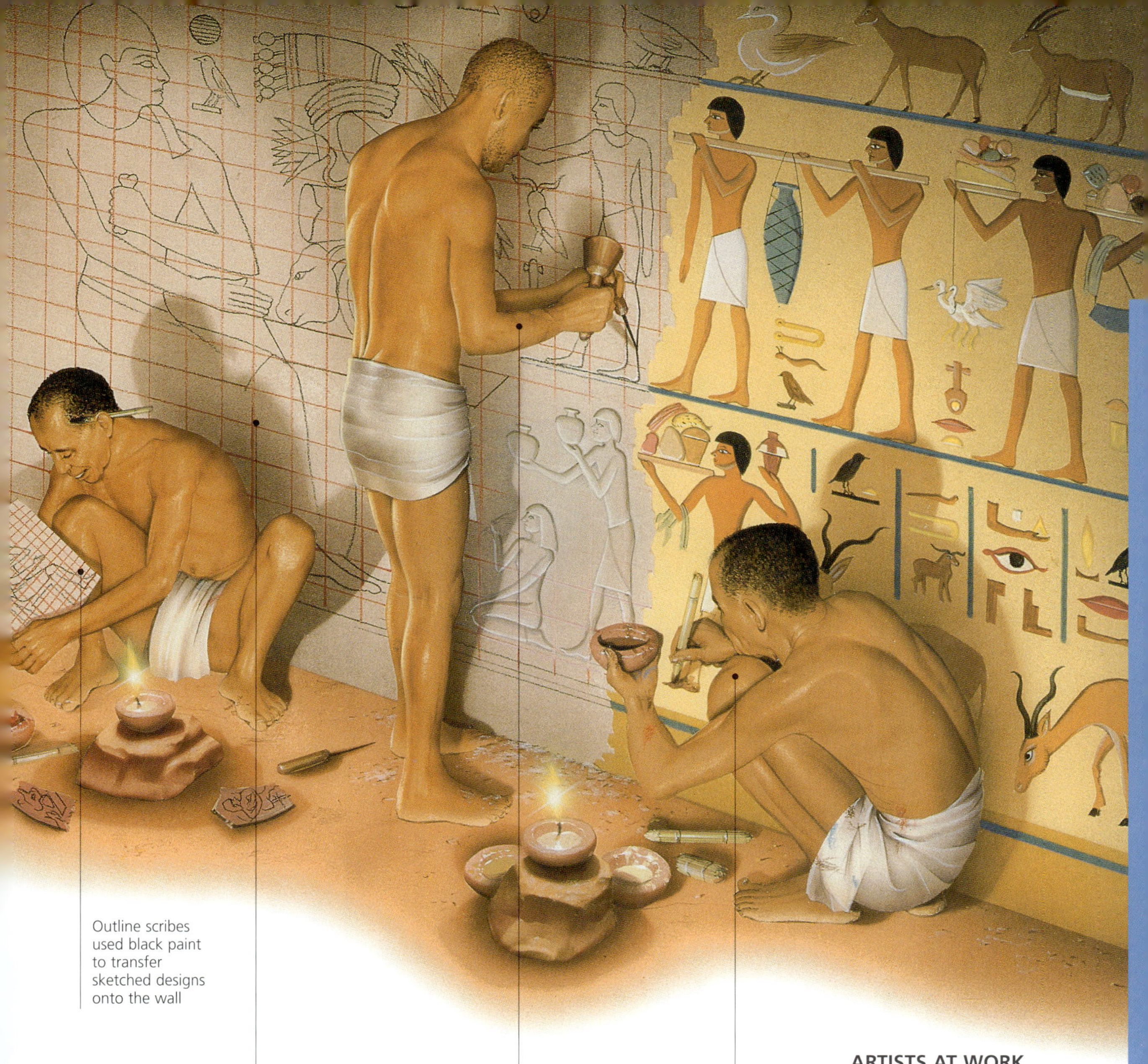

Outline scribes used black paint to transfer sketched designs onto the wall

The surface was marked with a square grid made by a string dipped in red paint

Stonemasons carefully chipped out the main figures from the background

Painters applied flesh tones and then filled in the background details on top of the base paint

ARTISTS AT WORK

Empire and Emperors

IMPERIAL PALACE

The Imperial Palace was called the Forbidden City because few people were allowed inside

The elaborate roof represented the heavens

The Hall of Supreme Harmony was built during the Ming dynasty (1368–1644) as part of the Imperial Palace

FIRST EMPEROR

Qin Shi Huangdi unified ancient China by making strict laws, taxing everyone in the country and introducing one script for writing.

DEFENDING THE EMPIRE

The Long Wall of ancient China snaked up and down mountains and across semi-desert plains. It was built to keep out invaders from the north.

The Emperor was called a Son of Heaven—the people believed he received heavenly approval to rule China

Society and Culture

SOCIAL ORDERS

Scholar

Peasant

Artisan

Merchant

CLOTHING

Woman

Short-sleeved upper garment

Flowing silk skirt

Man

Loose robes

Wide sleeves

MAGISTRATE'S COURT

A district magistrate was a low-ranking official who enforced law and order; collected taxes; registered births, deaths and marriages; supervised building programs; and judged court cases

When the court believed the evidence was enough to prove a person's guilt, the accused was encouraged to confess

Science and Communication

ACUPUNCTURE

Ancient Chinese physicians believed that life-giving energy flowed along 12 lines in the body called meridians

Doctors were able to ease pain and treat certain illnesses by sticking acupuncture needles just below the skin at points along the meridians

MEDICINAL HERBS

Cilantro (coriander)

Garlic

Ginseng

Star anise

CHINESE CHARACTERS

Ruler or king

Moon

Mouth

Sun

CALLIGRAPHY

Craft and Trade

BRONZE AGE CRAFT

THE SILK ROAD

SILK PRODUCTION

LACQUER ART

Sap from the lacquer tree is the oldest industrial plastic known to humans

The Greek World

GREEK COLONIES
The red areas indicate where Greeks settled around the edges of the seas.

LIGHTHOUSE AT ALEXANDRIA
Alexander the Great set up many new cities called Alexandria. The first one was in Egypt.

ANCIENT GREECE

MACEDONIA
Olympus
Aegean Sea
ASIA MINOR
Thermopylae
Delphi
Thebes
Marathon
Athens
Corinth
Ephesus
Olympia
Cyclades
Sparta
Rhodes
Mediterranean Sea
Knossos
Crete

Society and Culture

GREEK ALPHABET

GREEK GODS

Athena
Goddess of wisdom, art and war

Zeus
God of the sky and thunder

Aphrodite
Goddess of love and beauty

Hestia
Goddess of the family and the hearth

Poseidon
God of earthquakes, the sea, horses and bulls

Hermes
Messenger of the gods and protector of travelers

Ares
God of war

THEATRICAL MASKS

Ancient Greek actors performed wearing masks.

The large mouths helped carry the actor's voice.

Masks were made from fabric stiffened with plaster.

Actors changed masks every time they changed character.

There was a range of theatrical masks.

Daily Life

GREEK CLOTHING

Women wore a long tunic made of wool or linen, fastened on the shoulder with brooches or pins and tied at the waist and sometimes the hips

Men and boys wore thigh-length tunics; winter cloaks were often draped to leave one shoulder bare

INSIDE A GREEK HOUSE

Women's quarters
Women wove cloth in the loom room

Men's quarters
The head of the household entertained guests in a dining room furnished with couches

TUNIC STYLES

Folded over the top, usually made from wool

Fastened on the shoulders in several places, usually made from linen

Kitchen
Slaves baked bread in a pottery oven and cooked on an open fire—smoke escaped through a hole in the roof
Home furnishings
Couches, tables, stools, chairs, beds and storage chests were made from wood and bronze
Bathroom
Wealthy people had bathrooms in their homes and slaves filled the tubs with water

War and Warfare

HOPLITE

Greek foot soldiers, called hoplites, carried shields made of leather or bronze to protect them from neck to thigh

FIGHTING IN FORMATION

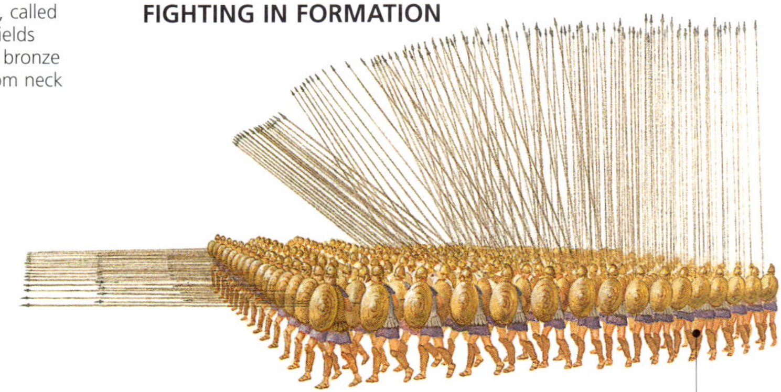

Phillip II of Macedon trained his hoplites to fight in a formation called a phalanx

BATTLE AT SEA

Soldiers wore bronze or leather breast and back plates joined on the shoulders and at the sides

Helmets protected soldiers' heads and faces

Athenian triremes were long, three-layered timber warships

Triremes were powered by 170 oarsmen

HOPLITE RACE

The hoplite race was part of the ancient Olympic games

Contestants were naked except for their leg-protectors and helmets, and they carried their shield as they raced

In 480 BC the Persians invaded Greece and destroyed Athens, after which the Greek fleet trapped the Persian fleet in the channel between the island of Salamis and the Greek mainland

At the Battle of Salamis Greek triremes rammed the larger Persian warships and forced them to retreat

The Roman World

ROMAN ARCHITECTURE

Hadrian's Arch

The Pantheon

The Colosseum

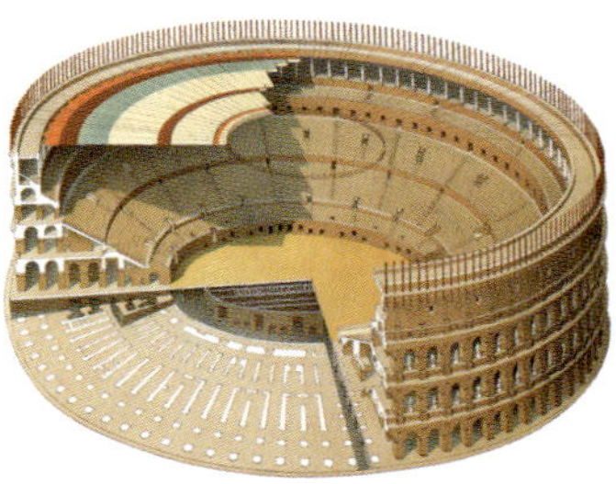

ROMAN EMPIRE

753 BC
The legendary founding date of Rome.
753–510 BC
Rome was ruled by a series of kings.
510–27 BC
The Roman Republic.
27 BC
The Roman Empire was established under Augustus.
AD 395
The Empire was split into West and East.
AD 476
The Western Empire collapsed.
AD 1453
The last city of the Eastern (Byzantine) Roman Empire was captured.
GERMANIA
DACIA
Black Sea
Ravenna
Constantinople
MACEDONIA
Adriatic Sea
ASIA
Rome
Ostia
sica
Pompeii
SYRIA
ACHAEA
inia
CYPRUS
Damascus
Ionian Sea
Aegean Sea
Sicilia
CRETA
Jerusalem
Carthage
JUDAEA
Mediterranean Sea
Alexandria
AEGYPTUS

Engineering and Science

ROMAN NUMERALS

BUILDER'S TOOLS

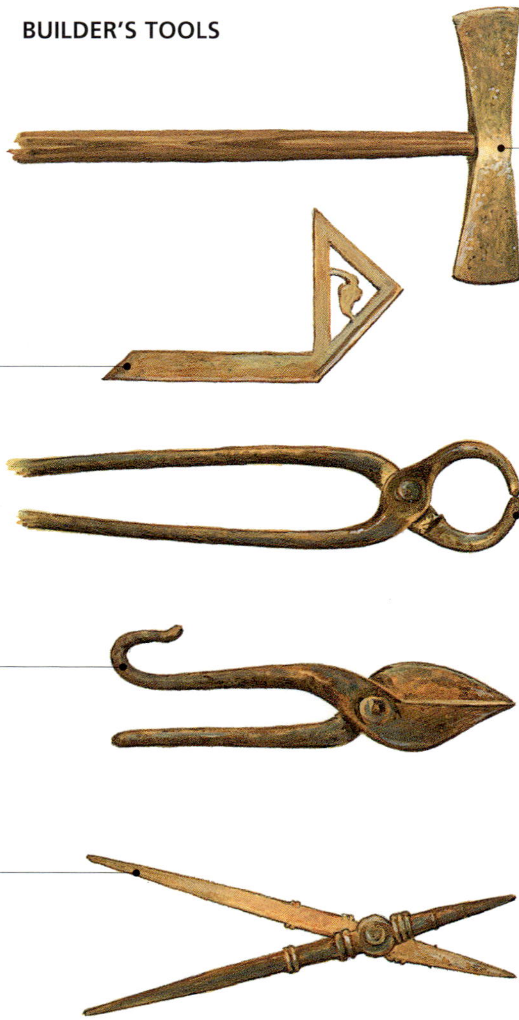

PANTHEON OF THE GODS
Rome's Pantheon honored all the state gods and still stands. Its domed roof, the largest of the time, represented the heavens; the circular opening stood for the sun.

Into Battle

GOING TO WAR

ROMAN LEGIONS

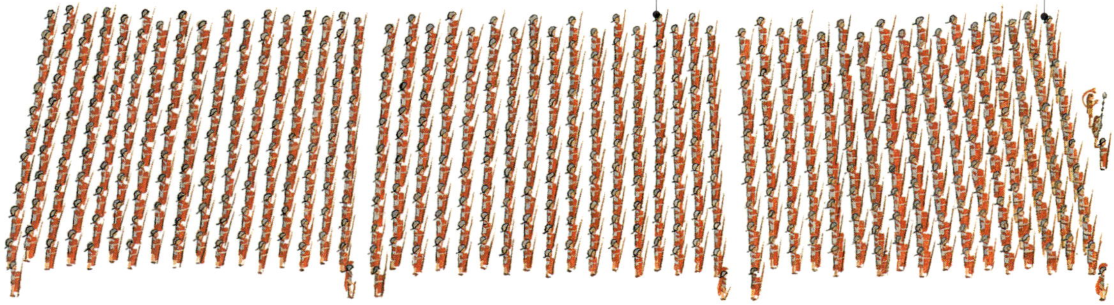

TORTOISE FORMATION

BATTERING RAM

ARMY CAMP

Armies on the march pitched a tent town each night. The camp was always arranged in the same way.

SIEGE WEAPONS

Catapult

Catapult

Onager

Roman Baths

BATHS OF CARACALLA

These baths were built in Rome between 211 and 217 by the Emperor Caracalla.

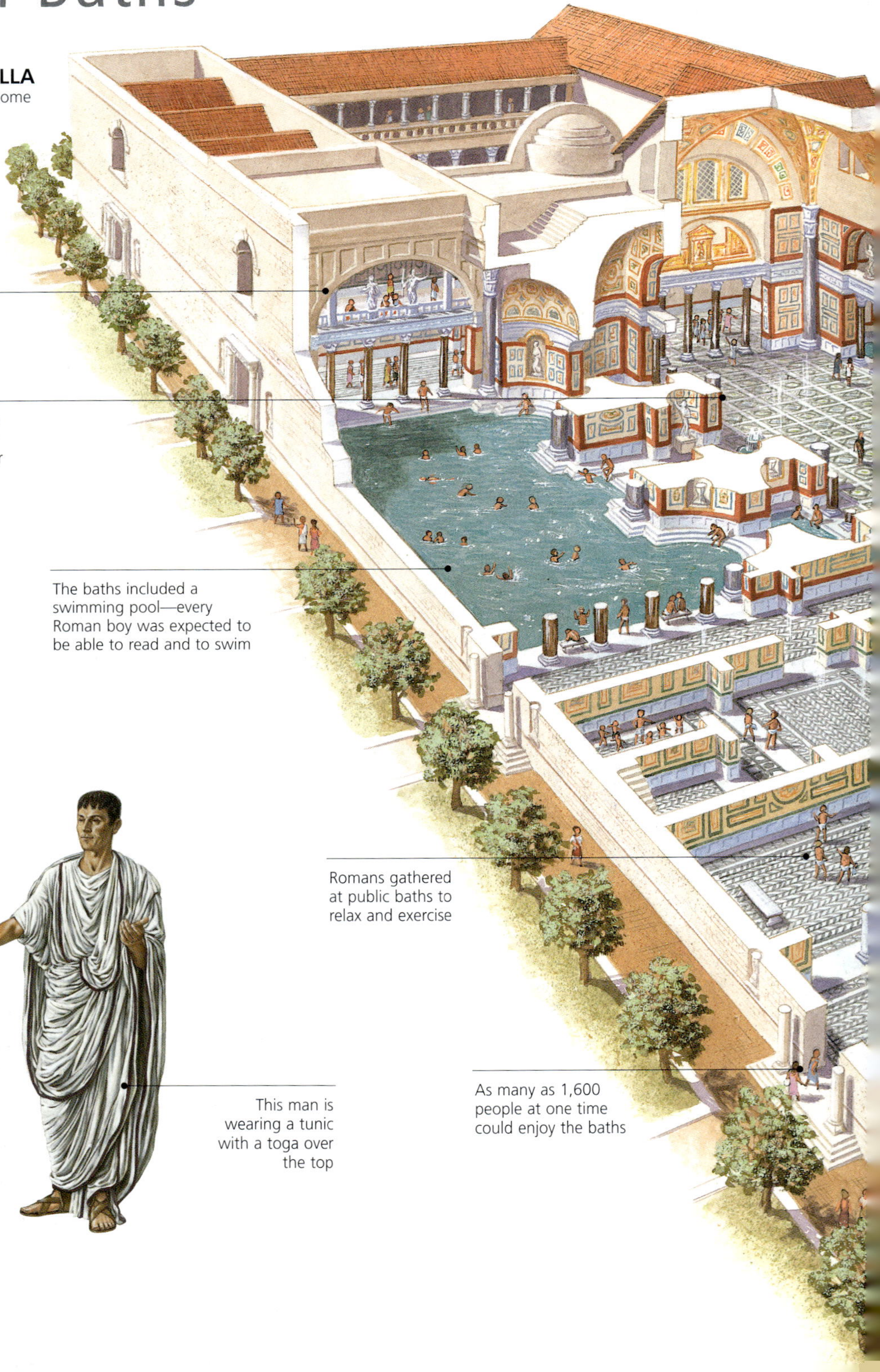

Take-out food shop and viewing gallery

The Frigidarium was at the center of the baths—four baths filled with cold water gave the room its name

The baths included a swimming pool—every Roman boy was expected to be able to read and to swim

Romans gathered at public baths to relax and exercise

As many as 1,600 people at one time could enjoy the baths

ROMAN FASHION

This woman is wearing a short tunic under a full-length one with a long robe

This man is wearing a tunic with a toga over the top

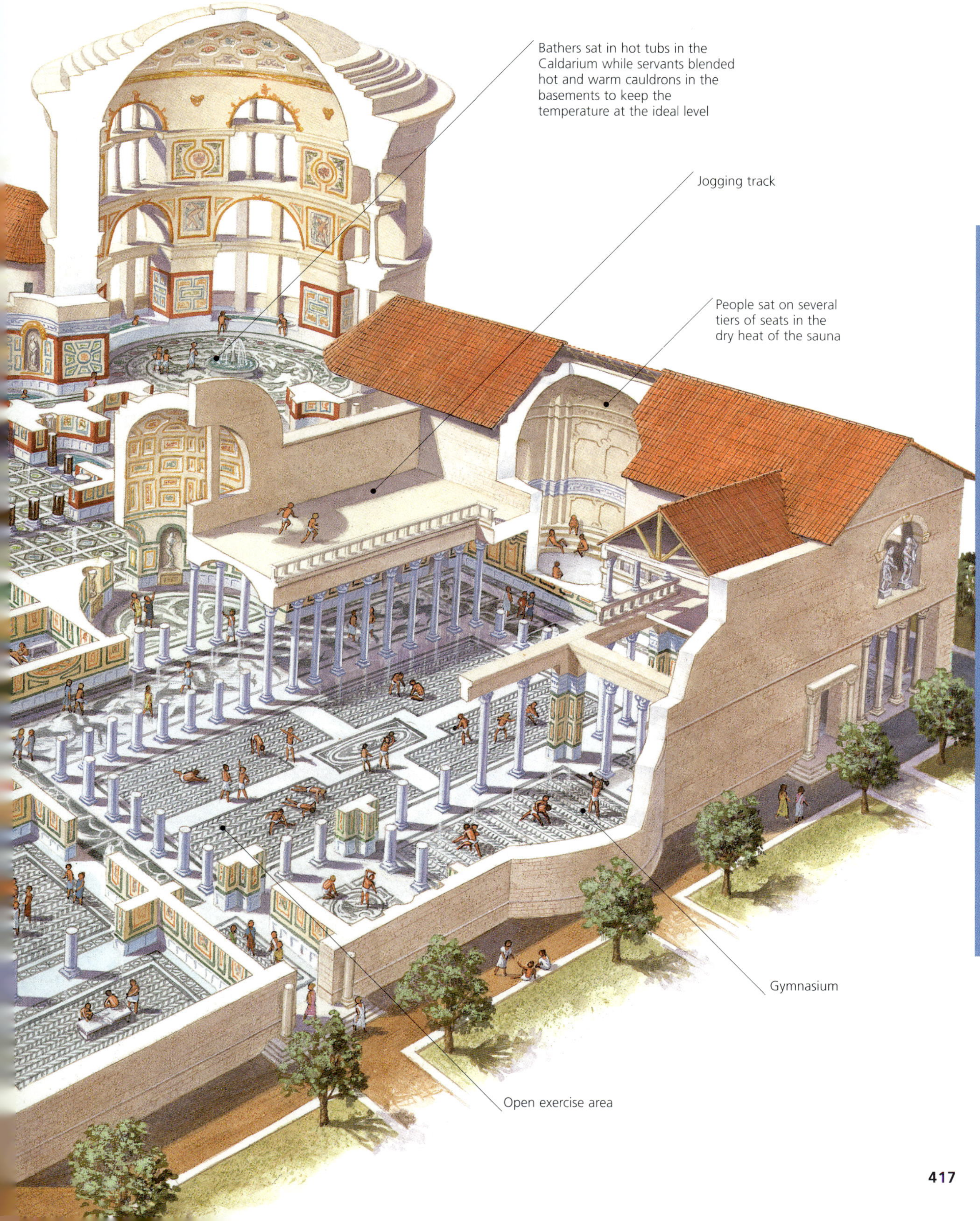
Bathers sat in hot tubs in the Caldarium while servants blended hot and warm cauldrons in the basements to keep the temperature at the ideal level
Jogging track
People sat on several tiers of seats in the dry heat of the sauna
Gymnasium
Open exercise area

Village Life

INSIDE A TEPEE

SIGN LANGUAGE

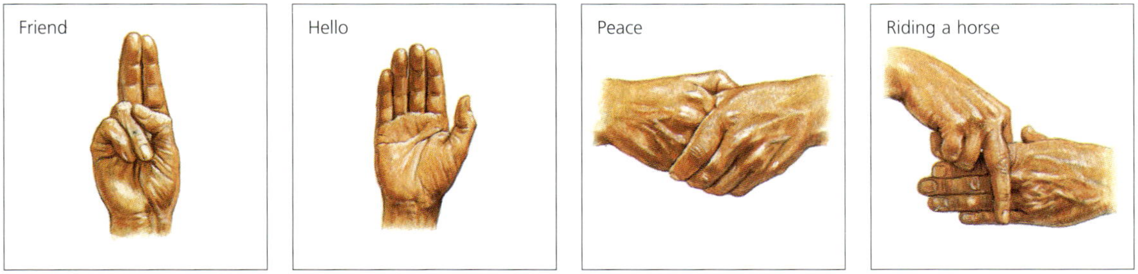

TARGET PRACTICE

TEPEE CAMP

PREPARING FOOD

Travel and Hunting

CEREMONIAL CANOE

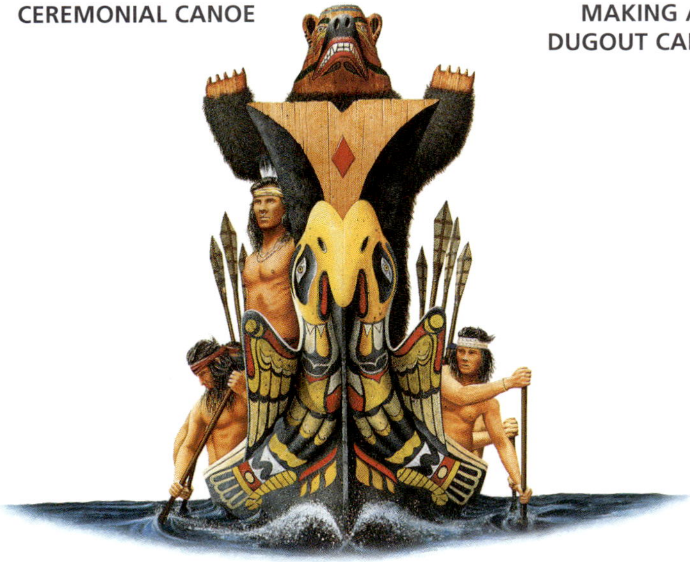

MAKING A DUGOUT CANOE

A cedar log was split lengthwise. Shaping began with stone tools.

The sides were chipped away to reach the required thickness.

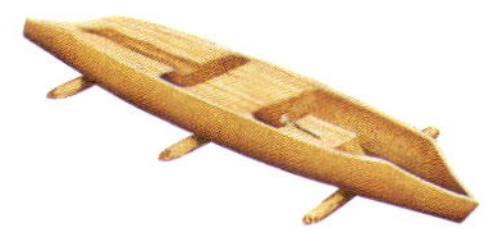

Hollowing the inside to the correct thickness took skill and time.

Water heated with hot rocks softened the wood. Thwarts were fitted to broaden the interior.

The bow and stern pieces were attached and the hull was sanded and decorated.

DOG SLEDDING

Arctic tribes trained huskies to pull sleds

Sleds were made by laying a platform of driftwood or caribou antlers on wooden or whalebone runners

DOG TRAVOIS

BUFFALO HUNT

Native Americans used buffalo hides for clothing and shelter, dung for fuel, fat for lamps, horns for spoons, bones for tools, stomachs for cooking pots, hooves for glue and meat for food

Plains Indians hunted buffalo from horseback

Culture and Ceremonies

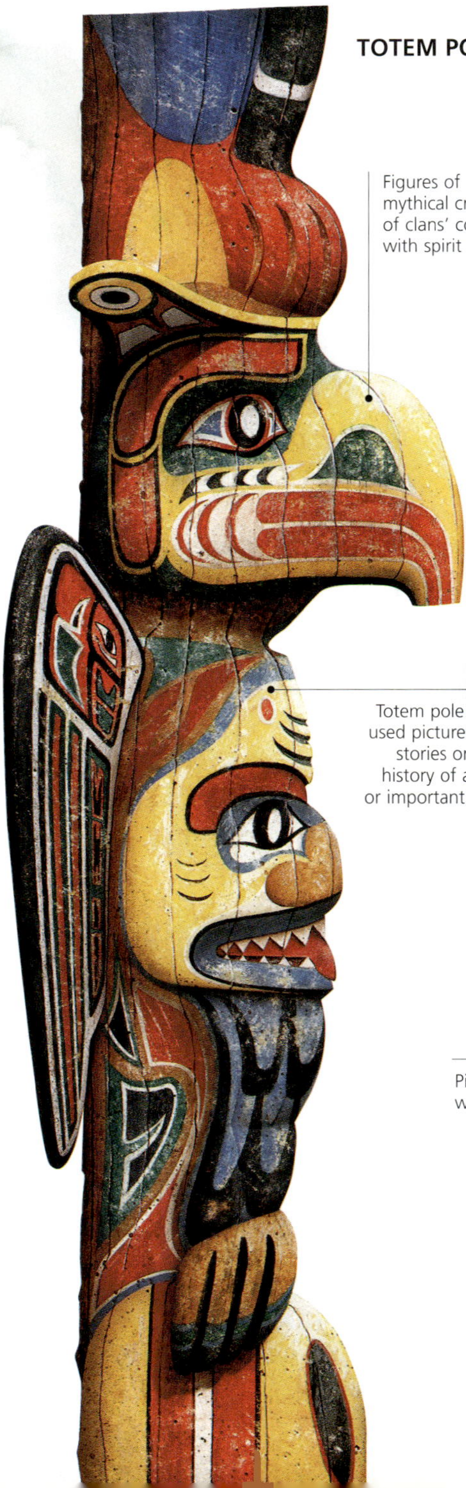

TOTEM POLE

Figures of animals or mythical creatures told of clans' connections with spirit ancestors

Totem pole carvers used pictures to tell stories or record history of a family or important person

SNOWSHOE DANCER

An Objibwa hunter rejoices after the first snowfall

PIPE CEREMONY

Pipes took several weeks to make

CEREMONIAL DANCE

Kwakiutl shamans wore bark costumes and painted wooden masks to represent birdlike friends of the fearsome Cannibal Spirit

Native Americans used solemn pipe-smoking rituals to ask for the spirits' help to make war, peace, rain, to hunt successfully, or to seal a good trade bargain

EUROPE

United Kingdom 428
Spain and Portugal 430
France 432
The Low Countries 434
Western Central Europe 436
Italy 438
Southeastern Europe 440
Eastern Europe 442
Northern Europe 444

NORTH AMERICA

Western Canada and Alaska 446
Eastern Canada 448
Northeastern United States 450
Central United States 452
Southern United States 454
Western United States 456
Central America and the Caribbean 458

SOUTH AMERICA

Northern South America 460
Southern South America 462

ASIA

Russia 464
Central Eurasia 466
The Middle East 468
Southern Asia 470
Southeast Asia 472
Eastern Asia 474
Japan 476

AFRICA

Northern Africa 478
Southern Africa 480

AUSTRALIA AND OCEANIA

Australia and Papua New Guinea 482
New Zealand and the Southwestern Pacific 484

United Kingdom

BAGPIPE PLAYER

STONEHENGE
Wiltshire, England

BRIGHTON PAVILION
Brighton, England

COLDSTREAM GUARD

BLARNEY CASTLE
Blarney, Ireland

CRICKET PLAYER

HAMMER THROWER

Spain and Portugal

BULLFIGHTER

TORRE DE BELEM
Lisbon, Portugal

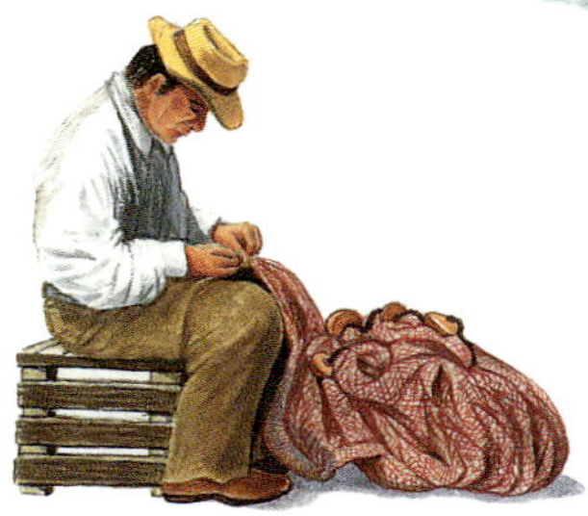

FISHERMAN

FLAMENCO DANCER

THE ALCAZAR
Segovia, Spain

Bay of Biscay
FRANCE
N
W
E
S
La Coruña
Gijón
Oviedo
Santander
Bilbao
Donostia–San Sebastián
Santiago
CANTABRIAN MOUNTAINS
PYRENEES
Pamplona
Pico de Aneto 11,168 ft (3,404 m)
ANDORRA
ANDORRA LA VELLA
Vigo
Ebro
Saragossa
COSTA BRAVA
Barcelona
Valladolid
Douro
Porto
Salamanca
Segovia
PORTUGAL
SPAIN
MADRID
Mondego
Coimbra
Minorca
Majorca
Palma
Balearic Islands
Alcántara Reservoir
Toledo
Tagus
MESETA
Valencia
Ibiza
Ibiza
LISBON
Badajoz
Guadiana
Setúbal
Evora
Alicante
Mediterranean Sea
Murcia
SIERRA MORENA
Guadalquivir
Córdoba
Cartagena
Seville
ALGARVE
Granada
Faro
Mulhacén 11,407 ft (3,477 m)
Almería
CAPE ST. VINCENT
Jerez
Málaga
Cádiz
COSTA DEL SOL
Gulf of Cádiz
Algeciras
GIBRALTAR (U.K.)
ALGERIA
Ceuta (SPAIN)
Melilla (SPAIN)
MOROCCO
SCALE
MILES
0 25 50 75 100
0 50 100 150
KILOMETERS

LOCATION

France

TGV TRAIN

BOULES PLAYER

CAFE

FASHION MODEL

EIFFEL TOWER
Paris

CAMEMBERT CHEESE

ENGLAND
English Channel
BELGIUM
LUXEMBOURG
GERMANY
SWITZERLAND
ITALY
SPAIN
ANDORRA
MONACO
CORSICA
Ajaccio
FRANCE
ATLANTIC OCEAN
Bay of Biscay
Mediterranean Sea
N
E
S
W
SCALE
MILES
0 25 50 75 100
0 50 100 150
KILOMETERS
Calais
Dunkerque
Boulogne
Lille
Dieppe
Amiens
Cherbourg
Le Havre
Rouen
Reims
Metz
PARIS
Nancy
Strasbourg
Brest
Quimper
Rennes
Troyes
St-Nazaire
Nantes
Tours
Dijon
Besançon
Bourges
La Rochelle
Lyon
St-Étienne
Grenoble
Mont Blanc
15,771 ft (4,807 m)
ALPS
Bordeaux
Avignon
Nice
Cannes
Marseille
Biarritz
Toulouse
Montpellier
Perpignan
PYRENEES
Seine
Loire
Meuse
Moselle
Saôn
Saône
Doubs
Rhone
Durance
Garonne
LOCATION

The Low Countries

FOLK DANCERS
The Netherlands

WINDMILL

WOODEN CLOGS

ZUIDER ZEE FOLK COSTUME
The Netherlands

DAMME CANAL
Damme, Belgium

N
W
E
S
SCALE
MILES
0
10
20
30
0
10
20
30
40
50
KILOMETERS
Ameland
Terschelling
West Frisian Islands
Vlieland
Waddenzee
Texel
Groningen
Leeuwarden
Ijsselmeer
Alkmaar
THE NETHERLANDS
Haarlem
AMSTERDAM
Apeldoorn
Utrecht
THE HAGUE
Arnhem
Lek
Rhine
Rotterdam
Nijmegen
Waal
Dordrecht
Maas
Breda
Tilburg
Eindhoven
North Sea
BAARLE-HERTOG
(BELGIUM)
Ostende
Brugge
Antwerp
GERMANY
Ghent
FLANDERS
BRUSSELS
BELGIUM
Liège
Meuse
Sambre
FRANCE
LUXEMBOURG
LUXEMBOURG
Esch-sur-Alzette
LOCATION

Western Central Europe

ALPENHORN PLAYER
Swiss Alps, Switzerland

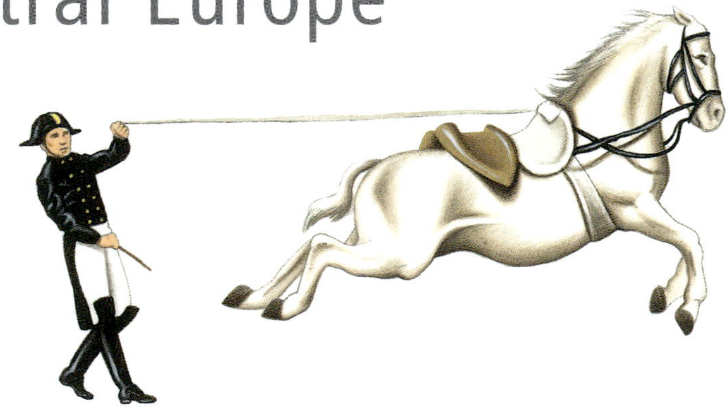

LIPIZZANER HORSE AND TRAINER
Vienna, Austria

FOLK COSTUME
Switzerland

HURDY-GURDY PLAYER
Germany

VIENNA PHILHARMONIC ORCHESTRA
Austria

NEUSCHWANSTEIN CASTLE
Bavaria, Germany

BAVARIAN BRASS BAND
Germany

DENMARK
North Sea
Baltic Sea
N
S
W
E
SCALE
MILES
0
25
50
75
0
25
50
75
100
125
KILOMETERS
Nord-Ostsee Canal
Kiel
Rostock
Lübeck
Hamburg
Elbe
THE NETHERLANDS
Oldenburg
Bremen
Oder
BERLIN
POLAND
Hannover
Brunswick
Magdeburg
Münster
HARZ MOUNTAINS
Duisburg
Essen
Dortmund
Düsseldorf
RUHR VALLEY
Cologne
Elbe
Leipzig
Bonn
Erfurt
Dresden
Chemnitz
ELGIUM
Rhine
GERMANY
Moselle
Wiesbaden
Frankfurt
Mainz
Main
XEMBOURG
CZECH REPUBLIC
Mannheim
Heidelberg
Nuremburg
BOHEMIAN FOREST
FRANCE
Stuttgart
Rhine
BLACK FOREST
Danube
Augsburg
Munich
Linz
Danube
VIENNA
Basel
Salzburg
JURA MOUNTAINS
Zürich
LIECHTENSTEIN
Salzach
AUSTRIA
BERN
Luzern
VADUZ
ALPS
Innsbruck
Mur
HUNGARY
Lausanne
SWITZERLAND
BRENNER PASS
Grossglockner
12,470 ft (3,801 m)
Graz
Jungfrau
13,642 ft
(4,158 m)
ITALY
SLOVENIA
Matterhorn
14,691 ft (4,478 m)
LOCATION

Italy

WINE MAKER

LEANING TOWER OF PISA

CHIANTI WINE

PIZZA MAKER

RIALTO BRIDGE
Venice

VATICAN GUARD

SWITZERLAND
AUSTRIA
FRANCE
SLOVENIA
CROATIA
ITALY
Mont Blanc 15,771 ft (4,807 m)
Matterhorn 14,691 ft (4,478 m)
Monte Rosa 15,203 ft (4,634 m)
ALPS
DOLOMITES
APENNINES
Lake Maggiore
Lake Como
Lake Garda
Po
Arno
Tiber
Bolzano
Turin
Milan
Brescia
Verona
Padua
Venice
Trieste
Parma
Genoa
Ferrara
Modena
Bologna
La Spezia
Ravenna
Gulf of Venice
Ligurian Sea
Florence
Rimini
Pisa
Livorno
SAN MARINO
SAN MARINO
Arezzo
Siena
Ancona
Elba
Perugia
Corsica (FRANCE)
Giglio
Adriatic Sea
Pescara
VATICAN CITY
ROME
Sassari
SARDINIA
Foggia
Naples
Ischia
Capri
Salerno
Bari
Mt. Vesuvius 4,190 ft (1,277 m)
Cagliari
Tyrrhenian Sea
Taranto
Brindisi
Strait of Otranto
Gulf of Taranto
Cosenza
Ustica
Stromboli
Palermo
Lipari Islands
Messina
Reggio di Calabria
Ionian Sea
SICILY
Mt. Etna 10,902 ft (3,323 m)
Syracuse
Mediterranean Sea
MALTA
VALLETTA
N
W
E
S
SCALE
MILES
0 25 50 75
0 50 100 150
KILOMETERS
LOCATION

Southeastern Europe

FOLK COSTUME
Romania

GORENJSKA FOLK COSTUMES
Slovenia

EVZONES GUARDS
Athens, Greece

CITY OF DUBROVNIK
Croatia

CITY OF BLED
Slovenia

CASTLE OF VLAD TEPES
Transylvania, Romania

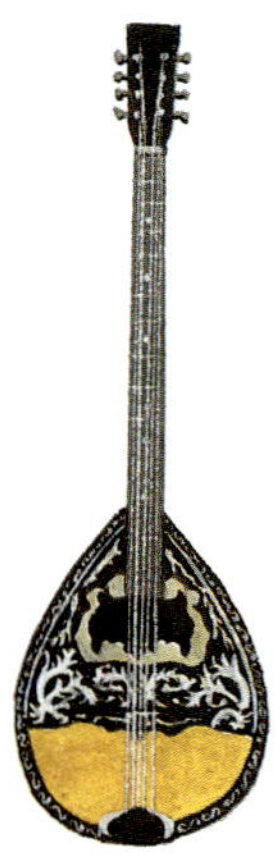

BOUZOUKI
Greece

KING AGAMEMNON'S DEATH MASK
Mycenae, Greece

UKRAINE
MOLDOVA
AUSTRIA
HUNGARY
SLOVENIA
LJUBLJANA
ZAGREB
CROATIA
Drava
Rijeka
Pula
Osijek
VOJVODINA
Novi Sad
Danube
Bosna
Banja Luka
DALMATIA
DINARIC ALPS
BOSNIA AND HERZEGOVINA
BELGRADE
SERBIA
SARAJEVO
Split
Mostar
YUGOSLAVIA
Morava
Niš
MONTENEGRO
Dubrovnik
Podgorica
Priština
KOSOVO
Shkodër
SKOPJE
MACEDONIA
Vardar
Durrës
TIRANE
ALBANIA
Bitola
Korçë
Vlorë
ROMANIA
Oradea
Cluj-Napoca
Iaşi
Prut
Siret
CARPATHIAN MTS.
Arad
Timişoara
Mureş
Sibiu
Braşov
Galaţi
TRANSYLVANIAN ALPS
Ploieşti
Craiova
BUCHAREST
Constanţa
Danube
BULGARIA
Varna
BALKAN MOUNTAINS
SOFIA
Mt. Musala
9,596 ft (2,925 m)
Burgas
Plovdiv
Struma
RHODOPE MTS.
Black Sea
TURKEY
Alexandroupolis
Thásos
Samothrace
Thessaloníki
Mt. Olympus
9,570 ft (2,917 m)
Lemnos
Corfu
GREECE
Volos
Northern Sporades
Skyros
Euboea
Aegean Sea
Lesbos
TURKEY
Chios
Levkás
Ionian Islands
Cephalonia
Khalkís
Patras
Zákinthos
ATHENS
Piraeus
PELOPONNESE
Tripolis
Ándros
Sámos
Tínos
Mykonos
Cyclades
Naxos
Páros
DODECANESE
Kíthira
Thíra
Rhodes
Sea of Crete
Canea
Iráklion
Crete
Kárpathos
Ionian Sea
Mediterranean Sea
Adriatic Sea
N
W
E
S
SCALE
MILES
0 25 50 75 100
0 50 100 150
KILOMETERS
LOCATION

Eastern Europe

FOLK COSTUME
Poland

CITY OF RIGA
Latvia

STRAW FIGURES
Belarus

FOLK DANCERS
Ukraine

HORTOBAGY HORSEMAN
Hungary

COSSACK DANCER
Belarus

Northern Europe

SAMI (LAPP) PEOPLE
Northern Scandinavia

BERGEN WHARF
Norway

ICE FISHING

KICK-SLEDDING

LITTLE MERMAID STATUE
Copenhagen, Denmark

ARCTIC CIRCLE PYRAMID
Norway

KALMAR CASTLE
Sweden

ICELAND
Akureyri
VATNAJOKULL
REYKJAVIK
ATLANTIC OCEAN
MILES
0 50 100 150
0 100 200
KILOMETERS
NORTH CAPE
Hammerfest
Barents Sea
N
E
S
W
Tromsø
Lake Inari
LAPLAND
Lofoten Islands
Narvik
Kemi
Kebnekaise
6,965 ft (2,123 m)
Torne
Bodo
Gällivare
Norwegian Sea
FINLAND
RUSSIA
Luleå
Skellefte
Oulu
Ume
Oulujärvi
SWEDEN
Umeå
Gulf of Bothnia
Trondheim
Indal
Kuopio
Joensuu
Vaasa
Jyväskylä
Nordfjord
Galdhøpiggen
8,100 ft (2,469 m)
Sundsvall
Sognefjord
JOTUNHEIM MOUNTAINS
Pori
Tampere
Lake Saimaa
Lahti
Österdal
Bergen
Turku
HELSINKI
NORWAY
Aland Islands
OSLO
Uppsala
Drammen
STOCKHOLM
Stavanger
Fredrikstad
Karlstad
Orebro
Gulf of Finland
ESTONIA
Lake Vänern
Norrköping
Lake Vättern
Linköping
Kristiansand
Skagerrak
SCALE
MILES
0 25 50 75 100 125
0 50 100 150 200
KILOMETERS
Borås
Goteborg
Jönköping
Gotland
Alborg
North Sea
DENMARK
Oland
LATVIA
Arhus
Hälsingborg
Baltic Sea
Esbjerg
COPENHAGEN
Malmö
Odense
Sjaelland
Fyn
Bornholm
Lolland
LOCATION
GERMANY
POLAND

Western Canada and Alaska

ALASKAN FERRY

IDITAROD MUSHER AND DOG TEAM
Alaska

SNOWMOBILE RIDER

INUIT ICE-FISHERMAN
Canada

TRADITIONAL CHURCH
Northwest Territories, Canada

ALASKAN BROWN BEAR

Eastern Canada

ICE HOCKEY PLAYERS

TRADITIONAL CHURCH
Newfoundland

CAP-DES-ROSIERS LIGHTHOUSE
Gaspé Peninsula, Québec

CN TOWER
Toronto

CHATEAU FRONTENAC
Québec City

ROYAL CANADIAN MOUNTED POLICE (MOUNTIES)

N
S
E
W
SCALE
MILES
0
50
100
150
200
0
100
200
300
400
KILOMETERS
Ivujivik
Hudson Strait
Hudson Bay
PÉNINSULE D'UNGAVA
(UNGAVA PENINSULA)
Ungava
Bay
Labrador Sea
ATLANTIC OCEAN
Feuilles
Belcher
Islands
Nain
QUEBEC
James
Bay
Réservoir de
la Grande
Deux
LABRADOR
Smallwood
Reservoir
NEWFOUNDLAND
Churchill
Happy
Valley —
Goose Bay
Albany
Lac Sakami
Moosonee
Hearst
Lac
Mistassini
Ile d'Anticosti
(Anticosti Island)
ult Ste. Marie
Lac
Saint-Jean
Saguenay
PENINSULE
DE LA GASPESIE
(GASPE PENINSULA)
Gulf of St. Lawrence
Newfoundland
Sudbury
NEW
BRUNSWICK
Lake
Huron
St. Lawrence
Québec
Prince
Edward
Island
St. John's
OTTAWA
Montréal
St-Pierre and
Miquelon
(FRANCE)
Fredericton
Charlottetown
Toronto
Saint John
London
Lake Ontario
Bay of Fundy
NOVA
SCOTIA
Halifax
sor
e Erie
UNITED STATES
OF AMERICA
LOCATION

Northeastern United States

AMISH PEOPLE
Pennsylvania

LIBERTY BELL
Philadelphia, Pennsylvania

STATUE OF LIBERTY
New York City

CHRYSLER BUILDING
New York City

KENTUCKY DERBY

CAPITOL BUILDING
Washington, D.C.

BASKETBALL PLAYER

Central United States

SIOUX HEADDRESS

AMERICAN FOOTBALL PLAYER

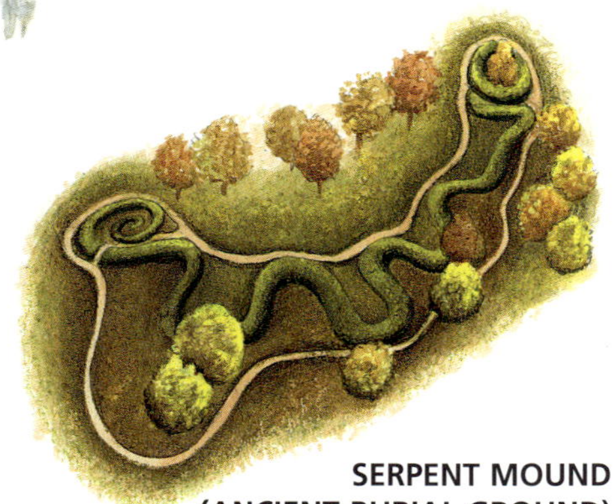

SERPENT MOUND
(ANCIENT BURIAL GROUND)
Adams County, Ohio

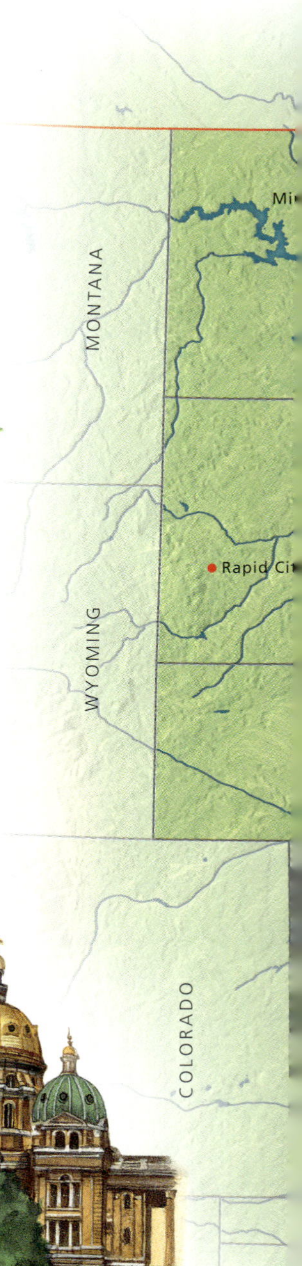

WINDMILL

ABRAHAM LINCOLN'S HOUSE
Springfield, Illinois

CAPITOL BUILDING
Des Moines, Iowa

CANADA
CANADA
CANADA
SCALE
MILES
0 50 100 150
0 50 100 150 200 250
KILOMETERS
N
E
S
W
Lake of the Woods
Lake Superior
Lake Huron
Lake Michigan
Lake Erie
MINNESOTA
NORTH DAKOTA
SOUTH DAKOTA
WISCONSIN
MICHIGAN
IOWA
NEBRASKA
ILLINOIS
INDIANA
OHIO
KANSAS
MISSOURI
WEST VIRGINIA
KENTUCKY
OKLAHOMA
ARKANSAS
Grand Forks
Fargo
Moorhead
Duluth
Superior
Marquette
Sault Ste. Marie
Escanaba
Minneapolis
St. Paul
Pierre
Green Bay
Appleton
Bay City
Saginaw
Rochester
La Crosse
Sioux Falls
Madison
Milwaukee
Grand Rapids
Lansing
Detroit
Dubuque
Sioux City
Chicago
Gary
Toledo
Cleveland
Fort Wayne
Davenport
Rock Island
Des Moines
Omaha
Council Bluffs
Platte
Grand Island
Lincoln
Peoria
Columbus
Springfield
Indianapolis
St. Joseph
Hannibal
Cincinnati
Topeka
Kansas City
Salina
Jefferson City
St. Louis
East St. Louis
Evansville
Dodge City
Wichita
Springfield
Cairo
Red
Mississippi
St. Croix
James
Minnesota
Missouri
Wabash
Illinois
Ohio
Kansas
Arkansas
OZARK PLATEAU
LOCATION

Southern United States

COUNTRY MUSICIAN

THE ALAMO
San Antonio, Texas

RODEO

MISSISSIPPI RIVER PADDLE STEAMER

JAZZ MUSICIAN

BASEBALL PLAYER

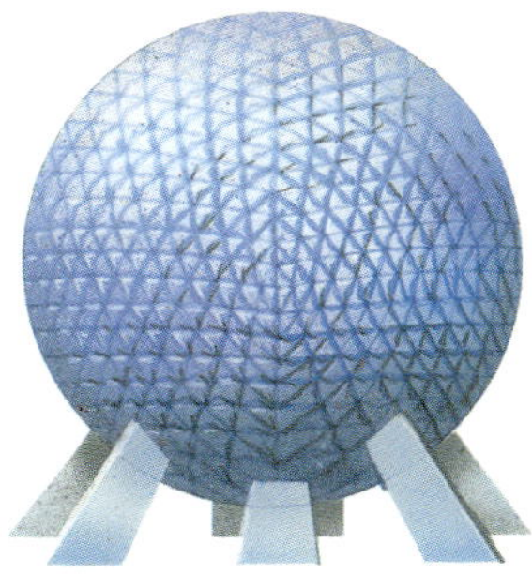

EPCOT CENTER
Orlando, Florida

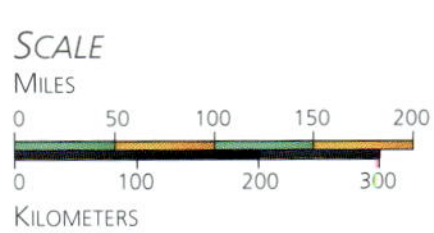

LOCATION

Western United States

IN-LINE SKATER

HULA DANCER
Hawaii

NAVAJO WEAVER
Arizona

GOLDEN GATE BRIDGE
San Francisco

PUEBLO POTTERY
New Mexico

DISNEYLAND
Anaheim, California

TAOS PUEBLO (NATIVE VILLAGE)
Taos, New Mexico

CANADA
MEXICO
PACIFIC OCEAN
WASHINGTON
OREGON
IDAHO
MONTANA
WYOMING
NEVADA
UTAH
COLORADO
CALIFORNIA
ARIZONA
NEW MEXICO
NORTH DAKOTA
SOUTH DAKOTA
NEBRASKA
KANSAS
TEXAS
Seattle
Tacoma
Olympia
Spokane
Mt. Rainier 14,410 ft (4,392 m)
CASCADE RANGE
Columbia
Portland
Salem
Eugene
Snake
Boise
Idaho Falls
Twin Falls
Missoula
Helena
Great Falls
Missouri
Billings
Yellowstone
Casper
Cheyenne
Rock Springs
ROCKY MOUNTAINS
Great Salt Lake
Ogden
Salt Lake City
Provo
Green
Eureka
Winnemucca
Humboldt
Reno
Carson City
Lake Tahoe
SIERRA NEVADA
Sacramento
San Francisco
Oakland
GREAT BASIN
COLORADO PLATEAU
Cedar City
Lake Powell
Grand Junction
Boulder
Denver
Colorado Springs
Pueblo
Arkansas
Fresno
Mt. Whitney 14,495 ft (4,418 m)
DEATH VALLEY
COAST RANGES
Las Vegas
Lake Mead
Santa Fe
Albuquerque
Flagstaff
Santa Barbara
Los Angeles
Colorado
Phoenix
Gila
Rio Grande
Roswell
San Diego
Tucson
HAWAII (U.S.A.)
Kauai
Lihue
Niihau
Oahu
Honolulu
Molokai
Lahaina
Lanai
Maui
Kahoolawe
Hawaii
Hilo
Mauna Kea 13,796 ft (4,205 m)
Mauna Loa 13,680 ft (4,170 m)
MILES 0 50 100
KILOMETERS 0 100 200
SCALE
MILES 0 50 100 150 200
KILOMETERS 0 100 200 300
LOCATION
N
E
S
W

Central America and the Caribbean

FOLK DANCER
Mexico

METROPOLITAN CATHEDRAL
Mexico City, Mexico

OLMEC STONE CARVING
Mexico

STEEL BAND
The Caribbean

TRADITIONAL FARMER
Guatemala

THATCHED CORNCRIB
Mexico

MARIACHI BAND
Mexico

Northern South America

QUECHUA MAN
Peru

CARNIVAL DANCER
Rio de Janeiro, Brazil

KAYAPO MAN
Brazil

TXUKAHAMAI HUNTERS WITH ANACONDA
Brazil

NOSSO SENHOR DO BOMFIM CHURCH
Salvador, Brazil

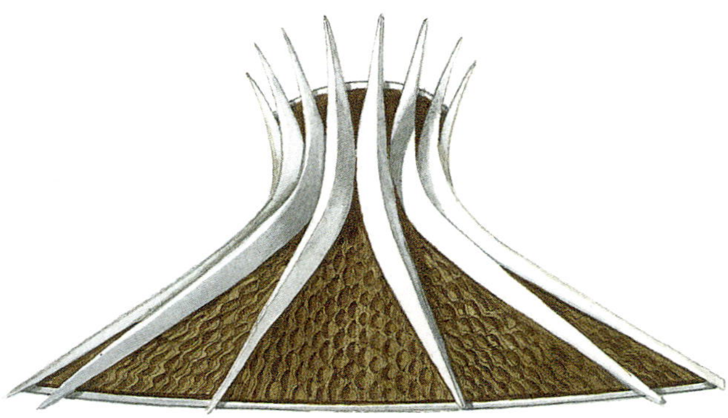

BRASILIA CATHEDRAL
Brasília, Brazil

TRINIDAD AND TOBAGO
ATLANTIC OCEAN
PACIFIC OCEAN
N
E
S
W
SCALE
MILES
0 100 200 300
0 100 200 300 400 500
KILOMETERS
PANAMA
VENEZUELA
COLOMBIA
ECUADOR
PERU
BRAZIL
BOLIVIA
PARAGUAY
CHILE
ARGENTINA
URUGUAY
GUYANA
SURINAME
FRENCH GUIANA (FRANCE)
CARACAS
BOGOTÁ
QUITO
LIMA
GEORGETOWN
PARAMARIBO
BRASILIA
Barranquilla
Cartagena
Bucaramanga
Medellín
Cali
Lake Maracaibo
Orinoco
Ciudad Bolívar
Cayenne
Amazon Delta
Belém
São Luís
Fortaleza
Recife
Salvador
Manaus
Negro
Amazon
Xingu
Tapajós
Madeira
Purus
Putumayo
Marañón
Iquitos
Leticia
AMAZON BASIN
Magdalena
ANDES
Chimborazo
20,702 ft
(6,310 m)
Trujillo
Huascarán
22,205 ft
(6,768 m)
Cuzco
Arequipa
Guaporé
MATO GROSSO PLATEAU
Tocantins
BRAZILIAN HIGHLANDS
São Francisco
Belo Horizonte
Paraná
São Paulo
Rio de Janeiro
Uruguay
Pôrto Alegre
Lagoa dos Patos
GALAPAGOS ISLANDS
(ECUADOR)
Pinta
Marchena
Genovesa
PACIFIC OCEAN
San Salvador
Fernandina
Santa Cruz
San Cristóbal
Puerto Ayora
Isabela
Puerto Baquerizo Moreno
Santa María
Española
MILES
0 20 40
0 25 50 75
KILOMETERS
LOCATION

Southern South America

VILLAGE MUSICIANS
Bolivia

FOLK COSTUME
Bolivia

TANGO DANCERS
Argentina

PRESIDENTIAL PALACE
Asunción, Paraguay

CONGRESO NACIONAL
Buenos Aires, Argentina

TRADITIONAL JESUIT CHURCH
Argentina

GIANT BROMELIAD
The Andes, Bolivia

GUANACOS
Argentina

PERU
BOLIVIA
BRAZIL
BRAZIL
PARAGUAY
URUGUAY
ARGENTINA
CHILE
PACIFIC OCEAN
ATLANTIC OCEAN
Guaporé
Mamoré
Trinidad
Lake Titicaca
LA PAZ
Mt. Illimani 21,201 ft (6,462 m)
Cochabamba
Santa Cruz
Arica
Lake Poopó
SUCRE
Iquique
ATACAMA DESERT
Antofagasta
ANDES
Pilcomayo
GRAN CHACO
ASUNCION
Paraguay
Cerro Ojos del Salado 22,664 ft (6,908 m)
San Miguel de Tucumán
Corrientes
Copiapó
Río Salado
Bonete 22,546 ft (6,872 m)
Paraná
La Serena
Córdoba
Uruguay
Aconcagua 22,834 ft (6,960 m)
San Juan
Mendoza
PAMPAS
Rosario
Valparaíso
SANTIAGO
BUENOS AIRES
MONTEVIDEO
La Plata
ANDES
Concepción
Colorado
Mar del Plata
Bahía Blanca
Negro
Puerto Montt
VALDES PENINSULA
PATAGONIA
Comodoro Rivadavia
Puerto Deseado
Falkland Islands (U.K.)
Stanley
Río Gallegos
Strait of Magellan
Punta Arenas
Tierra del Fuego
Ushuaia
Cape Horn
N
S
E
W
SCALE
MILES
0
100
200
300
0
100
200
300
400
500
KILOMETERS
LOCATION
EASTER ISLAND
(CHILE)
Mataveri
PACIFIC OCEAN
MILES
0
5
10
15
0
10
20
KILOMETERS

Russia

KHANTY TRIBESMEN

BALLET DANCERS

FARM WORKERS

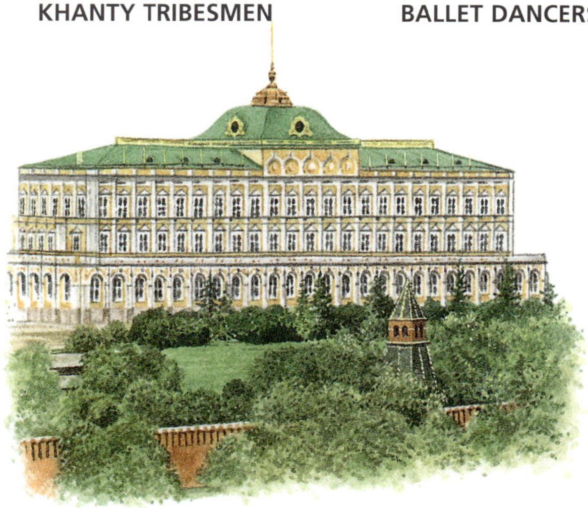

THE KREMLIN
Moscow

MATRESHKA DOLLS

TROIKA HORSES AND SLED

EVENKI MOTHER

TRANS-SIBERIAN RAILROAD

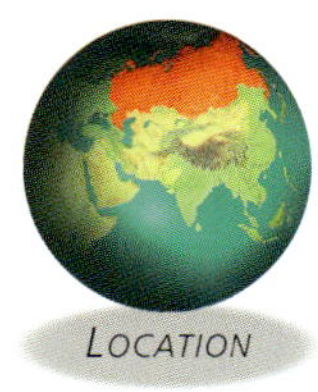

Central Eurasia

STREET VENDOR
Kazakstan

FOLK COSTUME
Georgia

WHIRLING DERVISH
Turkey

BLUE MOSQUE
Istanbul, Turkey

LONGHORN MUSICIAN
Tajikistan

SARSEMBEK HERDER
Kazakstan

EARLY VILLAGE OF CAPPADOCIA
Turkey

BORDER FORTRESS
Dogubayazit, Turkey

LOCATION

The Middle East

BEDOUINS

VEILED WOMAN

MEN WITH NARGHILE PIPE

WALLED CITY
Bam, Iran

ISRAELI MAN
Western Wall, Jerusaleum

CITY OF AL HAJRAH
Yemen

TRADITIONAL MUSICIAN
Iran

ARMENIA
AZERBAIJAN
TURKMENISTAN
TURKEY
Caspian Sea
Araks
Tabrīz
Rasht
Mosul
Aleppo
Latakia
Euphrates
CYPRUS
SYRIA
LEBANON
BEIRUT
DAMASCUS
TEHRAN
Mashhad
DASHT-E KAVIR
(GREAT SALT DESERT)
PLATEAU
OF IRAN
AFGHANISTAN
ZAGROS MOUNTAINS
DASHT-E LUT
BAGHDAD
Tigris
IRAQ
Eşfahān
IRAN
West Bank
AMMAN
JERUSALEM
Gaza
ISRAEL
JORDAN
Al Basrah
Abādān
Kermān
KUWAIT
Shīrāz
PAKISTAN
HEJAZ
Persian
Gulf
BAHRAIN
Ad Dammām
AL MANAMA
QATAR
AD DAWHAH
Strait of Hormuz
Dubai
Gulf of Oman
AN NAFUD
DESERT
RIYADH
ABU DHABI
MUSCAT
Medina
Red Sea
UNITED ARAB
EMIRATES
Sūr
SAUDI
ARABIA
OMAN
Jiddah
Mecca
SUDAN
RUB' AL-KHALI DESERT
(EMPTY QUARTER)
ASIR
Arabian Sea
Salālah
YEMEN
ERITREA
SANAA
Al Hudaydah
Ta'izz
Aden
Socotra
(YEMEN)
DJIBOUTI
SCALE
MILES
0 50 100 150 200 250
0 100 200 300 400
KILOMETERS
LOCATION
N
E
S
W

Southern Asia

FOLK DANCER
Bhutan

HERATI WOMAN
Afghanistan

SIKH MEN

SNAKE CHARMER
India

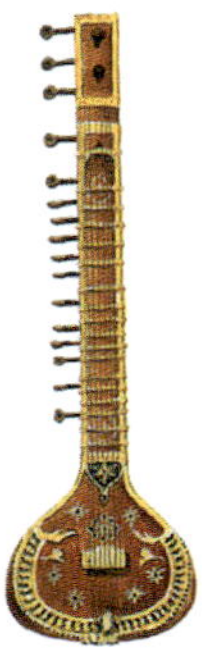

SITAR
India

TAJ MAHAL
Agra, India

PAINTED PALACE ELEPHANT
Jaipur, India

MEENAKSHI TEMPLE
Madurai, India

LINE FISHERMEN
Sri Lanka

UZBEKISTAN
TURKMENISTAN
TAJIKISTAN
IRAN
Herāt
KABUL
AFGHANISTAN
HINDU KUSH
KARAKORAM RANGE
K2 28,250 ft (8,611 m)
Peshawar
ISLAMABAD
Srinagar
Kandahar
CHINA
Lahore
Amritsar
HIMALAYAS
PAKISTAN
Indus
GREAT INDIAN DESERT
Annapurna 26,504 ft (8,078 m)
Mt. Everest 29,035 ft (8,850 m)
NEPAL
Delhi
NEW DELHI
KATHMANDU
Darjeeling
THIMPHU
BHUTAN
Agra
Jaipur
Jodhpur
Hyderabad
Karachi
Kanpur
Lucknow
Brahmaputra
Varanasi
Ganges
BANGLADESH
DHAKA
Arabian Sea
Ahmadabad
Bhopal
INDIA
Kolkata (Calcutta)
Chittagong
MYANMAR (BURMA)
Nagpur
Bhubaneswar
Mumbai (Bombay)
DECCAN
Bay of Bengal
Hyderabad
Panaji (Goa)
Andaman Islands
Bangalore
Chennai (Madras)
MALDIVES
MALE
MILES
0 100 200 300
0 200 400
KILOMETERS
Ernakulam (Cochin)
Jaffna
Nicobar Islands
Thiruvananthapuram (Trivandrum)
SRI LANKA
COLOMBO
LOCATION
INDIAN OCEAN
N
W
E
S
SCALE
MILES
0 100 200 300
0 100 200 300 400 500
KILOMETERS

Southeast Asia

FOLK COSTUME
Borneo

SINGKIL DANCER
The Philippines

BUDDHIST MONKS

JEEPNEY BUS
The Philippines

TOWN HALL
Ho Chi Minh City (Saigon), Vietnam

SHADOW PUPPET
Indonesia

SINGAPORE

FLOATING MARKET
Bangkok, Thailand

N
W
E
S
SCALE
MILES
0 100 200 300 400
0 150 300 450 600
KILOMETERS
CHINA
Hong (Red)
HANOI
Haiphong
VIETNAM
LAOS
VIENTIANE
Mekong
Hue
Da Nang
THAILAND
BANGKOK
CAMBODIA
PHNOM PENH
Ho Chi Minh City (Saigon)
Gulf of Thailand
South China Sea
Hat Yai
George Town
Ipoh
Kuala Terengganu
MALAYSIA
KUALA LUMPUR
Johor Baharu
SINGAPORE
SINGAPORE
Padang
Sumatra
Palembang
Java Sea
Pontianak
Kuching
SARAWAK
BANDAR SERI BEGAWAN
BRUNEI
SABAH
Kota Kinabalu
Mt. Kinabalu 13,455 ft (4,101 m)
Sandakan
Borneo
KALIMANTAN
Balikpapan
Banjarmasin
Luzon
Baguio
MANILA
Legazpi
Mindoro
PHILIPPINES
Panay
Samar
Palawan
Bacolod
Cebu
Negros
Mindanao
Davao
Sulu Sea
PACIFIC OCEAN
Celebes Sea
Manado
Halmahera
Sulawesi
Ujung Pandang
Buru
Ceram
Ambon
Banda Sea
Kai
Aru
Jayapura
IRIAN JAYA
Puncak Jaya 16,535 ft (5,040 m)
NEW GUINEA
JAKARTA
INDONESIA
Java
Yogyakarta
Surabaya
Flores Sea
Bali
Lombok
Sumbawa
Flores
Sumba
DILI
EAST TIMOR
Kupang
Timor Sea
Tanimbar
Arafura Sea
CEAN
AUSTRALIA
LOCATION

Eastern Asia

TIBETAN MONKS

CYCLISTS

FOLK COSTUME
South Korea

TAJIKIST

PAKIST

IND

JUNK
Hong Kong

TEMPLE OF HEAVEN
Beijing, China

GIANT PANDA

POTALA PALACE
Lhasa, Tibet

HERDING DUCKS

Japan

GEISHA PREPARING TEA

SUMO WRESTLERS

NINJA

CARP STREAMERS

TEMPLE OF THE GOLDEN PAVILION
Kyoto

KOKECHI DOLL

BULLET TRAIN

SHIOGAMA FESTIVAL BOAT

AYUKYU ISLANDS
East China Sea
Amami Islands
Okinawa Islands
Naha
MILES
0 25 50 75
0 50 100 150
KILOMETERS
RUSSIA
Sea of Okhotsk
Rebun
Rishiri
Wakkanai
RUSSIA
Hokkaidō
Asahikawa
Kushiro
Otaru
Sapporo
Hakodate
Tsugaru Strait
Aomori
N
E
W
S
SCALE
MILES
0 25 50 75 100
0 50 100 150
KILOMETERS
Morioka
Akita
Sendai
Sea of Japan (East Sea)
Sado
Fukushima
Niigata
Shinano
Utsunomiya
Kanazawa
JAPAN
TOKYO
Kawasaki
Yokohama
Honshū
Oki Islands
Nagoya
Shizuoka
Hamamatsu
SOUTH KOREA
Matsue
Kyōto
Korea Strait
Kōbe
Osaka
Okayama
Wakayama
Hiroshima
Inland Sea
Tokushima
Tsushima
Tsushima Strait
Matsuyama
Kōchi
Kitakyūshū
Shikoku
PACIFIC OCEAN
Fukuoka
Kumamoto
Nagasaki
Kyūshū
Gotō Islands
Miyazaki
Kagoshima
Osumi Islands
Tokara Islands
LOCATION

Northern Africa

ELEPHANT AND CALF

ALGERIAN NOMAD

BORORRO MAN
Niger

POUNDING MILLET
Senegal

CARRYING PALM WINE
Côte d'Ivoire

GIRAFFES

KOUTTOUBIA MOSQUE
Morocco

GIZA PYRAMIDS
Egypt

MALI MAN WITH FISHING TRAPS

LOCATION

EQUATORI
GUINEA

SAO TOM
AND PRINC

SAO TOM

Southern Africa

WATA WOODCARVERS
Kenya

TRADITIONAL DANCERS
Zaire

MASAI WARRIOR
Kenya

NINGA DRUMMERS
Zaire

HERERO WOMAN
Namibia

ZULUS
South Africa

KHOISAN HUNTERS
Southern Africa

CENTRAL AFRICAN REPUBLIC
SUDAN
ETHIOPIA
CAMEROON
SOMALIA
UGANDA
KENYA
Lake Turkana
LIBREVILLE
ABON
rt-Gentil
CONGO
DEMOCRATIC REPUBLIC OF THE CONGO (ZAIRE)
Margherita Peak 16,763 ft (5,109 m)
KAMPALA
Mt. Kenya 17,058 ft (5,199 m)
Lake Victoria
NAIROBI
KIGALI
RWANDA
Mwanza
BUJUMBURA
BURUNDI
Mt. Kilimanjaro 19,341 ft (5,895 m)
Mombasa
BRAZZAVILLE
KINSHASA
-Noire
BINDA
NGOLA)
Matadi
Congo (Zaire)
Kasai
Lualaba
Lomami
Kananga
Mbuji-Mayi
Lake Tanganyika
DODOMA
Zanzibar
DAR ES SALAAM
Mafia
TANZANIA
LUANDA
Cuanza
Seychelles
ANGOLA
Likasi
Lubumbashi
Lake Nyasa
Ruvuma
Luangwa
COMOROS
MORONI
Benguela
Huambo
Ndola
MALAWI
LILONGWE
MAYOTTE (FRANCE)
ZAMBIA
LUSAKA
Nampula
Cunene
Okavango
Zambezi
Lake Kariba
HARARE
Zambezi
Mozambique Channel
NAMIBIA
ZIMBABWE
Beira
Toamasina
ANTANANARIVO
Bulawayo
MOZAMBIQUE
Francistown
MADAGASCAR
WINDHOEK
BOTSWANA
Walvis Bay
KALAHARI DESERT
Limpopo
NAMIB DESERT
GABORONE
PRETORIA
Johannesburg
MAPUTO
MBABANE
SWAZILAND
Vaal
Orange
BLOEMFONTEIN
MASERU
DRAKENSBERG MTS.
Durban
LESOTHO
SOUTH AFRICA
INDIAN OCEAN
East London
CAPE TOWN
Port Elizabeth
Cape of Good Hope
N
E
S
W
SCALE
MILES
0 100 200 300 400
0 100 200 300 400 500 600
KILOMETRES
LOCATION

Australia and Papua New Guinea

SURF LIFESAVERS
Australia

MUD-MASKED WARRIOR
Papua New Guinea

RED KANGAROO
Australia

ULURU (AYERS ROCK)
Central Australia

SPIRIT HOUSE
Papua New Guinea

ABORIGINAL DANCERS
Australia

OPERA HOUSE AND HARBOR BRIDGE
Sydney, Australia

INDONESIA
EAST TIMOR
INDONESIA
PAPUA NEW GUINEA
N
W
E
S
SCALE
MILES
0
100
200
300
0
100
200
300
400
500
KILOMETERS
Arafura Sea
Torres Strait
Timor Sea
Melville Island
Darwin
ARNHEM LAND
Groote Island
Gulf of Carpentaria
CAPE YORK PENINSULA
Great Barrier Reef
KIMBERLEY PLATEAU
Broome
Derby
Fitzroy
Cairns
NORTHERN TERRITORY
Townsville
GREAT DIVIDING RANGE
Port Hedland
GREAT SANDY DESERT
Mount Isa
Mackay
QUEENSLAND
MACDONNELL RANGES
Alice Springs
GIBSON DESERT
Rockhampton
SIMPSON DESERT
Fraser Island
WESTERN AUSTRALIA
Maryborough
AUSTRALIA
GREAT VICTORIA DESERT
SOUTH AUSTRALIA
Brisbane
Toowoomba
Gold Coast
Lake Eyre
Geraldton
NULLARBOR PLAIN
Lake Torrens
NEW SOUTH WALES
Darling
Kalgoorlie-Boulder
Lake Gairdner
Port Augusta
Broken Hill
Perth
DARLING RANGE
Whyalla
Newcastle
Great Australian Bight
Sydney
Wollongong
Bunbury
Adelaide
CANBERRA
AUSTRALIAN CAPITAL TERRITORY
Albany
Kangaroo Island
Murray
Mt. Kosciuszko
7,310 ft
(2,228 m)
VICTORIA
INDIAN OCEAN
Ballarat
Melbourne
Geelong
Bass Strait
King Island
Flinders Island
Launceston
TASMANIA
Hobart
PAPUA NEW GUINEA
BISMARCK ARCHIPELAGO
Manus
Bismarck Sea
New Hanover
New Ireland
INDONESIA
Madang
Mt. Wilhelm
14,762 ft
(4,500 m)
New Britain
Bougainville
Lae
Solomon Sea
Solomon Islands
PORT MORESBY
Coral Sea
MILES
0
100
200
300
0
200
400
KILOMETERS
LOCATION

New Zealand and the Southwestern Pacific

RUGBY PLAYER

TAHITIAN SURFER

TRADITIONAL MAORI
New Zealand

SCUBA DIVER

KIWI
New Zealand

CHRISTCHURCH CATHEDRAL
Christchurch, New Zealand

WALKING ON HOT COALS
Fiji

PARLIAMENT HOUSE
Wellington, New Zealand

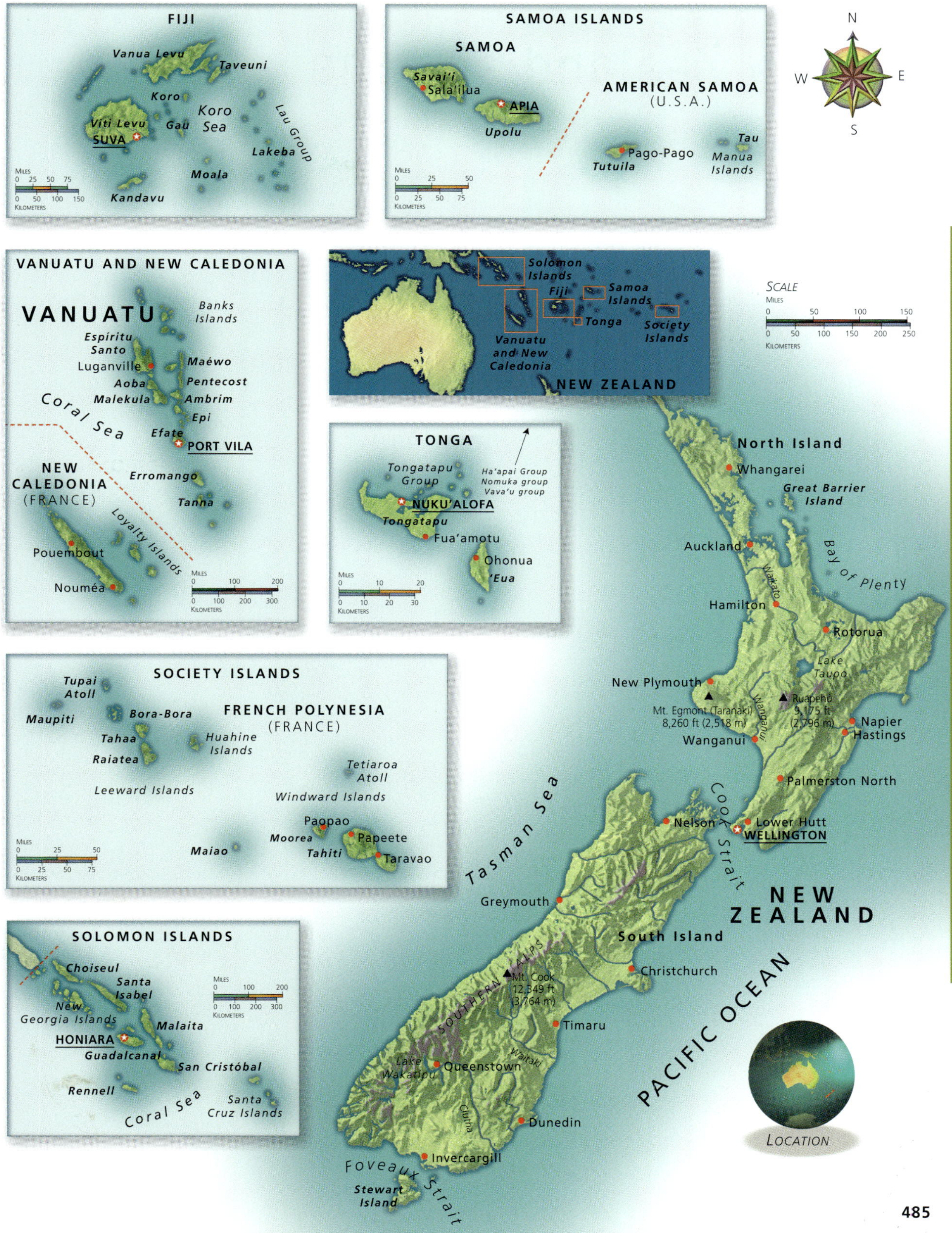

FIJI
Vanua Levu
Taveuni
Koro
Koro Sea
Viti Levu
SUVA
Gau
Lau Group
Lakeba
Moala
Kandavu
MILES 0 25 50 75
0 50 100 150 KILOMETERS
SAMOA ISLANDS
SAMOA
Savai'i
Sala'ilua
APIA
Upolu
AMERICAN SAMOA
(U.S.A.)
Pago-Pago
Tutuila
Tau
Manua Islands
MILES 0 25 50
0 25 50 75 KILOMETERS
N
W
E
S
VANUATU AND NEW CALEDONIA
VANUATU
Banks Islands
Espiritu Santo
Luganville
Maéwo
Aoba
Pentecost
Malekula
Ambrim
Epi
Coral Sea
Efate
PORT VILA
NEW CALEDONIA
(FRANCE)
Erromango
Tanna
Loyalty Islands
Pouembout
Nouméa
MILES 0 100 200
0 100 200 300 KILOMETERS
Solomon Islands
Fiji
Samoa Islands
Tonga
Vanuatu and New Caledonia
Society Islands
NEW ZEALAND
SCALE
MILES 0 50 100 150
0 50 100 150 200 250 KILOMETERS
TONGA
Tongatapu Group
Ha'apai Group
Nomuka group
Vava'u group
NUKU'ALOFA
Tongatapu
Fua'amotu
Ohonua
'Eua
MILES 0 10 20
0 10 20 30 KILOMETERS
North Island
Whangarei
Great Barrier Island
Auckland
Bay of Plenty
Waikato
Hamilton
Rotorua
Lake Taupo
New Plymouth
Mt. Egmont (Taranaki)
8,260 ft (2,518 m)
Ruapehu
9,175 ft
(2,796 m)
Wanganui
Napier
Hastings
Palmerston North
SOCIETY ISLANDS
Tupai Atoll
Maupiti
Bora-Bora
FRENCH POLYNESIA
(FRANCE)
Tahaa
Huahine Islands
Raiatea
Tetiaroa Atoll
Leeward Islands
Windward Islands
Paopao
Moorea
Papeete
Maiao
Tahiti
Taravao
MILES 0 25 50
0 25 50 75 KILOMETERS
Tasman Sea
Nelson
Cook Strait
Lower Hutt
WELLINGTON
Greymouth
NEW ZEALAND
South Island
SOLOMON ISLANDS
Choiseul
Santa Isabel
New Georgia Islands
Malaita
HONIARA
Guadalcanal
San Cristóbal
Rennell
Coral Sea
Santa Cruz Islands
MILES 0 100 200
0 100 200 300 KILOMETERS
Christchurch
SOUTHERN ALPS
Mt. Cook
12,349 ft
(3,764 m)
Timaru
PACIFIC OCEAN
Waitaki
Lake Wakatipu
Queenstown
Clutha
Dunedin
Invercargill
Foveaux Strait
Stewart Island
LOCATION

ARCHITECTURE

PLACES OF WORSHIP

Classical Style 490

Gothic Tradition 492

St Peter's Basilica 494

Religious Buildings of Europe 496

Mosques of the World 498

PUBLIC BUILDINGS

Early American Buildings 500

Statues and Monuments 502

Tombs and Memorials 504

Adventurous Shapes 506

Leisure Spaces 508

CASTLES, PALACES AND HOUSES

Early Settlement 510

Traditional Houses 512

Castles 514

Classical Influence 516

Classical Style

GREEK COLUMNS

THE PARTHENON
Athens, Greece

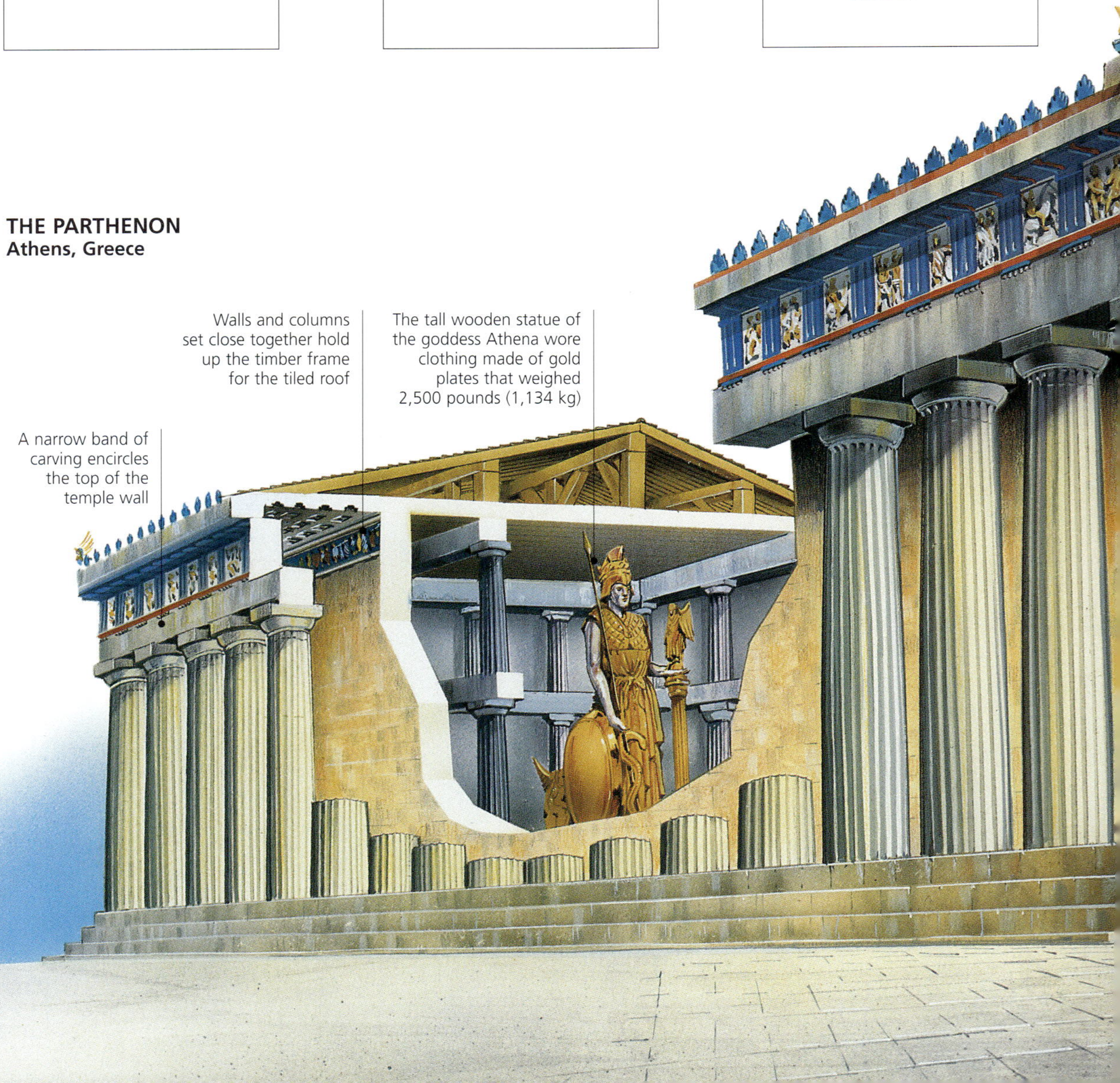

THE PANTHEON
Rome, Italy

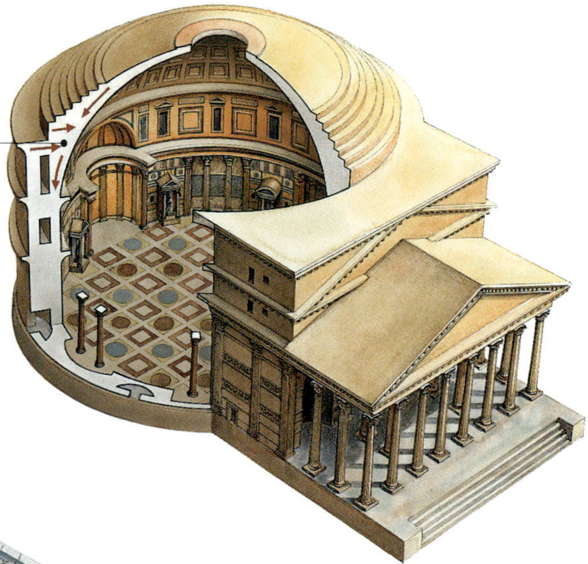

The dome is made of concrete that becomes lighter as it gets higher because each level is mixed with lighter stones such as volcanic pumice

Painted sculpture adorns the tympanum

Parthenon frieze depicts the procession of Athena

Athena's marble temple is surrounded by 46 Doric columns

Gothic Tradition

GOTHIC WINDOW TRACERIES

FLOOR PLAN

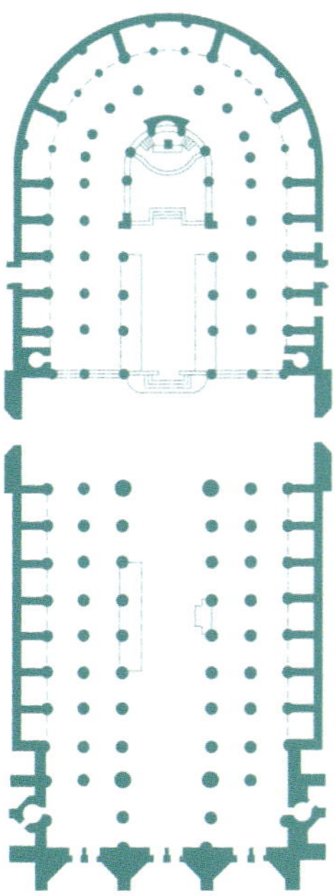

NOTRE DAME CATHEDRAL
Paris, France

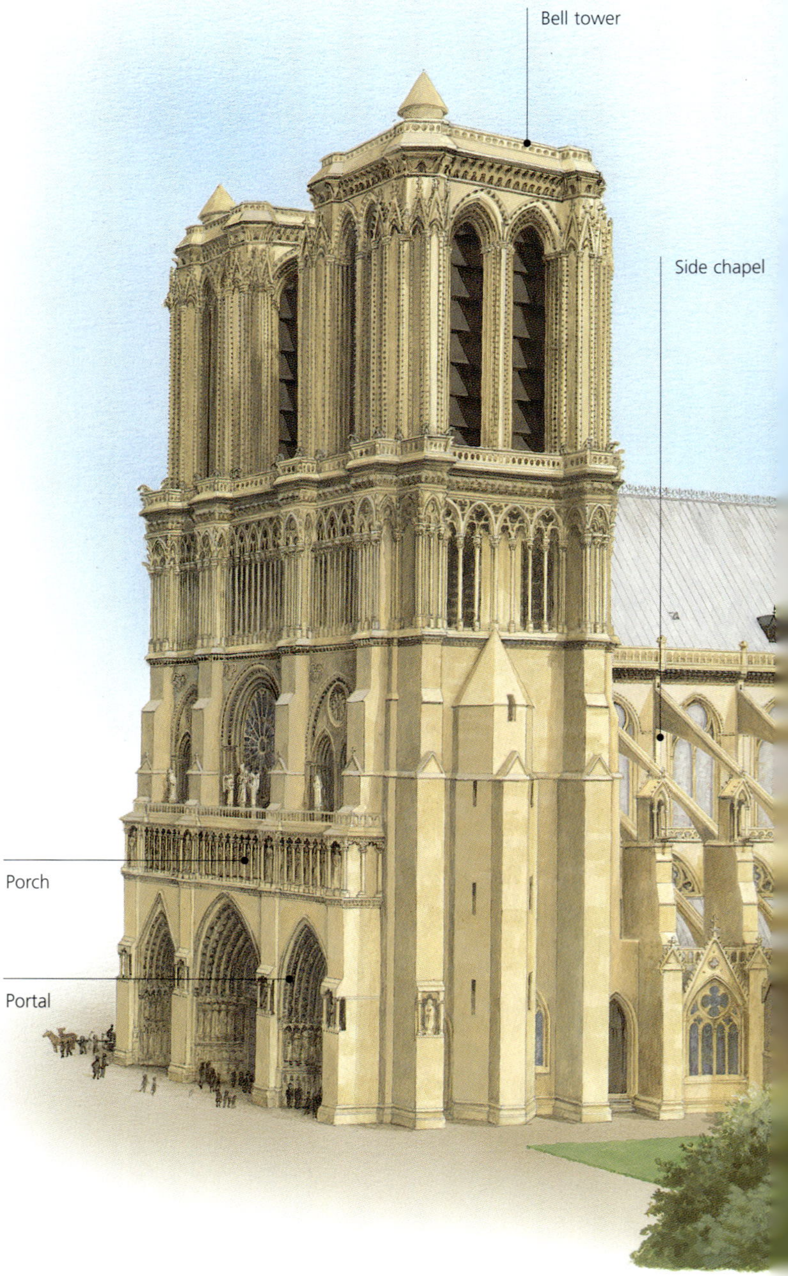

VAULT

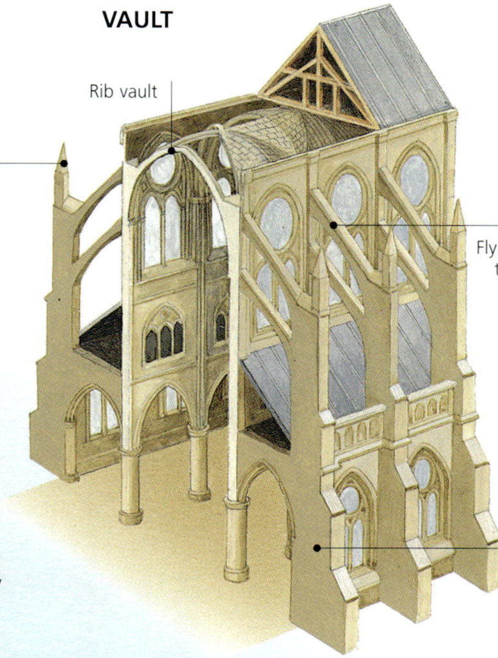

Rib vault
Carved pinnacles at the end of the flying buttresses help to buttress the vault
Flying buttresses for the vaults outside the cathedral support the stone ceiling
Buttress

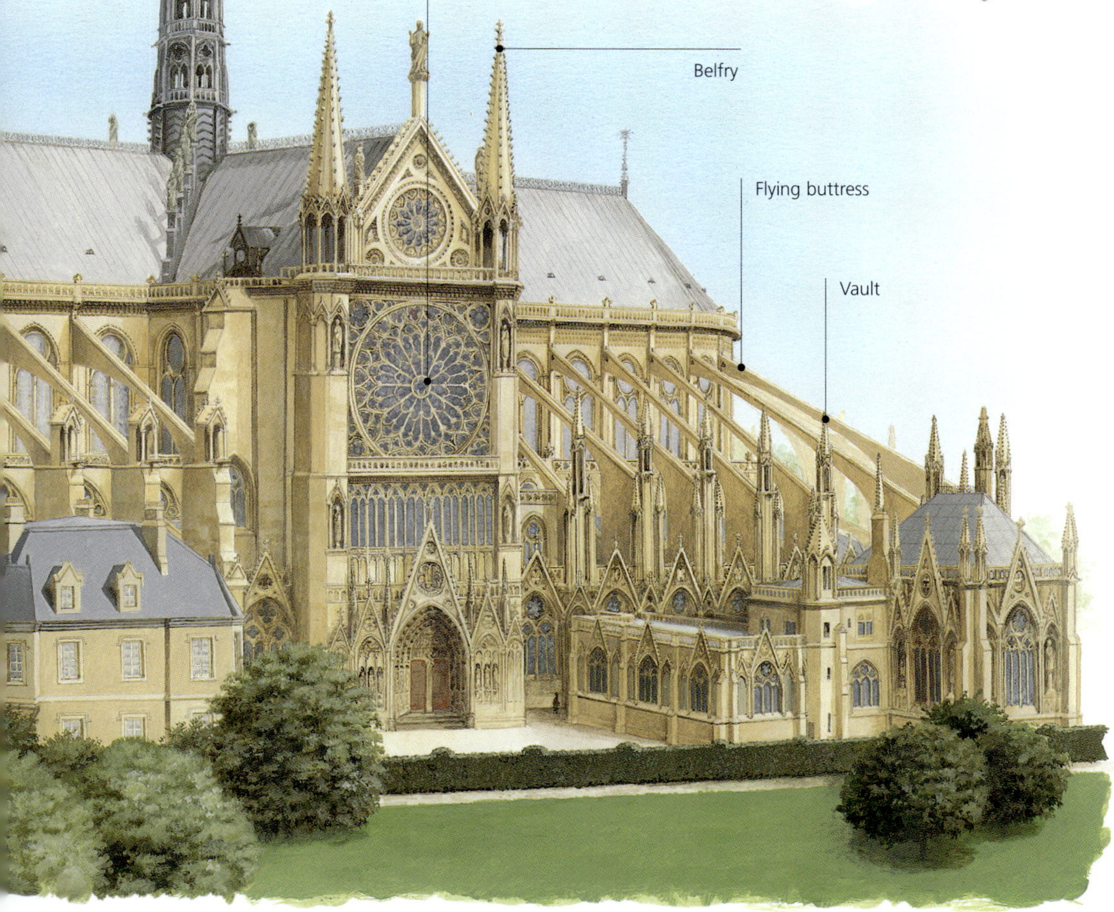

The spire is 298 feet (91 m) high
Stained glass window known as a rose window
Belfry
Flying buttress
Vault

St Peter's Basilica

ROME, ITALY

BRAMANTE'S FLOORPLAN

MICHELANGELO'S FLOORPLAN

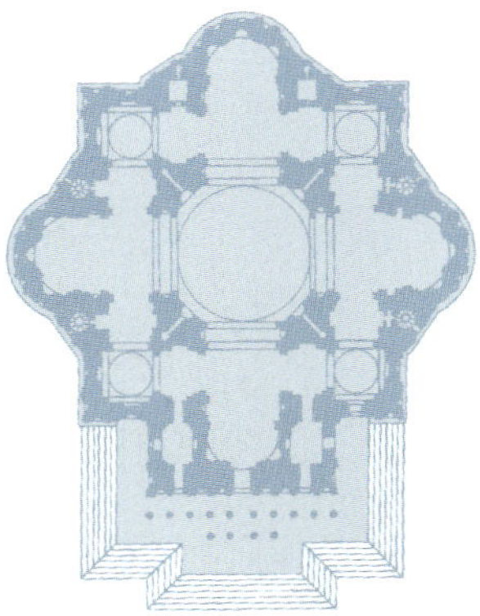

VATICAN CITY

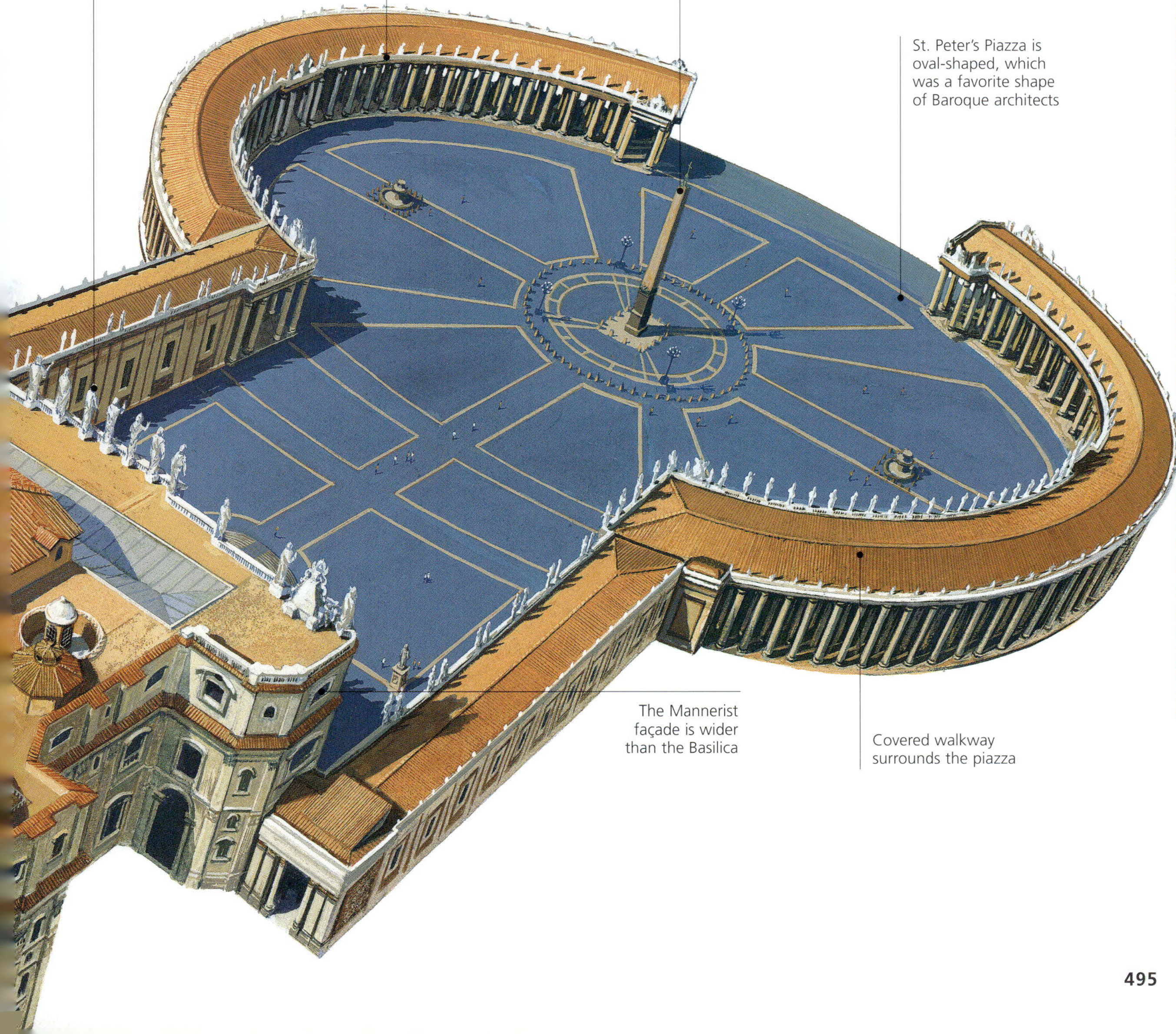

Religious Buildings of Europe

CSEMPESZKOPACS CHURCH
Csempeszkopacs, Hungary

KECSKEMET CHURCH
Kecskemet, Hungary

LA SAGRADA FAMILIA
Barcelona, Spain

COLOGNE CATHEDRAL
Cologne, Germany

PARMA BAPTISTRY
Parma, Italy

MILAN CATHEDRAL
Milan, Italy

THIRA CHURCH
Santorini, Greece

SHIPKA MEMORIAL CHURCH
Shipka, Bulgaria

ST. SOPHIA'S CATHEDRAL
Kiev, Ukraine

CHARTRES CATHEDRAL
Chartres, France

DOM CATHEDRAL TOWER
Utrecht, The Netherlands

CHURCH OF SAN VITALE
Ravenna, Italy

BAVARIAN CHURCH
Bavaria, Germany

ALEXANDER NEVSKY CATHEDRAL
Sofia, Bulgaria

EASTERN ORTHODOX CHURCH
Lake Ohrid, Macedonia

Mosques of the World

DOME OF THE ROCK
Jerusalem, Israel

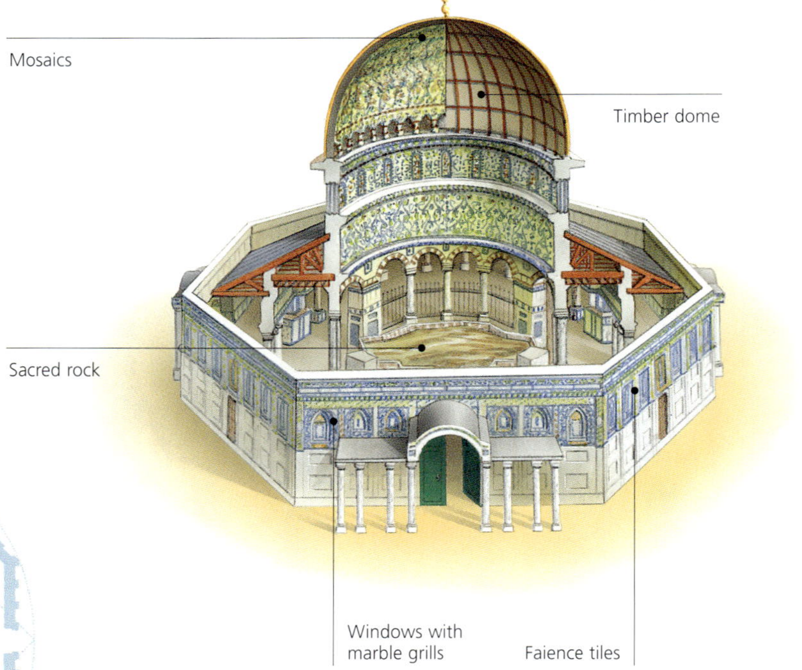

FLOOR PLAN

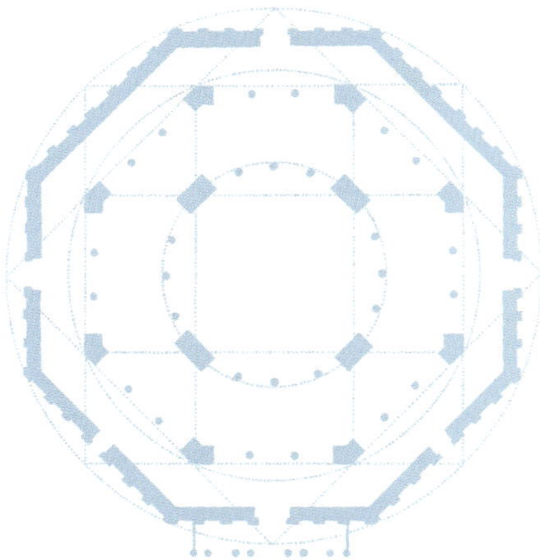

MOSQUE FEATURES

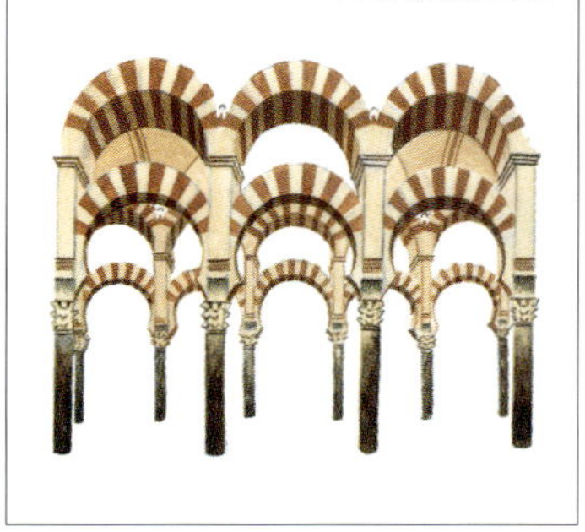
Arch decoration

Minaret

Dome

MASJID UBUDIAH
Kuala Kangsar, Malaysia

BLUE MOSQUE
Istanbul, Turkey

AL KHUWAIR MOSQUE
Al Khuwair, Oman

ROYAL MOSQUE
Eşfahān, Iran

GOL GUMBAZ MOSQUE
Bijapur, India

IMPERIAL MOSQUE
Lahore, Pakistan

Early American Buildings

GREAT PLAZA
Tikal, Guatemala

TAOS PUEBLO
New Mexico, USA

EL CASTILLO
Chichen Itza, Mexico

CITY OF TEOTIHUACAN
Mexico, AD 1— 200

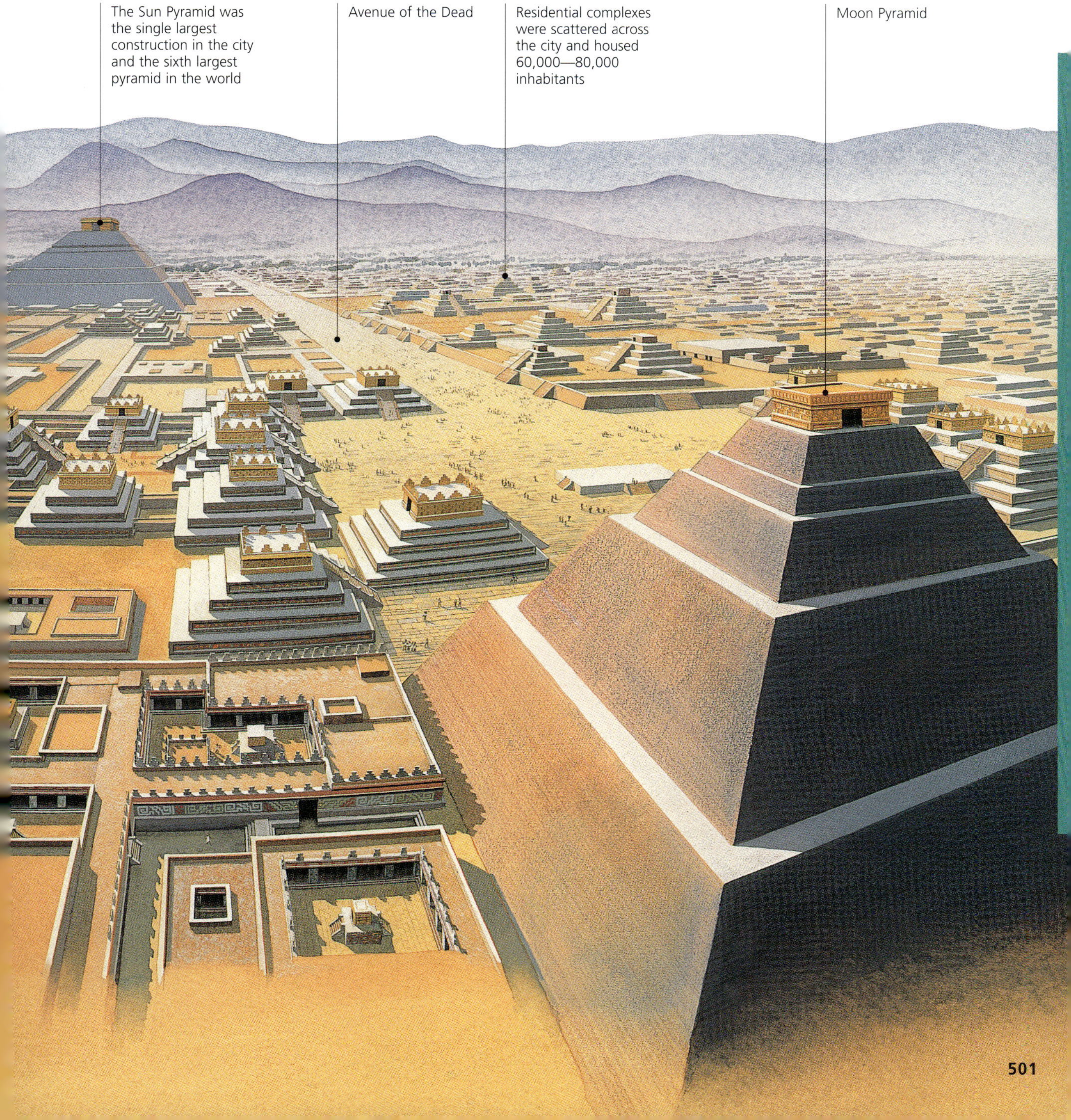

Statues and Monuments

MOAI STATUES
Easter Island

TOLTEC STATUE
Mexico

STATUE OF THE LION
Ethiopia

MOUNT RUSHMORE
South Dakota, USA

TERRA-COTTA WARRIORS
Xi'an, China

GIZA SPHINX
Giza, Egypt

STATUE OF LIBERTY
New York, USA

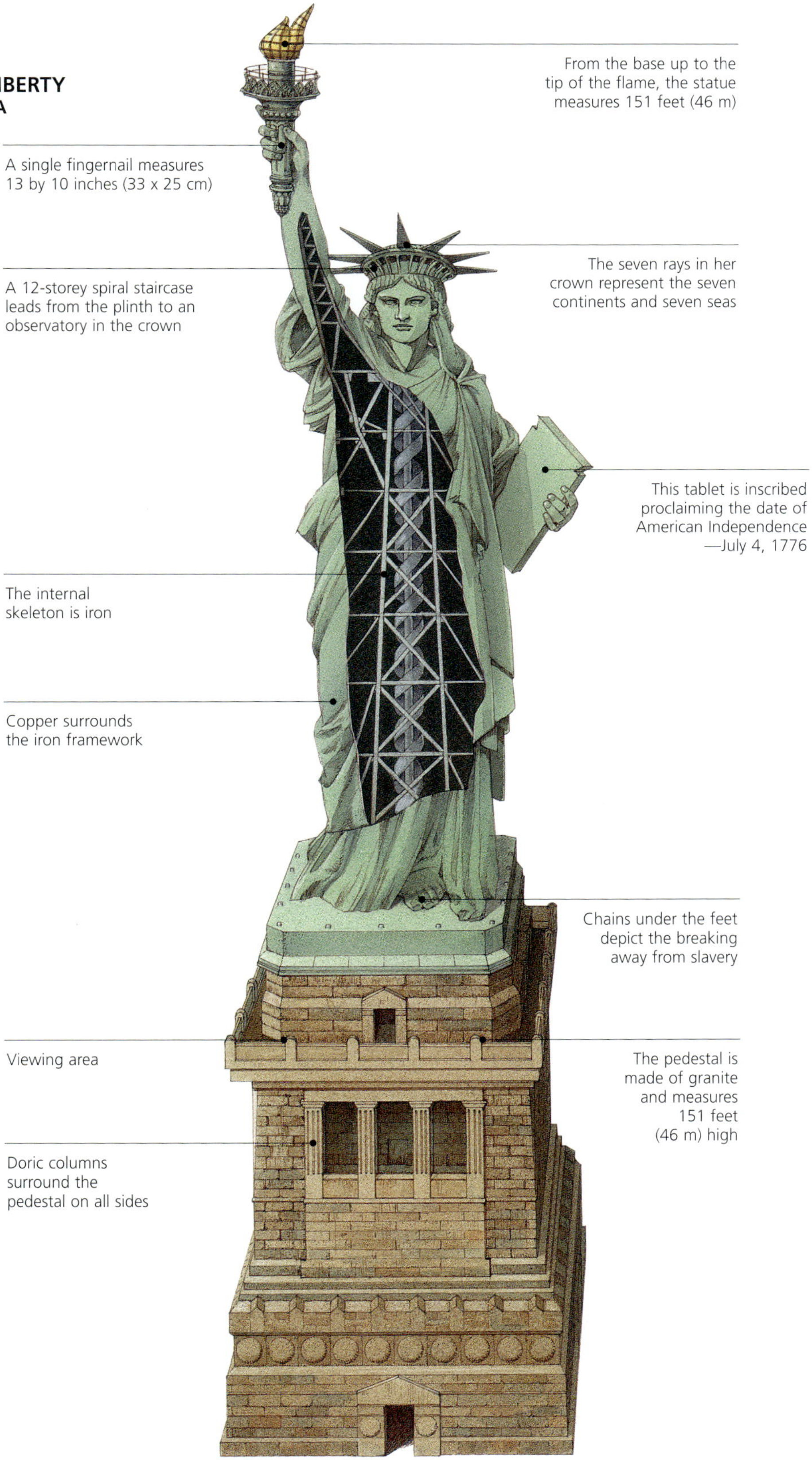

Tombs and Memorials

PREHISTORIC BURIAL GROUND
Newgrange, Ireland

ROCK TOMBS
Madain Salah, Saudi Arabia

BEEHIVE TOMB
Mycenae, Greece

ATOMIC DOME
Hiroshima, Japan

TOMB OF BIBI JAIWINDI
Uch Sharif, Pakistan

APAK HOJA TOMB
Kashgar, China

CROSS SECTION

GREAT PYRAMID
Giza, Egypt

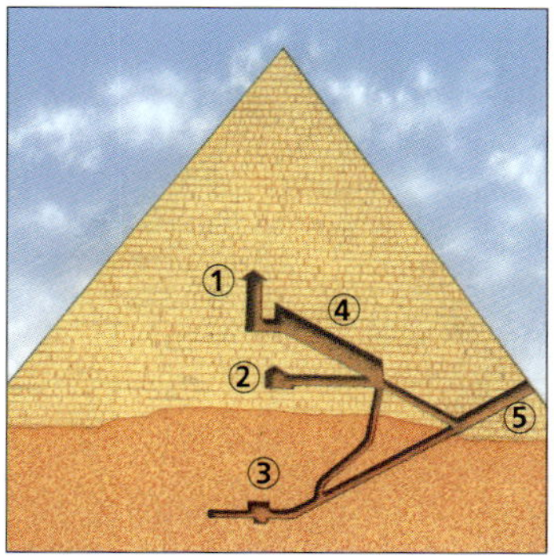

1 King's chamber

2 Queen's chamber

3 Underground chamber

4 Grand gallery

5 Entrance

Adventurous Shapes

CASA MILA
Barcelona, Spain

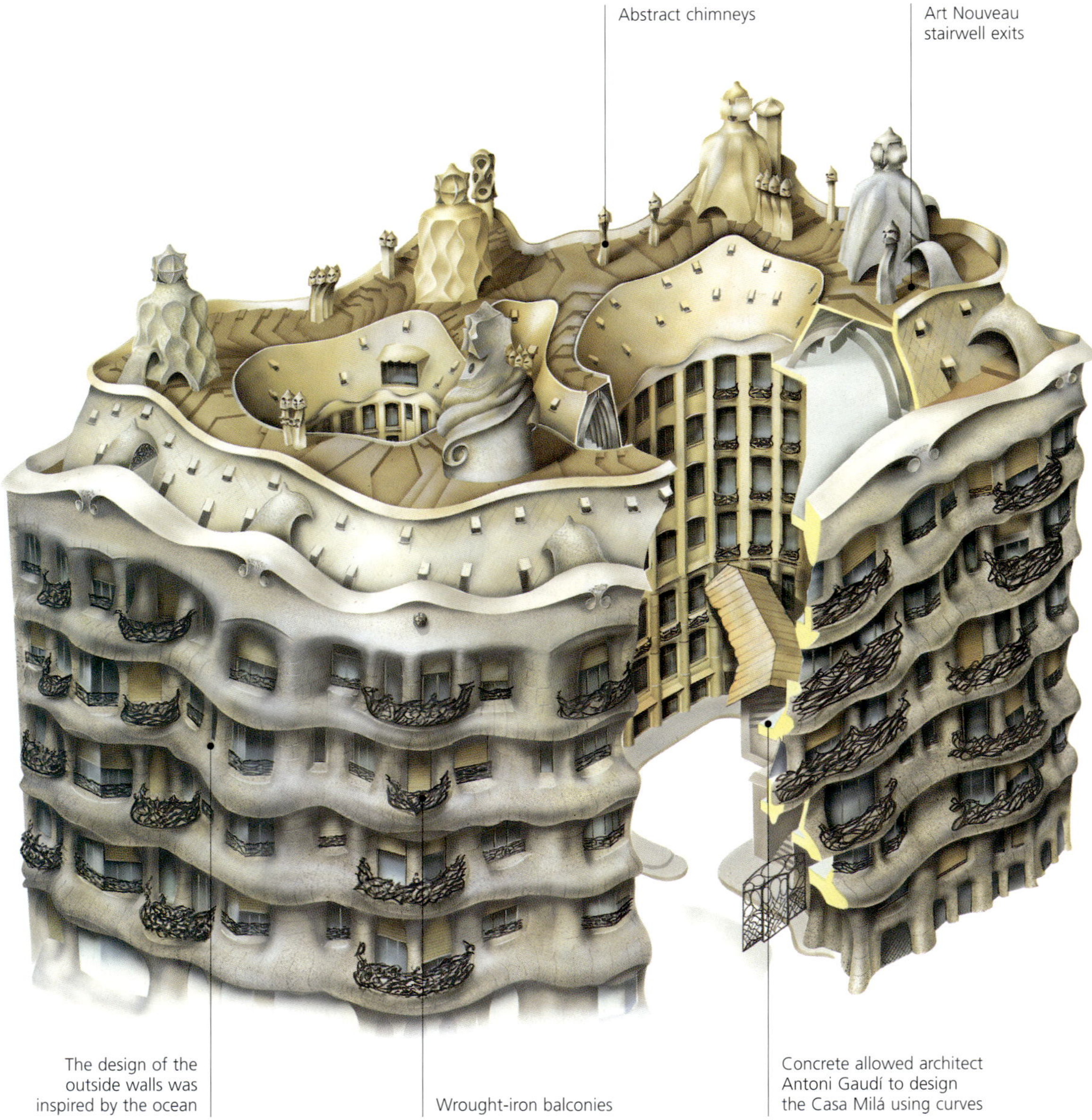

NOTRE DAME DU HAUT
Ronchamp, France

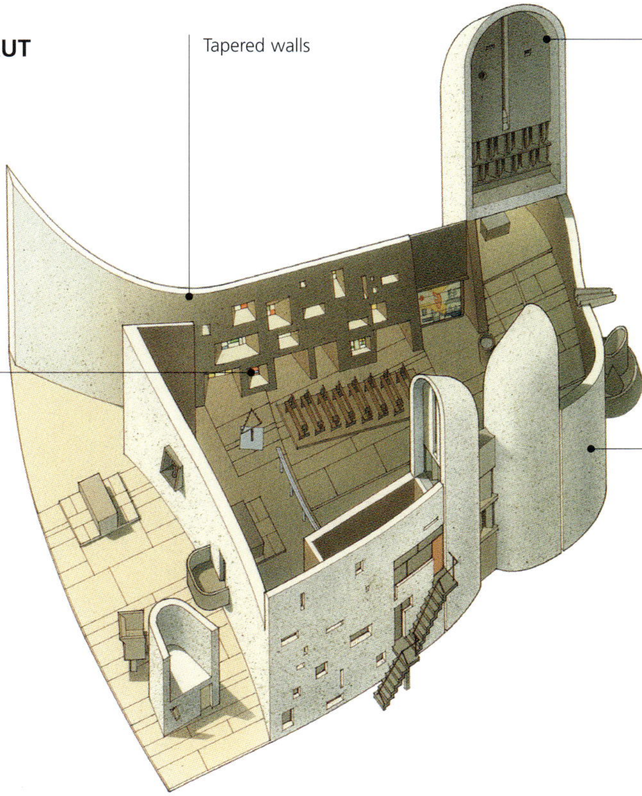

GUGGENHEIM MUSEUM
New York, USA

Leisure Spaces

COLOSSEUM
Rome, Italy

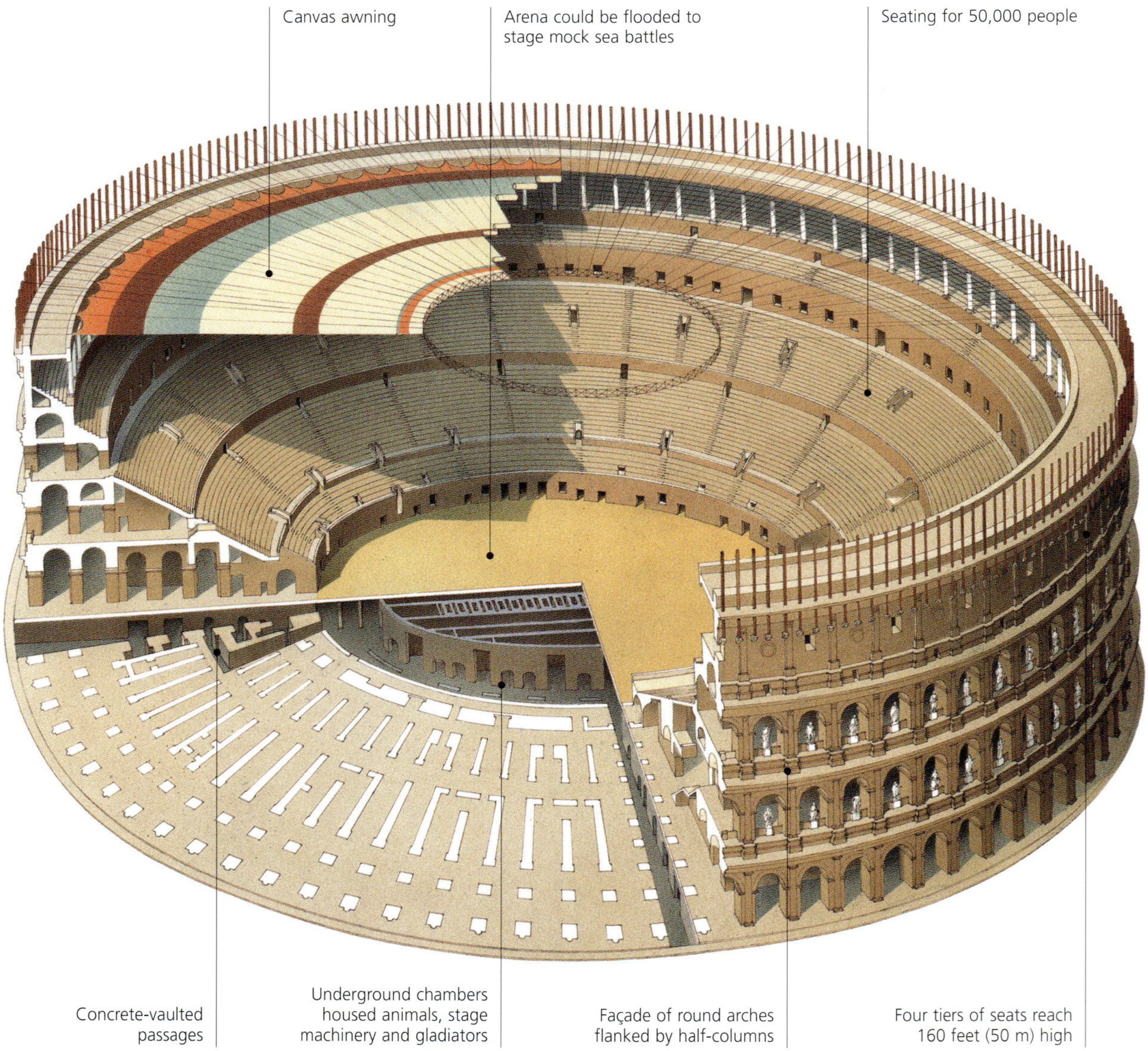

THE SKYDOME
Toronto, Canada

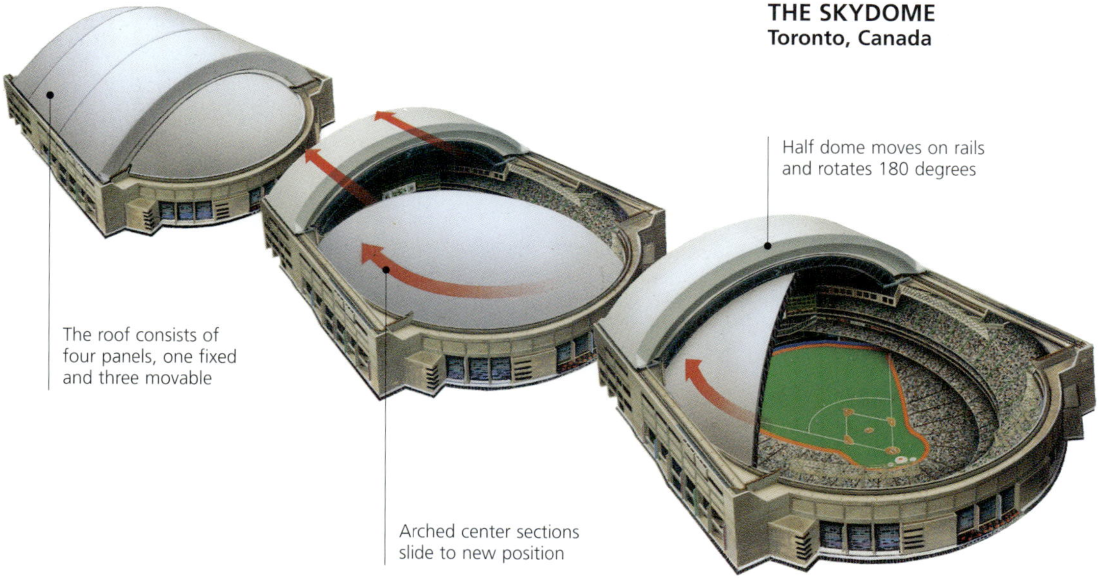

Early Settlement

CITY OF CATAL HUYUK
Turkey, 6500—5400 BC

Sprawling mudbrick buildings were laid out like modern apartment complexes. Each family lived in an almost identical three-room unit—complete with a sleeping space, sitting nooks, a storage area and a kitchen

Houses were built directly against one another—sometimes with intervening courtyards. There were no streets or lanes through the city

Access to the buildings was from the roofs

The site covered 32 acres (13 ha) and housed 6,000 inhabitants —making it the most populated city on earth at the time

One out of every three rooms at Catal Hüyük was a shrine. Each of these worship rooms was different, but all had a similar bull motif

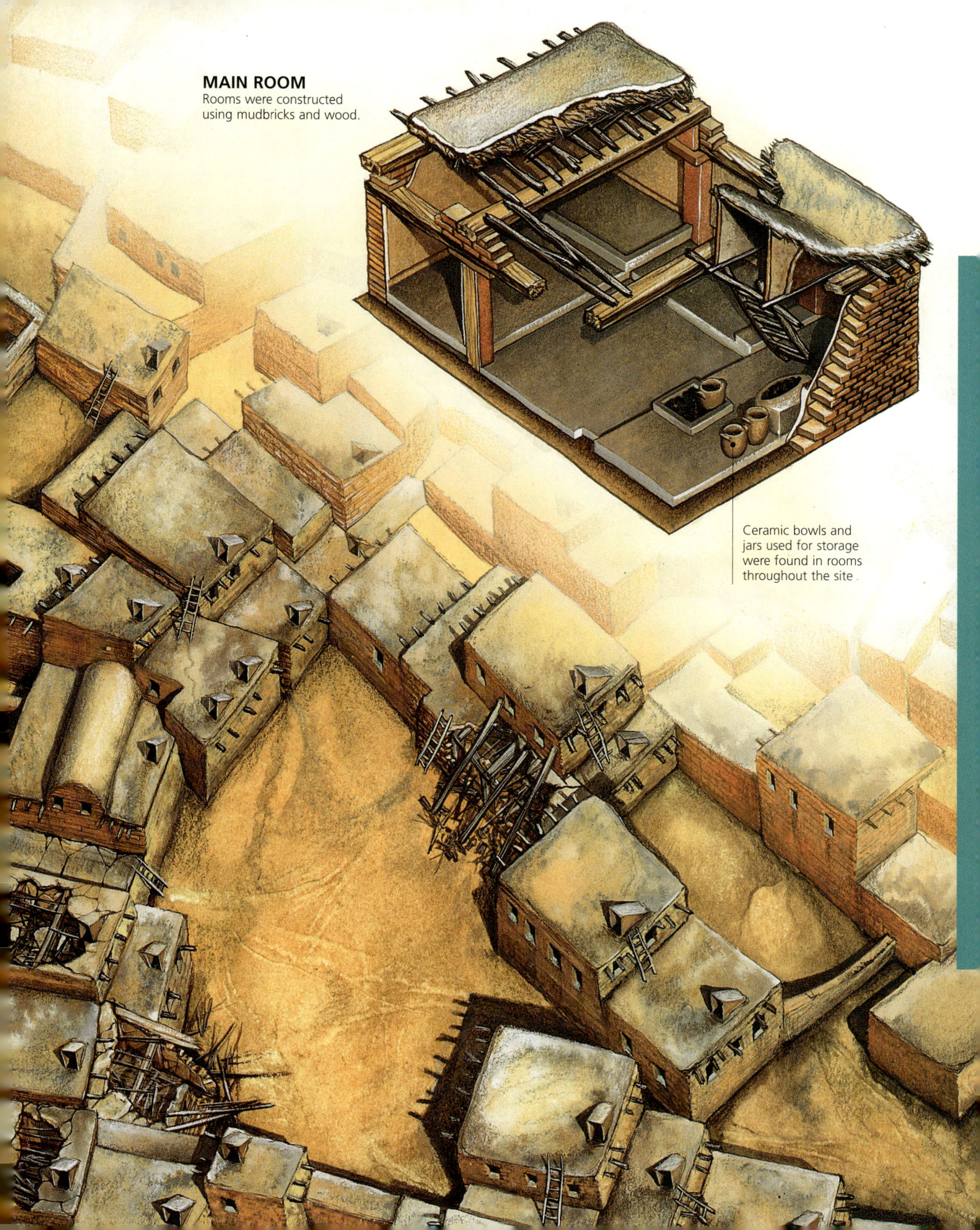
MAIN ROOM
Rooms were constructed using mudbricks and wood.
Ceramic bowls and jars used for storage were found in rooms throughout the site.

Traditional Houses

CHIAPAS HUT
Mexico

TRADITIONAL FARMHOUSE
China

TRADITIONAL HUT
Zimbabwe

NUNAVUT HOUSE
Canada

THATCHED COTTAGE
England

CROFTER'S COTTAGE
Ireland

LESOTHO HUT
South Africa

CHIPAYA SOD HUT
Peru

IGLOO
Canada

STILT HOUSE
Solomon Islands

WOVEN HUT
South Pacific

Castles

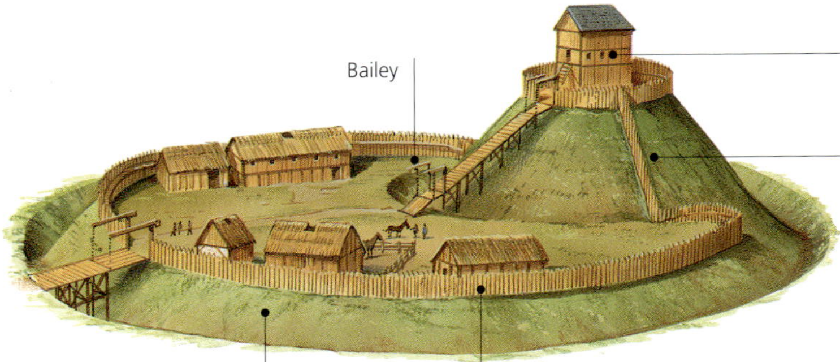

EARLY CASTLES

ROYAL CASTLE
Warsaw, Poland

CHATEAU DE CHAMBORD
Chambord, France

CONWAY CASTLE
Conway, Wales

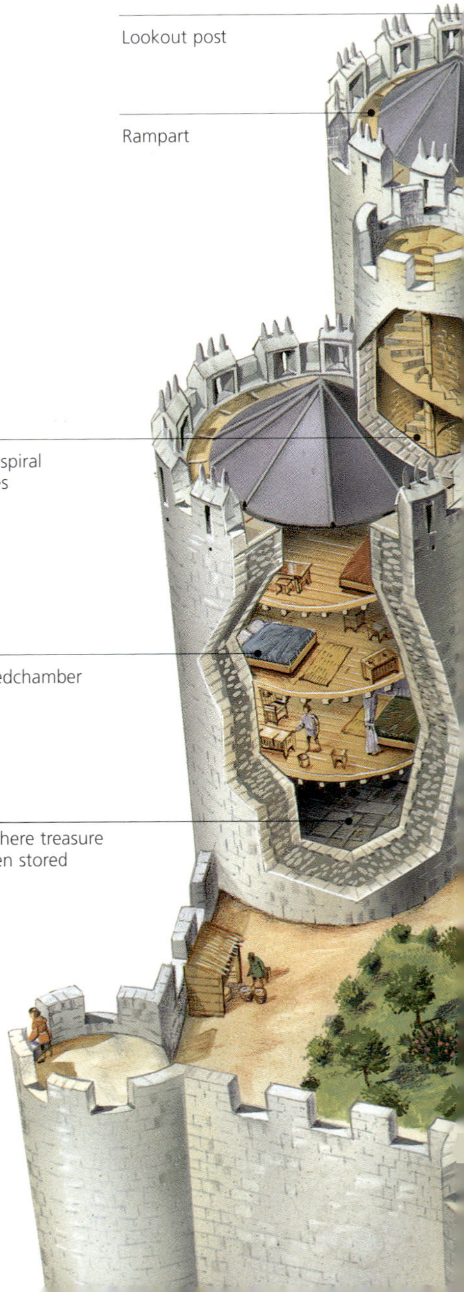

Great Hall
Portcullis
Arrow loops
Stone walls
16 feet (5 m) thick
Drawbridge
Guards on duty
A series of wheels and pulleys was used for lifting heavy objects

Classical Influence

ATHENAEUM
Bucharest, Romania

CAPITOL BUILDING
Washington, USA

MONTICELLO HOUSE
Charlottesville, USA

OPERA HOUSE
Manaus, Brazil

CONGRESO NACIONAL
Buenos Aires, Argentina

PRESIDENTIAL PALACE
Asunción, Paraguay

LEGISLATIVE BUILDING
Regina, Canada

VILLA CAPRA
Vincenza, Italy

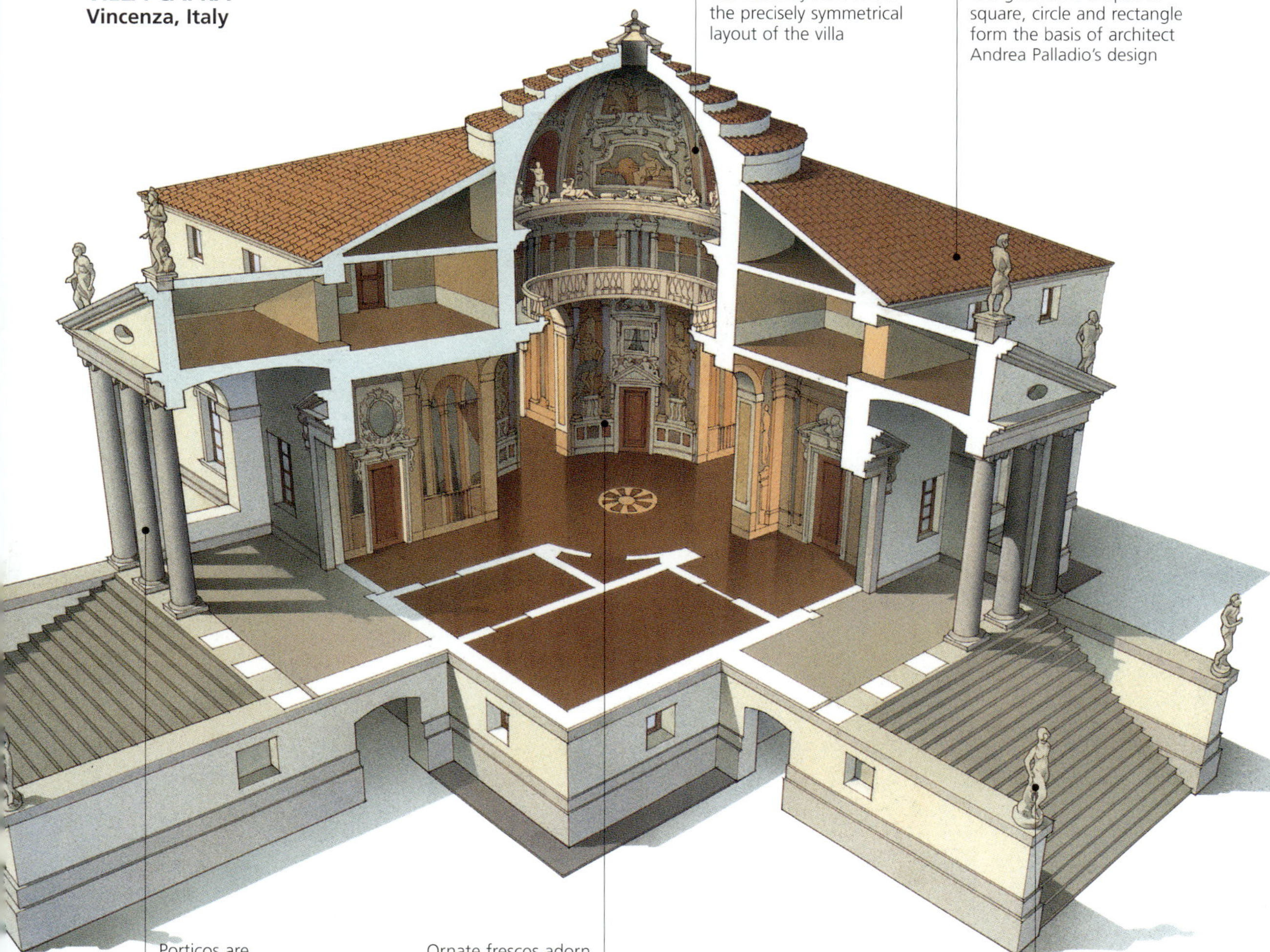

TECHNOLOGY AND INVENTIONS

11
12
10
9
8
7
6

TRANSPORT

Land Transport 522

Steam Trains 524

Water Transport 526

Flight 530

Passenger Aircraft 532

Military Aircraft 534

Supersonic Flight 536

EVERYDAY TECHNOLOGY

Forces at Work 538

Home Appliances 540

Computers 542

Medical Technology 544

COMMUNICATIONS AND INDUSTRY

Communications 546

Optics 548

Sound 550

Power and Energy 552

Land Transport

AUTOMOBILE

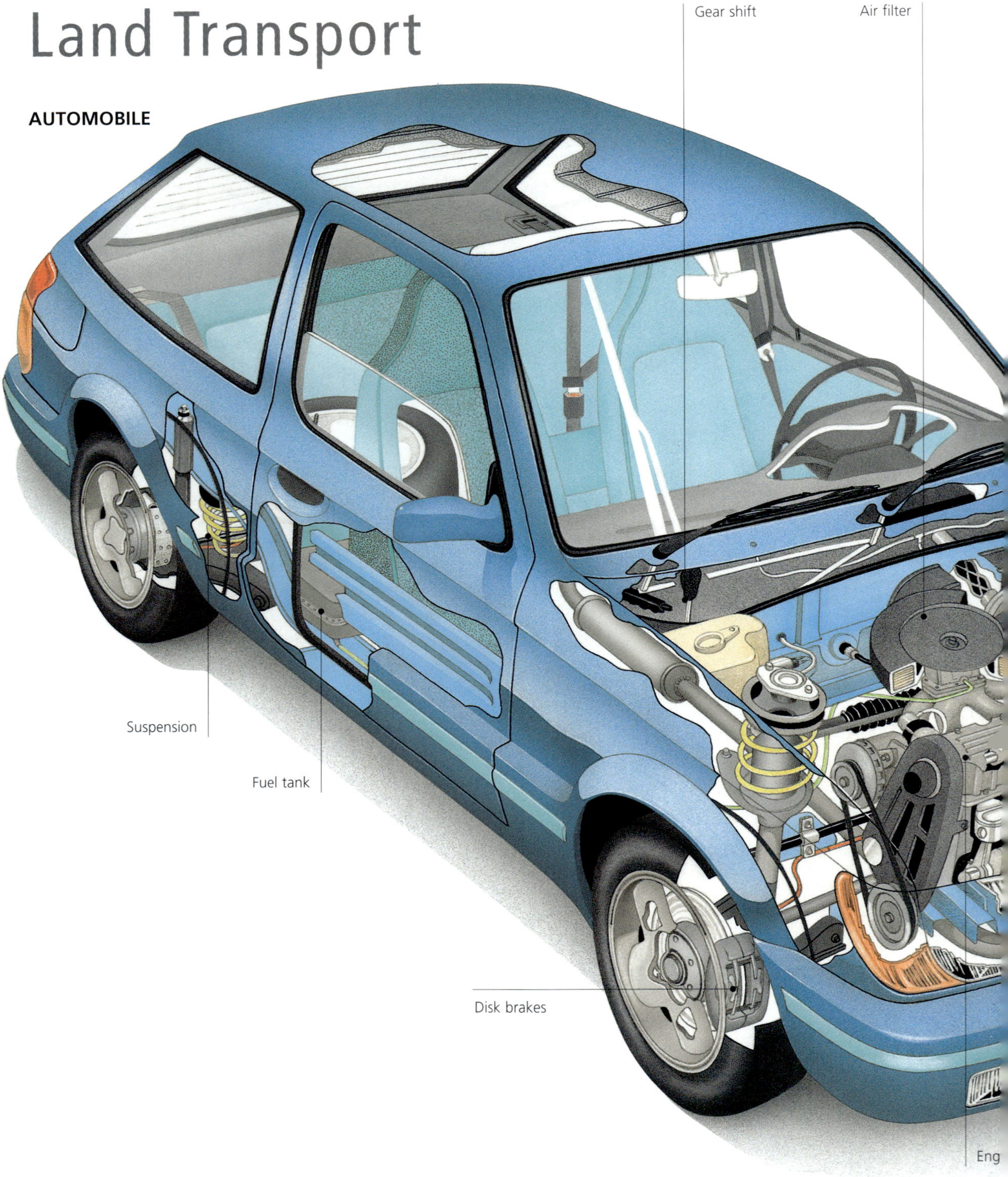

A HISTORY OF BICYCLES

Dandy horse
1790

Penny-farthing
1870

Safety bike
1879

Aerodynamic bike
Early 1980s

SEMITRAILER TRUCK

LONG DISTANCE PASSENGER COACH

Steam Trains

MALLARD STEAM TRAIN

HOW STEAM ENGINES WORK

HOW PISTONS TURN WHEELS

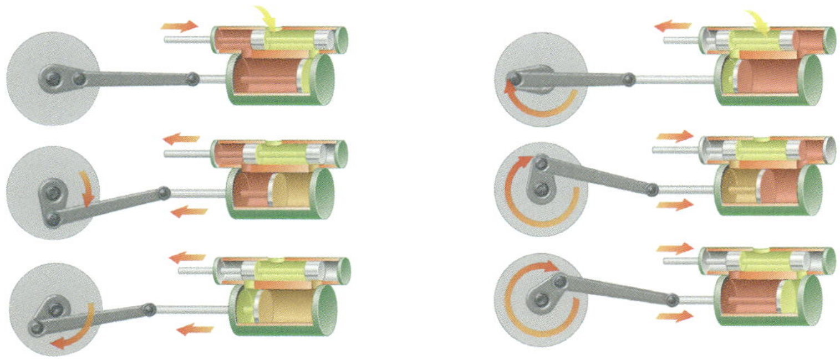

Inlet valve admits steam under pressure in front of piston.

Valve closes. Steam in cyclinder expands.

Steam almost spent. Piston nears one extreme.

Rear inlet valve opens. Steam enters at rear of piston.

Exhaust valve lets expanded steam out.

Two cycles complete one revolution of driving wheels.

Water Transport

A HISTORY OF SAILING VESSELS

CHINESE JUNK
Mid-15th century

CLIPPER
1845 to 1890s

STEAMSHIP
1800 to 1900s

Egyptian trading vessel
3000 BC to 500 BC

Phoenician trading vessel
1000 BC to 300 BC

Viking knorr
AD 800 to AD 1070

Polynesian canoe
Early AD onward

Hanseatic cog
1350–1450

Caravel
1430–1520

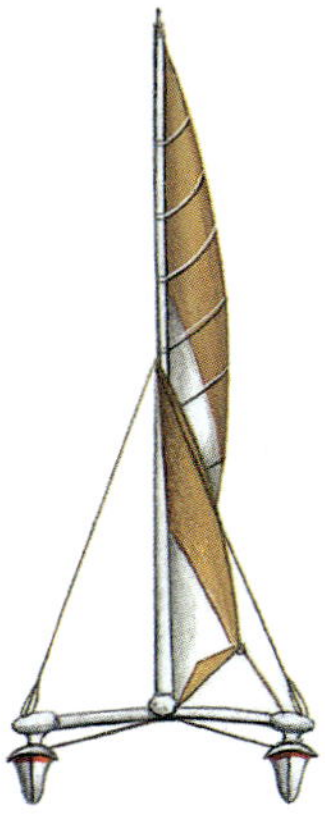

CATAMARAN
Twin hulls

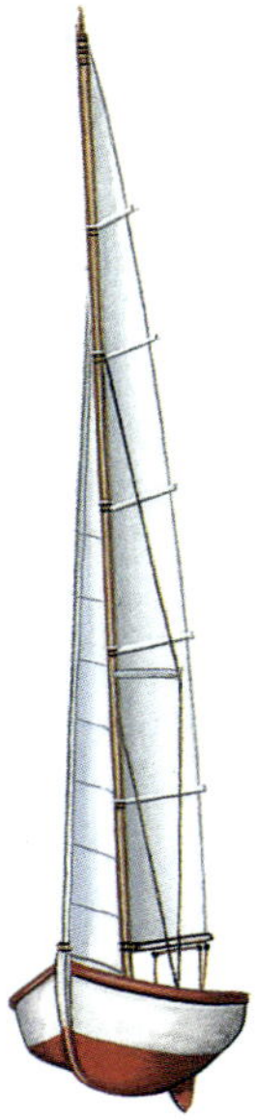

YACHT
Single hull

TRIMARAN
Three hulls

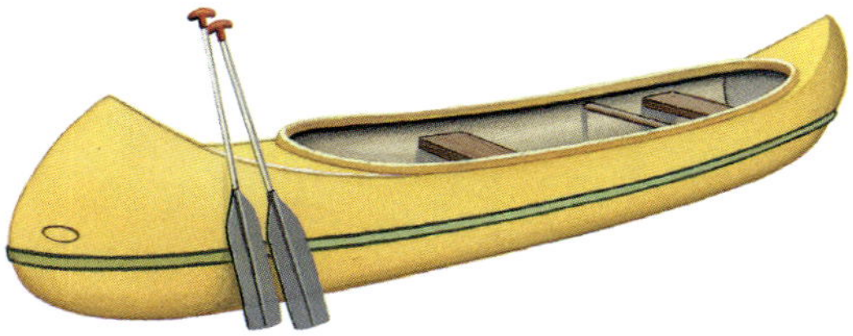

CANOE
Open boat with single-bladed paddle

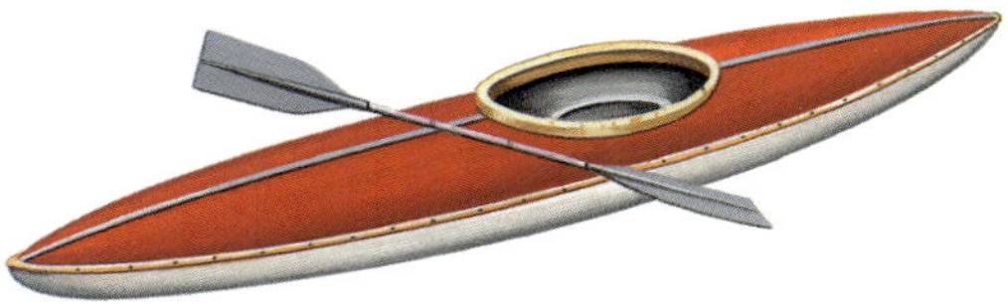

KAYAK
Enclosed craft with double-bladed paddle

ESKIMO ROLL
This maneuver allows a paddler to roll the kayak over if it capsizes.

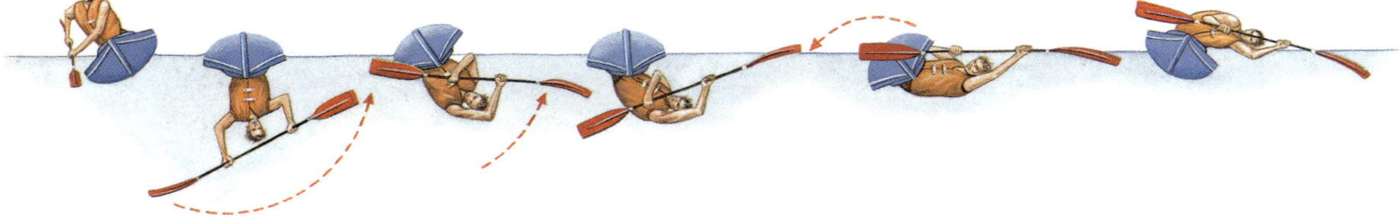

Water Transport

PASSENGER LINER

HOW A CANAL LOCK WORKS

Boat enters lock.

Gates close.

Water from higher level flows in.

Gates at higher end open and boat moves through.

Flight

PROPELLER PLANE IN FLIGHT

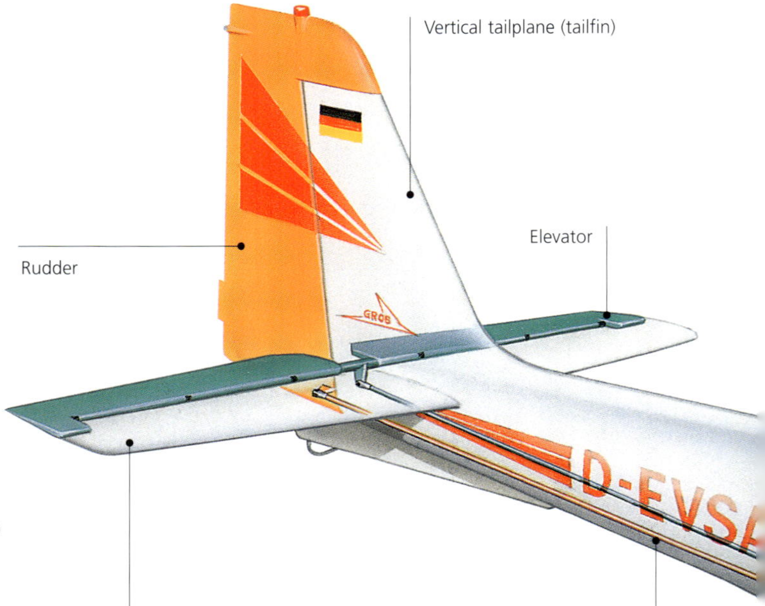

Banking

Pitching

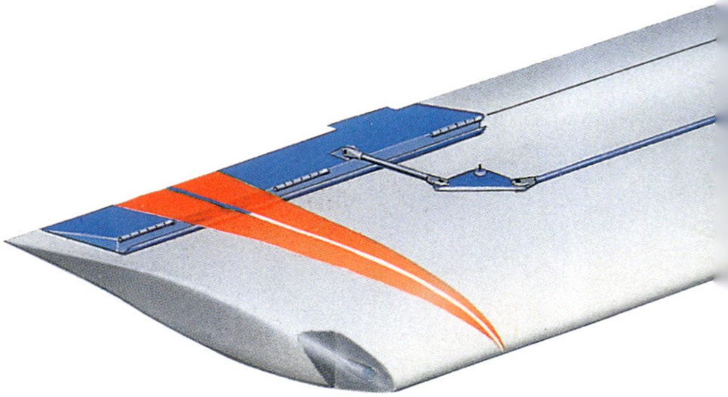

Turning

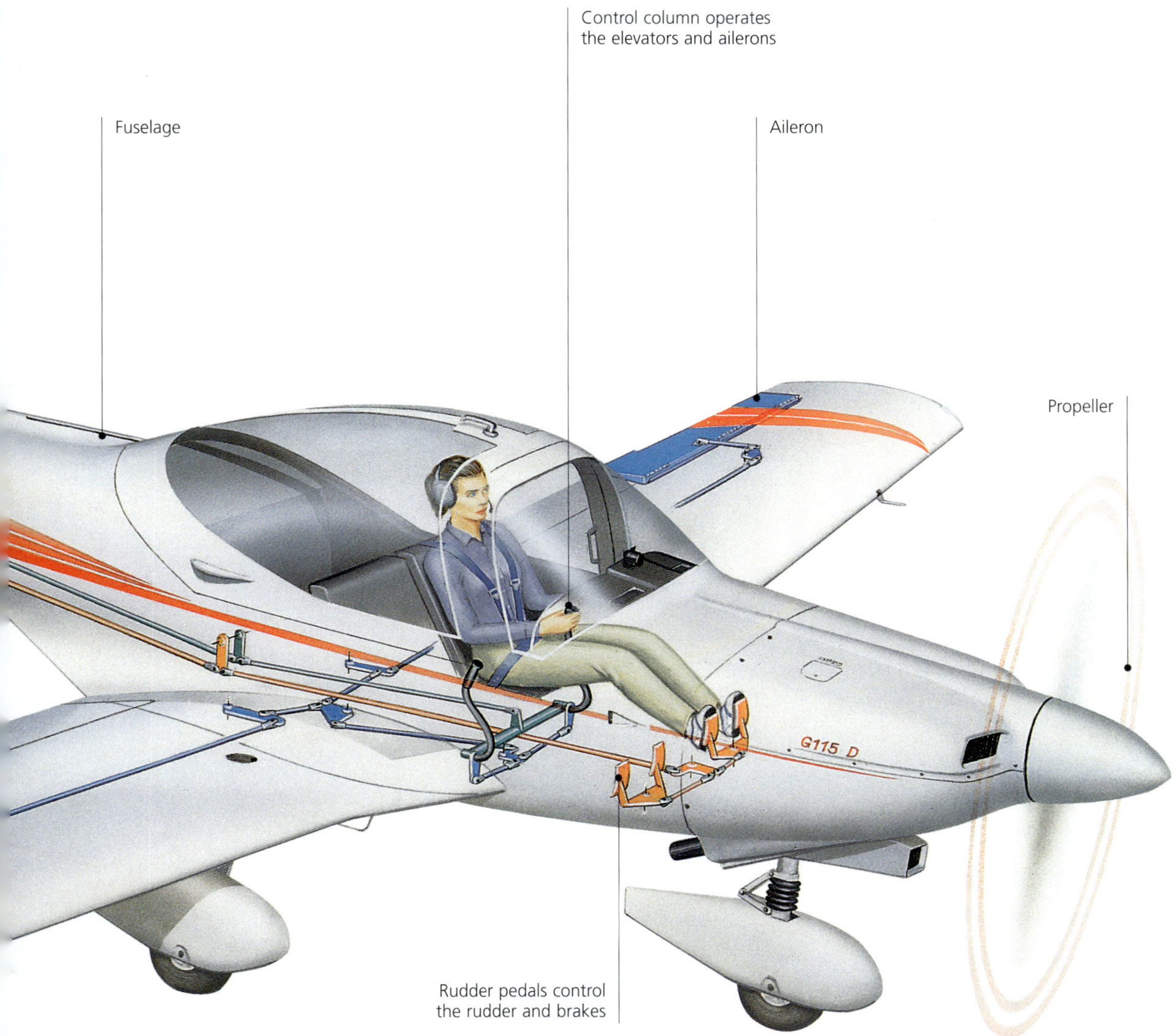

HELICOPTER FLIGHT

Ascending
Rotor blade angle is raised.

Descending
Rotor blade angle is lowered.

Flying forward
Rotor is tilted down.

Flying sideways
Rotor is tilted sideways.

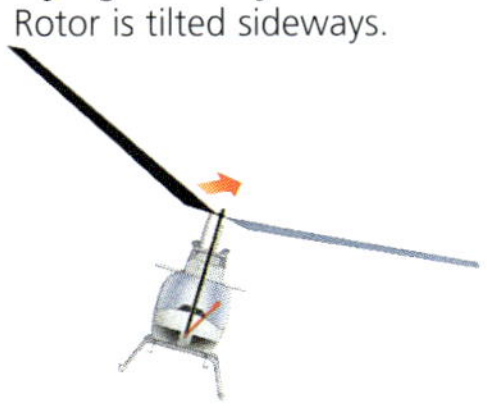

Passenger Aircraft

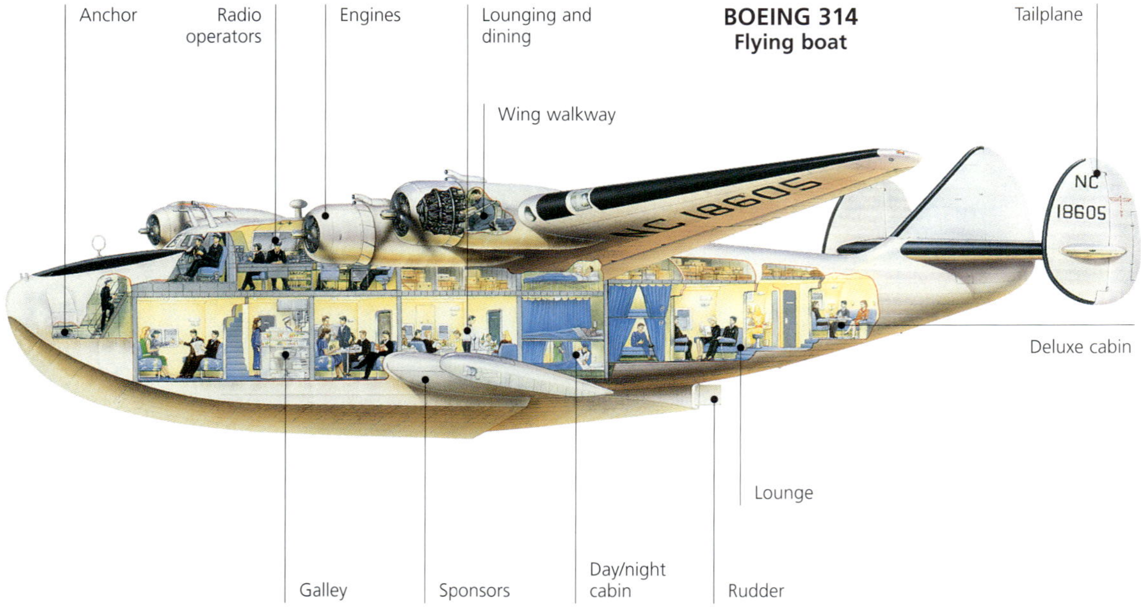

AIRSHIPS

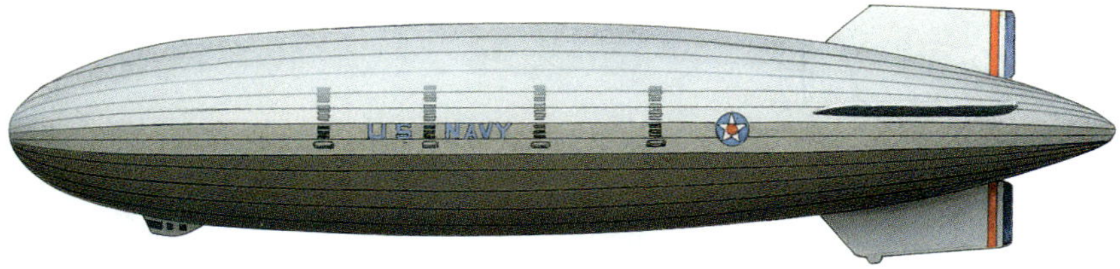

USS *Macon*
This US Navy airship was built in 1933 as a patrol carrier.

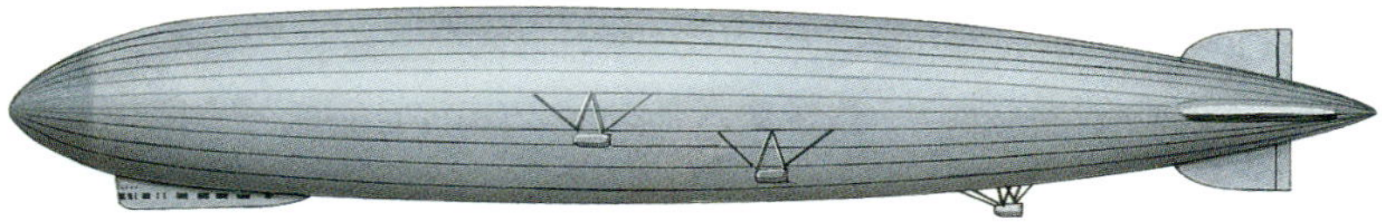

Graf Zeppelin
This airship made its first flight in 1928 and could carry 20 passengers.

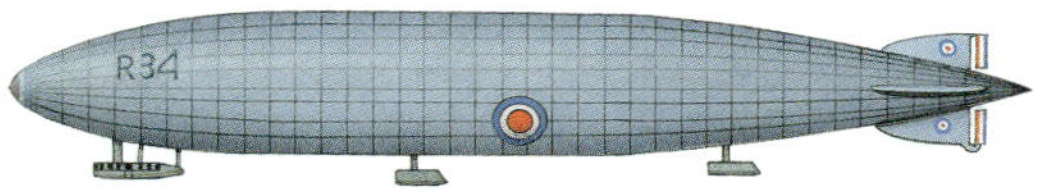

R-34
In 1919, this became the first airship to cross the North Atlantic.

Norge
Explorers Nobile and Amundsen traveled to the North Pole in this airship in 1926.

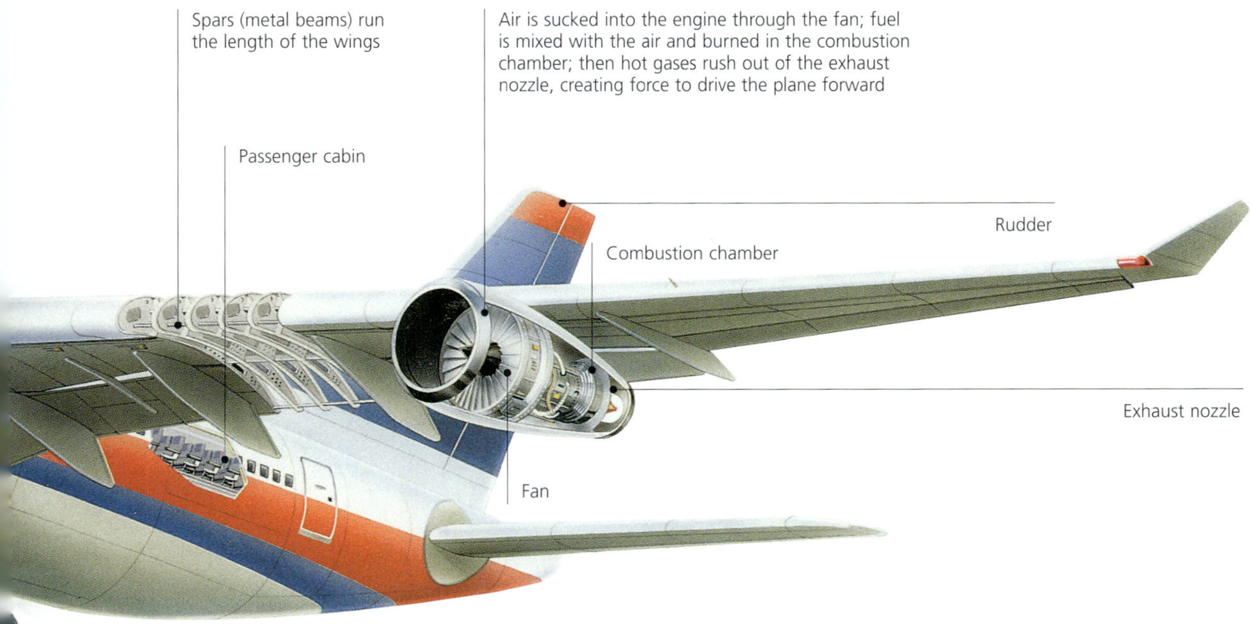

Military Aircraft

JUMP JET
McDonnell Douglas AV-8B

A HISTORY OF MILITARY AIRCRAFT

1915 German Fokker E.1 Eindecker
This fighter plane flew at 79 miles (128 km) per hour.

1917 French Spad X11
This biplane fighter flew at 129 miles (208 km) per hour.

1917 English Handley Page 0/400
This bomber could carry 2,002 pounds (906 kg).

1938 English Supermarine Spitfire
This fighter plane flew at 357 miles (576 km) per hour.

AIRWING OF AIRCRAFT CARRIER USS *AMERICA*

Intruder

Hawkeye

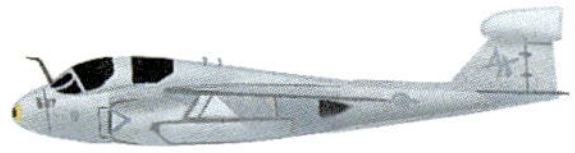

Prowler

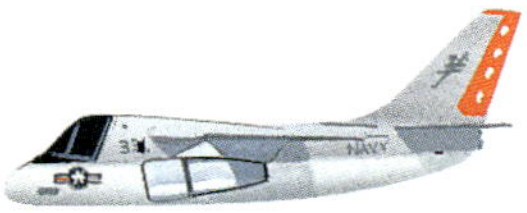

Viking

Tomcat

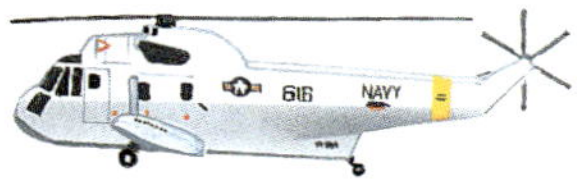

Sea King

STEALTH FIGHTER
Lockheed F-117A

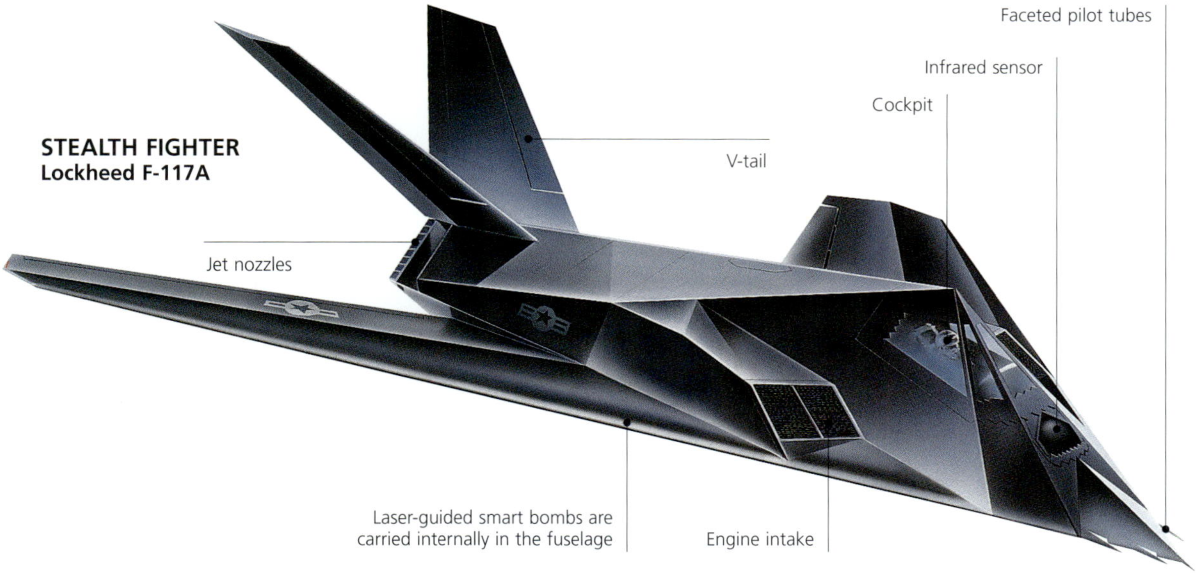

1943 English Gloster Meteor
The first British jet fighter flew at 600 miles (969 km) per hour.

1952 US Boeing B-52 Stratofortress
This bomber flew at 595 miles (960 km) per hour.

1974 German, English and Italian Panavia Tornado
This strike aircraft flies at 1,446 miles (2,333 km) per hour.

1978 US McDonnell Douglas F/A 18C Hornet
This fighter flies at 1,317 miles (2,124 km) per hour.

Supersonic Flight

SUPERSONIC WING SHAPES

Short thin wing
F-104 Starfighter, 1954

Delta wing
Mirage 111 AO, 1956

Swing-wing
Tupelov Tu-26, 1969

CONCORDE

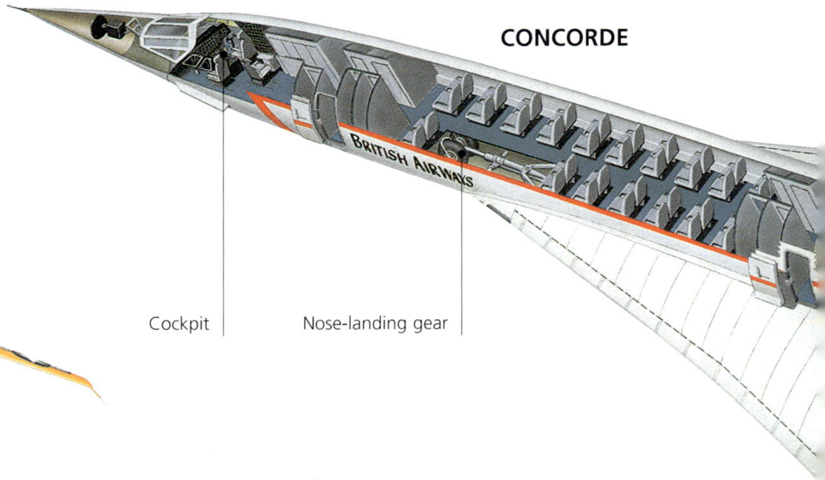

BELL AIRCRAFT

First aircraft to break the sound barrier

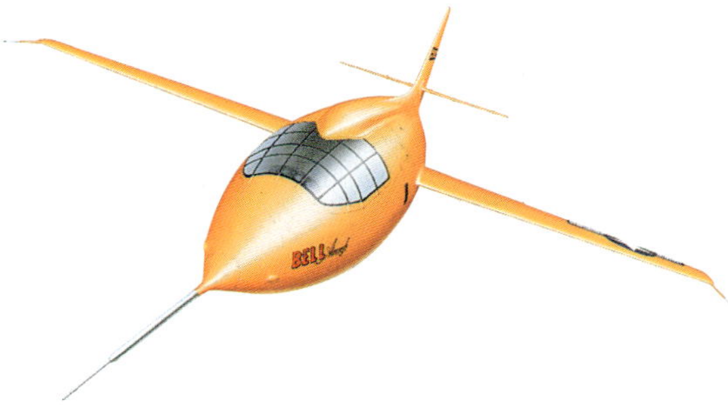

THE SOUND BARRIER

Subsonic Flight: Below Mach 1
Pressure waves radiate in front of and behind the aircraft.

Transonic Flight: At Mach 1
The aircraft catches up with its own pressure waves.

Supersonic Flight: Above Mach 1
Shock waves form a cone. This causes a sonic boom when it hits the ground.

CONCORDE'S NOSE

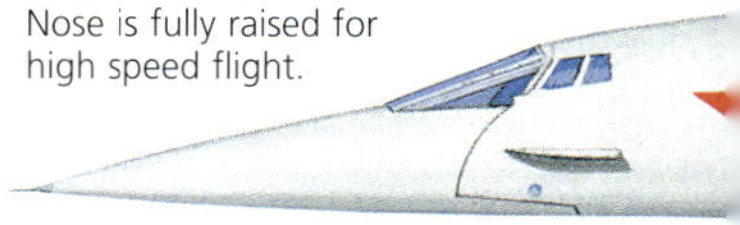

Nose is fully raised for high speed flight.

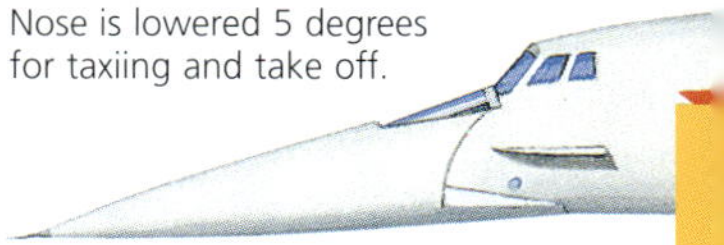

Nose is lowered 5 degrees for taxiing and take off.

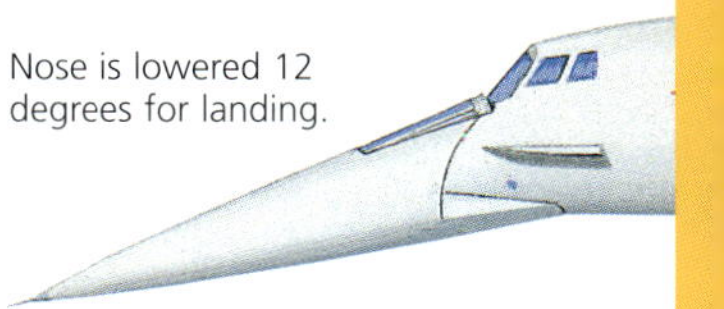

Nose is lowered 12 degrees for landing.

Sweep-back wing
Super Etendard, 1974

Swept-forward wing
Grumman X-29A, 1984

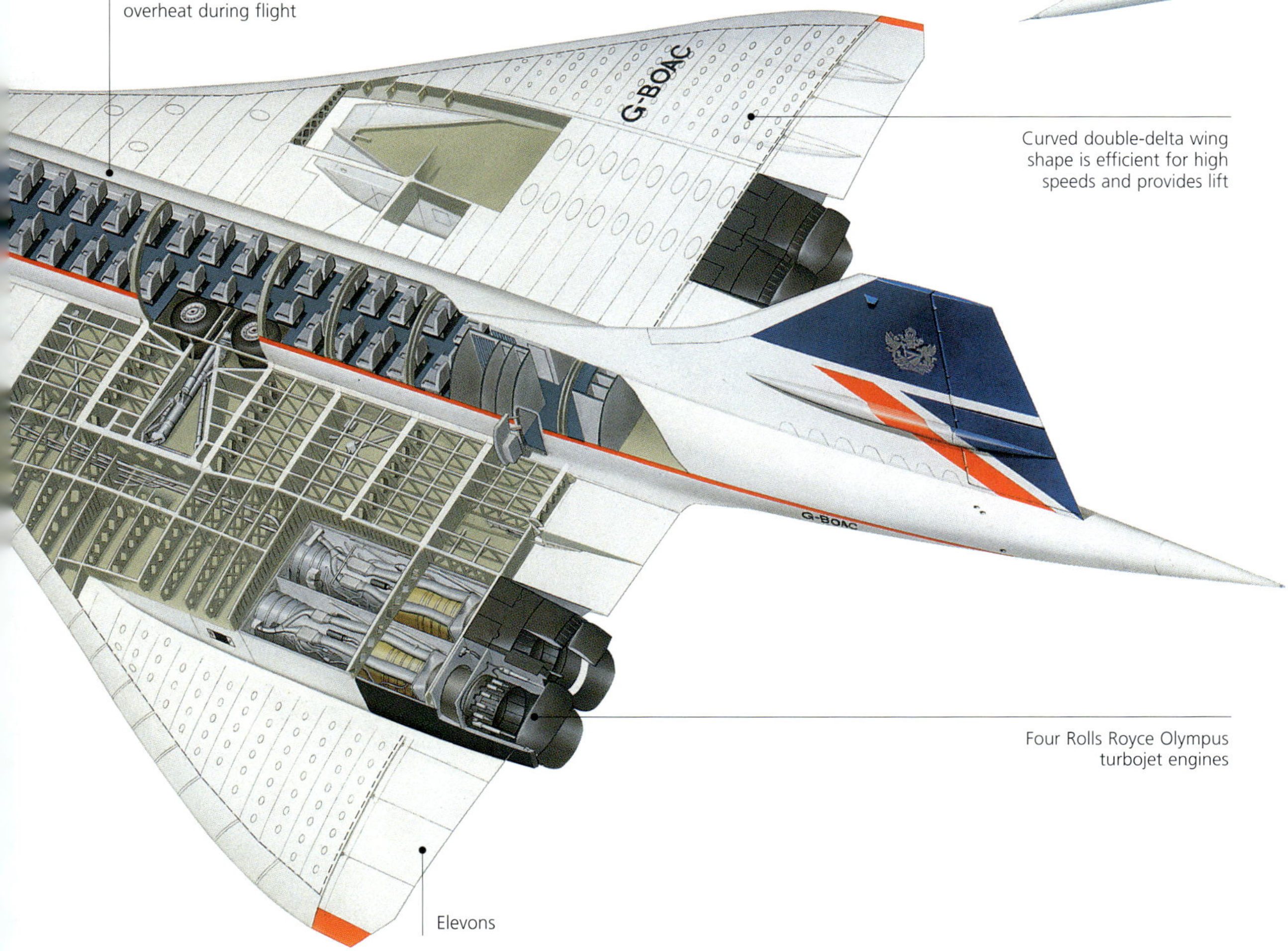

Forces at Work

PERMANENT MAGNET

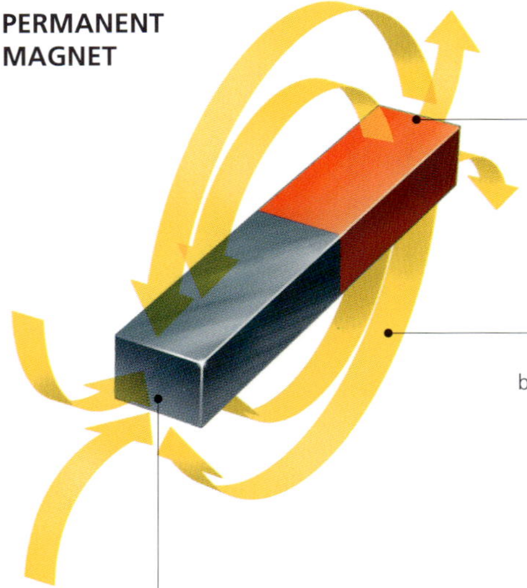

MAGNETISM AND ELECTRICITY

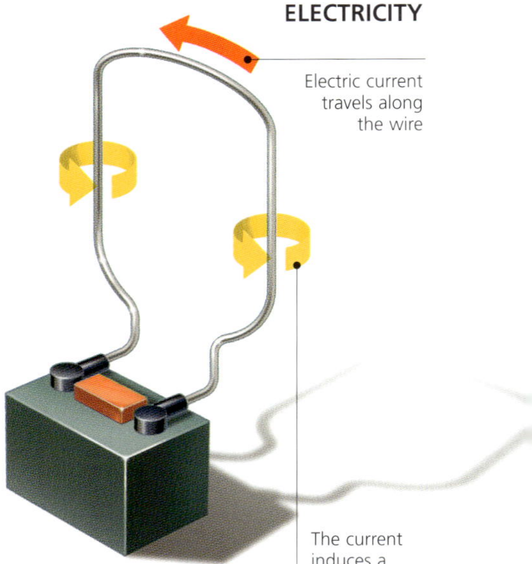

ATTRACTION

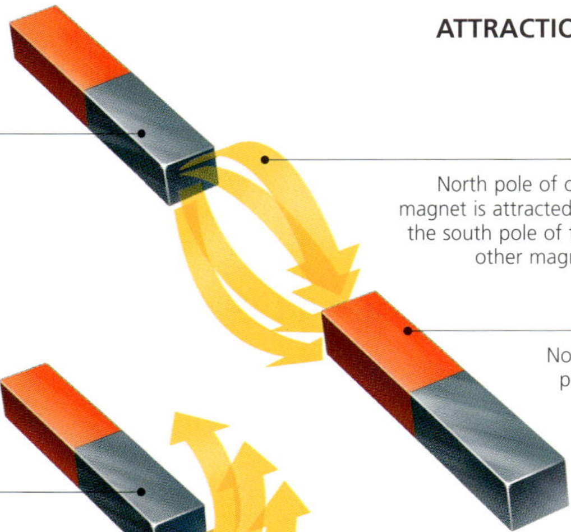

FINDING THE WAY

A compass needle always faces north because it is attracted to Earth's magnetic pole near the geographic north pole

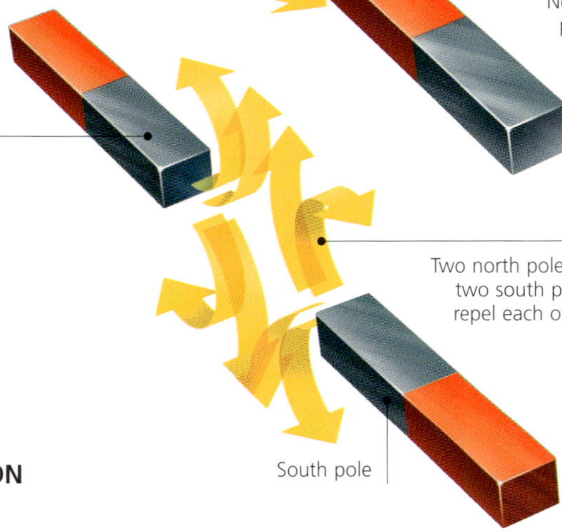

REPULSION

USING AN INCLINED PLANE

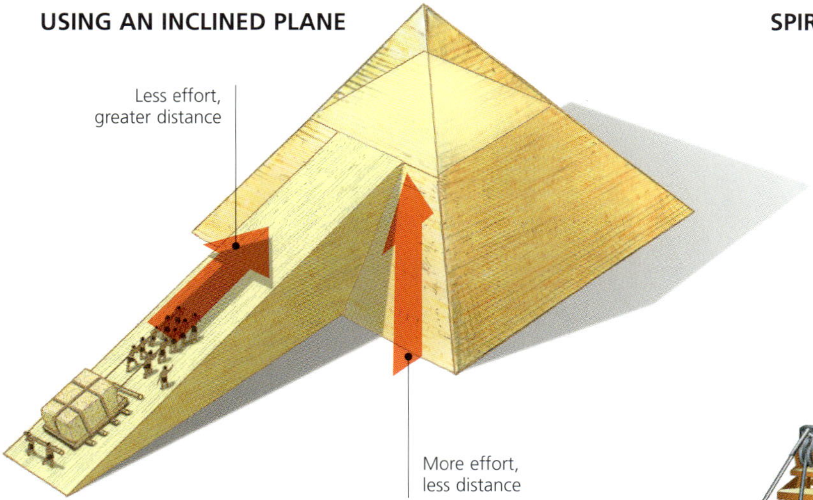

SPIRAL INCLINED PLANE

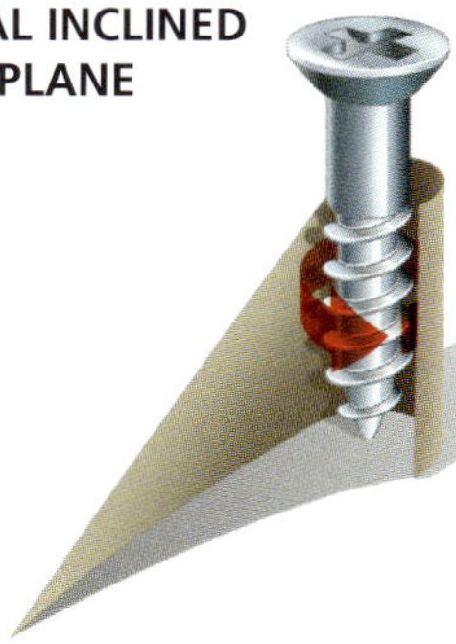

USING A WEDGE

TOWER CRANE

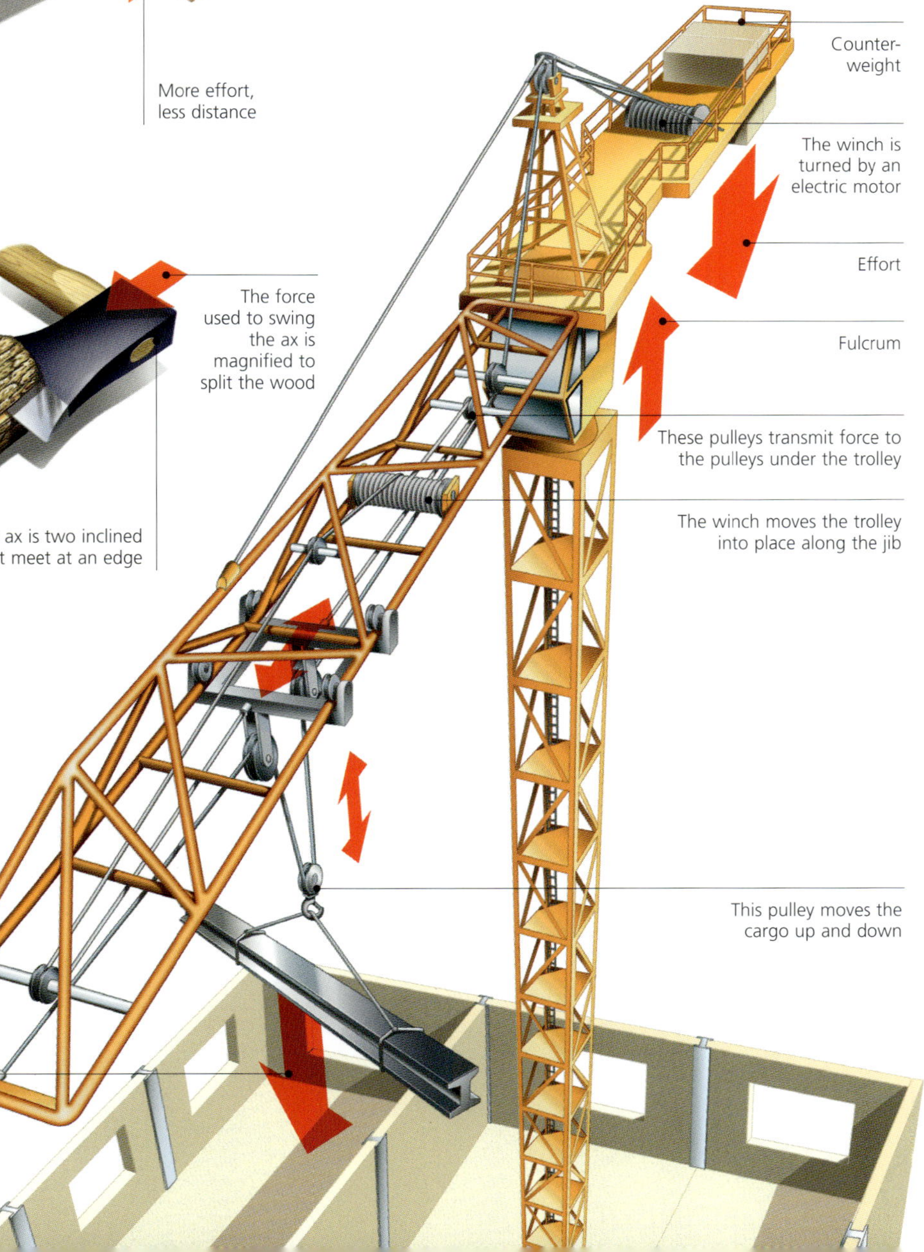

Home Appliances

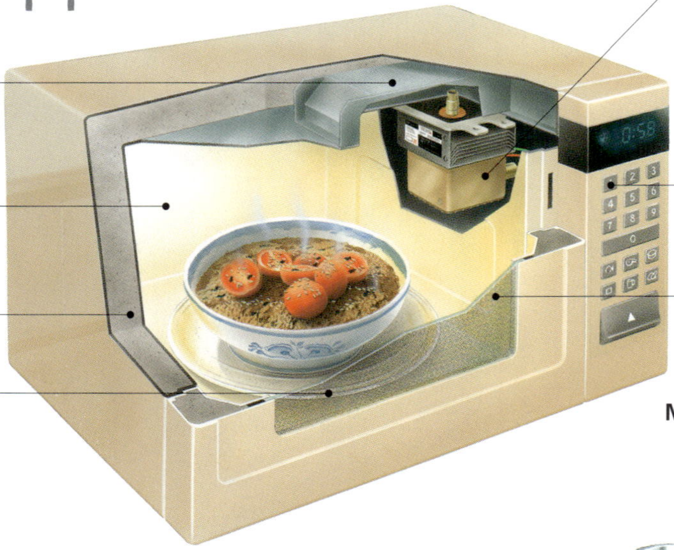

MICROWAVE OVEN

TELEVISION

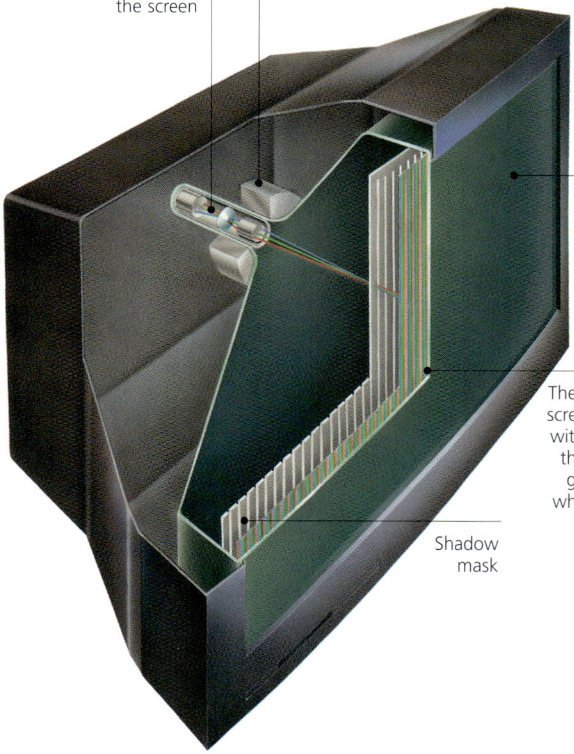

FOOD PROCESSOR

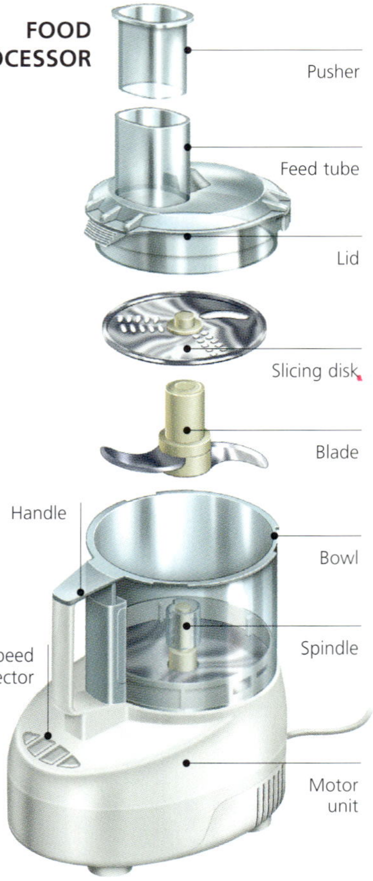

WASHING MACHINE

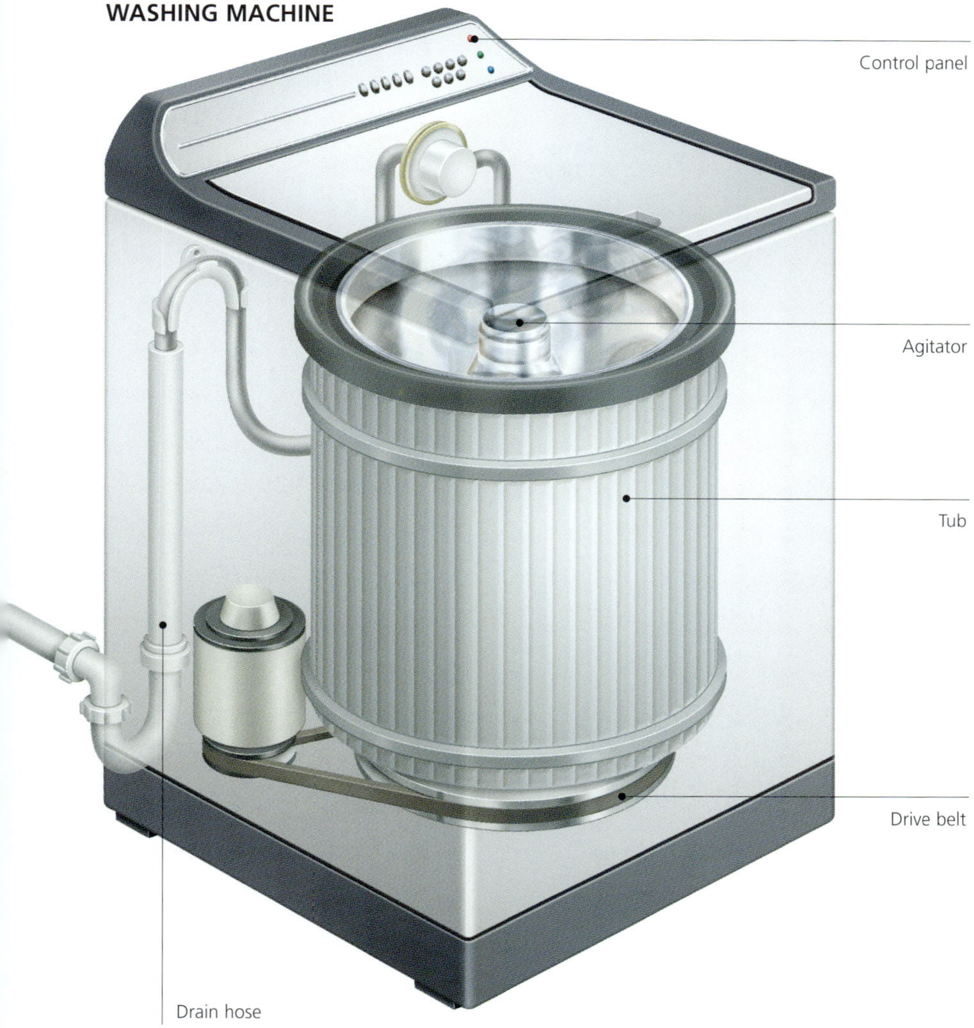

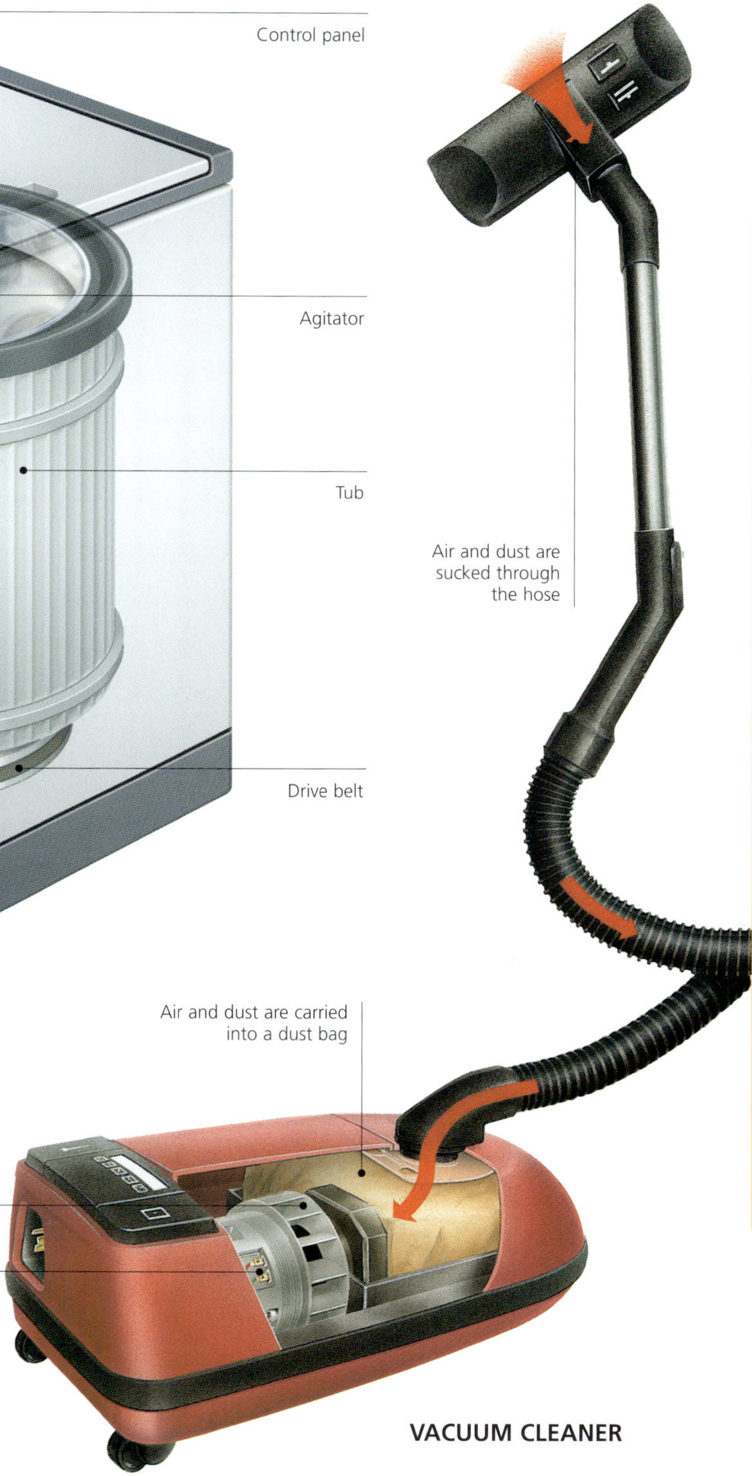

VACUUM CLEANER

Computers

PERSONAL COMPUTER

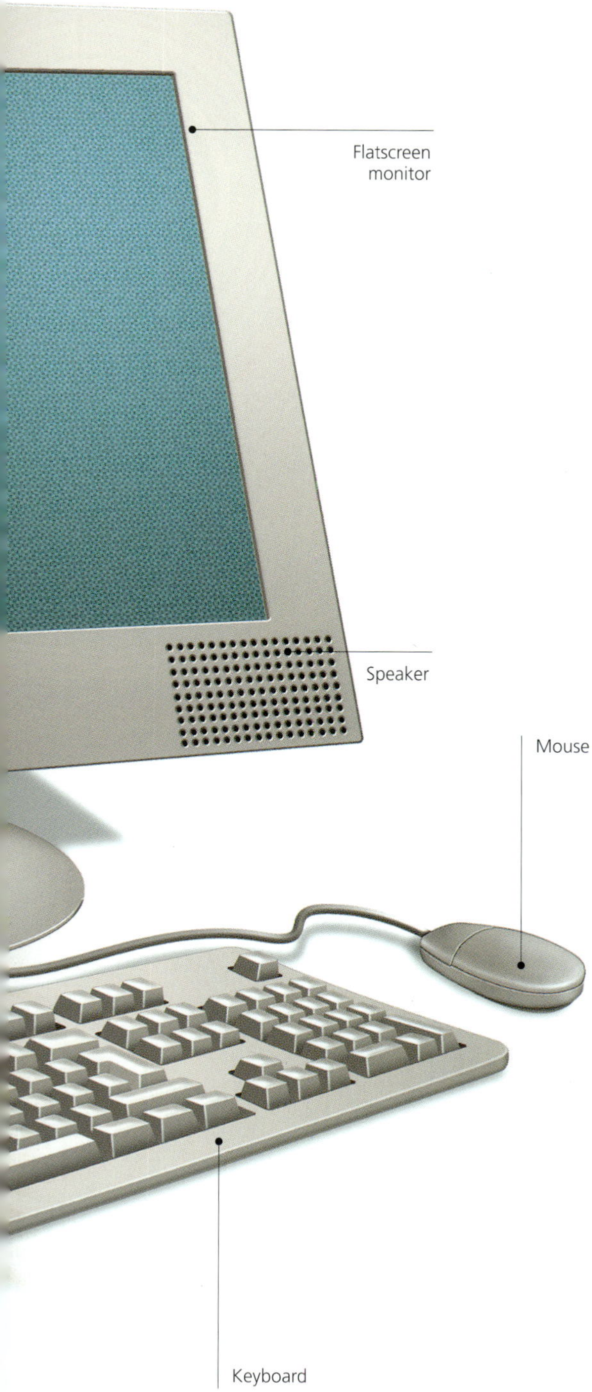

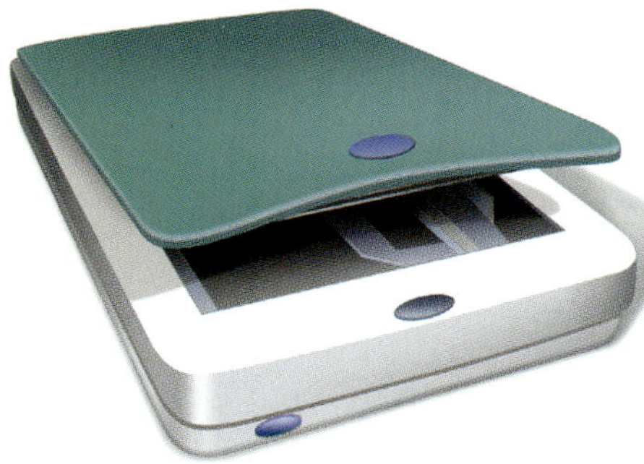

FLATBED SCANNER

LASER PRINTER

PERSONAL ORGANIZER

Medical Technology

X-RAY MACHINE

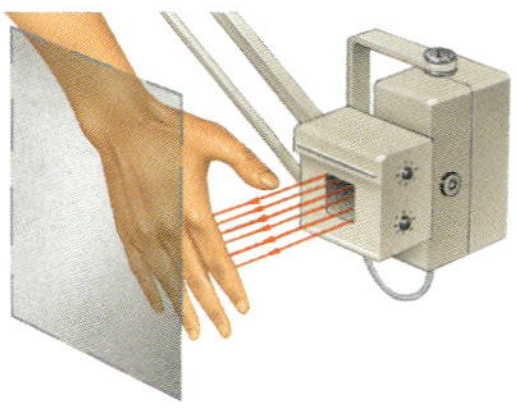

X-ray gun takes an image of a hand.

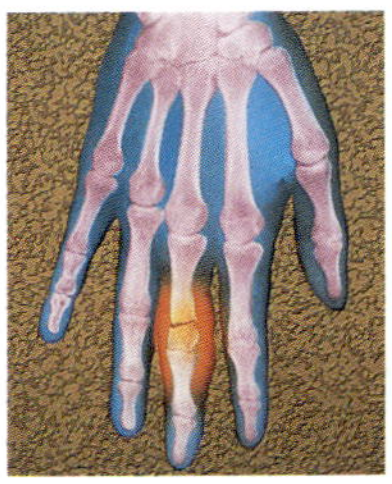

Processed x-ray image

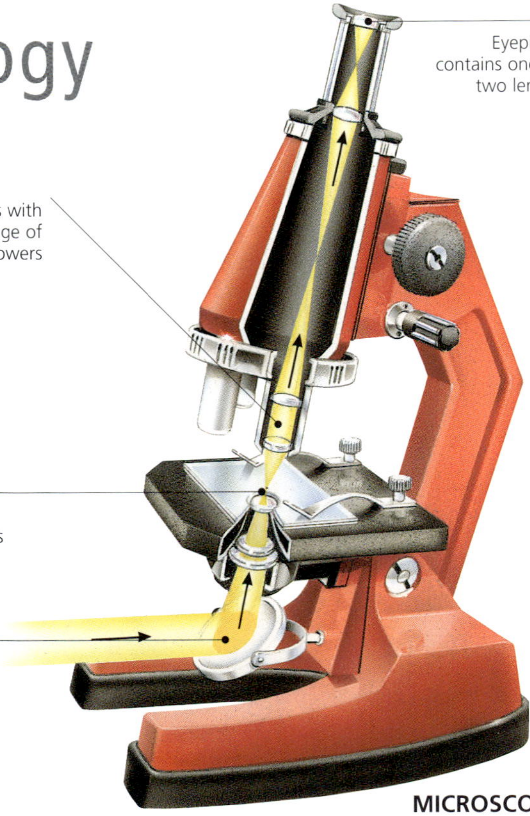

MICROSCOPE

ULTRASOUND MACHINE

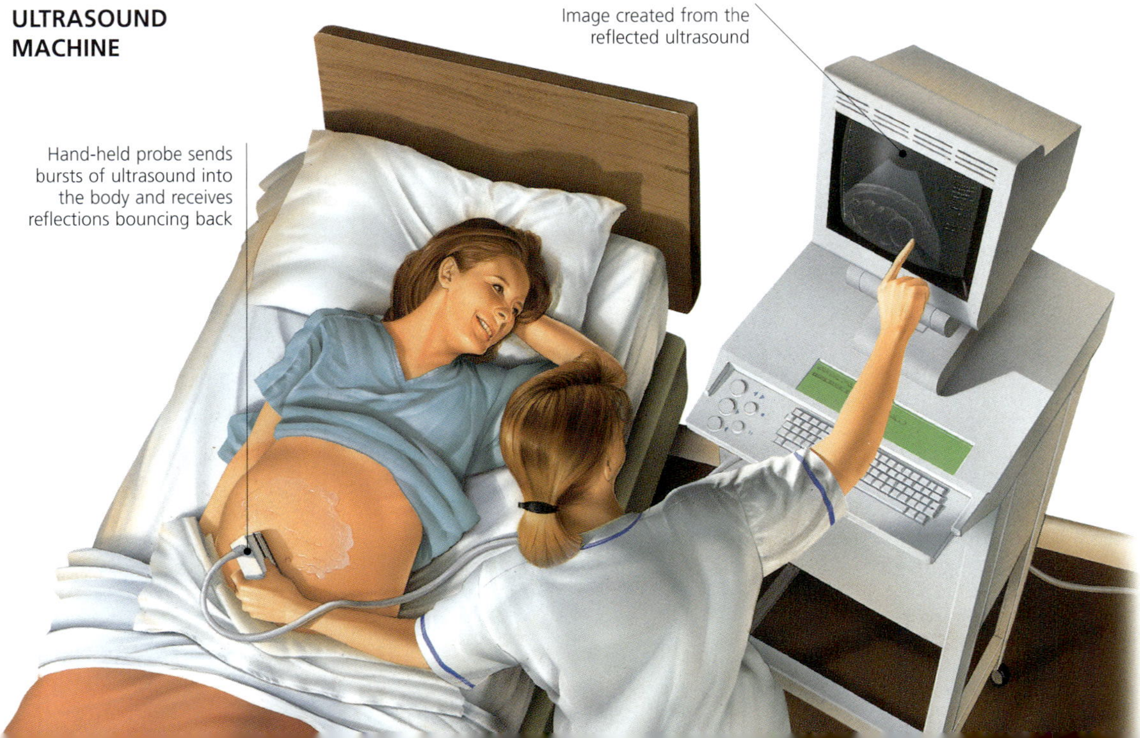

STETHOSCOPE

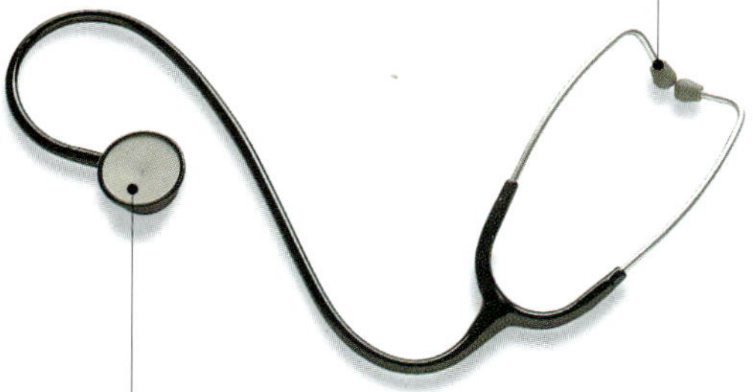

DIGITAL THERMOMETER

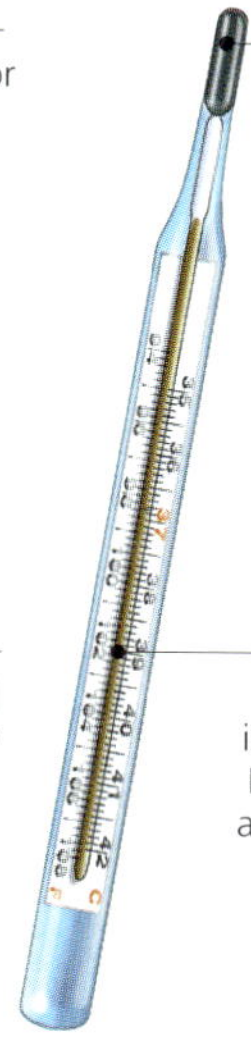

MERCURY THERMOMETER

COCHLEAR IMPLANT

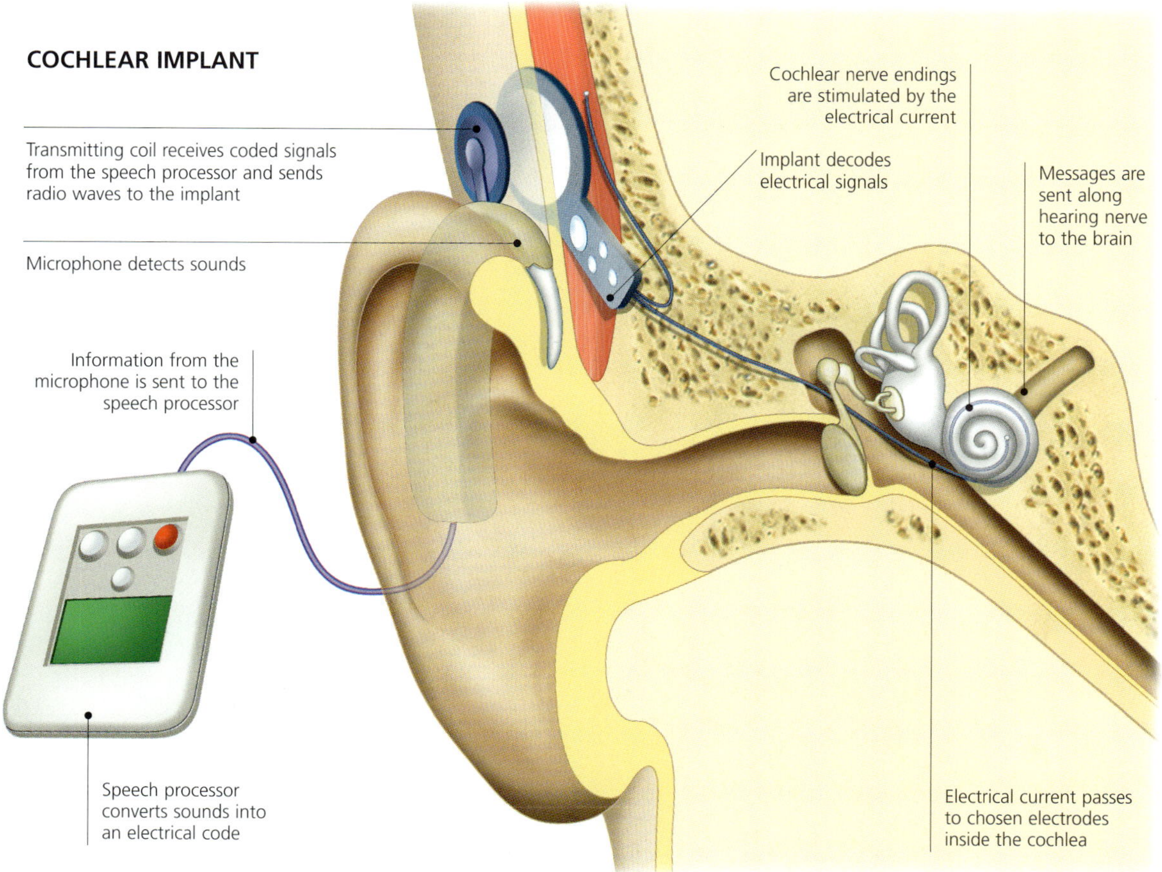

Communications

TELEPHONE

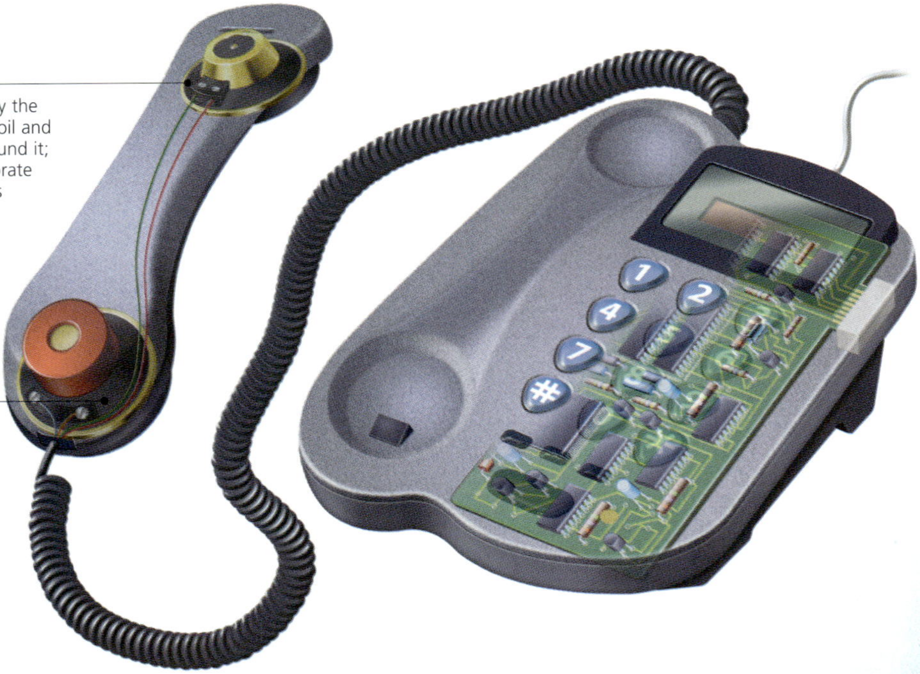

VIDEO CONFERENCE

COMMUNICATION SATELLITES

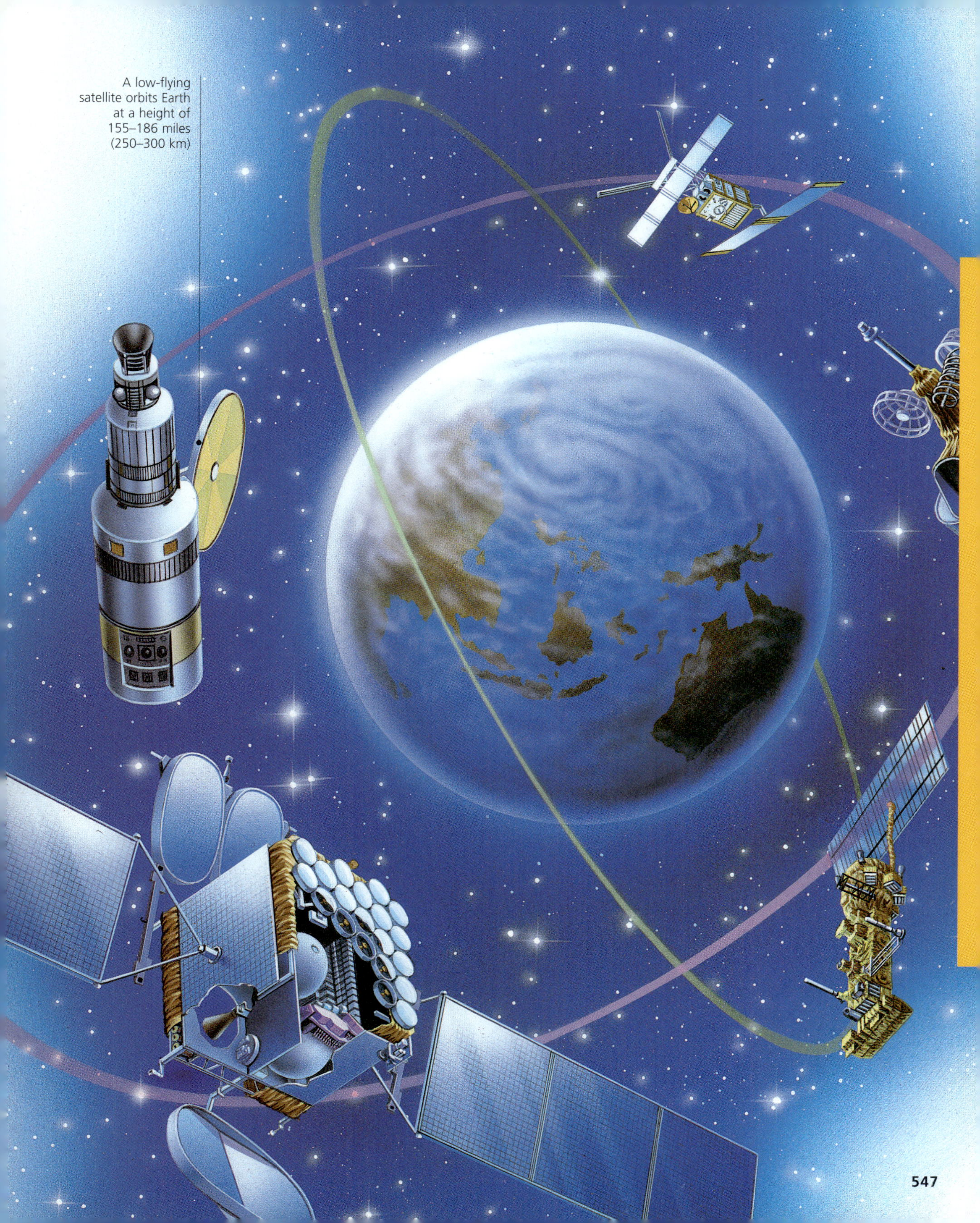
A low-flying satellite orbits Earth at a height of 155–186 miles (250–300 km)

Optics

BINOCULARS

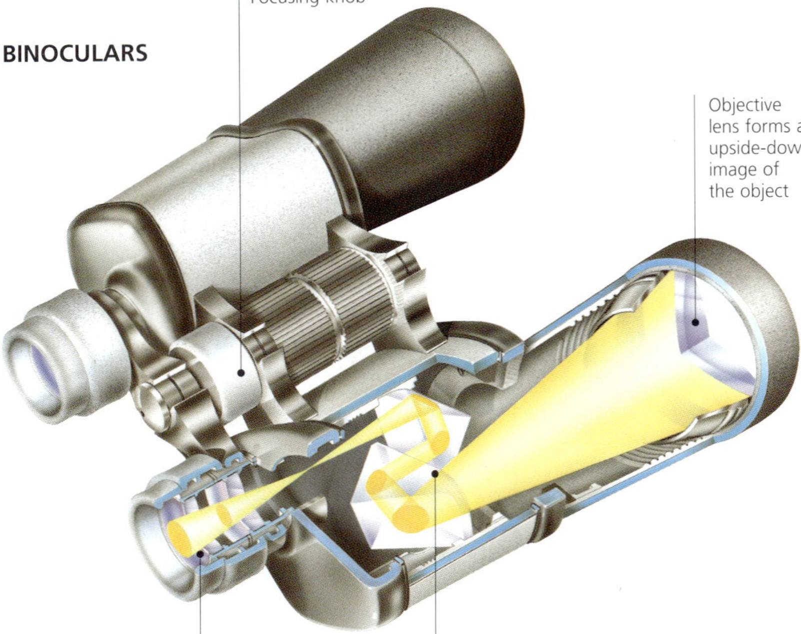

LENSES

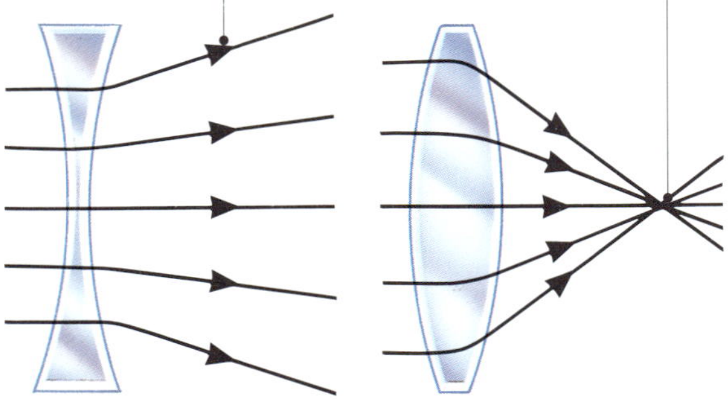

Concave lens **Convex lens**

SINGLE LENS REFLEX CAMERA

Sound

GRAND PIANO

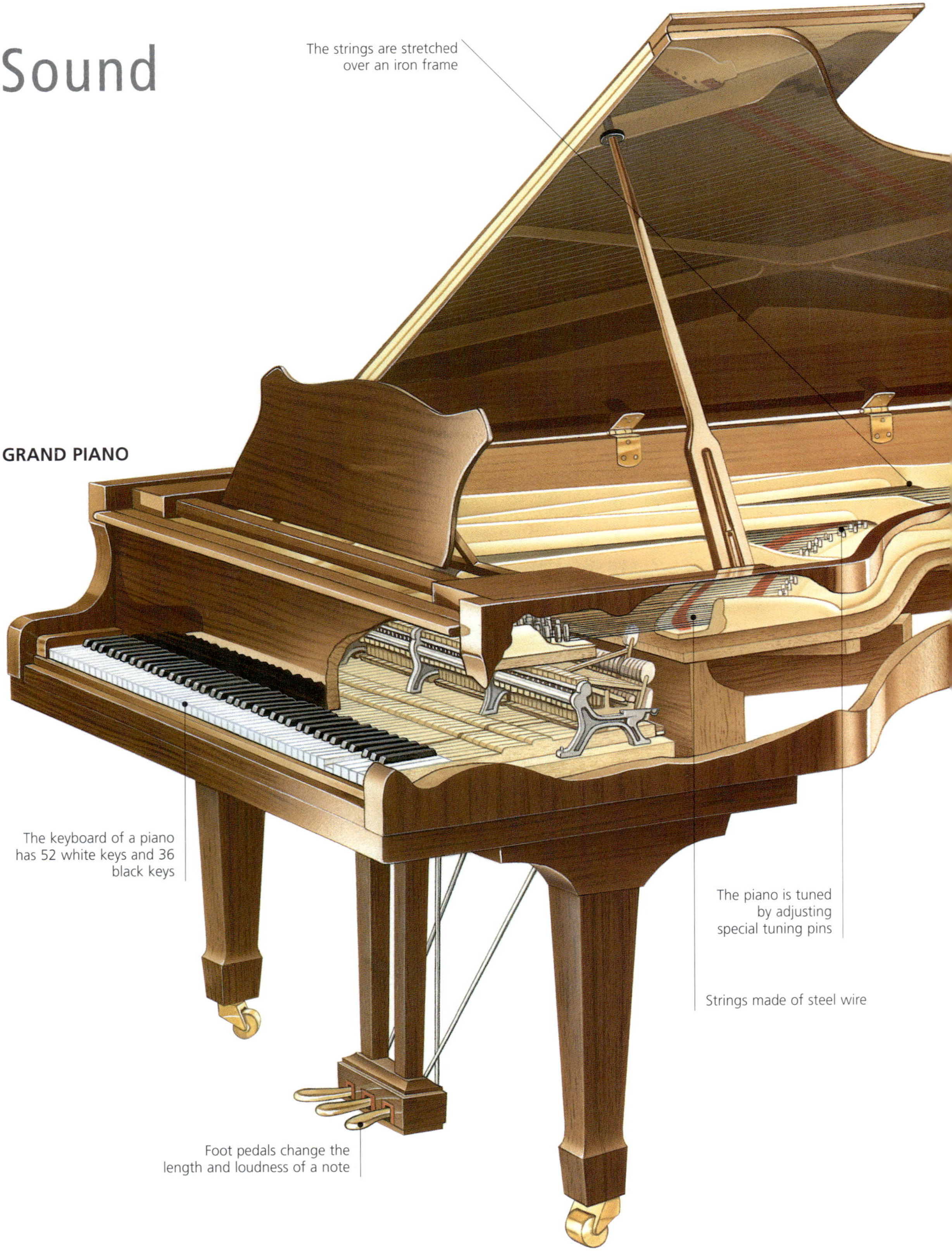

GUITAR

SOUND VIBRATIONS

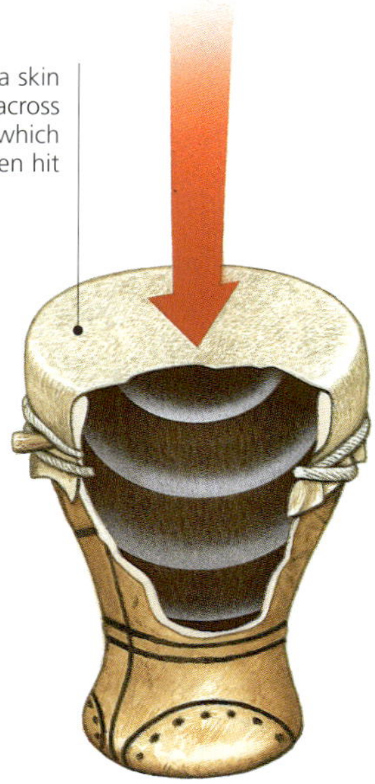

PIANO KEYS

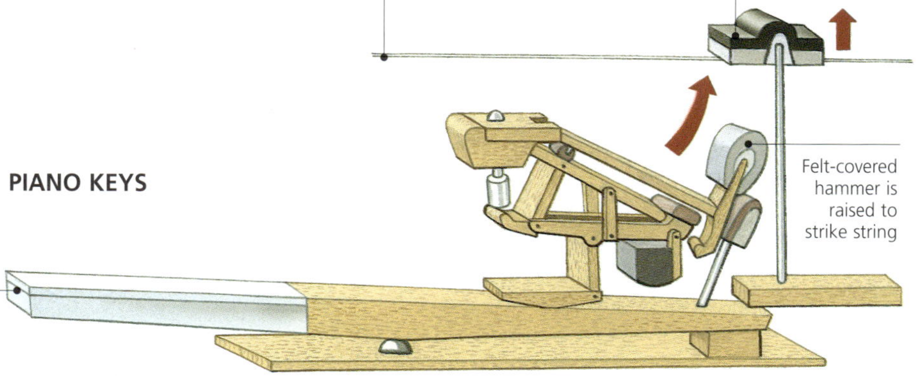

Power and Energy

TURBOGENERATOR

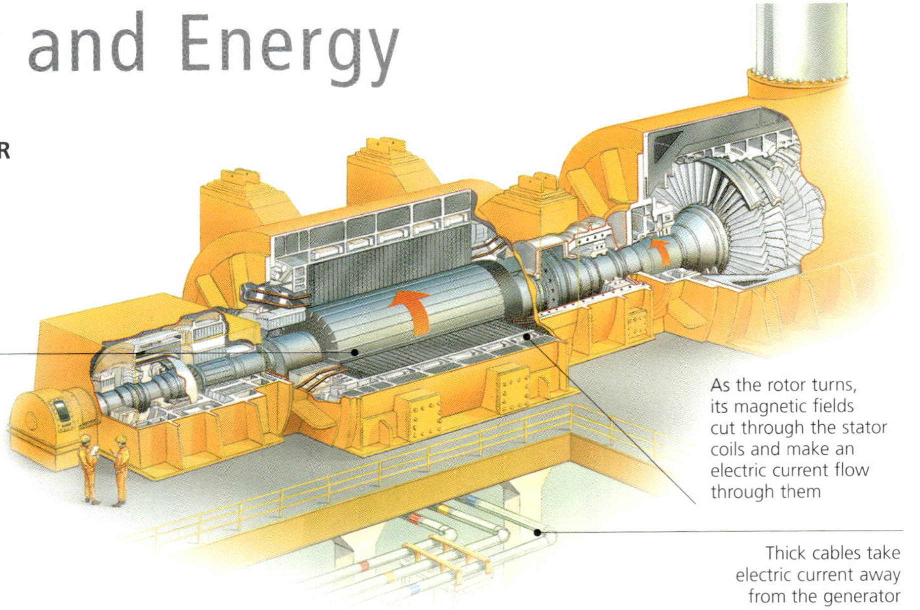

STEAM POWER

Steam-powered merry-go-round

Steam engine

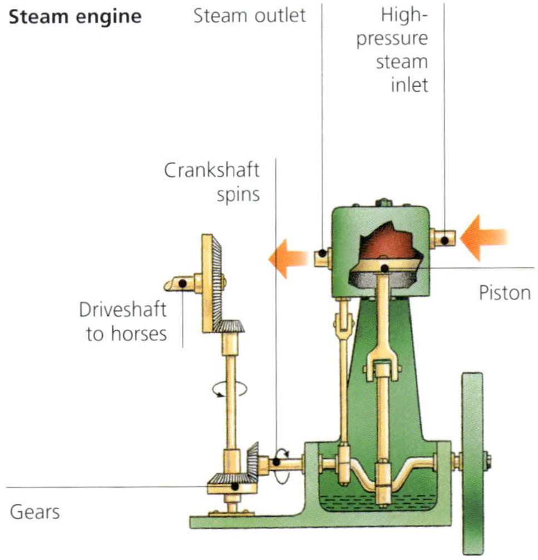

WIND FARM

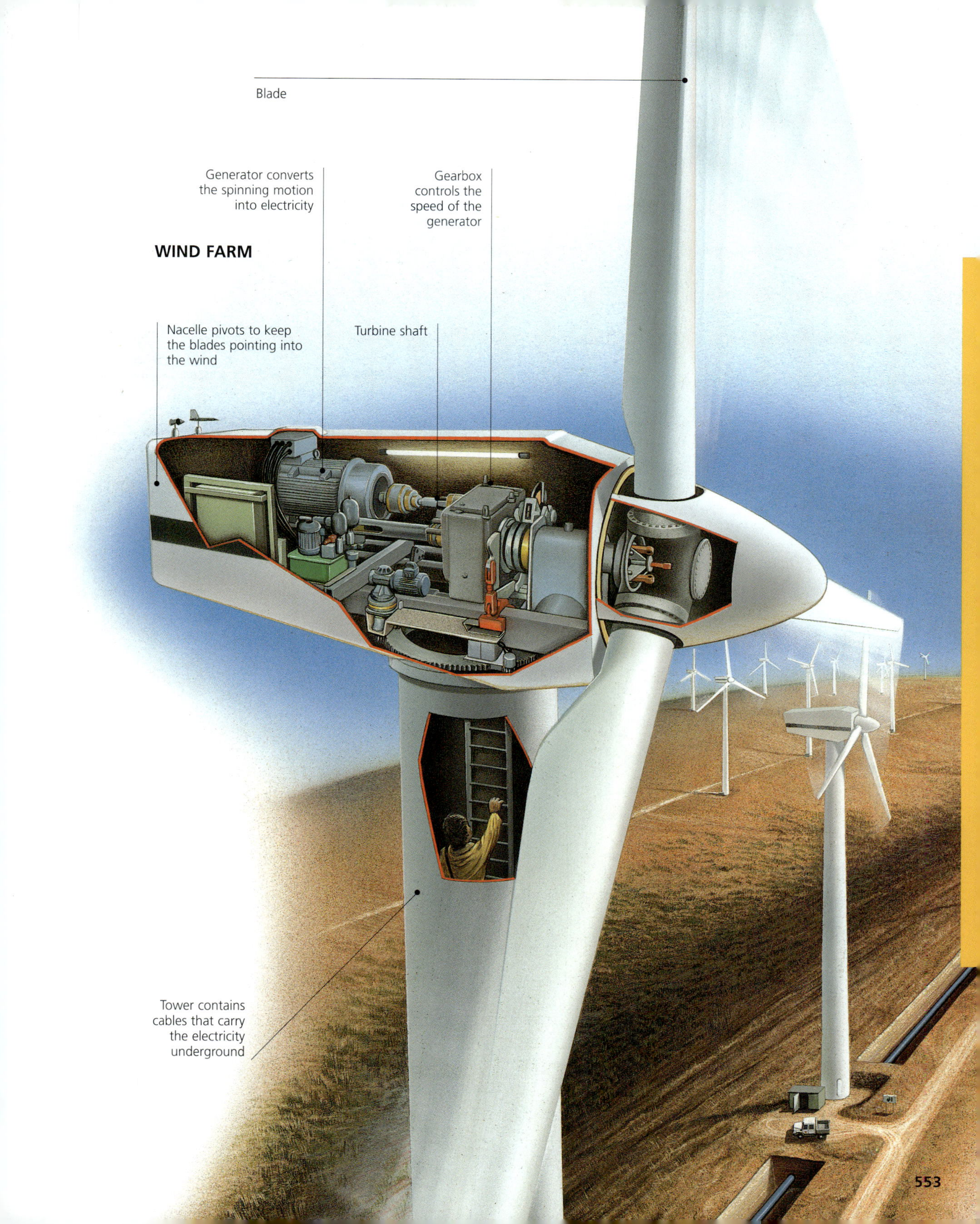
Blade
Generator converts the spinning motion into electricity
Gearbox controls the speed of the generator
Nacelle pivots to keep the blades pointing into the wind
Turbine shaft
Tower contains cables that carry the electricity underground

FACT FILE

World Map

COUNTRY FORMATION

Early on, people lived in small family groups and their ways of life, or cultures, were shaped by the physical demands of the regions they lived in. Eventually, as the family groups grew larger, relations between the groups helped form the regions into countries. Today, there are 193 independent countries and a small number of territories or dependencies of those countries.

KEY TO NUMBERED COUNTRIES

1	The Netherlands
2	Belgium
•3	Luxembourg
4	Czech Republic
5	Slovakia
6	Switzerland
•7	Liechtenstein
8	Slovenia
9	Croatia
•10	Andorra
•11	Monaco
•12	San Marino
•13	Vatican City
14	Bosnia-Herzegovina
15	Moldova
16	Yugoslavia
17	Albania
18	Macedonia
•19	Gibraltar (U.K.)
20	Armenia
21	Azerbaijan
22	United Arab Emirates
23	Rwanda
24	Burundi

ARCTIC OCEAN
SVALBARD (NORWAY)
JAN MAYEN ISLAND (NORWAY)
FAEROE ISLANDS (DENMARK)
SWEDEN
FINLAND
NORWAY
ESTONIA
LATVIA
LITHUANIA
DENMARK
UNITED KINGDOM
IRELAND
RUSSIA
BELARUS
POLAND
GERMANY
UKRAINE
FRANCE
AUSTRIA
HUNGARY
ROMANIA
ITALY
BULGARIA
PORTUGAL
SPAIN
GREECE
MALTA
TURKEY
GEORGIA
CYPRUS
SYRIA
LEBANON
ISRAEL
JORDAN
IRAQ
KUWAIT
BAHRAIN
QATAR
SAUDI ARABIA
OMAN
YEMEN
IRAN
AFGHANISTAN
PAKISTAN
TURKMENISTAN
UZBEKISTAN
KYRGYZSTAN
TAJIKISTAN
KAZAKSTAN
MONGOLIA
CHINA
NORTH KOREA
SOUTH KOREA
JAPAN
TAIWAN
NEPAL
BHUTAN
BANGLADESH
INDIA
SRI LANKA
MYANMAR (BURMA)
LAOS
THAILAND
VIETNAM
CAMBODIA
PHILIPPINES
MALAYSIA
BRUNEI
SINGAPORE
INDONESIA
EAST TIMOR
PAPUA NEW GUINEA
TUNISIA
MOROCCO
ALGERIA
LIBYA
EGYPT
MAURITANIA
MALI
NIGER
CHAD
SUDAN
ERITREA
DJIBOUTI
ETHIOPIA
SOMALIA
SENEGAL
BURKINA FASO
GUINEA
SIERRA LEONE
LIBERIA
GHANA
TOGO
BENIN
NIGERIA
CENTRAL AFRICAN REPUBLIC
CAMEROON
CÔTE D'IVOIRE (IVORY COAST)
EQUATORIAL GUINEA
SÃO TOMÉ AND PRÍNCIPE
GABON
CONGO
DEMOCRATIC REPUBLIC OF THE CONGO (ZAIRE)
UGANDA
KENYA
RWANDA
BURUNDI
TANZANIA
ANGOLA
ZAMBIA
MALAWI
MOZAMBIQUE
ZIMBABWE
NAMIBIA
BOTSWANA
SWAZILAND
LESOTHO
SOUTH AFRICA
MADAGASCAR
COMOROS
MAYOTTE (FRANCE)
MAURITIUS
REUNION (FRANCE)
SEYCHELLES
ASCENSION (U.K.)
ST. HELENA AND DEPENDENCIES (U.K.)
GOUGH ISLAND (U.K.)
BOUVET ISLAND (NORWAY)
LACCADIVE ISLANDS (INDIA)
MALDIVES
ANDAMAN ISLANDS (INDIA)
NICOBAR ISLANDS (INDIA)
BRITISH INDIAN OCEAN TERRITORY (U.K.)
CHRISTMAS ISLAND (AUSTRALIA)
COCOS (KEELING) ISLANDS (AUSTRALIA)
INDIAN OCEAN
AMSTERDAM ISLAND (FRANCE)
ST. PAUL ISLAND (FRANCE)
PRINCE EDWARD ISLANDS (SOUTH AFRICA)
CROZET ISLANDS (FRANCE)
KERGUÉLEN ISLANDS (FRANCE)
HEARD AND McDONALD ISLANDS (AUSTRALIA)
PACIFIC OCEAN
MIDWAY ISLANDS (U.S.A.)
NORTHERN MARIANA ISLANDS (U.S.A.)
WAKE ISLAND (U.S.A.)
GUAM (U.S.A.)
MARSHALL ISLANDS
JOHNSTON ATOLL (U.S.A.)
PALAU
FEDERATED STATES OF MICRONESIA
NAURU
KIRIBATI
SOLOMON ISLANDS
TUVALU
TOKELAU (N.Z.)
SAMOA
AMERICAN SAMOA (U.S.A.)
WALLIS AND FUTUNA (FRANCE)
VANUATU
FIJI
TONGA
NIUE (N.Z.)
NEW CALEDONIA (FRANCE)
AUSTRALIA
NORFOLK ISLAND (AUSTRALIA)
KERMADEC ISLANDS (N.Z.)
NEW ZEALAND
CHATHAM ISLANDS (N.Z.)
AUCKLAND ISLANDS (N.Z.)
MACQUARIE ISLAND (AUSTRALIA)
CAMPBELL ISLAND (N.Z.)
PACIFIC OCEAN
ANTARCTICA

NORTH AMERICA

CANADA

Pronunciation: KA-nuh-duh
Area: 3,851,809 sq. miles (9,976,185 sq. km)
Population: 31,902,268
Capital: Ottawa
Currency: 100 cents = 1 Canadian dollar (CAD)
Official Languages: English, French
Main Religion: Christianity 82%
Exports: Newsprint, wood pulp, timber, crude petroleum, machinery, natural gas, aluminum, motor vehicles and parts, telecommunications equipment, electricity

UNITED STATES OF AMERICA

Pronunciation: yoo-NEYE-tuhd STAYTS of uh-MEHR-uh-kuh
Area: 3,717,800 sq. miles (9,629,091 sq. km)
Population: 280,562,489
Capital: Washington, D.C.
Currency: 100 cents = 1 United States dollar (USD)
Official Language: English
Other Language: Spanish
Main Religions: Christianity 84%, Judaism 2%
Exports: Motor vehicles, raw materials, consumer goods, agricultural products, industrial supplies

Territories and Dependencies

American Samoa: South Pacific Ocean; 76 sq. miles (197 sq. km); population 68,688
Guam: Western Pacific Ocean; 209 sq. miles (541 sq. km); population 160,796
Midway: Central Pacific Ocean; 2 sq. miles (5 sq. km); no permanent population
Northern Mariana Islands: North Pacific Ocean; 184 sq. miles (477 sq. km); population 77,311
Puerto Rico: Caribbean Sea; 3,515 sq. miles (9,104 sq. km); population 3,888,000
Virgin Islands of the United States: Caribbean Sea; 133 sq. miles (345 sq. km); population 123,498
Wake Island: North Pacific Ocean; 3 sq. miles (7.7 sq. km); population 124

MEXICO

Pronunciation: MEK-si-koh
Area: 761,600 sq. miles (1,972,544 sq. km)
Population: 103,400,165
Capital: Mexico City
Currency: 100 centavos = 1 Mexican peso (MXN)
Official Language: Spanish
Other Languages: Regional languages
Main Religion: Christianity 95%
Exports: Crude oil, oil products, coffee, silver, engines, motor vehicles, cotton, electronic goods

GUATEMALA

Pronunciation: gwah-tuh-MAH-luh
Area: 42,042 sq. miles (108,889 sq. km)
Population: 13,314,079
Capital: Guatemala
Currency: 100 centavos = 1 Guatemalan quetzal (GTQ)
Official Language: Spanish

Other Languages: Quiche, Cakchiquel, Kekchi, other regional languages
Main Religions: Christianity 99%, traditional Mayan religions
Exports: Coffee, bananas, cotton, sugar, minerals, textiles, petroleum

BELIZE

Pronunciation: buh-LEEZ
Area: 8,867 sq. miles (22,966 sq. km)
Population: 262,999
Capital: Belmopan
Currency: 100 cents = 1 Belizean dollar (BZD)
Official Language: English
Other Languages: Spanish, Maya, Garifuna, Creole
Main Religion: Christianity 92%
Exports: Sugar, molasses, citrus fruit, bananas, clothing, fish products, timber

HONDURAS

Pronunciation: hahn-DER-uhs
Area: 43,277 sq. miles (112,087 sq. km)
Population: 6,560,608
Capital: Tegucigalpa
Currency: 100 centavos = 1 lempira (HNL)
Official Language: Spanish
Other Languages: Regional languages
Main Religion: Christianity 97%
Exports: Sugar, coffee, textiles, clothing, timber and timber products

EL SALVADOR

Pronunciation: el SAL-vuh-dor
Area: 8,260 sq. miles (21,393 sq. km)
Population: 6,353,681
Capital: San Salvador

Currency: 100 centavos = 1 Salvadoran colón (SVC)
Official Language: Spanish
Other Language: Nahua
Main Religion: Christianity 92%
Exports: Coffee, sugarcane, shrimp, raw materials

NICARAGUA

Pronunciation: ni-kuh-RAH-gwuh
Area: 49,998 sq. miles (129,494 sq. km)
Population: 5,023,818
Capital: Managua
Currency: 100 centavos = 1 gold cordoba (NIO)
Official Language: Spanish
Other Languages: English, regional languages
Main Religion: Christianity 100%
Exports: Coffee, cotton, sugar, bananas, seafood, gold, beef, tobacco

COSTA RICA

Pronunciation: kaws-tuh REE-kuh
Area: 19,652 sq. miles (50,899 sq. km)
Population: 3,834,934
Capital: San José
Currency: 100 centimos = 1 Costa Rican colón (CRC)
Official Language: Spanish
Other Language: English
Main Religion: Christianity 92%
Exports: Coffee, bananas, sugar, textiles, pineapples

PANAMA

Pronunciation: PA-nuh-mah
Area: 33,659 sq. miles (87,177 sq. km)
Population: 2,882,329
Capital: Panama
Currency: 100 centesimos = 1 balboa (PAB)
Official Language: Spanish
Other Languages: English, regional languages
Main Religion: Christianity 100%
Exports: Bananas, shrimp, sugar, coffee, clothing

THE BAHAMAS

Pronunciation: the buh-HAH-muhz
Area: 5,386 sq. miles (13,950 sq. km)
Population: 300,529
Capital: Nassau
Currency: 100 cents = 1 Bahamian dollar (BSD)
Official Language: English
Other Language: Bahamian creole
Main Religion: Christianity 95%
Exports: Pharmaceuticals, cement, rum, crayfish, refined petroleum products

CUBA

Pronunciation: KYOO-buh
Area: 42,804 sq. miles (110,862 sq. km)
Population: 11,224,321
Capital: Havana
Currency: 100 centavos = 1 Cuban peso (CUP)
Official Language: Spanish
Main Religion: Christianity 85%
Exports: Sugar, fish and shellfish, citrus fruit, coffee, tobacco, nickel, medical products

JAMAICA

Pronunciation: juh-MAY-kuh
Area: 4,243 sq. miles (10,990 sq. km)
Population: 2,680,029
Capital: Kingston
Currency: 100 cents = 1 Jamaican dollar (JMD)
Official Language: English
Other Language: Jamaican creole
Main Religion: Christianity 65%
Exports: Bauxite, sugar, bananas, rum, alumina

HAITI

Pronunciation: HAY-tee
Area: 10,714 sq. miles (27,749 sq. km)
Population: 7,063,722
Capital: Port-au-Prince
Currency: 100 centimes = 1 gourde (HTG)
Official Languages: French, Haitian creole
Main Religion: Christianity 96%
Exports: Clothing, coffee, sugar, manufactured goods, oils, mangoes

DOMINICAN REPUBLIC

Pronunciation: duh-MI-ni-kuhn ri-PUH-blik
Area: 18,657 sq. miles (48,322 sq. km)
Population: 8,721,594
Capital: Santo Domingo
Currency: 100 centavos = 1 Dominican peso (DOP)
Official Language: Spanish
Main Religion: Christianity 95%
Exports: Minerals, coffee, cocoa, gold, tobacco

ANTIGUA AND BARBUDA

Pronunciation: an-TEE-guh and bar-BOO-duh
Area: 171 sq. miles (443 sq. km)
Population: 67,448
Capital: St. John's
Currency: 100 cents = 1 East Caribbean dollar (XCD)
Official Language: English
Other Languages: Regional languages
Main Religions: Christianity 97%, indigenous religions 3%
Exports: Petroleum products, manufactured goods, machinery and transportation equipment, food and livestock

ST. KITTS–NEVIS

Pronunciation: saynt KITS NEE-vuhs
Area: 104 sq. miles (269 sq. km)
Population: 38,736
Capital: Basseterre
Currency: 100 cents = 1 East Caribbean dollar (XCD)
Official Language: English
Main Religion: Christianity 86%
Exports: Machinery, food, beverages, electronics, tobacco

DOMINICA

Pronunciation: dah-muh-NEE-kuh
Area: 289 sq. miles (749 sq. km)
Population: 70,158
Capital: Roseau
Currency: 100 cents = 1 East Caribbean dollar (XCD)
Official Language: English
Other Language: French patois
Main Religion: Christianity 92%
Exports: Bananas, grapefruit, oranges, vegetables, soap, bay oil

ST. LUCIA

Pronunciation: saynt LOO-shuh
Area: 238 sq. miles (616 sq. km)
Population: 160,145
Capital: Castries
Currency: 100 cents = 1 East Caribbean dollar (XCD)
Official Language: English
Other Language: French patois
Main Religion: Christianity 100%
Exports: Bananas, clothing, cocoa, coconut oil, fruit and vegetables

BARBADOS

Pronunciation: bar-BAY-dohs
Area: 166 sq. miles (430 sq. km)
Population: 276,607
Capital: Bridgetown
Currency: 100 cents = 1 Barbadian dollar (BBS)
Official Language: English
Other Language: Barbadian creole
Main Religion: Christianity 71%
Exports: Sugar and molasses, rum, chemicals, foods and beverages, electrical components, clothing

ST. VINCENT AND THE GRENADINES

Pronunciation: saynt VIN-suhnt and the gren-uh-DEENZ
Area: 150 sq. miles (389 sq. km)
Population: 116,394
Capital: Kingstown
Currency: 100 cents = 1 East Caribbean dollar (XCD)
Official Language: English
Other Language: French patois
Main Religion: Christianity 75%
Exports: Bananas, taro, tennis rackets, arrowroot

GRENADA

Pronunciation: gruh-NAY-duh
Area: 133 sq. miles (344 sq. km)
Population: 89,211
Capital: St. George's
Currency: 100 cents = 1 East Caribbean dollar (XCD)
Official Language: English
Other Language: French patois
Main Religion: Christianity 100%
Exports: Bananas, fruit and vegetables, cocoa, nutmeg, clothing, mace

TRINIDAD AND TOBAGO

Pronunciation: TRI-nuh-dad and tuh-BAY-goh
Area: 1,980 sq. miles (5,128 sq. km)
Population: 1,163,724
Capital: Port-of-Spain
Currency: 100 cents = 1 Trinidad and Tobago dollar (TTD)
Official Language: English
Other Languages: Hindi, French, Spanish, Chinese
Main Religions: Christianity 44%, Hinduism 24%, Islam 6%
Exports: Petroleum and petroleum products, chemicals, steel products, fertilizer, sugar, cocoa, coffee, citrus fruit, flowers

SOUTH AMERICA

COLOMBIA

Pronunciation: kuh-LUHM-bee-uh
Area: 439,735 sq. miles (1,138,914 sq. km)
Population: 41,008,227
Capital: Bogota
Currency: 100 centavos = 1 Colombian peso (COP)
Official Language: Spanish
Main Religion: Christianity 90%
Exports: Petroleum, coffee, coal, bananas, flowers

VENEZUELA

Pronunciation: ve-nuh-ZWAY-luh
Area: 352,143 sq. miles (912,050 sq. km)
Population: 24,287,670
Capital: Caracas
Currency: 100 centimos = 1 bolivar (VEB)
Official Language: Spanish
Other Languages: Regional languages
Main Religion: Christianity 98%
Exports: Petroleum, bauxite and aluminum, steel, chemicals, agricultural products, basic manufactured goods

GUYANA

Pronunciation: geye-AH-nuh
Area: 83,000 sq. miles (214,970 sq. km)
Population: 698,209
Capital: Georgetown
Currency: 100 cents = 1 Guyanese dollar (GYD)
Official Language: English
Other Languages: Local languages, Hindi, Urdu
Main Religions: Christianity 50%, Hinduism 33%, Islam 9%
Exports: Sugar, molasses, bauxite, rice, shrimp

SURINAME

Pronunciation: SUR-uh-nah-muh
Area: 63,039 sq. miles (163,270 sq. km)
Population: 436,494
Capital: Paramaribo
Currency: 100 cents = 1 Surinamese guilder or florin (SRG)
Official Language: Dutch
Other Languages: English, Sranang Tongo, Hindustani, Javanese
Main Religions: Christianity 48%, Hinduism 27%, Islam 20%, indigenous religions 5%
Exports: Aluminum, fish, shrimp, timber, rice, bananas, crude oil

ECUADOR

Pronunciation: E-kwuh-dor
Area: 109,483 sq. miles (283,561 sq. km)
Population: 13,447,494
Capital: Quito
Currency: 100 cents = 1 United States dollar (USD)
Official Language: Spanish
Other Languages: Quechua, other regional languages
Main Religion: Christianity 95%
Exports: Petroleum, bananas, shrimp, cocoa, coffee, flowers, fish

PERU

Pronunciation: puh-ROO
Area: 496,222 sq. miles (1,285,215 sq. km)
Population: 27,949,639
Capital: Lima
Currency: 100 centimos = 1 nuevo sol (PEN)
Official Languages: Spanish, Quechua
Other Language: Aymara
Main Religion: Christianity 90%
Exports: Copper, zinc, petroleum products, lead, coffee, cotton, fish and fish products, sugar

BRAZIL

Pronunciation: bruh-ZIL
Area: 3,284,426 sq. miles (8,506,663 sq. km)
Population: 176,029,560
Capital: Brasília
Currency: 100 centavos = 1 real (BRL)
Official Language: Portuguese
Other Languages: Spanish, English, French
Main Religion: Christianity 80%
Exports: Iron ore, soybean bran, coffee, sugar, footwear, manufactured goods

BOLIVIA

Pronunciation: buh-LI-vee-uh
Area: 424,162 sq. miles (1,098,579 sq. km)
Population: 8,445,134
Capitals: La Paz (seat of government), Sucre (legal and judicial)
Currency: 100 centavos = 1 boliviano (BOB)
Official Languages: Spanish, Quechua, Aymara
Main Religion: Christianity 100%
Exports: Natural gas, soybeans, zinc, gold jewelry, timber

CHILE

Pronunciation: CHI-lee
Area: 292,257 sq. miles (756,946 sq. km)
Population: 15,498,930
Capital: Santiago
Currency: 100 centavos = 1 Chilean peso (CLP)
Official Language: Spanish
Other Languages: Regional languages
Main Religion: Christianity 99%
Exports: Copper, metals and minerals, timber products, fish, fruit, chemicals

PARAGUAY

Pronunciation: PAR-uh-gweye
Area: 157,043 sq. miles (406,741 sq. km)
Population: 5,884,491
Capital: Asunción
Currency: 100 centimos = 1 guarani (PYG)
Official Languages: Spanish, Guarani
Main Religion: Christianity 97%
Exports: Cotton, soybeans, timber, vegetable oils, meat products, coffee, electricity, feed for livestock

ARGENTINA

Pronunciation: ar-juhn-TEE-nuh
Area: 1,068,296 sq. miles (2,766,884 sq. km)
Population: 37,812,817
Capital: Buenos Aires
Currency: 100 centavos = 1 Argentine peso (ARS)
Official Language: Spanish
Other Languages: English, Italian, German, French
Main Religions: Christianity 92%, Judaism 2%
Exports: Manufactured goods, meat, wheat, corn, vegetable oil, fuel and energy

URUGUAY

Pronunciation: OOR-uh-gweye
Area: 68,039 sq. miles (176,221 sq. km)
Population: 3,386,575
Capital: Montevideo
Currency: 100 centesimos = 1 Uruguayan peso (UYU)
Official Language: Spanish
Other Language: Brazilero
Main Religions: Christianity 68%, Judaism 1%
Exports: Wool, textiles, beef and other animal products, leather, rice

DISPUTED TERRITORIES WORLDWIDE

GAZA STRIP (PALESTINE)
Location: Middle East
Disputed By: Israel and Palestine, Palestinian interim self-government
Size: 139 sq. miles (360 sq. km)
Population: 1,225,911

KASHMIR
Location: Southern Asia
Disputed By: India and Pakistan
Size: 85,085 sq. miles (222,236 sq. km)
Population: 7,718,700

TURKISH FEDERATED STATE OF CYPRUS
Location: Mediterranean Sea
Disputed By: Turkey and Cyprus
Size: 1,295 sq. miles (3,355 sq. km)
Population: 177,120

WEST BANK (PALESTINE)
Location: Middle East
Disputed By: Israel and Palestine, Palestinian interim self-government
Size: 2,263 sq. miles (5,860 sq. km)
Population: 1,612,000

WESTERN SAHARA
Location: Northwestern Africa
Disputed By: Morocco and separatist movement
Size: 102,703 sq. miles (266,001 sq. km);
Population: 256,177

EUROPE

UNITED KINGDOM

Pronunciation: yoo-NEYE-tuhd KING-duhm
Area: 94,525 sq. miles (244,820 sq. km)
Population: 58,836,700
Capital: London
Currency: 100 pence = 1 British pound (GBP)
Official Language: English
Other Languages: Welsh, Scottish Gaelic, Irish Gaelic
Main Religions: Christianity 90%, Islam 3%, Sikh 1%, Hinduism 1%, Judaism 1%
Exports: Manufactured goods, machinery, fuels, chemicals, food and beverages, tobacco

Territories and Dependencies

Anguilla: Caribbean Sea; 35 sq. miles (91 sq. km); population 12,446
Bermuda: North Atlantic Ocean; 20 sq. miles (52 sq. km); population 63,960
British Indian Ocean Territory: Indian Ocean; 23 sq. miles (60 sq. km); no permanent population
British Virgin Islands: Caribbean Sea; 59 sq. miles (153 sq. km); population 21,272
Cayman Islands: Caribbean Sea; 118 sq. miles (306 sq. km); population 36,273
Falkland Islands and Dependencies (South Georgia and South Sandwich Islands): South Atlantic Ocean; 4,700 sq. miles (12,173 sq. km); population 2,967
Gibraltar: Southern Spain; 2.25 sq. miles (6 sq. km); population 27,714
Guernsey: English Channel; 30 sq. miles (78 sq. km); population 64,587
Isle of Man: Irish Sea; 221 sq. miles (572 sq. km); population 73,873
Jersey: English Channel; 45 sq. miles (116 sq. km); population 89,775
Montserrat: Caribbean Sea; 40 sq. miles (104 sq. km); population 8,437
Pitcairn Islands: South Pacific Ocean; 18 sq. miles (47 sq. km); population 47
St. Helena and Dependencies (Ascension Island and Tristan da Cunha): South Atlantic Ocean; 158 sq. miles (410 sq. km); population 7,317
Turks and Caicos Islands: Caribbean Sea; 166 sq. miles (430 sq. km); population 18,738

IRELAND

Pronunciation: EYER-luhnd
Area: 26,600 sq. miles (68,894 sq. km)
Population: 3,883,159
Capital: Dublin
Currency: 100 cents = 1 euro (EUR)
Official Languages: English, Irish Gaelic
Main Religion: Christianity 94%
Exports: Chemicals, data processing equipment, industrial machinery, livestock, animal products, pharmaceuticals

PORTUGAL

Pronunciation: POR-chi-guhl
Area: 35,383 sq. miles (91,642 sq. km)
Population: 10,084,245
Capital: Lisbon
Currency: 100 cents = 1 euro (EUR)
Official Language: Portuguese
Main Religion: Christianity 98%
Exports: Clothing, footwear, machinery, cork, paper products, animal hides, chemicals

SPAIN

Pronunciation: spayn
Area: 194,881 sq. miles (504,742 sq. km)
Population: 40,077,100
Capital: Madrid
Currency: 100 cents = 1 euro (EUR)
Official Language: Castilian Spanish
Other Languages: Catalan, Galician, Basque
Main Religion: Christianity 99%
Exports: Motor vehicles, manufactured goods, food, machinery, consumer goods

ANDORRA

Pronunciation: an-DOR-uh
Area: 180 sq. miles (482 sq. km)
Population: 68,403
Capital: Andorra la Vella
Currencies: 100 cents = 1 euro (EUR)
Official Language: Catalan
Other Languages: French, Castilian Spanish
Main Religion: Christianity 95%
Exports: Electricity, tobacco products, timber, furniture

FRANCE

Pronunciation: frans
Area: 211,209 sq. miles (547,030 sq. km)
Population: 59,765,983
Capital: Paris
Currency: 100 cents = 1 euro (EUR)
Official Language: French
Other Languages: Occitan, Breton, Catalan, Basque, Arabic, Corsican, Flemish, Alsatian
Main Religions: Christianity 92%, Judaism 1%, Islam 3%
Exports: Machinery and transportation equipment, chemicals, food, agricultural products, iron and steel, textiles, clothing, pharmaceuticals

Territories and Dependencies

French Guiana: Northern South America; 35,126 sq. miles (90,976 sq. km); population 182,333
French Polynesia: South Pacific Ocean; 1,609 sq. miles (4,167 sq. km); population 257,847
Guadeloupe: Caribbean Sea; 852 sq. miles (1,507 sq. km); population 435,739
Martinique: Caribbean Sea; 425 sq. miles (1,101 sq. km); population 422,277
Mayotte: Mozambique Channel, Africa; 144 sq. miles (373 sq. km); population 170,879
New Caledonia: South Pacific Ocean; 7,367 sq. miles (19,081 sq. km); population 207,858
Réunion: Indian Ocean; 969 sq. miles (2,510 sq. km); population 743,981
St-Pierre and Miquelon: North Atlantic Ocean; 93 sq. miles (241 sq. km); population 6,954
Wallis and Futuna Islands: South Pacific Ocean; 106 sq. miles (275 sq. km); population 15,585

MONACO

Pronunciation: MAH-nuh-koh
Area: 0.58 sq. miles (1.5 sq. km)
Population: 31,987
Capital: Monaco
Currency: 100 cents = 1 euro (EUR)
Official Language: French
Other Languages: English, Italian, Monégasque
Main Religion: Christianity 95%
Exports: Pharmaceuticals, perfumes, clothing

THE NETHERLANDS

Pronunciation: the NE-ther-luhndz
Area: 16,033 sq. miles (41,525 sq. km)
Population: 16,067,754
Capitals: Amsterdam (official); The Hague (seat of government)
Currency: 100 cents = 1 euro (EUR)
Official Language: Dutch
Main Religions: Christianity 52%, Islam 4%
Exports: Metal products, chemicals, processed food, tobacco, agricultural products, machinery and equipment

Territories and Dependencies

Aruba: Caribbean Sea; 69 sq. miles (179 sq. km); population 70,441
Netherlands Antilles: Caribbean Sea; 371 sq. miles (961 sq. km); population 214,258

BELGIUM

Pronunciation: BEL-juhm
Area: 11,781 sq. miles (30,513 sq. km)
Population: 10,274,595
Capital: Brussels
Currency: 100 cents = 1 euro (EUR)
Official Languages: Dutch (Flemish), French
Other Language: German
Main Religion: Christianity 100%
Exports: Iron and steel, machinery and equipment, chemicals, diamonds, petroleum products

LUXEMBOURG

Pronunciation: LUK-suhm-berg
Area: 999 sq. miles (2,587 sq. km)
Population: 429,100
Capital: Luxembourg
Currency: 100 cents = 1 euro (EUR)
Official Languages: Luxembourgish (Letzeburgesh), German, French
Other Language: English
Main Religions: Christianity 99%, Judaism 1%
Exports: Steel products, chemicals, rubber products, glass, aluminum, machinery and equipment

GERMANY

Pronunciation: JER-muh-nee
Area: 137,735 sq. miles (356,734 sq. km)
Population: 83,251,851
Capital: Berlin

Currency: 100 cents = 1 euro (EUR)
Official Language: German
Main Religions: Christianity 72%, Islam 2%
Exports: Machines and machine tools, motor vehicles, chemicals, iron and steel products, textiles, agricultural products, raw materials

SWITZERLAND

Pronunciation: SWIT-suhr-luhnd
Area: 15,941 sq. miles (41,287 sq. km)
Population: 7,301,994
Capital: Bern
Currency: 100 centimes = 1 Swiss franc (CHF)
Official Languages: German, French, Italian
Other Language: Romansch
Main Religion: Christianity 86%
Exports: Machinery, precision instruments, metal products, food, textiles, chemicals

LIECHTENSTEIN

Pronunciation: LIK-tuhn-shteyen
Area: 62 sq. miles (161 sq. km)
Population: 32,842
Capital: Vaduz
Currency: 100 centimes = 1 Swiss franc (CHF)
Official Language: German
Main Religion: Christianity 87%
Exports: Machinery, dental products, stamps, hardware, pottery

AUSTRIA

Pronunciation: AWS-tree-uh
Area: 32,375 sq. miles (83,851 sq. km)
Population: 8,169,929
Capital: Vienna
Currency: 100 cents = 1 euro (EUR)
Official Language: German
Main Religion: Christianity 82%
Exports: Machinery, electrical equipment, iron and steel, lumber, textiles, paper and paper products, chemicals, foodstuffs, metal goods

ITALY

Pronunciation: IT-uh-lee
Area: 116,313 sq. miles (301,251 sq. km)
Population: 57,715,625
Capital: Rome
Currency: 100 cents = 1 euro (EUR)
Official Language: Italian
Other Languages: German, French, Slovene
Main Religion: Christianity 98%
Exports: Textiles, clothing, machinery, motor vehicles, transportation equipment, chemicals, food products, minerals

SAN MARINO

Pronunciation: san muh-REE-noh
Area: 24 sq. miles (62 sq. km)
Population: 27,730
Capital: San Marino
Currency: 100 cents = 1 euro (EUR)
Official Language: Italian
Main Religion: Christianity 95%
Exports: Building stone, lime, timber, chestnuts, wheat, wine, baked goods, animal skins, ceramics

VATICAN CITY

Pronunciation: VA-ti-kuhn city
Area: 0.17 sq. miles (0.44 sq. km)
Population: 900
Capital: Vatican City
Currency: 100 cents = 1 euro (EUR)
Official Languages: Italian, Latin, French
Main Religion: Christianity 100%
Exports: None

MALTA

Pronunciation: MAWL-tuh
Area: 122 sq. miles (316 sq. km)
Population: 397,499
Capital: Valletta
Currency: 100 cents = 1 Maltese lira (MTL)
Official Languages: Maltese, English
Main Religion: Christianity 98%
Exports: Machinery and transportation equipment, clothing, footwear

SLOVENIA

Pronunciation: sloh-VEE-nee-uh
Area: 7,819 sq. miles (20,251 sq. km)
Population: 1,932,917
Capital: Ljubljana
Currency: 100 stotins = 1 tolar (SIT)
Official Language: Slovenian
Other Language: Serbo-Croatian
Main Religions: Christianity 72%, Islam 1%
Exports: Motor vehicles, furniture, machinery, manufactured goods, chemicals, textiles, food, raw materials

CROATIA

Pronunciation: kroh-AY-shuh
Area: 21,829 sq. miles (56,537 sq. km)
Population: 4,390,751
Capital: Zagreb
Currency: 100 lipas = 1 Croatian kuna (HRK)
Official Language: Serbo-Croatian
Main Religions: Christianity 88%, Islam 1%
Exports: Machinery and transportation equipment, other manufactured goods, chemicals, food, livestock, raw materials, fuels, textiles

BOSNIA AND HERZEGOVINA

Pronunciation: BAHZ-nee-uh and hert-suh-goh-VEE-nuh
Area: 19,740 sq. miles (51,129 sq. km)
Population: 3,964,388
Capital: Sarajevo
Currency: 100 pfenniga = 1 marka (BAM)
Official Languages: Serbo-Croatian, Bosnian
Main Religions: Christianity 50%, Islam 40%
Exports: Timber, furniture

YUGOSLAVIA

Pronunciation: yoo-goh-SLAH-vee-uh
Area: 39,449 sq. miles (102,173 sq. km)
Population: 10,656,929
Capital: Belgrade
Currency: 100 paras = 1 Yugoslav new dinar (YUM)
Official Language: Serbo-Croatian
Other Language: Albanian
Main Religions: Christianity 70%, Islam 19%
Exports: Manufactured goods, raw materials, food

ROMANIA

Pronunciation: roh-MAY-nee-uh
Area: 91,699 sq. miles (237,500 sq. km)
Population: 22,317,730
Capital: Bucharest
Currency: 100 bani = 1 leu (ROL)
Official Language: Romanian
Other Languages: Hungarian, German
Main Religion: Christianity 82%
Exports: Metals and metal products, minerals and fuels, textiles and footwear, electrical goods, machinery and equipment

BULGARIA

Pronunciation: buhl-GAIR-ee-uh
Area: 42,823 sq. miles (110,912 sq. km)
Population: 7,621,337
Capital: Sofia
Currency: 100 stotinki = 1 lev (BGL)
Official Language: Bulgarian
Main Religions: Christianity 86%, Islam 13%, Judaism 1%
Exports: Machinery and equipment, fuels, minerals and raw materials, metals, clothing, footwear

ALBANIA

Pronunciation: al-BAY-nee-uh
Area: 11,100 sq. miles (28,749 sq. km)
Population: 3,544,841
Capital: Tiranë
Currency: 100 qintars = 1 lek (ALL)
Official Language: Albanian (Tosk dialect)
Other Language: Greek
Main Religions: Islam 70%, Christianity 30%
Exports: Asphalt, metals and metallic ores, electricity, crude oil, fruit and vegetables, tobacco

MACEDONIA

Pronunciation: ma-suh-DOH-nee-uh
Area: 9,928 sq. miles (25,714 sq. km)
Population: 2,054,800
Capital: Skopje
Currency: 100 deni = 1 Macedonian denar (MKD)
Official Language: Macedonian
Other Languages: Albanian, Turkish, Serbo-Croatian
Main Religions: Christianity 67%, Islam 30%
Exports: Manufactured goods, machinery and transportation equipment, food, beverages, tobacco, iron and steel

GREECE

Pronunciation: grees
Area: 50,944 sq. miles (131,945 sq. km)
Population: 10,645,343
Capital: Athens
Currency: 100 cents = 1 euro (EUR)
Official Language: Greek
Other Languages: English, French
Main Religions: Christianity 98%, Islam 1%
Exports: Manufactured goods, food, petroleum

ESTONIA

Pronunciation: e-STOH-nee-uh
Area: 17,413 sq. miles (45,100 sq. km)
Population: 1,415,681
Capital: Tallinn
Currency: 100 cents = 1 Estonian kroon (EEK)
Official Language: Estonian
Other Languages: Russian, Ukrainian, English
Main Religion: Christianity 99%
Exports: Textiles, food, machinery, timber

LATVIA

Pronunciation: LAT-vee-uh
Area: 24,938 sq. miles (64,589 sq. km)
Population: 2,366,515
Capital: Riga
Currency: 100 santims = 1 Latvian lat (LVL)
Official Language: Latvian (Lettish)
Other Languages: Lithuanian, Russian
Main Religion: Christianity 100%
Exports: Timber, metals, dairy products, furniture, textiles, machinery and equipment

LITHUANIA

Pronunciation: li-thuh-WAY-nee-uh
Area: 25,174 sq. miles (65,201 sq. km)
Population: 3,601,138
Capital: Vilnius
Currency: 100 centas = 1 Lithuan litas (LTL)
Official Language: Lithuanian
Other Languages: Polish, Russian
Main Religion: Christianity 98%
Exports: Machinery, minerals, chemicals, textiles and clothing, food

BELARUS

Pronunciation: be-luh-ROOS
Area: 80,154 sq. miles (207,599 sq. km)
Population: 10,335,382
Capital: Minsk
Currency: Belarusian rubel (BYR)
Official Language: Belarusian
Other Language: Russian
Main Religion: Christianity 80%
Exports: Machinery and equipment, chemicals, food, metals, textiles

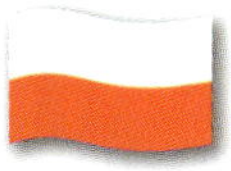

POLAND

Pronunciation: POH-luhnd
Area: 120,756 sq. miles (312,758 sq. km)
Population: 38,625,478
Capital: Warsaw
Currency: 100 groszy = 1 zloty (PLN)
Official Language: Polish
Main Religion: Christianity 95%
Exports: Machinery and transportation equipment, manufactured goods, food and livestock, fuels

CZECH REPUBLIC

Pronunciation: chek ri-PUH-blik
Area: 30,450 sq. miles (78,866 sq. km)
Population: 10,256,760
Capital: Prague
Currency: 100 haleru = 1 Czech koruna (CZK)
Official Language: Czech
Main Religion: Christianity 47%
Exports: Manufactured goods, raw materials and fuels, machinery and transportation equipment, chemicals, agricultural products

SLOVAKIA

Pronunciation: sloh-VAH-kee-uh
Area: 18,923 sq. miles (49,011 sq. km)
Population: 5,422,366
Capital: Bratislava
Currency: 100 halierov = 1 Slovak koruna (SKK)
Official Language: Slovak
Other Language: Hungarian
Main Religion: Christianity 73%
Exports: Machinery and transportation equipment, chemicals, minerals and metals, manufactured goods, agricultural products

UKRAINE

Pronunciation: yoo-KRAYN
Area: 233,089 sq. miles (603,701 sq. km)
Population: 48,396,470
Capital: Kiev
Currency: 100 kopiykas = 1 hryvnia (UAH)
Official Language: Ukrainian
Other Languages: Russian, Romanian, Polish, Hungarian
Main Religions: Christianity 90%, Judaism 2%
Exports: Metals, chemicals, machinery and transportation equipment, grain, meat, fuel and petroleum products

HUNGARY

Pronunciation: HUHNG-uh-ree
Area: 35,919 sq. miles (93,030 sq. km)
Population: 10,075,034
Capital: Budapest
Currency: 100 filler = 1 forint (HUF)
Official Language: Hungarian
Main Religion: Christianity 93%
Exports: Raw materials, machinery and transportation equipment, manufactured goods, food products, agriculture, fuels, energy

MOLDOVA

Pronunciation: mawl-DOH-vuh
Area: 13,012 sq. miles (33,701 sq. km)
Population: 4,434,547
Capital: Chişinău
Currency: Moldovan Leu (MDL)
Official Language: Moldovan
Other Languages: Russian, Gagauz
Main Religions: Christianity 98%, Judaism 2%
Exports: Food, wine, tobacco, textiles, footwear, machinery, chemicals

ICELAND

Pronunciation: EYES-luhnd
Area: 39,702 sq. miles (102,828 sq. km)
Population: 279,384
Capital: Reykjavík
Currency: 100 aurar = 1 Icelandic krona (ISK)
Official Language: Icelandic
Main Religion: Christianity 99%
Exports: Fish and fish products, animal products, minerals

NORWAY

Pronunciation: NOR-way
Area: 125,181 sq. miles (324,220 sq. km)
Population: 4,525,116
Capital: Oslo
Currency: 100 oere = 1 Norwegian krone (NOK)
Official Language: Norwegian
Other Languages: Finnish, Sami
Main Religion: Christianity 89%
Exports: Petroleum and petroleum products, metals, fish and fish products, chemicals, ships, machinery and equipment, natural gas

Territories and dependencies

Bouvet Island: South Atlantic Ocean; 22.6 sq. miles (58.5 sq. km); no permanent population
Jan Mayen Island: North Atlantic Ocean; 144 sq. miles (373 sq. km); no permanent population
Svalbard: Arctic Ocean; 23,958 sq. miles (62,052 sq. km); population 2,868

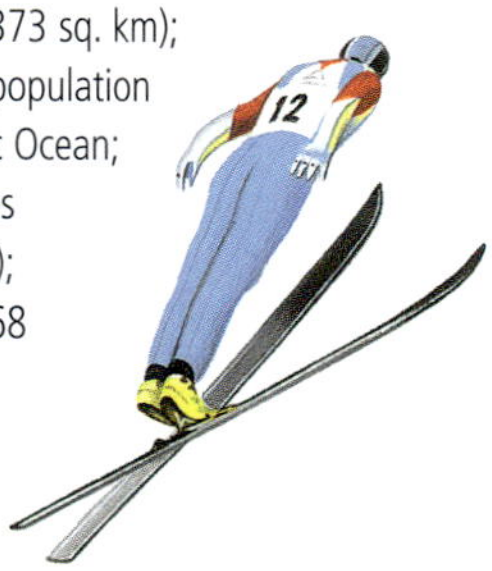

SWEDEN

Pronunciation: SWEE-duhn
Area: 173,665 sq. miles (449,792 sq. km)
Population: 8,912,000
Capital: Stockholm
Currency: 100 oere = 1 Swedish krona (SEK)
Official Language: Swedish
Other Languages: Finnish, Sami
Main Religion: Christianity 96%
Exports: Machinery, motor vehicles, paper products, pulp and wood, iron and steel products, chemicals, petroleum products

FINLAND

Pronunciation: FIN-luhnd
Area: 130,128 sq. miles (337,032 sq. km)
Population: 5,183,545
Capital: Helsinki
Currency: 100 cents = 1 euro (EUR)
Official Languages: Finnish, Swedish
Other Languages: Sami, Russian
Main Religion: Christianity 90%
Exports: Paper and pulp, machinery and equipment, chemicals, metals, timber

DENMARK

Pronunciation: DEN-mark
Area: 16,629 sq. miles (43,069 sq. km)
Population: 5,368,854
Capital: Copenhagen
Currency: 100 ore = 1 Danish krone (DKK)
Official Language: Danish
Other Languages: Faroese, Greenlandic, German
Main Religion: Christianity 98%
Exports: Meat and meat products, dairy products, ships, fish, chemicals, machinery and instruments, furniture, windmills

Territories and dependencies

Faroe Islands: North Atlantic Ocean; 540 sq. miles (1,399 sq. km); population 46,011
Greenland: North Atlantic Ocean; 836,326 sq. miles (2,166,086 sq. km); population 59,900

ASIA

RUSSIA

Pronunciation: RUH-shuh
Area: 6,592,812 sq. miles (17,075,383 sq. km)
Population: 144,978,573
Capital: Moscow
Currency: 100 kopecks = 1 Russian ruble (RUR)
Official Language: Russian
Main Religions: Christianity 75%, Islam, Buddhism
Exports: Petroleum and petroleum products, natural gas, timber and timber products, metals, chemicals, manufactured goods

TURKEY

Pronunciation: TER-kee
Area: 301,380 sq. miles (780,574 sq. km)
Population: 67,308,928
Capital: Ankara
Currency: 100 kurus = 1 Turkish lira (TRL)
Official Language: Turkish
Other Languages: Kurdish, Arabic, Armenian
Main Religion: Islam 99%
Exports: Manufactured goods, food, textiles and clothing, transport equipment

CYPRUS

Pronunciation: SEYE-pruhs
Area: 3,572 sq. miles (9,251 sq. km)
Population: 767,314
Capital: Nicosia
Currency: 100 cents = 1 Cypriot pound (CYP); 100 kurus = 1 Turkish lira (TRL)
Official Languages: Greek, Turkish
Other Language: English
Main Religions: Christianity 78%, Islam 18%
Exports: Citrus fruit, potatoes, grapes, wine, cement, textiles and clothing, shoes

GEORGIA

Pronunciation: JOR-juh
Area: 26,911 sq. miles (69,699 sq. km)
Population: 4,960,951
Capital: T'bilisi
Currency: 100 tetri = 1 lari (GEL)
Official Language: Georgian
Other Languages: Russian, Armenian, Azeri
Main Religions: Christianity 83%, Islam 11%
Exports: Citrus fruit, tea, wine, machinery, metals, textiles, chemicals, fuel re-exports

ARMENIA

Pronunciation: ar-MEE-nee-uh
Area: 11,506 sq. miles (29,800 sq. km)
Population: 3,330,099
Capital: Yerevan
Currency: 100 luma = 1 dram (AMD)
Official Language: Armenian
Other Languages: Russian, Azeri
Main Religion: Christianity 94%
Exports: Diamonds, scrap metal, machinery and equipment, brandy, copper ore

AZERBAIJAN

Pronunciation: a-zuhr-beye-ZHAHN
Area: 33,436 sq. miles (86,599 sq. km)
Population: 7,798,497
Capital: Baku
Currency: 100 gopiks = 1 Azerbaijani manat (AZM)
Official Language: Azerbaijani
Other Languages: Russian, Armenian
Main Religions: Islam 94%, Christianity 5%
Exports: Oil, gas, chemicals, oil field equipment, textiles, cotton, foodstuffs

KAZAKSTAN

Pronunciation: kuh-zahk-STAHN
Area: 1,049,150 sq. miles (2,717,300 sq. km)
Population: 16,741,519
Capital: Astana
Currency: 100 tiyn = 1 tenge (KZT)
Official Languages: Kazak, Russian
Main Religions: Islam 47%, Christianity 46%
Exports: Oil, metals, chemicals, grain, wool, cotton, machinery, ferrous and non-ferrous metals, meat and livestock, coal

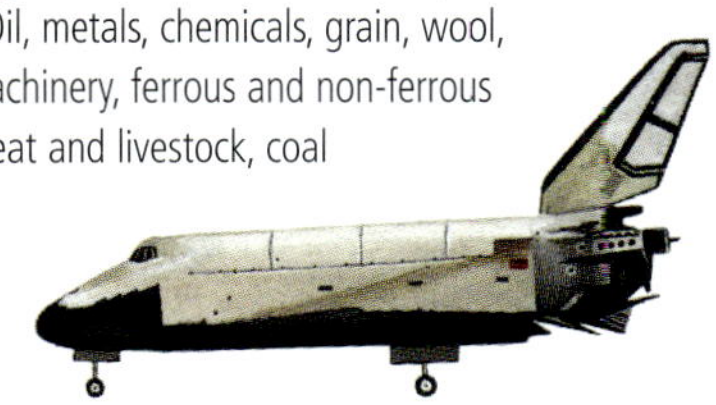

UZBEKISTAN

Pronunciation: uz-be-ki-STAN
Area: 172,741 sq. miles (447,400 sq. km)
Population: 25,563,441
Capital: Tashkent
Currency: Uzbekistani Sum (UZS)
Official Language: Uzbek
Other Languages: Russian, Tajik
Main Religions: Islam 88%, Christianity 9%
Exports: Cotton, gold, natural gas, mineral fertilizer, metals, textiles, food, automobiles

TURKMENISTAN

Pronunciation: terk-me-nuh-STAN
Area: 188,455 sq. miles (488,098 sq. km)
Population: 4,688,963
Capital: Ashkhabad
Currency: 100 tenesi = 1 Turkmen manat (TMM)
Official Language: Turkmen
Other Languages: Russian, Uzbek
Main Religions: Islam 89%, Christianity 9%
Exports: Natural gas, cotton, petroleum products, textiles, carpets

KYRGYZSTAN

Pronunciation: kihr-gi-STAN
Area: 76,641 sq. miles (198,500 sq. km)
Population: 4,822,166
Capital: Bishkek
Currency: 100 tyiyn = 1 Kyrgyzstani som (KGS)
Official Languages: Kyrgyz (Kirghiz), Russian
Main Religions: Islam 75%, Christianity 20%
Exports: Wool, chemicals, cotton, metals, shoes, machinery, tobacco, potatoes, fruits, vegetables, sheep, goats, cattle

TAJIKISTAN

Pronunciation: tah-ji-ki-STAN
Area: 55,251 sq. miles (143,100 sq. km)
Population: 6,719,567
Capital: Dushanbe
Currency: 100 diram = 1 somoni (TJS)
Official Language: Tajik
Other Language: Russian
Main Religion: Islam 85%
Exports: Cotton, aluminum, fruits, vegetable oil, textiles, electricity

SYRIA

Pronunciation: SIHR-ee-uh
Area: 71,498 sq. miles (185,180 sq. km)
Population: 17,155,814
Capital: Damascus
Currency: 100 piastres = 1 Syrian pound (SYP)
Official Language: Arabic
Other Languages: Kurdish, Armenian, Aramaic, Circassian, French, English
Main Religions: Islam 90%, Christianity 10%
Exports: Petroleum, textiles, raw cotton, fruit and vegetables, live sheep, phosphates

IRAQ

Pronunciation: i-RAHK
Area: 168,927 sq. miles (437,521 sq. km)
Population: 24,001,816
Capital: Baghdad
Currency: 1,000 fils = 1 Iraqi dinar (IQD)
Official Languages: Arabic, Kurdish (in Kurdish regions)
Other Languages: Assyrian, Armenian
Main Religions: Islam 97%, Christianity 3%
Exports: Crude oil and refined products, fertilizer, sulfur

IRAN

Pronunciation: i-RAHN
Area: 635,932 sq. miles (1,647,064 sq. km)
Population: 66,622,704
Capital: Tehran
Currency: 100 dinars = 1 Iranian rial (IRR)
Official Language: Farsi (Persian)
Other Languages: Turkic, Kurdish, Luri
Main Religion: Islam 99%
Exports: Petroleum, carpets, fruit, nuts, iron and steel, chemicals

LEBANON

Pronunciation: LE-buh-nuhn
Area: 3,949 sq. miles (10,228 sq. km)
Population: 3,677,780
Capital: Beirut
Currency: 100 piastres = 1 Lebanese pound (LBP)
Official Language: Arabic
Other Languages: Armenian, English, French
Main Religions: Islam 70%, Christianity 30%
Exports: Agricultural products, chemicals, paper, textiles, metals, jewelry, electrical products

ISRAEL

Pronunciation: IZ-ray-uhl
Area: 7,992 sq. miles (20,699 sq. km)
Population: 6,029,529
Capital: Jerusalem
Currency: 100 new agorot = 1 new Israeli shekel (ILS)
Official Languages: Hebrew, Arabic
Other Language: English
Main Religions: Judaism 80%, Islam 15%, Christianity 2%
Exports: Machinery, cut diamonds, chemicals, textiles, agricultural products, metals, software

JORDAN

Pronunciation: JOR-duhn
Area: 35,637 sq. miles (92,300 sq. km)
Population: 5,307,470
Capital: Amman
Currency: 1,000 fils = 1 Jordanian dinar (JOD)
Official Language: Arabic
Other Language: English
Main Religions: Islam 92%, Christianity 6%
Exports: Phosphates, fertilizer, agricultural products, potash, manufactured goods

SAUDI ARABIA

Pronunciation: SOW-dee uh-RAY-bee-uh
Area: 756,981 sq. miles (1,960,582 sq. km)
Population: 23,513,330
Capital: Riyadh
Currency: 100 halalas = 1 Saudi riyal (SAR)
Official Language: Arabic
Main Religion: Islam 100%
Exports: Petroleum and petroleum products

KUWAIT

Pronunciation: koo-WAYT
Area: 6,880 sq. miles (17,819 sq. km)
Population: 2,111,561
Capital: Kuwait
Currency: 1,000 fils = 1 Kuwaiti dinar (KD)
Official Language: Arabic
Other Language: English
Main Religions: Islam 85%, Christianity 8%, Hinduism and Zoroastrianism 2%
Exports: Oil and refined products, fertilizers

BAHRAIN

Pronunciation: bah-RAYN
Area: 255 sq. miles (661 sq. km)
Population: 656,397
Capital: Manama
Currency: 1,000 fils = 1 Bahraini dinar (BHD)
Official Language: Arabic
Other Languages: English, Farsi, Urdu
Main Religion: Islam 100%
Exports: Petroleum and petroleum products, aluminum

QATAR

Pronunciation: KAH-tuhr
Area: 4,400 sq. miles (11,395 sq. km)
Population: 793,341
Capital: Doha
Currency: 100 dirhams = 1 Qatari rial (QAR)
Official Language: Arabic
Other Language: English
Main Religion: Islam 95%
Exports: Petroleum products, steel, fertilizer

UNITED ARAB EMIRATES

Pronunciation: yoo-NEYE-tuhd a-ruhb EM-uh-ruhts
Area: 32,000 sq. miles (82,880 sq. km)
Population: 2,445,989
Capital: Abu Dhabi
Currency: 100 fils = 1 Emirati dirham (AED)
Official Language: Arabic
Other Languages: Persian, English, Hindi, Urdu
Main Religion: Islam 96%
Exports: Crude oil, natural gas, dried fish, dates

OMAN

Pronunciation: oh-MAHN
Area: 82,000 sq. miles (212,380 sq. km)
Population: 2,713,462
Capital: Muscat
Currency: 1,000 baiza = 1 Omani rial (OMR)
Official Language: Arabic
Other Languages: English, Baluchi, Urdu, Indian languages
Main Religions: Islam 86%, Hinduism 13%
Exports: Petroleum, fish, metals, textiles

YEMEN

Pronunciation: YE-muhn
Area: 203,849 sq. miles (527,969 sq. km)
Population: 18,701,257
Capital: Sanaa
Currency: 100 fils = 1 Yemeni rial (YER)
Official Language: Arabic
Main Religion: Islam 99%
Exports: Crude oil, cotton, coffee, animal skins, vegetables, dried and salted fish

AFGHANISTAN

Pronunciation: af-GA-nuh-stan
Area: 250,775 sq. miles (649,507 sq. km)
Population: 27,755,775
Capital: Kabul
Currency: 100 puls = 1 afghani (AFA)
Official Languages: Afghan, Persian (Dari), Pashtu
Other Languages: Uzbek, Turkmen, Balochi
Main Religions: Islam 99%, Hinduism and Judaism 1%
Exports: Opium, fruit, nuts, handwoven carpets, wool, cotton, animal skins, precious and semiprecious gemstones

PAKISTAN

Pronunciation: pa-ki-STAN
Area: 310,403 sq. miles (803,944 sq. km)
Population: 147,663,429
Capital: Islamabad
Currency: 100 paisa = 1 Pakistani rupee (PKR)
Official Languages: Urdu, English
Other Languages: Punjabi, Sindhi, Siraiki Pashtu, Balochi, Hindko
Main Religion: Islam 97%
Exports: Cotton, textiles, clothing, rice, yarn, leather, carpets, agricultural products

INDIA

Pronunciation: IN-dee-uh
Area: 1,269,338 sq. miles (3,287,590 sq. km)
Population: 1,045,845,226
Capital: New Delhi
Currency: 100 paise = 1 Indian rupee (INR)
Official Languages: Hindi, English, Bengali, Telugu, Marathi, Tamil, Urdu, Gujarati, Malayalam, Kannada, Oriya, Punjabi, Assamese, Kashmiri, Sindhi, Sanskrit
Other Languages: Hindustani, Rajasthani
Main Religions: Hinduism 81%, Islam 12%, Christianity 2%, Sikh 2%
Exports: Clothing and textiles, engineering equipment, gemstones and jewelry, chemicals, leather goods, cotton yarn, fabric

NEPAL

Pronunciation: nuh-PAHL
Area: 54,362 sq. miles (140,798 sq. km)
Population: 25,873,917
Capital: Kathmandu
Currency: 100 paisa = 1 Nepalese rupee (NPR)
Official Language: Nepali
Main Religions: Hinduism 86%, Buddhism 8%, Islam 4%
Exports: Carpets, clothing, leather goods, jute goods, grain

BHUTAN

Pronunciation: boo-TAHN
Area: 18,147 sq. miles (47,000 sq. km)
Population: 2,094,176
Capital: Thimphu
Currency: 100 chetrums = 1 ngultrum (BTN); 100 paise = 1 Indian rupee (INR)
Official Language: Dzongkha
Other Languages: Tibetan and Nepali
Main Religions: Buddhism 75%, Hinduism 25%
Exports: Timber, handicrafts, cement, fruit, electricity, gemstones, spices, gypsum

BANGLADESH

Pronunciation: bahng-gluh-DESH
Area: 55,598 sq. miles (144,000 sq. km)
Population: 133,376,684
Capital: Dhaka
Currency: 100 paisa = 1 taka (BDT)
Official Language: Bengali (Bangla)
Other Language: English
Main Religions: Islam 83%, Hinduism 16%
Exports: Clothing and textiles, jute and jute goods, leather, frozen fish and seafood, agricultural products

MALDIVES

Pronunciation: MAWL-deevz
Area: 115 sq. miles (298 sq. km)
Population: 320,165
Capital: Male
Currency: 100 laari = 1 rufiyaa (MVR)
Official Language: Maldivian Dhivehi
Other Language: English
Main Religion: Islam 100%
Exports: Fish, clothing

SRI LANKA

Pronunciation: sree LAHNG-kuh
Area: 25,332 sq. miles (65,610 sq. km)
Population: 19,576,783
Capital: Colombo
Currency: 100 cents = 1 Sri Lankan rupee (LKR)
Official Languages: Sinhala, Tamil
Other Language: English
Main Religions: Buddhism 70%, Hinduism 15%, Christianity 8%, Islam 7%
Exports: Textiles, tea, diamonds and other precious gemstones, petroleum products, rubber products, agricultural products, marine products

MYANMAR (BURMA)

Pronunciation: MYAHN-mar (BER-muh)
Area: 261,789 sq. miles (678,034 sq. km)
Population: 42,238,224
Capital: Yangon (Rangoon)
Currency: 100 pyas = 1 kyat (MMK)
Official Language: Burmese
Other Languages: regional languages
Main Religions: Buddhism 89%, Christianity 4%, Islam 4%, animism 1%
Exports: Clothing, foodstuffs, rice, precious stones, timber

LAOS

Pronunciation: lows
Area: 91,428 sq. miles (236,799 sq. km)
Population: 5,777,180
Capital: Vientiane
Currency: 100 at = 1 kip (LAK)
Official Language: Lao
Other Languages: French, English, regional languages
Main Religions: Buddhism 60%, animism 34%, Christianity 2%
Exports: Electricity, timber products, coffee, tin, textiles and clothing

VIETNAM

Pronunciation: vee-et-NAHM
Area: 127,243 sq. miles (329,560 sq. km)
Population: 81,098,416
Capital: Hanoi
Currency: 100 xu = 1 new dong (VND)
Official Language: Vietnamese
Other Languages: French, Chinese languages, English, Khmer, tribal languages
Main Religions: Buddhism 55%, Christianity 7%, Daoism (Taoism), indigenous religions, Islam
Exports: Crude oil, rice, clothing and footwear, rubber, tea, coffee marine products

THAILAND

Pronunciation: TEYE-land
Area: 198,455 sq. miles (513,998 sq. km)
Population: 62,354,402
Capital: Bangkok
Currency: 100 satang = 1 baht (THB)
Official Language: Thai
Other Languages: English, Chinese languages, Malay, regional languages
Main Religions: Buddhism 95%, Islam 4%
Exports: Computers and parts, textiles, integrated circuits, rice

CAMBODIA

Pronunciation: kam-BOH-dee-uh
Area: 69,898 sq. miles (181,036 sq. km)
Population: 12,775,324
Capital: Phnom Penh
Currency: 100 sen = 1 new riel (KHR)
Official Language: Khmer
Other Languages: French, English
Main Religions: Buddhism 95%, Islam 2%
Exports: Timber, rubber, clothing, rice, fish

MALAYSIA

Pronunciation: muh-LAY-zhuh
Area: 127,316 sq. miles (329,750 sq. km)
Population: 22,662,365
Capital: Kuala Lumpur
Currency: 100 sen = 1 ringgit (MYR)
Official Language: Malay (Bahasa Melayu)
Other Languages: English, Chinese languages, Tamil, Telugu, regional languages
Main Religions: Islam 53%, Buddhism 17%, Confucianism 12%, Christianity 9%, Hinduism 7%
Exports: Electronic equipment, petroleum, liquified natural gas, palm oil, timber and timber products, rubber, textiles

PHILIPPINES

Pronunciation: FI-luh-peenz
Area: 115,651 sq. miles (299,536 sq. km)
Population: 84,525,639
Capital: Manila
Currency: 100 centavos = 1 Philippine peso (PHP)
Official Languages: Filipino, English
Other Languages: Regional languages
Main Religions: Christianity 92%, Islam 5%, Buddhism 3%
Exports: Electronics, machinery and transport equipment, textiles, coconut products, copper, fish

SINGAPORE

Pronunciation: SING-uh-por
Area: 200 sq. miles (648 sq. km)
Population: 4,452,732
Capital: Singapore
Currency: 100 cents = 1 Singapore dollar (SGD)
Official Languages: Chinese, Malay, Tamil, English
Main Religions: Buddhism 28%, Islam 15%, Christianity 13%, Taoism 13%, Hinduism 5%
Exports: Computer equipment, chemicals, mineral fuels, telecommunications equipment

BRUNEI

Pronunciation: broo-NEYE
Area: 2,226 sq. miles (5,765 sq. km)
Population: 350,898
Capital: Bandar Seri Begawan
Currency: 100 cents = 1 Bruneian dollar (BND)
Official Language: Malay
Other Languages: English, Chinese languages
Main Religions: Islam 67%, Buddhist 13%, Christianity 10%, indigenous religions
Exports: Crude oil, liquefied natural gas, petroleum products

INDONESIA

Pronunciation: in-duh-NEE-zhuh
Area: 741,096 sq. miles (1,919,440 sq. km)
Population: 216,109,000
Capital: Jakarta
Currency: 100 sen = 1 Indonesian rupiah (IDR)
Official Language: Bahasa Indonesian
Other Languages: English, Dutch, Javanese, regional languages
Main Religions: Islam 88%, Christianity 8%, Hinduism 2%, Buddhism 1%
Exports: Manufactured goods, oil and gas, textiles, rubber, plywood

EAST TIMOR

Pronunciation: EEST TEE-mor
Area: 7,000 sq. miles (19,000 sq.km)
Population: 952,618
Capital: Dili
Currency: 100 cents = 1 United States dollar (USD)
Official Language: Tetum, Portuguese
Other Languages: Bahasa Indonesian, English
Main Religion: Christianity 93%, Islam 4%
Exports: Coffee, sandalwood, marble

CHINA

Pronunciation: CHEYE-nuh
Area: 3,705,386 sq. miles (9,596,960 sq. km)
Population: 1,284,303,705
Capital: Beijing
Currency: 10 jiao = 1 yuan (CNY)
Official Language: Mandarin
Other Languages: Cantonese, Shanghaiese, Fuzhou, Hokkien-Taiwanese, regional languages
Main Religions: Daoism (Taoism) 20%, Buddhism 6%, Islam 3%, Christianity 1%
Exports: Textiles and clothing, shoes, toys, machinery and equipment, mineral fuels

MONGOLIA

Pronunciation: mahn-GOHL-yuh
Area: 604,247 sq. miles (1,565,000 sq. km)
Population: 2,694,432
Capital: Ulaanbaatar
Currency: 100 mongos = 1 togrog/tugrik (MNT)
Official Language: Khalkha Mongol
Other Languages: Turkic, Russian, Chinese
Main Religions: Buddhism 95%, Islam 4%
Exports: Copper, livestock, animal products, cashmere, wool, animal skins, non-ferrous metals

NORTH KOREA

Pronunciation: north kuh-REE-uh
Area: 46,609 sq. miles (120,717 sq. km)
Population: 22,224,195
Capital: P'yŏngyang
Currency: 100 chon = 1 North Korean won (KPW)
Official Language: Korean
Main Religions: Chondogyo 14%, Buddhism 2%, Christianity 1%
Exports: Minerals, metal products, agricultural and fishery products, manufactured goods

SOUTH KOREA

Pronunciation: sowth kuh-REE-uh
Area: 38,022 sq. miles (98,477 sq. km)
Population: 48,324,000
Capital: Seoul
Currency: 100 chon = 1 South Korean won (KRW)
Official Language: Korean
Other Language: English
Main Religions: Christianity 49%, Buddhism 47%, Confucianism 3%
Exports: Electronic and electrical equipment, machinery, steel, motor vehicles, ships, textiles, clothing, shoes, fish

TAIWAN

Pronunciation: TEYE-wahn
Area: 13,887 sq. miles (35,967 sq. km)
Population: 22,548,009
Capital: Taipei
Currency: 100 cents = 1 New Taiwan dollar (NTD)
Official Language: Mandarin
Other Languages: Taiwanese, Hakka dialects
Main Religions: Buddhism 43%, Daoism (Taoism) 21%, Christianity 5%, Confucianism
Exports: Electrical machinery, electronic goods, textiles, metals, plastics, chemicals

JAPAN

Pronunciation: juh-PAN
Area: 145,882 sq. miles (377,835 sq. km)
Population: 126,974,628
Capital: Tokyo
Currency: 100 sen = 1 yen (JPY)
Official Language: Japanese
Main Religions: Shinto and Buddhism 84%, Christianity 1%
Exports: Machinery, motor vehicles, consumer electronics, chemicals, semiconductors

AFRICA

MOROCCO

Pronunciation: muh-RAH-koh
Area: 172,413 sq. miles (446,550 sq. km)
Population: 31,167,783
Capital: Rabat
Currency: 100 centimes = 1 Moroccan dirham (MAD)
Official Language: Arabic
Other Languages: French, Berber dialects
Main Religions: Islam 99%, Christianity 1%
Exports: Food, beverages, consumer goods, phosphates and fertilizers, minerals

ALGERIA

Pronunciation: al-JIHR-ee-uh
Area: 919,590 sq. miles (2,381,740 sq. km)
Population: 32,277,942
Capital: Algiers
Currency: 100 centimes = 1 Algerian dinar (DZD)
Official Language: Arabic
Other Languages: French, Berber dialects
Main Religions: Islam 99%, Christianity and Judaism 1%
Exports: Petroleum products, natural gas

TUNISIA

Pronunciation: too-NEE-zhuh
Area: 63,378 sq. miles (164,149 sq. km)
Population: 9,815,644
Capital: Tunis
Currency: 1,000 millimes = 1 Tunisian dinar (TND)
Official Language: Arabic
Other Language: French
Main Religions: Islam 98%, Christianity 1%, Judaism 1%
Exports: Agricultural products, chemicals, textiles, mechanical goods, phosphates

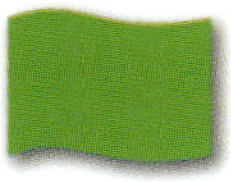

LIBYA

Pronunciation: LI-bee-uh
Area: 679,360 sq. miles (1,759,540 sq. km)
Population: 5,368,585
Capital: Tripoli
Currency: 1,000 dirhams = 1 Libyan dinar (LYD)
Official Language: Arabic
Other Languages: Italian, English
Main Religion: Islam 97%
Exports: Crude oil, refined petroleum products

CAPE VERDE ISLANDS

Pronunciation: kayp VAIRD islands
Area: 1,557 sq. miles (4,033 sq. km)
Population: 408,760
Capital: Praia
Currency: 100 centavos = 1 Cape Verdean escudo (CVE)
Official Language: Portuguese
Other Language: Cape Verde creole (Crioulo)
Main Religion: Christianity 97%
Exports: Fish, bananas, animal skins, clothing, fuel

EGYPT

Pronunciation: EE-juhpt
Area: 386,660 sq. miles (1,001,450 sq. km)
Population: 70,712,345
Capital: Cairo
Currency: 100 piasters = 1 Egyptian pound (EGP)
Official Language: Arabic
Other Languages: English, French
Main Religions: Islam 94%, Christianity 6%
Exports: Crude oil and petroleum products, cotton, textiles, metal products, chemicals

MAURITANIA

Pronunciation: maw-ruh-TAY-nee-uh
Area: 397,955 sq. miles (1,030,807 sq. km)
Population: 2,828,858
Capital: Nouakchott
Currency: 5 khoums = 1 ouguiya (MRO)
Official Languages: Hasaniya Arabic, Wolof
Other Languages: French, Pular, Soninke
Main Religion: Islam 100%
Exports: Iron ore, fish and fish products, gold

MALI

Pronunciation: MAH-lee
Area: 478,652 sq. miles (1,239,709 sq. km)
Population: 11,340,480
Capital: Bamako
Currency: 100 centimes = 1 CFA franc (XOF)
Official Language: French
Other Languages: Bambara, regional languages
Main Religions: Islam 90%, indigenous religions 9%, Christianity 1%
Exports: Cotton, livestock, gold

BURKINA FASO

Pronunciation: ber-KEE-nuh FAH-soh
Area: 105,869 sq. miles (274,201 sq. km)
Population: 12,603,185
Capital: Ouagadougou
Currency: 100 centimes = 1 CFA franc (XOF)
Official Language: French
Other Languages: Tribal languages
Main Religions: Islam 50%, indigenous religions 40%, Christianity 10%
Exports: Cotton, gold, animal products

NIGER

Pronunciation: NEYE-juhr
Area: 459,073 sq. miles (1,188,999 sq. km)
Population: 10,639,744

Capital: Niamey
Currency: 100 centimes = 1 CFA franc (XOF)
Official Language: French
Other Languages: Hausa, Djerma
Main Religions: Islam 80%, indigenous religions 14%, Christianity 1%
Exports: Uranium ore, livestock, cowpeas, onions

CHAD

Pronunciation: chad
Area: 495,752 sq. miles (1,283,998 sq. km)
Population: 8,997,237
Capital: N'Djamena
Currency: 100 centimes = 1 CFA franc (XOF)
Official Languages: French, Arabic
Other Languages: Sara, Sango, tribal languages
Main Religions: Islam 50%, Christianity 25%, indigenous religions and animism 25%
Exports: Cotton, cattle, textiles

SUDAN

Pronunciation: soo-DAN
Area: 967,500 sq. miles (2,505,825 sq. km)
Population: 37,090,298
Capital: Khartoum
Currency: 100 girsh = 1 Sudanese dinar (SDD)
Official Language: Arabic
Other Languages: Nubian, Ta Bedawie, Nilotic, Nilo-Hamitic, regional languages, English
Main Religions: Islam 70%, indigenous religions 25%, Christianity 5%
Exports: Oil, livestock, cotton, sesame, peanuts

ERITREA

Pronunciation: ehr-uh-TREE-uh
Area: 46,842 sq. miles (121,320 sq. km)
Population: 4,465,651
Capital: Asmara
Currency: 100 cents = 1 nafka (ERN)
Official Languages: Arabic, Tigrinya, Tigre
Other Languages: Regional languages
Main Religions: Islam 50%, Christianity 50%
Exports: Livestock, sorghum, textiles, food

ETHIOPIA

Pronunciation: ee-thee-OH-pee-uh
Area: 435,184 sq. miles (1,127,127 sq. km)
Population: 67,673,031
Capital: Addis Ababa
Currency: 100 cents = 1 birr (ETB)
Official Languages: Amharic, Tigrinya, Oromigna, Guiragigna, Somali
Other Languages: Arabic, English
Main Religions: Islam 45%, Christianity 35%, animism 12%
Exports: Coffee, leather products, gold, oilseeds, qat

DJIBOUTI

Pronunciation: ji-BOO-tee
Area: 8,494 sq. miles (22,000 sq. km)
Population: 472,810
Capital: Djibouti
Currency: 100 centimes = 1 Djiboutian franc (DJF)
Official Languages: French, Arabic
Other Languages: Somali, Afar
Main Religions: Islam 94%, Christianity 6%
Exports: Animal skins, coffee

SOMALIA

Pronunciation: soh-MAH-lee-uh
Area: 246,154 sq. miles (637,539 sq. km)
Population: 7,753,310
Capital: Mogadishu
Currency: 100 cents = 1 Somali shilling (SOS)
Official Language: Somali
Other Languages: Arabic, Italian, English
Main Religion: Islam 99%
Exports: Bananas, livestock, fish, animal skins

SENEGAL

Pronunciation: sen-i-GAWL
Area: 75,749 sq. miles (196,190 sq. km)
Population: 10,589,571
Capital: Dakar
Currency: 100 centimes = 1 CFA franc (XOF)
Official Language: French
Other Languages: Wolof, Pulaar, Jola, Mandinka
Main Religions: Islam 92%, indigenous religions 6%, Christianity 2%
Exports: Fish, peanuts, petroleum products, phosphates, cotton

GAMBIA

Pronunciation: GAM-bee-uh
Area: 4,363 sq. miles (11,300 sq. km)
Population: 1,455,842
Capital: Banjul
Currency: 100 bututs = 1 dalasi (GMD)
Official Language: English
Other Languages: Mandinka, Wolof, Fula
Main Religions: Islam 90%, Christianity 9%, indigenous religions 1%
Exports: Peanuts, fish, palm kernels, cotton lint

GUINEA-BISSAU

Pronunciation: gi-nee-bi-SOW
Area: 13,948 sq. miles (36,125 sq. km)
Population: 1,345,479
Capital: Bissau
Currency: 100 centimes = 1 CFA franc (XOF)
Official Language: Portuguese
Other Languages: Crioulo, tribal languages
Main Religions: Indigenous religions 50%, Islam 45%, Christianity 5%
Exports: Cashews, shrimp, palm kernels, peanuts, timber

GUINEA

Pronunciation: GI-nee
Area: 94,925 sq. miles (245,856 sq. km)
Population: 7,775,065
Capital: Conakry
Currency: 100 centimes = 1 Guinean franc (GNF)
Official Language: French
Other Languages: Tribal languages
Main Religions: Islam 85%, Christianity 8%, indigenous religions 7%
Exports: Bauxite, alumina, diamonds, gold, coffee, fish, agricultural products

SIERRA LEONE

Pronunciation: see-EHR-uh lee-OHN
Area: 27,699 sq. miles (71,740 sq. km)
Population: 5,614,743
Capital: Freetown
Currency: 100 cents = 1 leone (SLL)
Official Language: English
Other Languages: Mende, Temne, Krio
Main Religions: Islam 60%, indigenous religions 30%, Christianity 10%
Exports: Diamonds and other minerals, coffee, cocoa, fish

LIBERIA

Pronunciation: leye-BIHR-ee-uh
Area: 43,000 sq. miles (111,370 sq. km)
Population: 3,288,198
Capital: Monrovia
Currency: 100 cents = 1 Liberian dollar (LRD)
Official Language: English
Other Languages: Tribal languages
Main Religions: Indigenous religions 40%, Christianity 40%, Islam 20%
Exports: Iron ore, rubber, timber, coffee, diamonds

COTE D'IVOIRE (IVORY COAST)

Pronunciation: koht dee-VWAR
Area: 124,503 sq. miles (322,463 sq. km)
Population: 16,804,784
Capitals: Abidjan (seat of government), Yamoussoukro (official)
Currency: 100 centimes = 1 CFA franc (XOF)
Official Language: French
Other Languages: Regional languages
Main Religions: Christianity 34%, Islam 27%, animism 15%
Exports: Cocoa, coffee, timber, petroleum, cotton, bananas, pineapples, palm oil, fish

GHANA

Pronunciation: GAH-nuh
Area: 92,100 sq. miles (238,539 sq. km)
Population: 20,244,154
Capital: Accra
Currency: 100 pesewas = 1 new cedi (GHC)
Official Language: English
Other Languages: Regional languages
Main Religions: Indigenous religions 38%, Islam 30%, Christianity 24%
Exports: Cocoa, gold, timber, tuna, bauxite, aluminum, manganese ore, diamonds

TOGO

Pronunciation: TOH-goh
Area: 21,853 sq. miles (56,599 sq. km)
Population: 5,285,501
Capital: Lomé
Currency: 100 centimes = 1 CFA franc (XOF)
Official Language: French
Other Languages: Regional languages
Main Religions: Indigenous religions 59%, Christianity 29%, Islam 12%
Exports: Phosphates, cotton, cocoa, coffee

BENIN

Pronunciation: buh-NEEN
Area: 43,483 sq. miles (112,621 sq. km)
Population: 6,787,625
Capitals: Cotonou (seat of government), Porto-Novo (official)
Currency: 100 centimes = 1 CFA franc (XOF)
Official Language: French
Other Languages: Fon, Yoruba, tribal languages
Main Religions: Indigenous religions 50%, Islam 20%, Christianity 30%
Exports: Cotton, crude oil, palm products, cocoa

NIGERIA

Pronunciation: neye-JIHR-ee-uh
Area: 356,669 sq. miles (923,773 sq. km)
Population: 129,934,911
Capital: Abuja
Currency: 100 kobo = 1 naira (NGN)
Official Language: English
Other Languages: Regional languages
Main Religions: Islam 50%, Christianity 40%, indigenous religions 10%
Exports: Oil and petroluem products, cocoa, rubber

CAMEROON

Pronunciation: ka-muh-ROON
Area: 183,591 sq. miles (475,501 sq. km)
Population: 16,184,748
Capital: Yaoundé
Currency: 100 centimes = 1 CFA franc (XOF)
Official Languages: English, French
Other Languages: Regional languages
Main Religions: Indigenous religions 40%, Christianity 40%, Islam 20%
Exports: Crude oil, petroleum products, timber, cocoa beans, aluminum, coffee, cotton

EQUATORIAL GUINEA

Pronunciation: e-kwuh-TOR-ee-uhl GI-nee
Area: 10,825 sq. miles (28,037 sq. km)
Population: 498,144
Capital: Malabo
Currency: 100 centimes = 1 CFA franc (XOF)
Official Languages: Spanish, French
Other Languages: Pidgin English, Fang, Bubi, Ibo, other regional languages
Main Religion: Christianity 85%
Exports: Timber, cocoa, petroleum

CENTRAL AFRICAN REPUBLIC

Pronunciation: SEN-truhl AF-ri-kuhn ri-PUH-blik
Area: 240,534 sq. miles (622,984 sq. km)
Population: 3,642,739
Capital: Bangui
Currency: 100 centimes = 1 CFA franc (XOF)
Official Language: French
Other Languages: Sangho, Arabic, Hunsa, Swahili
Main Religions: Christianity 50%, indigenous religions 24%, Islam 15%
Exports: Diamonds, timber, cotton, coffee, tobacco

SAO TOME AND PRINCIPE

Pronunciation: SOW tuh-MAY and PRIN-suh-pee
Area: 372 sq. miles (963 sq. km)
Population: 170,372
Capital: São Tomé
Currency: 100 centimos = 1 dobra (STD)
Official Language: Portuguese
Main Religion: Christianity 80%
Exports: Cocoa, copra, coffee, palm oil

GABON

Pronunciation: ga-BOHN
Area: 103,346 sq. miles (267,667 sq. km)
Population: 1,233,353
Capital: Libreville
Currency: 100 centimes = 1 CFA franc (XOF)
Official Language: French
Other Languages: Regional languages
Main Religions: Christianity 60%, animism 40%, Islam 1%
Exports: Crude oil, timber, manganese, uranium

CONGO

Pronunciation: KAHN-goh
Area: 132,047 sq. miles (342,002 sq. km)
Population: 2,958,448
Capital: Brazzaville
Currency: 100 centimes = 1 CFA franc (XOF)
Official Language: French
Other Languages: Lingala, Monokutuba
Main Religions: Christianity 50%, animism 48%, Islam 2%
Exports: Petroleum, timber, sugar, cocoa, coffee, diamonds

DEMOCRATIC REPUBLIC OF THE CONGO (ZAIRE)

Pronunciation: de-muh-KRA-tik ri-PUH-blik of the KAHN-goh
Area: 905,356 sq. miles (2,344,872 sq. km)
Population: 55,225,478
Capital: Kinshasa
Currency: Congolese franc (CDF)
Official Language: French
Other Languages: Lingala, Kingwana, Kikongo, Tshiluba
Main Religions: Christianity 70%, Islam 10%, Kimbanguism 10%, indigenous beliefs 10%
Exports: Copper, coffee, diamonds, crude oil

UGANDA

Pronunciation: yoo-GAN-duh
Area: 91,134 sq. miles (236,037 sq. km)
Population: 24,699,073
Capital: Kampala
Currency: 100 cents = 1 Ugandan shilling (UGX)
Official Language: English
Other Languages: Ganda or Luganda, Swahili, other regional languages
Main Religions: Christianity 66%, indigenous religions 18%, Islam 16%
Exports: Coffee, cotton, tea, fish, iron and steel

KENYA

Pronunciation: KEN-yuh
Area: 224,960 sq. miles (582,646 sq. km)
Population: 31,138,735
Capital: Nairobi
Currency: 100 cents = 1 Kenyan shilling (KES)
Official Languages: English, Kiswahili
Other Languages: Regional languages
Main Religions: Christianity 66%, indigenous religions 26%, Islam 7%
Exports: Tea, coffee, petroleum products, fish

RWANDA

Pronunciation: ruh-WAHN-duh
Area: 10,169 sq. miles (26,338 sq. km)
Population: 7,398,074
Capital: Kigali
Currency: 100 centimes = 1 Rwandan franc (RWF)
Official Languages: Kinyarwanda, French, English
Other Language: Kiswahili
Main Religions: Christianity 87%, indigenous religions 7%, Islam 2%
Exports: Coffee, tea, animal skins, tin ore

BURUNDI

Pronunciation: boo-RUN-dee
Area: 10,759 sq. miles (27,866 sq. km)
Population: 6,373,002
Capital: Bujumbura
Currency: 100 centimes = 1 Burundi franc (BIF)
Official Languages: Kirundi, French
Other Language: Swahili
Main Religions: Christianity 67%, indigenous religions 23%, Islam 10%
Exports: Coffee, tea, cotton, animal skins, sugar

TANZANIA

Pronunciation: tan-zuh-NEE-uh
Area: 364,900 sq. miles (945,091 sq. km)
Population: 37,187,939
Capitals: Dar es Salaam (seat of government), Dodoma (official)
Currency: 100 cents = 1 Tanzanian shilling (TZS)
Official Languages: Swahili, English
Other Languages: Arabic, regional languages
Main Religions: Christianity 45%, Islam 35%, indigenous religions 20%
Exports: Coffee, cotton, tobacco, cashews, minerals

ANGOLA

Pronunciation: ang-GOH-luh
Area: 481,351 sq. miles (1,246,699 sq. km)
Population: 10,593,171
Capital: Luanda
Currency: 100 lwei = 1 kwanza (AOA)
Official Language: Portuguese
Other Languages: Bantu, other regional languages
Main Religions: Christianity 53%, indigenous religions 47%
Exports: Crude oil, diamonds, gas, refined petroleum products, coffee, sisal (fiber), fish and fish products, timber, cotton

ZAMBIA

Pronunciation: ZAM-bee-uh
Area: 290,585 sq. miles(752,615 sq. km)
Population: 9,959.037
Capital: Lusaka
Currency: 100 ngwee = 1 Zambian kwacha (ZMK)
Official Language: English
Other Languages: Regional languages
Main Religions: Christianity 62%, Islam and Hinduism 36%, indigenous religions 1%
Exports: Copper, cobalt, electricity, tobacco

ZIMBABWE

Pronunciation: zim-BAH-bway
Area: 150,820 sq. miles (390,624 sq. km)
Population: 11,376,676
Capital: Harare
Currency: 100 cents = 1 Zimbabwean dollar (ZWD)
Official Language: English
Other Languages: Shona, regional languages
Main Religions: Syncretic (part Christianity, part indigenous religions) 50%, Christianity 25%, indigenous religions 24%, Islam 1%
Exports: Tobacco, manufactured goods, metals, cotton, gold

MALAWI

Pronunciation: muh-LAH-wee
Area: 45,747 sq. miles (118,485 sq. km)
Population: 10,701,824
Capital: Lilongwe
Currency: 100 tambala = 1 Malawian kwacha (MWK)
Official Languages: English, Chichewa
Other Languages: Regional languages
Main Religions: Christianity 75%, Islam 20%, indigenous religions 5%
Exports: Tobacco, tea, sugar, cotton, coffee, peanuts, timber products

MOZAMBIQUE

Pronunciation: moh-zahm-BEEK
Area: 309,494 sq. miles (801,590 sq. km)
Population: 19,607,519
Capital: Maputo
Currency: 100 centavos = 1 metical (MZM)
Official Language: Portuguese
Other Languages: Regional languages
Main Religions: Indigenous religions 50%, Christianity 30%, Islam 20%
Exports: Shrimp, cashews, cotton, sugar, citrus fruit, timber, bulk electricity

NAMIBIA

Pronunciation: nuh-MI-bee-uh
Area: 318,694 sq. miles (825,418 sq. km)
Population: 1,820,916
Capital: Windhoek
Currency: 100 cents = 1 Namibian dollar (NAD); 100 cents = 1 rand (ZAR)
Official Language: English
Other Languages: Afrikaans, German, Herero, Oshivambo, Nama

Main Religions: Christianity 85%, indigenous religions 15%
Exports: Diamonds, metals, cattle, processed fish

BOTSWANA

Pronunciation: bawt-SWAH-nuh
Area: 231,803 sq. miles (600,370 sq. km)
Population: 1,591,232
Capital: Gaborone
Currency: 100 thebe = 1 pula (BWP)
Official Language: English
Other Language: Setswana
Main Religions: Indigenous religions 50%, Christianity 50%
Exports: Diamonds, copper and nickel, meat

SOUTH AFRICA

Pronunciation: sowth AF-ri-kuh
Area: 471,008 sq. miles (1,219,912 sq. km)
Population: 43,427,000
Capitals: Pretoria (administrative), Bloemfontein (judicial), Cape Town (legislative)
Currency: 100 cents = 1 rand (ZAR)
Official Languages: Afrikaans, English, Ndebele, Pedi, Sotho, Swazi, Tsonga, Tswana, Venda, Xhosa, Zulu
Main Religions: Christianity 68%, animism 29%, Islam 2%, Hinduism 1%
Exports: Gold, diamonds and other minerals and metals, machinery and equipment

SWAZILAND

Pronunciation: SWAH-zee-land
Area: 6,705 sq. miles (17,366 sq. km)
Population: 1,123,605
Capital: Lobamba (royal and legislative), Mbabane (official)
Currency: 100 cents = 1 lilangeni (SZL)
Official Languages: English, Swazi
Main Religions: Christianity 60%, indigenous religions 30%, Islam 10%
Exports: Sugar, wood pulp, cotton, refridgerators

LESOTHO

Pronunciation: luh-SOH-toh
Area: 11,716 sq. miles (30,344 sq. km)
Population: 2,207,954
Capital: Maseru
Currency: 100 licente = 1 loti (LSL)
Official Languages: English, Sesotho
Other Languages: Zulu, Xhosa
Main Religions: Christianity 80%, indigenous religions 20%
Exports: Wool, mohair, food and livestock, clothing, footwear, road vehicles

COMOROS

Pronunciation: KAH-muh-rohz
Area: 719 sq. miles (1,862 sq. km)
Population: 614,382
Capital: Moroni
Currency: 100 centimes = 1 Comoran franc (KMF)
Official Languages: Arabic, French
Other Language: Comoran
Main Religions: Islam 98%, Christianity 2%
Exports: Vanilla, cloves, perfume oil, copra

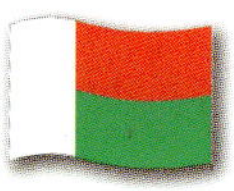

MADAGASCAR

Pronunciation: ma-duh-GAS-kuhr
Area: 226,657 sq. miles (587,042 sq. km)
Population: 16,473,477
Capital: Antananarivo
Currency: 100 centimes = 1 Malagasy franc (MGF)
Official Languages: French, Malagasy
Main Religions: Indigenous religions 52%, Christianity 41%, Islam 7%
Exports: Coffee, vanilla, shellfish, chromite, sugar, petroleum products, cotton cloth

SEYCHELLES

Pronunciation: say-SHELZ
Area: 176 sq. miles (455 sq. km)
Population: 80,098
Capital: Victoria
Currency: 100 cents = 1 Seychelles rupee (SCR)
Official Languages: English, French
Other Language: Seychelles creole
Main Religion: Christianity 98%
Exports: Fish, cinnamon bark, copra, petroleum products

MAURITIUS

Pronunciation: maw-RI-shuhs
Area: 720 sq. miles (1,865 sq. km)
Population: 1,200,206
Capital: Port Louis
Currency: 100 cents = 1 Mauritian rupee (MUR)
Official Language: English
Other Languages: Mauritian creole, French, Hindi, Urdu, Hakka, Bojpoori
Main Religions: Hinduism 52%, Christianity 28%, Islam 17%
Exports: Textiles and clothing, sugar, cut flowers, molasses

AUSTRALIA AND OCEANIA

AUSTRALIA

Pronunciation: aw-STRAYL-yuh
Area: 2,967,909 sq. miles (7,686,884 sq. km)
Population: 19,546,792
Capital: Canberra
Currency: 100 cents = 1 Australian dollar (AUD)
Official Language: English
Other Languages: Aboriginal languages
Main Religion: Christianity 76%
Exports: Coal, gold, meat, wool, wheat, alumina, iron ore, machinery and transportation equipment

Territories and dependencies

Christmas Island: Indian Ocean; 52 sq. miles (135 sq. km); population 474
Cocos (Keeling) Islands: Indian Ocean; 9 sq. miles (23 sq. km); population 632
Heard and McDonald Islands: Indian Ocean; 159 sq. miles (412 sq. km); no permanent population
Norfolk Island: South Pacific Ocean; 13 sq. miles (34 sq. km); population 1,866

PAPUA NEW GUINEA

Pronunciation: PA-pyoo-uh noo GI-nee
Area: 178,703 sq. miles (462,840 sq. km)
Population: 5,172,033
Capital: Port Moresby
Currency: 100 toea = 1 kina (PGK)
Official Languages: English, pidgin English, Motu
Other Languages: Regional languages
Main Religions: Christianity 66%, indigenous religions 34%
Exports: Gold, copper ore, oil, lumber, palm oil, coffee, cocoa, lobster, crayfish

NEW ZEALAND

Pronunciation: noo ZEE-luhnd
Area: 103,736 sq. miles (268,676 sq. km)
Population: 3,908,037
Capital: Wellington
Currency: 100 cents = 1 New Zealand dollar (NZD)
Official Languages: English, Maori
Main Religion: Christianity 67%
Exports: Wool, lamb, mutton, beef, fish, cheese, chemicals, forestry products, fruit and vegetables, manufactured goods

Territories and dependencies

Cook Islands: South Pacific Ocean; 92 sq. miles (238 sq. km); population 20,811
Niue: South Pacific Ocean; 100 sq. miles (259 sq. km); population 2,134
Tokelau: South Pacific Ocean; 4 sq. miles (10 sq. km); population 1,431

SOLOMON ISLANDS

Pronunciation: SAH-luh-muhn islands
Area: 10,985 sq. miles (28,450 sq. km)
Population: 494,786
Capital: Honiara
Currency: 100 cents = 1 Solomon Islands dollar (SBD)
Official Language: Melanesian pidgin
Other Languages: English, regional languages
Main Religions: Christianity 96%, indigenous religions 4%
Exports: Fish, timber, palm oil, cocoa, copra

SAMOA

Pronunciation: suh-MOH-uh
Area: 1,100 sq. miles (2,850 sq. km)
Population: 178,631
Capital: Apia
Currency: 100 sene = 1 tala (WST)
Official Languages: Samoan (Polynesian), English
Main Religion: Christianity 99%
Exports: Coconut oil and cream, taro, fish, beer, copra

VANUATU

Pronunciation: van-wah-TOO
Area: 4,710 sq. miles (12,200 sq. km)
Population: 196,178
Capital: Port-Vila
Currency: 100 centimes = 1 vatu (VUV)
Official Languages: English, French

Other Language: Bislama (pidgin)
Main Religions: Christianity 77%, indigenous religions 8%
Exports: Copra, kava, beef, cocoa, timber, coffee

FIJI

Pronunciation: FEE-jee
Area: 7,055 sq. miles (18,272 sq. km)
Population: 856,346
Capital: Suva
Currency: 100 cents = 1 Fijian dollar (FJD)
Official Language: English
Other Languages: Fijian, Hindustani
Main Religions: Christianity 52%, Hinduism 38%, Islam 8%
Exports: Sugar, clothing, gold, processed fish, timber

TONGA

Pronunciation: TAHNG-guh
Area: 270 sq. miles (699 sq. km)
Population: 106,137
Capital: Nuku'alofa
Currency: 100 seniti = 1 pa'anga (TOP)
Official Languages: Tongan, English
Main Religion: Christianity 70%
Exports: Squash, vanilla, fish, root crops, coconut oil

KIRIBATI

Pronunciation: kihr-uh-BAH-tee
Area: 277 sq. miles (717 sq. km)
Population: 96,335
Capital: Tarawa
Currency: 100 cents = 1 Australian dollar (AUD)
Official Language: English
Other Language: I-Kiribati
Main Religion: Christianity 94%
Exports: Copra, coconuts, seaweed, fish

MARSHALL ISLANDS

Pronunciation: MAR-shuhl islands
Area: 70 sq. miles (181 sq. km)
Population: 73,630
Capital: Majuro
Currency: 100 cents = 1 United States dollar (USD)
Official Language: English
Other Languages: Marshallese, Japanese
Main Religion: Christianity 98%
Exports: Coconut oil, fish, trochus shells

FEDERATED STATES OF MICRONESIA

Pronunciation: FE-der-ayt-ed STAYTS of meye-kruh-NEE-zhuh
Area: 266 sq. miles (689 sq. km)
Population: 135,869
Capital: Palikir
Currency: 100 cents = 1 United States dollar (USD)
Official Language: English
Other Languages: Regional languages
Main Religion: Christianity 97%
Exports: Fish, clothing, bananas, black pepper

NAURU

Pronunciation: nah-OO-roo
Area: 8.5 sq. miles (22 sq. km)
Population: 12,329
Capital: None. Government offices in Yaren district
Currency: 100 cents = 1 Australian dollar (AUD)
Official Language: Nauruan
Other Language: English
Main Religion: Christianity 100%
Export: Phosphates

PALAU

Pronunciation: puh-LOW
Area: 191 sq. miles (495 sq. km)
Population: 19,409
Capital: Koror
Currency: 100 cents = 1 United States dollar (USD)
Official Language: English
Other Languages: Palauan, Sonsorolese, Angaur, Japanese, Tobi
Main Religions: Christianity 67%, Modekngei religion 33%
Exports: Shellfish, tuna, trochus shells, copra

TUVALU

Pronunciation: too-VAH-loo
Area: 9 sq. miles (23 sq. km)
Population: 11,146
Capital: Funafuti
Currency: 100 cents = 1 Tuvaluan dollar (TVD); 100 cents = 1 Australian dollar (AUD)
Official Languages: Tuvaluan, English
Main Religions: Christianity 98%, Baha'i 1%
Exports: Copra

Astronomy Timeline

30,000 BC Lunar phases scratched on bone—the oldest astronomical record?

4000 BC Sumerians of Mesopotamia make the first records of Leo, Taurus, and Scorpius, the oldest constellations still used today.

600 BC Greek philosopher Thales probably knows the cause of solar and lunar eclipses.

525 BC Greek philosopher Pythagoras recognizes that Earth is round.

350 BC Greek philosopher Aristotle provides a scientific explanation of why Earth is round.

325 BC Greek mathematician Eudoxus explains celestial motions in terms of several crystal spheres with Earth at their center.

300 BC Greek astronomer Aristarchus proposes a Sun-centered model for the universe. But his ideas are ignored until Copernicus's time, almost 2,000 years later.

200 BC Greek astronomer Eratosthenes measures the circumference of Earth, getting a result close to the modern one.

150 BC Greek astronomer Hipparchus creates system of magnitudes to measure star brightness, discovers a slow wobble in Earth's axis (precession), and compiles the first star catalog.

AD 150 Greek astronomer Claudius Ptolemy publishes the *Almagest,* a detailed summing-up of all the ancient world's astronomical knowledge. It dominates the subject for more than 1,000 years.

AD 165 Chinese astronomers make the first accurately dated observations, recording sunspots on the face of the Sun.

AD 635 A Chinese scholar records the rule that a comet's tail always points away from the Sun.

1543 Nicolaus Copernicus publishes his book *On the Revolutions of the Celestial Spheres,* proposing a Sun-centered solar system.

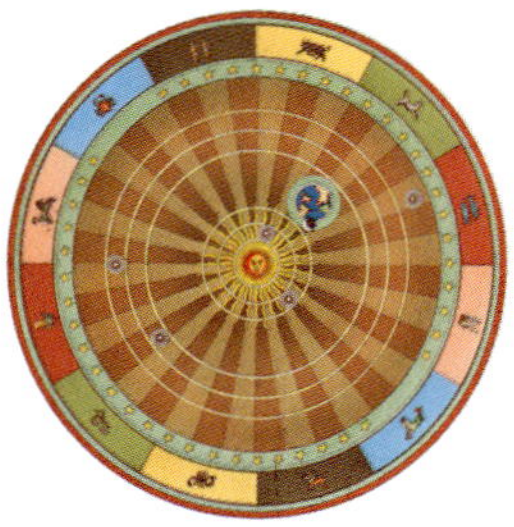

1572 Tycho Brahe sees a supernova in Cassiopeia and determines that it lies beyond the Moon. This discovery conflicts with ancient ideas of the heavens being unchangeable, and it encourages Tycho to make a whole new set of accurate observations.

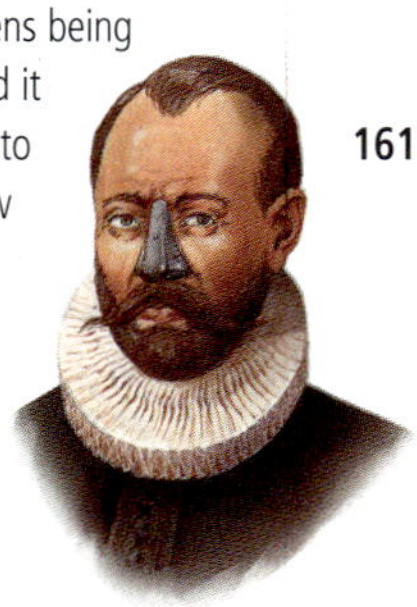

1576 Tycho builds his Uraniborg observatory on an island in the Baltic Sea and begins compiling the world's most accurate observations of the motions of stars and planets.

1600 Tycho Brahe hires Johannes Kepler as his mathematical assistant to work on the observations.

1608 Hans Lippershey in the Netherlands invents the telescope.

1609 Using Tycho Brahe's observations, Kepler determines that Mars's orbit is elliptical, a key advance over ancient astronomy, which had insisted on circular orbits. Galileo Galilei hears of the telescope and, following the reported description, builds his own. He is the first person to use the telescope for astronomy.

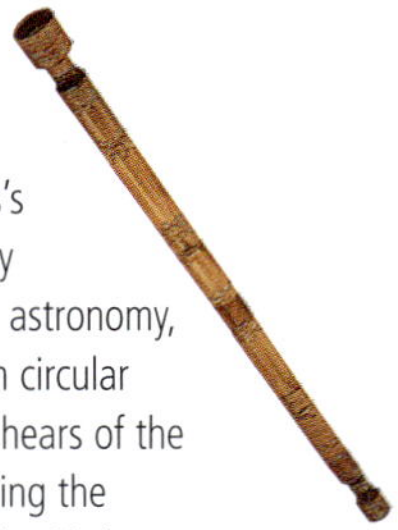

1610 Galileo publishes his telescope discoveries of moons orbiting Jupiter, craters on the Moon, and stars in the Milky Way. He starts promoting a Copernican model of the solar system.

1616 The Roman Catholic Church bans Copernican ideas as "false and absurd."

1619 Kepler discovers a simple mathematical relationship between the length of a planet's year and its distance from the Sun.

1633 Galileo is put under house arrest by the Church for promoting Copernican ideas.

1665 Isaac Newton starts developing mathematical physics.

1687 Newton publishes his book *The Mathematical Principles of Natural Philosophy,* which links astronomy with physics and puts both on firm mathematical ground.

1727 James Bradley discovers the aberration of starlight, an apparent shift in the positon of a star caused by the motion of Earth. It is the first physical proof that Earth moves around the Sun.

1758 Comet Halley returns as forecast by Edmond Halley, the first predicted return of a comet.

1781 William Herschel discovers seventh planet, Uranus. This is the first planet to be discovered since prehistoric times.

1833 A spectacular Leonid meteor shower shows astronomers that meteors come from space and do not originate in the atmosphere.

1835 The Roman Catholic Church removes books by Copernicus and Galileo from its list of banned works.

1838 Friedrich Bessel measures the parallax of 61 Cygni, the first direct measurement of a star's distance.

1846 Johann Galle and Heinrich d'Arrest find the eighth planet, Neptune, following predictions made by Urbain Leverrier (and, independently, by John C. Adams).

1860s The spectroscope begins to show astronomers what stars and nebulas are made of.

1880s Photography becomes an important tool for astronomy because it can detect things in the sky that people cannot see and it provides a permanent record.

1905 Albert Einstein's special theory of relativity is published.

1908 Ejnar Hertzsprung divides the population of stars into two groups, giants and dwarfs. It is the first step in learning how stars change as they age.

1910 The return of comet Halley creates the world's first media event.

1912 Henrietta Leavitt discovers that Cepheid variable stars with long periods of variation are systematically brighter than those with shorter periods.
Vesto Slipher discovers that most "spiral nebulas" are flying away from Earth, the first detection of an expanding universe.

1916 Einstein publishes his general theory of relativity, which predicts that the universe is expanding.

1917 100-inch (2.5-m) Hooker reflector telescope completed at Mount Wilson, California, USA.

1919 Einstein's general theory of relativity is confirmed by observations of a total solar eclipse seen from Brazil and West Africa.

1923 Edwin Hubble uses Cepheid variables to show that "spiral nebulas" are galaxies lying outside the Milky Way.

1929 Hubble presents observational evidence for an expanding universe and provides the first estimates of its age and rate of expansion.

1930 Clyde Tombaugh discovers the ninth planet, Pluto.

1931 Karl Jansky builds a rotating aerial and discovers radio waves coming from space. These radio waves had been predicted in the 1880s but were not found because astronomers had no way to detect them.

1937 Grote Reber discovers radio waves coming from the center of the Milky Way, using a radio telescope built in his own backyard.

1938 Hans Bethe publishes a theory explaining how the Sun and other stars shine because of nuclear reactions.

1942 John Hey and colleagues discover radio noise coming from the Sun.

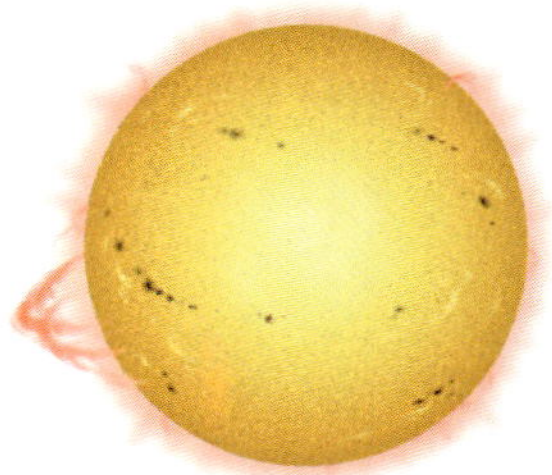

1946 Hey and colleagues identify the most powerful radio source in the sky, the radio galaxy Cygnus A.

1948 George Gamow, Ralph Alpher, and Robert Herman describe how chemical elements were formed in the Big Bang.

1948 200-inch (5-m) Hale Telescope is completed at Palomar Mountain, California, USA. Jan Oort proposes that comets come from a vast cloud orbiting far beyond Pluto.

1952 Walter Baade announces that galaxies are twice as far away as astronomers had previously assumed.

1957 Launch of Sputnik 1 satellite by the Soviet Union (now Russia) starts the Space Age.

1959 First photographs of the Moon's farside returned by Soviet probe, Luna 3.

1961 Yuri Gagarin from the Soviet Union is the first person to fly in space.

1962 Mariner 2 spacecraft flies past Venus, first probe to visit another planet, discovers dense atmosphere and verifies hot surface.
Orbiting Solar Observatory, the first astronomical satellite, is launched.

1963 Maarten Schmidt discovers that quasars are objects with big redshifts and must lie very far away.

1965 Arno Penzias and Robert Wilson discover the cosmic background radiation—the faded glow of the Big Bang explosion in which the universe began. Mariner 4 spacecraft is the first to fly past Mars. It discovers lots of craters.

1967 Jocelyn Bell-Burnell discovers pulsars, which are soon identified as neutron stars, one of the objects that massive stars can finish as.

1969 Apollo 11 astronauts Neil Armstrong and Edwin Aldrin make the first manned landing on the Moon.

1971 Mariner 9 is the first spacecraft to orbit another planet, Mars. Finds evidence of past water.

1973 Pioneer 10 makes first flyby of Jupiter and detects powerful radiation belts.

1974 Mariner 10 makes first two of three flybys of Mercury (third in 1975). Finds evidence of massive iron core and giant impacts.

1975 Venera 9 takes the first photos from the surface of Venus.

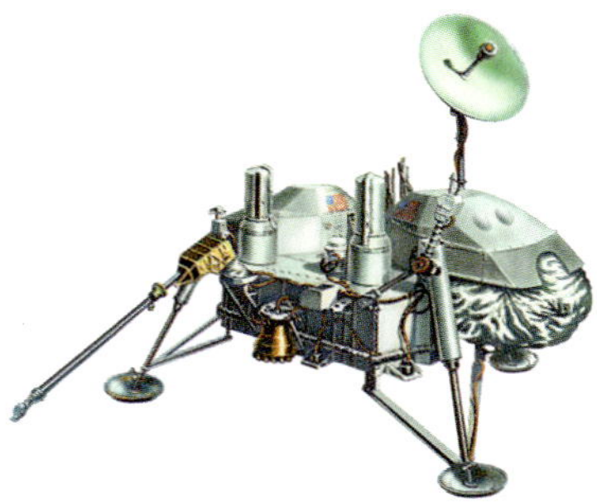

1976 Viking 1 and 2 land on Mars. They find no signs of life.

1977 Charles Kowal finds comet Chiron, the first in the outer solar system.

1977 Uranus's rings are discovered by astronomers aboard the Kuiper Airborne Observatory.

1978 James Christy discovers Charon, Pluto's moon.

1979 Voyager 1 and 2 spacecraft fly past Jupiter. Make detailed survey of planet and moons and find its rings. Pioneer 11 makes first flyby of Saturn.

1980 Alan Guth proposes a period of extremely fast expansion in the early history of the universe, which he calls cosmic inflation.
Voyager 1 spacecraft makes first detailed study of Saturn system.
Very Large Array radio telescope starts working in New Mexico, USA.

1983 Infrared Astronomical Satellite (IRAS) completes the first full survey of the infrared sky.

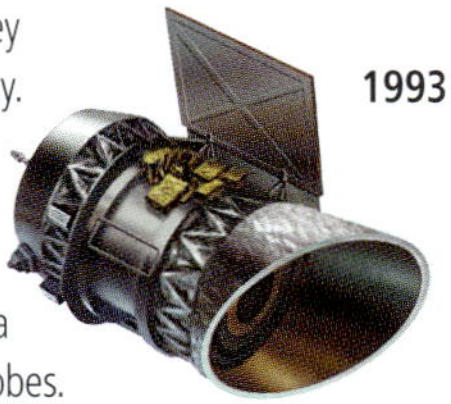

1985/6 Comet Halley's return is met by a fleet of space probes.

1986 Voyager 2 makes first flyby of Uranus.

1987 Supernova 1987A appears in the Large Magellanic Cloud.

1989 Voyager 2 spacecraft makes first flyby of Neptune. Captures details of the planet and its moons—and its rings, suspected to exist since 1981.
Margaret Geller and John Huchra announce evidence for walls and voids in the distribution of galaxies in the universe.

1990 Hubble Space Telescope is launched.

1991 Galileo spacecraft on the way to Jupiter makes first asteroid flyby, passing 951 Gaspra.
Compton Gamma-Ray Observatory begins survey of universe at high-energy wavelengths, seeking cause of mysterious bursts of high energy.

1992 COBE satellite observatory confirms predictions of Big Bang theory.

1993 First 394-inch (10-m) Keck telescope begins operation on Mauna Kea, Hawaii.
Hubble Space Telescope repaired and upgraded in orbit.

1994 Comet Shoemaker-Levy 9 crashes into Jupiter.

1995 Discovery of first planet to orbit ordinary star other than the Sun, orbiting 51 Pegasi.
Galileo spacecraft sends probe into Jupiter's atmosphere, begins tour of Jupiter's moons.

1996 Black hole confirmed at center of Milky Way galaxy.

1997 Burst of gamma rays tracked to source far from Milky Way, perhaps caused by colliding neutron stars.
Mars Pathfinder lands on Mars with Sojourner Rover.

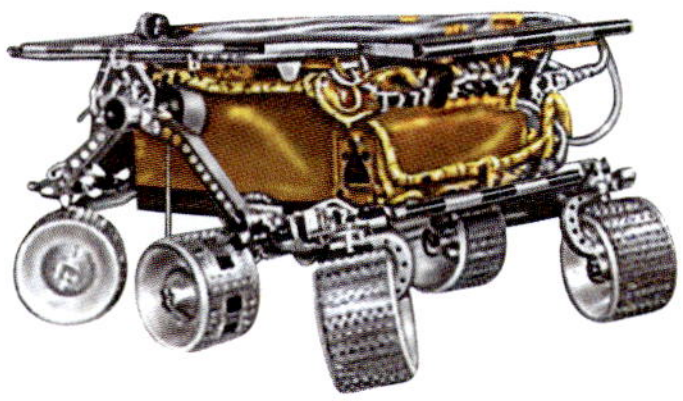

1999 Chandra X-Ray Observatory is launched to look for X-rays from distant objects.

Universe Fact File

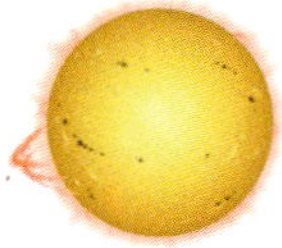

SUN

Apparent magnitude: –26.8
Absolute (actual) magnitude: 4.8
Rotation time: 25 Earth days at equator, 34 Earth days near poles
Diameter: 865,000 miles (1,392,000 km)
Mass: 332,946 x Earth's
Density: 1.4 x water's density
Surface gravity: 27.9 x Earth's
Composition: 92.1% hydrogen, 7.8% helium, 1% other elements
Surface temperature: 9,900°F (5,500°C)
Core temperature: 27,900,000°F (15,500,000°C)
Magnetic field strength: up to 10,000 x Earth's

MERCURY

When discovered: prehistoric
Who discovered it: unknown
How we can see it: naked eye
Apparent magnitude: –2 to +3
Distance from Sun: 0.4 AU, or 36 million miles (58 million km)
Length of year: 88 Earth days
Average speed: 30 miles per second (48 km/s)
Inclination of orbit: 7.0°
Eccentricity of orbit: 0.21
Tilt of axis: 0.5°
Rotation time: 59 Earth days
Solar day: 176 Earth days
Diameter: 3,029 miles (4,875 km)
Mass: 55% x Earth's
Density: 5.4 x water's density
Surface gravity: 0.38 x Earth's
Composition: iron and rock
Atmosphere: essentially none
Average temperature: –280°F to 800°F (–173°C to 427°C)
Magnetic field strength: 0.5% x Earth's
Number of moons: none
Number of rings: none
Number of probe visits: 1

VENUS

When discovered: prehistoric
Who discovered it: unknown
How we can see it: naked eye
Apparent magnitude: –4.0 to –4.6
Distance from Sun: 0.7 AU, or 67 million miles (108 million km)
Length of year: 225 Earth days
Average speed: 22 miles per second (35 km/s)
Inclination of orbit: 3.4°
Eccentricity of orbit: 0.01
Tilt of axis: 177.4°
Rotation time: 243 Earth days
Solar day: 117 Earth days
Diameter: 7,521 miles (12,104 km)
Mass: 82% x Earth's
Density: 5.2 x water's density
Surface gravity: 0.90 x Earth's
Composition: mostly rock
Atmosphere: 97% carbon dioxide, 3% nitrogen
Pressure of atmosphere: 96 x Earth's
Average temperature: 880°F (470°C)
Magnetic field strength: less than 0.05% x Earth's
Number of moons: none
Number of rings: none
Number of probe visits: 31

EARTH

When discovered: prehistoric
Who discovered it: unknown
Distance from Sun: 1.0 AU, or 93 million miles (150 million km)
Length of year: 365.25 days
Average speed: 18.5 miles per second (30 km/s)
Inclination of orbit: 0°
Eccentricity of orbit: 0.02
Tilt of axis: 23.5°
Rotation time: 23 hours 56 minutes
Solar day: 24 hours
Diameter: 7,926 miles (12,756 km)
Mass: 6×10^{24} tons (5.5×10^{24} tonnes)
Density: 5.5 x water's density
Composition: mostly rock
Atmosphere: 78% nitrogen, 21% oxygen, plus water, argon, carbon dioxide
Average temperature: 63°F (17°C)
Number of moons: 1
Number of rings: none

MARS

When discovered: prehistoric
Who discovered it: unknown
How we can see it: naked eye
Apparent magnitude: –2.6 to +1.8
Distance from Sun: 1.5 AU, or 142 million miles (228 million km)
Length of year: 687 Earth days
Average speed: 15 miles per second (24 km/s)
Inclination of orbit: 1.9°
Eccentricity of orbit: 0.09
Tilt of axis: 25.2°

Rotation time: 24 hours 37 minutes
Solar day: 24 hours 40 minutes
Diameter: 4,213 miles (6,780 km)
Mass: 64% x Earth's
Density: 3.9 x water's density
Surface gravity: 0.38 x Earth's
Composition: mostly rock
Atmosphere: 95% carbon dioxide, 2.7% nitrogen, 1.6% argon, plus others
Pressure of atmosphere: 0.6% x Earth's
Average temperature: –74°F (–59°C)
Magnetic field strength: less than 0.1% x Earth's
Number of moons: 2
Number of rings: none
Number of probe visits: 23

JUPITER

When discovered: prehistoric
Who discovered it: unknown
How we can see it: naked eye
Apparent magnitude: –2.5 to –1.2
Distance from Sun: 5.2 AU, or 483 million miles (778 million km)
Length of year: 11.9 Earth years
Average speed: 8 miles per second (13 km/s)
Inclination of orbit: 1.3°
Eccentricity of orbit: 0.05
Tilt of axis: 3.1°
Rotation time: 9 hours 55 minutes
Solar day: same as rotation time
Diameter: 88,846 miles (142,984 km)
Mass: 317.8 x Earth's
Density: 1.3 x water's density
Gravity at cloudtops: 2.6 x Earth's surface gravity
Composition: mostly gaseous
Atmosphere: 86% hydrogen, 13.6% helium, plus methane, ammonia, water
Average temperature at cloudtops: –162°F (–108°C)
Magnetic field strength: 7.1 x Earth's
Number of moons: 39
Number of rings: 3
Number of probe visits: 5

SATURN

When discovered: prehistoric
Who discovered it: unknown
How we can see it: naked eye
Apparent magnitude: 0.6 to 1.5
Distance from Sun: 9.6 AU, or 890 million miles (1,432 million km)
Length of year: 29.4 Earth years
Average speed: 6 miles per second (10 km/s)
Inclination of orbit: 2.5°
Eccentricity of orbit: 0.05
Tilt of axis: 26.7°
Rotation time: 10 hours 39 minutes
Solar day: same as rotation time
Diameter: 74,896 miles (120,533 km)
Mass: 95.2 x Earth's
Density: 0.7 x water's density
Gravity at cloudtops: 1.1 x Earth's surface gravity
Composition: mostly gaseous
Atmosphere: 96% hydrogen, 3.3% helium, plus methane, ammonia, and others
Average temperature at cloudtops: –218°F (–139°C)
Magnetic field strength: 0.34 x Earth's
Number of moons: at least 30
Number of rings: 7
Number of probe visits: 4

URANUS

When discovered: March 1781
Who discovered it: William Herschel
How we can see it: barely visible to the naked eye, but easy to see with a telescope
Apparent magnitude: 5.5 to 5.9
Distance from Sun: 19.2 AU, or 1,784 million miles (2,871 million km)
Length of year: 84.1 Earth years
Average speed: 4 miles per second (7 km/s)
Inclination of orbit: 0.8°
Eccentricity of orbit: 0.04
Tilt of axis: 97.9°
Rotation time: 17 hours 14 minutes
Solar day: same as rotation time
Diameter: 31,763 miles (51,118 km)
Mass: 14.5 x Earth's
Density: 1.3 x water's density
Gravity at cloudtops: 0.90 x Earth's surface gravity
Composition: mostly gaseous
Atmosphere: 83% hydrogen, 15% helium, 2% methane
Average temperature at cloudtops: –323°F (–197°C)
Magnetic field strength: 0.38 x Earth's
Number of moons: 21
Number of rings: 11
Number of probe visits: 1

NOTES ON PLANET FACTS

Apparent magnitude: How bright an object looks in the sky. Brighter objects have smaller numbers than dimmer ones.

Distance from Sun: The planet's average distance from the Sun.

Inclination of orbit: The angle of the planet's orbit relative to the plane of Earth's orbit.

Accentricity of orbit: How elliptical the planet's orbit is. The larger the number, the more elliptical the orbit is.

1 AU (astronomical unit): The average distance between Earth and the Sun, about 93 million miles (150 million km).

NEPTUNE

When discovered: September 1846
Who discovered it: Urbain Leverrier, John Couch Adams, Johann Galle, and Heinrich d'Arrest
How we can see it: telescope
Apparent magnitude: 7.9
Distance from Sun: 30.1 AU, or 2,795 million miles (4,498 million km)
Length of year: 164.9 Earth years
Average speed: 3.5 miles per second (5.5 km/s)
Inclination of orbit: 1.8°
Eccentricity of orbit: 0.01
Tilt of axis: 29.6°
Rotation time: 16 hours 7 minutes
Solar day: same as rotation time
Diameter: 30,775 miles (49,528 km)
Mass: 17.2 x Earth's
Density: 1.6 x water's density
Gravity at cloudtops: 1.1 x Earth's surface gravity
Composition: mostly gaseous
Atmosphere: 80% hydrogen, 19% helium, 1% methane
Average temperature at cloudtops: –330°F (–201°C)
Magnetic field strength: 22% x Earth's
Number of moons: 8
Number of rings: 6
Number of probe visits: 1

PLUTO

When discovered: February 1930
Who discovered it: Clyde Tombaugh
How we can see it: telescope
Apparent magnitude: 13.7
Distance from Sun: 39.5 AU, or 3,675 million miles (5,914 million km)
Length of year: 248 Earth years
Average speed: 3 miles per second (5 km/s)
Inclination of orbit: 17.1°
Eccentricity of orbit: 0.25
Tilt of axis: 122.5°
Rotation time: 6.4 Earth days
Solar day: same as rotation time
Diameter: 1,432 miles (2,304 km)
Mass: 0.2% x Earth's
Density: 2.1 x water's density
Surface gravity: 0.065 x Earth's
Composition: rock and ice
Atmosphere: methane, nitrogen
Pressure of atmosphere: about 3 millionths x Earth's
Average temperature: –387°F (–233°C)
Magnetic field strength: unknown
Number of moons: 1
Number of rings: none
Number of probe visits: none

COMET FACTS

NAME	FIRST RECORDED	FARTHEST FROM SUN	CLOSEST TO SUN	TYPE	ORBIT TIME	ORBIT INCLIN.	ORBIT ECCENT.
Encke	1786	4.1 AU	0.3 AU	short period	3.3 yrs	11.9°	0.85
Wirtanen	1954	5.1 AU	1.1 AU	short period	5.5 yrs	11.7°	0.65
Wild 2	1978	5.3 AU	1.6 AU	short period	6.4 yrs	3.2°	0.54
d'Arrest	1851	5.6 AU	1.4 AU	short period	6.5 yrs	19.5°	0.61
Tempel-Tuttle	1866	19.5 AU	1.0 AU	short period	32.9 yrs	163°	0.90
Halley	239 bc	35.0 AU	0.6 AU	short period	76.0 yrs	162°	0.97
Swift-Tuttle	1862	52.3 AU	1.0 AU	short period	137.3 yrs	113°	0.96
Bennett	1970	281.8 AU	0.5 AU	long period	1,678 yrs	90.0°	0.99
Donati	1858	311.6 AU	0.6 AU	long period	1,950 yrs	117°	0.99
Hale-Bopp	1995	370.6 AU	0.9 AU	long period	2,529 yrs	89.4°	0.99
Hyakutake	1996	2,006 AU	0.2 AU	long period	31,781 yrs	125°	0.99
Ikeya-Seki	1965	4,000 AU	0.01 AU	long period	89,443 yrs	129°	0.99

Name: Comets are named for their discoverers.
Orbit Time: All years listed are Earth years.
Orbit Inclin.: The inclination of the comet's orbit, relative to the plane of Earth's orbit.
Orbit Eccent.: The eccentricity of the comet's orbit. The larger the number, the more elliptical the orbit.

LUNAR ECLIPSES

DATE	TYPE	BEST SEEN FROM
May 16, 2003	total	North & South America
Nov 9, 2003	total	Europe, west Africa, North & South America
May 4, 2004	total	west Asia, Africa, Europe
Oct 28, 2004	total	North & South America
Oct 17, 2005	partial	central Pacific Ocean
Sept 7, 2006	partial	Indian Ocean, Asia, east Africa
Mar 3, 2007	total	Africa, Europe
Aug 28, 2007	total	central Pacific, west North & South America
Feb 21, 2008	total	North & South America, west Europe
Aug 16, 2008	partial	west Asia, Europe, Africa
Dec 21, 2009	partial	Asia, Indian Ocean, Africa, Europe
June 26, 2010	partial	central Pacific Ocean, west North & South America
Dec 21, 2010	total	North America, west South America
June 15, 2011	total	southwest Asia, Africa, Indian Ocean
Dec 10, 2011	total	west Pacific Ocean, east Asia, Alaska, Yukon
June 4, 2012	partial	central Pacific Ocean, west North & South America
Apr 15, 2014	total	North America, west South America, Pacific Ocean
Oct 8, 2014	total	Pacific Ocean, west North & South America
Apr 4, 2015	total	Pacific Ocean, west North & South America
Sept 28, 2015	total	west Europe & Africa, North & South America

MANNED MISSIONS TO THE MOON

NAME	CREW	LAUNCH DATE	ARRIVAL DATE	LANDING SITE	SAMPLES RETURNED
Apollo 8	Frank Borman, James Lovell, William Anders	Dec 21, 1968	Dec 24, 1968	no landing	no samples
Apollo 10	Thomas Stafford, John Young, Eugene Cernan	May 18, 1969	May 22, 1969	no landing	no samples
Apollo 11	*Neil Armstrong, Edwin Aldrin,* Michael Collins	July 16, 1969	July 20, 1969	Mare Tranquillitatis	49 pounds (22 kg)
Apollo 12	*Charles Conrad, Alan Bean,* Richard Gordon	Nov 14, 1969	Nov 19, 1969	Oceanus Procellarum	76 pounds (34 kg)
Apollo 13	James Lovell, John Swigert, Fred Haise	Apr 11, 1970	Apr 14, 1970	no landing	no samples
Apollo 14	*Alan Shepard, Edgar Mitchell,* Stuart Roosa	Jan 31, 1971	Feb 5, 1971	Fra Mauro highlands	93 pounds (42 kg)
Apollo 15	*David Scott, James Irwin,* Alfred Worden	July 26, 1971	July 30, 1971	Hadley Rille	171 pounds (77 kg)
Apollo 16	*John Young, Charles Duke,* Thomas Mattingly	Apr 16, 1972	Apr 21, 1972	Descartes highlands	213 pounds (96 kg)
Apollo 17	*Eugene Cernan, Harrison Schmitt,* Ronald Evans	Dec 7, 1972	Dec 11, 1972	Taurus-Littrow valley	247 pounds (111 kg)

* The names of the astronauts who landed on the Moon are in *italics*.

Universal Records

Hottest Planet Surface in our Solar System

The surface of Venus, 880°F (470°C). At its hottest, Mercury comes pretty close: 800°F (427°C). Venus's thick atmosphere traps the Sun's heat, so midnight temperatures are as hot as those at noontime. (And the rocks are hot enough to glow dull red.)

Coldest Planet Surface in our Solar System

Pluto when farthest from the Sun. The actual temperature at that point has not yet been measured because Pluto has not made a full orbit since it was discovered in 1930. Pluto will reach the farthest point in its orbit in February 2114. At present, Pluto's surface temperature is –387°F (–233°C)—and it is slowly falling!

Biggest Crater in our Solar System

South Pole-Aitken Basin on the Moon, roughly 1,600 miles (2,500 km) in diameter. This ancient impact scar is so heavily marked with smaller craters that it was not discovered until the Clementine probe visited the Moon in 1994. Scientists used data from Clementine to carefully map the Moon's surface. This mapping revealed the basin, a broad depression in the lunar farside that is more than 7 miles (12 km) deep.

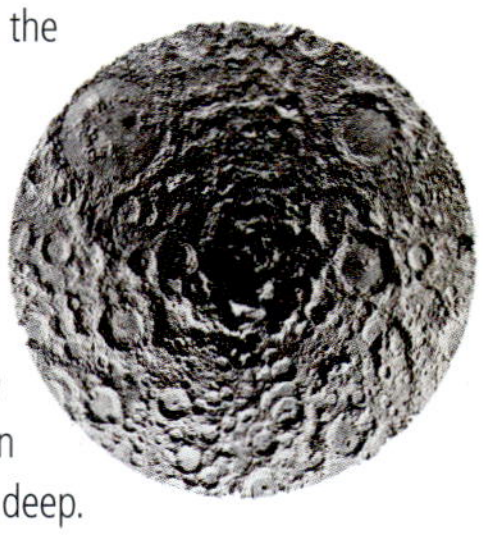

Tallest Mountain in our Solar System

Olympus Mons on Mars, rising 15 miles (24 km) above its base. The second tallest is Maxwell Montes on Venus, which rises 7 miles (11 km) above the planet's average surface. Earth's officially tallest peak is Mount Everest, 5.5 miles (8.8 km) above sea level. However, Hawaii's Mauna Kea can also claim to be the tallest on Earth, since it rises about 5.6 miles (9 km) above the ocean floor it stands on.

Biggest Canyon in our Solar System

Valles Marineris on Mars, roughly 2,500 miles (4,000 km) long, with a maximum width of about 370 miles (600 km) and a maximum depth of 5 miles (8 km). If it were in the United States, this canyon could extend from San Francisco on the west coast to the Appalachian Mountains in Virginia near the east coast. In Europe, it would stretch from Paris, France, to Russia's Ural Mountains.

Biggest Moon in our Solar System

Jupiter's Ganymede, 3,273 miles (5,268 km) in diameter. If Ganymede orbited the Sun instead of Jupiter, it would easily qualify as a planet. It is larger than either Mercury or Pluto.

Biggest Planet in our Solar System

Jupiter, with 317.8 times the mass of Earth, and about 11 times its diameter. Jupiter contains more mass than all the rest of the planets, moons, comets, and asteroids put together.

Biggest Known Planet

An unnamed planet orbiting the star HD 114762. This planet appears to have 11 times the mass of Jupiter, but some astronomers think it may actually be a brown dwarf, an object that is like a small, dim, cool star. If it is a brown dwarf, then the most massive planet would be one with 6.6 times Jupiter's mass that orbits the star 70 Virginis. (This Universal Record is very likely to change as research continues.)

Greatest Meteor Shower

The Leonids on November 13, 1833, with up to 200,000 meteors per hour. Onlookers said that the meteors "fell like snowflakes," and many uneducated people thought the world was about to come to an end. The remarkable display helped astronomers realize that meteors were entering Earth's atmosphere from outer space, and were not just an Earth-based event like rain.

Biggest Meteorite

Hoba meteorite in Namibia, weighing 65 tons (60 tonnes)—about as heavy as nine elephants! Discovered in 1920, this iron meteorite almost 10 feet (3 m) long still lies in the ground where it landed. It was originally even larger—the discolored soil surrounding it shows that part of the meteorite has weathered away.

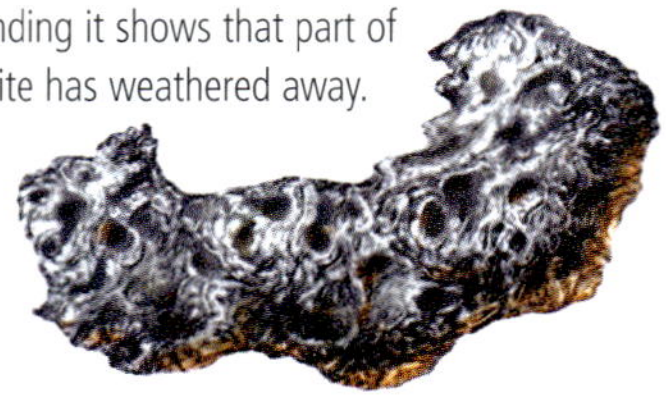

Biggest Asteroid

1 Ceres, 567 miles (913 km) in diameter. This largest of all asteroids was also the first one to be found—and its discovery came on the first day of the 19th century: January 1, 1801. The discoverer of Ceres was Giuseppe Piazzi (1746–1826) and the place was the Palermo Observatory in Sicily.

Closest Comet to Earth

Comet Lexell in 1770, at a distance of 1.4 million miles (2.2 million km) from Earth—less than six times the distance to the Moon. Despite coming so close, this comet never developed much of a tail and its head looked no bigger than five times the size of the Moon in our night sky.

Longest Comet Tail
Great Comet of March 1843, 190 million miles (300 million km) long. This tail was long enough to reach from the Sun to well past the orbit of Mars. When it passed closest to the Sun, the comet was only about 80,000 miles (130,000 km) above the Sun's surface. Planetary scientists call such comets "sungrazers."

Brightest Star in our Night Sky
Sirius, −1.46 magnitude. Sirius is actually a double star, and its dim companion was the first white dwarf star to be discovered.

Broadest Star
Betelgeuse in Orion, about 800 times the Sun's diameter. If it replaced the Sun in our solar system, this bloated red supergiant star would reach past the orbit of Jupiter.

Most Massive Star
Eta Carinae, about 150 times as massive as the Sun. Astronomers are not certain if Eta Carinae is really one star or two.

Least Massive Star
Gliese 105C, about 10 percent as massive as the Sun. This is about as small as a star can be and still be a true star (an object that fuses hydrogen into helium).

Nearest Star
Proxima Centauri, third member of the Alpha Centauri system. This cool red dwarf star lies about 4.2 light-years away, about 0.1 light-year closer to us than the other two stars in the system.

Globular Star Cluster with the Most Stars
Omega Centauri, with 1.1 million stars. This globular cluster measures about 180 light-years in diameter.

Most Massive Galaxy
Giant elliptical M87 in the constellation of Virgo, with at least 800 billion Suns worth of mass. M87 is a member of the Virgo cluster of galaxies.

Least Massive Galaxy
The Pegasus II dwarf elliptical, about 10 million solar masses. Smaller galaxies may exist, but because they are not very luminous, astronomers cannot detect them unless they also lie close to us.

Nearest Galaxy
Sagittarius dwarf elliptical, 80,000 light-years away. This galaxy is the current record holder, but surveys find new dwarf elliptical galaxies every year or so, and an even closer galaxy may yet be found.

Most Distant Object Visible to the Naked Eye
Andromeda galaxy (M31), 2.5 million light-years away. When you look at this galaxy, you are seeing light that left the galaxy when the most recent great Ice Ages were beginning on Earth.

Most Distant Object Detected
An unnamed galaxy in Ursa Major, 12.6 billion light-years away. This galaxy may not hold the record for very long. Astronomers working with giant telescopes on Earth and the Hubble Space Telescope find a new and more distant record-holder once or twice a year.

ASTEROID FACTS

NAME	DISCOVERY	DISTANCE FROM SUN	ORBIT TIME	ROTATION TIME	DIAMETER
1 Ceres	Piazzi, 1801	2.76 AU	4.6 yrs	9h 5m	567 miles (913 km)
2 Pallas	Olbers, 1802	2.77 AU	4.6 yrs	7h 49m	325 miles (523 km)
4 Vesta	Olbers, 1807	2.36 AU	3.6 yrs	5h 21m	323 miles (520 km)
10 Hygeia	De Gasparis, 1849	3.14 AU	5.6 yrs	27h 40m	267 miles (429 km)
511 Davida	Dugan, 1903	3.18 AU	5.7 yrs	5h 8m	209 miles (337 km)
704 Interamnia	Cerulli, 1910	3.06 AU	5.4 yrs	8h 44m	207 miles (333 km)
253 Mathilde	Palisa, 1885	2.65 AU	4.3 yrs	17h 24m	41 miles (66 km)
243 Ida	Palisa, 1884	2.86 AU	4.9 yrs	4h 38m	37 miles (60 km)
433 Eros	Witt & Charlois, 1898	1.46 AU	1.8 yrs	5h 18m	21 miles (33 km)
951 Gaspra	Neujmin, 1916	2.21 AU	3.3 yrs	7h 3m	11 miles (18 km)

Distance from Sun: The asteroid's average distance from the Sun.
Orbit Time: All years listed are Earth years.

Robot Missions

IMPORTANT MISSIONS TO THE PLANETS

MISSION	COUNTRY	TYPE*	LAUNCH	ARRIVAL	ACHIEVEMENTS
Mercury					
Mariner 10	USA	F	Nov 3, 1973	Mar 29, 1974	first close-up images show cratered surface
Venus					
Mariner 2	USA	F	Aug 27, 1962	Dec 14, 1962	first flyby finds heavy atmosphere, hot surface
Venera 4	Soviet Union	L	June 12, 1967	Oct 18, 1967	measures atmosphere, fails on descent
Mariner 5	USA	F	June 14, 1967	Oct 19, 1967	improves atmospheric measurements
Venera 5	Soviet Union	L	Jan 5, 1969	May 16, 1969	studies atmosphere
Venera 6	Soviet Union	L	Jan 10, 1969	May 17, 1969	studies atmosphere
Venera 8	Soviet Union	L	Mar 27, 1972	July 22, 1972	sends back first data from surface
Mariner 10	USA	F	Nov 4, 1973	Feb 5, 1974	flies past on way to Mercury, photographs clouds
Venera 9	Soviet Union	OL	June 8, 1975	Oct 22, 1975	first images of surface show volcanic rocks
Venera 10	Soviet Union	OL	June 14, 1975	Oct 25, 1975	photographs surface rocks and dirt
Pioneer Venus Orbiter	USA	O	May 20, 1978	Dec 4, 1978	first global radar map of landscape, studies clouds
Pioneer Venus Probes	USA	EP	Aug 8, 1978	Dec 9, 1978	five probes sample atmosphere
Venera 11	Soviet Union	OL	Sept 9, 1978	Dec 25, 1978	photographs surface, analyzes atmosphere
Venera 12	Soviet Union	OL	Sept 14, 1978	Dec 21, 1978	photographs surface, analyzes atmosphere
Venera 13	Soviet Union	OL	Oct 30, 1981	Mar 1, 1982	photographs surface, analyzes atmosphere
Venera 14	Soviet Union	OL	Nov 4, 1981	Mar 5, 1982	photographs surface, analyzes atmosphere
Venera 15	Soviet Union	O	June 2, 1983	Oct 10, 1983	radar mapping of northern hemisphere
Venera 16	Soviet Union	O	June 7, 1983	Oct 14, 1983	radar mapping of northern hemisphere
Vega 1	Soviet Union	LB	Dec 15, 1984	June 11, 1985	surveys atmosphere and winds with balloon
Vega 2	Soviet Union	LB	Dec 21, 1984	June 16, 1985	surveys atmosphere and winds with balloon
Magellan	USA	O	May 4, 1989	Aug 10, 1990	surveys geology over Venus using radar
Galileo	USA	F	Oct 18, 1989	Feb 10, 1990	flies past on way to Jupiter, studies clouds
Cassini	USA	F	Oct 15, 1997	Apr 26, 1998	flies past on way to Saturn, studies clouds
Cassini	USA	F	Oct 15, 1997	June 24, 1999	second Venus flyby, studies clouds
Mars					
Mariner 4	USA	F	Nov 28, 1965	July 14, 1965	first close-up images show craters, thin atmosphere
Mariner 6	USA	F	Feb 24, 1969	July 31, 1969	returns 75 photos, increases geological knowledge
Mariner 7	USA	F	Mar 27, 1969	Aug 5, 1969	returns 126 photos, increases geological knowledge
Mars 3	Soviet Union	OL	May 28, 1971	Dec 3, 1971	some data and few photos
Mariner 9	USA	O	May 30, 1971	Nov 12, 1971	first survey of surface, finds water channels, volcanoes
Mars 5	Soviet Union	O	July 25, 1973	Feb 12, 1974	lasts a few days
Mars 6	Soviet Union	OL	Aug 5, 1973	Mar 12, 1974	little data return
Mars 7	Soviet Union	OL	Aug 9, 1973	Mar 9, 1974	little data return
Viking 1	USA	OL	Aug 20, 1975	June 19, 1976	Survey from orbit, unsuccessful search for life
Viking 2	USA	OL	Sept 9, 1975	Aug 7, 1976	Survey from orbit, unsuccessful search for life
Mars Global Surveyor	USA	O	Nov 7, 1996	Sept 12, 1997	maps entire planet at high resolution
Mars Pathfinder	USA	LR	Dec 2, 1996	July 4, 1997	explores geology of a once-flooded landscape
Nozomi (Planet-B)	Japan	O	July 4, 1998	Dec 2003	studies upper atmosphere, magnetosphere, solar wind

MISSION	COUNTRY	TYPE*	LAUNCH	ARRIVAL	ACHIEVEMENTS
Mars					
Mars Climate Orbiter	USA	O	Dec 11, 1998	Sept 23, 1999	crashes on arrival, no data returned
Mars Polar Lander	USA	L	Jan 3, 1999	Dec 3, 1999	fails upon arrival, no data returned
Deep Space 2	USA	I	Jan 3, 1999	Dec 3, 1999	travels with Polar Lander, searches for subsurface ice
Jupiter					
Pioneer 10	USA	F	Mar 3, 1972	Dec 3, 1973	first detailed study of a gas-giant planet
Pioneer 11	USA	F	Apr 6, 1973	Dec 3, 1974	studies polar regions of Jupiter, magnetic environment
Voyager 1	USA	F	Sept 5, 1977	Mar 5, 1979	first detailed images of planet & moons, discovers rings
Voyager 2	USA	F	Aug 20, 1977	July 9, 1979	follow-up on Voyager 1's discoveries
Galileo	USA	OEP	Oct 18, 1989	Dec 7, 1995	first atmosphere probe, orbital tour of planet & moons
Saturn					
Pioneer 11	USA	F	Apr 6, 1973	Sept 1, 1979	first spacecraft visit, discovers new rings
Voyager 1	USA	F	Sept 5, 1977	Nov 12, 1980	detailed portraits of clouds, rings, and moons
Voyager 2	USA	F	Aug 20, 1977	Aug 25, 1981	follow-up on Voyager 1's discoveries
Cassini	USA	F	Oct 15, 1997	July 2004	orbital tour of planet and moons, lander for Titan
Uranus					
Voyager 2	USA	F	Aug 20, 1977	Jan 24, 1986	first visit, studies rings and moons, finds new moons
Neptune					
Voyager 2	USA	F	Aug 20, 1977	Aug 25, 1989	first visit, studies storms, finds geysers on Triton
Pluto					
no mission yet flown					

**Key to type* F: flyby; L: lander; O: orbiter; B: balloon; I: impactor; R: rover; EP: entry probe

MARINER 10

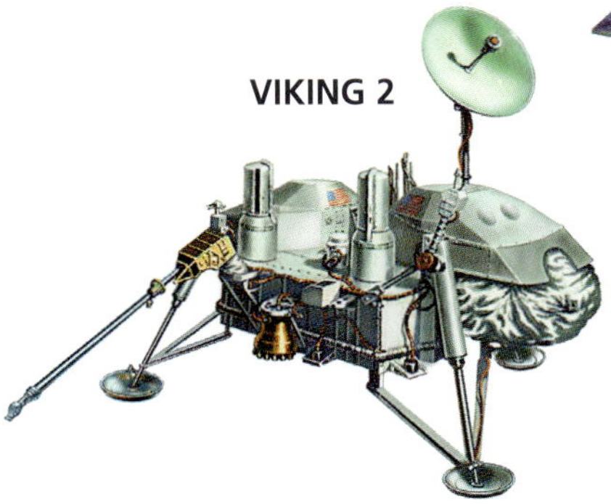

VIKING 2

MARS POLAR LANDER

Index

A

Aardvark, African 245
Aboriginal dancers 482
Abraham Lincoln's House (USA) 452
Acupuncture 398
Adonis asteroid 36
Afghanistan 471, 571
Africa 478–81
African pygmy falcon 223
Agamids 288–9
Aircraft
  military 534–5
  passenger 532–3
Al Hajra (Yemen) 468
Al Khuwair (Oman) 499
Alamo, the (USA) 454
Alaska 446
Alaska blackfish 321
Albania 441, 566
Albertosaurus 163
Alcazar, the (Spain) 430
Alexander Nevsky Cathedral (Bulgaria) 497
Alexandria Lighthouse (Egypt) 402
Algeria 479, 575
Alligators 284–5
Allosaurus 154, 160, 162
Alpenhorn player 436
Amish People 450
Amphisbaenians 286
Anaconda 295, 460
Andean condor 221
Andorra 430–1, 563
Angola 481, 580
Anise 196
Antelope 276–7
Antigua and Barbuda 459, 560
Ants 200, 333
Apak Hoja tomb (China) 504
Apatosaurus 158–9, 167
Apollo asteroid 36
Archaeopteryx 173
Architecture. *See also by name of building or structure*
  castles 514–15
  classical 490–1, 516–17
  early American 500–1
  early settlement 510–11
  Gothic 492–3
  houses 512–13
  religious 446, 448, 494–9
  Roman 508
  sporting 508–9
  tombs 504–5
Arctic Circle Pyramid (Norway) 444
Argentina 463, 562
Arizona coral snake 297
Armadillo, three-banded 245
Armenia 467, 569
Artery 350
Arthur's paragalaxias 321
Asparagus 197
Asteroids 15, 21, 36–7, 89, 592
Astronomy 82–3, 584–7
Athenaeum (Romania) 516
Atlantic puffin 215
Atmosphere 122–3
  frontal systems 134–5
  pressure movement 134–5
Atomic Dome (Japan) 504
Australia 482–3, 582
Australian pineapplefish 323
Austria 436–7, 565
Automobile 522–3
Avalanche 128
Aye-aye 248, 249
Azerbaijan 467, 569

B

Bacteria 348
Bagpipe player 428
Bahamas 459, 559
Bahrain 469, 571
Ballet dancers 464
Banded duiker 277
Banded lapwing 214
Banded pipefish 322
Banded pitta 235
Bangladesh 471, 572
Barbados 459, 560
Barosaurus 166, 167
Barred cuckooshrike 236
Baryonyx 163, 172, 174–5
Baseball player 455
Basil 196
Basketball player 451
Bateleur 222
Baths of Caracalla 416–17
Bats 246–6
Batswing coral-tree 186
Bavarian brass band 436
Bavarian Church (Germany) 497
Bears 262–5, 447
Bedouins 468
Beech, common 186
Bees 332–3
Beetles 328–9
Belarus 443, 567
Belgium 434–5, 564
Belize 459, 558
Benin 479, 578
Bergen Wharf (Norway) 444
Bhutan 471, 572
Bicycles 523
Bilby 242
Binoculars 549
Birch, silver 187

Birds 206–9. *See also by species*
diving for fish 230
extracting nectar 228
feathers 210–11
flight 211
flightless 218–19
land 243–5
sea and shore 214–15
songbirds 236–7
water 212–13
Birth 360
Black and white colobus 250
Black-capped lory 226
Black dragonfish 320
Black-headed blenny 325
Black holes 60–1, 587
Black korhaan 218
Black skimmer 215
Blarney Castle (Ireland) 428
Bled (Slovenia) 440
Blood 350–1
Blotched pipe snake 297
Blue-crowned motmot 231
Blue-footed booby 215
Blue jay 210
Blue Mosque (Turkey) 466, 499
Bluebanded goby 325
Blunt-headed tree snake 297
Boa constrictor 295, 296
Boats 526–9
Bobcat 258
Bolivia 463, 562
Bones 366–7. *See also* Skeleton
Bongo 277
Bontebok 277
Border fortress (Turkey) 467
Bororro man 478
Bosnia and Herzegovina 441, 566
Botswana 481, 581
Boules player 432
Bouzouki 440
Brachiation 249
Brachiosaurus 164, 165
Brain 372–3
Brasília Cathedral (Brazil) 460
Brazil 461, 561
Breathing 354
Brighton Pavilion (England) 428
Bristlemouth 320
Broccoli 197
Bromeliads 199
Brunei 473, 573
Brussel sprouts 197
Buddhist monks 472
Bugs 328–9
Bulbs 191
Bulgaria 441, 566
Bullfighter 430
Burkina Faso 479, 575
Burundi 481, 580
Bus 523
Buttercup 190
Butterflies 327, 330–1
Butterflyfish 312, 314
Byronosaurus 162

C

Cabbage 197
Caecilians 298–9
California quail 218
Calligraphy 399
Caloris Basin (Mercury) 16, 17
Camarasaurus 158, 166
Cambodia 473, 573
Camel, dromedary 274
Camembert cheese 432
Camera 548–9
Cameroon 479, 578
Camptosaurus 154
Canada 446–9, 558
Canal lock 529
Canoe 420, 526, 527
Cap-des-Rosiers Lighthouse (Canada) 448
Cape Verde Islands 479, 575
Capillary 350
Capitol Building (USA)
Des Moines 452
Washington 450
Cappadoccia (Turkey) 466
Capybara 278
Caracal 258
Caribbean trumpetfish 322
Carnival dancer 460
Carnosaurs 153
Carp streamers 476
Carrot 197
Casa Mila (Spain) 506
Castles 514–15
Catal Hüyük (Turkey) 510–11
Caterpillars 330
Cats 256–61
Caulilflower 197
Cedar, atlas 187
Celebes macaque 250
Cells 348–9
Central America 458–9
Centrosaurus 168
Ceratorsaurus 159
Chad 479, 576
Chameleons 288–9
Channel-billed cuckoo 234
Chartres Cathedral (France) 497
Chasmosaurus 168, 169
Château de Chambord (France) 514
Château Frontenac (Canada) 448
Cheetah 257
Chicken 206
Chile 463, 562
Chimaeras 310–11
China 475, 574
China, Ancient
craft and trade 400–1
empire 394–5
magistrate's court 397
science and medicine 398–9
social orders 396
writing 399

Chipmunk, least 278
Chive 196
Christchurch Cathedral (New Zealand) 484
Chrysler Building (USA) 450
Church of San Vitale (Italy) 497
Churches. *See by name*
Circumpolar burbot 321
Climate 136, 140–1
arctic 140, 141
desert 140, 141
dinosaurs, disappearance of 172
forest 140
high altitude 141
mountain 141
Clipper 526
Clogs 434
Cloning 348
Clouds 126–7
Clown killifish 318
Clown knifefish 313
Clown triggerfish 325
Clusters. *See* Stars
CN Tower (Canada) 448
Coastal she-oak 186
Cobra, spitting 296
Cochlear implant 545
Cockatoo, palm 207
Cockatoo waspfish 323
Cockchafer 327
Cockroach 155
Coelacanth 312
Coelophysis 152
Coelurosaurs 153
Coelurus 154
Coldstream Guard 428
Cologne Cathedral (Germany) 496
Colombia 461, 561
Colosseum (Italy) 508
Comets 15, 38–9, 584, 586, 590, 592–3
Encke 39, 590
Hale-Bopp 39, 590
Halley 39, 585, 590
Comoros 481, 581
Compass 538
Compsognathus 163, 173
Computers 542–3
Congo 481, 579
Congreso Nacional (Argentina) 462
Conifers 157, 188–9
Constellations
Antlia 65, 67, 77, 79
Apus 73, 75, 77, 79
Aquarius 69, 71, 72, 74
Aquila 69, 70, 71, 72, 74
Ara 73, 75, 79
Aries 64, 65, 71, 74, 76
Auriga 63, 64, 65, 66, 70, 76
Boötes 63, 66, 67, 68, 69, 72, 78
Caelum 65, 75, 77, 79
Camelopardalis 63, 64, 66, 68, 70
Cancer 65, 67, 76, 78
Canes Venatici 63, 64, 66, 67, 68, 78
Canis Major 65, 75, 76, 77, 79
Canis Minor 65, 67, 76, 78
Capricornus 69, 71, 73, 74, 75
Carina 75, 77, 79
Cassiopeia 62, 63, 64, 66, 68, 70, 74
Centaurus 67, 73, 77, 79
Cepheus 62, 63, 64, 66, 68, 70
Cetus 65, 71, 74, 76, 77
Chamaeleon 73, 75, 77, 79
Circinus 73, 77, 79
Columba 65, 77, 79
Coma Berenices 64, 67, 68, 72, 78
Corona Australis 69, 73, 75, 79
Corona Borealis 63, 66, 67, 69, 72, 78
Corvus 67, 73, 77, 78
Crater 67, 73, 77, 78
Crux 62, 73, 75, 77, 79
Cygnus 63, 64, 66, 68, 69, 70, 71, 72
Delphinus 69, 71, 72, 74
Dorado 75, 77, 79
Draco 63, 64, 66, 68, 70, 72
Equuleus 69, 71, 72, 74
Eridanus 65, 71, 73, 74, 75, 76, 77
Gemini 63, 65, 66, 70, 76, 78
Grus 71, 73, 75, 77
Hercules 63, 66, 68, 69, 70, 72, 78
Horologium 75, 77, 79
Hydra 65, 67, 69, 73, 76, 77, 78, 79
Hydrus 73, 75, 77, 78, 79
Indus 73, 75, 77, 79
Lacerta 63, 64, 66, 68, 70, 74
Leo 64, 67, 68, 76, 78, 584
Leo Minor 64, 65, 67, 68, 76, 78
Lepus 65, 75, 76, 79
Libra 67, 69, 72, 73, 79
Lupus 69, 73, 79
Lynx 63, 64, 66, 68, 70, 76, 78
Lyra 66, 68, 69, 70, 72
Mensa 73, 75, 77, 79
Microscopium 71, 73, 75
Monoceros 65, 67, 76, 78
Musca 73, 75, 77, 79
Norma 73, 75, 79
Octans 73, 75, 77, 79
Ophiuchus 63, 66, 67, 69, 70, 72, 75, 78, 79
Orion 63, 65, 66, 70, 71, 74, 75, 76, 79
Pavo 73, 75, 77, 79
Pegasus 64, 68, 69, 71, 72, 74
Perseus 63, 64, 65, 66, 68, 70, 74, 76
Phoenix 71, 73, 75, 77
Pictor 75, 77, 79
Pisces 64, 65, 68, 69, 71, 72, 74, 76
Piscis Austrinus 71, 73, 74, 75, 77
Puppis 65, 67, 75, 77, 79
Pyxis 65, 67, 77, 79
Reticulum 75, 77, 79

Sagittarius 69, 72, 73, 75, 79
Sagitta 69, 71, 72, 74
Scorpius 67, 69, 72, 73, 75, 79, 584
Sculptor 71, 73, 74, 75, 77
Scutum 69, 71, 72, 74, 75
Serpens Caput 67, 69, 72, 78
Serpens Cauda 69, 71, 72, 74, 75, 79
Sextans 65, 67, 76, 78
Taurus 57, 63, 65, 66, 70, 71, 74, 76, 584
Telescopium 73, 75, 79
Triangulum 64, 71, 74, 76
Tucana 73, 75, 77, 79
Ursa Major 62, 63, 64, 66, 67, 68, 70, 78
Ursa Minor 62, 63, 64, 66, 68, 70
Vela 67, 73, 75, 77, 79
Virgo 67, 69, 72, 78
Volans 75, 77, 79
Vulpecula 69, 70, 72, 74
Continental drift 98–9
Conway Castle (Wales) 515
Corythosaurus 156, 171
Cossack dancer 443
Costa Rica 459, 559
Country musician 454
Coyote 254, 255
Cranes 539
Crested caracara 222
Cretaceous period 156–7, 173
Cricket player 428
Crickets 336–7
Croatia 441, 566
Crocodiles 172, 284–5
Crow 211
Crowned crane 213
Crusafontia 156
Csempeszkopacs Church (Hungary) 496
Cuatro ojos 319
Cuba 459, 559
Cuban brown anole 288
Curlew, far-eastern 207
Currents 142–3
Cuscus, common spotted 242
Cuvier's dwarf caiman 284
Cycads 152, 154, 189
Cypress 187, 189
Cyprus 467, 569
Czech Republic 443, 567

D

Damme Canal (Belgium) 434
Day and night 136
Decorated fire-goby 324
Deep-space tracking antenna 19
Deer 276, 277
Deinonycheirus 162
Deinonychus 162
Denmark 445, 568
Diana guenon 251
Digestive system 356–7
Dilophosaurus 171
Dinosaurs. *See also by species*
anatomy 158–9, 160–1
armored 168–9
birds, relationship to 173
disappearance 172–3
duck-billed 170–1
food 152, 155, 165
footprints 175
fossils 174–5
long-necked 166–7
meat eaters 162–3
plant eaters 164–5
sites 153, 154, 156
Diplodocus 155
Disneyland (USA) 456
Djibouti 479, 577
DNA molecule 349
Dogs 254–5
sled 421, 446
Dolphins 266–71
Dom Cathedral (Netherlands) 497
Dome of the Rock (Israel) 498
Dominica 459, 560
Dominican Republic 459, 559
Doria's bumblebee goby 324
Dragonfly 152, 155, 327, 335
Dubrovnik (Croatia) 440
Dwarf siren 299

E

Eagles 207, 221, 224–5
Ear 376
pressure 377
Earth 15, 20–1, 34, 36, 39, 44, 45, 96, 100, 584, 588
Earthquakes 114–15
East Timor 473, 574
Eastern Orthodox Church (Macedonia) 497
Eastern ribbon snake 297
Eastern rosella 226
Eastern spinebill 237
Eating 357
Echidna, short-beaked 241
Echinacea 196
Echolocation 247
Ecuador 461, 561
Edelweiss 195
Edmontonia 169
Edmontosaurus 161, 171
Eels 298, 323, 317
Egypt 479, 575
Egypt, Ancient 386–7
art 392–3
boats 526
burial and afterlife 390–1
Giza pyramid 478, 505
gods 388–9
writing 392
Eiffel Tower (France) 432
El Castillo (Mexico) 500

El Salvador 459, 558–9
Electric catfish 316
Electricity 538
Elephantfish 311
Elephantnose 313
Elephants 272–3, 478
Elm, American 186
Emu 219
Epcot Center (USA) 455
Equatorial Guinea 479, 577
Eritrea 479, 575
Eros asteroid 36
Erosion 100, 146
Estonia 443, 567
Ethiopia 479, 576
Eucalyptus flowers 191
Eudimorphodon 153
Euoplocephalus 156, 168, 169
Eurasian griffon 223
Evenki mother 464
Evzones guards 440
Extinction, dinosaurs 172–3
Eyes 374–5

F

Fault lines 102–3
Feathers 210–11, 216
Federated States of Micronesia 583
Ferns 184–5
  tree 152, 155, 165, 184
Fertilization, human 361
Fig 186, 200
Fiji 485, 583
Finches 206, 238, 239
Finland 445, 568
Fir, balsam 187
Fish. *See also by species*
  bony 312–15
  freshwater 316–19
  ocean 320–5
  sex reversal 324
Fishers 430, 444, 446
Flamenco dancer 430
Flamingo 206
Flashlight fish 323
Flies 327, 334–5
Flight 530–1
  birds 210–12, 229
  military aircraft 534–5
  passenger aircraft 532–3
  supersonic 536–7
Floating market (Thailand) 472
Fog 124–5
Folk costume 434, 436, 440, 442, 462, 466, 468, 470, 472, 474
Food processor 540
Football (American) 452
Forbidden City (China) 394–5
Forests 198
Fossils
  dinosaurs 174–5
  footprints 175
  formation 175
  fuels 144
  plants 174
Foxes 255
Foxglove 195
France 432–3, 564
French Guiana 461
French Polynesia 485
Frogs 300–5
Frullania liverwort 184

G

Gabon 481, 579
Galaxies 60–1, 81, 586, 593
  Andromeda 58, 64, 68, 70, 71, 74, 593
  Fornax 58, 65, 71, 75, 77
  Large Magellanic Cloud 58, 62, 73, 75, 77, 79, 81
  Pinwheel 58
  Small Magellanic Cloud 58, 62, 73, 79, 81
Gallimimus 163
Gambia 479, 577
Garlic 197
Gaur 275
Gazelle 276, 277
Geckos 290–1
Geisha 476
Gelada 251
Gemsbok 277
Geology. *See also Rocks*
  continental drift 98–9
  erosion 100–1
  fault lines 102–3
  Grand Canyon (USA) 97
  natural sculpture 101
  sea floor 101
  shore 147
Georgia 467, 569
Gerbil 278
Gerenuk 276
Germany 436–7, 564–5
Germs 348
  fighting 350–1
Ghana 479, 578
Gharial 284, 285
Giant bromeliad 462
Giant grouper 315
Gibbon, Lar 248
Ginger 197
Gingko tree 152, 155, 165, 189
Giraffes 478
Goat, wild 275
Gol Gumbaz Mosque (India) 499
Golden agouti 279
Golden-crowned kinglet 236
Golden-fronted leafbird 236
Golden Gate Bridge (USA) 456
Golden potto 248
Gondwana 154
Gorilla 248

Gothic windows 492
Grasshoppers 336–7
Great auk 215
Great kiskadee 234
Great Plaza (Guatemala) 500
Great Wall of China 395
Greater moonrat 244
Greater raquet-tailed drongo 239
Greater roadrunner 234
Greece 441, 566
Greece, Ancient 402–3
  Agamemnon's death mask 440
  architecture 490–1
  clothing 406
  colonies 402
  drama 405
  gods 404–5
  houses 407
  war and warfare 408–9
  writing 404
Green broadbill 235
Green figbird 239
Greenhouse effect (Venus) 19
Grenada 459, 560
Guanacos 462
Guatemala 459, 558
Guggenheim Museum (USA) 507
Guiana cock-of-the-rock 235
Guinea 479, 577
Guinea-Bissau 479, 577
Guitar 551
Guitarfish 311
Guyana 461, 561

H

Hail 129
Haiti 459, 559
Hammer thrower 429
Haramiya 152
Harlequin tuskfish 324
Hatshepsut, Queen 386
Hawks 225
Hearing 376
  cochlea implant 545
Heart 352–3
Hedgehog, Algerian 245
Herati woman 470
Herbs 196, 399
Herero woman 480
Heron, purple 213
Herrerasaurus 153
Heterodontosaurus 165
Hibiscus 190
Hidalgo asteroid 36
Hieroglyphs 392
Himalayan tahr 275
Homolocephale 171
Honduras 459, 558
Hoopoe 206
Hoplite 408, 409
Hormones 380
Hornet 332
Horsetail 154, 184
Hortobagy horseman 442
Houses 407, 512–13
Hula dancer 456
Humingbirds 228–9
Hungary 443, 568
Hurdy-gurdy player 436
Hurricanes 130, 131
Hypsilophodon 158

I

Ice hockey player 448
Iceland 445, 568
Iguanas 288–9
Iguanodon 164
Imperial Mosque (Pakistan) 499
India 471, 572
Indian muntjac 277
Indonesia 473, 574
Indri 248, 249
In-line skater 456
Insects 326–7. *See also by species*
Iran 469, 570
Iraq 469, 570
Ireland 428–9, 563
Irritator 163
Israel 469, 570
Italy 438–9, 565
Ivory Coast 479, 578

J

Jaguar 258
Jamaica 459, 559
Japan 476–7, 574
Java sparrow 239
Javanese ricefish 319
Jazz musician 454
Jeepney bus 472
Jesuit Church (Argentina) 462
Jordan 469, 571
Judas tree 190
Junk 474, 526
Jupiter 15, 24–5, 34, 36, 38, 49, 586–7, 589, 592
Jurassic period 154–5

K

Kakapo 219
Kalmar Castle (Sweden) 444
Kangaroo 240, 482
Kannemeyeria 153
Kayapo man 460
Kazakstan 467, 569
Kecskemet Church (Hungary) 496
Kentrosaurus 168
Kentucky Derby 450
Kenya 481, 579

Kestrel 221, 222, 223
Khanty tribesmen 464
Khosian hunters 480
Kidneys 358
King eider 213
Kingfishers 230, 231
Kiribati 583
Kites 221, 222
Kiwi 218, 484
Klipspringer 277
Koala 242
Kodkod 261
Kohlrabi 197
Kokechi doll 476
Komodo dragon 292
Korea 475, 574
Kouttoubia Mosque (Morocco) 478
Kremlin (Russia) 464
Kritosaurus 171
Kronosaurus 156
Kuiper Belt 33
Kuwait 469, 571
Kyrgyzstan 467, 570

L

La Sagrada Familia (Spain) 496
Ladybird 328, 329
Lake Malawi zebra cichlid 314
Lambeosaurus 165, 171
Lanternfish 320
Laos 473, 573
Laser printer 543
Latvia 443, 567
Laurasia 154
Leaning Tower of Pisa (Italy) 438
Lebanon 469, 570
Legions (Roman) 415
Legislative Building (Canada) 516
Lemurs 248
Lenses 83, 549
Leopard 257, 259
Lesotho 481, 581
Lesser golden plover 214
Lettuce 197
Liberia 479, 577
Liberty Bell 450
Libya 479, 575
Licorice gourami 315
Liechtenstein 437, 565
Lightning 131
Lilac 194
Lilac-breasted roller 231
Lilies 195
Lion 258
Lipizzaner horse 436
Lithuania 443, 567
Little Mermaid Statue (Denmark) 444
Liver 359
Lizards 288, 289, 292–3
Locust, desert 337
Longhorn musician 466
Long-horned beetle 327
Lotus 386
Louse, human 327
Lumpsucker 323
Lungfish 313
Lungs 355
Luxembourg 434–5, 564
Lynx 258

M

Macedonia 441, 566
Machu Picchu (Peru) 500
Madagascar 481, 581
Madain Salah tombs (Saudi Arabia) 504
Magnetism 538
Magnolias 157, 165
Majungatholus 163
Malawi 481, 580
Malayan halfbeak 318
Malaysia 473, 573
Maldives 471, 572
Mali 479, 576
Mali man 479
Malta 439, 565
Mamenchisaurus 167
Mammals. *See also by species*
  hoofed 274–7
  insect-eating 244–5
Mandarin fish 323
Mandarin ratsnake 297
Mandrill 250
Mantis 327
Maori 484
Marbles hatchetfish 316
Margay 260
Mariachi band 458
Marigold 195
Marmot, hoary 278
Mars 15, 22–3, 34, 36, 48, 89, 586, 588–9, 592–3
Marshall Islands 583
Marsupials 240–3
Masai warrior 480
Masjid Ubudiah (Malaysia) 499
Matreshka dolls 464
Mauritania 479, 575
Mauritius 581
Meadowsweet 196
Meenakshi Temple (India) 470
Mercury 15, 16–17, 34, 36, 88, 586, 588, 592
Mesa Verde (USA) 500
Meteoroids 36–7, 585, 592
Metropolitan Cathedral (Mexico) 458
Mexico 458–9, 558
Micronesia 583
Microscope 544
Microwave oven 540
Midge 335
Milan Cathedral (Italy) 496
Milky Way 56–7, 58–9, 80–1, 585–6
Minerals 106–7

Mohs scale of hardness 106
Mississippi River Paddle Steamer 454
Moai statues (Easter Island) 502
Moldova 443, 568
Mole, European 245
Monaco 433, 564
Mongolia 475, 574
Monkeys 250–3
Monotremes 240–1
Monticello House (USA) 516
Moon
Earth's 40–5, 584, 586, 592
eclipses 44–5, 591
missions 90–1, 586, 591
planetary 46, 47
Moorish idol 314
Moose 276
Morocco 479, 575
Mosques 498–9. *See also by name*
Mosquito 327, 334
Moths 327, 330–1
Mount Rushmore (USA) 502
Mountain anoa 275
Mozambique 481, 580
Mud-masked warrior 482
Mudpuppy 299
Mummification 390–1
Muscles 368–9
Musk ox 275
Musky rat-kangaroo 242
Myanmar (Burma) 473, 572
Mycenae (Greece) 504

N

Nails, human 371
Namibia 481, 580–1
Narghile pipe 468
Native Americans
ceremonies 422–3
food 419
sign language 419
Nauru 583
Navajo weaver 456
Near-Earth asteroid orbit 15
Nepal 471, 572
Neptune 14, 30–1, 35, 39, 48, 585, 587, 590
Nerves 380–1
Netherlands 434–5, 564
Neuschwanstein Castle (Germany) 436
New Guinea 473
New Zealand 484–5, 582
Newgrange burial ground (Ireland) 504
Newts 298
Nicaragua 459, 559
Nicobar pigeon 226
Niger 479, 576
Nigeria 479, 578
Night and day 136
Ninga drummers 480
Ninja 476
Northern flicker 233
Northern screamer 213
Norway 445, 568
Nosso Senhor do Bomfim Church (Brazil) 460
Notre Dame Cathedral (France) 492–3
Notre Dame du Haut (France) 507
Numbat 242
Nuts 197

O

Oak, English 186
Ocelot 261
Olmec stone carving 458
Oman 469, 571
Oncilla 260
Onion 197
Opah 323
Opossum 243
Optics 548–9
Orange 197
Orange chat 237
Ores 107
Ornithischians 161
Ostrich 206
Othneilia 165
Ouranosaurus 159
Oviraptor 163
Owl, barn 222
Ozone layer 122

P

Pachycephalosaurus 156
Pachyrachis 156
Painted bunting 237
Pakistan 471, 572
Palau 583
Panama 459, 559
Panda
giant 264, 474
red 265
Pangea 99, 153
Pangolin 244
Pantheon (Italy) 410, 413, 491
Papua New Guinea 483, 582
Paraguay 463, 562
Parasaurolophus 170
Parliament House (New Zealand) 484
Parma Baptistry (Italy) 496
Parrotfish 324
Parrots 226, 227
Parthenon (Greece) 490–1
Passenger liner 528–9
Patagonian mara 279
Paxton's whipnose angler 323
Peach, reproduction 192
Peacock 211
Pelican, brown 214
Penguins 206, 216–17

Peregrine falcon 221
Personal organiser 543
Peru 461, 561
Pharoah, crowns of 286
Pheasant 207, 218
Philippines 473, 573
Photosynthesis 182–3
Piano, grand 550–1
Pileated woodpeacker 207
Pine 189
Pine cone 165
Pin-tailed sandgrouse 227
Pirate perch 319
Pitcher plant 182
Pizza 438
Plains viscacha 279
Planets. *See also by name*
  size comparison 34–5
Plants 182–3. *See also by species*
  anatomy 190
  edible 196–7
  flowering 190–5
  inflorescence 191
  medicinal 196
  root systems 198
  storing food 182
  water, saving 182
Platypus 241
Pleiades 57
Pluto 14, 32–3, 35, 48, 585–7, 590, 592
Polacanthus 169
Poland 443, 567
Pollution 122
Polyglyphanodon 156
Poppy 194
Porcupine 279
Porpoises 266–71
Portugal 430–1, 563
Potala Palace (Tibet) 474
Potato 197
Prenocephale 157
Presidential Palace (Paraguay) 462
Primates 248–9
  New World monkeys 252–3
  Old World monkeys 250–1
Primrose, thrum-eyed 190
Probes, space. *See* Spacecraft
Procompsognathus 153
Protoceratops 157, 165
Pudu 277
Pueblo pottery 456
Pufferfish 325
Puma 257
Pumpkin 191, 197
Purple gallinule 213
Purplequeen 314
Pyrenean desman 244, 245
Python 295, 296, 297

Q

Qatar 469, 571
Quechua man 460

R

Rain 129
Rainbow bee-eater 231
Rainbowfish 319
Rainforests 198, 200–1
Raptors 220–3. *See also by species*
Rat 279
Rattlesnake 294–5, 296
Rays 310–11. *See also* Skates
Red bishop 239
Red uakari 252
Red-and-yellow barbet 232
Red-bellied piranha 316
Red-billed leithrix 236
Red-breasted goose 213
Red-capped robin 237
Red-legged honeycreeper 237
Regal sunbird 236
Regent honeyeater 237
Reproductive system 360–1
  female 361
  male 360
Reptiles. *See by species*
Respiratory system 354–5
Resplendent quetzal 235
Rhinoceros 274
Rialto Bridge (Italy) 438
Ribbonfish 322
Riga (Latvia) 442
Rocks 97, 104–5
  erosion 100–1
Rodents 278–9
Rodeo 454
Romania 441, 566
Rome, Ancient
  architecture 410, 413
  baths 416–17
  builder's tools 412
  clothing 416
  empire 410–11
  numerals 412
  war and warfare 414–15
Roses 194
Rough-legged buzzard 221
Royal Canadian Mounted Police 448
Royal Castle, Warsaw (Poland) 514
Royal Mosque (Iran) 499
Rufous-backed shrike 237
Rufous-billed niltava 236
Rufous-tailed jacamar 232
Rugby player 484
Russia 464–5, 569
Rwanda 481, 579

S

Saddled hillstream loach 316
Saiga 277
St Kitts-Nevis 459, 560

St Lucia 459, 560
St Peter's Basilica (Italy) 494–5
St Sophia's Cathedral (Ukraine) 496
St Vincent and the Grenadines 459, 560
Sailfin pimelodid 317
Salamanders 299
Salivary glands 357
Salmon 321
Saltasaurus 156, 164, 167
Saltopus 153
Sami (Lapp) People 444
Samoa 485, 582
San Marino 565
São Tomé and Príncipe 481, 579
Sarsembek herder 466
Satellites 84, 88, 585–6
communication 547
Saturn 15, 26–7, 35, 39, 46, 587, 589
Saudi Arabia 469, 571
Saurischians 160
Saurolophus 171
Sauropelta 169
Sauropods 166
Scanner 543
Scarlet ibis 207
Scarlet minivet 211
Scipionyx 163
Scuba diver 484
Scutellosaurus 169
Sea floor 101, 102, 144–5
Seahorse, pot-bellied 322
Seasons 136–7
plants 192–3
wet and dry 139
Secretarybird 221
Semitrailer truck 523
Senegal 479, 577
Senses. *See under individual names*
Serpent Mound burial ground (USA) 452
Serval 260
Seychelles 481, 581
Shadow puppet 472
Shantungosaurus 171
Sharks 306–9
Sheep 275
Shipka Memorial Church (Bulgaria) 496
Shiogama festival boat 476
Shore 146–7
birds 214–15
blowholes 147
dunes 147
erosion 146
filters 147
sediment 147
Shrike-tit 236
Sierra Leone 479, 577
Sight 374–5
Sikh men 470
Silk Road 400–1
Singapore 472, 473, 573
Singkil dancer 472
Sioux headdress 452
Sistrum 388
Sitar 470
Sixline soapfish 315
Skate 311. *See also* Rays
Skeleton, human 362–4
Skin 370–1
color 370
Skull, human 365
Sky color 123
Skydome (Canada) 509
Slimy loach 317
Slovakia 443, 567
Slovenia 441, 565
Small intestine 356, 357
Smell 379
Snake charmer 470
Snakes 294–7. *See also by species*
Sneezing 378
Snow 128
Snowmobile 446
Society Islands 485
Solar System 14–15, 80
Solomon Islands 485, 582
Somalia 479, 577
Sound 550–1
Sound barrier 536
South Africa 481, 581
South American cora pipe snake 296
Southeast Asian pikehead 315
Southern blue gum 187
Southern roughy 323
Spacecraft 19, 23, 24, 42, 87–90, 586–7. *See also Satellites*
Space travel 90–1
Moon, journey to 90–1, 586, 591
Spain 430–1, 563
Spangled kookaburra 230
Sparrowhawk, little 221
Spectacled monarch 236
Speech 377
Sphinx (Egypt) 502
Spiders 338–43
Spine-cheek anemonefish 324
Spirit House (PNG) 482
Splendid fairy-wren 237
Splendid toadfish 322
Spookfish 311
Spoonbill, African 207
Spotted gar 313
Spotted harlequin snake 297
Spotted harrier 224
Spotted oreo 323
Spotted pardalote 237
Spotted-tailed quoll 243
Squirrel glider 242
Squirrels 278, 279
Sri Lanka 471, 572
Starling, superb glossy 239
Stars 52–7, 62, 588–93. *See also* Astronomy; Constellations; Galaxies
clusters 56–7, 81
double-star supernova 55
life cycle 52–3
Local Group 81
maps 62–79

Stars *continued*
neutron 54
planetary nebula 53
pulsars 54
red giant 52, 53
starbirth nebula 52
supernovas 54–5, 584
white dwarf 53, 55
Statue of Liberty (USA) 450, 503
Statue of the Lion (Ethiopia) 502
Statues and monuments 502–3. *See also by name*
Steam power 552
Steamship 526
Steel band 458
Steel-blue killifish 318
Stegoceras 171
Stegosaurus 154, 169
Sterlet 313
Stethoscope 545
Stomach 356
Stonehenge (England) 428
Stork, painted 213
Storms 130–1
Strawberry 197
Striped headstanter 316
Striped Julie 314
Sturt's desert pea 194
Sudan 479, 576
Sugar maple 187
Sulfur-breasted toucan 206, 233
Sumo wrestlers 476
Sun 15, 36, 39, 45, 50–1, 53, 80, 89, 584, 588, 592–3
Sunflower 195
Superb fruit dove 227
Superb tanager 237
Surf lifesavers 482
Suriname 461, 561
Swan, mute 212
Swaziland 481, 581
Sweden 445, 568
Switzerland 436–7, 565
Swordtail 319
Sydney (Australia) 482
Synoptic chart 132–3
Syria 469, 570

T

Tahitian surfer 484
Taiwan 475, 574
Taj Mahal (India) 470
Tajikistan 467, 570
Takahe 219
Tamandua 245
Tango dancers 462
Tanzania 481, 580
Taos Pueblo (USA) 456, 500
Tarsier 248, 249
Taste 378
Telephone 546
Telescopes 82–4, 584–5. *See also* Satellites
Television 540
Temple of Heaven (China) 474
Temple of the Golden Pavilion (Japan) 476
Teotihuacan (Mexico) 501
Tepee 418, 419
Terra-cotta warriors 502
Thailand 473, 573
Thatched corncrib (Mexico) 458
Thermometers 545
Thira Church (Greece) 496
Thrip 327
Tibet 475
Tibetan monks 474
Tides 142–3
Tiger 258
Tiger rockfish 323
Toads 300–5
Togo 479, 578
Toltec statue 502
Tomato 197
Tomb of Bibi Jaiwindi (Pakistan) 504
Tombs and memorials 504–5
Tonga 485, 583
Torre de Belem (Portugal) 430
Tortoises 280–3
Totem pole 422
Town Hall, Ho Chi Minh City (Vietnam) 472
Trains
bullet 476
steam 524–5
TGV 432
Trans-Siberian 465
Transport
air 530–7
land 522–5
water 526–9
Tree fern 152, 155, 165
Trees 186–7. *See also by species*
conifers. *See* Conifers
seasons 192–3
Triassic period 152–3
Triceratops 156, 168, 169
Trinidad and Tobago 459, 560
Troika horses and sled 464
Tsunamis 116–17
Tuataras 286–7
Tunisia 479, 575
Turbogenerator 552
Turkey 467, 569
Turkmenistan 467, 570
Turtles 155, 280–3
Tuvalu 583
Txukahamai hunters 460
Tyrannosaurus 156, 162

U

Uganda 481, 579
Ukraine 443, 567
Ultrasound 544
Uluru (Ayers Rock) (Australia) 482
United Arab Emirates 469, 571

United Kingdom 428–9, 563
United States of America 450–7, 558
Uranus 15, 28–9, 35, 38, 47, 585, 587, 589
Urchin clingfish 322
Urinary system 358
Uruguay 463, 562
Urutu 296
Uzbekistan 467, 569

V

Vacuum cleaner 541
Vanuatu 485, 582–3
Variegated lizardfish 320
Vatican City 494–5, 565
  guard 438
  St Peter's Basilica 494–5
Vegetables 197
Vein 350
Velociraptor 157, 162
Velvet cichlid 315
Venezuela 461, 561
Venus 15, 18–19, 34, 36, 86, 586, 588, 592
Video conferencing 546
Vienna Philharmonic Orchestra 436
Vietnam 473, 573
Villa Capra (Italy) 517
Vine snake 294
Violaceous trogon 235
Vipers 295, 296
Viruses 348
Vlad Tepes' Castle 440
Voicebox 377
Volcanoes
  chain formation 109
  dinosaurs, disappearance of 172
  eruptions 110–11
  famous 112
  hotspot 108–9
  pyroclastic flow 110
Vultures 206, 221
Vulturine guinea fowl 218

W

Waldrapp 213
Wallaby, forest 240
Walled City (Iran) 468
Wapiti 276
Washing machine 541
Wasp 326, 327, 332
Wata woodcarvers 480
Water
  cycle 124–5
  plants and 182
  precipitation 128–9
Waves 142–3, 147
Weather
  climate 136, 140–1
  clouds 126–7
  fog 124–5
  frontal systems 134–5
  hail 129
  hurricane 130–1
  lightning 131
  mapping 132–3
  monsoon 139
  pressure movement 134–5
  rain 129
  rain shadow 139
  seasons 136–7, 139
  snow 128
  storms 130–1
  water cycle 124–5
  waves, tides and currents 142–3
  winds 138–9
  zones 140
Weevil 328
Weka 218
Whales 266–71
Whirling dervish 466
White-cheeked turaco 234
White-rumped shama 237
White's thrush 237
Wielandiella 152
Wildebeest, blue 276
Windmill 434, 452
Winds 138–9
  Coriolis effect 139
  global air flow 138
  mountain 139
  wind farm 553
Wine
  Chianti 438
  palm 478
Wire-tailed manakin 207, 235
Wolves 254
Wood duck 213
Woodpeckers 232–3

X

X-ray 544

Y

Yellow-bellied sea snake 295
Yellow-billed hornbill 231
Yellow-lipped sea krait 297
Yemen 469, 571
Yew 189
Yugoslavia 441, 566

Z

Zaire 481, 579
Zambia 481, 580
Zanclodon 153
Zebra 274
Zebra danio 316
Zimbabwe 481, 580
Zuider Zee folk costume 434
Zulus 480

Acknowledgments

Weldon Owen would like to thank the following people for their assistance in the production of this book: Philippa Findlay and Sarah Plant at Puddingburn Publishing Services, Jacqueline Richards at Pinchme Design, Lithoteam, Greg Browne, Jessica Cox

The following illustrations are reproduced from *Anatomica: The Complete Reference Guide to the Human Body and How It Works*, Global Book Publishing, Australia: 351tl, 352t, 352b, 353tr, 353bl, 353br, 353tl, 354b, 355tl, 355tr, 355b, 356tr, 356cl, 356c, 356cr, 356bl, 356br, 357bl, 358t, 358bl, 358br, 362c, 362c, 364r, 365t, 365b, 373bl, 373br, 377tr, 377br, 381c (t=top, b=bottom, c=center, r=right, l=left)

Illustrators: Susanna Addario, Mike Atkinson/illustrationweb.com, Paul Bachem, Kenn Backhaus, Cy Baker/Wildlife Art Ltd., Alistair Barnard, Julian Baum, Andrew Beckett, Richard Bonson/Wildlife Art Ltd., Stuart Bowey, Anne Bowman, John Bull, Peter Bull Art Studio, Danny Burke, Martin Camm, Dan Cole/Wildlife Art Ltd., Leslye Cole/Wildlife Art Ltd., Sam and Amy Collins, Tom Connell, Marcus Cremonese, Marjorie Crosby-Fairall, Barry Croucher/Wildlife Art Ltd., Claire Davies/Wildlife Art Ltd., Fiammatte Dogi, Sandra Doyle/Wildlife Art Ltd., Levent Efe, Simone End, Christer Eriksson, Alan Ewart, Nick Farmer/Brihton Illustration, Rod Ferring, Cecilia Fitzsimons/Wildlife Art Ltd., Giuliano Fornari, Chris Forsey, Lloyd Foye, John Francis/Bernard Thornton Artists UK, Luigi Gallante/Wildlife Art Ltd., Lee Gibbons/Wildlife Art Ltd., Tony Gibbons/Bernard Thornton Artists UK, Jon Gittoes, Mike Gorman, Ray Grinaway, Terry Hadler, Langdon G. Halls, Gino Halser, Lorraine Hannay, David A Hardy/Wildlife Art Ltd., Tim Hayward, Phil Hood/Wildlife Art Ltd., Adam Hook/Bernard Thornton Artists UK, Christa Hook/Bernard Thornton Artists UK, Richard Hook/Bernard Thornton Artists UK, Robert Hynes, Mark Iley/Wildlife Art Ltd., Inklink, Ian Jackson/Wildlife Art Ltd., Gillian Jenkins, Janet Jones, Steve Kirk/Wildlife Art Ltd., David Kirshner, Frank Knight, Mike Lamble, Alex Lavroff, Connell Lee, John Mac/Folio, David Mackay, Iain McKellar, James McKinnon, Martin Macrae/Folio, Stuart McVicar/Geocart, Robert Mancini, David Mathews, Peter Mennim, Siri Mills, David Moore/Linden Artists, Colin Newman/Bernard Thornton Artists UK, Kevin O'Donnell, Nicola Oram, Matthew Ottley, Darren Pattenden/illustrationweb.com, Jane Pickering/Linden Artists, Sandra Pond/Wildlife Art Ltd., Marilyn Pride, Tony Pyrzakowski, Oliver Rennert, Luis Rey/Wildlife Art Ltd., John Richards, Edwinna Riddell, Steve Roberts/Wildlife Art Ltd., Trevor Ruth, Claudia Saraceni, Michael Saunders, Peter Schouten, Peter Scott/Wildlife Art Ltd., Stephen Seymour/Bernard Thornton Artists UK, Christine Shafner/K.E. Sweeny Illustration, Nick Shewring/illustrationweb.com, Chris Shields/Wildlife Art Ltd., Ray Sim, Marco Sparaciari, R. Spencer Phippen, Kevin Stead, Roger Stewart/Brihton Illustration, Irene Still, Roger Swainston, Kate Sweeney/K.E. Sweeny Illustration, Sharif Tarabay/illustrationweb.com, Steve Trevaskis, Thomas Trojer, Chris Turnbull/Wildlife Art Ltd., Glen Vause, Jane Walkins/Wildlife Art Ltd., Genevieve Wallace, Ross Watton/illustrationweb.com, Trevor Weekes, Rod Westblade, Steve Weston/Linden Artists, Laurie Whiddon, Simon Williams/illustrationweb.com, Ann Winterbotham, David Wood, David Wun

Countries of the World Maps: Digital Wisdom Publishing Ltd
Star Maps: Wil Tirion
Flags: Flag Society of Australia